Lecture Notes in Computer Science 14034

Founding Editors

Gerhard Goos
Juris Hartmanis

The series Lecture Notes in Computer Science (LNCS), including its subseries Lecture Notes in Artificial Intelligence (LNAI) and Lecture Notes in Bioinformatics (LNBI), has established itself as a medium for the publication of new developments in computer science and information technology research, teaching, and education.

LNCS enjoys close cooperation with the computer science R & D community, the series counts many renowned academics among its volume editors and paper authors, and collaborates with prestigious societies. Its mission is to serve this international community by providing an invaluable service, mainly focused on the publication of conference and workshop proceedings and postproceedings. LNCS commenced publication in 1973.

Aaron Marcus · Elizabeth Rosenzweig ·
Marcelo M. Soares
Editors

Design, User Experience, and Usability

12th International Conference, DUXU 2023
Held as Part of the 25th HCI International Conference, HCII 2023
Copenhagen, Denmark, July 23–28, 2023
Proceedings, Part V

 Springer

Editors
Aaron Marcus
Aaron Marcus and Associates
Berkeley, CA, USA

Elizabeth Rosenzweig
World Usability Day and Bubble Mountain
Consulting
Newton Center, MA, USA

Marcelo M. Soares
Southern University of Science
and Technology – SUSTech
Shenzhen, China

ISSN 0302-9743   ISSN 1611-3349 (electronic)
Lecture Notes in Computer Science
ISBN 978-3-031-35704-6 ISBN 978-3-031-35705-3 (eBook)
https://doi.org/10.1007/978-3-031-35705-3

This Springer imprint is published by the registered company Springer Nature Switzerland AG
The registered company address is: Gewerbestrasse 11, 6330 Cham, Switzerland

Foreword

Human-computer interaction (HCI) is acquiring an ever-increasing scientific and industrial importance, as well as having more impact on people's everyday lives, as an ever-growing number of human activities are progressively moving from the physical to the digital world. This process, which has been ongoing for some time now, was further accelerated during the acute period of the COVID-19 pandemic. The HCI International (HCII) conference series, held annually, aims to respond to the compelling need to advance the exchange of knowledge and research and development efforts on the human aspects of design and use of computing systems.

The 25th International Conference on Human-Computer Interaction, HCI International 2023 (HCII 2023), was held in the emerging post-pandemic era as a 'hybrid' event at the AC Bella Sky Hotel and Bella Center, Copenhagen, Denmark, during July 23–28, 2023. It incorporated the 21 thematic areas and affiliated conferences listed below.

A total of 7472 individuals from academia, research institutes, industry, and government agencies from 85 countries submitted contributions, and 1578 papers and 396 posters were included in the volumes of the proceedings that were published just before the start of the conference, these are listed below. The contributions thoroughly cover the entire field of human-computer interaction, addressing major advances in knowledge and effective use of computers in a variety of application areas. These papers provide academics, researchers, engineers, scientists, practitioners and students with state-of-the-art information on the most recent advances in HCI.

The HCI International (HCII) conference also offers the option of presenting 'Late Breaking Work', and this applies both for papers and posters, with corresponding volumes of proceedings that will be published after the conference. Full papers will be included in the 'HCII 2023 - Late Breaking Work - Papers' volumes of the proceedings to be published in the Springer LNCS series, while 'Poster Extended Abstracts' will be included as short research papers in the 'HCII 2023 - Late Breaking Work - Posters' volumes to be published in the Springer CCIS series.

I would like to thank the Program Board Chairs and the members of the Program Boards of all thematic areas and affiliated conferences for their contribution towards the high scientific quality and overall success of the HCI International 2023 conference. Their manifold support in terms of paper reviewing (single-blind review process, with a minimum of two reviews per submission), session organization and their willingness to act as goodwill ambassadors for the conference is most highly appreciated.

This conference would not have been possible without the continuous and unwavering support and advice of Gavriel Salvendy, founder, General Chair Emeritus, and Scientific Advisor. For his outstanding efforts, I would like to express my sincere appreciation to Abbas Moallem, Communications Chair and Editor of HCI International News.

July 2023   Constantine Stephanidis

HCI International 2023 Thematic Areas and Affiliated Conferences

Thematic Areas

- HCI: Human-Computer Interaction
- HIMI: Human Interface and the Management of Information

Affiliated Conferences

- EPCE: 20th International Conference on Engineering Psychology and Cognitive Ergonomics
- AC: 17th International Conference on Augmented Cognition
- UAHCI: 17th International Conference on Universal Access in Human-Computer Interaction
- CCD: 15th International Conference on Cross-Cultural Design
- SCSM: 15th International Conference on Social Computing and Social Media
- VAMR: 15th International Conference on Virtual, Augmented and Mixed Reality
- DHM: 14th International Conference on Digital Human Modeling and Applications in Health, Safety, Ergonomics and Risk Management
- DUXU: 12th International Conference on Design, User Experience and Usability
- C&C: 11th International Conference on Culture and Computing
- DAPI: 11th International Conference on Distributed, Ambient and Pervasive Interactions
- HCIBGO: 10th International Conference on HCI in Business, Government and Organizations
- LCT: 10th International Conference on Learning and Collaboration Technologies
- ITAP: 9th International Conference on Human Aspects of IT for the Aged Population
- AIS: 5th International Conference on Adaptive Instructional Systems
- HCI-CPT: 5th International Conference on HCI for Cybersecurity, Privacy and Trust
- HCI-Games: 5th International Conference on HCI in Games
- MobiTAS: 5th International Conference on HCI in Mobility, Transport and Automotive Systems
- AI-HCI: 4th International Conference on Artificial Intelligence in HCI
- MOBILE: 4th International Conference on Design, Operation and Evaluation of Mobile Communications

List of Conference Proceedings Volumes Appearing Before the Conference

1. LNCS 14011, Human-Computer Interaction: Part I, edited by Masaaki Kurosu and Ayako Hashizume
2. LNCS 14012, Human-Computer Interaction: Part II, edited by Masaaki Kurosu and Ayako Hashizume
3. LNCS 14013, Human-Computer Interaction: Part III, edited by Masaaki Kurosu and Ayako Hashizume
4. LNCS 14014, Human-Computer Interaction: Part IV, edited by Masaaki Kurosu and Ayako Hashizume
5. LNCS 14015, Human Interface and the Management of Information: Part I, edited by Hirohiko Mori and Yumi Asahi
6. LNCS 14016, Human Interface and the Management of Information: Part II, edited by Hirohiko Mori and Yumi Asahi
7. LNAI 14017, Engineering Psychology and Cognitive Ergonomics: Part I, edited by Don Harris and Wen-Chin Li
8. LNAI 14018, Engineering Psychology and Cognitive Ergonomics: Part II, edited by Don Harris and Wen-Chin Li
9. LNAI 14019, Augmented Cognition, edited by Dylan D. Schmorrow and Cali M. Fidopiastis
10. LNCS 14020, Universal Access in Human-Computer Interaction: Part I, edited by Margherita Antona and Constantine Stephanidis
11. LNCS 14021, Universal Access in Human-Computer Interaction: Part II, edited by Margherita Antona and Constantine Stephanidis
12. LNCS 14022, Cross-Cultural Design: Part I, edited by Pei-Luen Patrick Rau
13. LNCS 14023, Cross-Cultural Design: Part II, edited by Pei-Luen Patrick Rau
14. LNCS 14024, Cross-Cultural Design: Part III, edited by Pei-Luen Patrick Rau
15. LNCS 14025, Social Computing and Social Media: Part I, edited by Adela Coman and Simona Vasilache
16. LNCS 14026, Social Computing and Social Media: Part II, edited by Adela Coman and Simona Vasilache
17. LNCS 14027, Virtual, Augmented and Mixed Reality, edited by Jessie Y. C. Chen and Gino Fragomeni
18. LNCS 14028, Digital Human Modeling and Applications in Health, Safety, Ergonomics and Risk Management: Part I, edited by Vincent G. Duffy
19. LNCS 14029, Digital Human Modeling and Applications in Health, Safety, Ergonomics and Risk Management: Part II, edited by Vincent G. Duffy
20. LNCS 14030, Design, User Experience, and Usability: Part I, edited by Aaron Marcus, Elizabeth Rosenzweig and Marcelo Soares
21. LNCS 14031, Design, User Experience, and Usability: Part II, edited by Aaron Marcus, Elizabeth Rosenzweig and Marcelo Soares

47. CCIS 1836, HCI International 2023 Posters - Part V, edited by Constantine Stephanidis, Margherita Antona, Stavroula Ntoa and Gavriel Salvendy

https://2023.hci.international/proceedings

Preface

User experience (UX) refers to a person's thoughts, feelings, and behavior when using interactive systems. UX design becomes fundamentally important for new and emerging mobile, ubiquitous, and omnipresent computer-based contexts. The scope of design, user experience, and usability (DUXU) extends to all aspects of the user's interaction with a product or service, how it is perceived, learned, and used. DUXU also addresses design knowledge, methods, and practices, with a focus on deeply human-centered processes. Usability, usefulness, and appeal are fundamental requirements for effective user-experience design.

The 12th Design, User Experience, and Usability Conference (DUXU 2023), an affiliated conference of the HCI International conference, encouraged papers from professionals, academics, and researchers that report results and cover a broad range of research and development activities on a variety of related topics. Professionals include designers, software engineers, scientists, marketers, business leaders, and practitioners in fields such as AI, architecture, financial and wealth management, game design, graphic design, finance, healthcare, industrial design, mobile, psychology, travel, and vehicles.

This year's submissions covered a wide range of content across the spectrum of design, user-experience, and usability. The latest trends and technologies are represented, as well as contributions from professionals, academics, and researchers across the globe. The breadth of their work is indicated in the following topics covered in the proceedings.

Five volumes of the HCII 2023 proceedings are dedicated to this year's edition of the DUXU Conference:

- Part I addresses topics related to design methods, tools and practices, as well as emotional and persuasive design.
- Part II addresses topics related to design case studies, as well as creativity and design education.
- Part III addresses topics related to evaluation methods and techniques, as well as usability, user experience, and technology acceptance studies.
- Part IV addresses topics related to designing learning experiences, as well as design and user experience of chatbots, conversational agents, and robots.
- Part V addresses topics related to DUXU for cultural heritage, as well as DUXU for health and wellbeing.

The papers in these volumes were included for publication after a minimum of two single–blind reviews from the members of the DUXU Program Board or, in some cases, from Preface members of the Program Boards of other affiliated conferences. We would like to thank all of them for their invaluable contribution, support, and efforts.

July 2023

Aaron Marcus
Elizabeth Rosenzweig
Marcelo M. Soares

12th International Conference on Design, User Experience and Usability (DUXU 2023)

The full list with the Program Board Chairs and the members of the Program Boards of all thematic areas and affiliated conferences of HCII2023 is available online at:

http://www.hci.international/board-members-2023.php

HCI International 2024 Conference

The 26th International Conference on Human-Computer Interaction, HCI International 2024, will be held jointly with the affiliated conferences at the Washington Hilton Hotel, Washington, DC, USA, June 29 – July 4, 2024. It will cover a broad spectrum of themes related to Human-Computer Interaction, including theoretical issues, methods, tools, processes, and case studies in HCI design, as well as novel interaction techniques, interfaces, and applications. The proceedings will be published by Springer. More information will be made available on the conference website: http://2024.hci.international/.

General Chair
Prof. Constantine Stephanidis
University of Crete and ICS-FORTH
Heraklion, Crete, Greece
Email: general_chair@hcii2024.org

https://2024.hci.international/

Contents – Part V

DUXU for Health and Wellbeing

DUXU for Cultural Heritage

Research on the Development of Spatial Model and Value Perceptions of Lingnan's "Water Cultural Heritage" in the Context of Generative Whole Theory

Yali Chen[✉] and Mingyu Sun

School of Design, South China University of Technology, Guangzhou, China
chenyali@scut.edu.cn

Abstract. With the rapid development of digital technology, digital protection has become an important technical means of cultural heritage and heritage space protection. This study uses digital technology protection and management strategies to study the organic development and protection of the "water cultural heritage" landscape of traditional water settlements. Through field investigation and literature research, this study will establish the identification model of the digital landscape information platform for the value and characteristics of the "water culture" landscape heritage, to solve the problem of avoiding one-way linear protection and to realize circular and gradual organic development in the sustainable development of the water town cultural heritage space. From the perspective of the protection framework, this study will establish a digital landscape information model for the heritage space of the water town, and construct three advanced procedures, namely "Data collection", "File management" and "Presentation and Communication", to solve the complexity and differences in the process of heritage protection. From the perspective of technology application, this study will build an information platform based on the dynamic characteristics of the digital landscape model to better integrate the heritage space information, which will provide reliable technical support for all stages of heritage landscape practice, including heritage landscape assessment, protection planning, daily management, impact monitoring and change evaluation.

Keywords: Lingnan Traditional Water Settlements · Water Cultural Heritage · Digital Landscape · Heritage Landscape Information Model

1 Introduction

Since we entered the digital era, information digitization has gained significant attention from scholars and has developed quickly. Scientific research now has accessible, adaptable, and effective technical tools because to the spread of digital information technology. At the same time, people's research on cultural heritage landscape has gradually changed from static environment to the dynamic evolution of multiple elements, such as nature and humanity [1]. As landscape research develops and deepens, the application demand for digital information management technology is becoming more and more urgent. The term "digital heritage landscape" refers to the use of digital technology to produce electronic data information on the heritage landscape, which is convenient for recording, storing, and applying to the landscape in order to achieve a more thorough and effective management and protection of cultural heritage landscape [2]. The Preservation of Digital Heritage Charter, which expanded on the idea of heritage and the digital representation of cultural information products, was published in 2003 by the United Nations Educational, Scientific, and Cultural Organization. Then, in 2011, Recommendation on the Historic Urban Landscape was made, shattering the conventional heritage concept [3], brought some columns and heritage space, intangible dimension preservation and display, innovative digital technology protection and management of cultural heritage landscape become a hot topic of contemporary cultural heritage research and emerging areas.

A water culture develops as a result of man and water interacting. A general term for various cultural phenomena formed by water as the carrier, water culture is the sum of the material and spiritual wealth created by water as the carrier in their practical activities [4]. "Water cultural heritage" is a more specific classification of "cultural heritage", which generally refers to a type of cultural heritage connected to "water." The attention and research on "water cultural heritage" is little and limited to the scope of water conservancy projects and water conservancy facilities, focusing on the definition, type and value system of water cultural heritage [5]. The Interpretation of the Definition, Features, Type, and Value of Water Cultural Heritage by Professor Xuming Tan once explored the characteristics of water cultural heritage. He separated the water cultural heritage into engineering and non-engineering assets, built two different types of water cultural heritage structures, and for the first time devised the water cultural heritage evaluation method. Projects, cultural artifacts, knowledge and technology, religion, cultural activities, and other categories make to the cultural legacy of water [6].

The Lingnan region is home to a distinctive water environment, and the complicated water system distribution in the lives of the locals creates unbreakable connections [7]. People have developed the concept of "water as the principle of water," the choice of geographical construction, the structure of buildings, national cultural beliefs [8], and the development of Lingnan production as a result of utilising water resources. Water and Lingnan Water Village go hand in hand. In Lingnan, the "water cultural heritage" landscape consists of three elements: Building a livable water town environment under the philosophy of "human-water symbiosis," manage water and accumulate wealth; Under the religious concept of "water law worship", landscape image is more related to water, meaning beautiful. Village landscape under the influence of "water first" site selection water law, water is closely related to natural ecology. The village landscape is formed between the river and water network, giving it a "earth atmosphere" and "vitality" due to the presence of water [9].

The current Lingnan water village hamlet has distilled thousands of years' worth of cultural attractiveness, serving as a testament to the success of water culture. It is very crucial to safeguard the "water cultural heritage" landscape in Lingnan given the significant urbanization intervention, ecological environment disruption, and rising homogeneity of settlement landscape characteristics. In addition, the "water cultural heritage" landscape of Lingnan is rich in characteristics and has distinctive cultural and humanistic values. The living environment and life philosophy formed by people through history, the planning concept of water settlement construction and the humanistic viewpoint are important components of the splendid Chinese culture. The model and digital research on the landscape space construction of "water cultural heritage" of Lingnan water settlement are carried out to better protect the cultural heritage, and provide certain references for research in related fields.

2 Methods

2.1 Bibliometric Analysis of the Status of Hydrological Heritage Conservation

In order to understand the current situation of water cultural heritage protection, this paper uses the bibliometric method to achieve the research purpose. The included literature's key words, historical patterns, and study areas were analyzed. In general, bibliometry can understand the current research progress without thoroughly reviewing all relevant research literature, and make an intuitive and objective display of the research characteristics and laws [10]. This paper creates bibliometric maps for macroscopic visual analysis using the VOSviewer software. It is not only a tool for text mining technology to realize visualization, but also a commonly used tool in scientific metrology analysis, among which keyword co-occurrence analysis can well reflect the current academic research hotspot, interrelation and development trend of this field [11, 12].

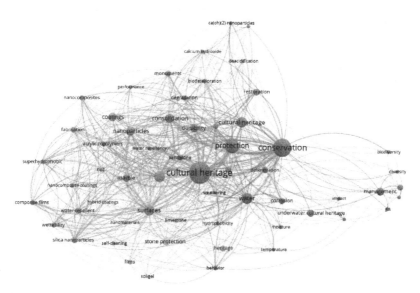

Fig. 1. VOSviewer keyword network visualization map of Cultural heritage land scapeprotection within the Web of Science (WoS) core collection database (devised by the authors). (Color figure online)

As shown in Fig. 1, this paper selected Web of Science as the data source and "Water cultural heritage protection" as the search topic, with a total of 267 literatures included. 59 keywords with a frequency greater than or equal to 5 were selected for visualization. In the figure, the larger the circular node is, the more frequent the keyword is, and the more it can represent the hot spots in the field. It can be seen from the figure that the larger nodes are cultural heritage, conservation, protection and water. It can be seen that under the study of cultural heritage landscape, protection and management have always been the focus of attention. Node lines represent correlation strength, and the thicker the lines are, the more times the two appear in the same literature. The closer the dots are, the closer the relationship is. Different colors represent different clusters. Among them, the literature in the blue cluster mainly focuses on the protection of natural environment of cultural heritage, and focuses on the degradation and restoration projects. The literatures in red cluster are more inclined to the protection of water cultural heritage, which is more in line with the research direction of this paper. This cluster focuses on hydrophobicity, management, underwater cultural heritage and biodiversity, including GIS, models and other research methods. The literatures in green cluster are mostly material terms, such as surfaces, nanoparticles, coatings, etc. It can be seen that the study of chemical materials plays an important role in the protection of cultural heritage landscape. Yellow clustering tends to be geological research, and the keywords include limestone and stone protection, etc., but there are few clusters and more overlapping parts with other clusters. As can be seen from Fig. 1, the overall distance between blue, green and yellow clusters is relatively close and closely related, indicating that in the study of cultural heritage protection, the research directions of natural environment, material research and geological protection have strong correlation and high co-occurrence frequency, which can be seen as a category. Thus, the whole network map is divided into two categories, as shown in Fig. 2.

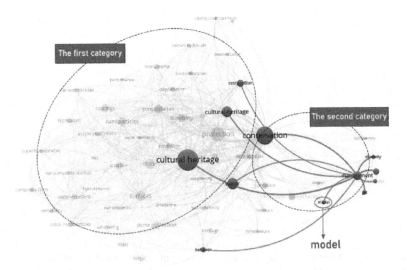

Fig. 2. Network visualization map with the theme of management in the WoS core collection database via VOSviewer (devised by the authors). (Color figure online)

The key words in this cluster can be divided into two categories, as seen in Fig. 2. The first category is the material research level of cultural heritage, such as material research, geological stone research, etc. The second category is the protection and management of water cultural heritage, which can be seen that the protection of water cultural heritage has a co-occurrence relationship with hydrology, management, diversity and technical means. In the management-related nodes, the emergence of the term model indicates that the method of model construction is widely recognized in the landscape protection of "water cultural heritage".

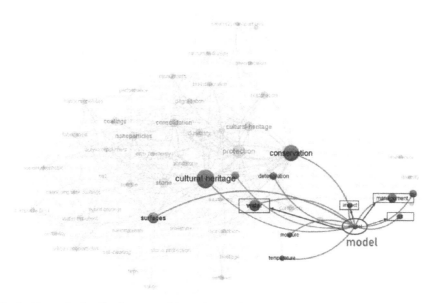

Fig. 3. Network visualization map with the theme of model in the WoS core collection database via VOSviewer (devised by the authors).

Focus model keywords are visible as shown in Fig. 3, model associated radiation far, but mainly used in water cultural heritage management and conservation. The correlation with temperature and hydrology can be regarded as component elements of model construction. The correlation with impact, management, deterioration and other words indicates that the model has management, monitoring and evaluation function for cultural heritage. The correlation with the word GIS reflects the interaction of digital technology methods in this field.

2.2 Digital Information Modeling Techniques and Methods of Heritage Landscape

The continuous development of digital technology promotes the acquisition, collection, management and performance of digital heritage landscape engineering.

Table 1 lists the relevant technologies that may be applied so far. With the development of science and technology, the parts of the digital practice of heritage landscape will

Table 1. Practical steps and technologies required for digitizing heritage landscapes.

Stage	Technology application
Data acquisition	Digital audio
	Digital image
	Data base
	Low altitude drone
	Scotograph
	Ladar
	Photographic surveying
	IR/multispectral imaging
File management	Multimedia database
	Text database
	Geographic information platform
	Building information model
	Video surveillance
	Cloud management
Presentation and communication	Internet of things
	Big data
	Virtual reality
	Holographic laser projection
	Public participation in the GIS
	Stereoscopic reproduction of the map
	Panoramic photography

be continuously optimized and developed [13, 14]. Current work on the digital heritage landscape presents the virtual construction of the realistic environment, and simulates the future development state of heritage landscape according to data processing [15]; Using virtual sensory technology to restore the past and modern material elements and construct the historical development line, three-dimensional landscape modeling technology is an indispensable link in heritage protection [16]. The concept of building information model (BIM) has developed rapidly and is widely used in various fields, including heritage landscape. However, the practice of cultural heritage landscape protection has obvious uniqueness: 1) the cultural heritage landscape management first considers cultural landscape extraction rather than design innovation; 2) the cultural heritage needs to protect the physical environment from the current quo, rather than demolition and reconstruction; 3) Different from the BIM concept in which construction is an important link, cultural heritage landscape does not need to be constructed in a large project, and only needs a small amount of restoration; 4) the cultural heritage landscape contains more elements, such as memory, myths and legends, aesthetic associations, etc., which are not included in the BIM framework [17, 18]. Based on obvious differences, professor Chen Yang proposed "Heritage Landscape Information Model" concept: heritage landscape information model is a digital information integration platform, representing the material and intangible elements of heritage landscape information. It will provide reliable technical support and knowledge resources for all stages of heritage landscape practice, and be applied to the assessment, monitoring, protection and management of heritage landscape [19].

However, the theory can not be fully applied to the practice of Lingnan water cultural heritage landscape. How to use digital technology to express the multi-value of water cultural heritage landscape? How to meet the needs of water cultural heritage for water characteristics, water development culture, water quality management and other aspects? Based on this, this paper attempts to use the concept of "heritage landscape information model" to study the digital spatial elements of Lingnan "water cultural heritage" landscape, and summarize innovative ideas, to provide a framework reference for the future digital water cultural heritage landscape practice.

3   Results

Based on the above methods, when collecting and archiving the information of Lingnan cultural heritage landscape, it is found that the current digital technology software is mostly designed for architecture majors, such as Sketchup and 3ds Max, which are physical features of construction, and few are specialized in serving the landscape garden profession. The construction of landscape information is rare to carry out, and it cannot be used in the management of cultural heritage landscape [20]. Therefore, under the concept of "heritage landscape information model", this paper tries to construct an information model conceptual framework applicable to Lingnan water cultural heritage landscape, improves the construction of information model framework of traditional water towns in Lingnan region, supplements the idea of digital information of "water cultural heritage" landscape, and provides certain references for more extensive practice of digital water cultural heritage landscape information. Analyze its value and future development trend.

As shown in Fig. 4, this paper divides the digitalization practice of water cultural heritage landscape into three steps: Data collection, File management, Presentation and Communication. The first step is to collect data on the constituent elements of heritage landscape. Professor Ervin believes that landscape includes six core elements: terrain, vegetation, water, structures, animals, and climate [21]. However, British Professor Carys Swanwick has constructed a new framework of landscape elements from the perspective of cultural heritage. She believes that landscape includes natural elements, cultural and social elements, and sensory and aesthetic elements [18]. Combined with the views of scholars, this paper classifies the data as: basic data information and special data information when collecting the elements of the heritage landscape, among which the basic data information is terrain, climate, hydrology, flora and fauna, structures and culture. Special data information refers to one or more data information that has advantages in basic data information by comparing the same data with other regions, namely regional cultural characteristics. In addition, special data information is characterized by large data amount, high value and strong attraction in the data collection

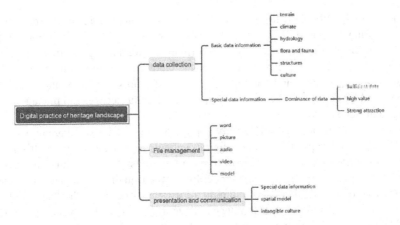

Fig. 4. Conceptual framework of landscape information model for water cultural heritage.

process. Document it emphatically and save it separately to facilitate resource allocation for subsequent protection work. The second step is to digitize the file and protect the data. When data collection reaches a certain amount, information should be timely input, multi-dimensional and multi-form digital filing, not limited to text, pictures, audio, video, models, etc., timely follow up platform development to facilitate the multiple storage of digital information to avoid loss. The third step is to present the dissemination of public digital information. The ultimate purpose of heritage landscape protection is to avoid the disappearance of heritage culture, to spread the digital cultural genetic landscape that can be publicized to the public, and to revitalize the cultural spirit is the highest achievement of heritage protection. Through the Internet, virtual reality and other technical means to break through the time and spread heritage landscape cultural characteristics, give new life to the landscape.

As shown in Fig. 5, it is known from the investigation and practice of water culture data in Lingnan that the human element in the water culture heritage landscape elements is a complex symbiosis with water, which is mostly the material or immaterial result of the interaction of water-related factors on people [22]. Humanistic elements generally include knowledge and culture, technology, scene senses, myths and legends, festival tradition, behavior system, etiquette system, art performance, spatial memory, religious belief and so on [18, 23]. This point is obvious in the humanistic characteristics of Lingnan. In the water town area, residents worship the natural god, and folk belief activities, farming activities and clan sacrifices are carried out together, generating unique cultural activities and forming a unique social life mechanism of the Lingnan water town settlement [24]. From the name of settlement landscape culture, we can also see many words related to water. For example, the scene of "hanging rainbow at the end of the village" in the eight scenes of Foshan in the Qing Dynasty, which depicts the landscape space memory of the sun slanting in the west reflected in the river, such as the rainbow rippling on the water [25]. For heritage landscape, intangible heritage information is the key factor constituting its cultural characteristics. However, the BIM framework does not contain the expression of intangible heritage elements, so the framework of

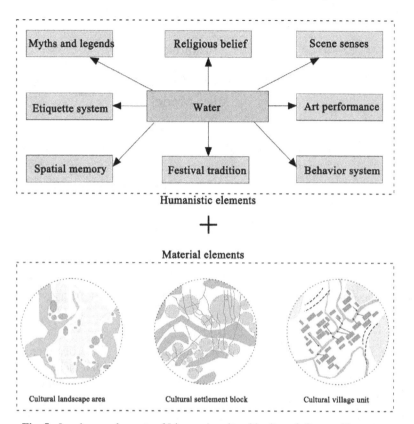

Fig. 5. Landscape elements of Lingnan's cultural heritage influenced by water.

humanistic elements is highlighted here. When obtaining the humanistic elements of heritage landscape elements, it should be clear that the humanistic elements focus on the immaterial information generated by human activities, so as to avoid overlapping with other elements. Intangible cultural heritage elements are important factors for the composition and uniqueness of heritage landscape, but they are difficult to be transformed into spatial information data. In the current incorporation process of computer spatial database, the immaterial elements need to have the corresponding material correlation, and with the change of time and environment, the non-material information that cannot be recorded is quickly disappeared or distorted. Therefore, it is a key link in the theoretical research of cultural heritage landscape information model to study the data acquisition and filing management of humanistic elements and to solve the difficulty of incorporating intangible information into the database.

4   Discussion

As shown in Fig. 6, the cultural heritage landscape information model, as an integrated platform, supports heritage landscape practice. Information model acts on cultural heritage landscape from space and time. In the spatial dimension, the integrity of the heritage

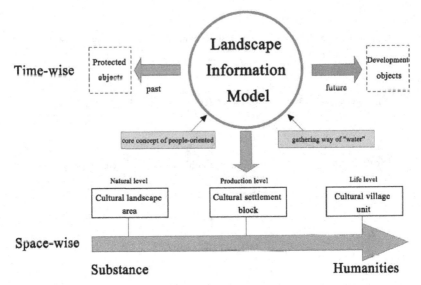

Fig. 6. A schematic framework for the role of the "Water Cultural Heritage" landscape information model.

landscape, from the objective presentation of material nature to the rich reproduction of humanistic scenes. For the construction of landscape information model of Lingnan water town, we should grasp the core concept of "people-oriented" and the gathering way of "water" [26], from the natural landscape area to the cultural landscape unit to the settlement living area, and explore the way between man and nature in different aspects of ecology, production and life. In the time dimension, the value of cultural heritage is continued. From the historical perspective of culture, heritage landscape is the core object of protection, the regional development context is sorted out, and the cognition of cultural heritage is improved to enhance cultural confidence. The accurate grasp of the relevant factors can provide the scientific basis and thinking methods for the repair and protection work in the later period, and promote the high efficiency, precision and digitalization of the daily management. And the digital landscape information model simulates the future development trend according to the existing data, and puts forward the optimal development path for the heritage landscape. The integrated data of the platform is convenient for the management to quickly monitor the change evaluation of relevant factors continuously, which is conducive to the powerful and credible evaluation of the status quo and development of the heritage landscape.

From the perspective of protection and management, the value of the future digital landscape information model is reflected in the following four aspects:

1) *Promoting the Systematic Management of Cultural Heritage and Landscape Information.* Digital landscape information reduces the technical threshold and data collection cost, and the systematic cloud data promotion of special research is inclined to online operation. With the continuous maturity and development of technology and theory, it is expected to establish an open and diversified cultural heritage landscape

information platform, break through the regional time restrictions, coordinate the fragmented information, and form a systematic management information platform. Systematic information management can better compare cultural heritage landscape information elements, refining special data information, within a certain range from different perspectives of hierarchical architecture, in special research provides targeted solutions, promote the characteristics of cultural heritage landscape research planning direction, further enhance the uniqueness of heritage landscape.

2) *Helping the Overall Coordinated Development of Cultural Heritage Landscape.* With the development and maturity of science and technology, data acquisition tends to be more efficient and fast, and the collection of data information can be expanded in both breadth and depth, which promotes the practice of heritage landscape digitization. In terms of data collection, the practical tools are more flexible and diverse, the information database is more abundant and accurate, which can better grasp special data information and more comprehensive standardized basic data information, facilitate the reasonable allocation of resources in the protection and research, and promote the coordinated development of cultural heritage landscape value. On archive management, the establishment of the digital landscape information model guaranteed under the guidance of theoretical heritage data comprehensive and rich, can targeted multidimensional corresponding related information properties and categories for data processing, so as to better reflect the uniqueness of cultural heritage landscape, provide professional data support for the final present spread, avoid the narrow vision. The digital presentation of heritage landscape is conducive to better integration with regional planning and fewer decision-making errors. On the other hand, when we protect landscape heritage, we adhere to maintaining the overall consistency of landscape culture and residents' life, increase residents' sense of participation and interest relevance, so that residents can spontaneously participate in landscape protection, and promote the sustainable development of cultural heritage landscape.

3) *Promoting Dynamic Monitoring and Scientific Evaluation of Heritage Landscape.* The dynamic evolution of cultural heritage landscape has become an important direction for the study of heritage landscape protection. Digital landscape information model provides dynamic and intelligent management means for heritage protection. With the help of high integration and intelligent analysis of data information, it further highlights the special data information in the heritage landscape and better identifies the landscape characteristics. Based on the periodically accumulated data information in the digital landscape information model, the changes of the heritage landscape are accurately captured to realize scientific and quantitative dynamic monitoring. Based on the heritage landscape information change research interaction and nature, break the simple preservation heritage "old tradition", the use of digital intelligent model system of cultural heritage landscape integrity authenticity assessment, according to the assessment of the adjustment management measures, promote the cultural heritage landscape "resurrection", and drive its continuous development with The Times [27].

4) *Enhance Understanding and Preserving the Values of the Diverse Cultural Landscape.* Digital landscape information model fully using digital tools, collection of multiple information form open information sharing platform, the forefront of digital communication means more attract different audience to participate in cultural

heritage landscape construction, the public can convenient access to heritage information, promote cultural data rich promotion, provide a solid power foundation for the revitalization of heritage landscape [28]. In addition, the open digital information platform promotes itself to become more open and democratic, and the increase of participation heat provides a strong data source, which will help enhance the value of cultural landscape diversification, and promote the diversified development and protection of cultural heritage landscape.

5 Conclusion

Based on the concept of "heritage landscape information model", this paper integrated landscape ecology, digital technology, architecture, human geography and unique aesthetics of Lingnan "water cultural heritage", studied the construction system of landscape spatial model of "water cultural heritage", and adopted digital technology protection and management strategies. This paper discusses the value cognition and future development of the construction of heritage landscape model to the conservation of "water cultural heritage" landscape. Water, spanning the gully of time, has nourished the landscape and scenery of Lingnan since ancient times and nurtured the unique water culture of Lingnan. Under the influence of time, the landscape style of Lingnan has shown its unique charm. The people in the water villages in Lingnan are also centered by the water and integrated with the natural environment, forming the unique living customs of the people in the water villages. This blend of material and immaterial, in the test of history run in with each other, continuous development, is a perfect combination of natural ecology and human ecology. The natural landscape and geographical resources of Lingnan water Township are the important support for the survival of the people of water township, and also the confidence for their continuous progress and development [29]. In the protection of Lingnan Water cultural heritage, it is necessary to balance the contradiction between environmental protection and the practical needs of social development, never stand on its own ground, always adhere to sustainable development, the common development of the city and the heritage, and allow the cultural heritage to develop, rather than retain it as a static natural architecture or style.

The new era brings new challenges as well as new opportunities. With the development of science and technology, the protection of cultural heritage has been standardized and detailed to a new level. Relying on 3S (RS, GPS, GIS) geographic data acquisition technology and the detailed architecture and landscape information model that BIM can support, the database of cultural landscape heritage has been thoroughly and dynamically supplemented. The settlement landscape research data is digitized, and different definitions and systems in various literatures are further clarified to carry out the accurate transformation of concept-data. So that it can provide important and timely guidance to the natural environment and adjust the protection method. Technology offers new forms of protection to the protectors of cultural heritage. Based on the development of science and technology, after the information modeling of the cultural heritage, this historical deposit with ancient charm will be presented to tourists and residents with a new look of modern flavor, endowed with new vitality. Science and technology bring the charm of culture to the eyes of the public more intuitively, so that people spontaneously fall in love with and appreciate culture, and then become stakeholders in the protection of cultural heritage.

In the protection of cultural heritage, it is also necessary to emphasize diversification and use a variety of ways to protect. With the help of the Internet, information platform, discussion forum, photography exchange and other sections can be provided to systematically increase the participation of residents and local people in cultural heritage protection, so that heritage protection can be deeply integrated into daily life. Or carry out offline folk story meetings and early childhood education. With government funding and social funding, special plans and subsidies are given to protectors, so as to form a protection pattern with orderly development and balanced progress. Therefore, when protecting and inheriting the water cultural heritage of Lingnan, it is necessary to always adhere to the holistic thinking and dynamic perspective, make use of cutting-edge technology to give overall consideration to the intangible cultural culture and material natural landscape, so that they can promote and fulfill each other, and continue to develop dynamically and make progress in the face of the historical test of the new era.

Funding. This research was funded by Guangdong province Philosophy and Social Science the 14th Five-Year Plan Project, grant number GD22CYS23. This research was funded by Guangzhou City Philosophy and Social Science Planning 2020 Annual Project: grant number 2020GZGJ19.

References

1. Han, F.: Explore the moving cultural landscape. Chin. Landsc. Archit. **28**(05), 5–9 (2012)
2. Chen, Y.: Digital heritage landscape: digital practice and innovation of urban historical landscape in Ballarat, Australia. Chin. Landsc. Archit. **33**(6), 83–88 (2017)
3. UNESCO: Recommendation on the Historic Urban Landscape. In: 10th Nov 2011 United Nations Educational, Scientific and Cultural Organisation. UNESCO, Paris (2010)
4. Fernand, B., Chao, X.: Histoire et civilizations, 1st edn. Guangxi Normal University Press, China (2003)
5. Yanhong, H.: Research on the Water Cultural Heritage Protection of the Beijing-Hangzhou Grand Canal Based on the Perspective of "Cultural Gene." Tianjin University, Tianjin (2017)
6. Xuming, T.: Interpretation of the definition, characteristics, types and values of water cultural heritage. China Water Resour. **21**, 1–4 (2012)
7. Biqi, L.: Natural Disasters in Guangdong, 1st edn. Guangdong People's Publishing House, Guangzhou (1993)
8. Zehong, C.: Guangfu Culture. Guangdong People's Publishing House, Guangzhou (2012)
9. Yali, C., Qi, L.: Lingnan water town traditional village camp scene based on the "water method." Huazhong Archit. **36**(02), 111–114 (2018)
10. Dias, G.P.: Smart cities research in Portugal and Spain: an exploratory biliometric analysis. In: Proceedings of the 2018 13th Iberian Conference on Information Systems and Technologies (CISTI), pp. 1–6, Caceres, Spain (2018)
11. Aimin, Z.: The cluster analysis of co-occurrence strength in the field of knowledge management in 2006. Mod. Inf. **28**, 30–33 (2008)
12. Yan, Y.: Research status of big data and education informatization in China–study based on biliometric and content analysis (2010–2019). In: Proceedings of the 2020 International Conference on Big Data and Informatization Education (ICBDIE), pp. 99–104. Zhangjiajie, China (2020)

13. Adamopoulos, E., Bovero, A., Rinaudo, F.: Image-based metric heritage modeling in the near-infrared spectrum. Heritage Sci. **8**(1), 1–12 (2020). https://doi.org/10.1186/s40494-020-003 97-w

14. Lombardo, L., Parvis, M., Corbellini, S.: Environmental monitoring in the cultural heritage field. Eur. Phys. J Plus **134**(8), 411 (2019)

15. Short, M.: Assessing the impact of proposals for tall buildings on the built heritage: England's regional cities in the 21st century. Prog. Plan. **68**(3), 97–199 (2007)

16. Jiang, X.: Research on digital landscape information model construction based on BIM technology. Sichuan Cem. **312**(08), 79–81 (2022)

17. UNESCO: Cultural Landscapes: the Challenge of a Conservation, 1st edn., Ferrara–Italy, Paris (2002)

18. Swanwick, C.: Landscape Character Assessment Guidance for England and Scotland. Natural England, UK (2002)

19. Chen, Y.: Discussion on the heritage landscape information model. In: Proceedings of the 2016 Annual Meeting of the Chinese Society of Landscape Architecture, pp. 428–432. China Architecture & Building Press, Guangxi (2016)

20. DesignIntelligence Homepage. https://www.di.net/articles. Accessed 9 Aug 2023

21. Ervin, S.M.: Digital landscape modeling and visualization: a research agenda. Landsc. Urban Plan. **54**(1–4), 49–62 (2001)

22. Yali, C., Pingwei, D.: Water cultural heritage and folk belief. Nat. Art Stud. **31**(04), 15–122 (2018)

23. Council of Europe: European landscape Convention. Council of Europe, Florence (2000)

24. Zhigang, Y.: Research on Chinese Etiquette System, 1st edn. East China Normal University Press, Shanghai (2000)

25. Dong, W.: A study on aesthetic culture of traditional villages in Guangzhou Prefecture in Ming and Qing dynasties. Ph.D. thesis, South China University of Technology, Guangdong (2017)

26. Guangsi, Y.: 100 Teaching Lesson of the World Settlement, 1st edn. China State Construction Press, Beijing (2003)

27. Chaohong, T.: Research on Value Assessment and Protection of Water Cultural Heritage in Yongding River (Beijing Daxing Section). Beijing University of Civil Engineering and Architecture (2021)

28. Xiaotong, G., Chen, Y., Han, F.: Digital recording and conservation innovation of cultural landscape heritage. Chin. Gardens **36**(11), 84–89 (2020)

29. Ruda, G.: Rural buildings and environment. Landsc. Urban Plan. **41**(2), 32–33 (1998)

Design of a Multi-user Collaborative Innovation Digital Resource Library for Miao Embroidery

Guoying Chen[1,2], Honglei Mo[1], Cheng Yin[1(✉)], and Can Cheng[3]

[1] Liuzhou Institute of Technology, Liuzhou 545000, Guangxi, China
achilles_c@126.com
[2] Bansomdejchaopraya Rajabhat University, Bangkok 10600, Thailand
[3] Guangxi University of Science and Technology, Liuzhou 545000, Guangxi, China

Abstract. The aim of this paper is to explore the construction and operation mode of a multi-user collaborative innovation digital resource library for Miao embroidery, and to provide new ideas and references for the design of digital resource libraries for traditional handicrafts. The project first studies and analyses the current situation and development trend of traditional handicraft repositories, and addresses the current problems of high development costs, low user participation and unsustainable development, and innovatively proposes a multi-user collaborative innovation system framework for Miao embroidery repositories, which consists of a primary basic digital resource library and a secondary derived resources and services platform, and encourages service providers to jointly construct and manage. The system is designed to bind multiple types of users for interactive experience and user creation. The results show that the multi-user collaborative innovation model of Miao embroidery digital resource library can give full play to the superiorities of multi-user innovation cost and dissemination sharing, and can effectively interact with different users, which helps the construction and interactive dissemination of traditional handicraft digital resource libraries.

Keywords: Multi-user · Collaborative innovation · Miao embroidery · Digital resource library · Interaction design

1 Introduction

Throughout their history, the Miao people have migrated several times, influencing and integrating with neighbouring ethnic groups, forming their unique cultural and artistic style, presenting a "mixture of diversity" and "symbiotic and complementary" cultural temperament. The Miao embroidery is the physical carrier of their culture and aesthetic awareness, and is a representative item of China's national intangible cultural heritage.

In October 2003, UNESCO adopted the Convention for the Safeguarding of the Intangible Cultural Heritage. Intangible cultural heritage itself is fragile and needs the participation of all aspects of human society to protect it. Subsequently, a great deal of research has been carried out on the safeguarding of intangible cultural heritage, and theories such as productive safeguarding, holistic safeguarding and living heritage

© The Author(s), under exclusive license to Springer Nature Switzerland AG 2023
A. Marcus et al. (Eds.): HCII 2023, LNCS 14034, pp. 17–26, 2023.
https://doi.org/10.1007/978-3-031-35705-3_2

have been put forward. At the same time, the ever-changing digital technology has brought unprecedented opportunities for the preservation and multimedia presentation of intangible cultural heritage, and digitisation has become an inevitable choice for continuation and revitalisation of intangible cultural heritage in contemporary times.

2   Current Status of Digital Resource Library for Traditional Handicrafts in China

2.1   Digital Resource Library are an Effective Way to Preserve Intangible Cultural Heritage

Since China launched the intangible cultural heritage protection project in 2003, the local intangible cultural heritage protection departments have registered, classified and established relevant archives of the intangible cultural heritage projects through field investigation, data collection and museum collection. However, the traditional way of archives establishment is relatively "isolated", the correlation between the data is not close enough, and the content is not rich enough. Its main function is to retain and manage the relevant data, and the users are basically limited to researchers. Therefore, it does not facilitate the dissemination, inheritance and development of intangible cultural heritage.

With the rapid development and wide use of digital technology, the development of digital acquisition technology, storage technology, remote sensing technology and virtual space presentation technology has provided a realistic basis and more possibilities for the protection of different types of intangible cultural heritage. Digital resource library can maximize cultural and artistic resources that are difficult to integrate in physical space, through the centralization and unification of digital information technology, and protect resources in the maximum extent, and provide support for cultural inheritance, communication, and even creative transformation. It is an effective path of the activation and inheritance of intangible cultural heritage.

2.2   Necessity of the Construction of Miao Embroidery Digital Resource Library

As an intangible cultural heritage of traditional handicrafts, compared with other intangible cultural heritages, Miao embroidery skills are easier to integrate into contemporary people's life through creative transformation, and have the possibility of innovative demand and industrialization development. However, due to the scattered distribution of the Miao population areas and the lack of effective communication between various branches and regions, the establishment of the archives related to the Miao embroidery skills is relatively isolated, unable to effectively contact and sort out these archival materials, and the overall research and inheritance and protection are more difficult. At the same time, it will also lead to the difficulty in the integration of its resources, unable to effectively transform and utilize and industrialization development. Combined with the functional and technical characteristics of the intangible cultural heritage digital resource library, the construction of the Miao embroidery digital resource library will be able to solve the above problems very well.

Digital resource library can provide different regional range, different kinds of data collection analysis. In the process of digital protection of intangible cultural heritage, an integrated database is needed to support it, and to reasonably integrate, manage and call the digital information resources of Miao embroidery skills, so as to improve the work efficiency and effect of intangible cultural heritage protection.

2.3 Problem Analysis of Traditional Handicraft Digital Resource Library

Through the analysis of the current traditional handicraft digital resource library by research team, and observation from the construction mode, operation mode, interactive way, found that there are problems mainly in high development cost, single function, low user usage and participation. The causes of these problems are as follows:

At present, the construction subject of the traditional handicraft digital resource library is usually the government cultural management department, and the construction mode is the project contracting system, that is, the service provider mastering digital technology is entrusted to develop the digital resource library. As Party A, the government cultural management department usually simply lists the functions and technical requirements of the digital resource library from the cognitive level of cultural management, while as Party B, the service provider only needs to respond to the functions and technical requirements proposed by Party A, and rarely develops the actual requirements of the digital resource library.

This mode has not realized the effective linkage between cultural management departments in different regions, forming the situation of their respective construction and management. On the one hand, It is owing to the duplication of construction among different places, and the service providers only assume the role of technical services of the project, that leading to the development cost of digital resource library is high. On the other hand, the construction process of "top-down" and decision-making by external forces rarely considers the use needs of local people, and lacks the two-way interaction between digital resource library builders and users, the official and the people. The needs of inheritors, practitioners and ordinary people as well as the needs of marketization are not well considered, and there is a one-sided and simplification, resulting in a single function and weak interaction of digital resource library. On the other hand, after the construction of most digital resource library, they are only preserved as digital archives, lacking of effective operation management, unable to carry out good dissemination and industrial transformation, which is not conducive to play the characteristics and role of digital resource library.

3   Design of a Multi-user Collaborative Innovation Digital Resource Library for Miao Embroidery

3.1 Construction Concept

Collaborative innovation takes knowledge appreciation as the core, It promotes the government, enterprises, universities and other institutions to play their respective advantages, integration of complementary resources, and realize the complementary advantages, accelerate technology application and industrialization, collaboration in industrial technology innovation and industrialization of scientific and technological achievements. It is a new paradigm of scientific and technological innovation.

Combined with the analysis of the problem of traditional handicraft digital resource library, the team believes that Miao embroidery digital resource library should adhere to the construction concept that "open cooperation, collaborative innovation", break the barriers, promote the government culture management departments, enterprises, universities and research institutes, inheritance, or Miao embroidery craftsmen, design institutions and designers, and even the common people of user participation and cooperation, jointly play their respective role, realize the complementary resources, complementary advantages, We should construct and use Miao embroidery digital resource library and build a digital interactive sharing, collaborative innovation, promotion, trade reciprocity platform.

3.2 System Construction

Based on the above construction concept and solving the existing problems, this digital resource library is constructed in the form of a two-tier database, with the primary basic digital resource library containing the basic digital archives of Miao embroidery and other contents; the secondary derived resources and services platform expands the derivative digital creative resources, data service platform, application development platform, exhibition and display platform, interactive experience and dissemination and promotion platform, cultural and creative products transformation platform, trading platform, research and study service platform and other modules on the basis of the primary basic digital resource library. The implementation path for the construction of the digital resource library system is proposed in accordance with the process of "data collection - classification and collation (review) - introduction and interpretation - development and operation - experience and purchase - dissemination and sharing" (Fig. 1).

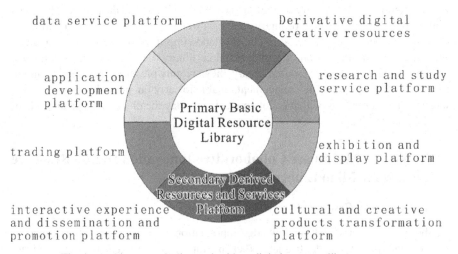

Fig. 1. Architecture of Miao embroidery digital resource library system.

Primary Basic Digital Resource Library. The primary basic digital resource library is the core module of the entire digital resource library, mainly used to store metadata information of Miao embroidery, and its basic function is similar to the traditional digital archive of intangible cultural heritage.

Data Collection and Classification. Data acquisition is the foundation of digital resource library construction. However, Owing to the multi-subjective sources of digital information of Miao embroidery, such as cultural management departments of governments at all levels, universities and research institutes, various archives, libraries and museums at all levels, as well as intangible cultural heritage inheritors. There are some problems in digital resources, such as inconsistent recording methods, scattered storage space, different logical modes of information storage, and heterogeneous data coding standards. Moreover, many data are scattered and have not been systematically sorted out.

Therefore, before the data collection of the primary basic digital resource library, the existing data need to be analyzed and sorted. Firstly, it is necessary to determine the data format and entry standard according to the functional requirements of the digital resource library and in combination with the analysis of the existing data information. Secondly, the data information needs to be sorted out and labeled accordingly, such as provenance, age, use, gender, applicable scenes, embroidery methods, patterns and other information. It is worth noting that the content of the data information may cross according to different classification standards, and the establishment of a scientific data storage and retrieval system is one of the core tasks in the construction of the digital resource library.

In addition, considering that the service provider needs to develop a Secondary Derived Resources and Services Platform based on the primary basic digital resource library at a later stage, the later development needs of service provider must be considered in the design of data structure (Table 1).

Table 1. Data Collection Classification Information Table of Primary Basic Digital Resource Library.

Provenance	Era	Use	Gender	Scenes of use	Embroidery method	Pattern
Entry based on actual origin	Entered according to actual age	Tops Trousers Skirts Back Fans Hats SHOES Waistbands	Male Female Neutral	Daily use Festivals Wedding	Flat embroidery Braid embroidery Drawstring embroidery Seed embroidery Yarn picking Patchwork Pile embroidery	Pendragon Flying Birds Butterfly Fish and shrimp Peony Pomegranate Peach blossom ......

After completing the above framework construction, we can start to enter new data. Data entry needs to follow the principle of convenience and modularity, to provide convenient data entry channels for different users. For example, researchers can collect data through fieldwork and enter it into the system; inheritors and collectors can enter data according to the system's instructions. When entering data, users can select the corresponding label for simple classification of data information, and then the data information can be formally entered into the digital resource library after being reviewed by the platform.

Introduction and Interpretation. At present, the digital protection of intangible cultural heritage has the phenomenon of that technology is more important than culture. However, in order to achieve effective dissemination and industrial application of digital resource library, it is necessary to do a good job in the construction of its cultural content. In addition to sorting out the data resources, managers should also make corresponding introduction and cultural interpretation of the data resources. This part should include the history and culture of the Miao nationality, the general overview of the Miao embroidery, and the detailed introduction of the specific classification content. The detailed introduction of the specific classification content can be modularized according to the label classification. After the data information enters the digital resource library, the management personnel need to confirm the data resource classification, and then link the introduction to the corresponding label or node location. If possible, the effect will be better if it is introduced with digital visual content demonstration.

Secondary Derived Resources and Services Platform. The secondary derived resources and services platform is the application port of the entire digital resource library. It will derive new digital creative resources based on the primary basic digital resource library, and form various service platforms based on the content of the repository. This is different from other digital resource libraries, and is also the key to the healthy and sustainable development of this digital resource library. If the digital resource Library is regarded as a big tree, the primary basic digital resource Library is the trunk of the big tree. The secondary derived resources and services platform will further enrich the digital resource library, spread branches and leaves on the main content of the primary basic digital resource library and bear fruit.

Development and Operation. The traditional intangible cultural heritage digital resource library is led by the government cultural management department, and service providers only participate in the construction of the project as technical service providers. The subsequent construction and operation and maintenance of the repositories need the continuous investment of the government cultural management departments, but this model is not conducive to the sustainable and healthy development of digital repositories. A mature digital resource library should be commercially operated by corporate capital and social forces. This digital resource library needs to be jointly led by service providers and government cultural management departments, and operated and developed by the service provider.

Currently, big data and artificial intelligence technologies are becoming more and more mature, Based on the development and application of the metadata of the Miao embroidery digital repositories and genetic algorithms, new digital creative content can be generated, bringing more possibilities for the operation and development of the digital resource library. Service providers can operate in the areas of digital interactive content development, intangible cultural heritage experience activities, study course development, handicraft and creative products sales, etc., and cooperate with data services and the concept of "metaverse", to form a complete digital creative system, thus achieving profitability.

This resource pool project will mobilize the enthusiasm of enterprises to participate, activate the hematopoietic function of the digital resource library, make the digital resource library develop healthily and sustainably, and promote the living inheritance of the intangible cultural heritage of Miao embroidery.

Experience Buying. In the era of digitalization and informatization, the interactive experience of digital resource library should make full use of advanced digital technology to present ideas, develop visual and dynamic experience content, and create an immersive scene interactive experience. Based on a clear interface hierarchy and good interaction design, a multi-layered, three-dimensional and coherent audience experience can be formed, which will lead to the purchase behaviour of users. At the same time, it can also combine the use of digital interaction technology and artificial intelligence technology, so that users can generate digital creative content in the interaction process, and provide cultural and creative product transformation services to enhance the user experience.

In addition, we should also use big data thinking, attach importance to the acquisition, management, analysis and improvement of information, and form an interactive experience neural network of Miao embroidery digital resource library based on data. While making use of advanced intelligent technology, through user-centered design and good user experience, we should help users to feel and understand the essence of Miao embroidery skills and culture, and help them carry out relevance-based learning and diversified interaction.

Spread the Word. The new features displayed by the information society have a wide and profound impact on people's attitudes, behavior habits, interpersonal interactions and ways of thinking. With the development of social media, users have become active information disseminators from passive information receivers, and mobile social networking has gradually become an important part of our daily lives. Users' dissemination and sharing can help digital repositories gain wide attention from social groups. Therefore, it is particularly important that the content of the platform is interesting and the sharing function is convenient. The multi-user collaborative and innovative construction model and interactive experience features help users to aggregate precisely, facilitate spontaneous sharing and community interaction, and form a fissile spread. The communication mode of "interaction, branding and mass distribution" is the key to the platform's growth and the promotion of the Miao embroidery technique and its cultural heritage. "Branding" is the recognition and protection of the intellectual property rights of the inheritors, and is also a measure to promote the value-added of intangible cultural heritage. The spread of "branding" will be beneficial to the building of intangible cultural heritage brands. "Segmentation" can be used to target different age groups and users with different needs, so that information can be disseminated accurately.

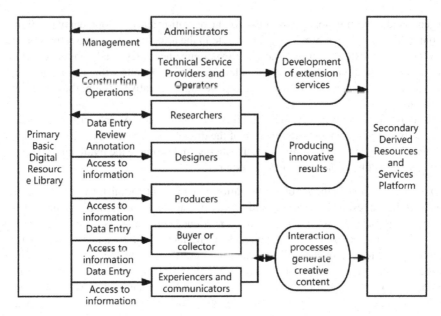

Fig. 2. Map of user roles in relation to the digital resource library.

3.3 Multi-user Role Positioning

Cultural Management Department. As the manager, the cultural management department is responsible for the construction and management of the primary basic digital resource library, To oversee the operation of the secondary derived resources and services platform (Fig. 2).

Service Providers. As the technical service provider and operator, the service provider is responsible for providing technical solutions and cooperating with the cultural management department to build and maintain the primary basic digital resource library, build and operate the secondary derived resources and services platform, and carry out commercial operations, such as trading platform, data service, application development, exhibition, dissemination, digital research, commercial transformation of cultural and creative products, etc.

Universities and Research Institutes. As researchers, universities and research institutes are responsible for the collation, review, classification of data resources, and the interpretation and introduction of cultural content, as well as the input of some data resources. It can also study, research and excavate the resources of the digital resource library, so as to realize the functions of talent training, scientific research, social service, cultural inheritance and innovation, and at the same time, achieve the purpose of knowledge innovation and value-added, and form scientific research results.

Inheritor or Miao Embroidery Craftsmen. As producers and collectors, inheritors or Miao embroidery craftsmen can upload original data resources, or upload and share

Miao embroidery handicraft products, which can be publicized and promoted through the platform to form transactions.

Design Agencies and Designers. As designers, design institutions and designers, can consult and obtain relevant information to facilitate innovative design, contact crafts-men for production through the platform, upload and share Miao embroidery creative products, promote and form transactions through the platform.

The Masses. As experiencers, disseminators and purchasers, the masses can experience, spread and share through the digital resource library and relevant activities organized by the operators, and can purchase relevant services and products.

4   Conclusion

In the era of information interconnection, digital resource library has become an inevitable choice for the protection of intangible cultural heritage. However, the digital resource library should not be a static and dusty archive, but a developing and open innovation platform. From the perspective of cultural inheritance, protection and innovation development, taking Miao embroidery as an example, this paper discusses the construction mode of Miao embroidery digital resource library for multi-user collaborative innovation, hoping to effectively integrate the resources of all parties, help the ancient handicraft of Miao embroidery to revive, carry forward its artistic charm, and inherit its cultural spirit.

Funding. Project to improve the basic research ability of young and middle-aged teachers in Guangxi universities "Research on the Application of Ethnic Minority Patterns in Film and Television Packaging in Northern Guangxi Region" (No. 2021KY1698); Guangxi Higher Education Undergraduate Teaching Reform Project "Research and Practice of Fabric Recreation and Innovative Application in the Perspective of Non-heritage Culture of Guangxi Ethnic Minority" (No. 2021JGZ183).

References

1. Jianghao, X., Huanian, W., Zhijun, W.: Construction of Xiangyu Nuo mask art database under the guidance of cultural creativity. Packag. Eng. **40**(24), 77–81 (2019). (in Chinese)
2. Qin, F.: Research on the digital survival and development of intangible cultural heritage (Doctoral dissertation, University of Science and Technology of China) (2017). (in Chinese)
3. Zhao, Y., Yaolin, Z.: Review of research on digital protection of international intangible cultural heritage. Library (8), 59–68 (2017). (in Chinese)
4. Liu, C., Lixin, Y.: Research review on digital protection of intangible cultural Heritage in China. Library **2**, 15–20 (2016). (in Chinese)
5. Weiling, Z.: Construction of the intangible cultural heritage database in the western ethnic minority areas based on the concept of "participatory digital protection" - Take the Ningxia region as an example. Libr. Theory Pract. (12), 110–114 (2016). (in Chinese)
6. Shanshan, Z., Xin, X., Yawei, S., et al.: Research on digital archive protection of intangible cultural heritage in the field of memory engineering. Books Intell. (4), 47–53 (2017). (in Chinese)

7. Ya, Z., Xin, X.: Review on the digital research of intangible cultural heritage. Libr. Inf. Work **61**(2), 6–15 (2017). (in Chinese)

8. Huanwen, C., Runhao, C., Peng, X.: Progress in the construction of library intangible cultural heritage database in the post-World Heritage Application era. Libr. Forum **38**(12), 1–7 (2018). (in Chinese)

9. Can, L.: Research on the archival management of the intangible cultural heritage of the folk art category. File Manage. (4), 70, 72 (2020). (in Chinese)

10. Duan, Z.: Analysis on the art characteristics of Miao nationality embroidery in Xiangxi. Art Time **3**, 71–74 (2010). (in Chinese)

11. Bingjie, Z., Yaqiong, Z., Jia, S.: Study on the art characteristics and digital inheritance of Miao ethnic clothing patterns. J. Jiamusi Univ. (Soc. Sci. Ed.) **39**(4), 162–165 (2021). (in Chinese)

12. Xiaochun, N., Rong, Z.: Thoughts on the construction of digital resource library of intangible cultural Heritage Archives. Arch. Commun. (02), 53–57 (2017). (in Chinese)

13. Liu, Y.: Application of digital technology in intangible cultural heritage protection. Mob. Inf. Syst. **2022**, 1–8 (2022)

14. Giannoulakis, S., Tsapatsoulis, N., Grammalidis, N.: Metadata for intangible cultural heritage. In: Proceedings of the 13th International Joint Conference on Computer Vision, Imaging and Computer Graphics Theory and Applications, pp. 634–645 (2018)

15. Wijesundara, C., Sugimoto, S.: Metadata model for organizing digital archives of tangible and intangible cultural heritage, and linking cultural heritage information in digital space. LIBRES: Libr. Inf. Sci. Res. Electron. J. **28**(2), 58–80 (2018)

Scenes, Interaction, Community and Values: A Service Experience Design Framework for Museum Public Space Based on the Theory of Experience Preference

Hailing Chen[1], Xiong Ding[1(✉)], and Lei Ding[2]

[1] Guangzhou Academy of Fine Arts, Guangzhou 510006, China
dingxiong@gzarts.edu.cn
[2] Guangdong Museum, Guangzhou 510623, China

Abstract. Focus on the development mode of museum public space service, exploring a sustainable service experience system and design strategy. This paper traces the origin and development of the theory of experience preference, and analyzes its concept, elements and application. Based on the summary of experience preference, audience needs and the status quo of museum public space, service design thinking is introduced to rebuild the internal correlation among the three. A "Scenes, Interaction, Community and Values (SICV)" service experience design framework of museum public space is established. This framework can build an open and social cultural service platform for the public space of museums. It is conducive to improving the audience's stereotype and evaluation of the museum's public space, promoting the "museum into the audience's life", and providing new ideas for the transformation and development of museums.

Keywords: Museum Public Space · Experience Preference Theory · SICV Framework · Service Experience Design

1 Introduction

In recent years, a surge in museum visits has occurred in China as a result of the dual influence of the rapid expansion of the cultural industry and the rise of people's spiritual and cultural needs. The conventional museum model has gradually been demolished, and museum's functions and values have shifted from cultural consumption centered on collection and display to activities and spatial experience. According to a survey of museum audience experience, many audiences experience "museum fatigue" when visiting exhibitions, resulting in audiences leaving after visiting exhibitions, and the lack of public space functions affects audience experience, which is not conducive to the transformation and development of museums. At the moment, domestic public space lacks an effective service system and strategy, and how to "integrate the museum into the audience's life" has emerged as the major issue to be addressed in the development of museums.

© The Author(s), under exclusive license to Springer Nature Switzerland AG 2023
A. Marcus et al. (Eds.): HCII 2023, LNCS 14034, pp. 27–39, 2023.
https://doi.org/10.1007/978-3-031-35705-3_3

In the user-led era, systematically incorporating experience design thinking and methods into the design of space, products, and service systems, as well as implementing all-around experience empowerment, will become an effective strategy for museums to gain decisive competitive advantages in transformation and upgrading [1]. This paper explains and defines the relevant concepts of museum public space, analyzes the development status of museums, the significance of combining public space and audience experience preferences, and the opportunity insight of intervention in audience service experience [2], and presents the research theme of this paper: the design strategy of museum public space service experience based on audience experience preference, and the construction of public space service experience that attaches importance to process and interaction. It is envisaged that this research proposal would contribute a microscopic viewpoint to the study of current museum public space architecture.

2 The Development Trend of Public Space Under the Transformation of Museums

Today's museums tend to be a place of experimentation and exploration of new opinions and ideas. Although we still frequently refer to the general public as "audience" in many museums operating under new models, this term is no longer appropriate. Instead, visitors are more accurately described as "experiencers of new wonders" "companions of new experiments" or "executors of new explorations" [3]. Scholarly research has identified six factors that influence visitors to museums: Interaction with others or social interaction, tendency to do meaningful activities, desire to stay in a comfortable and uninhibited environment, acceptance of new challenges and experiences, learning and research, and active participation in leisure behavior. Under such development demands, contemporary museums have become diversified places for education, leisure, entertainment and even the spirit of the public, and most of these non-exhibition activities occur in public spaces.

2.1 Definition of Public Space in Museums

"Public space" is an interdisciplinary concept, which scholars elaborate from the fields of architecture, sociology, museology. However simply opening the physical doors of museums cannot achieve a real sense of public space, and the study of museum public space must also need to pay attention to the physical and thinking space that can communicate with the public and produce consciousness. As a result, in this study, the "museum public space" in this study is defined as: the space accessible to the audience in addition to the exhibition and traffic space in the museum, which can provide the audience with a variety of services and carry out related public activities and exchanges, including audience behaviors such as rest, communication, consumption, and entertainment (As shown in Fig. 1, according to the division of museum areas and functional areas in the Architectural Design Collection) [4].

When the nature and concept of museums change, they will inevitably have an impact on new audiences, which may be classified into three categories. First, a single "viewing" is replaced by a pluralistic "experience"; Second, the enhancement of the sense of "exploration" that emphasizes personal participation means the transformation

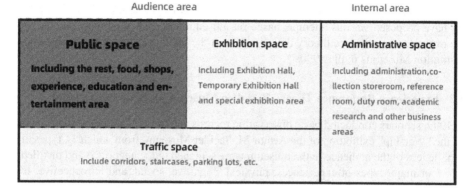

Fig. 1. The basic spatial composition of the museum and the research object of this paper

from passive to active, and obtains its own content, experience and results through one's own active thinking and behavior; Third, the nature of museum narratives has changed from a "publishing platform" to an "experimental field".

Museums have experienced a gradual evolution from "collection-centered" to "education-centered" and then to "audience-centered", How to play a good role, function and meet the needs of audiences has become a subject that every museum must think about [5]. Most museums are tangled up in genuine demands and pursue publicity and entertainment recklessly while investigating new methods of museum growth. Under such circumstances, public space, as the most direct window to the public, as a medium to trigger the public to carry out various activities in the museum [6], will inevitably face these issues, how to participate in shaping the audience's perspective and experience process, and building new relationships, new meanings and new experiences is a topic worth discussing.

Since the beginning of the 21st century, the traditional model of museum public space has been difficult to continue to suit the demands of museum operations and visitors. There are still significant issues with basic services in the public spaces of many museums in China. The Guangdong Provincial Museum has not designed its visiting routes and guidelines well, resulting in an issue where the audience is frequently confused about the route and does not know where to go, which is essentially a lack of consideration for the audience's visiting behavior. It can be noted that in the traditional museum-centered mode of exhibits, the public space only plays an auxiliary function to connect each space, showing the characteristics of a single function and monotonous space [7].

In the past, managers, operators and even designers have previously paid insufficient attention to public space, and the concept of "there is enough" has solidified the impression of public space to the audience, which is a lack of activities and leisure facilities, cookie-cutter memorial shops and a single simple catering area. For museum audiences, experience is the primary means of contacting museum knowledge. However, it is clear that most museums do not design the experience properly, and the lack of activities and services in the space reduces the experience of visitors, causing them to leave after the visit or even not to visit again. Therefore, creating a good experience is the ultimate goal of museum transformation, and it is also the top priority of public space design. Scholars have proposed various attempts based on museum audience experience, including the experience preference theory developed from the audience survey of Smithsonian Institution Museums in the 1990s.

2.2 Experience Preference Theory Based on Museum Audience Experience

In 1999, scholars conducted basic observation records and in-depth audience interviews on the "Worship" exhibition of the Arthur M. Sackler Museum, from which 14 types of experiences of the audience in the museum were screened out, categorized and distilled into four major types of experiences: physical, cognitive, social, and introspective. In the course of his long research interviews, Pekarik observed the existence of audience experience expectations, which led to the suggestion that the audience's museum experience is closely related to personal preferences. Subsequently, based on the results of audience research between 1999 and 2014, Pekarik and other scholars proposed the experience preference theory (IPOP theory) in 2014 [8], which classifies audience interests according to individual preferences, including ideas, people, objects and physical, and the primary research purpose is to provide museum audiences with better, unique and meaningful memorable museum services and experiences.

The IPOP theory developed by the museology field, has been extended to many aspects of museum exhibition design, renovation and audience evaluation. In China, however, this theory is still in its infancy, with scanty research and application. Peng Leiting (2020), Dean of the Field of Museum and Public Cultural Services at Wuhan University, pointed out in "Research on Optimizing Museum Audience Experience Service in China Based on IPOP Theory" [9] that the application of IPOP theory to museum audience service is an important attempt for museums to improve experience services. It is evident that the public space of the museum is not an independent individual, but is closely related to other aspects of the museum, and the experience of the audience is inseparable from the services in the museum space.

Among them, in the field of service, the audience experience becomes the design goal, the audience participates in the process of museum service transmission, can actively accept the services provided by the museum, so as to provide a unique experience, and is regarded as experience. So the museum public space should begin with the audience's point of view, attempting to shift from space construction thinking to user experience design, changing the audience's cognitive expectations, and providing a free and open leisure and cultural space where people can communicate and appreciate history and culture in harmony and happiness. The integration of heritage allows the audience to change from passive visitors to active participants in the space.

3 Insights into Opportunities to Intervene in the Audience Service Experience

In the context of interdisciplinary cross-fertilization, service design, as an emerging disciplinary way of thinking, is a design initiative to enhance the efficiency, experience and value of services by connecting multiple stakeholders in a user-centered manner, thus achieving systemic innovation in service delivery, processes and touchpoints. It focuses on the entire user experience process and employs applicable design methodologies to investigate user's true demands, which aligns with the objective of audience experience preference. Through the intervention of service design thinking, the service experience system in museum public space is considered. It is easy to see that with the transformation of museums, the needs of visitors have gradually changed, and active participation, exploration and co-creation have become the core motivation. How to provide visitors with the information they are interested in and how to meet their changing needs for offline experiences and online personalities are all factors that museums are considering. The composition of the scene area, the feasibility of equipment interaction, the communication of the circle, and the achievement of self-satisfaction are all service criteria that audiences are concerned about.

3.1 Building a New Service Perception: The Palace Museum

The evolution of the Forbidden City from "one man dominating the world" to the National Palace Museum, which attracts millions of visitors, exemplifies the enormous shift from imperial power to public service. How to interpret spatial relationships while bringing a new experience to the audience has become a challenge for the museum.

In recent years, the Palace has enhanced its service facilities while preserving its historic foundation, repairing seats and renewing palace lamps to suit the most basic rest demands of visitors. At the same time, additional dining and leisure space, such as the abandoned for many years "ice cellar" reuse, a creative method to convert it into a unique museum restaurant (Fig. 2). Whereas museums used to be more concerned with the exhibition halls, the public spaces through which visitors pass are now being given new significance. One such presence is the "Forbidden Academy" in the Forbidden City. The new academy model bridges the gap between the audience, culture, and space by combining conventional academy functions with modern cultural needs. At the same time, it promotes the recognition and satisfaction of groups with common interests in such a specific cultural context, giving the public space a new life and vitality. The Forbidden City in the new era can be said to build up a leisure lifestyle for the audience to spend their time.

3.2 Provide Multiple Experience Scenes: Nanjing Museum

The Nanjing Museum enjoys the reputation of being one of the "Top Three Museums in China" and has a distinctive overall layout of "one courtyard with six pavilions", namely the History Pavilion, the Special Pavilion, the Digital Pavilion, the Art Pavilion, the Non-Foreign Heritage Pavilion and the Republic of China Pavilion. In addition to the basic pavilions, there are several cultural and creative stores, providing visitors with a rich selection of cultural and creative products, Jiangsu specialties and non-foreign heritage souvenirs; at the same time, there are dessert stores, tea houses and cafes to meet the rich and diverse catering needs, and the reasonable and diverse scenes are of reference for the construction of other museums.

The immersive experience scenes of multiple venues are built to make the audience empathize with the exhibition and increase their stickiness. For example, the audience can

Fig. 2. The Palace Museum ice cellar leisure space

get close to the interaction with the non-hereditary inheritors, changing the impression of "treasures hidden in a glass enclosure" and experiencing the unique charm of the non-heritage products; for example, the regular performances of the Suzhou Folk Opera and Folding Opera, which exquisitely demonstrate the charm of non-heritage and give the audience the motivation to go there.

3.3 Enhancing the Interactive Experience of Visitors: Suzhou Museum

Situated in a classical garden, the Suzhou Museum, under the masterful work of the famous architect I.M. Pei, effectively blends the public and private spaces of modern architecture, preserving the design of the traditional Jiangnan dwelling group, making it an ideal place for local citizens to relax after tea and dinner. With its unique gardens and Soviet-style architecture, the museum attempts to use the public space to interact with its visitors intimately. Not only is the interactive installation "Water Screen": shaped as a ring of woolen glass (Fig. 3), cleverly set up to echo the exhibition, providing a variety of painting tools for visitors to freely create their painting screen, while allowing visitors to appreciate the audience created within the water screen, the cultural atmosphere is easily perceived; it also provides an official punch line, dividing the museum's public space into several scenic scenes on the public number It also provides an official punching guide, dividing the museum's public space into scenic scenes, showing the appropriate time, scenes, props and poses, guiding visitors to go to the photo experience according to the punching guide, integrating the cultural atmosphere of the museum's public space and playing an unexpected role.

3.4 A "Museum-Style" Consumer Space: Starbucks Workshop

In the era of the experience economy, branded "museum-style" consumer spaces [9] have gradually developed into a popular spot among young people, and compared with other

Fig. 3. Suzhou Museum "Water Screen" interactive installation

types of spaces, "museum-style" consumer spaces are more likely to meet people's demand for self-fulfillment and differentiation. In order to allow consumers to spend more time in their own spaces, some nodes are set up for the audience to interact and experience, spreading culture with the concept of "fun and education". For example, the Starbucks Select Roastery in Shanghai is a "museum-style" workshop that uses the coffee production line as a narrative display (Fig. 4). The display wall records the history of Starbucks and introduces the origin of the coffee beans, and the mobile service staff in the space acts like a museum docent to introduce the specific functions of each small scene in the space. Consumers learn about coffee and the Starbucks brand culture during their visit and experience. As advertised, it is a museum that educates consumers about the roasting process and coffee knowledge, so that consumers can have a pleasant experience in the brand's "museum-like" consumer space, whether they are engaged in consumer or non-consumer activities, consumers can have a pleasant experience in the brand's "museum-style" consumer space.

Although today's museum concept quietly places the needs of the audience first, how to meet their diverse needs in the space and recognize the role of museum public space in promoting social functions and values that cannot be ignored are still issues that need to be explored and practiced.

Fig. 4. Shanghai Starbucks "museum-style" space

4   SICV Service Experience Design Framework for Museum Public Space

Based on the above theoretical overview and case studies, it is easy to see that the process of visiting a museum is a multi-dimensional interactive experience, which fully integrates the spatial environment atmosphere, personal perception communication and human-computer interaction experience, and the transformation from spatial construction to audience perception emphasizes the importance of experience. Specifically, the real reason why visitors go to museums is to develop a diverse perception of the museum experience driven by different factors. This is precisely the result of the Smithsonian's study of museum visitors, which discovered a strong correlation between visitor's personal preferences and their experiences at museums. Therefore, using the idea of experience preference as an analytical framework, this study investigates the design strategies and paths of museum public space as a design object from the perspective of the observer.

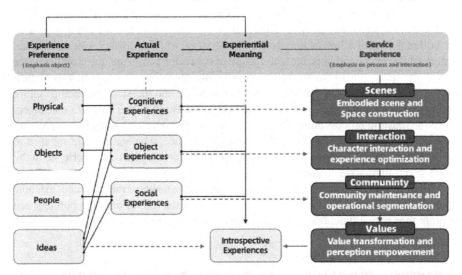

Fig. 5.   A service experience design framework for museum public space

In essence, museums are settings that provide "experiences" and ought to provide visitors with a range of emotional encounters [10]. From the analysis of the audience's focus, it is verified that they pay more attention to the four elements of the scene, interaction, community and value in the museum public space service experience. The framework of the museum public space service experience is produced after refinement based on the exploration of experience preference theory because the audience places more emphasis on the process and interactive transformation of the museum public space service experience than experience preference does (Fig. 5).

4.1 Museum Embodied Scene and Space Construction

According to the theory of museum experience preference, "Physical" emphasizes the formation of various senses through the five senses, while embodied cognition explores the generation of cognition in the trinity of body, brain and environment, which is consistent with the communication goal of museums that emphasize the generation of cognition through multiple senses in the space. Since the audience's experience in the museum space cannot be separated from the multi-sensory channels provided by the body, it is necessary to combine different scenes in the museum to form a multifaceted, flowing "flexible" space and set up reasonable flow and interaction areas, using partitions, steps, lighting and contrasting color signs to guide; for the virtual environment The design of the interface information elements for the virtual environment [11]; to meet the diverse experience needs of leisure and entertainment, dining and shopping, learning, etc., extends the leisure scenes of the audience in the museum in addition to the exhibition, and can attract more visitors to "enter the museum".

In the era of the experience economy, spatial scenes have added value. Based on museum research and user study to discover the gap in scenes, find suitable service scenes, construct and design reasonable consumption patterns, scenes combination schemes, improve audience satisfaction and recognition of the museum, and maximize the benefits of scene integration [12]. In addition to setting up relevant interactive communication scene nodes in the space, it is also possible to make full use of online scenes to build a platform for immediate audience communication and develop audience grouping links.

The physical communication of user groups in a meaningful "common scenario" will "awaken" user's perceptions, behaviors and emotions with spatial power and atmosphere, and users, products, spaces and services in the common scenario will empower each other in a The users, products, spaces and services in the common scenario will empower each other in an "in-body" way [1].

4.2 Character Interaction and Experience Optimization

The "Objects" in museum experience preference theory emphasizes the audience's desire for the aesthetics, craftsmanship, or visual language of the object itself, and through the use of interactive technology, the audience can interact effectively with the physical touch points of the museum public space, with the core goal of enhancing the immersive interactive experience of the audience and stimulating their interest and experience. A new interaction design concept often requires redefining participants, locating behavioral motives, planning behavioral processes, seeking new means, and creating new scenarios and environments [13]. The "4E theory" [14] points out that interactive experiences are multiple in nature, and different experiences bring different perceptions of value to the audience, and for museum public spaces, the audience places more emphasis on leisure and entertainment, and individual active participation in the experience. It should be emphasized that the interaction of the public space and the interaction of the exhibition hall are inseparable and should not be separated from each other, therefore, in the process of designing the corresponding interactive experience, the connection should be fully considered.

Unlike the previous museum experience, the audience is increasingly concerned about participation and accessibility, and should appropriately lower the threshold of experience, and enrich the experience scene and interactive play, so that the audience can pursue cultural experience in the form of lively and interesting activities, and eventually form a more profound memory experience.

The interactive process of existing museum exhibitions is usually designed with relevant VR and audiovisual interactive equipment and corresponding guidance staff to ensure that visitors can receive information in the act of interaction. It is worth mentioning that due to the advancement of technology and the hindrance of the epidemic, more and more museums are trying to explore online interactive experiences, as reflected in the dissemination and marketing of content such as metaverse digital collections and the application of digital exhibition halls. From the perspective constructed in this paper, the corresponding optimization of character interaction behavior and experience activities should also be built in each scene of public space, helping the audience integrate into the scene space to obtain a new perceptual experience beyond the exhibition, no longer limited to the design of offline scene interactive experience, and should enhance the audience's immersive "depth" experience under the premise of ensuring the basic service experience.

4.3   Community Maintenance and Operational Segmentation

The "People" aspect of museum experience preference theory emphasizes interpersonal relationships, emotional experiences, and the appeal of socialization to the audience, it focuses on the "sociality" of museums, which reflects that museums are not only places for exhibitions and collections, but also places for dialogue. It is a place where visitors can engage in cultural exchange and interaction with others, where each visitor is both a recipient and a transmitter of information about the museum's culture [15], and where culture is transmitted to foster community connections. Finding, linking, penetrating, and serving the community are the four elements of developing community relations in museums, and are an important way to shape the image of museums, as well as an effective connection point to expand museum boundaries and reach out to the community [16]. By exploring different needs through audience segmentation and then creating scenarios that fit together, audiences can develop deep emotional resonance and thus achieve increased stickiness. Some scholars point out that targeted "pan-social services" can be provided to different levels of viewers according to the user's knowledge structure, including interest-based social and professional social services [17]. Other scholars proposed the initiative of "scenario-based community operation" through "improvised social actions" [18], pointing out that while designing product and retail services, the brand culture and brand value construction of the services must be fully considered, and a system that conforms to the brand culture and fits with the inner pursuit of the target consumers must be established. It is pointed out that while designing product retail services, the brand culture and brand value construction of services must be fully considered, and a systematic service value system that conforms to the brand culture and matches the inner pursuit of consumers must be established, so as to enhance user's recognition of the brand and their participation in the brand community. And through online and offline improvised social actions, we can raise the emotional curve of users and guide them to experience the completion of goals to gain a sense of belonging and accomplishment. The operation and segmentation of the online community is to accurately identify the needs of users, and then plan, organize and push relevant information and activities, linking the audience with the audience, penetrating the museum culture into the audience's daily life, and thus developing a long-term community culture.

Whether it is pan-social or improvised social, it can be said to gather audiences by tapping into points of interest, not only to broaden the contact channels and stickiness between audiences and museums, but also to promote the dissemination of museum cultural values. In conclusion, the social nature of groups should be fully considered in the service experience of museum public space, so that museum culture can subconsciously penetrate into user's lives, connect the various channels between the audience and the museum, enhance the audience's stickiness to the museum, make them achieve cultural loyalty, and then attract more groups to know and understand the museum circle culture.

4.4 Value Transformation and Perception Empowerment

In museum experience preference theory, "Ideas" emphasizes the audience's interest in perceiving and forming a sense of belonging from a museum visit. As a term of focus and research in various disciplines, value by definition refers to the potential driving force behind the pursuit of something or a behavior. In this concept, experiential value perception can be understood as the value perception that the audience perceives from the experiential activities set up in the museum process, with the promotion and advancement of the museum culture concept as the core, which depends on the audience's subjective feelings, in the whole process of experience, sensory experience, scene feeling, discursive experience, emotional interaction, etc. may become the core elements affecting the audience's experiential value perception.

From the viewer's perceived value of museums, they attach more importance to the leisure experience value and place value of museums. The transformation of the museum's public space has led to the transformation of its functional and cultural values, and at the same time to a change in the audience's perception of the museum's role. Values, on the one hand, influence life goals and principles of life choices, and on the other hand, they change as individuals grow in their experiences [19]. Guiding museum design through values is a new attempt.

How cultural institutions of the museum type can reconnect with the public and demonstrate their value and relevance in contemporary life can, in a sense, be achieved by inviting the public to actively participate as cultural participants rather than passive consumers. The public wants to be able to discuss, share and remix what they consume. When the public can actively participate in cultural institutions and construct their own ideas of meaning from cultural experiences, museums become central to the activation of culture and community.

To sum up, museum public space design strategies focused on audience service experience can effectively promote value conversion among museums, and reasonable and sustainable strategic models provide practical guidance for the development of museum public spaces. The public service space of museums provides an invisible space for cultural exchange, and even becomes a popular mode of cultural exchange nowadays, providing rich cultural raw materials for people's dreams, behaviors and identities.

5   Conclusion

By providing qualitative analyses of the service experience of visitors in museum public spaces based on the experience preference theory in museology in the context of service design thinking, this paper adopts an interdisciplinary research approach to derive the SICV service experience design framework for museum public spaces. The framework can offer museums practical, exact recommendations on how to address visitor's requirements through scenarios, interactions, and communities, boosting visitor's perceptions of museum's worth and having repercussions for the modernization of conventional museums. It is worth noting, however, that this framework is still in its initial stages of exploration, and that differences in type, space, and audience size will affect the design of the corresponding solutions, which should be appropriately adjusted and optimized according to the museum's own conditions and development strategies. Museums are constantly updating and iterating to better respond to the times, and their subsequent operation and implementation still require collaborative innovation and joint efforts of multiple stakeholders, including museum institutions, supply chains, staff and audiences, to develop appropriate service experiences that will attract more attention and reshape the sense of museum public space experience. The exploration of this experience will give the public greater access and space to explore the culture of transmission and creation, strengthen pride in culture, and lead museum culture to new horizons.

Acknowledgment. This paper is supported by the 13th Five-Year Plan of Guangdong Education Science, which is "Research on the construction of knowledge system and teaching practice of service design under the interdisciplinary background (2020GXJK325)".

References

1. Lili, Y., Xiangyang, X.: A study of empowerment strategies driven by experience design: an example of Oodi library design. Zhuangshi **6**, 116–120 (2020)
2. Zidong, H.: Research on the Design Strategy of Contemporary Museum Public Space Based on the Analysis of Audience Behavior Pattern. Shenzhen University, Shenzhen (2020)
3. Degeng, L.: Mobile Museum. Culture and Art Publishing House, Beijing (2022)
4. Lu, D.: Planning and design of museum public space in the context of digitalization. Intell. Build. Smart City **10**, 24–26 (2019)
5. Siyi, W.: The development and practice of museum audience research: a case study of the audience survey of Wuxing Fu in Huzhou Museum. Sci. Popularization Res. **12**(01), 48–58 (2017)
6. Li, L., Xinyi, Y.: Research on the design strategy of museum public space that catalyzes daily activities. Contemp. Archit. **09**, 51–53 (2020)
7. Junjie, X.: Research on the Design of Contemporary Museum Traffic Space Polysemy. Harbin Institute of Technology, Harbin (2015)
8. Leiting, P., Wanna, L.: Research on optimizing museum visitor experience services in China based on IPOP theory. Chin. Mus. **03**, 68–74 (2020)
9. Xiaoyu, W., Longyuan, X.: Pan-Museum phenomenon: a new presentation of the social value of museums. In: China Museum Association Professional Committee of Museology. Proceedings of the 2016 Symposium on Social Value of Museums of the Professional Committee of Museology of China Museum Association (2016)

10. Zahava, D., Kai, Y., Siyi, W.: Stranger, guest or patron: visitor experience in museums. Sci. Educ. Mus. **3**(01), 59–66 (2017)
11. Cuiting, K., Husheng, P., Lie, Z.: Research on somatic interaction design of museums from the perspective of embodied cognition. Zhuangshi **03**, 90–93 (2020)
12. Yuchuan, X.: Research on New Retail Service Design Strategy Based on Scene Theory. Jiangnan University, Wuxi (2020)
13. Xiangyang, X.: Interaction design: from physical logic to behavioral logic. Zhuangshi **01**, 58–62 (2015)
14. Pine, B.J., Gilmore, J.H.: The Experience Economy. Machinery Industry Press, Beijing (2016)
15. Jixiang, S.: Re-discussing the museum public. Chin. Mus. **03**, 12–19 (2018)
16. Boya, L.: Pluralism and tolerance: a review of the relationship between museums and communities and communities in the context of harmony and sameness. Chin. Mus. **02**, 22–26 (2020)
17. Jun, L., Fengling, L.: Research on the design of Internet+ museum public services based on role cognition: taking the Palace Museum as an example. Zhuangshi **11**, 118–119 (2017)
18. Xiong, D., Qiaoling, Y., Hepeng, J.: Research on retail service design of winter Olympic cultural and creative products under BPC scenario architecture. Packag. Eng. **43**(06), 322–328 (2022)
19. Xiangyang, X.: The butterfly effect of design: When lifestyles become design objects. Packag. Eng. **41**(06), 57–66 (2020)

The Penta Model of Flow Experience: A Study on Service Design of Duan Inkstone Art Exhibition in Guangdong Museum

Xiong Ding[✉] and Hepeng Ji

Guangzhou Academy of Fine Arts, Guangzhou 510006, China
dingxiong@gzarts.edu.cn

Abstract. Under the transformation background of the social function from "research centers" to "education centers", museums around the world try to take public education as an important function, provide public services to the society, and the participation of the people is also unprecedented. However, there is still no clear design process and method for the public education service of museums. They facing the problems of single activity form, insufficient audience attraction, and low age education content, there is still a certain degree of "emphasis on exhibition, light on education". This study introduces the flow theory, discusses, refines and expands the basic elements of the museum's public education services that facilitate the audience or users to obtain the flow experience, reorders and constructs the "Penta Model" of flow experience in museum's public education services. Through exhibition planning, experience content, and educational games, the audience is promoted in the five flow stages of goal, challenge, integration, feedback and ability, and then gradually enter the flow status, so as to realize the purpose of the museum's immersive education service. Taking the service design of Duan Inkstone Art Exhibition in Guangdong Museum which named "Guanyan" as an example, the design verification of "Penta Model" of flow experience was carried out. Through value proposition design, service system construction, exhibition journey planning and service touchpoints design (display of the exhibition, offline experience activities, online education games), the five flow status are organically integrated into each link, including the theme atmosphere and display method of the exhibition, process and interactive of viewing, in order to meet the audience's dual needs for knowledge and entertainment. The design practice shows that the museum public education service designed based on the "Penta Model" of flow experience provides the audience with more attractive educational content and experience methods, and also provides new ideas and methods for the relevant functional departments of the museum.

Keywords: Museum · Service Design · Flow · Penta Model · Duan Inkstone Art Exhibition

A. Marcus et al. (Eds.): HCII 2023, LNCS 14034, pp. 40–57, 2023.
https://doi.org/10.1007/978-3-031-35705-3_4

1   Introduction

At the 21st Annual Conference of the International Council of Museums (ICOM) in 2007, the definition of a museum was revised as "museum open to the public for the purpose of public education, research of cultural objects and spread of culture, and the preservation, study, communication and presentation of the tangible and intangible cultural heritage of humanity" [1]. In this definition, "education" replaced "research" as the primary function of museums. Museums began to become the center of public education instead of the social research [2]. With the free museums and the enhanced education level of the general public, museums have become the main destination for recreation and learning, a "second classroom" for people to receive lifelong learning with an unprecedented level of participation. This has placed a high demand on the innovation of public education activities and services provided by museums in China.

Museum education is about launching teaching activities based on the museum objects in a museum, aiming to support the development of visitors (learners) [3]. Compared with foreign museums, domestic museums still fall behind which can be reflected in: a) Emphasis on exhibitions but not on education; b) The content of education is too easy or too professional which could not relate to the public education; c) Single form cannot meet diversified spiritual demands of the audience, and is not attractive enough. Specifically thinking, the current public education activities of museums in China basically consider edutainment (teaching through lively activities) as the goal, focusing on audience's pleasant visiting experience, comprehensive education and development. However, during the implementation, the entertainment, instead of the education, is often taken as a more important purpose, leading to the fact that museum ignores its education calling but only emphasis on its entertainment role. [4] In terms of the content design, the current domestic museum public education services (hereinafter referred to as MPES) show two extremes: under-aged and too professional. The latter one is far away from people's real life and audience can not apply what they have learned, thus affecting the effectiveness of public education. When it comes to the participants who served by museum public education, they come here out of their own interest on cultural relics and culture itself and have active motivation and interactive needs. In the past, most MPES have adopted a static approach, such as knowledge courses, heritage exhibitions, etc., where the audience are the only passive recipients. However, audience are more interested in dynamic forms in the current stage and they pay more attention to the interaction with the equipment, staff, or even cultural relics [5].

Under this background, this paper introduces the Flow Theory into the experience research of MPES, explores the possibility of obtaining flow experiences in MPES, and tries to construct a theoretical model of MPES on this basis, so as to provide guidance and reference for museums to make relevant public education services arrangement in the future.

2   Flow Experience Theory

When people concentrate their mind and devote all their energy to a certain activity, they will achieve a state of deep immersion which is called flow [6]. Mihaly Czikszentmihalyi, an American psychologist, proposed the flow theory. Based on the difficulty of the challenge and individual abilities, he classified the possible emotional and psychological states of people during the activity into eight categories: annoyance, worry, indifference, boredom, ease, control, flow, and inspiration. He also argues that nine elements are needed for flow experience: clear goals, timely feedback, balance between challenge and skill, integration of behavior and awareness, elimination of distractions from awareness, fearlessness of failure, loss of self-consciousness, ignorance of the time passage, and focus on the value of the activity itself [7]. During the state of flow, people are in a positive mental state and exclude all irrelevant emotions and thoughts. The immersive experience brought by complete concentration is an optimal experience [8]. And the elements that are needed to build an optimal flow experience include challenging activities that require skills, integration of action and awareness, clear goals and feedback, focus on the task at hand, mastery, loss of self-awareness, and loss of concept of time.

There have been various ideas on how flow arises. Schiefele states in his research that flow is a psychological experience that formed by the sole element [9]. Remy agrees with this view in his research and believes that flow is a state of experience that arises from the unification of behavior and thought. During this state, complete concentration, loss of time concept and other phenomenon will appear [10]. Rheinberg, Vollmeyer, and Engeser argue that the formation of flow consists of two elements, namely mental concentration and smooth operation. They also believe that the mental power of concentration is a more important condition [11]. Bakker hold the idea that three conditions are required to form flow: mental concentration, curiosity, and initiative, and he considers mental concentration and curiosity to be the two most important conditions [12]. On this basis, Engeser then changed the factors affecting the construction of flow from three to five: experiencing the goal, matching the thought with the behavior, mental concentration, ignoring one's own senses, and grasping the goal, and believed that the most important element was mental concentration. In conclusion, mental concentration is considered to be the main factor to form flow, whether it is a single condition or multiple conditions.

Flow theory can be applied to many fields from sports, art, work to human-computer interaction, games, and education. The current research on the application of flow theory is concentrated in public education, game design and addiction research [13]. a) The application of flow theory in public education can complement existing public education methods and approaches, promoting public education to a wider range of people to meet public expectations and enhance their interests and motivation. This can provide good experience for public and expand the design methods of public education services so as to drive new development of public education in China. b) In the field of game design, by studying the generation process of flow experience, it is integrated into the design of game's plot, levels and music to guide players to gradually form flow channels, gain flow experience and enjoy the game. c) When it comes to the addiction research, mobile phone addiction has become the focus for most psychologists. Studies show that an important manifestation of mobile phone addiction is the flow status [14]. It is worth thinking and paying attention to how to make good use of flow theory to reduce the social problem of mobile phone addiction.

3   The Construction of Penta-Model of Flow Experience in MPES

Since flow theory has been proposed, it has been considered as a way to enhance user experience and widely applied into game industry. The reason is that the three basic elements of the flow experience: goal, feedback and challenges that can match skills, which originally proposed by Czikszentmihalyi, can be perfectly implemented in games, especially online games (both PC and mobile). It is fair to say that game itself has these three elements naturally. Thus, game can fit in with flow theory. With the explosion of online games, educational games are getting more attention. Compared with ordinary games, the key of educational games is not to let players get the fun of it, but to learn by playing. The process of learning is a pleasant experience for learners [15]. However, as purposes are different, educational games could not attract players quickly. The reasons are as follows: First is about feedback. Most of the current educational games are in the QA form, which is a one-way and sluggish feedback. Different from the two-way interaction of internet games, educational games could not attract learner's attention in a long run and could not let people enter the flow experience; Second is about scenario. Not like ordinary games, the focus of education games is about delivering the knowledge, and unfortunately, it is the only thing that the current educational games can do. They ignore the point that whether learners can really receive the knowledge. In other words, the construction of education scenario (knowledge delivering and receiving) is not complete.

From another perspective, launching educational games with museum as the basic resources has its own advantages. Firstly, museums have rich collections which have extensive cultural objects and knowledge to share with the general public. The digital resource pool of cultural objects in recent years can be considered as the source of qualified education content. Secondly, museums are the right place for educational games. Learners can verify the knowledge based on the real objects they see in the real scenario. Besides, the combination of online and offline channels can enable the receiving of knowledge in practice. As for the public education services of museums, exhibitions, educational games and public education activities are the things audience can experience. And the physical exhibition can integrate games, activities and content into the same scenario, which is main character of flow and thus provide public education services that audience can experience in a deep way.

With the demands of MPES in mind, the author introduces the theory of flow to explore, refine and expand the basic elements that contribute to the flow experience of visitors or users in MPES, and reorder and build the Penta-model of flow experience in MPES. Through exhibition planning, experience content and educational games, audience can gradually experience 5 stages of flow from goals, challenges, integration, feedback to competencies, and finally enter the flow status. This can achieve the goal of immersive education services of museums. Penta-model has two parts. First, the five corners indict five stages of flow of MPES: goals, challenges, integration, feedback, and competences. Compared with the three basic elements that proposed by Czikszentmihalyi, Penta-model added challenges and integration, and clarifying the sequence based on the visiting and experience procedure of audience. The progressive relationship can be witnessed among five stages of flow which run through the whole process of user experience. Second, a flow status exists between each of the two adjacent flow stages, namely user attraction, user involvement, human-computer/objects interaction, content acquisition, and value co-creation. The dimensions of the flow status are quite abstract which describe the feelings of flow experience to some extent, implying how audience switch among these five flow stages (Fig. 1). User attraction, user involvement and value co-creation are derived from marketing and customer inclusion theory.

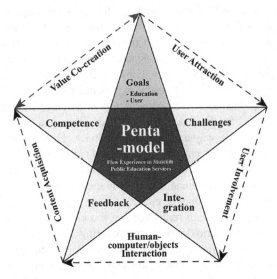

Fig. 1. Penta-model of flow experience in MPES

3.1 Goals and User Attraction

The goal of MPES have two layers. First is the education goal of service provider, and the second is the goal of service recipients. These two goals are different but are not contradicting with each other. The education goal of museums is to provide visitors with quality and in-depth public education services to promote and achieve enhanced national literacy. The goal of the user, i.e., audience, is to learn about cultural relics and historical knowledge, to be surprised and have a satisfying visiting experience. As for these two goals, educational goal is the result and user goal is the process, which is a cause-and-effect relationship.

Along with the goal, the flow status of audience is user attraction, which sourced from the customer attraction in marketing theory. It says if customers do not have experience on a certain product, store or environment, they may use their perception of image to gauge the quality of goods and services, including price range, product selection and variety, store layout, and environmental features that may trigger emotional responses from customers [16]. In MPES, user attraction relies on two main parts. The primary condition is audience's perception of the exhibition environment, and the second is the attraction of the viewing goal, and the goal is not imposed on the audience by the museum, but the interest and motivation that arise naturally from their perception of the environment. Therefore, the setting of user's goals must be clear, perceptible, and achievable. When audience are attracted by the goals, the first step of the flow experience begins.

3.2 Challenges and User Involvement

Generally speaking, providing challenges that can match visitors' competences and skills is an effective way to enhance participation. When the difficulty of the challenge is greater than the visitor's ability, the visitor will be anxious. When the difficulty of the challenge is less than the visitor's ability, the visitor will be bored. Both anxiety and boredom will prevent visitors from entering the state of flow, so the setting of challenge difficulty is particularly important.

In MPES, the definition of audience competence has changed. Instead of referring to an individual's comprehensive ability, it is more about achieving a balance between challenge and knowledge of the exhibition content by taking the audience's knowledge of the exhibition content as the standard. Due to the wide range of audience, the difficulty of challenges in public education services could not be set at a single level and need to be graded. The difficulty is not unchanged throughout the process, and should be gradually increased as the exhibition viewing process going.

During the challenge stage, the audience's flow status shifts from user attraction to user involvement. Involvement refers to the degree of participation of customers in marketing activities, which can influence customers' decision-making and communication behavior [17]. From user attraction to user involvement, audience are no longer the passive recipients but active participants. In addition to the visual stimulation of environment, the methods applied include stimulating visitors' desire to explore and fully concentrate on them through specific challenges, thus achieving the status of user involvement.

3.3 Integration and Human-Computer/Objects Interaction

When people reflect on their flow experience, they always mention the following features: fully concentrate, time passes quickly and immerse in their own world. During flow experience, people can fully concentrate on the activities and forget all unpleasant things. However, in the traditional public education activities, users always find it hard to stop thinking the judgement from others due to the distraction from staff and other participants (such as guidance, encouragement, suggestion and etc.) Here we can refer to the game and physical exercises which are easy for users to enter flow status. When people dedicate themselves to accomplish something hard but valuable, the best experience [18] or the state of immersion, usually occurs when the body or mind reaches its limit.

In museum public education activities, it is not easy for audience to fully immerse as it is hard to completely block out the distraction from the environment and other people. Therefore, it is not necessary to keep the audience in an immersion state constantly when it is about designing the exhibition process. Instead, audience should be guided to immerse in stages and unpleasant feelings of being interrupted by the outside should be reduced. For example, with the help of specific exhibits, VR devices, audio-visual terminals and other service touchpoints, audience can keep their attention focused through interesting human-computer interaction (audience and equipment) and human-objects interaction (audience and exhibits) to receive tasks and necessary information.

3.4 Feedback and Content Acquisition

As mentioned earlier, the immersion and integration stage can enable audience to keep the immersion state in stages, and build their awareness and feedback on artifacts through visualization. The main purpose of feedback is to inform participants of their performance and current progress, and to establish a feedback loop. Feedback from the audience in the Penta-model can be divided into immediate and cognitive feedback.

Immediate feedback is obtained through live human-computer/objects interaction which requires the audience to respond quickly. If audience have to wait a long time to realize what impact their actions may have, they will become distracted and lose focus on the task. Keeping the audience focused requires frequent feedback. The ideal feedback state is that audience can receive immediate feedback for each interaction. In addition, the accuracy of feedback is also very important, because frequent feedback will not leave much time for audience to react. When audience receive feedback that they cannot quickly understand, the state of integration and immersion will be disrupted. The accuracy of feedback rely on clear text, easy-to-use user interface, and appropriate sound cues. Cognitive feedback is related to cognitive problem solving, which provides an explanation for learning and cognitive immersion. Compared with immediate feedback, cognitive feedback focuses on the responses from audience. The cognition that audience continuously build up during the visit and the feedback given in the face of challenges or problems can be seen as the audience's mastery of the educational content. Cognitive feedback does not focus on timeliness. Audience need some time to digest the educational content, so cognitive feedback can be made during or after the end of the exhibition.

In the stage of feedback, the audience can immerse in the content and achieve the flow status. Content acquisition is the inevitable product of immediate and cognitive feedback as both of them need to be made by the audience based on the perceptions they made during their visiting. Content acquisition is the goal that both museums and audience want to achieve in public education activities, and it is the meaning of museum public education activities. Content acquisition does not occur only when the visitor completes the first four stages of flow, but at any of the stages of the Penta-model, only in fragmented form. At the end of the visit, the audience perceives and acquires the overall content through the cognitive integration of the entire educational activity.

3.5 Competence and Value Co-creation

In a typical flow experience "game", the acquisition of competence represents the process by which a player gradually becomes a skilled player from a novice. In this process, the player acquires a higher level of gaming skills, a richer gaming experience, and a higher social status in the virtual gaming world. In the public education service, the "competence" acquired by the audience differs due to the different "goals" of participation. In other words, different audience may obtain different knowledge and experiences. Competence, as the last flow stage of Penta-model, is not only a reward for all previous stages, but also a summary of the two goals in the first stage. As mentioned earlier, the educational goal of the museum is that audience can gain knowledge from it. The goal of the audience is to have a good visiting experience. Value co-creation will occur when these two goals achieved at the same time.

The concept of value co-creation in marketing means that in the process of value creation, enterprises and customers are the co-creators. In MPES, the audience is the customer and the museum is the enterprise. The process of audience's viewing is the process of value co-creation. The museum's educational goals are achieved through the achievement of users' goals. The audience gains immersive viewing experience and knowledge by visiting the museum and the museum realizes the function of public education services through exhibition planning and the provision of viewing activities. The museum and the audience jointly achieve the creation of public education service value.

4   Duan Inkstone Art Exhibition Public Education Services Design Based on Flow Experience of Penta-Model

Taking the Guangdong Museum Duan Inkstone Art Exhibition as the design practice object, we analyze the current problems faced by the Duan Inkstone Exhibition Hall. With the flow experience of Penta-model in MPES in mind, we initiate the service innovation practice and theoretical model verification.

4.1   The STQ of Duan Inkstone Art Exhibition in Guangdong Museum

Duan inkstone is known as the first of the four famous inkstones in China, and is also well-known as one of the "Scholar's Four Jewels" along with the Hu Pen, Hui Ink and Xuan Paper. Since the Tang Dynasty, Duan inkstones have appeared in Zhaoqing City, Guangdong Province. The stone used to make Duan inkstones is mainly produced near the Beiling Mountains in Zhaoqing City, and the three most famous ones are Laokeng, Mazikeng and Kengzaiyan [19]. The process of inkstone making is complicated. Dozens of procedures are required before a fine inkstone is made. The ink comes out quickly and the ink is delicate and smooth. Since its introduction, it had a high reputation among Chinese scholars ever since [20].

The Duan Inkstone Art Exhibition Hall is located on the third floor of Guangdong Museum, displaying hundreds of exquisite Duan Inkstone in different periods since the Tang Dynasty (Fig. 2). The display is divided into four parts: the first part is "The History and Culture of Duan Inkstone", which describes through texts and provides visitors with a background. It also exhibits some of the finest Duan inkstone from the Tang Dynasty to the present; The second part is "Stone Quality and Beauty", which introduces the quality of the pits and stones used to produce inkstones. The design of this exhibition hall also restore the mine pit scenario, displaying over 10 kinds of Duan Inkstone materials; The third and fourth part of the exhibition named "The Magic Artwork" and "Engraved Poems and Inscriptions", which are classified based on the shape, age, carving techniques and carving themes of Duan inkstone and displayed with the text introduction and scenes, implying close relationship between Duan Inkstone, ancient scholars and traditional culture [21].

Fig. 2. The STQ of Duan Inkstone Art Exhibition Hall of Guangdong Museum

4.2　User Research and Demand Insight

In order to better upgrade the design of exhibition services, the research group have launched user interview and questionnaire to understand users' needs, including audience's questions and feedback (like exhibition display and participation method) when they visit Duan Inkstone Art Exhibition and audience's interest on following public education activities after they have paid a visit to Duan Inkstone Art Exhibition, such as their further learning of related knowledge and their potential needs on future formats of public education activities. The questionnaire is conducted in two periods of weekdays and weekends by means of offline impromptu interview and online questions. The content of the research included audience's personal information, visiting time, visiting frequency, peers, information channels, motivation, purpose, feelings and expectation,s etc. 117 effective questionnaires were finally collected. Based on the interview feedback and questionnaire data analysis, the group found that the shortcomings of the current exhibition and viewing experience mainly include: a) the display content is informative but without many memorable highlights; b) the display is less interactive with few participation; c) the display route is vague without effective guidance. The main needs of the target users (interest-oriented Duan Inkstone enthusiasts, exploration-oriented Duan Inkstone novice, and learning-oriented users like parents and children) focus on: a) display content in the divided area and special area; b) display forms with game interaction and fun; c) display space that combines content and routes with echoes.

4.3　Guanyan: Curation and Visiting Services Design of Duan Inkstone Art Exhibition

According to the preliminary research and users' demand study, the research group takes the theme of Guanyan with flow experience of Penta-model in MPES to re-curate the exhibition and design the viewing service for the Guangdong Museum of Duan Inkstone Art Exhibition. Through value proposition design, service system construction, visiting journey planning and service touch points design (Duan Inkstone Art Exhibition, offline experience activities, online educational games), the five flow status are integrated into the exhibition's atmosphere, display, viewing process, interactive experience and other aspects to meet audience's dual demand for knowledge and entertainment.

Value Proposition Design. The value proposition canvas can visualize customers' needs quickly, build corresponding products or services through analysis. As shown in Fig. 3, the audience expects to have an immersive visiting process and interesting experience, and to enhance their knowledge of culture related to Duan Inkstone. They are bored with the one-way exhibition and expect to learn knowledge through interactions. Therefore, Guanyan defines the public education service with the theme of Duan Inkstone as a public education service that provides visitors with an immersive experience of Duan Inkstone art exhibition through plotted display and gaming interaction, thus achieving the purpose of learning by playing.

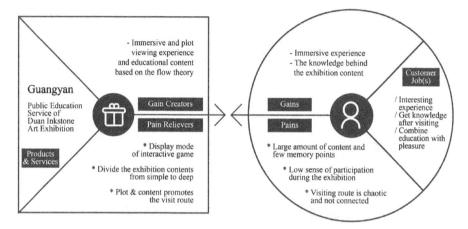

Fig. 3. Value Proposition Canvas of Guanyan

Service System Construction. The public education service built based on the Duan Ink-stone Art Exhibition of Guangdong Museum consider general public as target users. Different stakeholders in the public education service of Guanyan provide related services to the audience. As the main service recipient, the related stakeholders are museums, hardware and software providers, local suppliers, etc., including the museum staff.

Service System Map is a visual illustration of a service system that contains the participants involved in the service, the relationships among them and the flow of material, experience, money and information [22]. The Service System Map can show the relationship between different roles and departments in Guanyan system more comprehensively and directly. With the building of connection between information flow, funds flow and material flow, a balanced service ecosystem can be established. In Guanyan system, the exhibition provides four services for visitors, including interactive mini-programs, exhibition services, interactive experience games and related visiting materials (Fig. 4). Interactive mini-programs are platforms that provide online exhibition services and online educational games for visitors to access the exhibition content and related services at any time. It can also be used as service props in the exhibition. The remaining three services focus on the offline service experience. The exhibition hall is the place to provide and realize services for the audience. The interactive experience game is the specific content and service intermediary for the audience, and the related materials are the tools to realize the services. Guanyan system is mainly operated by different departments of Guangdong Museum and provide specific services such as tour guide, explanation and task release for the audience through staff and volunteers. During the service process, necessary props and products, such as simplified VR glasses, are purchased from suppliers to ensure a pleasant experience for visitors.

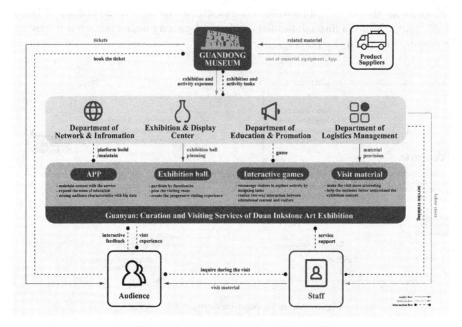

Fig. 4. Service System Map of Guanyan

Visiting Journey Planning. The consideration and planning of service stages, user goals, user behaviors, touch points, emotional changes, etc. during the viewing journey can be completed by using the tool of Customer Journey Map. It shows the process of a user receiving a service in a visual chart [23]. As shown in Fig. 5, in the journey of Guanyan, the service stages include online booking, check-in, enter the exhibition hall, start visit, leave, and follow information pushing, etc. In each service stage, users will have a series of actions under the corresponding goals, and then interact with several touchpoints (physical, digital and interpersonal touchpoints) on site, resulting emotional fluctuations with different effects. The service designers can plan the visiting journey reasonably based on the above content and apply methods including but not limited to increasing the touchpoints, raising the peaks and filling the troughs, etc.

During the pre-service stage, the App of Guangdong Museum can help audience know the exhibition content and experience activities arrangement in advance. Audience will also receive a customized invitation letter. At this moment, audience are curious about it and interested in the exhibition content. During the service stage, audience can view and experience the exhibition in an interactive way through the guidance provided by the staff when they enter the exhibition hall. These interactions, including scenario simulation, VR display, hands-on experience and online games can trigger audience emotions to the peak level and experience flow state. During the after-service stage, audience can still learn information of Duan Inkstone through online educational games after they left the exhibition hall. They will also receive posts on following activities and this can ensure the connection between audience and exhibition which triggers the future visiting motivation.

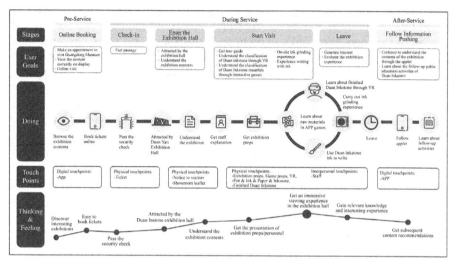

Fig. 5. Customer Journey Map of Guanyan

Service Touchpoints Design

Display Design of Duan Inkstone Art Exhibition. In recent years, the integration of story lines into the exhibition visiting process is a common method of exhibition design. Both clear and vague story lines can connect all areas of the exhibition hall and build a framework for the exhibition design. This can make the hall more integral and more attractive to audience [24]. Guanyan syetem have upgraded the scenario on the basis of original exhibition hall space and added a great number of interactive scenarios. Besides, the interactive educational gaming tasks can connect all areas into the visiting route, enabling audience to enter the flow status quickly and enjoy a better experience.

Figure 6 shows the correspondence between audience's journey and the flow state of the Penta-model. Specifically speaking, a) Explanation area at the entrance, corresponding to the "goal". The entrance is the first area that visitors access to. It is necessary to trigger audience's interest and desire for exploration in this area. The entrance is equipped with professional explanation, display video and VR interactive games and a variety of methods have been applied to stimulate the curiosity and interest of first-time visitors. At the same time, tasks will be released to visitors, who can experience the entire exhibition hall with questions and goals, enabling audiences to enter the immersion state. b) Display area of raw materials, corresponding to "goals, challenges and integration". After audience become interested in the entrance, following actions are needed to maintain the novelty for audience in order to transform curiosity into active participation. Through display of physical objects and live games, the audience is presented with raw materials of Duan Inkstone and memory about its types and characteristics can be formed. The interactive game is also a way to re-attract the audience who were not interested in the previous area. c) Display area of completed Duan Inkstone, corresponding to "challenge and feedback". In this area, visitors can learn about rich exhibits of Duan Inkstone and meet their expectations. At the same time, they can learn how a Duan Inkstone is transformed from a piece of stone to a fine inkstone through VR and video find it quite surprising. For first-time visitors, some interesting games such as "Know Inkstone through Silhouette" can help visitors quickly understand the finished inkstone. d) Experience area of Duan Inkstone, corresponding to "goals, challenges and competences". This is another surprise, where the audience can personally experience the grinding process and they can apply what they have learned in the previous areas into practice. They can also use the ink they grind to write and draw in the writing area. For visitors, the fun they can get by doing is much more just seeing. It is also easier to have the flow experience. e) Display area of use scenario, corresponding to "integration and feedback". Following the flow experience in the previous sections, audiences can experience multi dimensional sensory experience through the ancient calligraphy scenario, which can deepen users visiting memory and keep flow experience. As the last section of visiting journey, diversified scenarios can enable audiences to achieve peak experience.

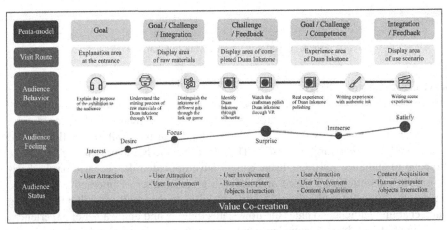

Fig. 6. The corresponding relationship between Guanyan and Penta-model

As for the space and scenario design of the exhibition hall, the visiting route was reset based on the Penta-model. The open structure was adopted. Thus, previously, a booth displaying multiple inkstones is replaced by a booth displaying only one inkstone, leading to a more focused sight and audience can observe it more closely in a more immersive environment. In order to help audience enter the immersive flow state, the exhibition hall adopts colorless warm colors, which is more in line with the style of Duan Inkstone. The overall lighting adopts darker light, with only partial lighting in the booth part to reduce the interference from the external environment. In addition to color and lighting, soft background music is also used. The multi-sensory viewing helps visitors to focus more on the exhibits, enter the flow state and immerse themselves in the exhibition atmosphere smoothly (Fig. 7).

Fig. 7. Renderings of Duan Inkstone Public Education Space

Design of Offline Activities. Most of the survey interviewees shared their idea that they hope more interesting interactive experience activities can be added in the visiting journey. According to the flow theory, the easiest way for people to enter flow experience is game. Because games meet the basic elements to construct flow experience, namely goals, challenges, integration, feedback and competence. The design of educational game itself does not necessarily require more techniques than ordinary games. The key is about content design [25]. In Guanyan system, the combination of Duan Inkstone's historical culture and physical objects can construct 5 different gaming activities to meet different audience's needs (Table 1). The games are distributed in the exhibition hall based on the clues, linking various areas. Visitors establish clear game objectives during the exhibition viewing process and interact with staff and exhibits to obtain clues or feedback. The offline game-like educational experience allows visitors to have a complete visiting journey and the expected knowledge of Duan Inkstone, and enter the flow state more easily.

Design of Online Educational Games. The goal of online educational games is to deliver digital educational content through game-like methods. Learners can learn in a more easy and pleasant way [26]. The App game in Guanyan system adopts a role-playing approach, allowing audience to play the role of ancient scholars. Players can find out different pieces of the Duan Inkstone in different game levels through clues in the offline exhibition hall. If they can collect all fragments and make it into a complete Duan Inkstone, they will be rewarded with "golden coins" which can be used to exchange souvenirs in the offline exhibition hall. In general, this online educational game has two features: a) The online

Table 1. Design checklist of Duan Inkstone Immersive Offline Experience Activities

Activities Name (Theme)	Game Clues	Content Intro	User Group
Duan Inkstone Exploration Manual	Pick up a strange stone	Play the role as geologist, and find out the type of the stone based on the pattern, material, color and other characteristics of the stone, then put on VR glasses to explore the origin of this stone	Parent-children Users & Duan Inkstone Novice
	What this stone can do	Decide on what type of the inkstone it can made based on the size of stones?	
	Stone's twin brother	Find a finished inkstone of the same material and similar size as this stone in the exhibition hall and experience the process of grinding ink with this stone	
	Astonished! The stone has transformed!	Watching the process of making inkstone and writing with the ink produced by the inkstone	
	Stone hidden in the history	Experience the using method of inkstone in the study	
The ever-changing Duan Inkstone	Duan Inkstone Factory	Identify the pattern features on the finished Duan inkstone and decide on its origin	Duan Inkstone Novice
	Traces of Duan Inkstone	Identify which exhibition hall the inkstone belong to based on the Duan inkstone silhouette	

(*continued*)

Table 1. (*continued*)

Activities Name (Theme)	Game Clues	Content Intro	User Group
	Master of complexity	Tell which inkstone in the exhibition hall has the most intricate craftsmanship based on patterns, carvings, inscriptions, etc	
Duan Inkstone Detector	Duan Inkstone searching guidance	Identify the oldest and youngest finished Duan Inkstone in the exhibition hall	Parent-children Users & Duan Inkstone Novice
	Duan Inkstone viewing guidance	Identify and count the number of shapes of finished Duan Inkstone in the exhibition hall	
Miners	Sharp eyes	Distinguishing the most similar inkstones produced in different pits	Duan Inkstone Lovers
	Make best use	Selecting the pit that produces the highest quality inkstone from more than ten pits	
	Identify Duan Inkstone	Find out the most valuable inkstone in the exhibition hall	
Writers and Poets	Engraved poem with inscription	Identify the Duan inkstones in the exhibition hall that have been inscribed with poems	Duan Inkstone Lovers
	The treasure of the exhibition hall	Finding the three main treasures of the exhibition hall and identifying the inkstone with the most inscriptions	
	The most popular inkstone	Find out the inkstone with most using traces	

game is closely related with offline clue collection and the difficulty is reasonable, leading to higher participation of audience and enable them to enter the flow experience more easily; b) The setting of interesting story can enhance the attractiveness of the game [27]. The game drives the plot development in a narrative way, guiding audience to explore the knowledge of Duan Inkstone material identification and production techniques in a more pleasant way. Viewers are no longer the passive receivers but active knowledge explorers. The interface design of the online educational game adopts an antique art style, as shown in Fig. 8, with traditional elements such as silk paper and scrolls, fitting the theme of Duan Inkstone. In this way, a light and elegant effect can be achieved. Different scenarios in the game are equipped with different background music, and the sound effects are designed to give audience the feedback on the game.

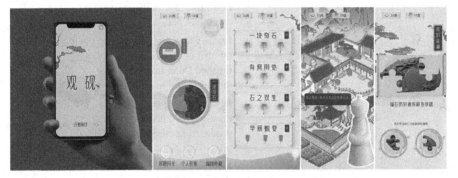

Fig. 8. Guanyan App Game

5 Conclusion

This study adopts an interdisciplinary approach and focuses on MPES based on the flow theory of positive psychology, to study how to improve visiting experience. Based on the theory of psychology, marketing, design and other disciplines, the study proposes Penta-model of flow experience. Five flow stages and five flow status can help audience to obtain flow experience in MPES. With this theory, the exhibition of Duan Inkstone Art Exhibition of Guangdong Museum is re-curated and re-designed. The original exhibition area and its display way are re-planned, connecting exhibition hall, offline experience activities and online educational games through story lines. Thus, a complete experience process is generated to meet needs of different levels of audience on exhibition visiting. Practice shows that the Penta-model of flow experience provides a new way of thinking for MPES as well as exhibition planning and presentation, which means it is user-centered and can facilitate audience's flow experience to achieve better participation, experience and immersion of public education.

References

1. The definition of a museum at the 21st Annual Conference of the International Council of Museums (ICOM) in Werna, Austria (2007). http://www.icommuseum/thevision/museum-definition. Accessed 30 Oct 2022

2. Xiangguang, S.: Museum definition and the development of contemporary museums. Chin. Mus. **04**, 1–6 (2003)
3. Xiangguang, S.: New trends in museum education. Chinese Museum **32**(01), 1–5 (2015)
4. Lanxiang, L., Yao, Z.: On the social and educational function of museums. Cult. Relics Southern China **1**, 135+14 (2007)
5. Shanwen, T.: Application of Interactive Design in Museum Display. Nanjing University of the Arts, Nanjing (2012)
6. Tianying, S., Jin, Y., Kaili, X., Jingbin, Z.: Overview of flow studies. Afterschool Educ. China **15**, 54+75 (2017)
7. Czikszentmihalyi, M.: Flow and the Psychology of Discovery and Invention. Harper Perennial, New York (1997)
8. Czikszentmihalyi, M.: Flow: The Psychology of Optimal Experience. Harper Perennial, New York (1991)
9. Schiefele, U.: Response to Engeser (2012): on the nature of flow experience. Psychol. Rep. **112**(2), 529–532 (2013)
10. Snyder, C.R., Lopez, S.J.: Handbook of Positive Psychology. Oxford University Press, Oxford (2005)
11. Stefan, E.: Comments on Schiefele and Raabe (2011): flow is a multifaceted experience defined by several components. Psychol. Rep. **111**(1), 24–26 (2012)
12. Bakker, A.B.: The work-related flow inventory: construction and initial validation of the WOLF. J. Vocat. Behav. **72**(3), 400–414 (2008)
13. Xin, C.: The review of the flow experience. Jiangsu Normal Univ. (Philosophy Soc. Sci. Edn.) **40**(05), 150–155 (2014)
14. Lin, Y., Dajun, Z.: Research on the relationship between internet addiction and flow experience. In: Chinese Psychological Society (eds.) Collection of Abstracts of the 10th Chinese Academic Conference of Psychology, pp. 276–277 (2005)
15. Webster, J., Trevino, L.K., Ryan, L.: The dimensionality and correlates of flow in human-computer interactions. Comput. Hum. Behav. **9**(4), 411–426 (1994)
16. Bell, S.J.: Image and consumer attraction to intraurban retail areas: an environmental psychology approach. J. Retail. Consum. Serv. **6**(2), 67–78 (1999)
17. Michaelidou, N., Dibb, S.: Consumer involvement: a new perspective. Mark. Rev. **8**(1), 83–99 (2008)
18. Grönroos, C.: Value co-creation in service logic: a critical analysis. Mark. Theory **11**(3), 279–301 (2011)
19. Duanyan, Z.: The metamorphosis from mediocrity to magic. PR World **01**, 96–97 (2015)
20. Xiaojing, W.: Ink and sea incense: Hebei Museum collection of Ming and Qing Duan inkstone treasures. Orient. Collect. **05**, 63–67 (2017)
21. Official website of Guangdong Museum. http://www.gdmuseum.com. Accessed 15 Sept 2022
22. Jiajia, C.: Service Design: Definition. Language and Tools. Jiangsu Phoenix Art Press, Nanjing (2016)
23. Guosheng, W.: Service Design and Innovation. China Construction Industry Press, Beijing (2015)
24. Jin, Z.: Research on the Development of Museum Display Design Thinking in China. Fudan University, Shanghai (2013)
25. Yi, T., Ruwei, Y.: Analysis and application of educational game design theory. J. Dist. Educ. **02**, 75–78 (2008)
26. Yonggu, W., Ting, Z., Wei, L., Biyu, H.: Research on the framework elements of educational game design based on Flow Theory: a case study of special Children's speech learning game. J. Dist. Educ. **32**(03), 97–104 (2014)
27. Shi, H., Zhaochen, D., Yanjie, C.: Digital Game Planning. Tsinghua University Press, Beijing (2008)

A New Transmission Mode of Chinese Neo-confucianism Combined with Digital Technology: A Case of Guanhai Lou

Shiqi Gong, Zhen Liu[✉], and Zhiya Tan[✉]

School of Design, South China University of Technology,
Guangzhou 510006, People's Republic of China
liuzjames@scut.edu.cn, 201930580475@mail.scut.edu.cn

Abstract. Chinese Neo-Confucianism (CNC) is one of the three trends of thought in modern China. It is a more appropriate Chinese philosophy for young people that draws on the essence of traditional Confucian culture and incorporates western culture with its emphasis on democracy and freedom. However, young people have a low grasp of CNC and have a misunderstanding of its culture and thought. Nowadays, most studies in the field of traditional cultural transmission focus on intangible cultural heritage techniques and historical relics, while few studies focus on traditional thoughts, among which the research on the transmission of CNC is still blank. In addition, no matter in the field of design, art, or transmission, the combination of traditional cultural inheritance and digital technology has become the future trend. Therefore, this study aims to publicize the philosophy of CNC through the combination of digital technology and CNC, to guide young people to explore, realize and understand the core views of CNC, and enhance their cultural confidence and cultural identity. In this paper, we select Guanhai Lou, the ancient architecture and former residence of CNC master Xiong Shili, located in Tangtou Village, Hualong Town, Panyu District, Guangzhou City, Guangdong Province, as the research object and use Double Diamond Model and Co-design are adopted to explore the propaganda pain points and design opportunities of CNC and to complete the subsequent design. This study not only integrates digital entertainment and cultural digitalization technology organically through the form of narrative design and orienteering and designs a complete set of user experience designs centered on CNC transmission. But it also combines digital technology, narrative design, and orienteering for the first time, which provides a design reference for more designers to design traditional ideological transmission modes in the future.

Keywords: Chinese Neo-Confucianism (CNC) · Transmission Mode · Double Diamond Model · Co-design · Digital Technology · Narrative Design · Orienteering · User Experience Design

A. Marcus et al. (Eds.): HCII 2023, LNCS 14034, pp. 58–73, 2023.
https://doi.org/10.1007/978-3-031-35705-3_5

1   Introduction

Together with Marxism and the School of Liberalism, modern Chinese Neo-Confucianism (CNC) is considered one of the three main social ideological trends in China. It is also the primary ideological representative of modern Chinese cultural conservatism [1]. Modern CNC especially refers to a kind of academic trend of thought or community, which advanced and enriched Chinese traditional culture, especially the essence of Confucianism, and integrated Western modern cultural spirit to create a new Chinese culture during the May Fourth Movement Period of the 20th century in China [2].

In this era, the passing down of traditional cultures has been interrupted. Committed to the in-depth exploration and illustration of the relationship between traditional culture and modernization from the philosophical perspective, modern CNC has managed to accumulate a considerable number of theoretical achievements. Even though some of its opinions and conclusions may fail to gain public agreement, it plays a significant guiding role in affirming the value of traditional culture and correctly handling the relationship between traditional culture and modernization, as well as Western culture. Young people are not only the earliest reflectors of social ideological trends but also the most active participants and practitioners. Their process of growth is constantly exposed to the influence and edification of social and ideological trends. Meanwhile, they also play a part in the formation and development of social ideological trends in their unique ways. Therefore, they have a close relevance to the spread of modern neo-Confucian thoughts, which leads to the necessity to spread among them modern neo-Confucian theories and views [3].

Unfortunately, CNC has been trapped in a dilemma of lacking recognition and appreciation in today's China. As German philosopher, Hegel once commented, "There is no philosophy in China." A mainstream opinion that CNC is a static, backward, and conservative theory also exists in the field of American Sinology [4]. Under the impact of political factors, CNC has stayed in a relatively passive situation for a period of time, making it hard to fully spread among people. Because of previous misleading propaganda, CNC has been labeled as "feudal dregs" and "old wine in a new bottle". Even the cultivation and dissemination of CNC can hardly affect the public [5]. Now, CNC is also facing the plight of a low popularity rate and an insufficient acceptance degree. Confucian classics and history are not only quite strange to the young generation in mainland China, but also unfamiliar to the older generation (except some professionals) [6]. All these phenomena urge people to consider how to solve the dissemination problem of CNC.

This paper studies how to realize the organic integration of digital technology, orienteering mode, and narrative design form. The aim is to break through the barriers between CNC and the public in a brand-new way of user experience, which enables the public to feel, understand and accept CNC philosophy and culture, and finally reaches the goal of disseminating CNC culture.

2 Literature Review

Traditional cultural diffusion is realized through four kinds of channels, namely cultural relics, museums or cultural institutions, mass media such as television, radio, and the Internet, as well as publications like print media, analog media, digital media, and souvenirs [7]. In the current era, people's communication process is more and more dependent on the mediation of digital technologies, which have formed new ways (including production ways, methods of connection with the world, and living styles). Based on them, new social systems are gradually built [8]. In this context, more and more cultural institutions, with museums as the leading ones, are striving to apply digital technology in the contact with visitors, to promote user engagement and attract new visitors in novel forms.

2.1 Digital Technology in Cultural Dissemination: Applications and Issues

As an emerging area, cultural computing applies computer technology and scientific methods to culture, art, and social sciences, aiming to show, strengthen, expand, and transform the process of creating products [9]. Since the mid-2000s, the application of enabling technologies in cultural heritage has been extended to immersive technologies, integrating augmented reality, virtual reality, and mixed reality technologies, which offer sensory experiences through varied combinations of real and digital content [10]. Nonetheless, this also brings a new and unavoidable problem: how to improve the attraction of cultural institutions without rendering them into a situation of seriously lacking content [8]? Despite the success in maintaining technological development, cultural institutions will still face reduced effectiveness of digital devices, if they have neither new communication strategies nor an understanding of their functions or immersive media ecology [7].

Based on study results, whatever method is applied, depending on digitalization alone is not efficient enough to boost cultural institutions' ability to create values [8], Given this, it is necessary to find more diversified cultural diffusion ways, enrich and deepen the conveyed contents with digital technology, and thereby increase the communication efficiency and depth of cultural institutions.

2.2 Orienteering in Cultural Dissemination: Applications and Issues

With the implementation of a nationwide sport policy, leisure sports are gradually welcomed and supported by the public. Orienteering being an emerging outdoor activity in leisure sports stands out with its rich contents and forms. Participants should go across unfamiliar landforms with a compass and a map, choosing a route by themselves to arrive at the checking point. The victory is determined by the time or the number of checking points arrived at. Now orienteering is more than a competition since many hosts integrate the local culture, which participants can learn about when taking part in the activity.

The Southern Guangdong Ancient Courier Route Directional Orienteering is a successful example of combining local cultures with sports tourism. Having been a passage from central China to the Lingnan Districts since the Qing Dynasty, the Southern

Guangdong Ancient Courier Route is mainly responsible for document delivery, cargo transportation, and population exchange. In history, it connected the entire system of transportation infrastructure in Lingnan Districts and presented the development tracks of the multinational cultures in Guangdong, and it is a precious historical and cultural resource of the province. With the progress of time, the ancient courier route has been deserted and replaced by the current national highway or greenway. The once splendid cultural heritage of China has been gradually forgotten. However, the Guangdong provincial government has applied the diversified integration mode of sports and tourist industry, a brand creative sports mode, which not only activates the Southern Guangdong Ancient Courier Route but also brings more visitors. Meanwhile, it popularizes the agricultural industry in surrounding villages and establishes the ancient route as a brand feature by advertising through the competition. Holding competitions promotes rural tourism, historic culture, the conservation and development of the ancient route and new construction, accelerating the development of ancient villages and offering a valuable reference to explore and utilize the Southern Guangdong Ancient Courier Route in the future [11].

Based on cultural heritage design challenging, interesting, and involving orienteering can activate and utilize the historic cultural heritage along the way to create a more novel and engaging cultural transmission mode. Nonetheless, there are many problems to be settled concerning such a new attempt. In specific, the exploration of the contents of existing cultural transmission orienteering is not deep enough since it only exhibits historic culture rather than inquiring thoroughly about it [12]. Despite the new form and strong sense of engagement, the culture embedded in it is restricted to receiving instead of transforming into internal thoughts. Besides, current activities of this category focus on "competition", which is highly competitive since users attach more importance to victory while neglecting the cultural content. As a brand way of culture transmission, such kind of orienteering should reduce the competitiveness and enhance the depth of content as well as participants' feedback to enable them to learn and reflect.

2.3 Narrative Design in Cultural Dissemination: Applications and Issues

The narrative plays an extremely important role in cognition and culture. Narrative-centric campaigns are receiving increasing attention. Given the inherent structure of narratives, a narrative-centered learning environment can provide an engaging world to motivate users to actively engage in story-building activities [13]. Narrative design is most often used in games. In the context of serious games and science education, more and more game designers are researching the role of narrative design in educational games. This new approach to science education de-emphasizes rote memorization of "facts" and coverage of vast amounts of knowledge, and instead focuses on problem-solving, core deep learning, and interdisciplinary concepts and processes [14]. In such games, narratives provide two main functions, motivation for problem-solving and cognitive framework [15].

When the narrative design is used in cultural communication educational games, it can indeed attract users and achieve a deep learning culture. However, the entire process is based on computers or virtual devices, and the experience is single, which cannot bring users a more realistic experience. Through the transformation from the online scene to the offline scene, a cultural communication institution combining reality and virtuality is created. Among them, narrative design runs through educational games to increase the immersive experience [16].

2.4 Analysis of the Complementary Advantages of Digital Technology, Orienteering, and Narrative Design

Based on the above literature analysis, the following conjectures are put forward:

Conjecture 1: Digital technology and orienteering activities can make up for the single experience of narrative design.

Conjecture 2: The orienteering activity can activate the purely online and pure virtual forms that make use of the historical and cultural heritage along the line to make up for digital technology and narrative design.

Conjecture 3: Narrative design can improve the depth of cultural communication and the degree of user acceptance in digital technology and orienteering activities.

Through the double diamond model, the advantages of the three are combined, and the disadvantages are complemented to design a new communication user experience model.

3   Method

The ancient architecture of Tangtou Village, Hualong Town, Panyu District, Guangdong Province, China, and the Guanhai Lou, the former residence of Xiong Shili, a master of philosophy, is chosen as a case study. The double diamond model is adopted (see Fig. 1). Based on the communication dilemma of Chinese Neo-Confucianism (CNC) obtained from the research, the mode of communication is innovated and new possibilities are explored. In the exploration stage, the status quo of cultural communication among young people was observed, and the pain points of CNC communication were summarized. According to the relevant research results, design breakthrough points are drawn. During the concept phase, design opportunities are translated into a user experience architecture, and stakeholder relationships are explored. During the realization phase, scene modeling and renderings are produced.

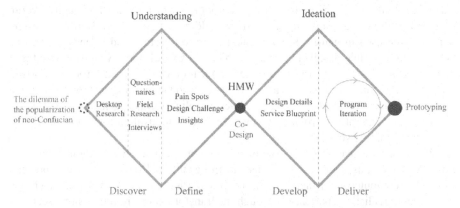

Fig. 1. Double diamond model design for the study.

3.1 Discover

Desktop Survey. The academic trend of Chinese Neo-Confucianism (CNC) has gone through four stages. The first stage is CNC after the May 4th Movement, with key figures Liang Shuming and Zhang Junmai. The second stage is CNC during the Anti-Japanese War, with key figures Feng Youlan and Xiong Shili. The third stage is Hong Kong and Taiwan CNC, with key figures Tang Junyi and Mou Zongsan. The fourth stage is overseas CNC, which returned to mainland China after the reform and opening up. The Guanhai Lou, located in Tangtou Village, Hualong Town, Panyu District, Guangzhou City, welcomed Xiong Shili, a 20th-century CNC figure in China in the autumn of 1948.

At the beginning of this year, several Chinese People's Political Consultative Conference (CPPCC) members jointly submitted the Proposal on Repairing the Former Residence of Xiong Shili in Panyu at the Fifth Session of the Twelfth CPPCC Guangdong Provincial Committee, calling for the restoration of the Guanhai Lou as soon as possible and the declaration of "Guangzhou Historic Buildings" for protection and utilization. In addition, representatives of the Guangzhou Municipal People's Congress also plan to jointly submit Suggestions on Repairing the Former Residence of Xiong Shili at the first session of the 16th Guangzhou Municipal People's Congress.

Field Observation and Field Interview. Through on-site visits (see Fig. 2), it can be found that there are many buildings around Guanhai Lou listed as cultural relics protection buildings in Guangzhou, such as Youwei Huang Ancestral Hall and Ruoquan Ancestral Room. There are gray and brick carvings of various shapes in these buildings during the Ming and Qing Dynasties. However, the overall conservation situation is poor. The local complex covers a large area, which is suitable for large outdoor activities.

Inside the Guanhai Lou, there are many historically unique carvings and some literati handwriting. Behind these elements are historical stories belonging to that era, which are worth developing.

In addition, the interviews with residents found that the current local cultural buildings are not strong enough, the protection effect is not good, and the local cultural atmosphere is lacking, resulting in little awareness of local cultural buildings and historical culture.

Fig. 2. Photos from the field trip (Left: surrounding buildings, middle: inside of the Guanhai Lou, right: field interview).

Questionnaire Survey. In this questionnaire survey, a total of 71 valid questionnaires are distributed, with the main users as college students. The purpose of the questionnaire survey is to understand college students' interest in and understanding of philosophy, their understanding of Chinese Confucian philosophy, and their expectations for future cultural and creative places. There are 9 questions in total, as shown in Table 1 below:

Table 1. The question in the questionnaire.

NO.	Question	
1	Have you ever voluntarily learned about philosophy?	
2	What do you think philosophy is?	
	a. A theory of inquiry into cognition	d. A theory of governance
	b. A theory of the origin of the world	e. A theory of nature unity
	c. A theory of empty and useless	f. A theory of social relations
3	How often have you been exposed to philosophy outside of class?	
4	Do you think Confucian culture belongs to philosophy?	
5	Do you find philosophy valuable to you in solving real-life problems?	
6	How do you learn about philosophy?	
7	In the process of philosophy dissemination, what are the factors that lead you to understand a philosophical idea deeply?	
8	Why don't you go into philosophy?	
9	What draws you to cultural places?	

The following information can be obtained from the questionnaire:

- 92% of people think that Confucian culture is philosophy in question 4, but 80% of them do not choose option e and option d (the core view of Confucian culture) in question 2. After the chi-square test $\chi^2 = 0.0172$, there is 90% confidence that even 92% of people think that Confucian culture is philosophy, but they do not understand the main content of Confucian culture.
- Most people know more about Western philosophy than Chinese philosophy.
- 66.2% of the people think that obscurity is the main reason that prevents them from understanding philosophy.
- The vast majority of people pay attention to the simplicity and practicality of philosophical ideas.
- The vast majority of people pay attention to the environment and cultural heritage of cultural places.
- Only 21.1% of people learn about philosophy through museums.

3.2 Define

Pain Point. Based on the above analysis, the pain point analysis shown in Table 2 is carried out.

Table 2. Pain points analysis.

Pain points from user research	
Philosophy lovers and cultural explorer	Few related resources and channels
	It is difficult to find like-minded philosophical friends
	A better understanding of Western philosophy than Chinese philosophy
	Most of them are spectators in Douban groups, and there is no interactive philosophy exchange platform
A beginner in Chinese philosophy	Pure text literature materials, high entry threshold
	Don't know the guiding meaning of philosophy to life
Residents and staff	Not much attention
	Think there is no culture and cultural atmosphere
	There is insufficient awareness of their cultural value and the importance of conservation
Pain points from the desktop survey and field trip analysis	
Guanhai Lou	In disrepair and need of repair and maintenance
	The site is hidden deep and needs to be extended drainage
	Its background and academic background are not transformed into visual collections
Surrounding buildings	No cultural relics and stories
	The ontology is well preserved but no related content is displayed
	It has history but it's mostly sitting idle
Government	It is difficult to carry forward and spread distinctive history and culture
	Failed to unite and protect the unused ancient buildings
	Cultural venues are deserted and the passenger flow is low

Challenge. Design challenges and design insights in Table 3 are obtained: with Xiong Shili as the hub, the core views of Chinese Neo-Confucianism (CNC) in China are interpreted. The Guanhai Lou becomes a window for the dissemination of Chinese CNC, which plays on historical value and jointly protects the surrounding area.

Table 3. Design insight.

Buildings	The Guanhai Lou and its surrounding buildings lack protective structures
	The interior was empty and dilapidated
	Lack of viewing and cultural atmosphere
	Lack of guide
Culture	CNC is not widely known and easily misunderstood
	The dissemination of traditional philosophy is not attractive
	Local residents lack knowledge of the relevant history and culture
Communication	Philosophy lovers lack a strong interactive philosophy exchange platform
	It is difficult to find like-minded philosophical friends
	Text-only documentation leads to a high threshold for entry

3.3 Co-create Workshop

Co-create Workshop Process. In the form of co-design workshops, potential users express their needs and innovative ideas (including but not limited to gameplay and experience routes) under the guidance of specific tools. Invited co-design participants need to be interested in outdoor sports, philosophical theory, or love to go to cultural places. The co-design process is shown in Fig. 3 and Fig. 4.

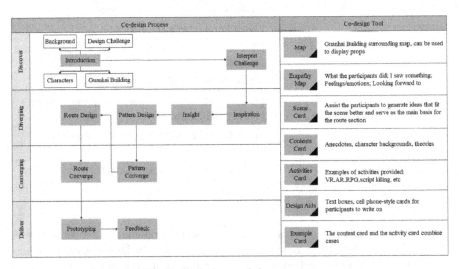

Fig. 3. Co-design workshop process.

After the co-design, the ideas generated in the co-design workshop are summarized, as shown in the following Table 4:

Fig. 4. Co-design workshop (Left: tools for co-design, middle: brainstorming, left: prototype output).

Table 4. Creative convergence.

Communication forms	Technical reference	Platform building
·Orienteering combined with cultural exploration ·Perceiving the historical timeline on the move ·Clue guide games ·Non-linear tour	·Digital media technology ·AR scanning ·Kinect V1 ·Metaverse ·Digital collection ·Digital twin	·Visualization of views ·Exchange insights ·Like-minded friends ·Philosophical temperament test

How Might We (HMW). Based on the above Insight and Creative convergence, we propose the following HMW:

- How to combine orienteering to jointly protect Guanhai Lou and its surrounding buildings?
- How to use digital technology to spread Chinese Chinese Neo-Confucianism represented by Xiong Shili?
- How to integrate narrative design into the culture to make communication more efficient and in-depth?
- How to build a communication platform for philosophy lovers around Guanhai Lou?

Experience Objectives. Based on the above analysis of user needs, existing technical means, and ideas put forward in co-design, a user experience design centered on experiencing Chinese Neo-Confucianism (CNC) philosophy and culture is proposed. In a modified form of orienteering, the plot is designed to guide visitors to explore and understand the core ideas of Chinese CNC, and to clarify the development of modern Chinese philosophy. The Guanhai Lou, the former residence of the philosopher Xiong Shili, has become a window for the dissemination of CNC in China to promote the cultural value of the historical buildings.

4   Results

4.1 Design Details

Based on the previous experience objectives, the specific design details of the product can be determined:

- Joint protection of buildings

- Promotion of Chinese Neo-Confucianism
- New technology in digital entertainment
- New experience with outdoor sports
- New presentation of narrative design

4.2 Prototype Design

To improve users' sense of immersion and engagement in the activation process, we have used a narrative design that enables them to be involved as a learner. Generally, the story is comprised of five stages (see Fig. 5): entry, first meeting Master Liang Suming, earnestly seeking Master Xiong Shi-li, visiting Master Mou Tsung-san, finishing

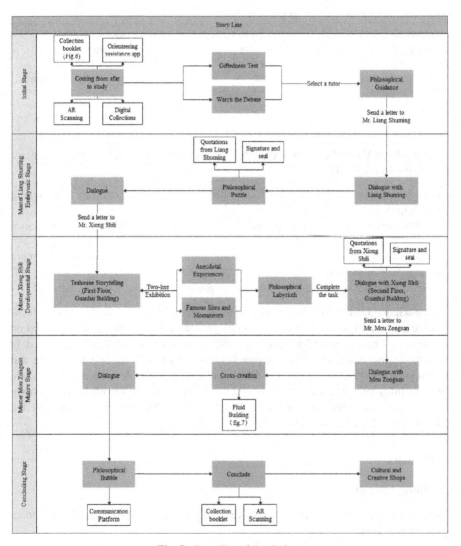

Fig. 5. Storyline of the design.

study, of which the three stories of visiting the three masters corresponds to the stage of germination, development, and maturity of Chinese Neo-Confucianism (CNC), respectively. In these three stories, users can better understand the comprehensive knowledge of the development route of CNC while they will receive two featured stuff including a collection book as well as a "fluid building" (see Fig. 6) as their unique souvenirs in the first and last stage.

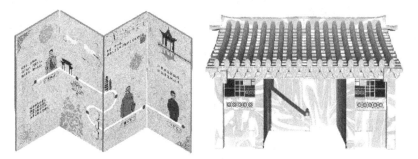

Fig. 6. Collection booklet and fluid building.

In this research, a series of interactive-device games are designed based on orienteering and they are integrated into all the plots. Ultimately, a service blueprint and a route diagram are developed as in Fig. 7 and Fig. 8 with a related supporting APP UI interface provided in Fig. 9.

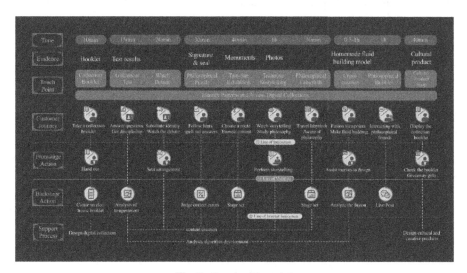

Fig. 7. Service blueprint.

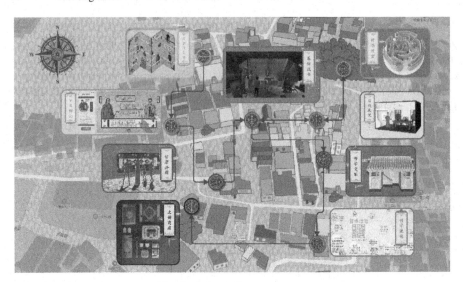

Fig. 8. Orienteering route map.

5   Discussion

In cultural transmission, digital technology has been widely applied, whereas there are some problems. In this paper, a new cultural transmission form is developed based on narrative design, orienteering design, and museum device design so that the defect of each can be remedied for spreading Chinese Neo-Confucianism (CNC). In the research, we have accidentally discovered the great potential of such a new transmission form in education, for instance, in philosophy popularization education of mid-school and primary students and the design of Chinese philosophy education bases. On account of the new digital entertainment mode teaching through lively activities and inspiring teenagers to be willing to learn deeply and efficiently based on "plots and outdoor activities", the mixed transmission way can grasp the interest of teenagers and construct an immersive intelligent philosophy education system which can be shared by different people.

In China, many ancient cultural architectures have been neglected or discarded in addition to Guanhai Lou. Based on the current research, a cultural propagating matrix can be established for similar buildings in the country so that all experiential products may be digitally shared without the barrier of location, historic culture, and platforms, realizing the limitless connection between digital entertainment and philosophy education user experiential mode and constructing a philosophy education ecosystem.

Fig. 9. APP interface design.

6 Conclusion

In this research, the forms and contents of Chinese Neo-Confucianism (CNC) have been improved. In forms, ordinary museums and visual games are replaced with nonlinear tours based on orienteering. In contents, the originally mere character exhibition gives way to cultural input instructed by plots and dialogues. Meanwhile, unified interactive forms and collecting elements are added to provide continuously new experiences all through the earlier, middle, and later periods. For the first time, cultural transmission is established on various designs, offering a precious example of propagating CNC. The research provides a design reference for future designers to develop products for inhering traditional ideology. However, the research is restricted by the huge system, which brings difficulties in probability tests. Therefore, the feasibility needs further discussion and the hypothesis should be verified by new models.

Acknowledgements. This research was funded by "2022 Constructing Project of Teaching Quality and Teaching Reform Project for Undergraduate Universities in Guangdong Province" Higher Education Teaching Reform Project **(project No. 386), 'Innovation and practice of teaching methods for information and interaction design in the context of new liberal arts'** **(project grant number x2sj-C9233001).**

References

1. Li, M., Qiao, T.: Characteristics and guidance of the network communication of neo-confucianism. Inner Mongolia Soc. Sci., 180–186+2 (2020). https://doi.org/10.14137/j.cnki.issn1003-5281.2020.05.025
2. Yang, Z.: A summary of the research of modern neo-confucianism since the 1990s. Chinese Culture Res., 32–44 (2016). https://doi.org/10.15990/j.cnki.cn11-3306/g2.2016.01.004
3. Qian, Y.: The communication of modern Neo-Confucianism trend and contemporary youth (2011)
4. Deng, L.: The academic practice of Dipeili, the founder of American Neo-Confucianism. J. Guangdong Univ. Foreign Stud. **31**, 113–119 (2020). https://doi.org/10.3969/j.issn.1672-0962.2020.05.011
5. Xu, J.: Take advantage of neo-Confucianism to strengthen the cohesion of the Chinese nation. People's Tribune., 136–137 (2017). https://doi.org/10.16619/j.cnki.rmlt.2017.01.067
6. Guo, R.: Modernization of Confucianism in the transition of modern Chinese society (2018)
7. Gándara, V.M.: Nuevas tecnologías y estrategias de comunicación para la divulgación del patrimonio cultural. Antropología. Revista interdisciplinaria del INAH, pp. 135–153 (2017)
8. Valverde Martínez, H.: When digitization is not enough. A perspective from the museum field in the digital age. Null **16**, 42–52 (2021). https://doi.org/10.1080/17447143.2020.1859518
9. Haydar, M., Roussel, D., Maïdi, M., Otmane, S., Mallem, M.: Virtual and augmented reality for cultural computing and heritage: a case study of virtual exploration of underwater archaeological sites (preprint). Virtual Reality **15**, 311–327 (2011). https://doi.org/10.1007/s10055-010-0176-4
10. Bekele, M.K., Pierdicca, R., Frontoni, E., Malinverni, E.S., Gain, J.: A survey of augmented, virtual, and mixed reality for cultural heritage. J. Comput. Cult. Heritage (JOCCH) (2018). https://doi.org/10.1145/3145534

11. Liao, P.: Study on the value of the ancient post road orienteering competition in Southern Guangdong Province. Contemp. Sports Technol. **9**, 196–198 (2019). https://doi.org/10.16655/j.cnki.2095-2813.2019.11.196
12. Wang, C.: Research on brand building of orienteering competition of Ancient Post Road in South Guangdong of China (2020). https://doi.org/10.27011/d.cnki.gdbsu.2020.001721
13. Mort, B., Callaway, C., Zettlemoyer, L., Lee, S., Lester, J.: Towards Narrative-centered learning environments (1999)
14. Quinn, H., Schweingruber, H., Keller, T.: A framework for K-12 science education: practices, crosscutting concepts, and core ideas (2011)
15. Dickey, M.: Game design narrative for learning: appropriating adventure game design narrative devices and techniques for the design of interactive learning environments. Educ. Tech. Res. Dev. **54**, 245–263 (2006). https://doi.org/10.1007/s11423-006-8806-y
16. Zhang, W.: Narration in product design based on the regional culture (2017)

Gamified Participatory Exhibition Design Research for Future Museums

Hao He[1](✉), Xiandong Cheng[2], Ziyang Li[2], and Qi Tan[1,2]

[1] Central Academy of Fine Arts, No. 8 Hua Jia Di Nan Street, Chao Yang District, Beijing, China
hehao@cafa.edu.cn

[2] Beijing City University, No. 269 Bei Si Huan Zhong Lu, Hai Dian District, Beijing, China

Abstract. This article discusses the potential of gamified participatory design to encourage ordinary visitors to participate in the early stages of museum exhibit design. The project borrows the idea of games to have students act as visitors to design games, serving as a way to design museum exhibits. The behaviour of participants in the game will be thoroughly observed and recorded to gauge their level of participation and achievement. The project will explore how gamified participatory design can transform the museum exhibition experience, potentially enhancing the sense of participation and making educational activities more appealing and useful, while also creating a more efficient flow of information and a shared environment. The study's findings will include an analysis of survey results and a practical guide for implementing the gamified participatory design in museums.

Keywords: Gamification Design · Participatory Design · Museum

1 Introduction

1.1 Why Museum as Study Focus?

At the beginning of the 20th century, with the development and maturity of modern society and urban culture, the awareness of museums serving the public continued to increase. The exhibition is one of the primary goals of museums. Its scientific and artistic nature has also received more and more attention. The investigation and research of the visitors also began to enter the scope of museology. The new museology movement in the 1970s not only put service to society into the new definition of museums but also believed that museum exhibition is not only a top-down education but also a cultural expression and a dialogue of values It plays an important role in creating group identity and values.

Our understanding of museums and their exhibitions is constantly changing. Nowadays, in museums, experts and designers are trying to match visitors' needs, including how to better display collections for visitors, how to present the value of collections, and encourage or guide visitors in their museum experience. All of those require the full participation of visitors, but how can museums build a good relationship with their visitors and understand their needs? Museums should shift from "collection-oriented" to "people-oriented". To be able to provide a better exhibition and education experience to visitors, museums are required to provide their materials and invite people to participate, create and share.

In the museum participatory experience, we prefer that visitors could be active participants rather than passive consumers. In museums, visitors should be able to create, share and connect with each other through exhibition collections. Creating means that visitors can contribute their ideas, expressions, and objects to the museum and each other. Sharing is that visitors can discuss and bring ideas home then they will integrate and recreate the content to re-share them. Connection is the social communication between visitors or museum staff and visitors to share interests between them.

1.2 Why Do We Provide Participatory Experience and Do Participatory Design in Museums?

The museum's participatory experience is an area of research that has developed with co-design and participatory design. Since the 1960s and 1970s museums have been concerned about the growth of their visitors and their goals and economic potential. They use new ways and methods to create a better visitor experience, and museums and designers gradually begin to pay more and more attention to the needs of visitors. Different participatory techniques and approaches foresee the possibility of visitors' participation as designers, and visitors are able to be engaged individually in different levels of participatory experiences in museums. We now have many successful cases of participatory experience in museums. Although they are very successful, in the exhibition design and visiting process, not all visitors are professional designers. So, there are full of challenges in communication and development for an exhibition design.

When visitors can become active participants in the museum exhibition design process, designers will need to shift their focus to the needs of the visitors and the motivation behind their behaviour. The greatest fortune of museums not only is their collections but also the creativity of visitors. No matter what the theme of the exhibition is, visitors will have a lot of brilliant ideas, and no matter what the topic is even if it is the most complex topic, many visitors want to be able to share their opinions. Especially for younger visitors, in particular, are more proficient at applying and mastering new technologies than older visitors, and use their own different abilities to express ideas and complete tasks that have been established. For younger visitors, their methods of gathering information and generating ideas for solutions can be influenced by their abilities. The younger visitors are more interactive, have a more international perspective, and are more dynamic. They are born to be participatory design partners. Lately, there is a lot of research including young people and children to carry out participatory design with a great number of amazing ideas.

In these documents, there are many methods and guidelines that can help designers to understand the needs and behaviours of the user in different contexts, and integrate ordinary users into the design process through appropriate approaches. Although adopting users into participatory experiences and participatory design is a very challenging task. Although adopting users into participatory experiences and participatory design is a very challenging task. But users as co-designers will contribute their own different creativity and perspectives, all of which can be valuable resources for participatory experiences and design.

2 How to Create a Museum Participatory Experience

Participatory experience is not simply a method or set of methodologies, it is a mindset and an attitude about people. It is the belief that all people have something to offer to the design process and that they can be both articulate and creative when given appropriate tools with which to express themselves Gamification Communication [1].

As Partners in the design process, users should be involved in the whole process of the design and create solutions. They are a part of the design. They can guide the design decisions and evaluate possible outcomes. For example, when designing, users should be seen as equal contributors and stakeholders. When we conduct experiments, users will have to truly become such a role that is possible for us to collect effective results and to inspire their ideas. Sanders found that when users accepted their role as design partners, they performed significantly better than when only taking them as providers of evaluation feedback or technical reference related to design [1].

2.1 Gamified Participatory Design

Games are definitely the best way for the most efficient participation, and through games, we can greatly engage participation. Many theories in design research, especially in the human-computer interaction field, agree with the entertainment-based design concept studied by Malone in the 1980s. It provides a good foundation and explanation for designing a fun and interesting user experience. First of all, we need to understand what a game is and what benefits it can bring to us. And we need to understand what game design is and the key issues in game design. Based on that, I carry out a more in-depth study of how to do the gamified participatory design with users.

Many researchers have spent a lot of time to define what is "game". In 2003, Salen and Zimmerman studied many definitions of the game, and they found out that most of the definitions are about descriptions of rules, objectives and how to play. In 2013, Adams came out with the definition of the game, which is "a type of play activity, conducted in the context of a pretended reality, in which the participant(s) try to achieve at least one arbitrary, nontrivial goal by acting in accordance with rules." [2].

Games have become a part of our modern culture and an important part of our lives. When the participants are playing the game, the game has its advantages which are giving participants positive influence. For example, it can promote cognitive skills, especially spatial cognitive skills. It is an effective way of motivating and stimulating emotions. It promotes the development of social skills. And it also can stimulate participants' ability to challenge, curiosity, discover, and learn to express themselves. In "Super Better", Jane McGonigal mentioned that "Traditional video games are more complex and harder to master, and they require that the player learn a wider and more challenging range of skills and abilities." [3].

If a game can be very well designed, it can promote participants' understanding and processing ability of concepts. It can also train participants' deeper understanding of cognition theory in the development of natural and scientific knowledge. Games can also stimulate a desire to engage players and increase their willingness to engage in scientific practice and discussion. McClarty and others described in their 2012 research report that they described the theoretical and experimental evidence of related games. They claim that the use of games in education offers the following advantages: 1, Study Principles. 2, Encourage participation in the study. 3, Make Learning Opportunities More Personal. 4, Understand modern learning skills. 5, Provide a real learning environment and relevant assessments [4]. Gee mentioned in 2003 that games are very interesting activities and that people can learn and grow by playing games [5].

Now, much of our research has included gamification. The reason behind this is that games are "a way of participation, interaction, entertainment and learning". Learning is a process of participation, which can benefit participants greatly by integrating the concept of games. The gamification of education or gamified learning, especially the transformation of the gamification concept into the learning process, allows learners or participants to relate their personal learning experience and environment of participation to encourage their active participation. The goal of gamification of learning is thus to "maximize enjoyment and engagement through capturing the interest of learners and inspiring them to continue learning" in their contexts [6].

There are some advantages of the game that we could adopt to engage visitors to get involved in design participation. First of all, a game is a goal-focused activity: the shared focus on achieving specific goals, is a means to increase the amount of time dedicated to learning tasks, and consequently, it increases engagement and motivation. Second is the reward mechanisms of the game, the use of leaderboards, and prizes can be powerful motivations to encourage participants. And the progress tracking in the game, it is crucial to record and track every step in the activity.

2.2 Adopt Gamified Participatory Design Approach to Form the Co-design and Learning

In previous research, we have learnt many participatory and gamification design concepts. If we want to do design activities in a certain environment such as a museum, which means that we have to deal with a lot of challenges. Our research goal is to adopt visitors as design partners in the design process. Our previous research on the approaches and skills will be implemented in the practice.

Hamari and some other researchers' study shows that depending on the context and type of players involved, gamified activities can stimulate participation and enthusiasm by encouraging participants [7]. And different motivation theories can explain why and how to use gamification to encourage participants [8]. In the study of Deci and Ryan in 2000, they defined a framework as a guideline to support ongoing engagement. The study also stated that a gamified activity needs to meet at least 3 basic requirements. Those are 1: The awareness of progress and abilities. 2: A sense of control. 3: Social-related content. When designing for participatory design through gamification, social-related content means encouraging and promoting cooperation in the process of participating in learning and working together [9].

Adopt gamified to encourage participation in the design and learning is an approach that can be used by museum experts and designers to plan, practice and evaluate the experience of putting visitors as designers in the early stage of museum exhibition design. At the same time, it is also possible to explore visitors' or users' expectations. In 2014 Gabriella Dedero proposed a theory and approach of Gamified Co-design with cooperative learning and then she carried out a number of experiments to revise his theory. We can find out more detailed information about her research from her document since she had the idea of gamified co-design then to her practical study from 2013 to 2014 [10].

In 2015, in the International Journal of Human-Computer Studies, Frauenberger, Fitzpatrick, and Iversen published an article "in pursuit of rigour and accountability in participatory design" which mentioned a summary of 4 lenses and starter questions in the conceptual framework. These lenses are epistemology, stakeholders, values, and outcomes [11].

Many studies have shown that playing games together or participating in gamified design activities can bring many benefits to learning. Games can help learners express their understanding of things in a specific and meaningful way. In addition, learners can learn how to ask questions and provide help to others. Games can not only encourage diverse ideas but also improve the awareness of the group of participants and encourage participation in learning through play. Finally, play can also generate effective social interaction, especially for young people and children.

If we want to better use the Gamification methods, the best way is to integrate the gamification mechanics into educational activities. Specifically, there are 3 basic elements of the game that we need to .3 give serious thought to. First, games are objective-based activities. Completing the specific tasks is a shared goal for participants. The purpose is to extend the time we spend in the learning process, and by doing so we can improve engagement and motivation. Second, it is the reward system. We can use the ranking list and prizes to stimulate a stronger motivation to participate. Third, is the tracking of the process. we will have to record and track every step of the activity. This is very important. Because all the materials of the tracking will provide a reference for the later work and make sure to get a better outcome.

The gamification design is a complicated process. A good understanding of education and participatory theory is crucial to forming the appropriate activity. Based on that, we can put on additional levels of activity to make the participation more effective. For example, an activity with a clear objective will have different stages in its entire process. By completing each stage of work, participants will have a clear sense of progress and find out how much work remains. But here we need to be very careful that the game mechanics will be only used to increase the motivation in participation, and should not be used to evaluate the learning of participation.

3   Organize and Conduct the Gamified Participatory Design Workshop for the Museum Exhibition

Before the workshop, I need students to understand the following concepts.

- In most museums, experiences are passive. (Visitors are not allowed to access collections and use them. What mostly they can do is read the tags beside the collection.)
- The research would like to swift the passive experience to an active experience by adopting visitors' needs. (How we can find out visitors' needs.)
- Museum exhibitions need to put visitors in the centre and adopt user-centred design principles.
- From UCD we need to move to the Participatory Design concept.
- To provide visitors participatory experience and do the exhibition design together.
- Gamified participatory design with visitors.
- Encourage Gamification

3.1   Phases to Conduct the Workshop

The First Phase

In the first phase, students will learn and do more research about Gamified Participatory Design in depth. Students will collect and organize their research about Participatory Experience and design, and museum documents. They will have a deep understanding of the Participatory experience and how Participatory Design is applied to the general public. Meanwhile, they will have to get a basic sense of how to encourage visitors to participate in activities. Reading and analyzing this research can greatly improve students' knowledge. And they will understand why museum needs to do exhibition design with visitors on another level.

The Second Phase

In the second phase, students will focus on their primary research problems which are as below:

- How can we include different ideas from participants? In other words, how can the professional exhibition design team work together with the visitors in order to encourage visitors to have their own voice for the exhibition?
- How can we encourage the visitors to participate in the design process? What approach can we adopt?
- Is it possible to encourage visitors' participation in the early and middle stages during the design of museum exhibitions so that in this way, the exhibition can be better designed?
- Is there a good way to help museum or museum exhibition design experts understand visitors' ideas in participatory design?

The Final Phase

In the final phase, students will carry out their workshops and experiments.

- Based on the research, students will learn the challenges and constraints of applying the Participatory Design Experience and Co-Design in museums. This will be carried out through case studies and workshop practices.

- Define the methodology: Learn the results and outcomes from the research of the Participatory Design and museum problems. We will define the value and methodology of applying the Gamified Participatory Design in museum exhibition design. To reach this objective, students will do experiments to testify their ideas.
- To evaluate the Gamified Participatory Design Activities
- To evaluate the gamification materials will be used
- To evaluate the gamification tasks.
- To evaluate the role of participants.
- To observe and evaluate the performance of visitors in the Gamified Participatory Design activities.
- To evaluate the relationship between participants' performance and emotions.
- To compose a guideline on how to organize the Gamified Participatory Design.

3.2   Carry Out the Workshop

Research and Case Study
Students did in-depth research on museum exhibition design to better understand the problem from both museums and visitors. Meanwhile, students did a case study of Gamification Design, Participatory Design. They learnt social penetration strategy from Tokyo Metropolitan Art Museum, End-user engagement and multi-stakeholder co-creation from U4IoT project, and a networked participatory design system (gamification participation) from Hybrid Space Lab. All the research and case studies helped students understand the concepts and benefitted them to carry out and organize the workshop for a gamified participatory exhibition design.

Preparation and Role Setup
Students published the exhibition design notice and collected ideas and themes for the exhibition. There were 5 students selected from different majors to participate in this workshop because they were the most active ones from the idea-collecting stage. They were the most active members of the idea-generation activities. A team host was responsible for explaining the rules and monitoring the whole workshop process. And there are 2 more roles in the team: timekeeper and recorder. Besides their work, they will assist the host in keeping the workshop running.

Materials
Designed card games for helping participants to generate ideas and encourage active participation. Forms and progressive boards to help participants maintain a sense of achievement and progress. Sketch paper, pens, and taps are for participants to visualize their thoughts. Stickers can be used to vote for the favourite ideas. Snacks are for creating a comfortable environment so that participants can relax and have fun.

Steps and Rules
First of all, it will be a preparation step. Each one of the participants will get a piece of white paper, they will design a personal logo or name to visualize themselves. The host will introduce the process and rules of the game so everyone will know what to do next (Fig. 1).

The first thing to do with participants will be brainstorm. Students get inspiration from Imaginaries Lab's New Metaphors tool kits and designed a card game to help participants break the social distance and generate ideas together (Fig. 2).

Fig. 1. Preparation and personal logo design to visualize participants.

Fig. 2. Adopt and redesigned the New Metaphors tool kits to engage participants.

Second, participants will share their ideas based on the 5 W questions (When, What, Where, Why, Who) cards. This 5 W will help participants to assess their ideas not to be too wild or too personal. When they got their ideas, they will share them and group together based on their interests. Participants will discuss each idea and approach and do a case study in charge of the host. The case study will give participants more inspiration. (This session will be limited to 20 min) (Fig. 3).

Fig. 3. 5 W card game developed to help idea generation.

Third, when participants are grouped, they will get into the next step of co-design. They will find out more in detail about the 5 W questions. Participants will be asked to finish some tasks given by the host. Tasks are question-based cards such as, what is the title of the exhibition? What is the meaning of this title? What will be the content of the exhibition? How do we present the exhibition? Etc. Participants finish these questions meanwhile they will make a pattern with these cards. After this step, each participant will have a score based on their answers. The highest one will get an extra reward. This highest one will be in the final step and everyone will be working together as one group (Fig. 4).

Fig. 4. Card game developed to encourage co-design (Gamification Participation)

The final step will be making the prototype. During this process, students will finish more question-based cards to polish their thoughts and the prototype. The prototype is a structured exhibition design flow board. All the answers to the exhibition design questions will be evolved from time to time (Fig. 5).

Fig. 5. Finished progressive board to visualize the results.

Every step of the workshop will be documented and analyzed to track the development of the participation. For example, how participants get involved in the gamified participation process. Are there any achievement emotions or negative emotions at any steps? How is the interaction between different roles?

Summary and Review. All participants believe that the brainstorming section was fun and inspiring. The card game helped participants to think about others' thoughts and had more inspiration by combining each other's questions. All participants thought that the case study and sharing section should be moved forward to the after-brainstorm section rather than the answering 5 W question section. It will help participants get more ideas. Museum design experts can get involved with participants from the beginning so that they can help participants because they are regular visitors instead of professionals. There should be more reward activities in the workshop to encourage participants and give them more achievement emotions to keep encouraging participation.

The collection of the samples has certain limitations because this workshop was held at school so the participants are all design students. They might have more experience than regular visitors from museums. The minimum size of the gamified participatory design workshop should be more than 4 participants which is including at least one museum exhibition design expert.

To Organize a Gamified Participatory Museum Exhibition Design Workshop

- Collect inspirations and ideas from all possible stockholders before the workshop which is including articles, images, and items as materials for the later brainstorming section.
- Invite participants to come over to design their ideal museum exhibition.
- Set up a comfortable environment for participants and prepare all essential gamification tool kits such as pens, cards, progressive boards, rewards, etc. The host will introduce the workshop background, the process of the workshop, time and rules for participants so they will understand what they will do and how to do it.
- The beginning stage is curial for inspiring participants' curiosity and bringing them closer together. In this workshop, the organizer adopted the New Metaphors tool kits from Imaginaries Lab and redesigned them by combining them with card games which helped participants generate ideas.
- Each participant will be paid equal attention because everyone is important in the workshop. We should minimize the competitive factors during the workshop so that participants can work as a group to contribute to one goal. Museum exhibition design is a complex project that we should encourage participants to play different roles in the design process to make different contributions.
- Monitoring every step of the participatory design process to give participants enough help to encourage their participation and get a good result.
- It is important to track the activities after the gamified participatory design workshop to analyze the result for future project development.

Tools and Materials

- The New Metaphors tool kit from Imaginaries Lab was adopted and redesigned into a card game to help participants to generate ideas and inspirations.
- Identity tag (designed by participants), markers, coloured pencils, sketch paper, 5 W question cards, and progressive board.
- The timer should be placed in an obvious place to remind participants to finish every section on time. The progressive board will show the progress of the workshop so everyone has a sense of achievement.
- Recording tools to record the whole process of the workshop which includes forms, words, images, voices and videos for future analysis.

Important Roles in the Design Team. There are some important roles for team members. Every one of them will have a specific role to help organize the workshop. The host will be in charge of the whole process including introducing the idea of the workshop, explaining the rules and controlling its progress. There is an observer in the team who is responsible for observing participants' questions and emotions. The observer will take record the process for future study and analysis. A timekeeper is important in the team. He or she will keep the workshop on track to avoid participants overthinking because they have too much time.

Professionals or design experts in the design team will answer questions from participants but cannot give them ideas to avoid interfering with their participation. Answers should be open-ended which can help participants to generate more interesting thoughts.

After the workshop, the design team should review the workshop including the materials used in the workshop. Are they efficient? Can we make them better? Collecting feedback, how do participants think about the workshop? Is there any misunderstanding? Do they have achievement emotions? We have to look at the whole structure of the workshop and details to find out the problems so that we can make the future workshop better (Fig. 6).

Fig. 6. Important roles in the design team (Host, Timekeeper, Observer)

4 The Contribution of Gamification

Normally, when we refer to the approach of gamification, we actually mean the proper use of the gamification element. For example, in a situation where a game or game activity is not the goal, we can use game stories and a progress map to encourage positive emotions and participation. Using the gamification strategy and method to carry out a participatory design which is adopting games to make the whole design process, control, and social related content tangible and can be tracked and evaluated through the process of the task. All of these can help us meet the basic needs of gamification activities.

When we use a gamification design-based approach to design a participation activity, we need to have clear and valuable goals for the participants. Because only in this way, all these mentioned needs earlier can be fulfilled. In the initial stage or the first task stage of a participatory design activity, the objectives must be simple and clear enough to create a relaxed environment for people to explore and participate. So that the whole task can be easily accepted and a trusting relationship between the participants and researchers or design experts can be established. Then in the follow-up tasks, they should be linked together, and gradually increase their interest and difficulty, in order to maintain the interest and sense of participation of the participants. In addition, according to the complexity of different participants, a task can be decomposed into different levels of challenges. In the process of gamification, we can show the progress of the participants through the progress map, which can remind the participants how the progress of the entire challenge so that the participants can have a sense of control rather than a sense of competition.

In addition, in the process of participatory design, the gamification approach can give participants a strong sense of control and autonomy. In the environment of participatory design, participants need to have the power to freely explore and choose. Through games, participants can be encouraged to feel a more real sense of control and autonomy in the process of co-design. Furthermore, rewards are a part of the gamification feedback system, which is a game element created through careful analysis and research on participatory design activities in a game-based approach. According to the concept of participation in learning and work, if rewards are only seen as a method of control, or have little value for the work, the result will be that the participants feel incompetent and lack control and power, therefore reducing the effectiveness of participation and disrupting creativity [12]. So, when we use gamification for participatory design, we need to regard rewards as a token, or some kind of reward for the design work. Graves explained in his research that in the tasks and challenges the rewards need to be controlled by the participants and to be customized to have exciting effects [13].

A gamified participatory environment can help foster and promote cooperation. And through a gamified environment can meet the principle of participatory design. For example, the gamified participatory design does not increase competition within the team. Through the reward mechanisms, we can achieve it by which can help the team promote internal interdependence and cooperation.

5 Conclusion

In this paper, I used gamified participatory methods to conduct research on participatory design. Everything was defined by design goals and carried out by design protocols. This task can only be accomplished in a corporation with stakeholders such as museum exhibition experts, psychology experts, and visitors or users. This gamified participatory design research was finally conducted in a non-museum environment but would be greatly beneficial for future museum exhibition design. The whole research includes 3 phases: ideation, transfer of ideas into structured documents, and prototype.

Generally speaking, in the experience of participatory design, the result would be the real thing we got at the end, to the design delivered at the end of the design activity. This outcome includes decision-making and thinking processes, so design knowledge it can bring researchers experience and insight into cognitive theory. For example, what types of gamification approaches might different actors prefer? Using gamification approaches to do participatory design was also identified as a tangible outcome. Epistemology is knowledge about product design that is helpful for professional designers. It is a challenge for us to use the gamification method to carry out the participatory design. Whether the results obtained through the gamified participatory design of the participants can be delivered to the museum and developed by professional designers into a real exhibition design is a question worthy of our study.

Using a gamification approach to carry out participatory design activities will make knowledge more valuable, and it can also enable participants to be better encouraged in gamified participatory design activities so that participants can participate better. This valuable knowledge includes the results achieved by the participants at the end of the gamified participatory design; Evaluate and discussing the quality of participants' design achievements in the whole process of gamification participatory design; The evaluation and discussion of the design achievements in the whole process of gamified participatory design; Furthermore, use knowledge as a means to judge if participants have learnt design skills or other knowledge through working together in the process of gamified participatory design [10].

Through gamified participatory design, it can help participants make their design more tangible and enhance their related knowledge. All of these will be reflected in the gamified participatory design process where participants were engaged in the activity. The outcome of the design and the enhancement of knowledge is part of the result. These results still need to be evaluated by effective methods, especially the participants' concentration, interest and enjoyment in the process of participation [14]. Through the evaluation of the emotion of achievement, we can understand whether the participants are positively related to emotions of happiness or enjoyment or negatively related to emotions of anxiety or boredom during the participation process [15]. Since the knowledge involved in participatory design is related to co-creation and contextual relations, and its background is quite complex, gamified participatory design tends to use mixed research methods for evaluation. We need to collect a large amount of data for analysis and interpret these data by using quality data analysis.

The user-centred design method and gamified participatory design are similar in evaluation in a lot of ways so they can depend on each other. When doing the evaluation, we may consider working with experts in some related research fields. Such as getting feedback from end users by observing how users experience the design. In this research, it would be better if experts are from museum exhibition design and some other design industries, and the users are from real museum visitors. In future research, I will correct the problems I have found now, and try to invite real museum exhibition design experts and visitors to do a real gamified participatory museum exhibition design.

References

1. Sanders, E.B.-N.: From user-centered to participatory design approaches. In: Design and Social Science (2002)
2. Adams, E.: Fundamentals of Game Design. 3rd edn. Pearson, Allyn (2013)
3. McGonigal, J.: SuperBetter: A Revolutionary Approach to Getting Stronger, Happier, Braver, and More Resilient - Powered by the science of Games. Penguin (2015)
4. McClarty, K., Orr, A., Frey, P., Dolan, R., Vassileva, V., McVay, A.: A literature review of gaming in education. Res. Rep. (2012)
5. Gee, J.P.: What video games have to teach us about learning and literacy. Compute. Entertain. 1(1), 20 (2003)

6. Huang, W., Soman, D.: A practitioner's guide to the gamification of education. Research Report Series Behavioural Economics in Action (2013)
7. Hamari, J., Koivisto, J., Sarsa, H.: Does gamification work? A literature review of empirical studies on gamification. In: Proceedings of 47th Hawaii International Conference on System Sciences (2014)
8. Kapp, K.M.: The Gamification of Learning and Instruction. Pfeiffer, San Francisco (2012)
9. Ryan, R.M., Dec, E.L.: Self-determination theory and the facilitation of intrinsic motivation, social development, and well-being (2000)
10. Dodero, G., Gennari, R., Melonio, A., Torello, S.: Gamified co-design with cooperative learning. In: Proceedings of In CHI 2014 Extended Abstracts on Human Factors in Computing Systems, pp. ages 707–718. ACM, New York (2014)
11. Frauenberger, C., Good, J., Fitzpatrick, G., Iversen, O.S.: In pursuit of rigour and accountability in participatory design. Int. J. Hum. Comput. Stud. **74**, 93–106 (2015). https://www.ncbi.nlm.nih.gov/pmc/articles/PMC4375798/
12. Deci, E.L., Ryan, R.M.: Intrinsic Motivation and Self-determination in Human Behavior. Plenum (1985)
13. Graves, T.: The controversy over group rewards in cooperative classrooms. Educ. Leadersh. **48**, 77–79 (1991)
14. Hamari, J., Shernoff, D.J., Rowe, E., Coller, B., Asbell-Clarke, J., Edwards, T.: Challenging games help students learn: an empirical study on engagement, flow and immersion in game-based learning. Comput. Hum. Behav. **54**, 170–179 (2016)
15. Kahu, E., Stephens, C., Leach, L., Zepke, N.: Linking academic emotions and student engagement: mature-aged distance students' transition to university. J. Furth. High. Educ. **39**(4), 481–497 (2015)

Play and Interpret in Art Museum's Games: A Systematic Review

Lin Lin[✉] ⓘ and Yuwei Tan

Nanfang College, Guangzhou, Guangzhou, China
llin65-c@my.cityu.edu.hk

Abstract. Games are gaining popularity in art museums as a form of communication that improves the visiting experience. However, little research has shed light on the influence of games on visitors' grasp of the museum narrative and their interpretation (as opposed to the acquisition of factual information) during the gameplay. In addition, few mature design methods can integrate games with museum content to reach games' full potential. How to combine the game with the exhibition to make a meaningful and inspiring play? What factors might influence the visitors' interpretation gained through the museum gameplay experience? Around these issues, this study aims to enrich this field of research by conducting a systematic review of game studies in art museums using the PRISMA protocol. Our review focuses on game design practices and their evaluation in art museums. The review results indicate a research gap in the evaluation method of visitors' interpretation during the art museum gameplay, and more research is needed in the field.

Keywords: Games in Museums · Museum Experience · Systematic Review

1 Introduction

Art museums are committed to enhancing the exhibition experience for educational and communication purposes by using multimedia. Among popular multimedia forms, games have been promising vehicles for academics, education, and learning [1]. Museums are ideal places for building games and activities because they offer applicable edutainment spaces (Nicholson [2] called them Ludic learning places) and abundant experience time. A museum game is developed based on museum contents and played by visitors during their visit and exploration. Usually, the museum visitors (also the players) follow the instruction in gameplay to search or observe the physical exhibits and complete some tasks [3] summarized the museum game tasks as observation tasks, which stimulate spatial reasoning and contextualized search in identifying parts of a painting; reflection tasks, which aim for the synthesis of clues and past information through quizzes; and arcade tasks, which stimulate fantasy as in the ancient world simulation games. Whichever game task or design serves the goal of the art museum experience: to bring visitors a fun experience with the hope that they can learn something from the play and, ideally, further make interpretations from a personal sense with prior knowledge.

A. Marcus et al. (Eds.): HCII 2023, LNCS 14034, pp. 88–100, 2023.
https://doi.org/10.1007/978-3-031-35705-3_7

However, there are problems and debates with games in art museums. On the one hand, in many cases, museum content is stiffly combined with game forms, such as old-fashioned jigsaw puzzles and quizzes, without considering how the interaction helps the learning process [4]. On the other hand, there are critiques that many art museum game designs focus too much on factual information and narration, and far too few possibilities are left for visitors through the game [5]. Moreover, the varying outcome measures and evaluation methods indicated a lack of standardization, leading to inconclusive results in the museum game's evaluation [6, 7]. These issues prompted us to explore the game design approach and its effectiveness in learning in the context of art museums. We hope to explore whether art museum games conduce to visitors' interpretation of the exhibition and figure that it is essential to have a comprehensive evaluation method and indicators to evaluate the degree of interpretation during the gameplay. Unlike the information in science museums, which is primarily facts and norms, the information in art museums is interwoven with social, humanistic, and personal understanding, thus putting forward higher demand for the evaluation process of learning effectiveness.

There are many game studies for art museums, but they rarely use mature game design methods and pay little attention to the visitors' interpretation during gameplay. Therefore, this paper systematically studies the game designs in art museums and the interpretation brought to visitors by art museum's games. Specifically, our review is based on two research questions (RQs): (1) What is the design guideline or method for designing art museum games? (2) What is the interpretation visitors gain by playing art museum games? In the rest of the article, we will introduce previous work, describe details of our review methodology, process, and result, discuss our findings regarding our research question, and conclude with a summary of future research direction.

2 Previous Work

In art museum games studies, learning effectiveness is a significant research factor. Many studies and scholars recognize the potential of museum games to promote learning. Play theorist Sutton-Smith proposed that game is a metaphor [8]. The statement emphasizes the metaphorical feature of games, which means the player could probability unfold the metaphor and learn something during the play, thereby gaining interpretation. According to game-based learning theory (GBL), games promote players' learning with their unique ways of conveying information, including providing an immersive virtual environment, instantaneous feedback, and continual encouragement to stimulate learning motivation, triggering empathy and provoking thoughts [9] argued that the uptake and adoption of learning resources often require supplemented understanding of different dimensions in an effective learning milieu and educational game as one approach for addressing the epistemological problem "through raising motivation, social and cognitive engagement, and cultural relevance of learning interactions, and the consequent improvement to players' cognition."

Art museum games provide an engaging way for visitors to learn during the exhibition. There is a great deal of research on art museum game experience. Most of them demonstrated that art museum games bring a fun experience to visitors, their storytelling immerses the visitors in museum narrative, and their incentive mechanisms such as points, bonuses, rewards, and tasks stimulate visitors learning motivation (see for examples [7, 9]). [13]conducted comparative experiences and discovered that cooperative games provide a social interaction context that facilitates visitor communication and discussion. The context, both from the virtual games and other players on site, enhances information retention and learning motivation.

However, art museum games' influence on learning effects has not been further explored, and there is controversy on the role of games in art museums. In art museums, learning is intertwined with "aesthetic experiences, prolonged and careful looking, personal recollections and reflections, and exploratory talk with friends and family" [14]. Art museums expect their visitors not only to grasp the authoritative art explanation but also to generate meaning beyond the art knowledge from a personal perspective. This is also a crucial purpose of art education—interpretation [15], a process of meaning-making with prior knowledge. However, as aforementioned, most art museum games focus on combining factual information, with little consideration of how games assist visitors' interpretation and the possible influencing factors.

Some studies have corroborated these concerns [11] discovered that in art museum games, visitors were capable of identifying and memorizing factual information such as names, numbers, and stories, but were weak in induction comparison and abstract generalization [16] found that although visitors were willing to explore exhibits according to the game instruction, they were disinclined to deepen the knowledge related to the exhibit's story and lacked confidence in the new knowledge gained in the game. Literature reviews and commentaries also demonstrated that art museum games still lack systematic methods, theory, and tools [5, 16], as well as the validation of their effectiveness in terms of art education [1]. Therefore, more exploration of art museum games design and learning outcome evaluation is needed, especially regarding factors that affect the interpretation-making process.

3 Methodology

We used the PRISMA review framework [18] to work on our review. PRISMA "primarily focuses on the reporting of reviews evaluating the effects of interventions" (prisma-statement.org). Although it was originally developed for healthcare, it has been more commonly used in other fields in recent years. [19] showed us its applicability in the game-related field by providing an exemplar of a clear, comprehensive, and extensible systematic review of the game topic that was. Thus, we used the PRISMA framework to achieve our review objectives: to prepare for our games design study for art museums in the next stage and hopefully provide an extensible and sustainable review for other related scholars and avoid duplication of effort.

Based on the PRISMA review framework, we conducted three rounds of systematic screening in the SpringerLink and ACM digital library databases. We chose these databases because they include articles from social science, technology, and education fields. We made three rounds of screening to get the final sample. First, we searched the determined keywords in these databases. Then, we screened the title and abstract with the eligibility criteria. Lastly, we screened the full text to ensure they met the same criteria. We retained articles from journals and conferences and excluded commentaries, proposals, dissertations, and columns. The theme of the papers included different types of games designed in an art museum and the evaluation of the visitors' game experience.

3.1 Keyword Search

We searched our pre-determined keywords from 28th December to 30th December 2022. We used sets of keywords ("game" OR "games") AND ("museum" OR "exhibition") to search the title and abstract in SpringerLink and ACM Digital library and got 38 papers and 41 papers, respectively. In total, we retrieved 79 records. After removing one duplicate, 78 papers were left for the second screening.

3.2 Titles and Abstracts Screening

In the second round of screening, we screened 78 papers with our exclusion criteria. The criteria were set according to the objectives of our systematic review. We considered studies that focus on art museum games design and evaluation. Therefore, we had the criteria below, and the paper that meets one of the criteria was excluded.

- C1: Not an empirical study (e.g., literature review, dissertation, thesis, proposal;
- $n = 10$)
- C2: Not a game (e.g., interactive settings that use a game development engine;
- $n = 14$)
- C3: Not a game to be played in a museum (e.g., a museum-themed game, an online museum game; $n = 1$)
- C4: Not art museum games (e.g., natural science museum game; $n = 12$)

After eliminating 37 papers against our criteria, 41 papers remained in the sample.

3.3 Full-Text Screening

With the result of the second round of screening, we went through the remaining 41 papers that we had access to and screened the full text with our criteria. In this round, 27 more papers were removed.

- C1: Not an empirical study (e.g., literature review, dissertation, thesis, proposal;
- $n = 7$)
- C2: Not a game (e.g., interactive settings that use a game development engine;
- $n = 1$)
- C3: Not a game to be played in a museum (e.g., a museum-themed game, an online museum game; $n = 2$)
- C4: Not art museum games (e.g., natural science museum game; $n = 10$)
- C5: Not evaluate the learning outcome (e.g., no evaluation or only test the view on technology; $n = 6$)

Finally, we have our sample: 5 papers and 9 papers from SpringerLink and ACM Digital library, totaling 14 papers. Following the PRISMA guidelines, the overview of the process of selecting papers is displayed in Fig. 1.

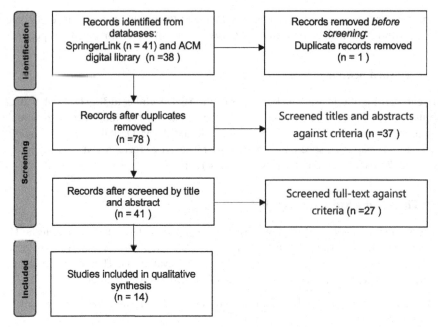

Fig. 1. The PRISMA selection process of relevant literature

4 Results

There are 79 papers in our initial search in two databases. After removing a duplicate and two rounds of screening by our screening steps and exclusion criteria, 14 papers remain as our final sample. The total number of papers screened by the criteria is listed in Table 1.

Table 1. Summary of the excluded articles

Exclusion criteria	Number
C1: Not an empirical study	17
C2: Not a game	15
C3: Not a game to be played in a museum	3
C4: Not art museum games	22
C5: Not evaluate the learning outcomes	7
Total	64

The papers were published between 2007 to 2023, and nearly half of the papers (6 out of 14) were published in the last five years, indicating that art museum games and related research have received increased attention in the recent decade. In addition, the sample reflected a tremendous interest in Europe ($n = 13$). However, there is only one study from another area (China, Taiwan). The studies were conducted in European countries, including Greece, Italy, Germany, Belgium, Athens, and the United Kingdom. The theme of these studies can be summarized as three themes: (1) to develop an educational game for art museums; (2) to use different interactive technology and explore the experience; (3) to make an evaluation of the game experience and learning outcomes. In general, all studies reported positive outcomes or potential benefits of art museum games on art museum experience and education.

Next, we collected the information from the final paper set. A coding framework with details of each paper is shown in Table 2 (game design part) and Table 3 (evaluation part). The analytic code includes (1) game genres, game design method or theory, and technology; (2) evaluation purpose and key findings.

As shown in Table 2, the game types included location-based games, escape room games, simulation games, story games, and critical games. In terms of game devices and technologies, most of the game interfaces were implemented on PAD or mobile phones, with the aim of allowing visitors to explore freely in the museum. Since the game tasks usually asked visitors to find and observe exhibits at specific locations in the exhibition hall, most of the games set up feedback mechanics to trigger specific information by location. These instant feedback mechanics used techniques such as image recognition scanning, NFC modules, Bluetooth modules, etc. Most studies presented their game design process and illustrated the design method. In general, these art museum games were developed using design methods or frameworks from the field of human-computer interaction design or based on learning models or information processing frameworks. In terms of evaluation methodology (see Table 3), the sample used quantitative and qualitative research methods, including questionnaires, semi-structured interviews, surveys, observation notes, field tests, video recordings, and focus groups. The participants covered teenagers, adults, and professionals in related areas, and the number of participants in the final sample's evaluation ranged from 2 to 156. The evaluations focused on two aspects: the game experience and the learning outcomes.

Table 2. Coding framework (Part I: Game design)

Paper	Game Genres	Design Method or Theory	Technology
[20]	Scrabble-like Game(group game)	Focuses on the principles of the educational design, on the use of mobile technology	PDA(Personal Digital Assistant), RFID tags
[21]	Serious Game (group game)	Follow the design thinking work process Based on contextual learning model Informal learning method	Virtual Reality, Hologram
[22]	Social Game (group game)	Not explicitly stated	PDA, XML parsers, IRDA signals
[16]	Location-Based Mobile Game, Story Game (single-player game)	Storytelling approach	Indoor positioning system based on the recognition of visual markers, AR
[23]	Serious Game (group game)	Based on contextual model of learning(CML) framework	Collaborative virtual environments (CVE), Projector
[24]	Simulation game, Serious Game (group game)	Based on contextual model of learning(CML) framework	Wireless Xbox controllers, Projector
[10]	Role-playing game (single-player game)	Research Through Design	Mobile phone camera, Artcode
[13]	Collaborative game (group game)	Based on contextual model of learning (CML) framework User-centered design (UCD)	PDA, Voice-over-IP (VOIP), Wi-Fi-based localization
[11]	Serious game (single-player game)	Use a descriptive model as a classification method for game Based on situated learning theory, constructive learning theory and game-based learning theory	Computer
[25]	Escape room (group game)	Mixed-method research Authorship Versus User-led Design, iterative constructivist approach and participatory action research	Microsoft HoloLens (VR), beacon technology
[26]	Escape room (single-player game)	Not explicitly stated	Web browser (html5, xml)
[12]	Simulation game (single-player game)	Not explicitly stated	Computer, simulation controller
[27]	Role-Playing Game (single-player game)	Information Theory and Rough Set	Smartphone app, PDA
[28]	Storytelling Game Card Game (group game)	User-centered design (UCD)	Paper prototype, digital cards to be designed in future

Table 3. Coding framework (Part II: Evaluation)

Paper	Evaluation Purpose	Key Findings
[20]	To test the functionalities and to observe how visitors respond to the game's characteristics	1) Children develop "a task-oriented way" of treating exhibit information; 2) Task-oriented practice help students to formulate a concrete and clear idea about the exhibits they play with
[21]	To test the game and issue a questionnaire to survey people's views on the game	1) Learning is optimized when parents and children share joint attention and respond to each other; 2) Students have a high memory rate of content directly included in the game
[22]	To survey people's views on the game	1) The games were judged amusing, intuitive, helping the learning process, and successful in pushing people collaborate and socialize; 2) Players less like the difficult task
[16]	To understand how the location-based mobile game influence visitors' behaviors and investigate whether it is effective in fostering enjoyment and learning	1) The game promotes an exploratory style of visiting museum; 2) Interacting with a digital interface is a difficult and time-/attention-consuming task
[23]	To test the game with different populations having diverse cultural backgrounds, interests, and motivation to learn about the topic; to assess the effects of these factors on the game experience and learning outcomes	1) The higher interactivity level leads to higher learning gain and the player's knowledge acquisition (more than two players participate together); 2) Tension in the interactive conditions negatively affects learning, while increasing collaboration opportunities elicit a higher sense of being together; 3) Learning gains are contingent on the profile of the visitors, with culture-specific learning style and cognitive development affecting the optimal means for information assimilation
[24]	To evaluate the understanding of the game content from three levels: factual information, conceptual knowledge of the domain, and understanding of the collaborative task	1) Expert guidance leads to more factual information and better understanding. Cooperation helps in understanding; 2) The controller scores higher on the quiz than others; 3) In multi-player games, players immerse in the social and gameplay and learn less; 4) Learning styles lead to poor performance of Greek students in game interaction; 5) Prior knowledge affects new knowledge interpretation; 6) Greek students lack discovery learning skills for game's learning, but gain more with discovery guide; 7) Collaborative culture makes students focus more on social relationships and equal opportunities for collaboration, which is not conducive to experience or learning

(continued)

Table 3. (*continued*)

Paper	Evaluation Purpose	Key Findings
[10]	To invest the feedback and insights gained from the game	Game 1: 1)Interesting and fun, stimulating thinking; 2) Interrupting the experience, being attracted by the mobile phone, a weak connection with the exhibits, lack of deep thinking and consideration of seriousness Game 2: 1)Spiritual, powerful, thoughtful resonance; 2)Some of the themes are belittled and experience are interrupted
[13]	To invest 1) the social interaction promoted by games; 2) the museum narrative delivery by experiencing the museum story again 3) the cognitive skills of learning history and visiting museums	1) Games promote social interaction even on unexpected parts (e.g. creating avatar); 2) The museum narrative is delivered; 3) Players process information from various sources and closely observing objects
[11]	To evaluate the games' educational potential and the ability to enhance visiting motivation	1) Players read additional text messages even when they weren't asked to; 2) Have a good memory for art forms (such as color); 3) Quiz help learns specific features but does not help understand categories and develop abstract thinking
[25]	To invest the intention to visit the museum, usefulness of receiving information, ease of use, and playability	1) AR installation encourage visit; 2) Have usability issue; 3) The device is hard for people who have not used it
[26]	To test the game's usability and educational potential	1) The game has potential in revealing the information behind the objects; 2) The games provides important training in spotting exhibits details; 3) Quiz questions lead to understanding important issues; 4) The easy level of the game might be difficult for people without relate knowledge
[12]	To test if players 1) understand the game and control; 2) like the game; 3) achieve the learning objectives (factual knowledge	1) All players understand the game and the control; 2) Shooting games are more popular for boys and the simulation game is only played by girls; 3) Not everyone achieved the learning goal; factual knowledge not applied in the game was not remembered very well
[27]	To test if: 1) visitors learned by play; 2) games make visitors spend more time in the museum; 3) knowledge retained through games last longer	All assumptions are proved
[28]	To investigates the visitors opinions and game experiences	1) The Game builds connection and familiarization with the artworks; 2) Good group interaction and stimulate diverse perspectives; 3) Trigger imagination and creativity

5 Discussion

5.1 Game Design

In terms of game design, many articles emphasized the importance of art museum content and considered connecting virtual game interaction with physical exhibition artefacts in physical places. However, in their design processes, it is rare to see discussion and consideration of how to design the game's interaction in terms of critical discussion, reasoning, or creative thinking. Most of them focused on reproducing ancient scenes, appropriating applicable game mechanics, and carrying factual information. It is noteworthy that in our sample of 16 papers, only two studies in their initial game design process focused on critical thinking and interpretation. [10] argued that art museum games should promote critical thinking and ask players to think about old things from a modern perspective, thus promoting critical dialogue between visitors and the story. When designing the game, [28] took a different direction by handing the story-making process to the visitors, actively involving them in the interpretation. In the other studies, only after the gameplay did [25] reflect that the education goal of art museum games should be heuristic and promote understanding based on game context rather than facts. The review of the game design indicated a general absence of considering the interpretation during the game design or to say, what the interpretation-related skill or knowledge should be developed was often unclear at the beginning of the game design. Considering the inadequacies of the existing game design method and tools, we believe that new game paradigms are urgently needed for art museums' game design.

5.2 Learning Outcome and Evaluation

Our review indicates that it is crucial to consider the visitors' interpretation during the art museum gameplay because it can, in turn, guide game design. In our sample, all the papers used gameplay as an experimental method for user studies. They mainly adopted evaluation frameworks from the digital product design field regarding user experience (UX) research, which usually assesses motivation, expectation, usability, information, entertainment, engagement, and overall assessment and satisfaction. Only three studies [23, 24, 28] adopted a method in game research, the Game Experience Questionnaire (GEQ) and Social Presence Questionnaire (SPGQ), to study player experiences. Most studies in the sample showed positive outcomes, whether on the game experience or learning effect. Nevertheless, it still reveals a huge gap in research on the evaluation of the interpretation visitors gain from the art museum games.

In the sample, evaluation regarding the learning outcome can be divided into two types: to evaluate the degree of gaining factual information and to evaluate other learning aspects, mainly cognition or understanding (see Table 4).

Table 4 indicates that most papers ($n = 13$) verified whether the game helped the visitors recall essential factual information and make the correct answers. Only 4 papers closely focused on the visitors' gain of understanding the story or concepts, diverse perspectives, and theme-related critical thinking. Regarding assessment methods, the criteria for assessing factual information were questionnaires, quizzes, time spent reading text information, and observations. At the same time, the methods for assessing

Table 4. Papers and their focus on learning outcomes evaluation

Learning Outcomes	Paper	Total
Focus on factual information (e.g., memory for shapes and colors, information about objects)	[11–13, 16, 20–28]	13
Focus on interpretation (e.g., understanding of exhibition concepts, stories, critical thinking, imagination)	[10, 11, 23, 28]	4

other learning aspects were usually semi-structured interviews and group discussions, usually without clear criteria in the analytics. As stated previously, art museum education emphasizes instructional understanding based on information. Therefore, learning and memorizing factual information can only partially represent the harvest of understanding. Measuring the learning outcomes might require not only traditional HCI performance metrics but also a combination of performance metrics in the field of games and learning. The analysis of our sample indicates that there is still a lack of effective frameworks and guidelines for assessing visitor interpretation in the context of art museum games.

5.3 Other Findings

We noticed that art museum game development and the learning outcome evaluation took a lot of time and effort. The study often requires the cooperation of game developers, scholars, museum experts, participants, and relevant institutions, as well as sufficient space and time, creating difficulties for art museum game research. It would be better to have mature design theory, framework, and tools available for art museum game practice. However, there is still no mature way. Art museums share similar educational purposes but vary in content, and they have to design their games from the beginning to the end. It seems impossible if a museum wants to quickly produce a fun and meaningful game within a short curatorial period.

This review has its limitations. First, to retain a large pool of sample in the first step, we only used the search terms "games" related to games but may have missed studies that use "gamification" or "edugames" to refer to museum games. Also, the search term "museum" is not exhaustive as it excludes papers that use "exhibition", "gallery" or "cultural heritage" instead of "museum". Moreover, due to time constraints, we only collected analysis papers from two databases. More articles from different databases would enrich this review.

6   Conclusions

The results of this systematic review present a research potential on design methods and the learning evaluation for games in art museums. Art museum games bring visitors knowledge, but only superficial. Admittedly, the way to assess learning outcomes is not comprehensive and pays little attention to changes from an interpretation perspective. This lack of attention has, in turn, affected game design. Very few art museum games have considered how art museum games can be inspiring and how they can fully assist in visitors' interpretation gains. As a result, the art museum game is still not living up to its potential. In future research, we are interested in new game design paradigms focusing on artwork interpretation and identifying factors influencing the interpretation process during the art museum game experience.

References

1. Nakatsu, R., Rauterberg, M., Ciancarini, P. (eds.): Handbook of Digital Games and Entertainment Technologies. Springer, Singapore (2017). https://doi.org/10.1007/978-981-4560-50-4
2. Nicholson, S.: A recipe for meaningful gamification', in Gamification in education and business, pp. 1–20. Springer (2015)
3. Bellotti, F., Berta, R., De Gloria, A., D'ursi, A., Fiore, V.: A serious game model for cultural heritage. J. Comput. Cult. Herit. **5**(4), 1–27 (2012). https://doi.org/10.1145/2399180.2399185
4. Madsen, K.M. : A critical literature review and discussion of gamification in museums, p. 18 (2020)
5. Kraemer, H.P.: On the way to the total amusement park. What Science Museums could learn from Art Museums (and vice versa). In: International Symposium of Science Museums 2018 (2018)
6. All, A., Castellar, E.P.N., Van Looy, J.: Measuring effectiveness in digital game-based learning: A methodological review. Int. J. Serious Games **1**(2) (2014)
7. Paliokas, I., Sylaiou, S.: The use of serious games in museum visits and exhibitions: a systematic mapping study. In: 2016 8th International Conference on Games and Virtual Worlds for Serious Applications (VS-GAMES), Barcelona, Spain, pp. 1–8 (Sep. 2016). https://doi.org/10.1109/VS-GAMES.2016.7590371
8. Sutton-Smith, B.: The ambiguity of play. Harvard University Press, Cambridge, Mass (1997)
9. Ravenscroft, A., McAlister, S.: Digital games and learning in cyberspace: A dialogical approach. E-Learn. Digit. Media **3**(1), 37–50 (2006)
10. Løvlie, A.S., et al.: Playing games with tito: designing hybrid museum experiences for critical play. J. Comput. Cult. Herit. **14**(2), 1–26 (2021). https://doi.org/10.1145/3446620
11. Antoniou, A., Lepouras, G., Bampatzia, S., Almpanoudi, H.: An approach for serious game development for cultural heritage: Case study for an archaeological site and museum. J. Comput. Cult. Herit. **6**(4), 1–19 (2013). https://doi.org/10.1145/2532630.2532633
12. Jenner, W., de Araújo, L.M.: Hanse 1380 - A learning game for the german maritime museum. In: Cress, U., Dimitrova, V., Specht, M. (eds.) EC-TEL 2009. LNCS, vol. 5794, pp. 794–799. Springer, Heidelberg (2009). https://doi.org/10.1007/978-3-642-04636-0_86
13. Schroyen, J.,et al.: Training social learning skills by collaborative mobile gaming in museums. In: Proceedings of the 2008 International Conference on Advances in Computer Entertainment Technology, Yokohama Japan, pp. 46–49 (Dec. 2008). https://doi.org/10.1145/1501750.1501760
14. Pierroux, P., Krange, I., Sem, I.: Bridging contexts and interpretations: Mobile blogging on art museum field trips. MedieKultur J. Media Commun. Res. 27(50) (2011). https://doi.org/10.7146/mediekultur.v27i50.2997
15. Bockemühl, M.: 'Zu Grundfragen der Betrachtung, der Kunstvermittlung und zur Zukunft der Museen', Zum Bedeut. Kunstmuseen Positionen Visionen Zu Inszenierung Dok. Vermittl. Verl. Für Mod. Kunst Nuremberg, pp. 102–117 (1998)
16. Rubino, I., Barberis, C., Xhembulla, J., Malnati, G.: Integrating a location-based mobile game in the museum visit: evaluating visitors' behaviour and learning. J. Comput. Cult. Herit. **8**(3), 1–18 (2015). https://doi.org/10.1145/2724723

17. Heilbrunn, B., Herzig, P., Schill, A.: Gamification analytics—methods and tools for monitoring and adapting gamification designs. In: Gamification, pp. 31–47. Springer (2017). https://doi.org/10.1007/978-3-319-45557-0_3

18. Shamseer, L., et al.: Preferred reporting items for systematic review and meta-analysis protocols (PRISMA-P) 2015: elaboration and explanation. BMJ **349**(1), g7647–g7647 (2015). https://doi.org/10.1136/bmj.g7647

19. Li, S., Li, E., Yuan, X.: Online social games in the eyes of children and teens: a systematic review. In: Fang, X., (ed.)HCI in Games, vol. 13334, pp. 245–255. Springer International Publishing, Cham (2022). https://doi.org/10.1007/978-3-031-05637-6_15

20. Yiannoutsou, N., Papadimitriou, I., Komis, V., Avouris, N.: Playing with museum exhibits: designing educational games mediated by mobile technology. In: Proceedings of the 8th International Conference on Interaction Design and Children, Como Italy, pp. 230–233 (Jun. 2009). https://doi.org/10.1145/1551788.1551837

21. Stanković Elesini, U., et al.: Mobile serious game for enhancing user experience in museum. J. Comput. Cult. Herit. **16**(1), 1–26 (2023). https://doi.org/10.1145/3569088

22. Dini, R., Paternò, F., Santoro, C.: An environment to support multi-user interaction and cooperation for improving museum visits through games. In: Proceedings of the 9th International Conference on Human Computer Interaction with Mobile Devices and Services

23. Apostolellis, P., Bowman, D.A.: Small group learning with games in museums: effects of interactivity as mediated by cultural differences. In: Proceedings of the 14th International Conference on Interaction Design and Children, Boston Massachusetts, pp. 160–169 (Jun. 2015). https://doi.org/10.1145/2771839.2771856

24. Apostolellis, P., Bowman, D.A., Chmiel, M.: supporting social engagement for young audiences with serious games and virtual environments in museums. In: Vermeeren, A., Calvi, L., Sabiescu, A. (eds.) Museum Experience Design. SSCC, pp. 19–43. Springer, Cham (2018). https://doi.org/10.1007/978-3-319-58550-5_2

25. Krzywinska, T., Phillips, T., Parker, A., Scott, M.J.: From immersion's bleeding edge to the augmented telegrapher: a method for creating mixed reality games for museum and heritage contexts. J. Comput. Cult. Herit. **13**(4), 1–20 (2020). https://doi.org/10.1145/3414832

26. Antoniou, A., Dejonai, M.I., Lepouras, G.: 'Museum escape': a game to increase museum visibility. In: Liapis, A., Yannakakis, G.N., Gentile, M., Ninaus, M. (eds.) GALA 2019. LNCS, vol. 11899, pp. 342–350. Springer, Cham (2019). https://doi.org/10.1007/978-3-030-34350-7_33

27. Chang, C., Chang, M., Heh, J.-S.: National palace museum adventure—a mobile educational role-playing game for museum learning. In: Kinshuk, Huang, R., (eds.) Ubiquitous Learning Environments and Technologies, pp. 201–223. Springer, Berlin Heidelberg (2015). https://doi.org/10.1007/978-3-662-44659-1_11

28. Vayanou, M., Ioannidis, Y., Loumos, G., Kargas, A.: How to play storytelling games with masterpieces: from art galleries to hybrid board games. J. Comput. Educ. **6**(1), 79–116 (2018). https://doi.org/10.1007/s40692-018-0124-y

29. Bauer, D., Pierroux, P.: Expert and adolescent interpretive approaches in a national art museum. Mus. Manag. Curatorship **29**(3), 260–279 (2014). https://doi.org/10.1080/09647775.2014.919162

Research on the Design of Interactive Installation in New Media Art Based on Machine Learning

Miao Liu[✉] [iD] and Jiayi Li

East China University of Science and Technology, Shanghai 200237, People's Republic of China
183787975@qq.com

Abstract. With the development of artificial intelligence technology and the change of information dissemination mode, the design concept of new media interactive device gradually changes to diversification and conceptualization. The main research of this paper is to explore the methods and development prospects of interaction design of new media interactive installation art under the premise of machine learning as the design method with the participation of algorithms. This paper summarizes the methods of using new media interactive installations in the context of machine learning, and explores the forms of expression of artificial intelligence technology in new media art. Starting with the new media interactive installation combining artificial intelligence and machine learning technology, this paper discusses the dynamic installation art based on machine learning from several aspects, including the presentation of interactive installation in mainstream application scenes, the current situation of artificial intelligence application in interactive installation art, and the specific application of machine learning at present.By understanding and mastering design methods based on machine learning technologies, using artificial intelligence as a new media tool and platform to bring out the creativity of human-machine collaborative creation.

Keywords: Machine learning · new media art · new media installation art

1 Introduction

With the emergence of Human-Computer Interaction Technology, 3D Interaction Technology and Virtual Reality Technology, new media art has entered the field of "digital". The greatest characteristic of the digital age is its immateriality, which does not rely much on a relatively fixed material carrier. Through the support of computer technology and tools, new media art can be disseminated in any electronic media space. Its unique characteristics of virtualization, infinite reproduction, rapid dissemination, and permanent preservation have changed the visual expression and information dissemination of new media art installations, and the concept of new media art has gradually shifted toward diversification and conceptualization.

New media interactive installation art, as installation art in the form of combining human-computer interaction technology and new media, has become a contemporary

A. Marcus et al. (Eds.): HCII 2023, LNCS 14034, pp. 101–112, 2023.
https://doi.org/10.1007/978-3-031-35705-3_8

trend in the art world. Camera technology, digital imaging, artificial intelligence, and virtual reality are often used in the work. New media interactive installation artworks are often designed with rich expressions that cross borders, such as music performance, audio-visual media, etc., giving it the emerging potential of sound and image creation. Artists combine independent and cross disciplinary art pieces together, thus triggering sensory sensations other than visual ones, and communicating and integrating art and thoughts and emotions.

With the continuous development of artificial intelligence technology in recent years, artificial intelligence and new media art have produced many combinations. In the era of artificial intelligence, AI technology has been used as an emerging art medium, not only as a tool for painting brushes, but also as an art creation mechanism for media art creators. Today, artificial intelligence is no longer used as a single tool to stimulate artistic creativity, but also extends the traditional medium of expression to achieve the purpose of human-computer collaborative creation, broaden the ideas and forms of creation, and realize the expression of various ideologies that cannot be achieved by traditional art creation.

The main research of this paper is to explore the methods and development prospects of interaction design of new media interactive installation art under the premise of machine learning as the design method with the participation of algorithms. This paper summarizes the methods of using new media interactive installations in the context of machine learning, and explores the forms of expression of artificial intelligence technology in new media art.

This paper focuses on the design of interactive installations in new media art based on machine learning, and carries out research on five sections. The first section introduces the current research and background information on artificial intelligence and new media art. This paragraph briefly introduces the intersection of artificial intelligence and technology and new media art with interactive installation art, analyzes the connection between them, and draws out the research purpose, significance and precise definition of the concept of this topic. The second section takes the application of new media art interactive installations as the main content, and systematically analyzes and explores the presentation of new media art interactive installations in the context of major applications in exhibition halls, public spaces, and commercial fields. The third section is oriented to the current state of application of artificial intelligence in interactive installation art, and selects dynamic installation art using a concentrated representative machine learning method as the research object, and conducts a comparative study of the presentation methods in traditional installation art and new media interactive installation art. The fourth section delves into the specific application of artificial intelligence and machine learning in the current design of interactive installations in new media art, exploring the new forms of artistic expression and positive promotion brought about by machine learning technology, and discussing the current development trend of new media installation art. Section five analyzes and summarizes the research, elaborates the application prospects of combining artificial intelligence and new media installations, and demonstrates the design methods of new media art interactive installations with certain aesthetic qualities and good visual effects in the context of machine learning [1].

With the development of nowadays technology, artists have more and more freedom in their creation and more integration of cross-media, which is the inevitability of the development of new media art. Starting with the new media interactive installation combining artificial intelligence and machine learning technology, this paper discusses the dynamic installation art based on machine learning from several aspects, including the presentation of interactive installation in mainstream application scenes, the current situation of artificial intelligence application in interactive installation art, and the specific application of machine learning at present. By understanding and mastering the design methods based on machine learning technology and using artificial intelligence as a new media tool and platform to display the interactive creativity of new media art, we can bring out the maximum creativity of human-machine collaborative creation. The development of artificial intelligence is of great significance for the future development of interactive installation design in new media art.

2 Background

2.1 Media Convergence in the Context of Digital Narrative

The concept of "media convergence" was first defined by Professor Boppel of the Massachusetts Institute of Technology as the tendency of various media to become multifunctional and integrated. Scholar Wang Fei points out that the end point of media convergence is information consumption, and its ultimate evolution process is to produce a composite media form from content to network convergence and terminal convergence. Andrew Nachison, director of the American Press Institute's Center for Media Studies, defines "media convergence" as "a strategic, operational, and cultural alliance between print, audio, video, and interactive digital media organizations," emphasizing that "Media convergence" refers more to the cooperation and alliance between various media.

In the new media context, the expression of digital expression is more abundant, the media platforms and carriers are diverse, and the expression methods and means of expression are more diversified. Through the combination of text, pictures, audio, video and artificial intelligence and other expressions, it effectively enhances the multi-faceted sensory experience of the audience.

2.2 New Media Interactive Device

New media is a form of communication that uses digital technology to provide information and services to users through computer networks, wireless communication networks, satellites and other channels, and with terminals such as computers, cell phones and TVs. New media is a media supported by digital compression and wireless network technology, and globalized by using its large capacity, real-time and interactivity.

New media installation art is an art form in which new media technology intervenes in installation art. Compared to traditional installations, new media installations integrate digital images, sculptural paintings, the Internet and other media, using new technologies such as algorithms, computer vision, virtual reality, augmented reality and artificial intelligence to empower them. It is used in mainstream scenarios such as exhibition displays in museums, display design in commercial fields, and live performances in public spaces. The new media interactive installation reflects its spatial, immersive, interactive and virtual characteristics through somatic interaction, robotic arm powered device, immersive space, augmented reality virtual simulation, mixed reality and many other ways [2].

As art and technology become increasingly connected and developed, new media installation art, which is more interactive and experimental, has gradually become one of the main media forms and expressions of contemporary art, and its development has provided a new context for the study of digital narratives.

3 Application of Artificial Intelligence in Interactive Installation Art

In recent years, with social development and technological innovation, intelligent interactive devices in the context of artificial intelligence have provided a new medium and design concept for new media devices. Simultaneously, the emergence of new media electronic media represented by virtual reality and augmented reality has also resulted in huge changes in people's lifestyles and habits. The new artistic development and new creative means have put forward higher requirements on the expression and creative means of contemporary interactive installation design. Under the background of emphasizing interactive experience, it is important to study the design of new media interactive devices based on artificial intelligence technology.

Technology and innovation are becoming increasingly important in today's cultural and artistic life, and technological advances and innovations have led to the emergence of interactive works that incorporate diverse elements. In recent years, with the development and popularity of new media technology, people have also begun to make full use of artificial intelligence and machine learning to improve the performance of new media interactive devices.

The Development of Traditional Installation Art to New Media Interactive Installation Art. The traditional art form is mostly static, and the distinction between abstract and figurative is the standard. The viewer can only view the artwork from a distance or touch it from a close distance, and it is difficult to understand the real thoughts and feelings that the artists want to express in the artwork. At the beginning of the twentieth century, a Hungarian artist named Laszlo Moholy Nagy proposed a reflection on the interaction between the work of art and the viewer's public. He argued that the viewer's participation in the work of art adds to the interactivity of the work, and therefore, more importantly, the work of art changes accordingly, so that the value of the work of art should not be limited to viewing only.

In the initial stage of the development of interactive installation art, physical and mechanical types of interaction were the most frequent. Artists often chose physical movement or mechanical transmission, using this principle to make the static installation art increase the movement behavior, this interactive way emphasizes the movement of the installation itself and the artistic concept that the artist wants to express through the work.

Since the 1990 s, AI has been involved in artistic practices involving computer art, generative art, cross-media art, augmented and virtual reality art, robotics and bioart, etc., forming a diverse and interdisciplinary ecological character.

Dutch artist Theo Jansen is best known for his 1990 moving installation Beach Monster. Theo Jansen simulated the behavior of a quadruped through computer calculations, consisting of PVC plastic pipes, wood, plastic water bottles and cloth, and converting wind energy into kinetic energy through natural wind power.

Since World War II, technology has developed rapidly, and many new materials and technological tools have emerged, breathing new life into traditional interactive installation art. More and more elements of life are being used in the creation of art. In the twenty-first century, interactive technology has become very mature, and interactive installation art has become more and more visible to people by virtue of its fun and technological nature. The installation art with its interactive specificity will certainly have an impact on the future development of art.

A Comparative Study of the Presentation of Traditional and New Media Interactive Devices.

Media Changing: Cross-Media and Multi-sensory. The system of new media installation consists of three parts: the expresser, the work and the visitor. With the development of computer graphics and the innovation of interactive media technology, installation art has developed from a single medium to cross-media expression. For example, virtual reality installation art can use VR technology to present multiple visual experiences [3], creating another world that extends beyond space and vision; augmented reality installation art can combine virtual and real images, allowing visitors to experience different environments through smart devices; sound installation art can work in concert with hardware and software to express artistic concepts through the recognition of sound changes, creating different Computer-assisted creation can help creators transform concepts into visual images through machine learning, etc. [4].

Subject Changing: The Viewer becomes a Participant. New media installation art allows the audience to transform the traditional approach of passive reception and participate in the interaction, leading the development of the plot and even determining the outcome. Mark Post has said that "digital literature allows each reader to write freely, and multiple authorship of texts seems inevitable."

By applying technologies such as Deep Learning, Natural Language Processing (NLP) and Pattern Recognition, interactive devices emphasize the viewer's initiative and participation, and the subject of expression in new media devices is no longer single and centralized. Deep learning can be used to build the user experience of new media interactive devices, helping to identify user behavior and personalize recommendations. Deep learning uses complex data models to identify and infer associative knowledge, thus assisting in the development of intelligent aspects of new media interactive devices. Natural language processing techniques can also be used in new media interactive devices, and NLP techniques can be used to process text data to provide new media interactive devices with more intelligent text processing capabilities and to define user needs more precisely, thus helping new media interactive devices to provide better user services. Pattern recognition can also be used to analyze user behavior to help new media interactive devices discover user needs in a timely manner and provide more intelligent predictive services [5].

In conclusion, the application of artificial intelligence and machine learning in new media interaction installations can help new media interaction installations identify users' needs and tastes more accurately and provide better personalized services, thus significantly improving user experience.

4 Application of Machine Learning Algorithms in New Media Interaction Devices

4.1 Application of Machine Learning Algorithms

Machine learning algorithms can effectively improve the accuracy of interactions and reduce the need for human intervention. Several algorithms that appear in new media devices, such as recommendation algorithms, search algorithms, and real-time user tracking algorithms, rely on the support of machine learning algorithms. New media interaction devices can use a variety of machine learning algorithms. For example, Bayesian classification and its derivative algorithms are used to distinguish the preference characteristics of different consumers and thus personalize the product recommendation services provided to consumers. New media interactive devices can also process linguistic information by using machine learning algorithms such as neural networks and Hidden Markov Models to achieve text sentiment analysis, speech perception, and other functions.

According to the process of creating new media interactive installation, we can divide the algorithms involved in AI into three stages. Firstly, it is the art-assisted creation stage, which can assist the creator to store and process the text and images quickly, and the creator is in the leading position in this stage. Secondly, the artistic style simulation stage, artificial intelligence through deep learning training neural network to independently complete the collection and collation of information, the creator through the machine computing to provide solutions to co-create combined to complete. The third stage is the independent creation stage. Artificial intelligence completely replaces the creator to run the program independently to process and create works. But in practical terms, artificial intelligence in the field of new media interactive devices is still in the transition stage from auxiliary intelligence to deep learning perception intelligence.

4.2 Expression of Machine Learning Applied to the Art of Interactive Installation

Generative art is the use of machine learning techniques to automatically generate artworks, including images, music, voice, non-linear video, text, etc. in a specific environment. It can be applied to dynamic installations, real-time music and visual effects, real-time rendering, generative forms, etc. The artist gives the computer autonomy according to the design concept by constructing a programming language and designing certain rules. The computer automatically writes programs to create artworks associated with visuals, resulting in works that cannot be replicated and have unique visual forms.

The commonality of human-computer collaboration makes computer-generated art more than a tool for interdisciplinary creation in the fields of art and technology. The artistic results it presents are also an important topic for aesthetic research in the age of artificial intelligence.

Image generation: DaDA: Design and Draw with AI. (Fig. 1). The AI-based interactive device is trained with landscape painting, a unique traditional Eastern art form. Using generative adversarial networks to train the model and build the web interaction interface to achieve the effect of drawing on the interface to present a real-time generated ink landscape painting (Fig. 2). Experience self-creation and expression of landscapes with the help of AI technology, exploring the possibilities of AI in a creative process traditionally dominated by humans in absolute terms [6].

Participants can sketch the landscape in their mind with a few strokes and draw the flowing green hills in the form of sketches [7], and the AI "Dada" will assist in creating a Chinese ink landscape [8].

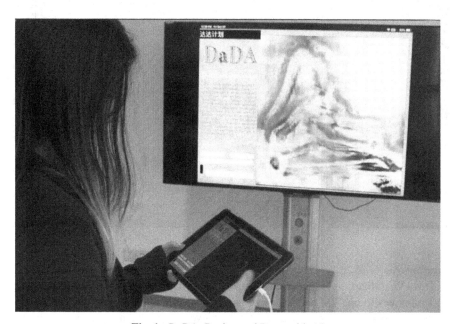

Fig. 1. DaDA: Design and Draw with AI

Interactive Image Generation: Kinetic Light (Fig. 3). The "Kinetic Light" installation, built by artists Adrien M. & Claire B. based on deep learning algorithms, adjusts its lighting in real time based on changes in music and sound [9]. The installation uses deep learning algorithms to track the harmonic beats and dynamics of the music and change the state of the lights based on this, providing a unique visual experience. In the Kinetic Light installations, visitors can interact with their work, for example by changing the hue or frequency of the light to reflect their movements as they dance around the room [10].

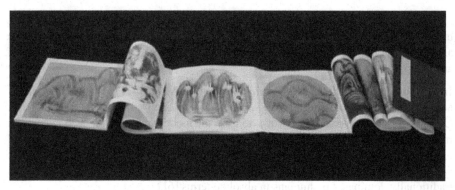

Fig. 2. DaDA: ink landscape painting

Fig. 3. Kinetic Light

Data Visualization Generation: Melting Memories (Fig. 4). Using machine learning techniques to analyze and visualize data, transforming large amounts of data into charts, flowcharts, and other forms to help achieve a comprehensive understanding of context, applications, and their relevance.

Born in Istanbul, Turkey in 1985, Refik Anado is a new media artist who has been very active in recent years. He holds a B.A. in Photography and Video, an M.A. in Visual Communication Design, and an M.F.A. in Media Arts from the University of California, Los Angeles (UCLA) in Istanbul. Arnaldo's main research areas include site-specific data painting and sculpture and immersive audio-visual performance, focusing on the relationship between media art and physical entities through the crossover application of big data visualization, neuroscience and machine intelligence technologies.

In 2018 Rafik Arnaldo collaborated with the Neuroscape Lab at the University of California, San Francisco to present Melting Memories, an exhibition of interdisciplinary work in the form of data painting and augmented data sculpture. The exhibition presents the results of several interdisciplinary projects in the form of data painting and augmented data sculpture [11].

The "Melting Memories" series of works captured 32 tracks of brain waves of long-term memories stored in the human brain and the functional processes in the corresponding areas of the brain at different locations of the volunteers (Fig. 5). The process of human memory retrieval is transformed into a sequence of data images, and convolutional neural networks are used to transform the data images into the basis for later construction of multidimensional visual structures, and then the VVVV visual programming platform and GPU extension libraries are used to generate dynamic images that can present the materiality of human memory. The exhibition reproduces the different operation mechanisms and processes of the brain when thinking and recalling through dynamic images. The gray-toned data sculptures slowly curl and undulate on the screen, and the audience feels the visualized operation of the brain with their senses, immersing themselves in the mysterious "memory illusion".

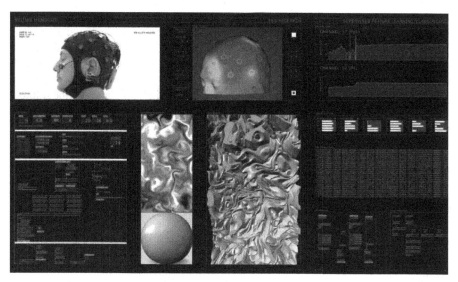

Fig. 4. Melting Memories

Virtual Interaction Generation: SKP-S 2020AW New Arrival Digital Campaign (Fig. 6). With the rise of products and technologies such as head-mounted virtual reality glasses and metaverse, interactive installations may take on a whole new dimension in the virtual world. "Maybe they use the latest technological achievements to create artworks, but these new technologies can also easily become obsolete. I hope that artists can transcend the shackles of technology, and that sometimes their imagination may be one step ahead of the development of technology." So says Richard Castelli, the renowned exhibition curator.

SKP-S 2020AW New Arrival Digital Campaign is a physical retail experience created with digital technology as a commercial space and an immersive exhibition space.

Fig. 5. Traces of Memory: The Past

Through 3D scanning and motion capture technologies, dancers and musicians are created as virtual 3D characters and placed in 3D virtual art installations and full-angle scenes for performances. Users and consumers can dress up the characters and switch interfaces to view clothing brands, prices and item details. The digital catalog is closely aligned with SKP-S' long-established brand image of "digital-simulation of the future", which enhances the consumer experience and helps SKP-S build its brand uniqueness in commercial real estate [12].

Fig. 6. SKP-S 2020AW New Arrival Digital Campaign

4.3 Development Trend of New Media Interactive Installation

Dynamic Expression and Diversified Development. The new media interactive installation shows a dynamic and diversified development. From the perspective of design, new media installations are gradually free from the shortcomings of the current design of mass technical reproduction and features being covered up by form and technology. From the level of digital industry development, new media installation is a field that is still emerging. Art research institutions such as MIT Media Lab, ZKM Karlsruhe Center for Media and Art in Germany, and ICC Media Art Center in Tokyo, Japan have been playing a bridge between new technology, new art, new media and people. These new media artworks with long-term significance and artistic vitality can be transformed into products with functional and economic value, which have great future commercial potential.

From the Physical World to the Future World. Technological progress is the fundamental driving force behind the development of new media installation art. The rapid iterative development of computer storage and computing power has brought a huge flood of data, and the ubiquitous Internet and mobile devices have blurred the boundary between physical space and digital space. Interactive image installation through artificial intelligence can use data and coding to reorganize the definition of reality and return to real life, allowing the experiencer to experience the world with a new dimension of cognition and achieve emotionally resonant artistic expression.

5 Conclusion and Future Work

Professor Philip Galanter of the Interactive Communication Project Institute at New York University believes that generative art is inclusive and that it provides the basis for theoretical developments in the integration of technology and art. With the development of contemporary installation art forms, mechanical devices, computer algorithms, program coding, intelligent materials, and robotic systems have all been introduced into the process of creating art. Such systems require that future creators no longer presuppose a given outcome, but rather unfold their creations within the system and extend the infinite possibilities of the creative medium. The construction of the creative act and process is as important as the outcome of the work.

In this paper, by studying the method and development prospect of interaction design of new media dynamic installation art under the premise of machine learning as design method and the participation of algorithmic system, we summarize the method of using new media dynamic installation in the context of machine learning, explore the expression form of artificial intelligence technology in new media art and research and think about the future development direction. Interactive devices are the carriers of information in future society, and we should fulfill the mission of information dissemination through artistic means by understanding and mastering the design methods based on machine learning technology and using artificial intelligence as new media tools and platforms. At a time when artificial intelligence is gradually moving from learning style to collaborative innovation, it is more necessary to cultivate the ability of interdisciplinary and diversified development to turn artificial intelligence technology into the most creative partner of new media interactive devices.

References

1. Kurosu, M. (ed.): HCI 2018. LNCS, vol. 10902. Springer, Cham (2018). https://doi.org/10.1007/978-3-319-91244-8

2. Muñoz, H.: The interaction in an interactive exhibition as a design-aesthetics-experience relationship. In: Stephanidis, C. (ed.) HCI 2016. CCIS, vol. 617, pp. 364–370. Springer, Cham (2016). https://doi.org/10.1007/978-3-319-40548-3_61
3. Kweon, Y., Kim, S., Yoon, B., Jo, T., Park, C.: Implementation of educational drum contents using mixed reality and virtual reality. In: Stephanidis, C. (ed.) HCI 2018. CCIS, vol. 851, pp. 296–303. Springer, Cham (2018). https://doi.org/10.1007/978-3-319-92279-9_40
4. Hong, J.S., Lee, J.W.: Picture book-based augmented reality content authoring system. In: Stephanidis, C. (ed.) HCI 2018. CCIS, vol. 851, pp. 253–257. Springer, Cham (2018). https://doi.org/10.1007/978-3-319-92279-9_34
5. Kurosu, M. (ed.): HCI 2018. LNCS, vol. 10901. Springer, Cham (2018). https://doi.org/10.1007/978-3-319-91238-7
6. Xue, A.: End-to-End Chinese Landscape Painting Creation Using Generative Adversarial Networks. In: 2021 IEEE Winter Conference on Applications of Computer Vision (WACV), Waikoloa, HI, USA, pp. 3862–3870 (2021). https://doi.org/10.1109/WACV48630.2021.00391
7. Zhou, J., Gao, F., Yang, X., Lin, W.: Chip-SAGAN: A self-attention generative adversarial network for Chinese ink wash painting style transfer. In: IECON 2022 – 48th Annual Conference of the IEEE Industrial Electronics Society, pp.1–8 (2022)
8. DaDA   Homepage.https://www.thisiscolossal.com/2015/11/movement-of-air-dance/,last a(Accessed 2 Sep 2023)
9. Balducci, F., Grana, C., Cucchiara, R.: Affective level design for a role-playing videogame evaluated by a brain–computer interface and machine learning methods. Vis. Comput. **33**(4), 413–427 (2016). https://doi.org/10.1007/s00371-016-1320-2
10. The Movement of Air: A New Dance Performance Incorporating Interactive Digital Projection from Adrien M & Claire B Homepage, https://cloud.tencent.com/developer/news/331070. (Accessed 2 Sep 2023)
11. Refik Anadol homepage. https://refikanadol.com/. (Accessed 2 Sep 2023)
12. SKP-S 2020AW New Arrival Digital Campaign homepage, https://m.skp-beijing.com/skps2020aw/index.html. (Accessed 2 Sep 2023)

A View of Chinese Character Design in Traditional Culture from the Perspective of Daily Articles

Qian Lu[(✉)]

Central Academy of Fine Arts, No. 8 Hua Jia Di Nan St., Beijing, Chao Yang, People's Republic of China
136794311@qq.com

Abstract. Chinese characters are the most important cultural symbol in the life of Chinese people as well as an important element in traditional creation activities and modern design practice. The design of daily articles in traditional Chinese culture carries much information associated with Chinese characters. "Thing as a carrier of characters" is a manifestation of combining Chinese characters with creation activities, embodying the "order of things" in our daily life. This paper stresses the complicated, diversified, vivid and stereoscopic interaction relations between Chinese characters and people, and traditional Chinese material space and daily life form. In the modern design context dominated by technologies, "things" and "characters" are still very important media, only needing to take on new relations and forms in a new scene of daily life. Therefore, the traditional Chinese creation concept of "thing as a carrier of characters" is of important value to modern design practice and the study of methodology.

Keywords: Chinese character design · utensil · daily life · traditional culture · materiality

1 Introduction

For Chinese people, Chinese characters are not only a medium and tool for conveying information, but also exist in every aspect of social life as an important cultural symbol. Chinese character symbols carrying rich cultural connotations are scattered in daily life, interwoven with things and space, and constructing meanings in the material world. In the traditional life of Chinese people, daily articles often serve as carriers of characters. The reason can be traced back to a long time ago and involves complicated cultural background. Gradually established in the long period of social development, the unique creation form of "thing as a carrier of characters" is a very vivid and wonderful part of traditional Chinese culture. The Chinese character design in the space of traditional material life discussed in this paper is a design problem concerning "thing as a carrier of characters". It should be noted that material forms such as inscriptions on beast shells, inscriptions on pottery and inscriptions on ancient bronze objects are only a character presentation form of carriers, and do not constitute a focal point of this paper. The material carriers as writing materials for Chinese characters such as bamboo slip, silk, Xuan paper, modern paper and electronic screen are not in the discussion scope of this paper. In addition, auspicious character patterns such as "福 (good fortune)", "禄 (position)", "寿 (longevity)" and "喜 (happiness)" in paper-cut art, sculpture and other crafts decorating living or public spaces, and plaques and calligraphy are not the research object of this paper. The paper mainly discusses those Chinese character design forms, which take daily articles as a medium, are firmly implanted into the daily life of Chinese people, and have continuous and profound interactions with their behaviors, thoughts and cultures.

Originating from ancient pictogram, modern Chinese characters were at first closely related to witchcraft. In Preface to Origin of Chinese Characters, Xu Shen associated the Eight Diagrams that "get inspirations by observing human bodies and the universe" with the generation of Chinese characters. Taking objective things as an object, pictogram directly describes things instead of words and concepts. They express personal, religious and social emotions, and so cannot be regarded as pure rational symbols. In the traditional thought of the Chinese, Chinese characters are closely related to human subject, and human subject is integrated with nature. It can be said that the development of the Chinese character culture is interwoven with the material world of the people all the time, and the Chinese characters themselves have evident "materiality". Through the long history, with the abstract and symbolic evolution of Chinese characters, their materiality seems to become more and more difficult to be identified. However, it has not disappeared but gradually changed into a recessive but more profound state. The "materiality" of Chinese character is an important condition for being able to produce interaction relations with material space and human embodiment activities in our daily life. The interaction relations are not simple, still and formatted, but are becoming increasingly complicated, diversified and stereoscopic with the development of society. The traditional creation form of "thing as a carrier of characters" is an intensive embodiment of these interaction relations. Therefore, to study it can provide a valuable thinking angle for our present design practice and exploration of design theories.

"Utensil for carrying norms of etiquette" is regarded as an important traditional Chinese design system. "Utensil" is originally a tangible thing, but is endowed with some abstract symbolic meaning due to "carrying norms of etiquette", connected with man's creation activities and imagination about ideal life. As a typical representative of Chinese ritual culture, bronze wares are not only luxuries of the rulers, but also ritual utensils symbolizing the state power. Apart from the profile and decorative patterns, inscriptions are also an important part of a bronze ware. Most of them record sacrificial rites of the nobility, national systems, important events or something about the casting of the utensil. Though bronze wares are articles in the life of the ruling class and most of them are serious ritual utensils, they once produced vivid sparks in the life from day to day through colliding with the users. According to the historical data, King Tang of the Shang Dynasty once engraved "If one can make things better for one day, he should make them better every day." in his own bathtub. The contents of the inscription formed an interesting interaction with the bathtub. A bronze wine flagon unearthed from Han Tombs in Mancheng District, Baoding City, Hebei Province is inscribed with "nourish the blood and skin, prolong life, prevent diseases, and live for more than ten thousand years", which is deemed associated with the traditional Chinese witched-doctors' treatment of diseases. (Fig. 1) From the above, it can be seen that the creation tradition taking utensils as a carrier for characters or decorating utensils with characters not only has a long history in China, but also the relationship between characters and the utensils carrying characters is not split. Instead, there are rich and vivid associations between them. Characters not only serve as a text for recording information, but also play a role of beautification as decorative patterns. The relationship between the connotations of characters and the utensils is also an important content worth noting. "Utensil for carrying norms of etiquette" embodies the Chinese cognition of theories, the assessment of correct behaviors and the pursuit for the meaning of life. With the development of the history, this thought is not restricted to ritual activities of the ruling class and noble life, but is gradually infiltrated into the daily life and creation activities of Chinese people, thus fully implementing a concept stressing order and harmony into the behaviors of the Chinese. It is intensively embodied in the making of utensils. As an important cultural symbol, characters have never been absent.

Fig. 1. Bronze pot engraved with bird characters (a decorated form of the Great Seal) of interlaced gold and silver threads unearthed from Han Tombs in Mancheng District, Baoding City, Hebei Province.

Daily articles have special meanings because they are a part of daily life, and are "things" at hand most intimate with people. The Analects of Confucius raised "inquiring with earnestness and reflecting with self-application". Reflections of Things of hand, which reflects neo-confucianism, also stresses a reflection on "things at hand". "Reflecting with self-application" refers to a pragmatic rather than over-ambitious life attitude. In the daily life of ancient Chinese people, the bronze mirror is an important private article. As an ornament liked by the people, it not only has practical functions, but also has very strong decorative nature and symbolic implications. On a bronze mirror are often engraved with inscriptions with a variety of contents. There are auspicious expressions such as "prosperous family situation", "descendants enjoying harmonious and orderly family life" and "everlasting happiness", as well as words for expressing emotions such as "everlasting longing" and "don't forget me". They have embodied the empathy of the maker or the user with things. The characters and the mirror itself have constituted abundant and complicated associations between men and life. In ancient China, there was also a light transmitting mirror. When facing the sun or lamplight, the characters on the back of the mirror can be projected on the wall. (Fig. 2) In the interactions between light, shadow and image, the mirror owner seems to communicate with a subject in the depth of his heart, and thus a very private small sacred space is formed. This scene has a very strong sense of picture, just like a freeze-frame on the drama stage. It is a poetic presentation of daily life. Therefore, a spatial dimension is added to the interaction relation with Chinese characters, utensils and men, making it more vivid and stereoscopic. In the life of Chinese people, there are numerous scenes of decorating daily articles with Chinese characters. Auspicious characters such as "福 (good fortune)", "禄 (position)", "寿 (longevity)" and "喜 (happiness)" can be seen everywhere, for example, on eating utensils, toilet boxes or furniture. Moreover, Chinese character patterns on many utensils are decorative subjects. (Fig. 3) Apart from family daily articles, in the past, some grain shops would stamp Chinese character symbols on the surface of rice in their granary with a kind of wooden utensil. (Fig. 4) On the one hand, it was a precaution against burglars. On the other hand, the stamped Chinese characters were often the name of the grain shop or had auspicious connotations, and embodied the owner's ingenuous ideas and nice wishes. Similarly, the Chinese have a custom of decorating foods with Chinese characters. Nowadays, there are still many tools for decorating foods such as pastries and cakes with characters among the people. (Fig. 5) They believe that eating these auspicious characters will produce a mysterious strength and bring good luck to themselves. Chinese characters have been deeply embedded into the life of Chinese people long before, decorating the details of life and symbolizing a nice life. Design and creation activities associated with that are a wonderful chapter in traditional Chinese material culture.

Of the eight words stressing personal cultivation in The Great Learning reflecting Confucian moral thoughts, the first is "格物 (investigation of things)". It is thought that "knowledge is acquired through investigation of things". According to traditional Chinese, "things" are not only "functional" to life, but also can exert influence at the spiritual level through "investigation of things", or probing into theories of things and rectifying men's behaviors. In our life, "investigation of things" can be deemed as a way of "learning rules". It is an "order of things" established in the life of Chinese people. As is said in Analects of Zhu Xi, "Dao means theory, and everything has a theory. Form means formality, and everything has a formality. Dao cannot be separated from form, and form cannot be separated from Dao. Everything must observe a rule." The tradition of

Fig. 2. "Light Transmitting Mirror" with inscriptions "Jian Ri Zhi Guang Tian Xia Da Ming (When the sun is seen, the world will be bright)", bronze mirror, collected by Shanghai Museum.

"thing as a carrier of characters" tells us that characters play an important role that can not be neglected in "investigation of things". The "order of things" constituted with Chinese characters in the daily life of Chinese people is a living culture associated with daily articles. In the traditional Chinese life, there is an interesting object made from characters, which is called double-nine diagram. (Fig. 6) It is a picture drawn by northern men of letters according to the traditional "count nine" custom (From Winter Solstice of the lunar calendar, take nine days as one unit, and count nine nine-day periods continuously. After eighty-one days are counted, the winter has passed.). As an object accompanying people through severe winter and greeting spring, it expresses a nice expectation for the arrival of warm spring, and is used from the populace to the nobility. Emerging in the Ming Dynasty, the double-nine diagram has different forms, for example, in the form of characters, in the form of circles or in the form of plum blossoms. One of the most typical double-nine diagrams is a calligraphic work of hollow strokes used for character tracing - "Ting Qian Chui Liu Zhen Zhong Dai Chun Feng (the drooping willows in front of the pavilion have sprouted, and so you must cherish the warmth of spring breeze)", all written in traditional Chinese. Each character has nine strokes, and there are eight-one strokes altogether. From Winter Solstice on, fill each stroke every day according to the sequence of the stokes. For each nine-day period, a character will be filled. When spring returns to the earth after nine nine-day periods, the double-nine diagram will be completed. Therefore, it is also called "write nine". The double-nine diagram has its function in agricultural production. As a reluctant action of ancient people to enjoy life in severe cold, it is an entertainment, and at the same time a way of combining

Fig. 3. Five-color pot with "福 (Fortune)" of the Qing Dynasty

Fig. 4. Pottery seal "Ju Wan Shi" used by a granary. Private collection.

education with recreation. In the double-nine diagram, the contour, pronunciation and meaning of characters are in their right positions as a comprehensive vocabulary for jointly completing one complete narration. With Chinese characters as a subject, the double-nine diagram has constituted a relationship of continuous interaction between

Fig. 5. Wooden mold for stamping "喜 (Happiness)" in cakes collected by Jilin Provincial Museum.

men and things in the material space of daily life, and endowed this interaction with rich cultural connotations, and even play a role of spiritual ballast.

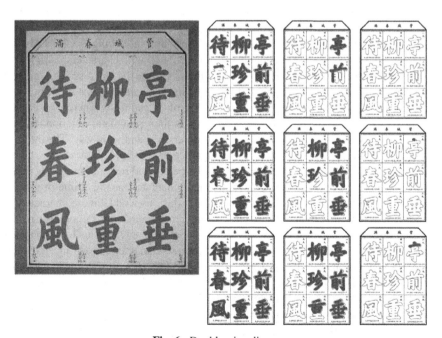

Fig. 6. Double-nine diagram

In constituting scenes of daily life, "things carrying characters" has an enormous space for playing its role. Relations between things and characters can be diversified. For example, sometimes, though they jointly make a meaning, they are not necessarily "present" at the same time. In the hall of a traditional Chinese dwelling house, there is a special space decoration design: On the middle section of a long narrow table is placed with a desk clock, at each side of the desk clock is placed with a hat container, to the east of the hat container is placed with a porcelain bottle, and to the west of the hat container is placed with a mirror, homophonic for "Zhong Sheng Ping Jing (bell tone, bottle and mirror)", with the implied meaning of "peaceful all life". (Fig. 7) The house owner pins his hope that his cause and family can be peaceful all the time on this design. It is a nice expectation about the survival environment. In such a spatial design, the contour of characters does not appear on the material carrier. Instead, Chinese characters are drawn forth from the names of the utensils, and then the authentic meaning is conveyed through the homophonic sound of Chinese characters. Sound, text and articles are intermingled in the hall, which is an important daily life space for the Chinese. The desk clock, porcelain bottle and mirror are decorating the hall as a material space while the propitious connotations conveyed by the characters are decorating the spiritual space of the Chinese. Therefore, a dual structure comprising material space and spiritual space is formed.

The traditional philosophic thought "What is above form is called Dao, and what is under form is called an object" reflects the traditional Chinese value "spirit is always higher than material". This value orientation will inevitably lead to a result that articles in daily life are endowed with more spiritual connotations. Spirit is always abstract, and the abstractness of spirit must be lodged in a certain place and converted into a symbol of things. Maybe by this way, a certain "correspondence between heaven and man" can be reached. People in daily life need to pin his thought by relying on this way of conveying "theories" through "things" or expressing "emotions" through "things". Characters are presented with things as a carrier, and things are decorated with characters, both jointly serving the Chinese cognition about life, nature, the world and the universe. This creation form is an objective existence in the daily life of Chinese people. Utensils are not only a physical carrier of characters, but also a carrier of "meanings". Therefore, articles are endowed with cultural significance in addition to their pragmatic function, and the meanings of characters are interpreted in a more diversified and vivid way. The tradition of "thing as a carrier of characters" may be regarded as a unique grammar of Chinese character design, by which, design can expand the perceptual realm of human beings.

There is no lack of design works with Chinese characters as the theme in modern design. For example, after the 1990 s, many poster designs with Chinese characters as the theme emerged in China, and Chinese character elements are frequently seen in the visual design of many important international events like Olympic Games. (Fig. 8, and Fig. 9) As an important cultural symbol, Chinese characters are an inexhaustible treasury of inspirations for contemporary Chinese design. However, through enormous social changes, affected by various modern thoughts and technologies, the material form of "thing as a carrier of characters" in the daily life of Chinese people is gradually disappearing, which is synchronous with the severe impact inflicted upon the traditional Chinese spiritual world and cultural system. The organization and form of the daily life of modern people are reconstituted through interactions with more extensive social

Fig. 7. Chengzhi Hall, Shot in Hongcun, Anhui Province

changes. In China's modern design practice, there are cases of making innovative practice by combining characters with utensils, and there are a lot of them. However, most take Chinese characters as decorative patterns or model elements, and the design language is far less abundant and vivid than in the past. While modernity is giving people a power to change the world, it is also changing the people themselves. Modern daily life is like a Montage Drama. Traditional life habits and soul orders are shredded and pieced together in disorder. People are forced to be trapped in trivial fragments, separated from the originally related things. The system or narration structure that gives people a sense of security has fully collapsed. Facing increasingly abstract and fragmented daily life and individuals, modern design may make a response by starting from constituting a scene of daily life that can gives people a sense of security. As mentioned earlier, the form of "thing as a carrier of characters" is of great significance to the establishment of a stable "order of things" in the traditional Chinese life. It provides people with hierarchical scenes of daily life, and is also a source of the sense of security. Therefore, for constituting scenes of daily life and individual identities in modern society, "things" and "characters" are still very important media, and "thing as a carrier of characters" can still be a unique and effectively way, just like what was manifested in the Chinese daily life for thousands of years, only needing some new changes in the form language.

Fig. 8. Emblem of 2008 Beijing Olympic Games, Zhang Wu, Guo Chunning & Mao Cheng

In 2020, She Luyun, a student of CAFA School of Experimental Art made a device called "contemporary art drive" from bare miniature circuit boards. (Fig. 10) It is a small machine of anti-art language system. The screen of each circuit board will randomly display a text composed of contemporary art "formulas" collected by the author. For example, "Forgive confident species", "Build a public sculpture that does not exist", "Overthrow an illegitimate revolution", "Fold a dusk that is full of confidence"… The original intention for She Luyun making this device was to satirize the exhaustion phenomenon of contemporary art interpretation and express her own art view. As a result, it unexpectedly aroused a strong response among the audiences, especially young people. Therefore, she made these circuit board devices into ornaments such as key chains and necklaces for sales, making them toys with a cyberpunk style that can be carried anytime and anyplace, or daily articles at hand. Those circuit boards, randomly-generated texts and fragmented expressions originally only had very abstract connotations. However, when claimed and worn by a certain individual, they are associated with that individual, and become a medium for self presentation of that individual in daily life. The combination of circuit boards with characters make us naturally think of discussions about technology, culture and modernity. It is an introspection brought by the contemporary form of "thing as a carrier of characters". Afterwards, She Luyun made a device called "2020 Did Exist" during the period of COVID-19 pandemic. (Fig. 11) It also takes circuit boards as the subject, and the core is a black-and-white display screen with the size of only two fingernails, and a button. Press the button once, and the time on the display screen will go forward by one day, and behind the date of each day is followed by a sentence associated with events that actually happened. From Jan. 1st to Dec. 31st, the personal experience and collective memory of 2020 will be shown in slightly absurd languages. For example, "Jan. 21st, suitable for feeling sick: People have found the chief criminal, which is the bat, with vigor and vitality! And made concerted efforts to expose all people that have eaten bats." "Mar. 28th, suitable for celebrating joyfully:

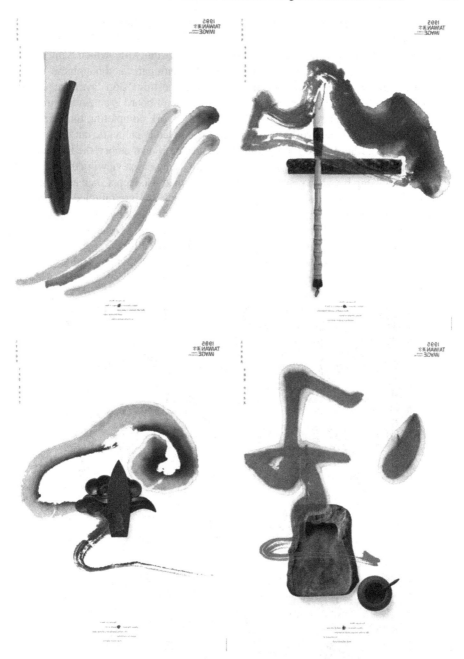

Fig. 9. Emotion for Chinese Characters - Mountain, Water, Wind & Cloud Series Posters, Kan Tian-Kueng, 1995

An important announcement of Sichuan Province: Mahjong clubs can be open to the public." "Oct. 29th, avoid makeup: Your face is being transacted." From the perspective of an onlooker, the artist is viewing the familiar and strange daily life, which is interlaced with the pandemic and other events, and intermingled with pains and happiness. When you press the button to the last, the machine will raise a question; "366 days have passed. Can you confirm 2020 did exist?" As a medium, the circuit board is an evident modern metaphor, and characters are the spiritual core for the work completing the narration. The news information in the work has constituted a completely authentic but fragmented scene of daily life. Based on common experience and historical memory, the information and characters can generate links and resonance with each person viewing them. In this way, the relationship between people and things is formed. Concepts such as electronic accessory, screen reading, fragmented text and cyberpunk are intermingled together to jointly complete the narration of this work about reflection on daily life. Maybe it can be regarded as a contemporary way to present "thing as a carrier of characters". Though the materials, starting point and intention of the creation are different, the form of constituting a certain meaning in daily life through continuous interactions with words day by day seems to be a little similar to the double-nine diagram.

Fig. 10. Contemporary *Art Drive* Ornament Design, She Luyun, 2020

Fig. 11. 2020 *Did Exist*, She Luyun, 2021

The generation of Chinese characters was based on the traditional Chinese thought of "abstracting images from viewing". According to a point of view, the Chinese grasp all things through Chinese characters. The Chinese character system itself is a symbol network, of which, the overlapped hermeneutics and semiotics reveal the "order of things". As a symbol of markers, Chinese characters cover every aspect of people's life, and serve as a medium for us to see invisible things. Design activities should first be based on the cognition of the objective material world, and then turn to creation. As a creation activity with people as the subject, design cannot be separated from the marking of semiotics and the narration of hermeneutics during the process. Design activities need originality. The overlapped action of hermeneutics and semiotics is an effective way to stimulating creativity, and will facilitate the generation of "invisible things", i.e. creative ideas. The traditional Chinese creation concept and practice of "thing as a carrier of characters" are of important reference value to design activities handling the relationship between people and the material world. Whether Chinese character decorative patterns that can be seen everywhere on daily articles or decorative stereotypes such as the double-nine diagram and "Zhong Sheng Ping Jing (bell tone, bottle and mirror)", have revealed the creativity and imagination in the traditional Chinese creation concept. The graphical features and metaphorical function of Chinese characters can stimulate people's inspiration, subconsciousness and imagination, all belonging to the category of intuitive thinking or non-logical thinking. The overtones or meanings beyond characters cannot be attained by the logic. Chinese characters are able to make a contribution to the world civilization through artistic works recording cultures and presenting wonderfulness, and more importantly, they are conveying the life ideal, world outlook and spirit of the Chinese. Through sorting out the creation form of "thing as a carrier of characters" in the traditional Chinese culture, it can be seen that design can not only make a graphic and functional creation to Chinese characters as a cultural symbol, but also can consciously participate in the abstract and imperceptible cultural information transmission based on Chinese characters and through more diversified and stereoscopic expressions. Design is a means of embedding Chinese characters into social life so that the traditional cultural genes carried by Chinese characters can be preserved in the Chinese daily life.

References

1. Translated and annotated by Tang Kejing, *Origin of Chinese Characters*. Zhong Hua Book Company, Beijing (2018)
2. Nan, C.: The History of Chinese Character Design. Hubei Fine Arts Press, Wuhan (2021)
3. Jiuying, H.: Chinese Character Culturology. Commercial Press, Beijing (2016)
4. Ling, L.: Changing: A Collection of Li Ling's Works about the History of Archaeological Art. SDX Joint Publishing Company, Beijing (2016)
5. [Germany] Lothar Ledderose, translated by Zhang Zong, etc, Ten Thousand Things. SDX Joint Publishing Company, Beijing (2020)

The Experience Design of Cultural Heritage Tourism in the Perspective of Gamification

Kexing Peng[1](✉), Xiaohui Tao[1], Jinchen Jiang[2], and Jingyu Zhai[1]

[1] Chongqing University, Chongqing 400030, China
254144620@qq.com
[2] Sichuan Fine Arts Institute, Chongqing 400030, China

Abstract. The abstract should summarize the contents of the paper in short terms, i.e. 150–250 words. Objective: To enable gamified learning for users through the experience of gamified cultural heritage tourism, the meaning configuration process of "experience-perception-introspection" is built up. Method: By means of field study and literature research, the "cultural standard" user demands are researched and a study in the perspective of gamification is carried out to explore the view and path of gamification experience design involving in the cultural heritage tourism project, then preliminary practical verification is conducted to take the tourism development project of the Song Dynasty Cultural Heritage Park, Huanghuacheng Island, Zhong County, Chongqing City as an example. Result: A gamification experience design strategy theory model targeted at "participants' sense of learning" is established and the questions of "What is the gamification of historical and cultural experience?", "How to integrate online and offline game contacts using narration as the thread?" and "How do users realize the transformation from sense of gameplay into sense of learning in their experience?" are answered. Significance: The study contributes new ideas to the theory system of experience design and provides new reference methods and innovated paths for the design, development and practice of cultural heritage tourism projects.

Keywords: Experience Design · gamification · immersive experience · cultural heritage tourism

1 Research Background

With the progress and development of the age, people are focusing more on the experience economy which is an economic activity and creates unforgettable living experience consistently mobilizing and developing the positivity and proactivity of the internal psychology and spirit of consumers from products to experience of services [1]. Nowadays, when the experience economy is on the rise, cultural heritage tourism has become an emerging developing mode for tourism [2]. Cultural heritage tourism is traveling to places with historical value and the legacy of the ancestor (such as temples, museums and palaces, etc.). It is a journey of tourists to explore historical value [3] and the purpose of its development is to protect and pass down the culture and historical heritage of an area or a city [4]. Compared to traditional tourism projects, cultural heritage tourism not only provides entertainment, but also enables tourists to experience local historical and humanistic landscape and to learn about related historical and cultural knowledge. However, the cultural heritage tourism projects at present have many problems such as lack of delights, chaotic cultural resources and absence of systematic integration, monotonous travel modes, and poor user experience, which greatly reduces tourists' learning efficiency in historical and cultural knowledge and eventually results in the loss of real value and significance of cultural heritage tourism projects.

Therefore, the paper concentrates on how to entertain users' traveling experience to make them learn history and culture highly-efficiently (namely the gamified learning) and a positive circulation result of "experience-perception-introspection" is obtained. In terms of the above problems of traditional cultural heritage tourism projects, the core contents of the study are as follows: (1) introducing the gamification thinking to the tourism experience design of users; (2) linking related resources of cultural heritage tourism projects by means of narration; (3) to enable immersive experience by means of online and offline interactive traveling; (4) to explore the real value and significance of cultural heritage tourism projects.

2 Target: To Realize Users' Cultural Standard Demands

Learning historical and cultural knowledge is both tourists' cultural standard demands and the basic target of cultural heritage tourism. Hence, how to make users learn about historical and cultural knowledge highly-efficiently becomes the direct target of the experience design study of cultural heritage tourism projects, whereas study and analysis are conducted to explore its realization. The "learning" mentioned above refers to the experiential learning firstly proposed by Kolb [5], a scholar in 1984. He stresses that knowledge is obtained and tested during the experience of learners, which means the process is completed by the interaction between learners and the environment. Such experience has objective and subjective meanings, the former indicating the external experience (for example, X has 10 years of working experience), the latter indicating the individual status (such as experience of delights), and the study focuses on the latter. Speaking of joyful experiential learning, people usually tend to think of the teaching theory of edutainment. The essence is to obtain knowledge through an entertaining and interesting learning process, in which the self-perception accompanied by interest of learning experience or process is defined as sense of learning [6]. In the experience of cultural heritage tourism, tourists' sense of learning is obtained by means of gamification which supports them in improving their interest and efficiency in learning historical and cultural knowledge so as to truly realize users' cultural standard demands. Therefore, during the experience design of cultural heritage tourism, sense of learning and gaming becomes a new view to study how users learn during traveling through gamification. In this view, sense of learning is a product of the gamified learning process and sense of gameplay is the product of gaming experience, and the study discusses the following contents in the construction of the latter advancing the former.

3   Method and Design: The Song Dynasty Cultural Heritage Park, Huanghuacheng Island Gamified Tourism Experience Project

The study of gamified learning starts from the design method of gamification. First of all, in terms of the broad definition of gamification, Deterding believes that it refers to the application of game design elements in the non-gaming context. In regard to the gamification for the purpose of learning, Kapp considers that in the teaching context, it is a process based on the gaming mechanism, aesthetics and thinking to attract people, stimulate actions, improve studying and problem-solving. In short, gamification generally makes the process more fascinating through the application of game design elements and gaming mechanism to arouse people's participation motivation. The paper conducts study and analysis on the gamification design process targeted at user experience and sense of learning, on the basis of users' cultural standard demands for historical and cultural knowledge in their cultural heritage tourism experience and two famous game design theories, namely "MDA gamification design framework" and "octagonal action analysis". Related resources of cultural heritage tourism projects are connected by means of narration to build up gamified elements, and gamified dynamic mechanism is established by online and offline interactive immersive traveling experience, to develop users' sense of gameplay in their traveling experience. The paper takes the tourism experience design project of the Song Dynasty Cultural Heritage Park, Huanghuacheng Island, Zhong County, Chongqing City as an example, and conducts preliminary verification.

Fig. 1. Huanghuacheng Island, Ancient Ruins of the Song Dynasty

Huanghuacheng Island, Ancient Ruins of the Song Dynasty (see Fig. 2) is a natural island located in the geographic center of the Three Gorge Reservoir and Chongqing section of Yangtze River. It was a defensive island keeping out enemies (Huns) during the Song Dynasty. The island covers an area of 170 hectares, with pleasant ecological environment and abundant species of animals and plants. Rich in historical and cultural deposits, the island retains a huge number of Song Dynasty remains of buildings, such as city gates, government offices, temples, folk houses, wells, and sculptures etc. Profound historical deposits and abundant historical remains make Huanghuacheng Island a place for searching for the past. Since ancient times, Huanghuacheng Island has been highly praised by many celebrities and writers. Wang Erjian, a poet during the Qing Dynasty described Huanghuacheng Island as "rivers and beaches from four sides are blended into a harmony, smoke and trees are diffused all over the island". Above all, Huanghuacheng Island is both a city, an island, and a natural-cultural heritage complex of prominent heritage value. Cultural heritage tourism should be greatly developed taking the opportunity of heritage protection to protect Yangtze River heritage. However, there are many existing problems for the historical and cultural communication of ancient city heritage tourist sights such as Huanghuacheng Island: The ancient city heritage is invaded by rapid development and transformation of commercial culture. The completeness, systematicness and comprehensiveness of historical and cultural heritage resources are so damaged that the cultural heritage becomes a "cultural island". The binary opposition thinking has long imprisoned and binded the protection of historical and cultural heritage, that is, a dilemma of protection first or development orientation has come forward. Cultural heritage encounters severe damages from economic development and natural forces. Designers for developing the cultural heritage tourism projects are lacking correct understanding for the value of cultural heritage. Those problems indirectly result in poor sense of delights and experience of users and low learning efficiency of historical and cultural knowledge, which further causes cultural heritage tourism projects lose their true value and significance. Targeted at the above pain spots, the paper brings up a gamification experience design strategy theory model for the purpose of "sense of learning of participants" for the guidance of developing the tourism experience design project of the Song Dynasty Cultural Heritage Park, Huanghuacheng Island.

3.1 A Gamification Experience Design Strategy Theory Model for the Purpose of "Sense of Learning of Participants"

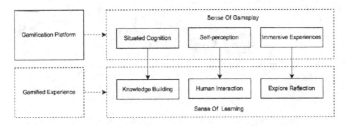

Fig. 2. Sense of gameplay and learning in the perspective of gamification

What is sense of learning? As mentioned above, sense of learning is an individual feeling along with the learning experience or process of the learner. Positive sense of learning is beneficial to improving learners' learning interest and achieving an result of "playing and gaining wisdom" during the experience of gamification (see Fig. 1). Sense of learning is obtained through knowledge construction, problem discussion and human interaction during the gamified learning. Such gamified learning contents completed by gaming experience respectively matches users' contextual awareness, self-perception and immersive experience in their experience [6]. Among them, contextual awareness and self-perception are reached by means of the construction of gaming elements and environments through the gamified design method. Immersive experience is connected with user participation gamified dynamic mechanism. Based on that, the paper conducts the following study of the experience design of cultural heritage tourism in the perspective of gamification.

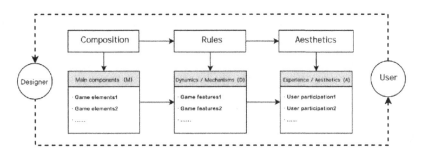

Fig. 3. Sense of gameplay and learning in the perspective of gamification

As to the definition of the gamified process in the study, the famous MDA gamified design theory is referenced. MDA gamified design theory devides a game into three parts, the composition, rules and aesthetics, and further defines their corresponding design forms: elements/modules, dynamic/mechanism, and experience/aesthetics [6]. The feature is to analyze a game from the perspective of designers and users, illustrating, decomposing and designing through the above three design forms. The gamified process design content selected by the paper is the construction of gaming elements and mechanism. However, the gamified design framework provided by MDA model fails to thoroughly explore the specific design path guidance or provide suitable design paths for the experience of cultural heritage tourism projects, namely how to use gaming elements, detailed methods and cases of gaming mechanism for the cultural heritage tourism (non-gaming context). Therefore, targeted at the existing problems of cultural tourism projects, an in-depth extensive study is conducted on the basis of basic gamified process in which gaming elements and mechanism are built up:

(1) Gaming elements: elements/modules of MDA framework refer to the specific parts of the game, namely the characters, background, actions and controls provided for players in a gaming environment, such as selection of character cards and house building in Monopoly. The study brings up an idea of building up methods and contents based on the narration thread, considering the design of gaming elements, chaotic cultural resources of cultural heritage tourism projects and lack of systematic integration. (2) Gaming mechanism: dynamic/mechanism of MDA framework refers to the operation mode of players for a game, which is the key rule of the game. In essence, it is a process of building up interaction mode under the limitation of gaming mechanism. For example, the same card game has different interaction gameplay ways when different rules are applied. The paper brings up methods and contents of enabling the immersive experience by online and offline interactive traveling mode, integrating the gaming mechanism to solve problems of poor user experience, monotonous traveling mode and lack of delights for cultural heritage tourism.

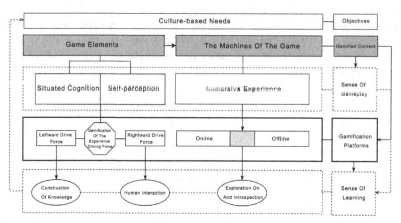

Fig. 4. A gamification experience design strategy theory model for the purpose of "sense of learning of participants".

Next, on the basis of the extended and upgraded gamified process and contents, a gamification experience design strategy theory model for the purpose of "sense of learning of participants" is established (see Fig. 3). First of all, it is designed to realize users' cultural standard demands (learning historical and cultural knowledge highly-efficiently), aimed at establishing sense of gameplay for users' cultural heritage tourism experience. A gaming element configuration platform based on the "octagonal action analysis" gamified experience driving force model and a gaming mechanism configuration platform for the immersive traveling experience integrating online and offline interaction mode are established, and these two platforms are called "the gamified platform". Secondly, users gain sense of learning by experiencing the service journey delivered by the gamified platform, and eventually form positive circulation meeting their initial cultural standard demands. The above sense of learning includes knowledge construction, problem discussion and human interaction during the experience. In brief, the core path of gamification experience design strategy theory model for the purpose of "sense of learning of participants" is to build up a gamified platform with gamified contents. By establishing sense of gameplay through cultural tourism service experience, users gain sense of learning and meeting their cultural standard demands.

In terms of the Song Dynasty Cultural Heritage Park, Huanghuacheng Island gamified tourism experience project, the cultural standard demands of users are learning about the cultural heritage and remains of local area, historical and cultural knowledge of the Song Dynasty. For this design purpose, the above design strategy theory model is used to guide the study on the user experience (see Fig. 4), and related design contents and achievements include: (1) service and visual design; (2) online game design; (3) traveling experience contact design; (4) cultural innovation and agricultural sideline product design, see specific design results in Schedule 1.

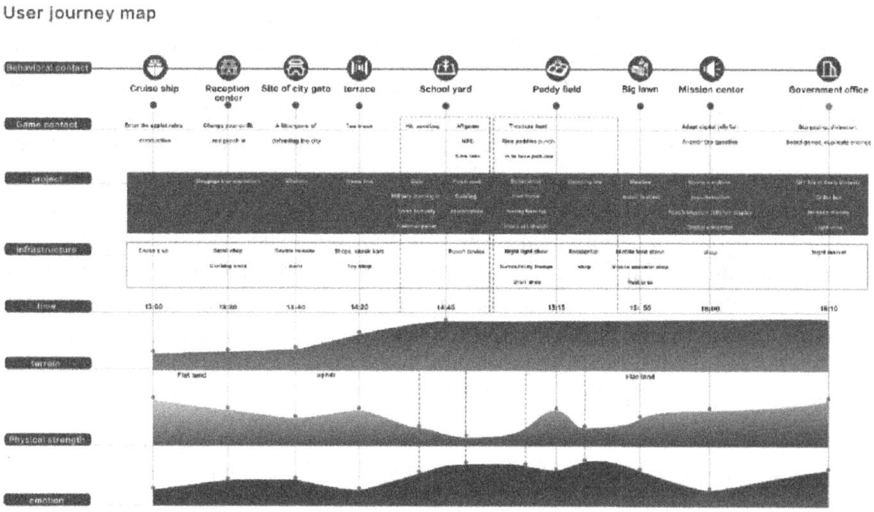

User journey map

Fig. 5. The user journey mapping for the Song Dynasty Cultural Heritage Park, Huanghuacheng Island tourism experience project

3.2 Gamified Contens 1: To Build up Gamified Elements and Contents Using Narration as the Thread

Fig. 6. Octagonal action analysis model

This part brings up an idea of building up methods and contents based on the narration thread, considering the chaotic cultural resources of cultural heritage tourism projects and lack of systematic integration. Narration refers to story telling. In the process of learning, the story context may better assist learners in acquiring the knowledge [7]. In order to strengthen users' sense of learning, the process applies narration method. The establishment of gamified elements refers to reinforcement of users' contextual awareness and self-perception during the traveling experience through the configuration of gaming elements. In this way, users will gain a high sense of gameplay, and such contextual awareness and self-perception respectively sources from objective external environments and subjective individual feeling. Yu-kai Chou, a Japanese game designer brings up a gamified design method called the "octagonal action analysis" [8]. In his research, he divides the eight core driving forces of gamification into the leftward drive and the rightward drive (see Fig. 5) classified by objective factors and subjective factors (rationality and sensibility). They respectively provide gamified external motivations and internal motivations, which corresponds to the contextual awareness (external) and self-perception (internal) of users' sense of gameplay in the research stage of this paper. Therefore, this phase of the paper conducts research based on the "octagonal action analysis" gamified design method. Related cultural resources are connected by means of narration to intensify users' sense of gameplay and experience to reinforce their historical and cultural knowledge construction and human interaction. Among them, the target-oriented leftward drive are realized by the online virtual platform, and the experience-oriented rightward drive are achieved by the offline real traveling experience. See the gamified element configuration sheet of historical and cultural knowledge learning orientation in Table 1.

Table 1. Gamified element configuration sheet based on the octagonal action analysis

Driving force	Sense of gameplay	Gaming element	Content	Sense of learning
Achievement	Context Cognition	Level, score, rank, combat, medal	Historical official position, historical medal of hero, Historical war and story background	Knowledge Construction
Object		Personal home, personal commodity, virtual pet Equipment, skin, virtual currency, membership	Historical architecture, commodity, costume, currency	
Scarcity		Lucky draw, guessing, reward, gift	Random draw, guanpu, medallion, Digitalized historical treasure	
Duty		Patriotism, the hero saving the beauty, righteousness above family royalty	Historical story, historical character, Traditional cultural spirit	

(*continued*)

Table 1. (*continued*)

Driving force	Sense of gameplay	Gaming element	Content	Sense of learning
Creation	Self Perception	Role play, footprinting, game mission, routine sightseeing	Inquiry, group activity	Interpersonal Interaction
Social contact		Relation binding, NPC interaction, match	Multiplayer interaction, character relationship establishment	
Unknown		Party, trap triggering, quick flashing	Ancient social contact pattern	
Escape		Tarot, fortune-telling, fortune stick	Historical and cultural communication	

Based on the theoretical research guidance of this part, namely the gamified element construction method using narration as the thread, related practice for the design of the Song Dynasty Cultural Heritage Park, Huanghuacheng Island tourism experience project is conducted. First of all, the paper conducts study targeted the local culture. Huanghuacheng Island, as a park with remains of the Song Dynasty anti-Hun history, is rich in local culture, such as the city gate remain, historical stories of the war between Song and Yuan, records of historical figures and craspedacusta. Based on those local cultural resources, according to the topographic distribution and functional zoning of the island, Huanghuacheng Island is divided into the dynamic area (sports area), farm area (catering area), and literature area (cultural and learning area). Three IP figures are designed, including Ma Kun (civil official), an anti-Hun historical figure and hero, Ma Ji (military officer) and craspedacusta (a rare local aquatic animal). They respectively corresponds to the literature area, dynamic area, and farm area. The IP stories are built up by means of narration to connect with users' online and offine interactive traveling experience and journey. Furthermore, these IP figures will be used for users to select their virtual characters on the online platform later and for offline real character experience. Moreover, the project conducts study in the purpose of providing the Song Dynasty living style for tourists. The contacts of various experiences will be designed from the aspect of social contact (drinking tea, liquor battle, joss stick making, and Cuju), dress culture (the Song Dynasty clothes) and catering culture (literati gathering, night fair and delicacy). As to the selection of related gaming elements for the design of various contacts, Table 1 should be referenced. See details and analysis in Table 3.

Fig. 7. The functional zoning for the Song Dynasty Cultural Heritage Park, Huanghuacheng Island tourism experience project

3.3 Gamified Content 2: Establishment of Online and Offline Interactive Gaming Mechanism

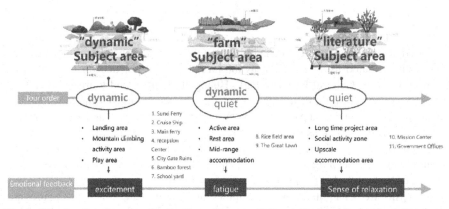

Fig. 8. The functional zoning for the Song Dynasty Cultural Heritage Park, Huanghuacheng Island tourism experience project

The paper brings up methods and contents of enabling the immersive experience by online and offline interactive gaming mechanism, targeted at problems of poor user experience, monotonous traveling mode and lack of delights for cultural heritage tourism of users. The paper, based on the online and offline gaming features and attributes, concludes the content as online and offline corresponding gaming mechanism design (see Table 2). Based on the theoretical research guidance of this part, the design for the Song Dynasty Cultural Heritage Park, Huanghuacheng Island tourism experience project is conducted and practiced. Eventually, "My Huanghuacheng", a hybrid experience game is launched. It is an experience game integrating the online virtual and offline real scene specially designed for Huanghuacheng Island tourism experience project. Themed with immersive Song Dynasty living experience, the game offers tourists of fancy visual and

Table 2. Online and offline corresponding gaming mechanism configuration table

Mode	Gaming mechanism	User participation mode
Online	Voting and contest, referral jackpot	Using social platforms to organize a "Like/Dislike" voting activity; allowing users to share through their social networks and awarding them if their followers' forwarding volume reaches a certain standard (tickets, vouchers, game skins)
	Consumption cumulative reward	Offering rewards to users if their payment reaches a certain level
	Virtual fitting	Providing virtual fitting services for users at online platforms and preparing related real clothes for them to try on offline
	Progress bar	Providing clear service experience progress and inspiring users to proceed
	Level system	Differentiating user levels through their accumulated data and usage to visualize user levels
	Reward mechanism	Duration cumulative reward, timing reward, level-up reward, and task reward
Offline	New mode unlocked	To unlock new scenes, clothes, equipment, game themes and maps
	Likes collecting and forwarding	To enable users to share, experience and comment on the social platform and offer them rewards if Likes are collected and reaching a certain level
	Exaggerated interaction	Applying exaggerated interaction gestures and behaviors to draw attraction and form representativeness
	Items collection	Encouraging users to collect cards, badges and digital collections to inspire their sense of achievements
	NPC tasks	Improving the interaction between users and NPC and inspiring them to unlock new tasks
	Game configuration	Game equipment providing specified interaction mode for users, such as the dancing machine
	Teamplay	Requiring users to make a team to take part and providing many experiences and choices (teams of 2, 4 or 6)

(continued)

Table 2. (*continued*)

Mode	Gaming mechanism	User participation mode
O2O	Sales package	Family package, lovers package, ladybro package
	Group purchase	Offering overall ticket price discount if purchasers exceed a certain number
	Special benefits	Students' special offer, birthday benefits, regular user rewards, new user gifts
	Vouchers	Users may purchase high discount vouchers in a lower price and operators may distribute vouchers randomly
	Lucky draw	"Lucky Dog" activity, users may obtain lucky draw chances if their payment exceeds a certain number
	Cross promotion	Cross promotion with real brands (peripheral products of local IP, local specialties), online forwarding and offline prize acceptance

joyful sensual experience through visualized online gaming screen, innovated theme and atmosphere, integrated with interactive design in the real scene, and enables tourists to learn about the culture and history of the Song Dynasty effectively. As to the selection of related gaming mechanism for the design of various contacts, Table 1 should be referenced. Eventually, related experience process is arranged, taking tourists' emotional changes as the research foundation (see Fig. 6). See details and analysis in Table 3.

3.4 Project Summary

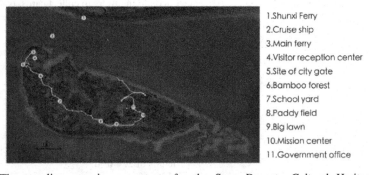

1.Shunxi Ferry
2.Cruise ship
3.Main ferry
4.Visitor reception center
5.Site of city gate
6.Bamboo forest
7.School yard
8.Paddy field
9.Big lawn
10.Mission center
11.Government office

Fig. 9. The traveling experience contacts for the Song Dynasty Cultural Heritage Park, Huanghuacheng Island tourism experience project

Please All in all, targeted at the problem that designers have a biased cognition of users' cultural heritage tourism demands and cause poor user experience, the writer conducts a field study in Huanghuacheng Island in the perspective of the principal by means of field study and user investigation, and forms insights over users' cultural standard demands. Based on the guidance provided by the above theoretical models, gamified experience contents of each phase are established and completed, and a complete experience path for the Song Dynasty Cultural Heritage Park, Huanghuacheng Island has been prepared (see Fig. 6). Among them, see Table 3 for the gamified design and analysis summary of various experience process contacts and see Schedule 1 for the design achievements. In addition, the evaluation prototype used by this study includes USE tests, namely in four standards: usability (UU), accessibility (EU), ease of learning (UL) and satisfaction (US) [3]. Questionnaires themed at presenting the project design concepts are prepared to investigate users' gameplay intention, and intensive analysis is conducted for the investigation result by means of the four above variables to form a preliminary testing result. In the future developing process of the project, game modes and contents will be further optimized according to the result to iterate new game tasks.

Table 3. Configuration of Huanghuacheng Island traveling experience of gamification experience design strategy theory model for the purpose of "sense of learning of participants"

Tourism area	Experience contacts	Gaming elements (M) Online — Form/function	Offline — Form/function	Gaming mechanism (D) Online — Input mode	Offline — Input mode	Sense of gameplay — Contextual awareness	Self-perception	Immersive experience	Sense of learning — Knowledge construction	Human interaction	Discussion and introspection
Dynamic area	Shunxi Ferry	Level, rank, personal commodity, equipment	Credit, membership	Login interface	Virtual fitting, special benefits	√	√		√		
	Cruise	Individual skin, Relationship binding	Gift	Character selection	Teamplay	√	√	√	√	√	√
	Main ferry	Game task	Trap triggering	AR scanning	Exaggerated interaction	√		√	√		√
	Tourist reception center	Relationship binding	Clothes and equipment	Clothes changing, equipment configuration, storyline selection, friend interconnection	Lucky draw, Teamplay	√	√	√	√	√	√
	City gate remain	Virtual currency	Vouchers	Knowledge contest	Game configuration	√		√	√	√	√
	Bamboo forest	Virtual pet	Trap triggering	AR scanning	Game configuration						
	Drill ground (battleground)	Badge, rank, drama	Battle	Competitive game	Competitive teamplay game	√	√	√	√	√	
	Drill ground (yamen)	Badge, rank, credit	Battle, competition, contest, NPC task	Sports game	NPC interaction	√	√	√	√	√	
Farm area	Rice field viewing area	Virtual pet, Badge	Trap triggering	Progress bar, reward Likes collecting and forwarding	Game configuration, exaggerated interaction	√	√	√		√	√
	Rice field living quarter	Virtual currency, Gift	Reward, gift, NPC task	New mode unlocked, Cumulative consumption	NPC interaction		√	√		√	
	Grand lawn	Virtual currency	Party, quick flashing	Node reward, Sales package	Sales package, group purchase		√	√		√	
Literature area	Publicity and education center	Individual commodity, Level	Guessing	Items collection, progress bar, level system	Sales package	√	√	√			√
	Yamen	Fortune stick	Fortune-telling, fortune stick, divination	Likes collecting and forwarding, group purchase, special benefits, vouchers	Game device, lucky draw		√	√	√	√	√

4 Conclusion

The primary purpose of the study is to explore a set of gamified design theory methods to instruct cultural heritage tourism service experience in a joyful way, that is, to focus on user demands with an idea of user first, according to the experience design. With insights over the cultural standard demands of users for the purpose of historical and cultural learning, the design strategy and method are explored for the gamified experience of related cultural heritage tourism projects. Based on that, the gamified experience design strategy model is established for the purpose of "sense of learning of participants" to guide the development of core contents of cultural heritage tourism experience projects. Gamified study brings up an idea of building up methods and contents based on the narration thread, providing solutions for the chaotic cultural resources of cultural heritage tourism projects and lack of systematic integration. The paper brings up methods and contents of enabling the immersive experience by online and offline interactive traveling mode, integrating the gaming mechanism to solve problems of poor user experience, monotonous traveling mode and lack of delights for cultural heritage tourism. The accessibility of the above theoretical research results is verified through the Song Dynasty Cultural Heritage Park, Huanghuacheng Island tourism experience project, providing new ideas and methods for designers, researchers and design practice in the future, offering new approaches for the historical and cultural inheritance, creating new purposes for participants to realize cultural and educational vision of edutainment through the gamified journey and cultural experience.

Table 4. The design achievements for the Song Dynasty Cultural Heritage Park, Huanghuacheng Island gamified tourism experience project

Category	Item	Picture
Service and visual design	User journey mapping	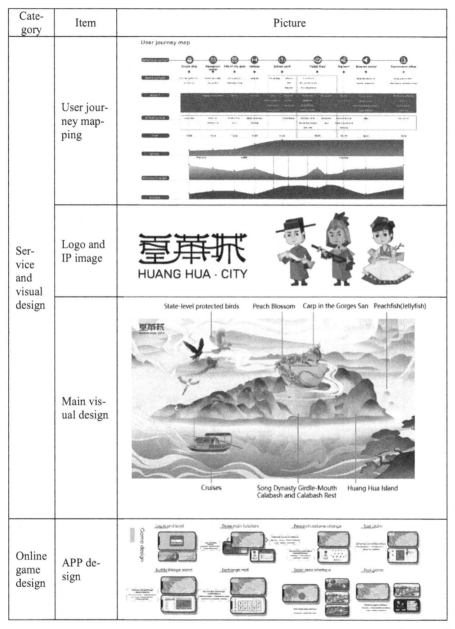
	Logo and IP image	
	Main visual design	
Online game design	APP design	

(continued)

Table 4. (*continued*)

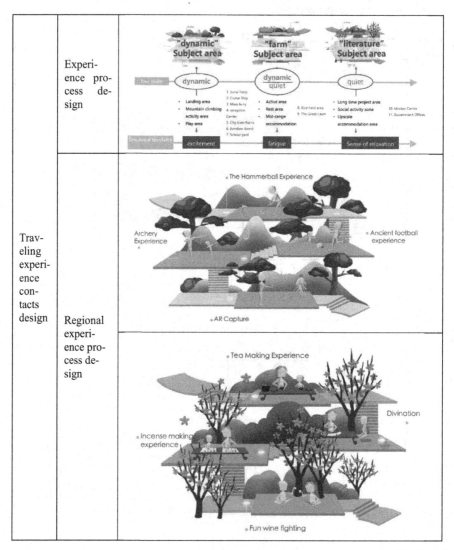

(*continued*)

Table 4. (*continued*)

	Part of contacts details design	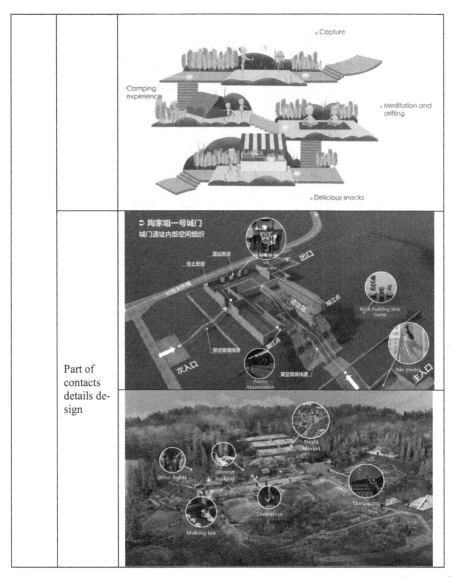

(*continued*)

Table 4. (*continued*)

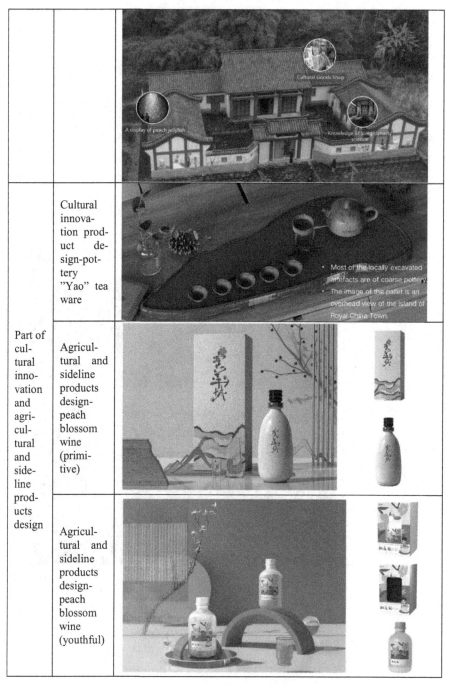

(*continued*)

Table 4. (*continued*)

Agricultural and sideline products design-peach blossom pastry	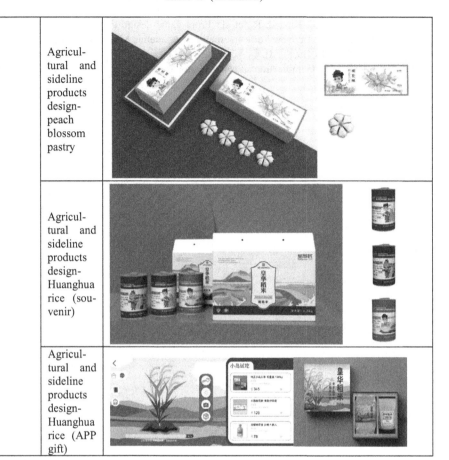
Agricultural and sideline products design-Huanghua rice (souvenir)	
Agricultural and sideline products design-Huanghua rice (APP gift)	

References

1. Pine, J., Gilmore, J.H.: The Experience Economy. China Machine Press, Beijing (2002)
2. 付璐, 体验型文化遗产旅游产品开发初探. 社会科学家, 2019(04): 第92–96页
3. E Widarti S Suyoto AWR Emanuel 2020 Mobile application design for heritage tourism uses gamification approach in Indonesia Int. J. Eng. Pedagogy (iJEP) 10 5 89 102
4. Marimin, M.: Cultural heritage as a tourist destination: a focus on Surakarta Kasunanan Palace in Indonesia. J. Environ. Manag. Tour. **7**(4), 723–732 (2016): https://doi.org/10.14505/jemt.v7.4(16).19
5. DA Kolb 2014 Experiential learning: experience as the source of learning and development 2 Pearson FT Press Upper Saddle River

6. 陶侃.从游戏感到学习感:泛在游戏视域中的游戏化学习. 中国电化教育, 2013(09): 第22–27页

7. Deterding, S., Dixon, D., Khaled, R., et al.: From game design elements to gamefulness: defining "Gamification". In: New York: International Academic Mindtrek Conference (2011)

8. 卡普, 2015. 游戏, 让学习成瘾[M]. 陈阵, 译. 北京: 机械工业出版社

9. Chou, Y.K.: Actionable Gamification: Beyong Points, Badges, and Leaderboards. New York: Octalysis Media (2015)

Research on the Application of Participatory Design in the Digitalization of Traditional Culture

Haoyue Sun, Ziyang Li[(✉)], Shengxian Chen, and Yifan Ma

Beijing City University, No. 269 Bei Si Huan Zhong Lu, Hai Dian District, Beijing, China
li.ziyang@bcu.edu.cn

Abstract. As the digital age is rapidly developing, people's requirements for design also have higher and higher cultural connotations. It is necessary and feasible to use emerging digital media technology to innovate the traditional culture and art. This paper introduces the participatory design concept into the digitalization of traditional culture. Based on the research of the application of digitalization of traditional culture, the artistic value of traditional culture is revitalized through digital technology and media, allowing more people to participate in the protection and inheritance of traditional culture. By involving users in the design process, emotional resonance is caused, and a digital protection system that meets user needs and local characteristics is jointly built, which shows and brings out the characteristics and advantages of traditional culture, while also satisfying the emotional needs of the audience. This not only has artistic research value but also has important significance for the historical value and cultural value of traditional culture inheritance and development.

This article studies the concepts of digitalization of traditional culture and participatory design, finds opportunities for the combination of the two, and investigates the application of participatory design in digitalization of traditional culture. By analyzing the participation methods and design strategies of participatory design in digitalization of traditional culture, it proposes a method for stakeholders' participation in design and uses this method to design an interactive design application for Yangzhen Dragon Lantern Festival, verifying the feasibility of the method. It also argues the importance of this method and opens up new paths for the inheritance and development of the Yangzhen Dragon Lantern Festival.

Keywords: Participatory design · Traditional culture · Digital dissemination · Yangzhen Dragon Lantern Festival

1 Background

Nowadays, we have entered the digital age and emerging digital media technologies are rapidly integrating into every aspect of our lives. With the rapid development of media such as short videos and live streaming, the forms of cultural communication have changed. At the same time, more and more people are becoming aware of the importance of Chinese traditional culture and realizing that strengthening our culture helps to improve the country's cultural soft power. However, how to use digital means to inherit Chinese traditional culture is a topic worth considering and researching.

This article deals with VR interactive design, which is different from ordinary VR games. It takes into account the digital presentation form of traditional culture, the user's understanding of traditional culture, and the acceptance of digital inheritance. Therefore, relying solely on designers to complete these tasks is not enough. Without understanding user preferences, the problems encountered in the current inheritance of Chinese traditional culture, and the ability to promote the understanding and love of traditional culture through VR games, the result will not be satisfactory. Therefore, it is necessary to involve users, inheritors, and dragon enthusiasts in the design process, and to call for participation and in-depth communication to find the right design direction and meet the needs of all parties.

The author based on the concept of "participatory design," plans to combine modern digital methods with Chinese traditional culture to create a deeper sense of pleasure in users, resulting in an emotional resonance, ultimately achieving the goal of protecting and inheriting traditional culture. The author selects some VR applications for students and dragon enthusiasts to experience, analyze, and record the experience through the visual, auditory, and cognitive senses, and organizes communication with stakeholders to participate in the project and design the Yangzhen Dragon Lantern Interactive Design together.

2　Digitalization of Traditional Culture

Digitalization of traditional culture refers to the use of new digital media and techniques to display traditional culture in a new and diverse way, in order to achieve the protection and dissemination of traditional culture in a more acceptable way. In December 2018, the Ministry of Industry and Information Technology proposed to promote the development of "VR + culture" key industries. Therefore, using virtual reality technology to transmit valuable Shunyi dragon lantern festival content is beneficial in fully showcasing the unique charm of the dragon lantern festival. As the absolute core of dissemination, the user experience and perception are all channels through the body, thus launching cognitive activities on the virtual environment. When the user connects to the virtual world of dragon lantern festival through wearable devices, an emotional resonance will be generated [1].

The article focuses on the use of VR interactive design to showcase the traditional cultural event of the Yangzhen Dragon Lantern Festival in Shunyi, Beijing.

The festival, which has over 200 years of history and is included in the second batch of Beijing's intangible cultural heritage list, is known for its rough and bold styling, and has been passed down through generations with minimal changes to adapt to the needs of folk performances. The author aims to use VR technology to transport users to the virtual world of the dragon lantern festival, allowing them to experience the unique charm of the traditional culture and create emotional resonance. Through the participation of users, dragon lantern enthusiasts, and heritage keepers, the author hopes to find the right design direction and ultimately achieve the goal of protecting and promoting traditional culture through digital means (Fig. 1).

Fig. 1. Yangzhen Dragon Lantern Festival performance(From the Internet)

When traditional Chinese culture meets digital technology, new sparks will be created, bringing a rich and different cultural experience. Digital display and dissemination expands the ways of cultural communication, updates the ways of cultural communication, and expands the scope of cultural communication, making traditional culture come alive, come alive and ignite in a "soaring as if startled by a swan" way. In order to further improve the design quality of traditional culture digitalization in the digital age, this study applies the participatory design concept to the research of traditional culture digitalization, takes the design practice of Yangzhen Dragon Lantern Festival in Shunyi District, Beijing as a verification, and provides a certain reference for the research of traditional culture digitalization.

3 Participatory Design

3.1 Introduction to Participatory Design

In the 1970 s, Participatory Design originated in the Scandinavian Peninsula and became a new design method. The emergence of Participatory Design is due to two reasons: first, in the 1970 s, "the union movement prompted new laws to give employees new powers to change the work environment"; second, manufacturers saw that cost reduction could increase productivity, increase profits and expand development, making design innovation more important [2].

By the late 1980 s, participatory design had developed into a widely used design method in the United States. User participation in design means that the end user also joins the design process, and design is no longer done solely by the designer, but by actively involving the user in the entire design process, from the initial stage to the final end. And the best way to meet user design needs is to attract them to participate in the design, users actively participate in design based on their environment and real feelings, and it is easier to express and meet their own personalized needs [3]. Participatory design is a process of mutual communication, coordination, collaboration, and sharing. As active participants in the design process, users become an important part of the design team. Therefore, everyone is both a designer and a user, and their participation directly impacts the outcome of the final product [4].

"Participatory design" concept, in essence, is a deeper development of the "user-centered" approach. It emphasizes the user's deeper integration into the design process. Currently, in the field of design, participatory design methods refer to inviting users and other stakeholders to actively participate in different stages of the design process, to work with designers and researchers to solve problems and design solutions. This design method allows people who are affected by the design to express their own interest needs and to provide creativity. Compared to traditional design methods, it is more open and flexible, able to provide multiple perspectives for problem-solving and make the design process continue to be efficient [5].

3.2 Participation Design Approach

As the objects of participation in the activity are different, the ways of participatory design need to be considered from various aspects such as organizational forms, application requirements, and degree of participation. The ways are also relatively flexible and can roughly be divided into three forms: group-based, one-on-one, and online open. [6]The choice of participatory method should be made based on the actual situation.

Group-Based Participation Design. The group-based participation method is similar to the focus group method. Users participate in the design activity process in the form of a group, and the number of group participants is generally 6–8. This method of design process is: First, select appropriate participating users, second, the organizer introduces the purpose and methods of participating in the activity to the participants, allowing them to understand it; then, the participating group members propose personal suggestions and plans based on their understanding and requirements of the design work; finally, the design team analyzes the users' ideas and requirements, and improves the final design by screening and summarizing these design ideas. This method gathers users together in the form of a group and can inspire more creative ideas through interaction and exchange of ideas among group members. By participating in the entire design process with users and with the premise of respecting their ideas, the final design is more in line with user requirements. However, this participation method also has certain difficulties in implementation. Due to the different requirements of different users and their knowledge and thinking levels, group-based participation method requires research and analysis of target users before recruiting and conducting design activities. This organizational method also has higher requirements for coordination, time, and venue compared to one-on-one methods, and is difficult to implement in practice.

One-on-one Participation Design. The one-on-one participation method is where only one user participates in the design process and the designer communicates directly with the user. During the communication, the designer observes the user's language, expressions, ideas, etc. and records them. One-on-one communication allows for sufficient exchange between the user and the designer, which helps to deeply understand the user's requirements. One-on-one operation is relatively easy to implement compared to group-based, and it can enhance the user's participation and motivation. Additionally, the participant is more professional in certain areas, which is conducive to design innovation.

This method is suitable for groups of users with fewer people and higher requirements, generally experts or inheritors, who have a good understanding of all aspects of the product and have unique insights.

Online Open-Style Participation Design. The online open method mainly allows users to participate in design through the internet, using online communication such as forums, and converting the participation method from offline to online. This method eliminates time and location constraints during participation and has a high degree of interactivity and freedom. It truly enables users to participate in the design decision-making process, and they have a stronger sense of initiative and participation while sharing their own experience. Additionally, this method does not have specific requirements for the user's gender or experience, and most users can participate [7].The open participation method is convenient for user experience and feedback, allowing users to express their opinions about their experience and share their views. In the process of collecting user opinions, this open participation method is relatively easy to implement compared to the first two methods, and the collected information is more extensive, which is beneficial for the final design to meet user needs and better spread. Its advantage is that it is easy to implement, the information collection is broader, but the workload of user needs analysis is large in later stage (Fig. 2).

Participation method	Features	Advantages	Disadvantages	Applicable scenarios
Group-based participation design	Participating in the design process in a group format, with group sizes generally ranging from 6 to 8 people	1.Face-to-face direct communication provides more intuitive feelings, and it is convenient to record the verbal and nonverbal expressions of participants 2.Group members can communicate and exchange ideas with each other 3.Cognitive collision can stimulate more creative ideas	1.Practice has a certain level of difficulty and is limited by factors such as participants, time, and location 2.The needs of different participants are different	Used to collect a large number of ideas from participants, such as brainstorming, group discussion, etc.
One-on-one participation design	Only one user participates in the design process during participation.	1.The operation is relatively easy to implement and can increase the enthusiasm of participation 2.One-on-one communication is targeted, which helps to deeply mine 3.Participants are professionals, which is conducive to design innovation	1.The requirements for participants are high, and they need to have professional literacy 2.Both parties need to have theoretical knowledge reserves in relevant areas	It is mostly targeted at expert users, inheritors, etc. who have a good understanding of a certain aspect and have their own unique insights
Online open-style participation design	Participating in the design process through the internet	1.Unrestricted by factors such as time and place, conducting online communication 2.Having strong interactivity and freedom. 3.Information collection is extensive, and most users can participate	1.Online communication may be subject to network delays 2.The workload for later information collection and analysis is large	Due to some objective factors, online communication through the internet is required, such as online meetings, forums, etc.

Fig. 2. Participation method

4   Participatory Design is a Design Strategy in the Digitalization of Traditional Culture

4.1   Participatory Design is a Design Principle in the Digitalization of Traditional Culture

The Principle of Unifying Culture and Technology. At present, the digital preservation and dissemination of traditional culture mostly focuses on the technical level, emphasizing technological research and development, and sometimes neglecting users' experience and needs of culture, resulting in some phenomena of "heavy technology, light culture", which affects the actual effect of the protection and dissemination of traditional culture, making traditional culture lose its original meaning and value, and easily causing deviation in users' understanding of traditional culture. Currently, the digital preservation and dissemination of traditional culture mostly relies on professional technical personnel, while ignoring the participation of inheritors and users. Due to the lack of understanding of traditional culture by technical personnel and the weakness of inheritors in technical ability [8], the dissemination of traditional culture is relatively weak.

Therefore, only by cooperating with inheritors, participants, users, designers and other parties to jointly participate in the digital preservation and dissemination of traditional culture, can the principle of unifying culture and technology be achieved.

Innovative Design Principle. Innovation is the first driving force, and the development of anything cannot be separated from innovation. Cultural heritage is the product created by people according to their own cultural level, production methods, and lifestyle at a certain period of human development. Every change in traditional culture is due to innovation, whether it is an adjustment change made in response to the development of the times or technological trends, it is achieved through innovation [9]. Participatory design requires that we innovate traditional cultural digital preservation and dissemination methods in a collaborative way during the process of participating in traditional cultural preservation and dissemination. In the process of participating in design, we should not only copy the traditional cultural form, but also pay attention to the cultural attributes of the differences, and conduct creative design.

Respect for Participants Principle. Inviting users and other stakeholders to actively participate in the design process, during the implementation of participatory design activities, we should prioritize the choices and opinions of the participants and allow them to fully participate. However, due to the cultural level, cognitive ability and personal experiences of each participant, there may be some communication barriers in the process of cooperation, at this time, we should fully respect each participant, listen to their ideas and suggestions. It is precisely because of these factors that they can gather wisdom in the whole design process, have their own thinking mode and ideas, and play the advantages of the participants, providing more aspects for the design team to solve the problems in the design. We should take the opinions and suggestions proposed by the participants seriously, record them one by one, respect the labor results of the participating subjects, and maximize the value of participation in design to promote the normal progress of the design work [5].

4.2 The Change of Method in Participatory Design for the Digitalization of Traditional Culture

The Transformation from Design Led by Designers to a More Collaborative Approach in the Digitalization of Traditional Culture. In traditional design patterns, the design process is generally led by designers, with audiences more likely to be passively accepting of design outcomes. This can sometimes lead to partiality in design results. Especially for traditional cultures with relatively less dissemination and less recorded information, it is easier to produce errors when researchers do not have knowledge of certain information. In this case, it is necessary to cooperate with inheritors, participants, local governments and media to ensure the accuracy of digital information. Therefore, in the entire design process, it is necessary to pay attention to the flow of information between people and the expansion of different design personnel, and to seek the best solution through continuous cooperation among different professional related personnel. Designers invite users and stakeholders to participate in the design process, forming a new design force composed of multiple stakeholders to assist designers in better design, and encouraging participants to continuously expand and provide support from multiple forces for design. This mode is conducive to designers opening their design thinking and improving work efficiency.

The Shift from Protection to Dissemination-Oriented. The protection and development of traditional culture also requires the active participation of the public. The goal of participatory design in digitalization of traditional culture is not to focus on the outcome, but rather on the process of design. The public is not only a beneficiary, but also a participant, who takes part in discussions about traditional culture, provides ideas for digital preservation and dissemination, and even helps to finalize design plans. The protection of a certain traditional culture is never a one-time accomplishment, but a continuous process. Building a platform for mutual communication and discussion, maintaining activity, keeping up with the times, and constantly listening to the public's opinions are essential for the widespread dissemination of traditional culture. Utilizing one's own resources and combining them with traditional culture, vigorously developing culture, strengthening propaganda efforts, updating ideas and concepts, and raising public awareness and enthusiasm for the protection and dissemination of traditional culture.

From Digital Display to Autonomous Participation. In digital application design, digital display is the foundation, and in order to maintain the longevity of traditional culture, constant innovation must be kept close to daily life. Innovation is keeping pace with the times, and the public is the largest group of innovators. Therefore, in order to change traditional design, under the premise of setting conditions, public self-design is advocated, and the public can, on the premise of understanding traditional culture, propose design strategies and innovate design according to their own understanding and willingness of the culture to achieve self-satisfaction. This not only achieves the protection and innovation of traditional culture, but also enhances the public's cultural self-confidence and spiritual satisfaction. The fusion of culture and era is the driving force to maintain the prosperity of culture, so it is important to let more people participate in the design process, which not only brings users closer to culture, but also has a good communication effect [10].

5 The Participatory Design Activity of Yangzhen Dragon Lantern Festival

Yangzhen Dragon Lantern Festival is a non-material cultural heritage in Beijing, which fully reflects the national characteristics of the Chinese nation, and has great artistic value, historical value and folk value. In communication with the inheritors of Yangzhen Dragon Lantern Festival, it has been expressed multiple times that there is a problem with the transmission of the heritage, lack of entertainment and innovation in the way of dissemination, and it is difficult to attract people's attention, especially among contemporary young people. Therefore, it is very necessary to design an application that can promote Yangzhen Dragon Lantern Festival and should meet the aesthetic needs of contemporary young people, expand the scope of promotion, and attract more people to participate in the protection and dissemination of Yangzhen Dragon Lantern Festival.

5.1 Research and Analysis

Current Situation Analysis. Through multiple exchanges with inheritors of the Yangzhen Dragon Lantern Festival, it was concluded that the current problems mainly include: 1) a lack of emphasis on traditional culture and inadequate core promotional planning and design for the protection of traditional culture, resulting in many people not understanding the Yangzhen Dragon Lantern Festival and unable to truly achieve the goal of culture promotion; 2) excessive reliance on traditional inheritance methods, with more "physical" protection and promotion of the Yangzhen Dragon Lanterns in the form of exhibitions, performances, etc., lacking innovation in content and form, weakening the ability of dynamic inheritance and lacking attractiveness; 3) due to the inheritors being older and physically and mentally exhausted, there is a problem of discontinuity, resulting in the festival being on the verge of extinction. It cannot be integrated into modern social life practice and sustained in life.

In response to the above phenomena, this research proposes three points as simultaneous innovations: first, user participation and integration. By using the concept of "participatory design," digital technology is integrated with the Yangzhen Dragon Lantern Festival, allowing stakeholders to participate in the design process and emphasizing active and proactive involvement in the design process, while ensuring that the design is usable and in line with their original design intentions. Second, emotional resonance is triggered. Meet the emotional needs of users, build digital communication methods that are in line with local culture and regional characteristics, and promote the protection and development of the Yangzhen Dragon Lantern Festival. Third, innovative ways of communication are adopted. Using the concept of "participatory design" as a principle, a new and innovative way of communication is used to attract more young people to pay attention to and promote the cultural connotations and characteristics of the Yangzhen Dragon Dragon Lantern Festival.

SWOT Analysis. SWOT analysis is a method for evaluating the strengths, weaknesses, opportunities, and threats of a project or business venture. By conducting a SWOT analysis, we can gain a general understanding of the situation and develop strategies accordingly. By utilizing our strengths and external opportunities in the SWOT analysis, we can continuously tap into the cultural value of the traditional culture and seek external cooperation to create more opportunities for the public to interact with culture. To address the threat of fast-changing user needs and weak international competitiveness, we can enhance user experience or integrate user needs with traditional culture. By uncovering the fun aspects of traditional culture and encouraging more professionals to participate in cultural inheritance, we can improve our design thinking and skills. To address the threat of not fully understanding user needs, we can continue to research and provide more connection points between user needs and culture through various forms of cultural promotion (Fig. 3).

Fig. 3. SWOT Analysis

Stakeholder Analysis. After the initial research and analysis, the author conducted a comprehensive sorting and summary of stakeholders, roughly divided into two levels: core stakeholders and other stakeholders. In this phase, further interviews and surveys were conducted on core stakeholders and representative other stakeholders (Fig. 4).

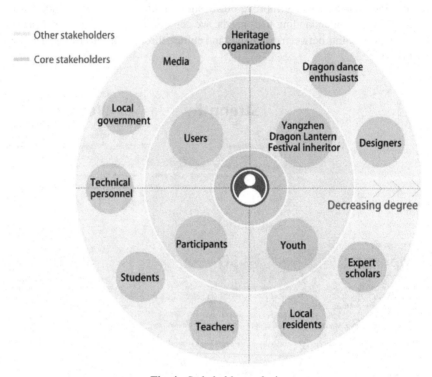

Fig. 4. Stakeholder analysis

Core Stakeholder: Heirs. With the support and help of the local government, several interviews and surveys were conducted with Mr. Liu Zhenbo, one of the inheritors of the Yangzhen Dragon Lantern Festival, to gain a detailed understanding of the historical origins, inheritance of skills, and development status of the Yangzhen Dragon Lantern Festival. Direct communication with the inheritors provided strong support for the subsequent design of the plan.

Core stakeholder: Users. In the initial research process, inheritors repeatedly mentioned the phenomenon of a gap caused by a lack of young people. Therefore, the user is positioned as young people, to attract more young people to join and better inherit and spread the traditional culture of the Yangzhen Dragon Lantern Festival. An initial interview was conducted with students from the dragon dance club at Beijing City University.

Other Stakeholders. In the research process of other stakeholders, some groups were selected for key research, in order to have a more comprehensive understanding of user needs. In this phase, research was conducted on other stakeholders such as the Yangzhen government, the designated inheritance unit of the Yangzhen Dragon Lantern Festival, Yangzhen primary school, and dragon dance enthusiasts (Fig. 5).

Fig. 5. Core Stakeholder and Other Stakeholders research

5.2 Plan Design

After analyzing the survey questionnaire, eye-tracking test data, and interviews with some groups, it was found that most people have a deep level of attraction to VR, and it is more popular among young people. Most people think that VR is interactive and relatively easy to accept. VR entertainment games are the most common in real life, but few people have played VR traditional culture games. In the research process, they said that if there is a traditional culture VR game, they would be willing to try it, because this not only allows them to learn about traditional culture knowledge in the game but also to use this digital way to protect and inherit traditional culture, breaking the boredom of traditional teaching methods and truly making education fun.

During the plan design phase, some users were invited to participate in a brainstorming session in a small group format. Through roundtable discussions, participants quickly got to know each other and the project background, objectives, and principles of "mutual communication, coordination, and sharing" were explained through conversation. After the brainstorming session, by combining similar information, word frequency search, and other methods, the information provided by the participants was obtained. High-frequency words and consistent views were selected, providing a foundation for the determination of the next design plan.

The creative plans proposed by the participants were collected, and the plans that can be further deepened were discussed and determined. All the information collected from the interests, expressions, important language, views, and creative ideas of the participants during the activity were sorted, summarized, and analyzed. The useful information was used as reference for the next game plan (Fig. 6).

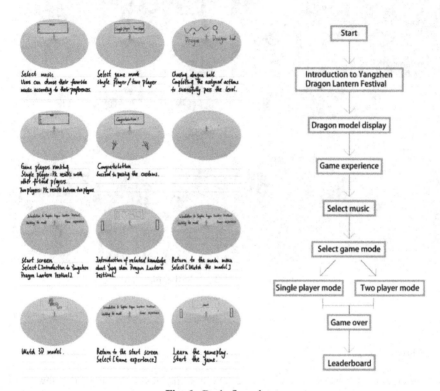

Fig. 6. Basic flow sheet

After using a small group participation method in the previous stage, this stage uses a combination of small group and one-on-one methods. As this stage involves cooperation from multiple parties, the background, objectives, and principles of the project must be explained before starting to ensure that the participants fully understand. Then, participants were given and explained the materials obtained in the previous stage, to understand the current progress and results of the project. Finally, discussions were held around related topics and creative ideas were presented in brief words. The views expressed by the participants were recorded in detail, and drawing tools such as paper and pens were provided to encourage participants to design and create based on their previous creative ideas (Fig. 7).

Fig. 7. Users participate in the design of the solution

In terms of determining some details, through online and offline communication with the inheritors, it was ultimately decided to initially select "Two dragons coming out of the water"、 "Two dragons playing with the pearl"、 "Dragon head raised three times" and "Dragon Jumping" four actions for design. Through repeated communication with participants, the game style, dragon style, regulation of movements and music were determined. Meanwhile, contacts were made with the school's dragon dance club, allowing more users to participate in the discussion (Fig. 8).

Fig. 8. Dragon dance

5.3 Application Design

The game includes two game modes: single player mode and double player mode, corresponding to single dragon dance and double dragon dance. Players follow the guidance of glowing points and touch them with the dragon ball in hand, completing the four dragon dance actions of "Two dragons coming out of the water"、 "Two dragons playing with the pearl"、 "Dragon head raised three times" and "Dragon Jumping" in order. Players can choose their favorite music style and perform the actions in time with the accompaniment. For players who are not familiar with dragon dance, they can watch the animation of the actions first. For players with some basic knowledge, they can also review and practice by watching the animation of the actions before starting the actual operation. Finally, the system will record the duration of each action flow and rank it accordingly.

By experiencing the game firsthand, players can improve their coordination while gaining a deeper understanding of the traditional Yangzhen Dragon Lantern Festival culture. This innovative interactive approach can attract more young people to join this group, increase their interest in traditional culture, experience the charm of Chinese culture, and enhance cultural self-confidence (Fig. 9).

Fig. 9. Application Design

6   Conclusion

This article studies "participatory design" by combining the concept of participatory design with the digitalization of traditional culture. It conducts research on the application of participatory design in the digitalization of traditional culture. The design guided by the concept of participatory design breaks the traditional design method and innovates the design of digitalized traditional culture through new thinking, improving the level of user participation. In the process of preliminary testing in the later stage, the overall feedback from users is relatively good, but there are also some areas that need improvement. In the next stage, we will continue to test and iterate the design. We will invite users to test, improve according to the suggestions and evaluations of users, and further explore and optimize the methods of participatory design, providing new design ideas for the application of participatory design in the digitalization of traditional culture.

References

1. Zhu, B.: Research on the Digital Communication of Dunhuang Culture. Henan University, Kaifeng (2020). https://doi.org/10.27114/d.cnki.ghnau.2020.000836
2. 张歌. 论参与式设计[D].西安美术学院,2014
3. Chen, Z.: Research on the application of clothing design based on the concept of user participatory design. Sichuan Fine Arts Institute, Chongqing (2020). https://doi.org/10.27344/d. cnki.gscmc.2020.000305
4. Li, Z., Cheng, X., Wang, L., He, H., Liang, B.: The Application of Student Participation in the Desigrof Virtual Reality Educational Products. In: Marcus,A. Wang,W. (eds) Design, User Experience, and Usability. Application Domains. HCII 2019.LectureNotes in Computer Science(),VOl 11585. SpringerCham (2019).https://doi.org/10.1007/978-3-030-23538334
5. Liu, J.: Research on the Theme of Regional History and Culture under the Concept of Participatory Design. University of Science and Technology Liaoning, Anshan (2021). https://doi. org/10.26923/d.cnki.gasgc.2021.000423
6. 许倩.基于用户思维的"参与式设计"[J].大众文艺,2017(24):103–104
7. Yao, L.: The digital protection about Yangzhou Lacquerware based on participatory design concept. Shaanxi University of Science and Technology, Shaanxi (2019)
8. Wei, K.: Study on The Protection of Intangible Cultural Inheritors'Rights. Northwest Normal University (2015)
9. 郜玉金.新疆非物质文化遗产数字化传播的现状、问题与对策[J].Journal of Xinjiang University (Philosophy,Humanities & Social Science), 2013,41(03):120–123. https://doi.org/10. 13568/j.cnki.issn1000-2820.2013.03.017
10. Zhao, Y.: Research on Digital Protection and Design of Yao Ethnic Clothing in North Guangdong Based on Participatory Design Concept. South China University of Technology (2020). https://doi.org/10.27151/d.cnki.ghnlu.2020.000739

Research on the Design of Red Cultural and Creative Products Based on Digitalization

Liang Tan[✉] and Rongnan Liang

Guangxi Normal University, Guilin 541000, China
434912456@qq.com

Abstract. Vigorously promoting red culture and inheriting red spirit should focus on integrating with science and technology, and continuously promoting the forward development of digital culture industry. Based on the combination of red culture and technologies such as big data, cloud computing and artificial intelligence, this paper takes the red cultural and creative products of Guangxi as the research object, firstly introduces the definition of interactive technology, red culture and digital cultural industry, researches and analyzes the mature and effective digital cultural products in reality, and gives a summary after comparison. Based on the red culture of Guangxi, the series of red cultural and creative products are designed by using immersive interactive experience and augmented reality technology, combining digital application with red culture, giving new connotation and promotion form to the cultural and creative products, continuously improving user experience, and positively influencing local cultural and creative products and public cultural life, in order to provide certain reference for red cultural and creative design, and to better display the red culture in the red We hope to provide some reference for red cultural and creative design, and to better display and spread the red spirit.

Keywords: digitalization · red culture · cultural and creative products · cultural experience

1 Introduction

With the continuous development of society, living in the era of peace, we should cherish the hard-won peace and strengthen education on patriotism, so we must vigorously promote the tradition of red culture and inherit the red gene. "Xi Jinping stressed that it is the common responsibility of the whole party and society to strengthen the protection and utilization of revolutionary cultural relics, carry forward revolutionary culture and inherit the red gene" [1]. In order to protect the red cultural resources and inherit the red revolutionary spirit, we closely combine red culture with modern technology and use modern means to continuously innovate design, making red culture burst out more dazzling sparks in the context of the new era. Most of the current red cultural and creative product designs still remain on the surface, and consumers can only understand red culture superficially through shapes or some words, but this is not in line with what we want. We hope to help consumers understand the values and spiritual core it contains in a deeper way through more advanced ideas and methods, innovate red expressions, and use AR, VR, etc. to understand and publicize red culture in an all-round way Red culture.

Among the vast group of visitors, the group that has the most difficulty in understanding red culture and is most hindered when visiting red culture memorials is children. We designed the AR children's guide mirror for it in the Xiangjiang Battle Memorial Museum, which is smaller and lighter in weight, convenient for children to carry, using the guide mirror to reduce part of the bloody war exhibits, while combining the exhibits that children can easily accept with some small stories, attracting children to watch through the form of animation, thus enhancing their interest in visiting and actively learning the knowledge of the museum. In addition, the game of breaking into the accumulation of fragments continues to enhance the fun of children, so that they can not only increase the knowledge of the red but also reduce the resistance to visit the memorial hall boring and tedious, technology and cultural creativity combined to better demonstrate the vitality of red culture.

1.1 Review of Related Studies

In Deng Lu's "Research on Guizhou Red Cultural and Creative Products Design Based on Digital Shaping Techniques," he introduces the interactive communication between cultural and creative products and buyers by "revitalizing" virtual static digital files through digital media technology, which constantly brings the distance between cultural and creative products and buyers closer, and closely links the content of integrated media communication (APP) with cultural and creative products to promote the sales of cultural and creative products. The "revitalization" of cultural and creative products has enabled interactive communication between cultural and creative products and purchasers, and has brought the distance between cultural and creative products and purchasers closer [2]. In Yu Tingting's "Research on the Development of Shaoshan Red Culture Digital Creative Products under the Perspective of Living Heritage", it is proposed to use augmented reality technology to reproduce some famous people's short stories to enhance the understanding of each other and immerse in the classic red revolutionary scenes, and to use the combination of red architecture and puzzle games to deepen the understanding of red architecture by collecting pieces and using the exploratory nature of the game to stimulate players' deep communion with Shaoshan culture. Shaoshan culture [3]. In Nong Qiuhong and Li Dongdong's "Research on the Integrated Development of Red Culture and Tourism in North Guizhou Region under the Background of Digital Economy - Taking Quanzhou County as an Example", it is proposed to play the advantages of digital propaganda, accurately classify the tourism crowd through big data technology, and accurately push the red culture and tourism resources and tourism programs of Quanzhou County on the premise that the whole platform has been linked to red culture programs, etc. to help tourists plan, and show dynamic news of red cultural tourism from multiple angles through multiple interactive self media platforms [4]. In Jiang Ye et al.'s "Research on Digital Dissemination and Innovative Development of Red Cultural Heritage Resources", it is argued that digital technologies such as VR technology can be used to combine with the protection and restoration of cultural relics to establish three-dimensional digital archives in a targeted manner to help the later precise restoration, and also to continuously promote the dissemination of red culture through digital technology recording giant screen films [5].

2 Basic Overview of Interactive Technology, Red Culture and Digital Culture Industry

2.1 Overview of Interactive Technologies

"Interactive technology is divided into virtual reality technology and augmented reality technology, which both belong to digital technology" [6]. "Augmented Reality (AR, for short), is a technology that can identify objects by tracking their position, object shape and object labeling in the real world, and superimpose three-dimensional models, pictures and images in the real world, and human-computer interaction can also be achieved through sound, gesture, touch, eye movement and other ways" [7]. Through the vivid reproduction of the real exhibits and the virtual environment inside the Xiangjiang Battle Memorial Hall, which are suitable for children to understand, the augmented reality technology leads children to return to the scene of the hard battle again, giving the audience a sense of visual reality, enhancing children's patriotism and sense of national mission, guiding children to face history and war and cherish peace, while filtering the bloody and violent scenes of war, reducing the impact of war on children. At the same time, the bloody and violent scenes of war are filtered out to reduce the negative consequences of war on children's psychology.

2.2 Overview of Red Culture

"Red culture refers to 'the red relics and the red spirit that coalesced during the process of achieving national independence and national prosperity during the revolution, construction and reform and opening-up period led by the Communist Party of China'." [8] "Red culture, as an important resource, includes both material and immaterial culture. 'Material culture refers to the historical relics, relics and sites left behind during the revolutionary period and the monuments, memorials and halls built later; immaterial culture refers to the historical records of the revolution including revolutionary deeds, revolutionary literature, revolutionary literature and art and the revolutionary spirit embedded in them'."[9] In the Xiangjiang Battle Memorial Hall, we can see the red relics of the Chinese Communist Party during the revolutionary period, and in those exhibits we can deeply appreciate the patriotic spirit of the Communist Party in the war years, which was dedicated to the country and the people, and in the material culture we can see the relics of the Xiangjiang Battle, and in the non-material culture we can understand the red revolutionary spirit through the revolutionary literature inside the Xiangjiang Battle Memorial Hall and some memory records left by the revolutionary veterans. In terms of non-material culture, you can understand the spirit of the Red Revolution in the memorial hall.

2.3 Overview of the Digital Culture Industry

"China Information Center defines digital culture industry as 'an emerging industry with cultural and creative content as the core, relying on digital technology for creation, production, dissemination and services, with convenient transmission, green and low-carbon, strong demand, interactive integration and other characteristics', which belongs to the current leading new supply and new consumption, The scale of high-speed growth of the digital creative industry is an important part" [10]. The development of digital culture industry has greater prospects, it is in line with the habits of young consumers, through digital technology to reproduce these historical exhibits, is the people can be in the memorial heritage is difficult to reach the case, through the means of technology to clearly, all-round feeling of cultural relics, the highest precision restoration makes the visitors as if they were there, this process is the digitization of cultural heritage. After filtering the cruelty of war through technical means, the science effectively follows the laws of physical and mental development of children while also allowing children to have a certain interest in war memorials, reducing children's disbelief and boredom.

3 Exploring the Feasibility of Red Culture in Digital Product Design

Through the observation of the series of products of "One Big Cultural Creation" in the Memorial Hall of the Communist Party of China, we chose the creative children's book "Kai Tian - "One Big Book" as the object of analysis, which is a combination of 3D origami art and VR animation to produce the red culture It is an enlightening reading book using 3D origami art and VR animation. By unfolding the three-dimensional book and scanning the three-dimensional scenes with a camera, VR animation can be viewed, which is convenient and simple to operate and easy to realize, and the bright colors and different shapes inside the children's book are conducive to stimulating children's curiosity about the book and then continuously understanding its contents. Through the scanning of the internal scenes of the books, audio, sensory and animation effects are used to attract children to understand the contents and help them understand the inner spirit of the red culture, and through the telling of red stories, the distance between the heavy history and children is narrowed. There are also rich interactive organs on paper to help children immerse themselves in reading, promote the continuous interplay of digital technology and red culture, and better make excellent cultural and creative products. However, there are also certain shortcomings, such as the high price of the book due to its high technological content, which is not conducive to the sale of books, as well as the book itself is thick in the reading process, if children are young in the book may be easy to open the three-dimensional structure of the internal bruises and other possibilities.

After the completion of the recent update of the Shanghai Urban Planning Exhibition Hall, we can see that more digital interactive content has been added to the hall. Next to the model of the Great Site of the Communist Party, you can scan it using the tablet next to it, light up fireworks on the virtual Bund to enhance the fun, and turn on the lights inside the house by clicking on the door of the Great Site of the Communist Party of China.

The interactive technology helps the cold venue to have a touch more fireworks, keeps getting closer to the distance between visitors and the venue, enhances visitors' interest in red culture, and helps the venue to keep improving its own exhibitions. In the City Lab on the second floor, you can feel the process of urban planning by placing different blocks based on interactive projection games, with real-time calculation and recognition technology giving instant feedback on the results. Visitors can also experience the urban planning process in the game, which will lead to a greater interest in urban planning and a deeper knowledge of urban planning in subsequent visits. The content is suitable for visitors of all ages to perceive the development needs of the city together, while the interior of the exhibition hall combines its own distinctive features with technological means, which not only conforms to the development ideas that the exhibition hall hopes to convey, but also brings new directions for visitors to think about the future.

3.1 Feasibility Summary

Through the analysis and comparison of the two exhibition halls, we had some thoughts on the combination of digital technology and red cultural and creative products. After combining the local red cultural resources of Guangxi, we selected the Xiangjiang Battle Memorial Hall as the basis of our design, and took children, who are less concerned about the visitors, as the design object. The design focuses on children's difficulty in understanding the introduction of the exhibits, their fear of the bloody war exhibits, their low concentration level, and the lack of interaction during the visit to reduce the efficiency of the visit, etc. In the design, we hope to solve these problems, and also to avoid the heavy and three-dimensional structure of the children's book may cause harm to children At the same time, we want to avoid the situation of heavy and three-dimensional structure in children's books, which may be harmful to children, and choose simple and easy-to-understand operations, such as clicking on the lights and turning the handle in the second venue, so that children can have a greater sense of fun and actively participate in the interactive facilities inside the venue, and improve their efficiency and enjoyment of visiting the venue, in order to continuously promote the spread and development of red culture.

4   Red Cultural and Creative Product Design Concept Based on Digital Technology

In the background of digital era, we explore the method of combining red culture and cultural creative products, and build the educational and awareness functions of red cultural and creative products from the perspective of design contexts, with the aim of bringing red culture closer to children. With the virtual character guiding and explaining, it brings immersive experience, stimulates their interest in exploring the red culture, and achieves educational purposes. It allows more children to understand the history of the Red Army and feel the red culture of Xiangjiang River.

4.1 Digital Technology for Red Cultural and Creative Product Design Ideas

Red culture is an excellent culture with national spirit, which is a product of China's historical development and is guided by Marxism and fused with Chinese traditional culture. Among the red resources in Guangxi, the Battle of Xiangjiang River is the key battle that influenced the development of Chinese Red Army Revolution. The design of this digital red cultural and creative product development is also for the dissemination of the red culture of Xiangjiang Battle and the inheritance of the red revolutionary spirit of Xiangjiang Battle, which is different from the general cultural and creative product design for commercial purposes, and pays more attention to the cultural communication function of the product. There are two basic conditions for the cultural communication function of cultural and creative products: first, the product has a high recognition as a carrier of a certain culture; second, the product is spread and used in a wide range. In the context of patriotic education activities, the design method of red cultural and creative products of the Xiangjiang Campaign is explored with children as the audience, aiming to design red cultural and creative products with educational significance, enhance the effectiveness of patriotic education in the new era, remember the history of the Xiangjiang Campaign, and inherit and carry forward the revolutionary spirit. Using the database of the Xiangjiang Battle Museum and the information of the cultural relics, we select the cultural relics with representative cultural value and connotation as the design theme and reconstruct and re-express the visual effects of the relics through AR and other digital technologies, so that children can experience a professional way of exploration in the simulated space, build up a deep understanding of the relics and gain an immersive experience.

4.2 Combining Digital Applications with Red Culture to Strengthen Users' Emotional Experience

Revolutionary history memorials are a carrier of national spirit and historical culture, showing the heroic deeds of revolutionary predecessors and the indomitable national spirit of the Chinese nation, and providing patriotic education to the people, especially minors. According to the survey, children under 14 years old generally lack interest and patience in visiting revolutionary memorials. Memorial museums should focus on grasping interactivity and freshness in display design. Improve the "graded education" for minors and children in memorials.

At present, the Xiangjiang River Battle Memorial Hall for children's social education activities, cultural relics exhibition display part of the distinction between adults and children is not obvious, the introduction of some exhibits simple content. Some children are resistant to some of the real battle exhibits that exist in the memorial museum due to their young age and the lack of appropriate reminders in the museum before and after the visit. The exhibits just put things on display and there is no follow-up interaction, which is less participatory. Based on the above shortcomings, we can design and develop the animation form of exhibit explanation and interaction for children, select exhibits as much as possible from the perspective of children, choose content that meets the cognitive level of children, and at the same time reduce children's sense of unfamiliarity through some small stories in the Xiangjiang River Battle, stimulate children's interest, and realize the two-way interaction between the memorial museum and children. Children often find it difficult to raise interest and establish a deeper emotional connection when faced with displays that only provide textual information such as cultural relics, and using digital technology to combine cultural relics with historical stories makes it easy for children to understand. Through immersive interactive experience and virtual technology role-playing to create a story situation in real time, the scene is arranged as an "archaeological site", children are called to conduct archaeological excavations, play the role of archaeological team members, dig out simulated artifacts in the archaeological site, put the object to the induction area, multimedia digital will explain the object. Children can experience the professional way of exploration in the simulated space, build up an understanding of "heritage excavation" and gain an immersive experience.

4.3 The Practice of Red Cultural and Creative Product Design with Digital Technology

Design digital products, such as AR children's guide mirror (Fig. 1, 2, 3), the use of AR technology development, the original exhibits based on the design of the card, so that the static exhibits move, children's guide mirror scan to the key cultural relics AR card, you can look at some specific scenes, such as the long road of the Red Army Long March, the Xiangjiang River battle of the beacon years and other virtual visual experience, in a vivid story and animation to obtain a more profound cultural and emotional appreciation.

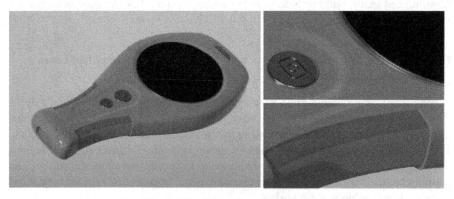

Fig. 1. AR children's guide mirror.

In addition, with the help of digital technology, red culture is combined with games, and game points are set up in the exhibition hall to find task markers through the AR children's guide mirror and perform game breakthroughs, interspersing the knowledge corresponding to the cultural relics flexibly in the game. After passing the levels, children are rewarded with a series of commemorative coins (Fig. 4). Digital technology is used to multi-design the content of the Xiangjiang Battle Museum, making the product design elements, purpose and value more easily accepted by children. The museum realizes a two-way interaction between "people - cultural relics - data" and can also rely on big data to provide personalized learning experiences for children in terms of education. For

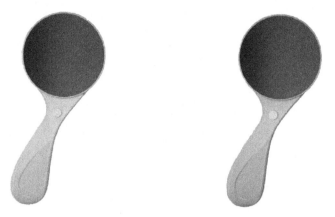

Fig. 2. Different styles of AR kids guide mirror.

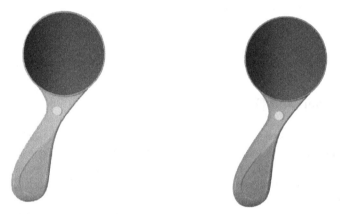

Fig. 3. Different styles of AR kids guide mirror.

example, for children visiting for the first time, information such as age and education is entered before the visit to provide children with information about the exhibition that meets their cognitive characteristics, record information about the child's visit to help them learn more deeply and progressively, and through information matching intelligent planning for children to visit the route and learning programs.

Under the background of digital technology, digital cultural and creative products are developing well, bringing more diversified visual effects to the public and enhancing the authenticity of users' product experience. In order to promote the coordinated and integrated development of digital technology and red cultural and creative products, people in related fields should cultivate their own innovative consciousness and design and develop more interesting and novel digital red cultural and creative products by using digital technology, so that more people can understand red history, promote red culture and inherit red spirit.

Fig. 4. Commemorative coin of Xiangjiang Battle Memorial Hall.

5   Conclusion and Outlook

The design idea of this project is to provide some reference for the research and development of digital red culture and creativity, hoping to better display and spread the red spirit in China. We designed and conceived the AR children's guide mirror and the supporting creative products, using digital technology to let children visit and learn the Xiangjiang Battle Museum in a more innovative and interesting way. We still have a shortage of methods to explore children's psychology and market demand, but we hope to use this to broaden our research on digital red cultural and creative product design, to help better improve children's understanding of red culture, to make cultural and creative design help red culture heritage, and to make the combination of red culture and cultural and creative products more modern.

6   Fund projects

1. Guangxi Normal University Innovation and Entrepreneurship Education Scientific Research Fund Project, Project No. CXCY2021005 Title "Research on Culture Innovation and Entrepreneurship Art and Design Talent Cultivation System under the Background of New Liberal Arts Construction. 2. The work originates from the project of Guangxi young and middle-aged scientific research basic ability improvement, "Research on the strategy and path of cultural innovation empowerment to help Dong rural revitalization", project number 2022KY0033.

Project:. 2022 Scientific Research Basic Ability Enhancement Project for Young and Middle-aged Teachers in Guangxi Universities, Project Name Guangxi Scientific Research Basic Ability Enhancement Project for Young and Middle-aged Teachers, Project Name Strategy and Path Research of Cultural and Creative Empowerment to Help Dong Rural Revitalization, Project No. 2022KY0033.

References

1. Jinping, X.: Stressed: the effective protection of revolutionary cultural relics to manage the good use of the spiritual power of the majority of cadres and masses. Chin. J. Radio Telev. (05), 1 (2021)
2. Deng, L.: Research on Guizhou red cultural and creative product design based on digital shaping techniques. Ind. Des. **12**, 145–146 (2018)
3. Tingting, Y.: Research on the development of Shaoshan red culture digital creative products under the perspective of living heritage. Chem. Fiber Text. Technol. **51**(07), 195–197 (2022)
4. Qiuhong, N., Dongdong, L.: Research on the development of red culture and tourism integration in northern Guizhou region in the context of digital economy: the case of Quanzhou County. Tourism Overview **24**, 159–161 (2022)
5. Ye, J., Jing, H., Cheng, Y.: Research on digital dissemination and innovative development of red cultural heritage resources. Shandong Libr. J. **05**, 39–44 (2022)
6. Yang, Z.Y.: Research on Digital Communication of Tangible Cultural Heritage. Hunan University, Changsha (2017)
7. Weicun, C., Heng, S.: Research on the application of AR technology in mass customization of home appliances. In: Proceedings of the 2019 China Household Appliance Technology Conference, pp.1161–1167 (2019)
8. Chengfei, S., Wenmei, L.: On the connotation and characteristics of red culture and its contemporary value. Teach. Res. **01**, 97–104 (2018)
9. Hongbing, T.: The Formation and Development of Red Culture in Xiang-Exi. Huazhong Normal University, Wuhan (2006)
10. Yaqin, Z., Jiemin, Z.: Report on the development of cultural industry in China's special economic zones. In: Report on the Development of China's Special Economic Zones (2017), pp. 163–175 (2018).

Research on Rural Cultural Tourism Service Design Based on Customer Perceived Value: Taking "TANXUN" Parent-Child Travel as an Example

Yizhuo Wang[1,2], Xiaomi Yi[1], and Xiong Ding[2(✉)]

[1] Sichuan Conservatory of Music, Chengdu 610000, China
[2] Guangzhou Academy of Fine Arts, Guangzhou 510006, China
dingxiong@gzarts.edu.cn

Abstract. The rural cultural tourism in China is booming against the backdrop of rural revitalization. However, problems in the tourism resources integration, planning and services still exist, leading to much potential improvement. Based on service design thinking and methods, combined with the Customer Perceived Value(CPV) theory, the functional value, cultural value, emotional value, safety value and green value in rural parent-child cultural travel services are studied. As for parent-child tourism, Guangzhou Huadu Gangtou Village is taken as an example. Through the integration of perceived objects, perceived values and rural resources, TANXUN service system with the idea of low-carbon is proposed. Parent-child group-travelling model can make tours more fun and connected through interesting, pleasant and diversified countryside vibe and low-carbon cultural tourism experiences, including TANXUN brand image and digital touch points design, TANXUN Nature space design, TANXUN Children's Fun game design. Thus, to demonstrate the feasibility and rationality of building a rural parent-child tourism service system based on CPV.

Keywords: Rural Cultural Tourism · CPV · Parent-child Tourism · Service Design · Low-carbon

1 Introduction

As a national strategy, rural revitalization is the most key strategy in the new era. Meanwhile, cultural tourism, which is a focus of rural revitalization, is an emerging industry to promote national economic development. Chinese rural and cultural tourism enjoys rich resources, facing unprecedented opportunities. In such a new era, it is important to transform historical, cultural and tourism resources into new economic products, find out the balancing point between rural culture and tourism, and explore innovative ideas.

This research starts from the relationship between service design and Customer Perceived Value(CPV), with service design as the basis, customer experience the intermediary, and customer value and value co-creation improvement as the goal to study the relationship among service design, customer experience and CPV. It also explores the design strategy of rural cultural tourism based on CPV, and enhances rural cultural tourism service design and experience through scenario, content and product.

2   Overview of Chinese Rural Cultural Tourism

Traditional villages has its unique cultural vibe. It is the best way for general public to be immersed in traditional culture. As alive cultural relics, traditional villages carry tremendous history, memory, humanity, ecosystem, architectural aesthetics and social development traces [1]. Tourist's needs for rural tourism is increasing due to the lift of travel restrictions during post-pandemic era as well as the popularity of mini-tourism. However, there are still a lot of problems in Chinese rural cultural tourism: a) Services lack uniqueness, special traits and diversity. The cultural tours are only about the combination of culture and tourism without further and deeper integration. The unique and special resources could not be transformed into special tourism products that can be sold; b) Lack of management and scientific guidance, thus leading to low participation; c) Lack of specialists and financial resources. The work division of cultural tourism department is not clear enough. The whole industry is quite fragmented without synergy [2]. It is fair to say the integration of rural tourism resources is poor, and the combination of culture and tourism is failed without reasonable planning and service system building. Overall speaking, the cultural tourism in rural area are not diversified and special without complete and sustainable products and services.

3   Rural Parent-Child Tourism Service System Based on CPV

The study on rural tourism in China is switching from macro to micro level. It mainly focuses on the unity of rural cultural service model and its importance analysis, brand building of rural tourism, improvement of service quality and service process, as well as emotional needs during rural tourism. The author tries to apply CPV into the optimization of rural tourism services, such as how CPV can help in prioritizing rural cultural tourism services, whether it is possible to add new perceived features, so as to identify new ways to build the system rural parent-child cultural tourism service.

3.1   Customer Perceived Value (CPV)

Drucker's study found that it is product's value, instead of product itself, that determines customer's purchasing behaviors. Customer Perceived Value is more about a balance between customer's perception of products and services and the efforts taken [3]. Momne believed that CPV equals to customer perceived quality (interests), or customer perceived cost. James C. Anderson proposed that CPV is customer's perception on products and services affected by subjective factors. The research of CPV mainly concentrates on new retailer, branding, marketing and other fields in recent years. Many scholars believed that the drivers of CPV is the source or elements of CPV. There are different ways to classify CPV. Sheth divides it into 5 dimensions: social value, emotional value, functional value, knowledge value and condition value [4]. Yang Xiaoyan and other researchers found that customers will take environmental protection into consideration when they make purchasing decisions, thus proposed a new dimension--green value. Suraman once said that the main driver of CPV is the quality of products and services as well as price [4]. Wang Wei's analysis on CPV's dimensions is quite complete and comprehensive. He has integrated all dimensions that previous researchers have proposed and divided CPV into functional value, emotional value, safety value, cultural value, social value, green value and perceived efforts [5].

Product value considers customer needs to upgrade products and services. It is a value system mainly dominated by the providers of products and services. Compared with product value, CPV on products and services is to consider whether the perceived benefits and perceived efforts are balanced. It is a trade-off process of payoffs and feedback, a value perception with the customer as the starting point. Customer value reflects subjective perceptions and is the process of passively accepting value. In contrast to customer value, customer perceived value is the overall evaluation of the utility of a product or service after weighing the benefits perceived by the customer against the costs paid to obtain the product or service [5]. It is a criterion for objectivity, a process in which customers give objective feedback and actively receive value through experiencing products and services (shown in Fig. 1).

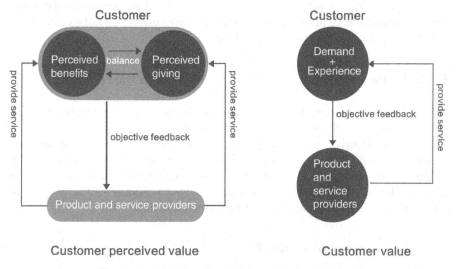

Fig. 1. Customer Perceived Value and Customer Value

3.2 Customer Perceived Value and Rural Cultural Tourism Resources Integrated Framework

The rural cultural tourism service system, which built on CPV, consists of service providers and service recipients (tourists). As mentioned above, the value the can be perceived by tourists include emotional, functional, safety, cultural, social and green value, as well as perceived pay-out. They are interconnected and different strategies should be applied to realize different perceived value. Rural areas, as the service provider, mainly include land, biodiversity and culture delivery [6], which needs to be designed based on the natural, cultural and human resources with the third-party resources combined. The system starts from the pay-out and pay-off perceived by customers, and build CPV as well as an integrated rural cultural tourism resources framework (shown in Fig. 2), to guide the innovation and design of rural cultural service experience.

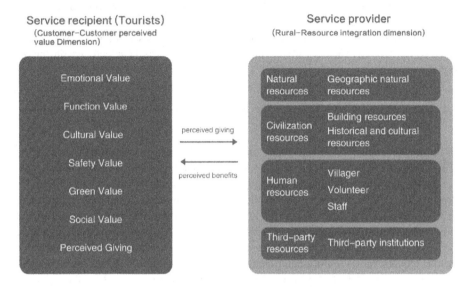

Fig. 2. CPV and rural cultural tourism resourced integrated framework

3.3 Explicit and Implicit Value in Rural Cultural CPV

Among all dimensions of CPV, functional value is the most valuable and key one. Rural cultural service should build a quite complete basic function system. Tourism cultural services base on the rural cultural tourism, and the cultural value is the priority among all values. Cultural value does not only represent the idea of the whole service system, but also play its role as a bridge in the service process. After the functional and cultural value, emotional value should be introduced and reinforce with each other. The safety measures in rural tourism is quite poor [7], which is a common pain point for tourists. During the rural parent-child tourism, safety value is considered as the most basic, and must-have value to tourists (parents in particular). As an integral part of sustainable development in 21st century, the sustainable development of rural areas began to attract people's attention worldwide [8]. Green services and green value are the added-value in rural cultural tourism. It represents a sustainable service mode, which can ensure the upgrade, innovation and iteration of tourism experience, thus leading to a sustainable business model.

Travelling with children has become a primary choice for many families during holiday to enhance communication. Compared with traditional tourism, parent-child tourism focuses more on children's features, travelling destinations and needs. Thus, people have higher standards on the safety, interest and educational effect of tourism products. Natural and cultural resources are the attractions carried by the rural areas. Such rural parent-child tourism can attract families to entertain, travel and consume [9].

In a nutshell, authors believes that within the service system of rural parent-child tourism, tourists could obtain pleasant feeling, knowledge and cultural immersion through participating functions, cultures, emotions and other service content from service providers. Through the mutual pay-off and pay-out, tourists could acquire explicit value. The safety and green ideas introduced in the whole service process and provided by the service providers are the implicit value that tourists can perceive during the experience.

3.4 Rural Parent-Child Tourism Service System Based on Customer Perceived Value

Customer Perceived Value has direct and positive influence on customer satisfaction [10]. Perceived objects, perceived value and rural resources are combed and collected in a systematic way to build a CPV-based rural parent-child tourism service system. As shown in Fig. 3, the perceived objects include service recipients like parents, children, and service providers like staff. Users in the rural parent-child tourism service system are not only parents and children. Service providers and service recipients can equally perceive the value dimension and content of the whole system to some extent. Perceived value include explicit values (emotional, functional, cultural) and implicit ones (safety, green) mentioned earlier. Parent-child cultural tourism services are planned based on the rural resources, including natural, cultural and human resources. In the countryside, natural and cultural resources are unique and relatively abundant; human resources consist of villagers and migrant workers; and third-party resources refer to the presence of brands and suppliers who will be involved in the provision of rural tourism services.

The author proposes the following design idea based on the service system: in the process of innovating rural cultural tourism system, is it possible to focus on green value and design based on the abundant natural resources in rural areas? Is it possible to introduce green value into the service content that shows core value, combining implicit and explicit value? The following part will take Gangtou Village, Guangzhou City in Guangdong Province as an example and conduct a design of rural parent-child cultural tourism system based on CPV.

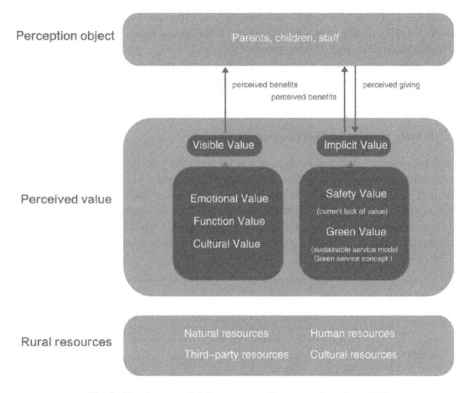

Fig. 3. Rural parent-child tourism service system based on CPV

4 Design Practice of Rural Parent-Child Cultural Tourism: Take TANXUN as an Example

4.1 Design Survey and User's Position

Gangtou Village is a traditional Chinese village with a rich base of natural, architectural and cultural resources. Gangtou Village is trying to build cultural tourism, but still faces great challenges. As for parent-child cultural tourism, we can identify the target users, through desktop research, as young and trendy parents in 80s or 90s with their children. The target group are mostly middle and high class households in high-tier cities, who have relatively high consumption power and pursue high-quality life; who love social life and have interest in recording their interesting life; who love to be involved into the circle of fancy and young moms; who are open in education during parent-child relationship; who favour education through practices and support their children during all sorts of outdoor activities. The author randomly selected five groups of urban parent-child families for interviews. Through field research in Gangtou Village and interviews with four villagers, it can be found that: a) The homogenization can be witnessed on the parent-child tourism products in the market and Gangtou Village, and most of the services are low-end ones.; b) Gangtou Village has too much transformation traces with insufficient use of resources; c) The position of users is vague, resulting a fact that targeted services could not be provided to build users' mindset; d) Problems exist in children's safety during parent-child tourism; e) The current rural cultural tourism do not have adequate interaction, making parents feel bored with low participation and leading to ineffective social connection; f) The existing services are fragmented. A complete and systematic cultural tourism service system with brand communication value has not been built yet.

4.2 Service Position and Service System Building

Value proposition is the core element of service ecosystem. It attaches great importance to the innovation on services against the complex environment [11]. Design team named the rural parent-child cultural tourism of Gangtou Village as TANXUN. Its services are defined as: a mini-vacation with the theme of zero-carbon in groups. Through diversified services, users can feel a more interesting and pleasant low-carbon life besides the unique countryside vibe. Thus, receiving the education in a fun way, as shown in Fig. 4.

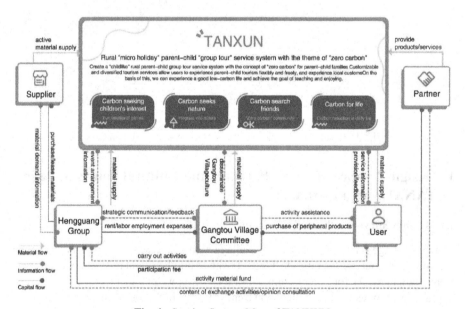

Fig. 4. Service System Map of TANXUN

The value proposition of Tanji shows in two modes. The first is mini-vacation mode, in which a service system is built based on the uniqueness of parent-child users. As Gangtou Village enjoys advantages in its geography, a short-distance and short-period vacation mode is built. Through frequent and systematic services, a sustainable service system is built to increase users' loyalty in a long run. The second is group-travelling mode. Through group-travelling, groups or organization in which members share the same interest can be built. This mode can also decrease the travelling cost and then achieve the zero-carbon life.

TANXUN is a diversified parent-child cultural tourism system, with dining, living, travelling, entertainment and shopping as the basic content. Two service modes-- Zero-carbon Life and Children's Fun are built. Zero-carbon life can lengthen the green value of CPV, and introduce the green value into the perception of users on the whole service system, delivering a sustainable life idea. A series of services with zero-carbon concept are built. Meanwhile, the countryside culture is embedded to provide cultural value for service recipients. As the emotional attachment and wisdom result of Chinese nature for thousands of years, countryside culture is a glimpse of people's needs for rural public spirit[12]. The introduction of rural culture adds unique tone to the services. Children's Fun is a display of core value of CPV. Through traditional Lingnan games with strong rural features, user's emotional and cultural resonance can be triggered, providing cultural and emotional value for parent-child users.

There are four themed services of TANXUN. TANXUN Children's Fun is about making use of time-honored architectural and natural resources in Gangtou Village and combining traditional games with Lingnan features to provide cultural and emotional value for parents and children during tourism. TANXUN Nature is about learning zero-carbon life concept and experiencing pleasant countryside life during the exploration of the nature. It is a green outdoor activity based on the natural resources in Gangtou Village. TANXUN Friends is an online platform of service system. No matter whether it is parents or children, they can meet and make friends on this platform and build their own social groups. They can have marking activities, shopping, customized services and get to know related information on the platform. TANXUN Life is about a series of services centering the countryside tourism, which includes dining, living, travelling and other considerate services.

4.3 Service Touch Points Design

In the cultural tourism system of TANXUN, the design of touch points include brand image of TANXUN and its digital touch points, TANXUN Nature space, TANXUN Children's Fun game and so on. As the places where services recipients and providers will interact with each other, touch points are key to optimize services design [13]. After the optimization of touch points and innovative design, users can participate in the diversified and entertaining services, thus experience CPV deeply.

Brand Image of TANXUN and Digital Touch Points Design. During people's daily life, at least 80% of the information is obtained through visual. Visual is the most important feeling to human beings [14]. The brand visual image of TANXUN service design echos the concept of zero-carbon. The LOGO is designed with the symbolic "C-O-2" as the main image and incorporates cute and funny expressions to cater to the parent-child users. The logo is in fresh green and named Carbon Member, implying that users who participate in the TANXUN service in Gangtou Village are active practitioners of low-carbon living. (shown in Fig. 5) TANXUN mini-program (digital points) is an online service platform for parents and children who travel in Gangtou Village. The mini-program design can reduce the information exchanging processes, simplify information framework and use cards as an interaction way. The overall visual design is derived from the LOGO and reflects green and zero-carbon concept. Based on the basic needs of tourism and four core modules of TANXUN, namely, TANXUN Nature, TANXUN Life, TANXUN Friends and TANXUN Children's Fun, the functional framework is constructed. The TANXUN is the core service module in the service system, in which the TANXUN Snap Taken section is to provide a community for users, satisfying users' needs for social connection. (shown in Fig. 6).

Fig. 5. Logo and the IP image of TANXUN

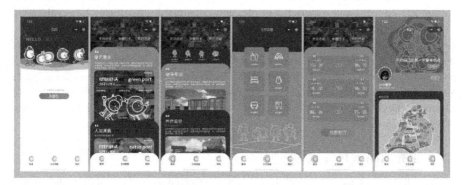

Fig. 6. Mini-program of TANXUN

TANXUN Nature Space Design. The outdoor space design follows openness and takes service content and service process into consideration. The overall design takes wooden structure and straw as main elements which are quite unique to the countryside, highlighting the rural visual style. With glass embedded, users can experience a fresh and natural feeling. According to the existing natural landscape and architectural resources of Gangtou Village, outdoor experience spaces such as TANXUN Sangji Fish Pond, Field Watch Tower, Field Farm and Stream Fishing are designed (shown in Fig. 7).

TANXUN Sangji Fish Pond is an entertaining activity for parents and children based on the Sanji Fish Pond Ecosystem that is unique to Lingnan. In the vicinity of the fish pond at the entrance of Gangtou Village, three major areas are set up: a small sericulture area, a mulberry tree observation platform and a fish feeding area. Parents and children can get a sense of the penetration of green concept in agriculture and be immersed in Lingnan's culture while knowing the agricultural culture that is special in Lingnan. The whole activity shows functional, cultural and green value of CPV, which builds an impressive and in-depth tourism experience for parents and children. Field Watch Tower is located in the middle of the field where people can appreciate the sunset. The space at the bottom of the tower is used as a souvenir store to realize the commercial function of the service system. The surrounding roads and the tower itself are equipped with many safe recreational facilities, making it a standing area for visitors to relax and enjoy the outdoors.

Field Farm is a co-creation space for green planting in the middle of the farmland of Gangtou Village, which is used to hold various types of Greenery Activities. Parents and children can enjoy the cultivating and planting in the farmland and learn rich zero-carbon knowledge in the Greenery Activities. Greenery Activities is a subdivision of the TANXUN Nature service module, including Green Restoration and Green Guardian. Parents and children should cooperate with each other to participate in the Greenery Activities, enhancing the parent-child relationship. Stream Fishing is a recreational space near the famous landmark of Gangtou Village, including a viewing platform and fishing platform in the shape of a fishing boat, which provides a good place for parents to relax.

Fig. 7. Nature space of TANXUN

Game Design of TANXUN CHildren's Fun. Lingnan is home to four or five thousand-year history with rich cultural essence and unique regional features, enjoying advantageous tourism resources [15]. Meanwhile, Lingnan folk sports and cultural objects have been passed from generation to generation with a long history [16], which are the important resources to develop cultural tourism in Guangdong Province. Based on the traditional games and folk sports activities in Lingnan's traditional culture, TANXUN Children's Fun has Arcade Playground and Dragon Boat Race in the nostalgic and ancient architecture and environment of Gangtou Village (Fig. 8). The arcade is an architecture that is special to Lingnan. The corridor under it is a natural playground and performance stage where traditional games such as rolling iron ring, playing marbles, hopscotch and lion dance can be set up for users to experience, creating a rich Lingnan Child fun atmosphere. Dragon Boat Race is set up along the streaming rivers next to the village and also requires parent-child cooperation. For parents, the game which is full of local flavor can recall their beautiful memories in the past and trigger strong emotional resonance. TANXUN Children's Fun allows parents to enjoy the colorful traditional culture of Lingnan while having fun, which enhances the cultural, emotional and functional value for parents and children during the travel.

Fig. 8. Arcade playground and dragon boast race game space

5 Conclusion

Based on service design thinking and methods, this paper discusses the correlation between customer perceived value and rural parent-child cultural tourism services, thus building a framework of rural parent-child cultural tourism service system. Parents in the new age not only focus on functional, cultural and emotional values, but also safety and green – the new driving engine of consumption when they travel with children. In the design of Gangtou Village's mini-vacation parent-child group-travelling, concepts such as zero-carbon, local flavour and children's fun are the combination of tradition and innovation which can trigger the emotional resonance and meet people's needs with enhanced tourism experience.

Acknowledgment. This paper is supported by the academic promotion program of Guangzhou Academy of Fine Arts, which is "Research on the Integration Innovation Strategy of Cultural Tourism in Guangdong-Hong Kong-Macao Greater Bay Area from the Perspective of Service Design (20XSA04)".

References

1. Haolong, Z., Jing, C., Chunshan, Z.: Review and prospect of traditional Chinese village research. Urban Plan. **41**(04), 74–80 (2014)

2. Na, W.: Research on the development strategy of rural cultural tourism industry. Guangzhou Sericult. **54**(10), 134–135 (2020)
3. Zeithaml, V.A.: Consumer perceptions of price, quality and value: a means-end model and synthesis of evidence. J. Mark. **52**(3), 2–22 (1988)
4. Gilly, M.C.: Book review: consumption values and market choice. J. Mark. Res. **29**(4), 487–489 (1992)
5. Wang, W., Jiping, Y., Shanshan, Z.: Customer perceived value: research review and prospect. J. Henan Univ. Technol. (Soc. Sci. Ed.) **14**(05), 33–41 (2018)
6. Yixiang, W.: Research on the Effective Development and Utilization of Rural Resources in China's Regional Tourism. Hefei University of Technology, Hefei (2016)
7. Shaochen, Z.: Research on the Development of Rural Parent-child Tourism Products. Zhejiang Normal University, Hangzhou (2017)
8. Yansui, L., Yuheng, L.: Revitalize the world's countryside. Nature **548**, 275–277 (2017)
9. Xiaolong, C., Kai, W.: The characteristics and new development strategies of rural parent-child tourism under the background of "strolling baby" era. J. Hebei Tour. Vocat. College **23**(03), 34–37 (2018)
10. Jianmin, H., Yongtao, P.: Empirical study on the relationship between customer perceived value, customer satisfaction and behavioral intention. Manag. Modern. **35**(01), 28–30 (2015)
11. Wang, L., Jianqiu, Z.: Warm: the impact of customer value proposition on service innovation performance - the intermediary role of customer participation. Econ. Manag. Res. **39**(08), 133–144 (2018)
12. Feng, J.: Research on Problems and Countermeasures in the Inheritance and Development of Chinese Local Culture. Jilin University, Jilin (2018)
13. Xiaoyu, X.: Design of Beidaihe Kangyang Riding Equipment Based on Service Contact Theory. Yanshan University, Qinhuangdao (2020)
14. Xiong, D.: The service system design of Nanhai tourism special train based on five senses experience. Packa. Eng. **38**(10), 24–30 (2017)
15. Yutian, T., Shulan, L.: Thoughts on the inheritance and innovation of Lingnan culture in the new era. Quest **03**, 111–116 (2019)
16. Jianlei, G.: Contemporary interpretation of Lingnan folk sports culture - taking foshan dragon boat race as an example. Contemp. Sports Sci. Technol. **4**(30), 146+148 (2014)

Study on the Digital Inheritance Path of Oral Literature Intangible Cultural Heritage

A Case Study of Minnan Nursery Rhymes

Wenyue Wang(✉) ⓘ and Ying He

Xiamen University of Technology, Xiamen 361024, China
wangwyxm@163.com

Abstract. In recent years, with the continuous evolution of VR, artificial intelligence, XR, ultra-high-definition and three-dimensional digital scanning technologies, the application of metauniverse technology in the field of intangible cultural heritage has attracted much attention. These cutting-edge digital technologies have brought a deeper sense of reality and a more immersive sense of interaction to the audiovisual industry. This "sense of presence" can provide strong support for the digital inheritance of intangible cultural heritage. This paper, through the method of case study, analyzes the protection and inheritance path of Minnan nursery rhymes through the construction of digital database of Minnan nursery rhymes, the application of digital technology of "presence+" in the meta-universe and the digital transmission of short video platform, so as to explore a new path of panoramic restoration and interactive inheritance of Minnan nursery rhymes, so as to ensure the vitality and sustainability of the inheritance of Minnan nursery rhymes. Through the study on the digital preservation and inheritance of nursery rhymes in southern Fujian, it opens a new idea to explore the non-genetic inheritance of oral literature.

Keywords: Oral Literature Intangible Cultural Heritage · Digital Technology · Metaverse · Minnan Nursery Rhymes

1 Introduction

The protection of intangible cultural heritage has become one of the hot topics in China and even the world in recent years. Under the background of China's vigorous development of cultural undertakings, people are constantly exploring new paths for the inheritance of intangible cultural heritage with the help of folk inheritors. Minnan nursery rhymes, which are children's rhymes chanted or sung in Minnan, are an important part of Minnan culture. As an important part of Minnan ballads, Minnan Tong is the crystallization of common people's collective wisdom creation [1]. As an oral literary intangible cultural heritage, it has been included in the second batch of national intangible Cultural Heritage list, which is of great significance to its protection and inheritance. Because oral literature relies heavily on oral language to inherit, coupled with the aging of the current art and other factors, the traditional oral literature of nursery rhymes in southern

© The Author(s), under exclusive license to Springer Nature Switzerland AG 2023
A. Marcus et al. (Eds.): HCII 2023, LNCS 14034, pp. 184–195, 2023.
https://doi.org/10.1007/978-3-031-35705-3_14

Fujian faces the dilemma of loss. Therefore, it is urgent to carry out the rescue and protection of this kind of intangible heritage. With the development of modern industry and science and technology, the concept of meta-universe has exploded on a large scale in recent years. Its tentacles are involved in all walks of life and have brought considerable effects. Cloud technology, multimedia technology, sensor technology, human-computer interaction technology, network technology, three-dimensional display technology and other digital technologies have a high degree of compatibility with the protection and inheritance of oral literature intangible cultural heritage [2]. Will become the Minnan nursery rhyme protection and inheritance of a sword. This provides a new idea for the protection and inheritance of oral literature intangible heritage such as Minnan nursery rhymes. This paper, through the method of case study, analyzes the protection and inheritance path of Minnan nursery rhymes through the construction of digital database of Minnan nursery rhymes, the application of digital technology of "presence+" in the meta-universe and the digital transmission of short video platform, and integrates the protection and inheritance of Minnan nursery rhymes with digital technology. This study can provide a new idea and open up a new perspective for the rescue and protection of oral literature intangible cultural heritage, expand the research on the digital protection of oral literature intangible cultural heritage, promote the sustainable development of oral literature intangible cultural heritage, and help the sustainable development of ethnic cultural industry.

2 Current Situation and Significance of Digital Inheritance of Oral Literature Intangible Cultural Heritage

2.1 Oral Literature Intangible Cultural Heritage is Facing Inheritance Crisis

Intangible cultural heritage in China is divided into five categories: oral traditions and forms of expression, including language as the medium of intangible cultural heritage; Performing arts; Social practice, ceremony, festival activities; Knowledge and practice of nature and the universe; Traditional handicrafts [3]. Among them, oral traditions and forms of expression, including as intangible cultural heritage media, rank first. As the first category of intangible cultural heritage defined in the Law of the People's Republic of China on Intangible Cultural Heritage, traditional oral literature and the language used as the carrier play an important role. However, due to the influence of region, national cultural background, dialect, language and other aspects, this kind of intangible cultural heritage shows a strong dependence on the oral and physical inheritance mode, especially the profound influence of folk songs, proverbs and other rhymes.

Oral literature intangible cultural heritage is more likely to be endangered in the process of inheritance because of its liveliness and integrity. The reasons are mainly reflected in two aspects: on the one hand, oral literature is not inherited in the process of oral expression. Taking nursery rhymes in southern Fujian as an example, it is difficult for Chinese characters to restore their authenticity, and the trans writers will show traces of The Times in the transmission process [4], which brings a gap between them and the original spoken language. In the classic Minnan nursery rhyme "Sky Black", different dialect versions appear, and an indispensable element of the Minnan nursery rhymes is the

Minnan language. The media language of the Minnan nursery rhyme is a crucial link in the inheritance process, which has a non-negligible influence on the correct continuation of the nursery rhyme from generation to generation. On the other hand, oral and physical inheritance depends on its cultural background, national folklore, form of expression and application context. The essence of oral literature based on ballads is the overall interpretation of the text rather than the simple oral pronunciation and interpretation of the text [5]. Combined with the context and cultural background, the text content is brought to life and presented. Thus, it can be seen that oral literature intangible cultural heritage is more dynamic, traditional and integrated. The fault caused by the aging of inheritors and the loss of some elements in the inheritance process make this kind of intangible cultural heritage face a crisis in inheritance.

2.2 The Lack of Overall Support for the Application of Digital Technology in Oral Literature Intangible Cultural Heritage

In recent years, the application of metauniverse technology in intangible cultural heritage and other fields has attracted much attention. Cloud computing, artificial intelligence, XR, ultra-high definition, three-dimensional sound and other technologies continue to evolve, driving profound changes in shooting, cloud production, rendering process, digital rights management and other aspects. These cutting-edge digital technologies have brought a deeper sense of reality and a more immersive sense of presence to the audiovisual industry, which can provide strong support for the digital inheritance of intangible cultural heritage. Digital technologies and platforms such as digital preservation library, virtual reality and digital streaming media are currently recognized worldwide strategies for the protection of intangible cultural heritage. Due to its vitality and integrity, oral literature needs more directional concept support and more diversified technical support in the process of inheritance. In terms of concept, oral literature intangible cultural heritage avoids the occurrence of duplication, avoids its separation from cultural background, and attaches importance to the integration with modern culture [6], so as to truly achieve cultural appreciation and compatible progress in inheritance [7]. In terms of technology, digital technology of intangible cultural heritage is widely used in 3D reconstruction, mixed reality, panoramic shooting and other related technologies in China, which tends to focus on technical packaging rather than the integration of technology, intangible cultural heritage and media. There is a problem that digital technology lacks the overall support for the protection and inheritance of intangible cultural heritage.

As an intangible cultural heritage of oral literature with Fujian characteristics, Minnan nursery rhymes have taken a series of measures in the early 21st century in Xiamen, China to save and protect Minnan nursery rhymes, including holding Minnan nursery rhymes performance competition and promoting Minnan culture on campus. A five-year plan for the protection of Minnan nursery rhymes was also formulated and implemented. In June 2009, Xiamen Minnan Nursery Rhyme Culture Research Association was established. In 2010, the construction of southern Fujian Nursery rhymes Cultural Activity Center began in Xiang 'an District, as the base and symbol of the key protection of southern Fujian nursery rhymes culture. In September 2010, the training class on teaching, investigation and creation of Minnan nursery rhymes was held in Xiamen Foreign Language Affiliated Primary School, which was sponsored by Xiamen Intangible Cultural

Heritage Protection Center and the Physical Health Department of Xiamen Education Bureau. Sixty-nine teachers and cadres of intangible cultural heritage protection from the city's middle and primary schools, kindergartens, youth palace and cultural centers attended the training. In November 2019, the List of National Intangible Cultural Heritage Representative Project Protection Units was published. Guankou Primary School of Jimei District, Xiamen City and Jimei Branch of Xiamen Experimental Primary School were granted the protection units of Minnan nursery rhyme Project. The country and society attach great importance to the nursery rhymes of southern Fujian, but the development of digital inheritance of nursery rhymes of southern Fujian is not mature at present. Most of them are technical packaging rather than technical integration, which is more manifested as formal innovation.

2.3   The Significance of Digital Inheritance of Oral Literature Intangible Cultural Heritage

Intangible cultural heritage is a "living fossil" that inherits human civilization, history and culture, and a red card that carries forward national culture. With the gradual withdrawal of the older generation of non-hereditary inheritors from the stage of history, the protection and inheritance of intangible cultural heritage is faced with a huge dilemma of intermittent loss, especially for the intangible cultural heritage of oral literature, because of its particularity, it is more difficult and urgent to protect and inherit. The main reason is that most of the nursery rhymes in southern Fujian are based on long-term experience accumulation, word-to-heart memorization, word-to-body teaching and other methods, with unique characteristics of vitality, inheritance, instability and so on. Once lost, it is difficult to make up for. As for the cultural industry, it is proposed in the 20th Report that a hundred flowers should bloom and a hundred schools of thought contend, creative transformation and innovative development should be upheld, core socialist values should be taken as the guide, advanced socialist culture should be developed, revolutionary culture should be carried forward, and fine traditional Chinese culture should be passed on to meet the growing spiritual and cultural needs of the people. We will increase the influence of Chinese civilization, stick to the position of Chinese culture, tell good stories about China, present a credible, lovely and respectable image of China, and promote Chinese culture to the world. Non-legacy works are important carriers of Chinese traditional culture, and their protection and inheritance are of great historical significance.

In recent years, the normal display of "presence+" from the perspective of Metaverse has further broadened the survival space of intangible cultural heritage and improved the intimacy and sense of reality. Especially for oral literature intangible cultural heritage, which has been endangered by word-of-mouth transmission based on specific cultural background, virtual reality technology under the requirements of "presence+" in the meta-universe can realize panoramic restoration, popular science and survival, enrich the collection, storage and inheritance of traditional Chinese culture, and solve the dilemma faced by the protection and inheritance of oral literature intangible cultural heritage. Under the perspective of "presence+" in the meta-universe, digital collection and storage technology provides a more comprehensive guarantee for the preservation of Minnan nursery rhymes, digital display technology provides a platform for its inheritance and extensive sharing, and digital virtual reality technology provides space for its development and utilization. The importance of transitioning from the protection and inheritance of technology packaging to the creative application and digital research paradigm, This paper studies the path of protection and inheritance of oral literature intangible cultural heritage by using 3I (Immersion, Interaction, Imagination) properties in digital virtual reality to realize panoramic collection and storage, so as to effectively practice the protection concept of cultural integrity and vitality. With the help of the digital technology of "presence+" in the meta-universe, the visualized virtual reality and somatosensory interactive shaping "across time and space" has practical, simulation and innovative experience, providing vivid, intuitive and efficient information dissemination services for the protection and inheritance of Minnan nursery rhymes [2].

At present, the research on the digitalization of intangible cultural heritage of oral literature in China focuses on technology research or visual design analysis of virtual reality, while the research on specific schemes and creation application is relatively immature. Most of them are technical packaging rather than technology integration, which is more manifested as formal innovation. The scene and interaction design also remain at a relatively superficial level, lacking a real sense of "presence", which shows that the overall support of digital technology for oral literature intangible cultural heritage is insufficient at present. The oral literature intangible cultural heritage and meta-universe "presence+" have a high degree of compatibility and strong integration. As one of the intangible heritage in urgent need to be saved, this paper explores the deep connection between the two, and uses digitalized audio-visual images, "presence+" and other concepts to seek a new path for the protection and inheritance of Minnan nursery rhymes.

3   On the Inheritance and Protection Path of Oral Literature Intangible Cultural Heritage Enabled by Digital Technology -- A Case Study of Minnan Nursery Rhymes

Facing the multi-cultural background and the general environment of advocating "telling Chinese stories well", nursery rhymes of southern Fujian, an excellent traditional intangible cultural heritage passed down from generation to generation in southern Fujian, are on the verge of disappearing. The increasingly mature and extensive application of digital technology provides a new path for the protection and inheritance of Minnan nursery rhymes. On the one hand, digital technology is used to collect, scan and store relatively complete and highly restored digital information, and 2D and 3D are combined to build digital protection database and ecological good interactive display platform and interaction mode. On the other hand, make full use of the communication channels of short video platform to carry out digital transmission of nursery rhymes in southern Fujian, expand its influence, stand in the spotlight of traffic, attract more people's attention, and provide a new channel for the inheritance of nursery rhymes in southern Fujian.

3.1 To Construct the Digital Protection Database of Oral Literature Intangible Cultural Heritage

In the context of the increasing perfection of meta-universe related technologies, it has become a general trend to reasonably use Internet big data to build historical data and sample databases of oral literature intangible cultural heritage and to properly and comprehensively preserve them. According to the data classification shown in Table 1, the Internet big data is combined with field investigation, and the literature, physical and digital data of Minnan nursery rhymes are comprehensively sorted out to build the database. This database will use reasonable and effective coding and preservation of the collected data, so as to preserve the Minnan nursery rhymes in multiple dimensions.

Table 1. Classification of oral literature intangible cultural heritage

Primary data	Secondary data	Tertiary data
diary	Book monograph	bibliography
memoir	textbook	dictionary
Folk story	Journal article	encyclopedia
photograph	magazine	Wikipedia
Video recording	Newspaper article	Baidu Baike
recording	biograph	Network data

Three-dimensional software technology provides quick and effective technical support for the construction of digital models of intangible cultural heritage in the current era, and it is an indispensable link for oral literature intangible cultural heritage. Three-dimensional software technology can not only accurately scan and save static objects, but also save the dynamic data of Minnan nursery rhymes in an all-round way with its motion capture technology. Through the scanning, recording and visualization processing of audio and video data, the digital model is built to provide comprehensive and visual teaching and scientific research materials for digital inheritance.

3.2 Build a Digital Browsing and Interactive Display Platform for Oral Literature Intangible Cultural Heritage

A two-dimensional digital tour display platform and a three-dimensional interactive platform can be built for oral literature intangible cultural heritage from the perspective of the meta-universe. The two-dimensional digital display will become the primary form of the digital display platform of southern Fujian nursery rhymes in the metauniverse. The display platform can demonstrate the extraordinary charm of southern Fujian nursery rhymes and the new development in the modern context in a multi-dimensional way by displaying the historical stories, rhythm and formula behind the nursery rhymes, inheritance status and derivative product development.

With the increasingly mature and widely used digital human technology, the public's acceptance of this kind of virtual character is gradually improving. Three-dimensional software technology is used to reprocess the materials provided by the digital library of Minnan nursery rhymes, and the non-genetic inheritors will interpret and explain the learned content, so as to construct the exclusive digital human image, adding fun, visibility and interactive learning platform for digital inheritance. This digital browsing display platform is equipped with online work such as exhibition, teaching and social communication. The "presence+" experience brought by the new requirements of virtual reality technology in the meta-universe has achieved a good interactive experience in the online learning platform. In the interactive display platform, learning content, environment and activities are reasonably integrated to design three-dimensional dynamic holographic inquiry content, recreated simulation environment with virtual-real integration and interactive experience activity integrating body and mind [8]. Under the premise of proper application, virtual reality digital technology can achieve the effect of cultural reproduction and expansion of reality, so as to guarantee users' Interaction, Immersion and Presence in the experience [9]. The VR design of Minnan nursery rhymes is mainly to redesign its learning content, application environment and specific interpretation methods to realize the transformation from "physical immersion" to "mental immersion", and to complete the upgrading of experience from "presence" to "presence+".

After completing the construction of the interactive experience platform of "presence+", the existing two-dimensional browsing platform for Minnan nursery rhymes and three-dimensional interactive display platform will be linked and integrated, that is, the transition from official display dominance to users' independent choice of the mode of dissemination of Minnan nursery rhymes. Inheritors, users and learners of Minnan nursery rhymes can log in to the interactive display platform as experiencers. Experiencers wear immersive interactive devices to directly experience the interactive teaching and singing of all nursery rhymes in the interactive display platform, as well as the communication and interaction of experience. With the improvement of meta-universe technology, virtual reality technology and interactive equipment can be upgraded continuously in practice, so that various interactive experience activities can be carried out conveniently and effectively in the future. This lays a foundation for building a digital virtual reality interactive display platform for intangible cultural heritage protection and inheritance.

3.3 Build a Digital Browsing and Interactive Display Platform for Oral Literature Intangible Cultural Heritage

Under the influence of digital browsing and virtual interactive display platform for oral literature intangible cultural heritage, non-inheritance opens new ideas. Reasonable use of new media communication channels and building an ecosystem with cross-border communication function can better improve the interactive communication of intangible cultural heritage. A good and sustainable interactive mode has a strong impact on the implementation and implementation of intangible cultural heritage digital inheritance. Since the nursery rhymes of southern Fujian are interesting to some extent, interactive communication is a very important part in the process of digital inheritance.

Firstly, the convenience, diversity and interactivity of media communication mode from the perspective of meta-universe should be reasonably utilized, and the "non-homogeneity" characteristics of blockchain technology should be fully utilized to provide users with an interactive experience platform, increase the vitality of Minnan nursery rhymes and expand the scope of influence. Specifically, we can use blockchain technology to create a special NFT (Non-Fungible Token) of Minnan nursery rhymes with a sense of "presence+" experience in the meta-universe environment. The form of NFT can tokenize the communication of traditional culture and make the communication of NFT of intangible cultural heritage more multi-dimensional. At the same time, it combines the new communication path of traditional media and new media to realize the intangible cultural heritage communication mode of digging pain points, creative expression, creating topics and hot spots, and accurately guiding target users from the perspective of the meta-universe.

Secondly, the content interactivity of the dissemination platform of Minnan nursery rhymes should be enhanced, and multi-sensory stimulation should be stimulated by relevant digital technologies in the meta-universe perspective to provide users with "presence+" interactive experience. In the interactive communication mode of nursery rhymes in southern Fujian, it can be developed from three aspects: first, create interactive experience of narrative games, construct interactive scenes from historical, social, cultural and artistic values, improve the audience's perceptual interest, and achieve the purpose of attracting users' attention to the culture of nursery rhymes in southern Fujian; The second is to create interactive experience in the teaching process of Minnan nursery rhymes. It can design interesting interactive learning process, and use interactive technologies such as dynamic capture and virtual human to enable users and inheritors or disseminators to have teaching interactive experience across time and space, so as to achieve the purpose of in-depth teaching for users. By singing ballads with digital people, interactive games are designed. For example, lulling game, users will choose to learn a Minnan nursery rhyme with virtual digital "mother". After completing the learning task, they will enter the test phase, which will use Minnan nursery rhyme to lull virtual "baby" to sleep, and the speed and depth of "baby" to sleep depends on the user's acquisition degree. After completing the task, you can get certain token rewards, which can be exchanged for derivatives around the platform; The third is to create the experience of interactive display effect of Minnan nursery rhymes. By integrating relevant interactive technologies from the meta-cosmic perspective and using diversified interactive experience methods, users can interact directly or indirectly, and create a close connection between intangible cultural heritage and the audience with interactive mechanism, so as to break the time-space restriction of display and create a way for users to turn from passive to active to receive information. To enhance the user immersion full of actual experience effect [10].

3.4 Promote the Dissemination of Short Video Platform

In the process of short video platform communication, attention should be paid to enrich the cultural connotation of Minnan nursery rhymes. According to the 50th Statistical Report on China's Internet Development, by June 2022, 99.6 percent of Chinese netizens used mobile phones to access the Internet, and the number of short video users reached

962 million, an increase of 28.05 million compared with December 2021 [11]. The dissemination of short video platform has gradually become one of the mainstreams. On the eve of the 17th Cultural and Natural Heritage Day, Douyin released the 2022 Intangible Heritage Data Report. According to the report, videos related to national intangible cultural heritage projects on Douyin reached 372.6 billion views and 9.4 billion likes in the past year, covering 99.74% of national intangible cultural heritage projects. With the help of Douyin's "Intangible Cultural Heritage Partnership Program" and "See the Handicraft Program", the number of live broadcasts of Douyin's intangible cultural heritage projects increased by 642% year on year, the number of anchors awarded by live streaming increased by 427% year on year, and the number of videos of endangered intangible cultural heritage increased by 60% year on year. It is worth noting that in the survey on the age distribution of Douyin intangible cultural heritage creators, creators born in the 1980s accounted for 35% and those born in the 1990s accounted for 26%, becoming the main force of short video platforms not inherited by heredity [12]. Many intangible cultural heritage talents have found a new stage for inheriting their skills in Douyin. However, there is no official certified account of Minnan nursery rhymes on this platform, and the attention of its inheritors is not high, and the videos released mainly focus on daily records and live performance videos. In the context of the rapid development of streaming media, it has become one of the important tasks to actively promote the digital streaming media communication, make the short video platform become the spotlight to expose the southern Fujian nursery rhymes, and let more people know the charm of the southern Fujian nursery rhymes.

Enrich the Cultural Connotation of Communication. Due to its fragmented dissemination content and vivid presentation methods, short video platforms have narrowed the distance with the public in terms of sharing and experience, and the use of short video platforms to spread intangible cultural heritage can be rapidly expanded.

Sphere of influence. Different from traditional media, the collection of intangible cultural heritage works in short videos shows obvious "decentralization". Instead of complete restoration, the elements with the most visual expression and emotional expression are disseminated, so as to open a door for intangible cultural heritage and lead the public to "walk in" and generate strong interest.

However, this "decentralization" approach is a double-edged sword. It is colorful in content, but it is also prone to problems such as uneven quality of works, deliberately seeking favor and taking advantage of opportunities. According to data from mainstream short video platforms such as Douyin, Kuaishou and BiliBili, the content of the videos released focused on singing at the event and clips of Minnan nursery rhymes intermingled with pop songs, while the relevant cultural background and historical information rarely appeared. These contents cannot maximize the dissemination of the cultural connotation carried by the nursery rhymes of southern Fujian, so we should dig deep into the familiar songs of the public to show the inherent cultural and historical information with regional characteristics of southern Fujian. At the same time, combined with digital technology, the intangible cultural heritage is presented in multiple ways, so that it is no longer "archaeology", and both the accurate expression of traditional culture and the modern expression of the characteristics of The Times.

Performance is a direct way to export the cultural connotation of oral literature intangible cultural heritage. Reasonable, accurate and innovative interpretation on short video platforms is the fast lane to expand the audience of this kind of intangible cultural heritage, and to load high-quality content on this fast lane to open up a new path for inheritance.

Optimize the Communication Subject. The characteristics of low threshold and low cost of short video platform have made essential changes in the communication pattern. All willing organizations and individuals are actively involved in the communication of intangible cultural heritage, and the communication subjects show unprecedented activity. According to the search, there are no official certified accounts of "Minnan nursery rhymes" and related on mainstream short video platforms such as Douyin, Kuaishou and BiliBili, which indicates that the main body of dissemination of Minnan nursery rhymes on short video platforms is not strong in integrity [13]. The information released by the communication subject is limited to the live video of the event, the mv of the early songs, the single episode recommendation of the "we media" person and the episode of the movie and TV drama, etc., showing the overall situation of scattered and not concentrated.

This activity of the subject is "limited activity". In the process of the real inheritor's identity as a disseminator, the accuracy of the communication content is relatively high, but the communication mode is not keeping pace with The Times, and the quality of the works is not high. However, most professional media organizations and "we media" are not familiar with the cultural connotation of nursery rhymes in southern Fujian, and they focus on the pursuit of entertainment while seldom showing the cultural connotation and historical information behind them. The temporary heat brought by this way of communication is not enough to achieve the ultimate goal of non-inheritance. In addition to inheritors and professional media personnel, there are also individual users. Such subjects mainly meet personal social needs and emotional expression, such as on-site video shooting, and lack value judgment.

The rise of short video provides a new opportunity for mainstream media to expand their influence in communication, and major media have taken it as a breakthrough in innovation and transformation. The reasonable use of short video platform to seek a new path of inheritance for Minnan nursery rhymes should adhere to the government's leading, establish a good order of short video platform communication subject, and cooperate with universities and enterprises to create a good communication ecological environment. At the government level, on June 10, 2022, the launch ceremony of the Cultural and Natural Heritage Day "Cloud Tour Intangible Cultural Heritage · Image Exhibition" and the "Intangible cultural Heritage Shopping Festival" was held in Beijing. China Performance Industry Association and eight online platforms jointly held the "Cloud Tour Intangible Cultural Heritage · Image Exhibition", and broadcasted more than 2,300 non-inherited videos and intangible cultural heritage documentaries online. Various activities such as short video topics, theme live broadcast and topic discussion will be carried out simultaneously [14]. At the enterprise and social level, Kuaishou has released the "Kuaishou Intangible Cultural Heritage Leader Plan", and Douyin has successively released the "Douyin Intangible cultural Heritage Partner Plan", which aims to explore China's intangible cultural heritage and establish an open exchange platform for intangible cultural heritage through urban cooperation, targeted poverty alleviation and traffic support, so as to comprehensively promote the inheritance of intangible cultural heritage. According to the White Paper of the 2022 Mega Engine on Intangible Cultural Heritage, from June 2021 to May 2022, the coverage rate of the 1,557 national intangible cultural heritage projects on Douyin reached 99.74%, and the total number of videos of national intangible cultural heritage projects exceeded 372.6 billion and the number of likes exceeded 9.4 billion. In addition, with the development of live broadcasting, many non-genetic inheritors choose to start their inheritance business online. From January to July 2022, the number of live streaming sessions of intangible cultural heritage increased by 109% year on year, and the total duration of live viewing increased by 126%. This also makes the growth rate of the user group of non-genetic bearers in all cities obvious and stable. Compared with the same period last year, the growth rate of non-genetic bearers is in the growth range of 35%-55% [15].

It makes the inheritance of folk intangible cultural heritage more extensive and creates more possibilities. The reconstruction of traditional culture and popular culture will also be another breakthrough in the dissemination of intangible cultural heritage in the future [13]. Minnan nursery rhymes should seize the opportunity to actively expand their influence on short video platforms.

4   Conclusion

As China attaches great importance to building cultural confidence in socialist construction in the new era, intangible cultural heritage as the "living fossil" of human history has been widely concerned. As one of the categories of intangible cultural heritage facing the endangered problem, oral literature non-legacy should conform to the development of The Times, seek adaptation channels with digital technology, the construction of two-dimensional and three-dimensional database in digital technology, the application of virtual interactive digital technology "presence+" in the meta-universe and digital transmission of short videos and other different display ways with the inheritance of oral literature intangible cultural heritage. However, in the process of integration, we should not blindly replace the old with the new. We should always take cultural connotation as the core and take digital technology as the means to carry out diversified inheritance and communication. As a treasure in the long river of Chinese traditional culture, southern Fujian culture has been endowed with a new era value and historical mission. Through the study of nursery rhymes in southern Fujian, it can be seen that the virtual reality technology under the concept of "presence+" can provide strong support for the non-genetic inheritance which obviously relies on oral and physical instruction, and the application of the mode of "digital technology + intangible cultural heritage" has strong operability. From the perspective of inheritance, this immersive interactive experience of "presence+" is consistent with the traditional inheritance concept of oral literature intangible cultural heritage. As digital technology becomes more and more mature, powerful interactive experience provides strong support for non-inherited inheritance. The combination of digital inheritance is played according to local conditions, providing new ideas and perspectives for the rescue and protection of oral literature intangible heritage, expanding the research on digital protection of oral literature intangible heritage, and promoting the sustainable development of oral literature intangible heritage. Promote the sustainable development of ethnic cultural industries.

Fundings. This research was funded by Study on the Digital Inheritance Path of Oral Literature Intangible Cultural Heritage - A Case Study of Minnan Nursery Rhymes (Grant No. YKJCX2022232); Research on Strengthening the Cooperation of Marine Strategic Emerging Industries in Fujian Province (Grant No. JAT21022); Research on the Innovative Training Model of Digital Publishing Talents under the Background of New Liberal Arts Construction (Grant No. FJJKBK21-039); Research on the Development Strategy of Xiamen Digital Culture Industry Chain under the Dual circulation (Grant No. JAS21300).

References

1. Wang, L., Xu, Z.: The Dynamic inheritance and media promotion of Minnan nursery rhymes from the perspective of social and cultural mentality. J. Fuzhou Univ. (Phil. Soc. Sci. Ed.) (04), 107–112 (2021). (in Chinese)
2. Lu, L., Lu, Y., Xu, X.: Popuaverselar science VR design of Oral Intangible Cultural Heritage from the perspective of Met. Library BBS, PP. 1–10 (2023). http://kns.cnki.net/kcms/detail/44.1306.g2.20220729.1741.002.html. (in Chinese)
3. Duan, X.Q.: Research on the classification of intangible cultural heritage and the construction of hierarchical element system of Intangible cultural heritage. Cult. Herit. (04), 9–16 (2018). (in Chinese)
4. Deng, Y., Yao, X.: Holistic and comparative vision: the existence characteristics, multidimensional literary view and its significance of minority oral literary theory. Inner Mongolia Acad. Soc. Sci. (01), 147–154 + 213 (2021). https://doi.org/10.14137/j.carol.carroll.nki.iss n1003-5281.2021.01.019. (in Chinese)
5. Hui, F.: Research on the "performance View" in the translation of Ethnic minority oral literature. Guizhou Ethnic Stud. (12), 133–136 (2018). (in Chinese)
6. Han, M., Zhou, X.: Review and Prospect of research on digital inheritance of Intangible cultural heritage in recent 20 years. J. South-Central Univ. National. (Human. Soc. Sci. Ed.) (01), 65–74 + 184 (2022). https://doi.org/10.1989/j.cnki.42-1704/C.20220109. (in Chinese)
7. Tan, G., He, Q.: Research status, predicament and development path of digital communication of intangible cultural heritage in China. Theor. Monthly (09), 87–94 (2021). (in Chinese)
8. Liu, G., Wang, X.: Virtual reality reshaping online education: learning resources, teaching organization and system platform. China Audio-Visual Educ. (11), 87–96 (2020). (in Chinese)
9. Qi, Z.: The Intangible cultural heritage universe: empowerment, integration, immersion. Media Today (09), 101–103 (2022). (in Chinese)
10. Han, T., Ma, Z.: Strategies for the protection and inheritance of Intangible cultural heritage from the perspective of meta-universe. Art Design (Theory) (10), 109–110 (2022). https://doi.org/10.1684/j.cnki.issn10082823.2022.10.033. (in Chinese)
11. China Internet Network Information Center. http://www.cnnic.net.cn/n4/2022/0914/c88-10226.html. Accessed 31 Aug 2022. (in Chinese)
12. This year, Douyin's intangible heritage answer paper. https://www.toutiao.com/article/710 7571378617844228/?%20channel=%20&source=search_tab. Accessed 10 June 2022. (in Chinese)
13. Wang, L.: Application of new media platforms in digital dissemination of Intangible cultural heritage. China New Commun. (19), 98–100 (2022). (in Chinese)
14. China Cultural Travel. https://baijiahao.baidu.com/s?id=1735045158878098103&wfr=spi der&for=pc. Accessed 08 June 2022. (in Chinese)
15. Douyin. https://v.douyin.com/B536fUS/. Accessed 27 Jan 2023. (in Chinese)

Research on the Aesthetic Connotation of New Media Ink Painting Art Based on Grounded Theory

Wenyi Xu ⓘ, Jinbo Xu ⓘ, and Zhipeng Zhang⁽✉⁾ ⓘ

Wuhan University of Technology, Wuhan 430070, Hubei, China
414609024@qq.com

Abstract. The combination of traditional Chinese ink art and new media technology has produced art with contemporary aesthetic value. In the collision of tradition and modernity, a brand-new aesthetic form is gradually emerging. Based on the traditional aesthetics of Oriental ink painting and nourished by modern new technology and craft aesthetics, it has developed rapidly. The new art form is currently in a transition period from the embryonic stage to the development stage, with various forms of works appearing rapidly and in large numbers, and relatively stable and unique aesthetic styles gradually emerging. However, with the rapid upgrading and iteration of technology, the aesthetic style of artistic works also appears the phenomenon of rapid iteration. How to remove the dross and take the essence in iteration after iteration? We use the rooted theory to study the aesthetic connotation of new media ink art. The aesthetic connotation is studied and summarized to form a theoretical framework of the aesthetic connotation of new media ink painting art, which can be used to guide the benign development of new media ink painting art under subsequent technological iterations, inject the vitality of the new media digital era into the traditional Chinese classic aesthetic forms and thoughts, and consolidate the excellent inheritance of traditional aesthetic thoughts.

This paper summarizes the theoretical model of the aesthetic connotation of new media ink painting art, which is divided into four levels from shallow to deep, namely, impression beauty, feeling beauty, human-computer interaction beauty and emotional reflection beauty.

Keywords: New media ink painting art · Aesthetic connotation · Grounded theory

1 Introduction

1.1 A Subsection Sample

In the field of new media art, China started late compared with the West, and the development of new media art in China is relatively slow. In the early stage of development, Chinese artists borrowed a lot from Western research results to create, and most of their works were imitative rather than original in the real sense.

A. Marcus et al. (Eds.): HCII 2023, LNCS 14034, pp. 196–214, 2023.
https://doi.org/10.1007/978-3-031-35705-3_15

With the accumulation of new media art practices in China, new media art with traditional ink art as its theme and carrier has emerged. This form has created the original creation of Chinese new media art, injected the soul of Chinese traditional aesthetics into Chinese new media art, and also provided Chinese inspiration for the world's new media art.

Throughout the development of Chinese new media ink painting art, it roughly includes these periods and nodes: in the early stage, image processing software such as photography and PS was used as the creation media for ink painting graphic design. The earliest ink animation - "Little tadpoles looking for their mother". Simulation and reproduction of ink painting dynamics and texture with dynamic software. The landscape world created through modeling. Interactive ink art achieved through various external recognition and sensing devices. Ai generates paintings drawn by ink paintings. Released early this year in the film "Deep Sea" top ink wind particle animation design [1]. The development of new media ink painting art covers various more subdivided art fields, and the application methods and presentation effects of ink painting elements are different in different fields and schools. Since they have the same root – Chinese traditional ink aesthetics, and its development is a great help to the new media art in China and the world, so the new aesthetic connotation generated by it is of high research value.

2   Related Concepts

2.1   Chinese Traditional Ink Art

Ink and wash art has been inherited in China ever since. The ink painting shows the origin of Chinese culture, which not only contains the ancient Chinese literati unfettered, happy and comfortable outlook on life, but also contains the cosmic law of Yin and Yang and the five elements, and everything in the world is endless. The long history of thousands of years and the unique political and cultural environment of China have created the ink painting spirit of literati. By externalizing this spirit and expressing delicate emotions, a unique visual symbol of ink painting has been formed.

Ink art is the portrayal of the inner world of literati in any era. It is also closely related to the characteristics of The Times at that time. It is the product of the combination of history, culture and the environment of The Times. Contemporary ink painting art was born in the new cultural and technological context, integrating the literati thought carried by traditional ink painting, and using the new media and forms of the information age to express.

2.2   New Media Ink Art

When we discuss how to make an ancient art form full of new vitality, we have to mention the medium exploration of ink painting [2]. We refer to the art forms that are different from traditional creation and expression media and created with relevant elements or features of ink art as new media ink art. This concept is broad and not limited to the features of new media art expressed in digital and optical forms. Compared with traditional ink art, new media ink art first innovates on media materials. Traditional ink art uses "pen, ink, paper and inkstone" as tools and materials for creation and expression, while contemporary ink painting new media art not only uses traditional media materials, but also introduces new media and tools such as Internet and computer. In the form of creation, traditional ink painting pays attention to various techniques, strokes and colors, lines, textures and forms, which complement each other with the tools and forms of creation and expression of new media art, greatly enriching the material base of new media art and allowing traditional ink painting to develop continuously in the context of The Times [3].

3   Research Design

3.1   Research Methods and Contents

Desktop Research Method. Through the literature and forum research analysis of the development of new media ink art, characteristics and types. By collecting the comments and analysis of various representative works of KOLs on various platforms and forums as the original materials for grounded theory research, six comments corresponding to six KOLs are specifically collected.

Ink animation "Little Tadpoles Looking for Their Mother" "Little Tadpoles Looking for Their Mother" is based on the images of fish and shrimp created by painter Qi Baishi. It is the first Chinese ink cartoon produced by Shanghai Art Film Studio in 1960, as in Fig. 1.

The biggest innovation and breakthrough of this film is to make the unique Chinese ink painting move. Different from Western painting, ink painting emphasizes spirit resemblance, vitality and charm. Ink painting is blended with ink and wash, resulting in different variations of shade, shade, emptiness and reality. These changes show rich colors, vivid expressions, appropriate forms, or near or far space [4].

In 1959, Xu Jingda wanted to try his hand at ink-style animation, and he approached photographer Duan Xiaoxuan. "Qi Baishi's painting can be printed on the washbasin. It looks very realistic. Could you make it into an animation?" Two people also found the United States film factory chief technician Qian Jiajun study together.

"Little Tadpole Looking for his mother" is the world's first cartoon in the form of ink painting. Its creation breaks through the previous animation mode both in art and technology and has epoch-making significance. In 1961, it won the first Chinese film "Hundred Flowers Award"; In the same year, he won the Silver Prize for Short Films in the 14th International Film Festival of Locarno, Switzerland. In 1962, he won the Children's Film Award at the 4th International Film Festival in Annecy, France. In 1964, won the 17th Cannes International Film Festival in France honorary Award; In 1978, he won the first prize of the 3rd Zagreb International Animation Film Festival in Yugoslavia. In 1981, he won the second prize in the 4th International Film Festival for Children and Youth in France.

From numerous international awards, we can see that the international cartoon industry to "Little Tadpoles looking for his mother" recognition and praise. It not only tells a popular science story in a popular form, telling people the right way to know things.

Fig. 1. Ink animation "Little Tadpoles Looking for Their Mother".

Moreover, it presents ink painting as a new art form, which is also the beginning of new media ink painting art. Its appearance opened the prologue of Chinese new media art.

Yang Yongliang – "Urban Landscape". With the development of ink painting art, contemporary artists are also innovative in the content of creation. In terms of creative intention, traditional ink painting pays more attention to the expression of aesthetic taste, while contemporary new media ink art goes beyond that. Contemporary artists are full of the sense of responsibility of The Times. They reflect on and expose various current problems, and worry about the living environment and future development of human beings. This also makes most of the new media art of ink painting reflect on the current ecological environment and social civilization [3].

Contemporary new media ink art, as a typical example of the combination of tradition and modernity, is also developing rapidly under the changes of The Times. Yang Yongliang, a famous contemporary new media ink artist, realizes the separation and contradiction between traditional landscape painting and the pursuit of urban modernization. In order to arouse people's reflection on the pursuit of urban modernization, Yang Yongliang retains the visual pattern and charm of traditional landscape painting in his series of works City Landscape, and replaces the detailed elements with those unique to modern cities. Combining the primitive, detached and secluded image of traditional landscape art with the secular, noisy and rigid image of modern urban machinery, this stark contrast is thought-provoking, a reflection on urban modernization and a reflection of traditional cultural spirit, as in Fig. 2 and 3.

The Application of Dynamic Graphics Software and Computer-Generated Art to Extract and Reproduce the Texture of Ink Painting. When digital image processing technology becomes more and more mature and graphics and dynamic software become more and more powerful, the representative type of new media ink painting art appears -- the

Fig. 2. Yang Yongliang -- "Urban Landscape"

Fig. 3. Details of "Urban Landscape".

dynamic ink painting art that is re-created by extracting the features of ink painting, such as color, form, texture and dynamics. In terms of color, most of these works extract the black and white features of ink and wash, but there are also color forms; In terms of form and texture, this kind of works uses computer to extract and simulate the characteristics of the physical properties of ink painting [4]. For example, the texture and dynamics of ink and water dyeing, and the texture and dynamics of ink dyeing on rice paper. The restoration and emphasis on the original physical characteristics of ink painting are the characteristics of this kind of works. Artist Aoooxixi's work "Ink Mark" reflects the smooth and graceful dynamic of ink in water. This wonderful dynamic and texture is fascinating, as in Fig. 4.

Fig. 4. Work of "Ink Mark".

Some works are innovative under the premise of preserving part of the nature of ink painting. Artist HWJU's work "Ink Rhyme" combines rational computer code art with perceptual ink painting art, and uses generated waveform to express the background music of classical music, which not only has a strong sense of form, but also retains the charm of ink painting, as in Fig. 5.

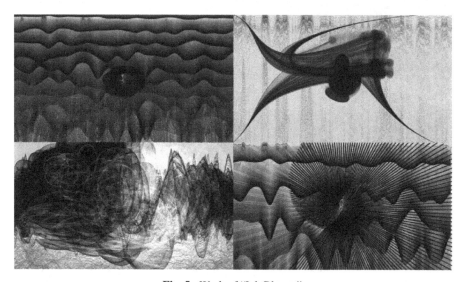

Fig. 5. Work of "Ink Rhyme".

Modeling Technology and Interactive Technology are Embedded in Ink Art. In the past two decades, the unprecedented progress of 3D scene modeling technology and image-based object recognition technology has laid an important foundation for the construction of 3D scene in Chinese painting. The research of 3D scene reconstruction based on virtual reality technology has been widely carried out. Using information technology to provide new solutions for the inheritance and development of Chinese painting. The object recognition, virtual scene modeling and rendering of Chinese painting will become the research hotspot in the future.

Through intelligent recognition and classification technology of landscape painting, three-dimensional model generation technology of landscape painting content, inter-active modeling technology of three-dimensional terrain, intelligent retrieval of three-dimensional model and intelligent synthesis technology of three-dimensional scene and other technologies, the creators overcame many difficulties to carry out the digital construction of ancient landscape painting. When this kind of digital three-dimensional art is displayed in museums or through VR glasses, it brings the audience a strong sense of immersion [5]. "Digital Map of Thousands of Miles of Rivers and Mountains" restores Zhang Daqian's map of thousands of miles of rivers and mountains, and displays it with a large LED screen, the effect is extremely shocking, as in Fig. 6 and 7.

Fig. 6. "Digital Map of Thousands of Miles of Rivers and Mountains".

When the model of ink painting scene is applied to the advertisement, it will produce special effect and add new interest to the advertisement design, as in Fig. 8. In this advertising video of "Yuanguo" wine, the creator not only uses the basic elements and style of ink painting, but also uses the technique of leaving blank space very cleverly [6]. The combination of white space and simple but strong style elements is very advanced, and also reflects the ancient Chinese "Zen", leaving the viewer space to think.

Fig. 7. "Digital Map of Thousands of Miles of Rivers and Mountains" (at night).

Fig. 8. Ink painting advertising video.

The development of interactive technology also injects new soul into new media ink painting art. Taking the above "digital map of Rivers and Mountains" as an example, visitors can change its dynamics by touching the light spots on the ground. With the changes of the main picture, strong interest is generated. For example, Riverside Scene at Qingming Festival 3.0 has been released by the Palace Museum since Northern Song Dynasty painter Zhang Zeduan's Riverside Scene at Qingming Festival was the first to use digital technology to show the characters and environment dynamics in the work at the Shanghai Expo in 2010, as in Fig. 9. With the help of 8K ultra high-definition digital technology, 4D dynamic image, interactive projection technology and many artistic forms. People can appreciate this work in front of the 8-m-long giant projection curtain, and interact with the figures in the Northern Song Dynasty through finger touch on the curtain, so as to have a deeper interaction, understand the customs at that time, feel the smell of fireworks on the street, and learn precious historical knowledge. In a simple exhibition process, the viewer has unwittingly brought themselves into it, and got an immersive viewing experience. Modern technology is used to make the exhibits "alive", and the distance between the exhibits and the viewers is further drawn through the four steps of association, transformation, fit and immersion, so as to truly realize the emotional communication between body and mind [7].

Fig. 9. Digital Riverside Scene at Qingming Festival.

AIGC'S Impact on Ink Art. Artificial intelligence has brought great changes to art and design. In today's information technology era, with the progress of technology represented by artificial intelligence, artistic creation is increasingly enriched, content expression is intelligent, interactive and data-driven, and the relationship between technology, art and people is increasingly close. Artificial intelligence technology aims to perfectly replicate the human mind by using natural responses based on the surrounding environment, decoding emotions, and recognizing human characteristics in the energy range [8]. However, artificial intelligence has a much higher working efficiency than human thinking, which makes it able to effectively improve the frequency of cognitive iteration in design [9], and expand the boundary of perceptual divergent thinking in artistic creation. As an auxiliary tool in design activities, AI effectively improves creative designs and produces "unexpected" new designs [10]. There is an irreversible trend for AI to intervene in art and design and disrupt existing paradigms [11].

The expression of new media art has subjectivity, diversity and complexity. Generally speaking, the characteristics considered by artists only partially describe the aesthetic thinking and emotional changes of artists and experiencers [12]. When people use Disco Diffusion to create ink paintings, they get unexpected results, as in Fig. 10. The elements produced are not the same as those in traditional paintings, but abstract and even grotesque. They break the norms of traditional ink and wash landscape painting, but have great charm and attract people, and provide inspiration for artists.

However, the works generated in this way are not all good aesthetic properties. Critics who support the experimental school intentionally deconstruct the traditional culture and aesthetic spirit behind ink painting, and emphasize the media characteristics of ink painting and artists' comprehensive use of different media, modes of display, space and scene. Their criticism is more about the problem consciousness and theoretical consciousness of contemporary art [13]. However, we should carry forward the ink art of new media and balance the two.

Compared with the unfettered generation, artist Cao Yuxi created the "artificial intelligence landscape map" according to the model with more strict training, as in Fig. 11 and 12. Which is more regular in aesthetic and has a stronger sense of form. At the same time, he fully displays the dynamics generated by artificial intelligence, integrating the dynamics of ink painting with the dynamics of algorithm.

Fig. 10. Ink painting created by Disco Diffusion.

Fig. 11. "Artificial intelligence landscape map".

Interview Method. Through the exhibition of representative works and the interview of the interviewees with certain artistic foundation and aesthetic accomplishment, the original materials are collected. The interview was conducted from the following three perspectives: 1. Perceptual and intuitive feelings about the work; 2. Recognition and reasons for the form and aesthetics of the works; 3. Reflection on the emotion or connotation of the work, as in Table 1. In the interview, the author guides the interviewees to actively express their experience and feelings through dialogues. Besides the interview outline, the author impromptu raises new questions according to the interviewees' answers, so as to ensure the comprehensiveness and richness of the interview materials.

Grounded Theory. After the survey and interview, the original data obtained from the desktop survey and interview are coded using the grounded theory method, from which the aesthetic connotation of the new media ink art is analyzed and summarized.

3.2 Data Collection

This study interviewed 13 users from December 5, 2022 to February 10, 2023. The interviews were all about half an hour long. The interviewees are all people with certain artistic foundation and aesthetic accomplishment, the ratio of men to women is balanced, and the age ranges from 19 to 60. The interviewees cover a comprehensive range of subjects, which ensures the scientific nature of the research. The 13 samples obtained

Fig. 12. "Artificial intelligence landscape map".

Table 1. Interview design.

Number	Purpose of interview	Interview question
1	The emotional, intuitive feeling of the work	What was your first impression of this work?
2	The form and aesthetic recognition of the work and reasons	Do you think the work is beautiful/interesting/attractive? Please elaborate on the reasons
3	A reflection on the emotion or connotation of the work	Does this work impress you? If so, what struck you about it?

from the interview and 6 KOL comments collected together constitute the original data. After excluding 3 invalid interview samples and 1 invalid comment sample, there are 15 valid samples for the study, 5 are randomly selected as the theoretical saturation test, and the remaining 25 are used as the coding basis. The specific interviewees are shown in Table 2:

Table 2. The information of interviewees.

Number	Pseudonym	Gender(Male/Female)	Age	occupation	nationality	Have you ever come into contact with traditional ink art	Have you ever come into contact with new media ink art
1	Xiao Wang	M	22	Graduate student in visual communication	China	Y	Y
2	Mr. Yang	M	30	Graphic designer	China	N	Y
3	Jerry	F	25	Graduate student in information arts	China	Y	Y
4	Mr. Liu	M	37	Art teacher/young painter	China	Y	N
5	Uncle Liu	M	60	Art teacher/famous painter	China	Y	N
6	Peter	F	25	Graduate student in digital media arts	China	Y	Y
7	Linag Liang	F	22	Graduate student in visual communication	China	Y	Y
8	Xiao Wen	F	20	Graduate student in industrial design	China	N	N
9	Xiao Li	F	19	An undergraduate, majoring in oil painting at the Academy of Fine Arts	China	Y	Y
10	Professor Bo	M	51	University design professor/famous painter	China	Y	Y
11	Doctor Chen	F	29	PhD in design	China	N	N
12	Caroline	F	53	University professor	Britain	Y	N
13	Martin	M	56	University professor	Britain	N	N

4 Data Analysis

4.1 Open Coding

Open coding of interview data refers to extracting several initial concepts from the original interview data, and then classifying the initial concepts to form several sub-categories. In order to ensure the true expression of the interviewees, this study only deleted meaningless pauses to compile the original sentences, and then refined them into Marine language as the initial concept. Due to the length and large amount of coding data, only the initial coding examples of part of original statements are shown, as shown in Table 3. The results show that 60 initial concepts and 30 sub-categories are obtained through open coding, as shown in Table 4 for details.

4.2 Spindle Coding

The main process of spindle coding is to logically connect and distinguish the categories formed by open coding, and then determine the main category by combining the same kind of generic block. On the basis of referring to related literature concepts and practical experience, this study conducted spindle coding on 30 categories and obtained 4 main categories, as in Table 5.

4.3 Selective Coding

Selective coding refers to further summarizing and refining the main category into a more comprehensive core model, analyzing its action path and relationship structure, and constructing a rooted theoretical model demonstrating the operation law of each main category. In this study, the core category is determined as "Aesthetic connotation of contemporary new media ink painting art" through thinking and analysis, as shown in Fig. 13.

Table 3. Sample initial encoding of partial original statement.

Original statement	Subcategory (Ai)
I was shocked by this work. It was very big, and the ancient paintings were actually restored to be more three-dimensional and dynamic. There were sounds and songs of nature, as well as wind, and I seemed to be one with it.	A1 Magnificent and shocking A2 dynamic A3 The beauty of multi-channel immersion
The movement of ink painting makes me unable to move my eyes at a glance. This movement effect is very simple and natural. So is the texture of ink painting, which makes people comfortable and contemplative.	A4 Natural A5 Peaceful and comfortable
I have never seen such an interesting Qingming River map, these little people can interact with me, I seem to enter the square city, the buildings here are really beautiful, here is so busy!	A6 Interesting interactions A7 Immersive interaction A8 The beauty of traditional architecture

Table 4. Open coding results.

Subcategory (Ai)	Original statement (concept)	Subcategory (Ai)	Original statement (concept)	Subcategory (Ai)
A1 Magnificent and shocking	change color, different weather, not on the earth, fairyland, the mountains are very beautiful, the scenery is also very beautiful. it seems to feel through the four seasons, and like the rain after the sunny	A12 The beauty of fantasy	painting ink and wash paintings for decades and I didn't know it could be done like this, Compared to all kinds of digital art, ink and wash art looks better	A23 Cultural affiliation
A2 dynamic		A13 The beauty of natural scenery		A24 Cultural confidence
A3 The beauty of multi-channel immersion		A14 The beauty of time		A25 The Beauty of Optimism
A4 Natural	glaciers thawed, mountains appeared green, "saw" the flowers in spring	A15 The beauty of synesthesia	like flying in the sicy, the scenery in front of me is constantly changing, feel more open-minded	A26 The beauty of a free soul
A5 Peaceful and comfortable	create unique images on my own,felt a sense of accomplishment	A16 Interaction with a sense of accomplishment		A27 Beauty of simplicity
A6 Interesting interactions	input my ideas, and the image generated by DiscoDiffusion amazed me, get inspiration from careful observation,want to make the next input	A17 Unexpected beauty	advertisement simple, and elegant	A28 Elegant
A7 Immersive interaction		A18 Curious interaction	only three meters high, like I was looking at a world.	A29 The beauty of vast space
A8 The formal/cultural beauty of traditional architecture	reminds me of when I was a child in the village and friends to catch grasshoppers, really beautiful	A19 The beauty of Remembrance	The shape of it caught my eye in the first place, so interesting	A30 An attractive form
A9 dynamic		A20 The beauty of children's Fun		
A10 The beauty of fusion and symbiosis	Ink painting and Guqin melody complement each other, and the rhythm of ink painting produces rhythmic beauty	A21 The beauty of rhythm		
A11 The beauty of algorithms		A22 Harmonious beauty		

4.4 Saturation Test

The number of samples in this study is determined according to the criterion of theoretical saturation. 2/3 of the original data (7 interviews and 3 forum comments) were randomly selected for coding analysis and model construction, and another 1/3 of the interview data (3 interviews and 2 forum comments) were randomly selected for theoretical saturation test. A new round of open coding, spindle coding and selective coding was conducted for the remaining 5 data in accordance with the coding process of grounded theory. It was

Table 5. Open coding results.

Principal category (Bi)
B1 Beauty of First Impressions (A1/4/5/17/30)
B2 Beauty of perception (A2/3/8/9/11/12/13/14/15/21/27/28/29)
B3 Beauty of Human-computer interaction(A6/7/16/18)
B4 Beauty of emotional reflection(A8/10/19/20/22/23/24/25/26)

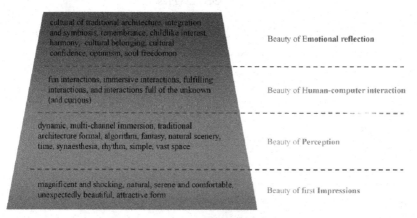

Fig. 13. "Aesthetic Connotation of contemporary new media ink painting art" grounded theoretical model.

found that there were no new concepts and categories, and the original logical relationship was in line with each category. Therefore, the grounded theory model of "Aesthetic connotation of contemporary new media ink painting art" passed the saturation test.

5 Model Interpretation

The grounded theoretical model of "Aesthetic connotation of contemporary new media ink painting art" consists of four levels, from the shallow to the deep: the beauty of impression, the beauty of sense, the beauty of human-computer interaction, and the beauty of emotional reflection. Its in-depth basis lies in the interactive course of human and artistic works. That is, the experiencer's instinctive impression at the first moment of contact with the work, the feeling at the sensory level, the interaction in behavior, and finally the emotional reflection after internalizing the previous information.

5.1 The Beauty of Impression

The beauty of impression is the first instinct feeling and impression that the new media ink painting art brings to the audience. It depends on the external form of new media ink painting art, namely "attractive shape". Influenced by traditional Chinese philosophy and ink painting gene, the subject matter and artistic conception of landscape painting, for example, create a "magnificent and shocking" feeling, while the ancient "pastoral spirit" and "secluded feelings" convey a "quiet and comfortable" feeling. It is also influenced by new technologies, such as the "unexpected beauty" brought by AIGC. Coincidentally, the "unexpected beauty" is also emphasized in the ink painting art of ancient literature. A poem describes that "there is no road after mountains and rivers, and there is a bright village", which is the expression of this aesthetic feeling.

5.2 Beauty of Perception

Beauty of perception is inevitable. The sensuous beauty of new media ink painting art mainly comes from three sources. 1. Traditional beauty: the formal beauty of traditional architecture, the beauty of natural scenery, the beauty of synaesthesia, the beauty of melody, the beauty of simplicity, the beauty of physical texture (supplement). 2. The beauty of technology: the beauty of logic and rationality of algorithm. 3. The beauty produced by the fusion of tradition and modernity: the beauty of multi-channel immersion, dynamic beauty, fantastic beauty, time beauty and vast space beauty.

In traditional thought, the idea of conforming to nature is the main basis of beauty, through the expression of nature's form, texture, rules to reflect the original beauty [14]. The beauty of synaesthesia and rhythm is born of Chinese classical literature and art [15]. The simplicity of beauty contains the core philosophy of ancient China: "Simplicity of the road" [6]. Technology itself has a logical, rational beauty. When new technology is combined with traditional ideas, more beauty is highlighted or produced. Multi-channel technology restores the immersive aesthetic of "people in painting"; dynamic technology and three-dimensional technology enhance the aesthetic feeling of time and space; various perceptual technology and dynamic technology reflect the dynamic beauty and restore the fantasy beauty.

5.3 Human-Computer Interactive Aesthetic

The interactive aesthetic of new media ink painting art is the product of the deep integration of ink painting art and modern technology. As a tool to assist human brain to extend, the interaction between machine and human produces special aesthetic characteristics. [16]. Technology breaks the limits of interaction, and many "tiny" interactions produce interesting interactive aesthetic [17]. When experiencers are immersed in the interactive workflow, they can feel the immersive interactive aesthetic [18]. When experiencers gain a lot in interactive tasks, they will feel a sense of achievement in interactive aesthetics, and the emergence of AI also enables more intelligent and deeper interactions. Many feedbacks generated by AI are often unpredictable by human beings, which is the unexpected interactive aesthetics. However, when a non-human thing is similar to human beings to a certain extent, Will cause the Uncanny Valley effect [19], so whether AI will bring beauty or fear to art in the future remains to be seen.

5.4 Beauty of Emotional Reflection

On the level of emotional reflection, aesthetic mainly comes from: 1. The pursuit of ancient Chinese literati, such as the beauty of freedom of soul, the beauty of optimism. 2. The principles of beauty advocated by ancient Chinese philosophy, such as the beauty of symbiosis and harmony. 3. The beauty of reminiscence and childlike beauty rooted in ancient literary thoughts. 4. Beauty based on cultural affiliation, such as the beauty of cultural affiliation and cultural confidence. Their essence is a part of Chinese culture conveyed by ink art, which is more brilliant through the reinforcement of modern new media technology.

6   Design Case

Based on the grounded theoretical model of "Aesthetic connotation of contemporary new media ink painting art", the author and the team designed and implemented the new media ink painting art.

This design uses TouchDesigner software for graphic programming, dynamic processing of ink paintings created by team members, and design interactive special effects followed by examples. The work depicts "populus euphratica", which is a kind of plant living in the arid desert, so we use the elements of water to create the deformation and dynamics of the picture, and the elements of light to express the vitality of the leaves. The interactive effect is small and unexpected, and the simulated runway scene makes people walk through the screen with a "sense of advanced experience", as shown in Fig. 14 and 15.

Fig. 14. Interactive ink screen based on TouchDesigner.

Fig. 15. Project field photos.

7   Conclusion

This research summarizes and refines the development of new media ink painting art, obtains the rooted theoretical model of "aesthetic connotation of contemporary new media ink painting art". The new media ink painting art is rooted in the traditional ink painting art and the ancient Chinese thought, which needs to be further studied at a deeper level. We should also constantly tapping the potential of technology to keep up with the changing times. The limitation of this research lies in the limitation of the original materials of the grounded theory. A larger sample size should be collected from a broader channel to further improve the comprehensiveness and reliability of the research.

References

1. Wang, X.: Searching for the Heart in "Particle Ink Painting". Wen Hui Po (2023). https://doi.org/10.28814/n.cnki.nwehu.2023.000288
2. Liu, X.J.: Review the current development State of Ink Painting from the Dimension of Modern Sociology. Chin. Fine Arts **06**, 15–16 (2022)
3. Liang, K., Jin, H.: Explore the application of ink and wash symbols in new media art under the trend of contemporary art. Sci. Technol. Commun. **12**(18), 53–54 (2020)
4. Zhang, X.: On the construction of artistic conception in chinese painting. Art Educ. **325**(09), 111–113 (2018)
5. Wang, J., Han, Z.: Research on Stylization of ink painting in VR interactive images. Contemp. Animat. **01**, 88–93 (2023)
6. Liu, Q.: "Trace, Return to the Root" -- the expression of calligraphy and ink elements in kan tai-keung's graphic design. Beauty Times (I)(12), 86–88 (2022). https://doi.org/10.16129/j.cnki.mysds.2022.12.020
7. Miao, L.: Application of virtual reality technology in narrative design of museums. Packa. Eng. **39**(04), 15–18 (2018)
8. Shen, Y., Yu, F.: The influence of artificial intelligence on art design in the digital age. Sci. Program. (2021)
9. Zhou, C., Chai, C., Yang, C.: Research on iteration of artificial intelligence aided design – taking graphic design as an example. Packa. Eng. **42**(18), 50–62 (2021)
10. Gao, F., Jiao, Y.: Aided creative design based on artificial intelligence. Zhuangshi **11**, 34–37 (2019)
11. Duan, Y., Zhang, J., Gu, X.: A novel paradigm to design personalized derived images of art paintings using an intelligent emotional analysis model. Front. Psychol. **12** (2021)
12. Yang, X.: Image modal analysis in art design and image recognition using AI techniques. J. Intell. Fuzzy Syst. **40**(4), 6961–6971 (2021)
13. Chen, Q.: The '"Field"' of ink painting: a research method of art sociology. Chin. Fine Arts Stud. **02**, 172–175 (2022)
14. Fang, J.: Discussion on the application of ink elements in graphic design. Pop. Literat. Art **545**(23), 35–37 (2022)
15. Zhao, L.: Powerful "Ink Sculpture" – Zhou Jingxin's ink painting. Fine Arts Observ. **328**(12), 118–119 (2022)
16. Wang, C.: Analysis on the influence of color aesthetics on modern interior design in chinese painting art. Ind. Arch. **52**(04), 259 (2022)
17. Yin, J., Yu, T.: On the "Micro" interest of interactive display under the background of digital age. Packa. Eng. **33**(18), 12–14+30 (2012). https://doi.org/10.19554/j.cnki.1001-3563.2012.18.004
18. Zhao, S., Shen, L.: Research on Interactive interface design of children's smartwatch based on Flow theory. Packa. Eng., 1–11 (2023)
19. Zhong, X., Wang, J., Liu, C., Jiang, G.: Based on the analysis of emotion fuzzy computing the uncanny valley effect cause. J. Packa. Eng. **33**(14), 190–196 (2018). https://doi.org/10.19554/cnki.1001-3563.2018.14.035

The Meta-universe Platform Roblox for the Conservation of the Globally Important Agricultural Heritage Systems (GIAHS): The Case of the Floating Garden Agricultural Practices

Man Zhang[1](✉), Zhen Liu[1] (iD), and Kaixin Lai[2]

[1] School of Design, South China University of Technology,
510006 Guangzhou, People's Republic of China
sdzhangman@mail.scut.edu.cn
[2] Escp Europe, 75020 Paris, France

Abstract. The World Important Agricultural Heritage Sites are essential cultural treasures that contain the wisdom of ancient human survival and potential solutions to promote a balance between human development and environmental protection. However, these heritage sites are under the impact of modern development. Their influence and importance are gradually forgotten by people, which will be detrimental to the sustainable development and transmission of agricultural cultural heritage sites. After the metaverse concept exploded, it provides new ideas for heritage site conservation. As such, the aim of this paper is to bring users a new look and experience about the heritage site through the new form of 3D modeling and game interaction, so that users can learn and understand the charm of the heritage site in a good experience. The method is to use the Roblox platform to design an experience game taking the floating garden agricultural cultural heritage site as an example. It fully demonstrates the potential of the floating garden agricultural practices in Bangladesh in coping with flood disasters. The results show that it will draw more attention to the current situation of the Globally Important Agricultural Heritage Systems (GIAHS) and ultimately promote their sustainable development.

Keywords: Floating Garden Agricultural Practices · GIAHS · Games Experience · Heritage Site Conservation

1 Introduction

1.1 The Globally Important Agricultural Heritage Systems (GIAHS)

The Globally Important Agricultural Heritage Systems (GIAHS) are scenic landscape systems that combine agrobiodiversity with a valuable cultural heritage. They meet the needs of local economic, social and cultural development and contribute to the sustainable development of the region [1]. GIAHS is a project promoted by the Food and

© The Author(s), under exclusive license to Springer Nature Switzerland AG 2023
A. Marcus et al. (Eds.): HCII 2023, LNCS 14034, pp. 215–226, 2023.
https://doi.org/10.1007/978-3-031-35705-3_16

Agriculture Organization of the United Nations to protect and support the world's agricultural cultural heritage systems [2]. Agricultural heritage sites are different from ordinary natural or cultural heritage sites because they combine multiple social, economic, and natural attributes and have multiple functions of landscape, production, and culture. It contains traditional agricultural knowledge, technology and agricultural landscapes, agricultural sites, agricultural biodiversity, etc. [3].

However, agricultural heritage sites face challenges from climate, industrial development, pollution, and many other sources, and many traditional agricultural systems are under threat of disappearance [4]. For example, the Floating Gardens Agricultural Heritage Site in south-central Bangladesh is facing serious environmental problems such as reduced arable areas due to flooding and land degradation as well as environmental pollution. The Ifugao terraces in the Philippines have seen many abandoned farmlands due to low returns from agricultural production. As a result, it is listed as a landscape in danger by the World Heritage Foundation [5]. This study hopes to draw attention to the sustainability issues facing agricultural heritage sites through design.

1.2 Digital Heritage Conservation

Digital conservation is well adapted to tangible heritage, providing objective, realistic, and comprehensive data recording of tangible heritage through images, videos, and 3D reconstructions, and providing the public with corresponding visual channels for dissemination, retrieval, and learning [6]. Digital heritage conservation has entered a new phase of development with the growth of digital media, virtual reality, augmented reality, and other smart platforms that combine reality and imagination. In particular, the rise of the metaverse concept is driving the rapid development of new technologies. Important technologies such as 3D modeling and rendering are becoming easier with the opening of various metaverse platforms, allowing ordinary people to build personalized virtual worlds through simple learning. This provides another effective tool for lay people to create and express themselves, and those involved in heritage conservation can use these tools to advance the cause of heritage conservation.

1.3 Roblox Metaverse Platform

The Roblox platform is an internet-based online game development platform that allows users to use tools and model resources already available. Users implement game development through simple programming, which made Roblox one of the hottest metaverse platforms for a while [7]. On the Roblox platform, users have the dual role of player and developer, creating an active online community. This makes the platform not only a tool for realizing game ideas, but also a good way of communicating the ideas behind the games or the messages the developers want to convey. In this project, a scenario-based experience game is designed on the Roblox platform. Through virtual world building and scenario building, the players on the forum will be able to recognize the potential of the floating garden agricultural heritage site in Bangladesh to address the global climate challenge through the game. It aims to promote awareness of conserving the world's agricultural heritage and the region's sustainable development.

2 Status and Challenges of Floating Garden Agricultural Practices in Bangladesh

2.1 Status of Floating Garden Agricultural Practices in Bangladesh

The cultivable area in southern Bengal is reduced due to frequent flooding during the rainy season (June to October) [8]. In ancient times, people started cultivating crops using floating gardens [9]. Firstly, people build rafts or water platforms with bamboo of the right size, collect water plants or hyacinths, and place them on the platforms to rot. After a period, they become a loose and fertile medium suitable for growing a wide range of vegetables and spices. The advantage of floating garden growing is that no additional nutrients or fertilizers are required [10], but the crops are more productive than those grown in the soil. When winter comes, the flood waters recede and the floating beds degrade, producing residues that are used as organic fertilizers for vegetable growing in the winter. This traditional farming practice makes clever use of local resources to improve the resilience of local people in the face of flooding, bringing economic, agricultural, and ecological benefits to the development of local communities [10].

Floating garden farming in Bangladesh is good for increasing people's income and is also more female-friendly. People who practice floating bed cultivation can earn a better income compared to those who do not, contributing to a better gender balance [11]. The medium on the floating platform is water hyacinth, which is one of the most dangerous invasive species [12], but in this agricultural system, it is transformed into the most efficient resource. The consumption of water hyacinth also prevents water eutrophication and water pollution [13], contributing to the growth of fish in the waters and preserving the biodiversity of this ecosystem. It also provides a favorable condition for residents to catch fish to increase their income.

2.2 The Challenges of Floating Garden Agricultural Practices in Bangladesh

Large-scale development is one of these threats. To avoid flooding humans, the government undertook a massive dam-building project after the modern era. This leads to a lack of fertile soil on farmland from flood deposits, while silt deposits in rivers clog local drainage systems, leading to flooding and inundation happening more often [14]. Another threat is salinity intrusion. Due to climate change, higher levels of salt water infiltrate rivers and streams. This not only affects crop production but also reduces the availability of water hyacinth [11], which may hurt local production systems.

More attention needs to be drawn to the importance of agricultural production in floating gardens for local communities and sustainable development. Its contribution in terms of food and livelihood security and foreseeable potential for future resilience to climate change. There is a need to strengthen efforts to protect and promote this important world agricultural heritage site. Also attract more businesses in tourism, smart farming, and marketing of agricultural products to promote the sustainable development of this heritage site.

3   Methodology

The study begins with a STEEP approach to assess the past and current situation of Bangladesh, where the floating garden agricultural heritage is located, using five perspectives: social, technological, economic, environmental, and policy dimensions. In this way, the background to the study is entirely constructed to understand better the challenges and development dynamics of the agricultural heritage of the floating gardens.

From the STEEP analysis, it is possible to conclude that the floating garden heritage site is facing social problems such as overpopulation, frequent natural disasters, and sea level rise [8, 10]. In particular, the shortage of arable land and overpopulation poses a threat to people's well-being [14]. Although floods have caused a shortage of arable land in Bangladesh, flood subsidence can make farmland more fertile. The government is also taking positive promotional action by initiating agricultural subsidy policies and vigorously promoting hydroponic projects [14].

The second step uses a user profile to construct the future identity of the agricultural heritage site. The information gathered during the secondary research phase was integrated to explore the essence of stakeholders who could contribute to the sustainable development of the heritage site. Based on this, some integration or modification was made and the final roles explored are shown in Fig. 1

BIO

Originally from Bangladesh, Nubi has a deep knowledge of climate issues. Mindful of the development situation in his hometown, he returned to develop and call for more attention to development of the Floating Gardens Heritage Site.

Connect

• Learn about smart agriculture, technology–based farming and other aspects to improve production efficiency.

• Open up the water trading market to enhance the sales of agricultural products to increase income.

• Growing high cash crops.

Ability

• Sensitive to weather changes and able to judge the timing of reinforcing the floating bed.

• Strong curiosity and desire to learn and stay on top of new business models and technological innovations.

• Good communication skills

Fig. 1. Future identity construction of the floating garden agricultural heritage site (Generated by authors).

The third step is to build the game's plot by envisioning a future incorporating the specific crops of the floating garden's agricultural heritage, distinctive cultivation methods, and local customs and geographical features. Build stakeholder characters and possible storylines to explore the plot development in the game. Figure 2 shows the three main scenes explored in the development of the storyline.

The fourth step was to complete an analysis of the stakeholders in the floating garden heritage site, using the "How Might We" tool to help assess which characters would be

Fig. 2. Exploring the game's plot (Generated by authors).

more suitable as game protagonists. This process focuses more on the positive impact that the actor can have on the heritage site, as shown in Fig. 3. The main character is eventually identified as a young intellectual concerned about climate issues. He devotes himself to finding solutions to severe climate problems. Still, he finds that the effective method turns out to be the floating garden planting technology that he considered backward as a child.

How Might We ?

In the future, () can () to ()

Game designers can develop interactive experience games to provide virtual teaching and growing experiences.

Designers can make the floating garden more beautiful to enhancing the benefits of heritage sites.

Engineer can Simplifying the planting process for floating gardens to promote floating garden planting.

Culture Lovers can through the sharing of local people to take a virtual tour at the Floating Gardens Heritage Site.

Local women can participate in floating garden labor to get more income for a better life.

Fig. 3. Game role exploration (Generated by authors).

4 Results

Combining the information from the preliminary secondary research and the vision of the future story of the heritage site, the game was initially determined to be based on the construction and conservation of the floating garden. The game vision will be realized on the Roblox platform, and the tools provided by the platform will be used to build the story scenario, guide the storyline, and render the emotions to realize the game vision.

4.1 Game Interaction Flow Building

Figure 4 illustrates the interaction flow of this game design. The game was originally designed to spread awareness of the potential of floating garden agricultural practices to resist disasters in flood-affected areas and after sea level rise. To enhance the player's sense of mission, the story background is interspersed at the beginning and in the game, giving players the mission to save the flood-affected people. The game guides the player through different living areas and landscapes in a way that collects materials to better understand and appreciate the local character of the Bangladeshi landscape. This will help the player to recognize the importance of floating gardens to the local productive life. Arrange some Non-Player Characters in the game scene. If players talk to them, they can understand the real impact that floating gardens have on their lives from the perspective of different stakeholders.

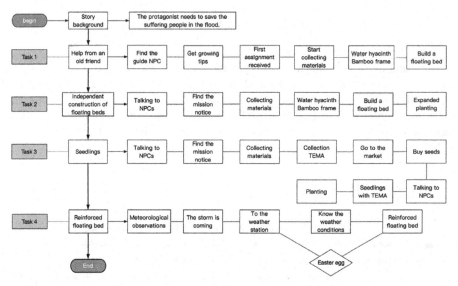

Fig. 4. Game interaction flow construction (Generated by authors).

4.2 Game Character and Scene Construction

According to the design of the game interaction flow, we arrange the important guiding roles for the game plot advancement. Players mainly through talking and interact with NPCs to obtain important information such as planting introduction, background introduction, and game guide. The main NPC characters in the game include Mirza, who enthusiastically provides planting guidance. Yusna, a kind neighbor who gives away seeds at the market. Hajina, a female nursery instructor. They are essential in guiding the player to continue the game and move forward.

The game scene is divided into three main areas: the living area, the planting area, and the trading market. It also includes a representative landscape of the snowy mountains and the weather tower, indicating climate change.

We recreated the local landscape of Bangladesh as much as possible in the construction of the scene. For example, the characteristic water market, which is a unique local form of trading in floods. The floating platforms with their regular arrangement of crops also create a beautiful landscape with an ornamental character, which is the origin of the name "garden".

Fig. 5. Game scenario layout (Generated by authors).

The operation interface of the game is shown in Fig. 5. Games developed on the Roblox platform can be run on both PC and mobile phones. The project uses the computer side as a showcase. The right side of the interface will display the materials and progress that players need to collect, divided into two parts: building a floating bed and cultivating seedlings, and displaying photos of the corresponding materials to be collected as clues for players to find. Users can use the "↑", "↓", "←", "→" keys to control the character movement and move the field of view by mouse movement. As shown in Fig. 7, if the player is close to the collection, the system will pop up the operation button, which presses and hold the "E" button to complete the collection, and press and hold the "F" button to complete the task.

4.3 Game Background Story

To make the players have empathy and mobilize their interest in the game, at the beginning of the game, the players will take on the role of aspirants with the vital mission of saving people from the flood. Due to industrial development, the ancient technique of floating garden growing has been forgotten. Still, in the face of increasingly severe flooding, people need to take action to get food in floods. So, players need to learn how to build floating beds, raise seedlings, expand their homes, observe the weather and protect the floating beds from flood damage in floods. The story's background is narrated by the player's memories, taking the flood as an opportunity to guide the player to take action to protect the heritage site. The game background unfolds with pictures and text, as shown in Fig. 6.

Fig. 6. Game story takes place in the background (Generated by authors).

4.4 Game Process

The game is divided into four main tasks: teaching newcomers, building a floating bed independently, planting seedlings, observing the weather, and reinforcing the floating bed. The middle of the game will also trigger the egg plot, which is used to strengthen the theme and render the atmosphere.

As shown in Fig. 7. Task I is to learn the technique of building a floating bed with the help of an old friend, Mirza. Players find the first task notice board and get the details of task one. Then he collects the water gourd and bamboo frame needed to build the floating bed and can create the floating bed after getting enough quantity.

Task 2 is completed in the same way as Task 1, but requires the player to complete it independently.

The third task is to cultivate seedlings. After expanding the floating bed waters, players need to collect seeds and Tema, a floating garden feature nursery tool, to complete the nursery and sow seeds. Seeds need to be purchased at the market, and once the seedlings are finished, they need to be planted on the floating platform and wait for maturity. As shown in Fig. 8, after the planting task is completed, the weather system will be triggered to produce floods and torrential rain as a weather signal to guide players to the weather tower to observe the weather conditions.

Task 4 is to protect the floating bed during flooding. When the weather becomes gloomy, and the current also becomes unusually fast, the player will be guided by the arrow to find the way to the weather tower. On the weather tower, players can observe the current weather warning and real-time weather parameters. When players judge that they need to reinforce the floating bed, they must go back to the planting area to find a partner NPC to strengthen the floating bed together. As shown in Fig. 9, the weather tower player on the snowy mountain will trigger the egg story about the weatherman, telling the story

1. First assignment received

2. Collecting bamboo frame

3. Collecting water hyacinth

4. Build floating beds

Fig. 7. Illustration of Task 1 (Generated by authors).

1. Find the mission notice

2. Buy seeds

3. Collecting Tema and Seeding

4. Planting

Fig. 8. Illustration of Task 3 (Generated by authors).

of the former weatherman who is always concerned about climate change to protect the villagers and the floating garden.

1. The storm is coming

2. Weather observation at the weather station

3. Find help from neighbors

4. Reinforced floating bed

Fig. 9. Illustration of Task 4 (Generated by authors).

5   Discussion

Besides the Floating Gardens Agricultural Heritage Site in Bangladesh, there are many other important agricultural cultural heritage sites in the world, such as the Fuzhou Jasmine Tea Agricultural Heritage Site in China. They have all been affected in one way or another by modernization and industrial development. Preserving and passing on the ancient wisdom of survival and promoting the sustainable development of important agricultural heritage sites can promote agrarian culture and the transmission of traditional farming civilizations, both for the development of local communities and the world. Fortunately, emerging immersive technologies can help to enrich our actions in conserving and promoting cultural heritage sites. This can facilitate the economic value of agro-cultural heritage beyond its agricultural production, bringing added value such as cultural heritage tourism, social awareness, and education.3D modeling techniques and technologies such as virtual reality and augmented reality can overcome the limitations of time and space. This can then be promoted to a broader audience through the metaverse platform, which will provide new opportunities for the development of local communities in heritage sites.

The limitation of this study is the lack of authentic reduction of the floating gar-den agricultural heritage site. Due to the inability to go to the site research and the lack of first-hand data, only partial simulation can be done through photos. If it can be truly restored, it can also provide users with a sense of immersion on top of the game, such as a virtual tour. The current development of cultural and heritage tourism will be influenced by the condition of the heritage sites that remain, and the relationship between the two is interdependent. The development of virtual tours with the help of emerging technologies allows players to play relaxedly. And this will not produce the destruction of excessive tourism, which is an essential direction for future development.

6   Conclusion

This paper explores the creation of experiential games on the Roblox platform, using the floating garden agro-cultural heritage site as a case study. The project publicizes the potential of the floating garden agro-cultural heritage site in addressing crucial global development issues in terms of both climate and food security. The integration of new technologies is the future direction of heritage site conservation. Virtual tourism, experience games, and so on will be potential application directions. This study explores the characteristics of the Floating Gardens Agricultural Heritage Site and the aspects that best reflect its values through secondary research and analysis. It enables agricultural production and food security during floods. The scenario building and plot design allow players to visualize the potential of floating gardens in dealing with the global sea level rise crisis. This study provides a reference for the future development of conservation and innovation of agricultural cultural heritage sites. In the future, more flexible technologies can provide opportunities for sustainable management and diverse applications of agro-cultural heritage sites, so that people have more exciting channels to understand the charm of cultural heritage sites and be willing to put in the effort to initiate conservation actions.

References

1. Globally Important Agricultural Heritage Systems (GIAHS) | Food and Agriculture Organization of the United Nations | Food and Agriculture Organization of the United Nations, https://www.fao.org/giahs/en/. (Accessed 19 Dec 2022)
2. Min, Q., Sun, Y.: The concept, characteristics and conservation requirements of agroculture heritage. Res. Sci. **31**, 914–918 (2009)
3. Altieri, M.A., Koohafkan, P.: Globally Important Ingenious Agricultural Heritage Systems (GIAHS): extent, significance, and implications for development. In: Proceedings of the second international workshop and steering committee meeting for the globally important agricultural heritage systems (GIAHS) project. FAO, Rome, Italy, pp. 7–9 (2004)
4. Zhang, Y., Min, Q., Li, H., He, L., Zhang, C., Yang, L.: A conservation approach of globally important agricultural heritage systems (giahs): improving traditional agricultural patterns and promoting scale-production. Sustainability. **9**, 295 (2017). https://doi.org/10.3390/su9020295
5. Zhang, Y., et al.: Traditional culture as an important power for maintaining agricultural landscapes in cultural heritage sites: A case study of the Hani terraces. J. Cult. Herit. **25**, 170–179 (2017). https://doi.org/10.1016/j.culher.2016.12.002

6. Chen, X., Miao, T., Tang, X., Chen, W., Wang, X.: Digital conservation and visualisation of cultural heritage. Packaging Eng. **43**, 26–37 (2022). https://doi.org/10.19554/j.cnki.1001-3563.2022.20.003

7. Yang, J.: Development and Application of High School Information Technology Educational Game Based on Roblox (2021). https://doi.org/10.27751/d.cnki.gjxkj.2021.000199

8. Anik, S.I., Khan, M.A.S.A.: Climate change adaptation through local knowledge in the north eastern region of Bangladesh. Mitig Adapt Strateg Glob Change. **17**, 879–896 (2012). https://doi.org/10.1007/s11027-011-9350-6

9. Islam, T., Atkins, P.: Indigenous floating cultivation: a sustainable agricultural practice in the wetlands of Bangladesh. Dev. Pract. **17**, 130–136 (2007). https://doi.org/10.1080/096145206 01092733

10. Kabir, K.H., et al.: Furthering climate-smart farming with the introduction of floating agriculture in Bangladeshi wetlands: Successes and limitations of an innovation transfer. J. Environ. Manage. **323**, 116258 (2022). https://doi.org/10.1016/j.jenvman.2022.116258

11. Chowdhury, R.B., Moore, G.A.: Floating agriculture: a potential cleaner production technique for climate change adaptation and sustainable community development in Bangladesh. J. Clean. Prod. **150**, 371–389 (2017). https://doi.org/10.1016/j.jclepro.2015.10.060

12. Téllez, T.R., López, E., Granado, G.L., Pérez, E.A., López, R.M., Guzmán, J.M.S.: The water hyacinth, Eichhornia crassipes: an invasive plant in the Guadiana River Basin (Spain). Aquat. Invasions **3**, 42–53 (2008)

13. Kutty, S.R.M., Malakahmad, A.: Nutrients removal from Municipal Wastewater Treatment Plant Effluent Using, vol. 10 (2009)

14. Bangladesh, M.: Globally Important Agricultural Heritage Systems (GIAHS) Site Proposal: Floating Garden Agricultural Practices in Bangladesh. Government of the People's Republic of Bangladesh, Ministry of Agriculture (2015)

Augmented Reality Technology in Painting Display

Yitong Zhang[1] and Yan Wang[2(✉)]

[1] South China Normal University Academy of Fine Arts,
Guangzhou 510631, People's Republic of China
[2] School of Design, South China University of Technology,
Guangzhou 510006, People's Republic of China
yanw@scut.edu.cn

Abstract. With the development of Internet technology, digital media technology has penetrated more and more into the lives of the masses. The traditional static display methods of art galleries and museums are being replaced by various digital multimedia interactive displays. Among them, augmented reality AR technology Combining reality and virtuality to create an immersive experience combining virtuality and reality has attracted widespread attention. This paper analyzes and introduces the cases of augmented reality display in art venues at home and abroad, and explores the feasibility and diversity of this display method. Although there are still many limitations in the interactive technology, it is believed that with the development of new technologies, it will become the future of painting. Important way of showing.

Keywords: Augmented reality · Interactive experience · Painting display

1 Basic Concepts and Characteristics of Augmented Reality Technology

Augmented reality literally means to strengthen the real world by some means, unlike the completely virtual world that VR presents to viewers, augmented reality technology Augmented Reality (AR) is to superimpose the information processed by the computer with the real scene, presented to the viewer at the same time. This computer-processed information includes real-time positioning, algorithms, and analysis techniques for corresponding images [1].To put it simply, AR technology can superimpose some virtual information in the real world environment, and update the position and angle of the virtual information on the computer device in real time, and superimpose the virtual information on the screen in the real environment and interact with it. Interaction, in order to provide users with richer visual experience and more convenient information acquisition. This multi-dimensional information can be perceived through images and sounds, and even taste, smell, temperature, etc. Users use corresponding equipment with cameras and displays to identify by scanning relevant markers. The "integrated" information images appear on the display, so as to achieve the display effect of "real and virtual", allowing users to obtain an unprecedented sensory experience, that is, enhancing the user's understanding of the real environment. Augmented reality technology can be widely used in military, medical, construction, education, engineering, film and television, entertainment and other fields.

"Augmented reality" was first used by ex-Boeing researcher Tom Caudell in 1990 [2], before that, AR was not clearly separated from VR. The commercial augmented reality experience was first introduced in the entertainment and game business. With the improvement of the computing power of electronic products, the use of augmented reality has become more and more extensive. After 2000, APPs using AR technology emerged as the times require and are widely used in The field of commercial entertainment.

There are currently two general definitions of augmented reality. The first was proposed by Ronald Azuma, a professor at the University of North Carolina in 1997. He believed that augmented reality includes three aspects: information integration of the real world and the virtual world; real-time interactivity; three-dimensional scale Add positioning virtual objects in the space [3]. These three aspects are as follows:

1.1 Fusion of Virtual and Reality

Emphasizing the coexistence of virtual and reality, AR technology does not place users in a completely virtual world, but superimposes computer-generated virtual objects and information into real-world scenes. The fusion of virtual and real is the most important feature of augmented reality technology. It is also the most important difference that distinguishes it from virtual reality. Through augmented reality technology, real scenes and objects can be better combined with computer-generated virtual digital information to achieve the characteristics of virtual and real fusion.

For example, when appreciating traditional easel paintings, viewers can use electronic devices to watch the virtual layers of various information superimposed on the paintings. These virtual layers contain the content related to this work, that is, enhanced It makes it possible for the audience to understand the paintings in multiple directions in a short period of time.

1.2 Real-Time Interaction

Real-time interaction refers to the corresponding instructions issued by the user through the computer, which can generate real-time interaction with the generated digital information, so as to enrich the user experience. With the development of technology, in the exploration of human-computer relationship, in addition to the traditional external device interaction, there are also emerging forms of interaction such as gestures and voice interaction.

1.3 Three-Dimensional Registration

"Registration" (here can also be interpreted as tracking and positioning) refers to the one-to-one correspondence between the computer-generated virtual objects and the real environment, and the user will continue to maintain the correct alignment relationship when moving in the real environment. In the real environment scene, in order to ensure the simulation of virtual digital information, the 3D registration technology is required to ensure real-time and stability, which is also an important index to evaluate the performance of augmented reality technology [4].

Another interpretation of augmented reality is the reality-virtuality continuum (Milgram's reality-virtuality continuum) proposed by Paul Milgram and Fumio Kishino in 1994. They regard the real environment and the virtual environment as two ends of a continuous system, and the one in the middle is called "mixed reality". Among them, the augmented reality (augmented reality) is close to the real environment, and the augmented reality is close to the virtual environment.

2 The Development History of Augmented Reality Technology

Augmented reality technology is a technology that can integrate virtual information generated by computer equipment (two-dimensional, three-dimensional, text, sound, etc.) Glasses, etc.) presents its fused result. The so-called augmented reality is to enhance the information of the real scene, so that users can obtain more information. Corresponding to it is virtual reality technology (referred to as VR technology). Compared with virtual reality technology that can only perceive virtual digital information, augmented reality technology can perceive real world information in addition to digital virtual information. Therefore, it is generally believed that the application of augmented reality technology will be more extensive than that of virtual reality technology.

In the early days, augmented reality technology was mainly used in high-tech fields such as military and aviation due to its high technical difficulty. With the continuous development of technology, the advancement of computer graphics technology and the improvement of related computer computing power, the cost of related hardware equipment has been continuously reduced., augmented reality technology has gradually entered the public life. After Ivan Poupyrev and others developed the open source system ARToolkit25 in 2002, related AR applications gradually blossomed in entertainment, education, art and other fields [5]. After that, more and more academic institutions began to invest in research related to AR technology, which also promoted the application of this technology in the field of life. In 2007, Otis Liarokapis and others developed a multimedia interactive platform based on augmented reality technology, which superimposes corresponding virtual information on the desktop environment, such as pictures, 3D models, text, etc., and can interact with virtual information. In 2012, Google's latest release of Googleglass was also called a milestone event by the industry.

2016 is known as the first year of AR. After years of exploration, the AR industry has ushered in a critical turning point and released unprecedented market forces. In 2019, in addition to Microsoft, Google and other giants that have been deeply involved in the AR field for many years, they are constantly launching iterative products, and many traditional non- AR companies have also begun to launch their own AR -related products. For example, both oppo and vivo released self-developed AR in 2019.

Glasses. In 2021, Zuckerberg announced that he would officially change Facebook 's name to Meta, and "Metaverse" suddenly became a keyword mentioned by high-frequency words. We don't know whether the metaverse is a hype, but there is no doubt that with the rise of the metaverse concept, AR and VR technologies have ushered in a further development climax, and some experts even believe that AR and VR technologies are likely to be released in 2007 as influential as the iPhone.

3 Development Trend of Augmented Reality Technology

AR technology, it has already reached the public. Whether it is education, industry, medicine or entertainment and business, we can all see the presence of AR technology. With the continuous innovation and progress of technology, AR plays an important role and is popularized in more and more fields. The application of AR technology in the field of education is a concept that has emerged in recent years. Due to some restrictions, it has not been widely used in the field of daily teaching. But we can see that in the future, there will be a wide range of applications. In September 2018, the Ministry of Education issued the "Opinions on the Implementation of the Excellent Teacher Training Program 2.0 ", pointing out that it is necessary to use information technology to reform teaching, and use VR, AR and other technologies to build a number of high-quality curriculum education resources [6].

In addition to course education, there are many offline education combined with AR technology. For example, most popular science museums at home and abroad have set up relevant exhibition areas, and by adding interactivity with the audience to AR technology, it plays a role of entertaining and teaching. In addition, there are AR picture books, AR picture books and other application methods to improve children's reading interest.

AR technology in the industrial field has gone through a period of time, from the initial application in the military and aviation fields to the application in civilian industry. AR can not only carry out virtual simulation design, but also carry out relevant skills training and learning for workers, which not only reduces training costs, but also plays a very good role in promoting the effect and efficiency of training and learning. It can also perform functions such as expert guidance and remote assistance to reduce enterprise costs.

Entertainment: When talking about the application of AR in the field of game entertainment, we have to talk about the classic AR game " Pokemon Go ". As the first AR interactive game, it is this game that brings AR into the world. The vision of the public, and provide a gameplay idea for the subsequent AR games. Today's AR games are also emerging in endlessly. There is no doubt that in terms of game experience, the immersive interactive experience brought by AR games is beyond the reach of ordinary games. In addition to AR virtual games, there are also real-life games such as AR script killing and AR secret room escape. The use of AR technology greatly improves the immersion of the game.

In addition, AR has also been widely used in the home furnishing field, such as the well-known IKEA dedicated software. By scanning the home environment with a mobile phone, furniture sold in stores can appear, and customers can place their homes in virtual spaces to help them better choose products suitable for their home. There are also trial fitting services in clothing stores, as well as a self-timer processor that is popular among young people and can synthesize changes in real time.

The cases mentioned above from the three aspects of education, industry and entertainment are only a small part of the many AR applications, but we can know from a glimpse that AR technology will be widely used now and in the future. All aspects of the game will be affected by AR technology, and the concept of the metaverse will also become a reality in the future with the innovation and development of technology.

4 Technical Requirements for Implementing Augmented Reality

Order to achieve AR effects, auxiliary equipment is an indispensable condition for AR technology at this stage. The most important thing is to recognize specific targets. The technical principles include optical tracking, mechanical tracking, content sensor tracking, ultrasonic tracking and magnetic tracking., and the most common is optical tracing [7].

For example, the scanning function of mobile devices we use can realize location tracking, and mobile phones and tablets are also the mainstream carriers of AR applications that are more commonly used at present. However, the image-triggered mode is easily affected by the environment and temperature, and has certain requirements for the GPS function of the smart device, so its application will be limited. In order to solve this problem, the orientation and the acceleration sensor of the device are often combined to further improve the accuracy of the displayed position. AR that can be activated by tapping the space recognition screen. Since the camera and sensors can recognize space, it is possible to display AR content with a size and depth that matches the real world. This technology is usually used in the configuration simulation of furniture and home appliances, and is also widely used in augmented reality displays in museums and art galleries.

5 The Application of Augmented Reality Technology in Painting Display

AR applications are constantly innovating, and its unique interactive features have been favored by museums and art galleries. In recent years, exhibitions with AR functions have entered the audience's field of vision, and with the increase in promotion, the technical effects are also constantly improving. An exhibition method that the audience loves to see. Many artists are also trying this new technology, combining their artistic creation with AR technology to create more connotative works of art that can bring a stronger impression to the audience.

Art exhibitions that incorporate AR technology are mainly divided into two exhibition modes: art exhibitions that use AR technology to recreate traditional classic artworks and art exhibitions that use AR technology to create new creations [8]. Use AR technology to recreate traditional classic works of art, that is, to scan classic works of art through AR, so that it can add dynamics, sounds, text, etc. to the original picture, in this way to break through the traditional static plane display method, in While bringing a novel visual experience to the audience, it also narrows the distance between these classic works of art and the audience [9].

5.1 Display of Augmented Reality Paintings Made on the Basis of Existing Paintings

Augmented reality technology is usually built on a technical platform in the application of painting exhibitions. Many foreign art museums use the Spark AR platform to present special effects. Spark AR is an AR tool developed by Facebook in 2017. Users use The camera in the Facebook APP has a dedicated environment to create AR special effects for works, and some art galleries and technology companies jointly develop software to assist in the production of augmented reality effects. An excellent example of this technique is shown below:

1. Art Gallery of Ontario, Toronto, Canada

Art Gallery of Ontario, an art gallery located in Toronto, Canada, collaborated with artist Alex Mayhew in 2017 to hold an exhibition called R eBink. Artist Alex Mayhew selected multiple works of art from the museum's collection for AR re-creation. Viewers can interact with the works through mobile phones or tablets. These classic paintings have changed their classic shapes on the mobile devices of the audience, presenting the normal life of contemporary people. In front of the paintings depicting chemical plants, figures in protective clothing appeared. The legendary goddess Marchesa Luisa Casat held up her mobile phone to communicate with the audience. Take a selfie.

2. London Museum of Modern Art (Tate Modern)

Tate Britain used the Facebook APP to select eight works of art in the collection. These works of art have unusual or little-known stories. After rearranging these paintings, AR special effects were created. Camera scanning activates Spark AR, and a new space for viewing artworks can be obtained within the software. Through AR technology, the story behind the painting can be re-presented in the virtual space.

3. Mauritshuis Museum, Netherlands

To commemorate the 350th anniversary of the death of Dutch painter Rembrandt, Mauritshuis Museum in the Netherlands and Capitola, a Dutch design agency, developed an APP called "Rembrandt Reality". In the painting "Anatomy Lesson of Dr. Nicholas Tour", come to the scene and watch the group of surgeons complete the anatomy lesson. In order to achieve the most authentic state of experience, the art museum invited actors to play the roles in the scene, and completely restored the costumes, layout, and light in the painting. After several scans and modeling, this 360-degree dissection room space was born. "This is a new way of viewing art, and it brings the way of viewing art into the future." Emilie Gordenker, curator of Mauritshuis Museum, commented on this [10].

4. Isabella Stewart Gardner, USA Museum " Hacking the Heist " Exhibition

The Isabella Stewart Gardner Art Museum located in Boston, USA is a large family collection art museum. In 1990, due to a theft, 13 works were lost, worth 500 million US dollars, becoming the most stolen art museum in the world. In order to pay tribute to the lost paintings and condemn the thieves, the art museum has kept the location where the original paintings were displayed vacant. Cuseum, a company dedicated to the digital technology of art museums, independently developed an APP with AR effects. Using this software, the camera is aimed at the frame of the stolen painting, and the stolen painting will appear on the display screen.

5.2 Creative Painting Display Using AR Technology

AR re-creation of classic works of art, there are also endless works created using AR technology. AR technology stimulates the imagination of artists to the greatest extent, breaks through the tradition, and creates one after another eye-catching works of art. AR technology also allows works of art to not only appear in art galleries, AR allows works of art to enter the streets and squares, and participate more in life scenes closely related to people.

1. Apple and the New Museum's [ar]t project

2019 Apple and the New Museum in the United States Co-launched a series of outdoor AR art exhibitions, and the AR works of seven artists including Nick Cave were released in six major cities around the world, including London and New York, and gained a wide range of influence [11]. The audience came to the Apple Store in the designated six cities, and by scanning the mobile phone in the store, they could see the artistic works created by the artist presented in the virtual space with the real-time status of the Apple Store as the background, and some of the works of the artists needed to be designated outdoors. Discovered on the Central Park hiking trails.

This art project has attracted a lot of attention due to the dual effects of Apple and well-known artists, but there are also comments that the fit between the virtual work and the outdoor real scene is not high, and participants need to constantly adjust the angle of the mobile phone to suit the real scene. It is pointed out that the GPS positioning technology of AR technology in the natural environment needs to be improved.

2. "Expanded Holiday" by KAWS and ACUTE ART in the UK

2020, the street trend artist KAWS and the British ACUTE ART studio jointly created the " Expanded Holiday " AR virtual exhibition, which caused quite a stir in the art world. This public art exhibition displays the floating COMPANION dolls in the public space of twelve cities in the world in a virtual form. The audience can use the APP of ACUTE ART studio, and then they can choose the designated location in these twelve cities. The location sees the COMPANION doll, which is very similar to the game of poketomosita. At the same time, the platform also introduces the form of paid purchase and rental. After purchasing the virtual doll, buyers can place COMPANION anywhere they want. At the same time You can also use social media to share, and the rental version is a paid short-term rental with a smaller-sized doll. During the rental period, you can place the virtual doll in any space you like, and take photos to share.

3. Louis Vuitton and Yayoi Kusama co-brand in 2023

In early 2023, luxury brands After Louis Vuitton and Japanese artist Yayoi Kusama cooperated for the first time in 2006, they teamed up again to create a joint series of products with polka dot elements. What is different from the past is that this product display uses a lot of technological means, especially a The AR applet allows artists to attract audiences into the AR experience. By taking a selfie with Yayoi Kusama's pumpkin hat and posting it online, it not only satisfies the entertainment psychology of the audience, but also promotes the business.

5.3 Advantages of Augmented Reality Technology Applied to Painting Display

About appreciating paintings that the average time people spend on appreciating the "Mona Lisa" will not exceed 15 s. Some scholars have found through a study of the audience of an art museum in Germany that those who have just finished watching the exhibition Among the audience, a quarter can't remember the works and creators they have seen at all, and more than half of them can remember only 4 or even fewer paintings [12]. It can be seen that if a painting wants to leave a deep impression on the audience during the display process, the time spent in front of the painting is the key. The emergence of AR technology provides a variety of choices for the audience to stay in front of the painting for a longer time. Its unique interactive function has a rich expansion level, which has changed the monotonous text description form in the past. Based on the original display Various levels of information can be added, such as short videos, animations, music, etc., and there are more attractive secondary creations for the displayed works. Attention plays a key role. At the same time, augmented reality technology not only allows the audience to stop and stay, but also reproduces the history and culture behind the work. Audiences of different ages can be inspired here. A new relationship with the audience.

Augmented reality technology is involved in the display of paintings and artworks, the situation that artworks were originally limited to professional exhibition spaces such as art galleries and galleries has begun to change. We have seen more and more commercial organizations begin to intervene in it, such as Apple and the New Museum. The urban public art project AR[T] Walk is planned, and the location of art appreciation is transformed into an Apple retail store in the city. This cooperation between art museums and technology companies has truly completed the integration of art and technology. The art museum also provides Apple users with online AR teaching and workshop courses, which expands the boundaries of art and perfectly integrates art projects with commercial projects. In the process of participation, the audience changes from the position of the viewer to the collector and then in the Participating in the creation of public art in the virtual space has realized multiple transformations of one's own roles, which is undoubtedly full of temptation for the younger generation growing up in the Internet age.

6 Epilogue

From the above, we can see that the participation of augmented reality technology in painting display has become an inevitable trend. The multi-dimensional design and interpretation of exhibits through digital AR technology creates a multi-sensory experience for the audience, thus expanding the time and space of exhibits. The above dimension brings a richer viewing experience to the audience. At the same time, artists will also create more works that incorporate AR technology, and even use AR to realize the role exchange between the artist and the audience, bringing about a revolution in the way paintings are displayed.

There are still some problems in the current way of displaying augmented reality paintings. For example, it needs to use software and hardware such as APP and mobile phone to realize interaction. It is not friendly to some people who are not good at using these electronic tools. In addition, there will be certain identification marks. Unclear, unclear intentions and other inconveniences in use, and it is easy to fall into a situation of homogeneity in the production of content. When the novelty dissipates, is it still attractive enough? In addition, there may be issues related to intellectual property rights and privacy. There are also those who hold opposing opinions that modern technology should not be forcibly added to painting art. How to develop and utilize AR technology more effectively is a challenge that designers will face.

Acknowledgements. This research is supported by "Quality Engineering" of Guangdong Province in 2019: Open Online Course-pulp Plastic Arts (project approval number x2sj/C2170110).

References

1. Rekimoto, J.: Future prospects of augmented reality technology. Video Inform. Media **66**(12), 1048–1053 (2012)
2. Lee, K.: Augmented Reality in Education and Training. TechTrends **56**(2): 13–21 (2012). ISSN 8756 -3894.doi:https://doi.org/10.1007/s11528-012-0559-3
3. Azuma, R.: A Survey of Augmented Reality (Presence: Teleoperators and Virtual Environments, pp. 355–385 (August 1997)
4. Wikipedia Editor. Augmented Reality [G/OL]. Wikipedia, (2022) (20220306) (6 March 2022)
5. Wang, G., Li, J., Yang, L.: Design and implementation of a digital sand table based on augmented reality technology. Gansu Sci. Technol. (2017)
6. Zhou, C.: Research on the design method of museum digital visual representation under the background of AR technology. Wuhan University of Technology (2019)
7. [Young Design Shop] Augmented Reality AR (2 Nov 2022). https://mp.weixin.qq.com/
8. Okada, N., Imura, J., Narumi, T., Tanikawa, T., Hirose, M.: Manseibashi reminiscent window: on-site ar exhibition system using mobile devices. In: Streitz, N., Markopoulos, P. (eds.) DAPI 2015. LNCS, vol. 9189, pp. 349–361. Springer, Cham (2015). https://doi.org/10.1007/978-3-319-20804-6_32
9. Tie, Z., Zhu, X.: Mixed reality design and realization of cultural heritage protection. School Art Design, Shanghai Univ. Eng. Technol. (2018)
10. [Philo Art] Before KAWS, these art museums had already started AR experiments, https://mp.weixin.qq.com/s/XGOLoxPjXS97cTEh6-Qagw [(20 April 2020)
11. Kitamura, K.: Case study of digital exhibition of japanese classical writings and drawings based on ar technology. 2In: 017 International Conference on Culture and Computing (Culture and Computing), pp.125–126 (2017). https://doi.org/10.1109/Culture.and.Computing.2017.43
12. [WenhuiDaily Whb.cn] Mona Lisa can only retain the audience for 15 seconds (10 May 2017). https://www.whb.cn/zhuzhan/yishu/20170510/91503.html2017-05-10 06:05:35 Author: Fan Xin

DUXU for Health and Wellbeing

Using the TURF Framework to Design an Enhanced Dosimetry Quality Assurance Checklist in an Academic Medical Center

Karthik Adapa[1,2(✉)] ⓘ, Gregg Tracton[2], Prithima Mosaly[3], Fei Yu[4] ⓘ,
Ross McGurk[2], Carlton Moore[5], John Dooley[2], Shiva Das[2], and Lukasz Mazur[1,2,3]

[1] Carolina Health Informatics Program, University of North Carolina, Chapel Hill, NC, USA
karthikk@live.unc.edu
[2] Department of Radiation Oncology, University of North Carolina, Chapel Hill, NC, USA
[3] Ben Allegretti Consulting, Inc., Stafford, VA, USA
[4] School of Information and Library Science, University of North Carolina, Chapel Hill, NC, USA
[5] Department of Medicine, School of Medicine, University of North Carolina, Chapel Hill, NC, USA

Abstract. Academic radiation oncology centers have a long history of developing in-house quality assurance (QA) checklists to promote patient safety. These checklists are designed without utilizing formal human-computer interaction methods and are deployed without robust usability evaluation. We applied the Task, User, Representation, and Function (TURF) framework to identify design changes to a dosimetry QA checklist currently deployed in our institution. We found that the TURF framework provided great insights to improve the usability of QA checklists.

Keywords: Quality assurance · Checklist · Radiation oncology

1 Introduction

Radiation therapy (RT) plays an important role in the curative and palliative management of many types of cancer. In the US, ~ 600,000 people receive RT annually [1] Errors in RT occur in 1–5% of patients, with harm occurring in 1 of 1,000–10,000 patients annually [2]. The predominant approach to minimizing errors is to perform well-established quality assurance (QA) processes such as pretreatment dosimetry and physics QA processes between treatment planning and delivery [3]. However, there are inter and intra-institutional variations in how these QA processes are performed, and checklists have been promoted by radiation oncology professional organizations such as the American Society of Radiation Oncology and the American Association of Physics in Medicine to facilitate standardization [4].

Multiple academic institutions have designed, developed, and implemented QA checklists and typically use in-house QA checklists to optimize cognitive workload and reduce human errors [5]. However, these QA checklists are often implemented in

© The Author(s), under exclusive license to Springer Nature Switzerland AG 2023
A. Marcus et al. (Eds.): HCII 2023, LNCS 14034, pp. 239–254, 2023.
https://doi.org/10.1007/978-3-031-35705-3_18

clinical settings without formal human-computer interaction (HCI) and human factors (HF) engineering evaluations.[6] In our previous study, we reported that our institutional dosimetry QA checklist has suboptimal usability and meets only 3 out of 9 recommended HCI standards [7]. The HCI field offers alternative approaches to improve QA checklists' usability, optimize users' cognitive workload, improve performance, and improve care coordination [8]. In a previous study, we used the human-centered participatory co-design process to design enhanced DQC [8].

2 Theoretical Framework

TURF stands for task, user, representation, and function, and these four components are used to evaluate the usability of an EHR system. The TURF framework is a human and work-centered design methodology that has been widely used to evaluate the usability of existing EHRs and also for redesigning EHRs for better usability [9]. Thus, the TURF framework guides the evaluation of the current DQC and the redesign of the enhanced ADC. Per the TURF framework, the steps for redesigning enhanced DQC are:

2.1 User Analysis

User analysis provides user information required to conduct function, representation, and task analyses. Analysis of users (dosimetrists/physicists) involves identifying their attributes such as technology readiness, motivation for change, computer expertise, understanding of QA procedures, and work experience to ensure that the interface design provides the best match to the user's characteristics [9, 10].

2.2 Function Analysis

The purpose of function analysis is to help identify the critical functions in the QA checklist without which the checklist will fail. The interface's functionality is analyzed by categorizing user interface widgets as objects (an interface widget that cannot cause another action or trigger an event) or operations (a widget that can cause another action to occur) [9, 10]. Operations are further classified as either overhead or domain operations. Overhead operations are not associated with the work domain, such as a "Next" button to move to a subsequent screen or window. Domain operations are necessary for the users to complete their work, like checkboxes to select symptoms [11]. The goal of functional analysis is to identify and eliminate the unwanted and unused processes/QA items in the current DQC that are considered overhead and to remove them from the checklist. Functions fall into three categories: a) functions that system implements (Designer model) b) functions that users want (User model) c) functions that get used to carry out the tasks to accomplish the goal (Activity model). The usefulness of the redesigned checklist is directly proportional to the overlapping regions of these three models. The discrepancies of functions across the three models shall be analyzed during function analysis as they offer opportunities for design improvement of enhanced DQC.

2.3 Task Analysis

Task analysis is a standard process in which a skill, movement, or cognitive process is broken into sub-tasks that a system operator must complete to accomplish the system's high-level goals [12]. To redesign a new QA checklist, it is important to evaluate individual QA tasks and task analysis facilitates the identification of sub-components of a task which can then be evaluated or modified independently [12]. Tasks that dosimetrists and physicists perform during pre-treatment dosimetry checks are cognitively challenging tasks, and therefore, we will conduct a cognitive task analysis (CTA). The CTA aims to identify the hidden and ineffective strategies that dosimetrists and physicists use and tasks that induce high cognitive demand. We will use the methodology suggested by Knisely et al. [13] as it integrates standard terminology from existing taxonomies for task classification to describe the expected operator CWL during task performance. For instance, this methodology uses Bloom's taxonomy of the cognitive domain [14] and Harrow's taxonomy of the psychomotor domain [15]. Bloom's taxonomy is a six-tiered model for the classification of cognitive skills, where each tier corresponds to increased cognitive complexity, thus providing a structure to identify tasks of increasing workload. Similarly, Harrow's taxonomy is a six-tiered model for the classification of psychomotor skills. The major advantage of this methodology is that it uses both these taxonomy classifications to identify and predict the workload experienced by operators during cognitive tasks. Bloom's taxonomy primarily addresses non-observable actions, starting at the lowest level of cognitive function in memory-based tasks (Knowledge). As the levels increase, the conscious control required to execute the task also increases, with each higher level composed of the lower-level tasks Table 1. Meanwhile, Harrow's taxonomy focuses primarily on observable tasks, moving from lower levels of complexity (Reflexive Movements) to higher levels (Non-Discursive Communication). Harrow's taxonomy also considers non-observable sensory tasks (Perceptual Abilities) Table 2. Thus, by combining Bloom's and Harrow's taxonomy, we can provide a comprehensive categorization of QA tasks that can be used to understand how cognitive workload and complexity are represented in a series of actions. Previous studies have used these taxonomies in conjunction with task analysis [16, 17].

To operationalize this, the procedure starts by identifying the overarching goal of each QA check on pre-MD and post-MD. For each QA check, the tasks performed by dosimetrists/physicists on the treatment planning system (RayStation), electronic health record (MOSAIQ), and the QA checklist will be presented using hierarchical task analysis format Table 3 and decomposed into cognitive tasks using Bloom's and Harrow's taxonomy as a guide.

2.4 Representational Analysis

In this method, the goal is to ensure that data is presented most effectively. Internal representations (such as propositions, schemas, mental images, etc.) are replaced by external representations (such as physical symbols, external rules, etc.), and visual cues that users find more intuitive and reduce cognitive workload are focused upon.

Heuristic evaluation. Heuristic evaluation is a technique to promptly identify a product's major usability problems at a reasonable cost. This provides an additional cross-check of the TURF evaluation and serves as the baseline for comparing improvement

Table 1. Bloom's Taxonomy listed in order of increasing cognitive complexity.

Taxonomy Level	Description	Example Verbs
1. Knowledge	Recall of specific facts or ideas	remember, define, list, memorize
2. Comprehension	Understanding and interpreting facts and ideas	classify, explain, discuss, identify
3. Application	The use of prior knowledge in novel situations	execute, solve, operate, respond
4. Analysis	Decomposing a system into its composite parts and examining those parts	compare, associate, contrast, test
5. Synthesis	Combining independent elements to form a new system	assemble, design, integrate, produce
6. Evaluation	Judging the value of a system based on evidence and certain criteria	judge, appraise, defend, critique

Table 2. Harrow's Taxonomy listed in order of increasing psychomotor complexity.

Taxonomy Level	Description	Example Verbs
1. Reflexive Movements	Involuntary movements evoked in response to some stimuli	flex, extend, stretch, react
2. Fundamental Movements	Basic movement patterns which build on reflexive movements	reach, grasp, walk, jump, crawl
3. Perceptual Abilities	Ability to receive information about oneself and the world via one of several sensory systems (vision, hearing, etc.)	sense, perceive, hear, see, feel
4. Physical Abilities	The functional characteristics of the body which govern the efficiency of skills in the psychomotor domain	exert endurance, exert strength, exert flexibility
5. Skilled Movements	Complex movement skills which require learning	dance, drive, juggle
6. Non-Discursive Communication	Learned movements and gestures used for communication	express, posture, gesture

in the enhanced interface [18]. Per this framework, Nielsen's ten heuristics [19] and Schneiderman's eight golden rules [20] have been combined to form fourteen principles customized to HIT and have also been applied in different healthcare settings. The fourteen principles are as follows: consistency, visibility, match, minimalist, memory, feedback, flexibility, message, error, closure, undo, language, control, and documentation. Three evaluators independently evaluated the redesigned enhanced DQC and separated

Table 3. Cognitive Task Analysis format

Procedural task	Information System (MOSAIQ/ RayStation / QA checklist)			
Name of task	Cognitive task level 1	Cognitive task level 2	Cognitive task level 3	Taxonomy classification (Bloom/Harrow)

the results into a list of violations. Each evaluator independently rated the violation for its severity on a scale of 0 to 4 (0 = no usability problem, 1 = cosmetic problem only, need not be fixed unless extra time is available; 2 = minor usability problem, fixing should be given low priority; 3 = major usability problem, important to fix and should be given priority; 4 = usability catastrophe, imperative to fix before the product can be released) and ratings were then averaged [21].

Thus, the objectives of this study are:

1. To apply the Task, User, Representation, and Function (TURF) framework to design the enhanced DQC.
2. To identify the design changes to the current DQC in an academic radiation oncology clinic and develop a user-focused functional prototype of an enhanced DQC

3   Methods

3.1   Participants

Dosimetrists are the primary users of the DQC. Therefore, five dosimetrists working in the department of radiation oncology at an academic medical center were invited for this study. Physicists are the secondary users of the DQC as they use DQC to review the work of the dosimetrists. Both dosimetrists and physicists were actively recruited for this study. Dosimetrists are involved in designing a treatment plan specifically for each patient. They carefully select the treatment technique, radiation beam orientations, beam aperture shapes, and beam weights to deliver a therapeutic radiation dose to the tumor while sparing healthy tissues and organs to the best extent possible.

3.2   Study Settings

We conducted the study in a radiation oncology clinic to account for interruptions and collaborations between interdisciplinary care team members. We obtained approval from the Institutional Review Board at the University of North Carolina for this study.

3.3   Pre-treatment QA Process

In radiation oncology, QA processes are critical in minimizing errors in treatment planning before the delivery of radiation to patients. Dosimetrists perform the following QA tasks in the pre-treatment QA process, which includes a varying number of checks:

- *Pre-planning task (4 QA checks)*: Dosimetrist investigates electronic medical records to assess the physician's intent and planning note.

- *Planning task (5 QA checks):* During designing a radiation therapy (RT) plan, dosimetrists check isocenters (ISO) and verify parameters in plan design.
- *Pre-MD approval task (3 QA checks):* Before submitting a plan for approval to physicians, dosimetrists perform additional checks such as set up beams.
- *Post-MD approval task (21 QA checks):* After the physician's approval, dosimetrists perform most of the checks along with crosschecking data from the treatment planning system and record and verify systems.

3.4 Current DQC

We have described the design features and components of the current DQC in our previous publication [8]. This work is an extension of our previous research efforts [7, 8].

3.5 Data Collection

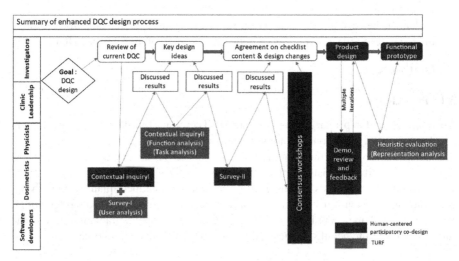

Fig. 1. Enhanced DQC co-design process

The key stakeholders involved in the DQC design process of this study were: (1) dosimetrists (n = 5) as the primary users of the DQC (2) physicists (n = 9) who review the plan designed by dosimetrists to improve the safety and quality of the plan as secondary users of DQC (3) the design team (including two human factors experts and an experienced software developer), (4) clinic leadership which oversaw the project management (including the chair of the physics division), (5) experienced software developers (n = 2) involved in designing and developing enhanced DQC. The design process involved methods from both human-centered participatory co-design and TURF but in this work, we will describe only methods from TURF. The goal was to redesign the enhanced DQC by involving all key stakeholders. We also reviewed the checklist content and key design ideas in the current DQC and approached to improve the usability and effectiveness of DQC further. We will use methods from Fig. 1 to describe the enhanced DQC co-design and data collection efforts.

User Analysis. We administered online a 10-item validated Technology Readiness Index (TRI) 2.0 scale (5-point scale with 1 for strongly agree and 5 for strongly agree) to classify dosimetrists and physicists by their propensity to adopt or embrace technology at home and work. Permission was sought by the authors to administer this copyrighted scale for research purposes (https://rockresearch.com/techqual/). [22].

Contextual Inquiry. We conducted contextual inquiries with dosimetrists and physicists to perform functional and cognitive task analyses.

Function Analysis. As recommended by TURF, we used contextual inquiries to assess the desired functionality and examine them against implemented and used functions. Contextual interviews were conducted with dosimetrists (n = 5) and physicists (n = 4) to integrate the user model (information regarding functions that dosimetrists want in the enhanced DQC), activity model (functions in current DQC that are used during pre-treatment QA check), and designer model (functions that are available in current DQC).

After observations, we used a semi-structured interview for the study participants to assess the desired functionality (and weigh them against implemented and used functions in the current DQC). During the interview, participants were asked about the current DQC as well as what functionalities they wanted to see implemented in the enhanced DQC. They were specifically asked about ways in which they conducted QA checks and how they used information in Mosaiq and RayStation to complete the pre-treatment QA process. A careful capture of data from participants proved useful in listing their problems, expectations, and recommendations for the enhanced DQC.

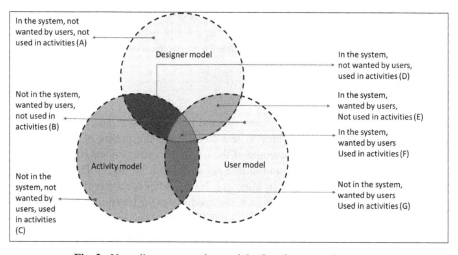

Fig. 2. Venn diagram to understand the function saturation metrics

We calculated two function saturation metrics previously used in other studies using the TURF framework to assess the usefulness of enhanced and current DQC. [43, 45] These metrics provide a quantitative assessment of the overlap portions of implemented functions in the current DQC (Designer model) that the users want in enhanced DQC (User model) and which were used by users to accomplish QA tasks (Activity model).

Within-Model Domain Function Saturation: This metric quantifies the functions covered by the implementation of the current DQC and is computed as the ratio of domain functions to total functions in the designer model. This is calculated as the sum of number of functions in D, E, and F divided by the sum of the number of functions in the regions of A, D, E, and F.

Across-Model Domain Function Saturation: This metric is computed as the ratio of domain functions in the designer model to the domain functions in all three models (designer, user, and activity). It is calculated as the sum of the numerators in the regions of A, D, E, and F divided by the count of all domain functions in all three models Fig. 2.

Task Analysis. In the TURF framework, task analysis aims to develop a comprehensive understanding of the tasks performed by the dosimetrists during pre-treatment dosimetry checks. We performed CTA as described in 2.3. It was, therefore, important to understand how dosimetrists perform tasks in QA checklists, Ray Station and Mosaiq. Participants were observed as they performed QA checks using the current DQC. To further improve and redesign the enhanced DQC, during interviews, participants were asked to explain the kind of information they would like to see from Mosaiq and RS for each QA check.

Heuristic Evaluation. In addition to user comments and reviews, three independent evaluators conducted a heuristic evaluation of the enhanced DQC prototype. Evaluators used a validated heuristic evaluation checklist that includes Nielsen's ten usability heuristics and Schneiderman's golden rules [23].

Functional Prototype. In this phase, the development team used agile software development methods to release small functional pieces of software. Subsequently, a user-focused functional prototype (v3.3) was built as a script using Python and JavaScript, which included all the key design changes that the participants suggested during TURF.

3.6 Data Analysis

User Analysis. Responses from dosimetrists and physicists were analyzed as distinct groups. We used the Mann-Whitney U test to examine the means of TRI between dosimetrists and physicists. The average of the five positive statements (from the Optimism and Innovativeness scale and the five negative items (from the Discomfort and Insecurity scales) were computed in Microsoft Excel. After reversing the mean of the negative items by subtracting them from 6, the average for the two dimensions (positive and negative) was calculated to calculate a total TRI score. The lowest possible score is 1.0 and the highest is 5.0 with a higher score indicating higher techno-readiness.

Contextual Inquiry Analysis (Functional and Task Analysis). The observation notes and interview transcripts were coded and analyzed using NVivo 11 plus. Similarly, notes written by observers were used for CTA. The CTA for each QA task was verified with multiple users to confirm the decomposition of each QA task.

Heuristic Analysis. We assessed the average ratings for evaluators for a violation based on a severity scale of 1 to 4 (1 = cosmetic; 2 = minor; 3 = major; 4 = catastrophic) for enhanced and current DQC.

4 Results

4.1 User Analysis

4 dosimetrists (n = 5, 80% participation rate) and 6 physicists (n = 10, 60% participation rate) responded to the survey. Mann-Whitney U test indicates that the mean technology readiness score of physicists (mean = 4.25, SD = 0.55) is statistically significantly higher than the mean technology readiness score of dosimetrists (2.25, SD = 0.75; p-value < 0.05).

4.2 Function Analysis

After observing all participants, analyzing their responses to interview questions, and filtering the overhead functions, 40 distinct functions were identified Fig. 3 shows the function coverage. The current DQC implemented 16 out of 19 domain model functions, resulting in 84% coverage for within-model function saturation. The across-model saturation was 48%, wherein the current DQC implemented 19 out of 40 identified functions.

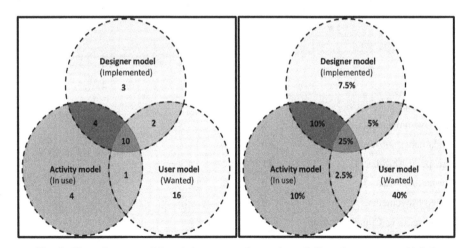

Fig. 3. Venn diagrams of function coverage (in numbers (left) and percentages (right))

4.3 Task Analysis

We analyzed representative and key QA tasks performed pre-MD and post-MD. Since the pre-plan and in-plan tabs of the enhanced DQC were largely identical to the dosCheckv2 component of the current DQC, tasks in those pre-treatment QA processes were not analyzed. Firstly, the sub-tasks for each QA check in pre-and post- MD were analyzed on Mosaiq, RayStation, and QA checklist. The detailed CTA for pre-MD QA tasks is available in Appendix I. Each procedural task has been decomposed into cognitive task levels in Mosaiq, RayStation, and the QA checklist and the relevant taxonomy (Bloom/Harrow) have been presented.

When users perform tasks in Mosaiq and RayStation, both in pre-MD and post-MD, most of the tasks are at the knowledge level of cognitive complexity. Also, only a limited number of tasks in both pre-MD and post-MD have higher order cognitive complexity - comprehension (6), application (3), analysis (4) and synthesis (1). However, in the QA checklist, tasks are primarily in the higher form of cognitive complexity – synthesis and evaluation. Regarding psychomotor complexity, all tasks involve perceptual abilities which are of middle-level psychomotor complexity. Tables 4 and 5 provide a high-level overview of the cognitive complexity and psychomotor complexity of QA tasks in pre-MD and post-MD.

Table 4. Taxonomy level analysis of pre-MD QA tasks

Taxonomy level	MOSAIQ	RayStation	QA checklist
Cognitive complexity			
Knowledge	**10**	**5**	
Comprehension	4	2	
Application	2		
Analysis	2		
Synthesis	2		3
Evaluation	0		4
Psychomotor complexity			
Reflexive movements	0		
Fundamental movements	0		
Perceptual Abilities	21	5	
Physical Abilities	0		
Skilled Movements	0		
Non-Discursive Communication	0		

Table 5. Taxonomy level analysis of post-MD tasks

Taxonomy level	MOSAIQ	RayStation	QA checklist
Cognitive complexity			
Knowledge	**13**	**3**	
Comprehension	0		
Application	1		
Analysis	2		
Synthesis	0		2
Evaluation	0		2
Psychomotor complexity			
Reflexive movements	0		
Fundamental movements	0		
Perceptual Abilities	20	7	
Physical Abilities	0		
Skilled Movements	0		
Non-Discursive Communication	0		

4.4 Heuristic Evaluation

The average severity of problems related to each of the heuristic principles is shown in Fig. 4.

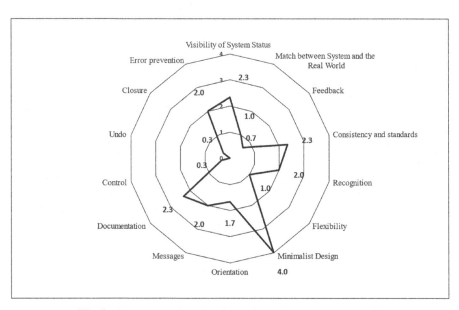

Fig. 4. Average severity of problems identified for each heuristic.

5 Discussion

This study demonstrates that TURF can be used to design an enhanced DQC. This involved user analysis, function analysis, task analysis, heuristic evaluation, and a developed functional prototype of enhanced DQC. The function analysis and CTA have added further insights for designing enhanced DQC.

This study uses methods from TURF theoretical framework for a comprehensive understanding of the users, their context, their preferences, the tasks they perform, the currently implemented, and the functions they would like to see in the enhanced DQC. To our best knowledge, this is the first study that uses TURF framework to redesign an enhanced version of DQC. These methods are generalizable and may be used by other radiation oncology medical centers to redesign suboptimal HIT tools.

A significant contribution of this study is how we used task analysis to help us understand information necessary for dosimetrists to conduct QA checks comprehensively. CTA demonstrated that when users perform tasks in Mosaiq and RayStation, they memorize this information which explains the high knowledge level of cognitive complexity in both pre-MD and post-MD. Further, users synthesize and evaluate this memorized information, before taking an appropriate decision on the QA checklist. This explains why the cognitive complexity is of higher order in QA checklist in the form of synthesis and evaluation while it is of lower cognitive complexity level (knowledge) in Mosaiq and RayStation. This has important design implications for the enhanced DQC. Dosimetrists and physicists can effectively synthesize and evaluate only when the relevant information from Mosaiq and RayStation is provided to check against each QA check. CTA also provides insights into the nature and kind of information that dosimetrists/physicists would like to see for each QA check. Thus, providing information from both Mosaiq and RayStation, an important design feature of the enhanced DQC was further augmented by the findings from CTA.

Function analysis metrics provide insight into the usefulness of the current DQC and also offer insight into additional functionalities that users want in the enhanced DQC. Our study results are comparable with previous studies that suggest that 80–95% coverage for within-model function saturation and 20–30% across-model saturation indicate better function coverage or usefulness of an interface.[43,45] The function analysis metrics of the current DQC meet both the requirements and have higher across-model saturation (48%). This also provides evidentiary justification to utilize the key design elements of the current DQC and to develop the enhanced DQC after including all the critical functions available in the current DQC.

This study has several limitations. First, this study is based on participants from a single academic medical center. Second, there are inter-institutional differences in how QA processes and checks are performed. Third, this checklist has only undergone heuristic evaluation and its integration into the clinical environment would require comprehensive testing. Third, we have not evaluated the checklist in the clinical environment though we gathered feedback from multiple stakeholders throughout the design process.

6 Conclusion

Improving the usability of a current DQC and designing an enhanced DQC requires an understanding of users, the critical functions in the QA checklist, and an evaluation of the key individual QA tasks that impact the usability and effectiveness of the QA checklist. We used generalizable methods from the TURF framework which may be used by other radiation oncology medical centers to redesign suboptimal HIT tools. Future research will assess the enhanced DQC's usability, users' cognitive workload, performance, and patient safety.

Acknowledgments. We thank the dosimetrists, physicists, and clinic leadership of our department for their support of our research efforts.

Appendix I

Procedural QA task	MOSAIQ (MQ)		Taxonomy Clf. **	RayStation (RS)			Taxonomy Clf. **	QA checklist		Taxonomy Clf. **
	CT level 1	CT level 2		CT level 1	CT level 2	CT level 3		CT level 1	CT level 2	
DOB and Age: Check if DOB of the patient is same in both Mosaiq and RS	1.Select patient	1.1 Click on Facesheet	Perceptual ability	1. Select patient data management	1.1 Click patient information		Perceptual ability	1.Compare DOB information from MQ and RS	1.1 Select appropriate option	Analysis
		1.2 Retain the patient's DOB in working memory	Knowledge		1.2 Retain the patient's DOB in working memory		Knowledge			
Pacemaker: Check if pacemaker is assessed as present? If pacemaker present is ROI contoured?	1. Select assessments	1.1 View simulation directive	Perceptual ability	1. Select ROI tab	1.1 Skip targets		Perceptual ability	1.Compare most recent pacemaker assessment in MQ with presence of ROI and contours for pacemaker in RS	1.1 Select appropriate option	Evaluation
		1.2 Check if pacemaker has been assessed	Comprehension		1.2 Look for pacemaker in OARs	1.2.1 If pacemaker ROI exists, check for contours	Perceptual ability			
		1.3 Retain the date of assessment	Knowledge		1.3 Look for pacemaker in unknowns	1.3.1 If pacemaker ROI exists, check for contours	Perceptual ability			
		1.4 Only the most recent date of assessment is important	Evaluation		1.4 Retain informatiion about ROI and contours		Knowledge			

(continued)

K. Adapa et al.

(continued)

Procedural QA task	MOSAIQ (MQ)		Taxonomy Clf. **	RayStation (RS)			Taxonomy Clf. **	QA checklist		Taxonomy Clf. **
	CT level 1	CT level 2		CT level 1	CT level 2	CT level 3		CT level 1	CT level 2	
Rx vs Planning note: Check if prescription is MQ is identical to plan information on RS	1. Select navigator	1.1 Click Tx plan	Perceptual ability	1. Select plan design	1.1 Select the beamset		Perceptual ability	1.Compare the Rx in MQ with dose, fractions, energy and modality in RS and see if dose constraints has been met	1.1 Select appropriate option	Evaluation
		1.2 Retain the content of the note in working memory (dose, fraction, primary site, secondary site etc.)	Knowledge		1.2 Look for dose, fraction, energy and modality (all located in different tables) Retain the content about fraction,		Perceptual ability			
					1.3 Retain the information about fraction, dose, fraction, energy and modality (all located in different tables) in working memory		Knowledge			
				2. Select plan evaluation	2.1 Look for PTV and see if dose constraints were met		Perceptual ability			
QCL Finance: IMRT/SBRT pre-auth	1. Select QCL or navigator	1.1 Add filter for pre-auth	Perceptual ability					1.Ensure QCL is complete, assessment is recent and completed by authorized user	1.1 Select appropriate option	Analysis
		1.2 Double click or scan the entire breadth of list of columns	Perceptual ability							
		1.3 Confirm that information is complete, and date is fresh for this QCL	Analysis and Knowledge							

*CT – Cognitive Task.
* * Taxonomy cf. – Taxonomy Classification.

References

1. Marks, L.B., Jackson, M., Xie, L., et al.: The challenge of maximizing safety in radiation oncology. Pract Radiat Oncol. **1**(1), 2–14 (2011). https://doi.org/10.1016/j.prro.2010.10.001
2. Adapa, K.: Unifying evidence-based frameworks to design, develop, implement, and evaluate health information technology tools in radiation oncology (Order No. 29393143). Available from Dissertations & Theses @ University of North Carolina at Chapel Hill; ProQuest Dissertations & Theses Global (2022). (2760194888). http://libproxy.lib.unc.edu/login?url=https://www-proquest-com.libproxy.lib.unc.edu/dissertations-theses/unifying-evidence-based-frameworks-design-develop/docview/2760194888/se-2
3. Ford, E.C., Terezakis, S., Souranis, A., Harris, K., Gay, H., Mutic, S.: Quality control quantification (QCQ): a tool to measure the value of quality control checks in radiation oncology. Int. J, Radiat. Oncol. Biol. Phys. **84**(3), e263–e269 (2012). https://doi.org/10.1016/j.ijrobp.2012.04.036
4. Adapa, K., Mosaly, P., Yu, F., Moore, C., Das, S., Mazur, L.: Exploring association between perceived usability of dosimetry quality assurance checklist and perceived cognitive workload of dosimetrists in clinical settings. Proc. Hum. Factors Ergon. Soc. Annu. Meet. **65**(1), 771–775 (2021). https://doi-org.libproxy.lib.unc.edu/10.1177/1071181321651285
5. Tracton, G.S., Mazur, L.M., Mosaly, P., Marks, L.B., Das, S.: Developing and assessing electronic checklists for safety mindfulness, workload, and performance. Pract. Radiat. Oncol. **8**(6), 458–467 (2018). https://doi.org/10.1016/j.prro.2018.05.001
6. McGurk, R., et al.: Multi-institutional stereotactic body radiation therapy incident learning: evaluation of safety barriers using a human factors analysis and classification system. J. Patient Saf. **19**(1), e18–e24 (2023). https://doi.org/10.1097/PTS.0000000000001071
7. Adapa, K., et al.: Human-centered participatory co-design of a dosimetry-quality assurance checklist in an academic cancer center. In: Duffy, V.G. (ed.) Digital Human Modeling and Applications in Health, Safety, Ergonomics and Risk Management. Health, Operations Management, and Design. HCII 2022. LNCS, vol. 13320, pp. 3–20. Springer, Cham (2022). https://doi.org/10.1007/978-3-031-06018-2_1
8. Adapa, K..: Hhuman-, centered, participatory co-design of a dosimetry-quality assurance checklist in an academic cancer, center, ., indigital, human, modeling, and applications in health, safety, ergonomics, and risk management. health, operations management, and design. In: 13th international conference, DHM: Held as Part of the 24th HCI International Conference, HCII 2022, Virtual Event, June 26–July 1, 2022, Proceedings, Part II 2022 Jun 16, pp. 3–20. Springer International Publishing, Cham (2022). https://doi.org/10.1007/978-3-031-06018-2_1
9. Zhang, J., Walji, M.F.: TURF: toward a unified framework of EHR usability. J. Biomed. Inform. **44**(6), 1056–1067 (2011). https://doi.org/10.1016/j.jbi.2011.08.005
10. Zhang, J., Butler. K.: UFuRT : A work-centered framework and process for design and evaluation of information systems. In: Proceedings of HCI International 2007 (2007)
11. Zhang. Z., Walji, M.F., Patel, V.L., Gimbel, R.W., Zhang, J.: Functional analysis of interfaces in U.S. military electronic health record system using UFuRT framework. In: AMIA Annual Symposium Proceedings 2009, pp. 730–734 (2009)
12. Moreira, M., Peixoto, C.: Qualitative task analysis to enhance sports characterization: a surfing case study. J. Hum. Kinet. **42**, 245–257 (2014). https://doi.org/10.2478/hukin-2014-0078
13. Knisely, B.M., Joyner, J.S., Vaughn-Cooke, M.: Cognitive task analysis and workload classification. MethodsX. **8**, 101235 (2021). https://doi.org/10.1016/j.mex.2021.101235
14. Bloom, B.S.: Taxonomy of educational objectives : The classification of educational goals. Published online, Cognitive domain (1956)

15. Harrow, A.J.: A Taxonomy of the Psychomotor Domain: A Guide for Developing Behavorial Objectives
16. Anwar, F., Sulaiman, S.: P.D.D.Dominic. Cognitive Task Analysis: A Contextual Inquiry Study on Basic Computer and Information Literacy Skills among Physicians. ISICO 2013. Published online (2013)
17. Chan, C.V., Kaufman, D.R.: A framework for characterizing eHealth literacy demands and barriers. J. Med. Internet Res. **13**(4), e94 (2011). https://doi.org/10.2196/jmir.1750
18. Nielsen J. Usability inspection methods. In: Plaisant, C., (ed.) Conference Companion on Human Factors in Computing Systems - CHI 1994, pp. 413–414 ACM Press (1994).:https://doi.org/10.1145/259963.260531
19. Usability Engineering - Jakob Nielsen - Google Books
20. Shneiderman, B.: Designing the user interface strategies for effective human-computer interaction. SIGBIO Newsl. **9**(1), 6 (1987). https://doi.org/10.1145/25065.950626
21. Zhang, J., Johnson, T.R., Patel, V.L., Paige, D.L., Kubose, T.: Using usability heuristics to evaluate patient safety of medical devices. J. Biomed. Inform. **36**(1–2), 23–30 (2003). https://doi.org/10.1016/S1532-0464(03)00060-1
22. Parasuraman, A., Colby, C.L.: An updated and streamlined technology readiness index. J. Serv. Res. **18**(1), 59–74 (2015). https://doi.org/10.1177/1094670514539730
23. Dowding, D., Merrill, J.A.: The development of heuristics for evaluation of dashboard visualizations. Appl. Clin. Inform. **9**(3), 511–518 (2018). https://doi.org/10.1055/s-0038-1666842

Towards Co-design with Day Care Teachers Based on In-Situ Behavioral Data: A Case Study of a Workshop for Reflection Based on Video Recordings

Sawako Fujita[1]([✉]), Yuki Taoka[1] [ID], Shigeru Owada[2] [ID], Momoko Nakatani[1] [ID], and Shigeki Saito[1] [ID]

[1] Tokyo Institute of Technology, 2-12-1 Ookayama Meguro-ku, Tokyo 152-8550, Japan
`fujita.s.an@m.titech.ac.jp`
[2] Sony Computer Science Laboratories, Inc., 3-14-13 Higashigotanda Shinagawa-ku, Tokyo 141-0022, Japan

Abstract. In designing products and services that improve the quality of childcare, it is necessary for designers to empathize deeply with people involved in childcare (i.e., day care teachers) to understand context-dependent know-how. For that purpose, co-design, a collaborative design activity involving designers and non-designers, is essential. To conduct co-design, in-situ data can provide a common understanding for discussion. However, the types of data that are useful and how they can support co-design for childcare is unclear. Therefore, the objective of this study is to explore the potential usage of behavioral data in day care centers for co-design. We conducted a two-hour workshop with day care teachers. The results of the workshop showed that the video recordings effectively supported the teachers' reflections. In addition, they also pointed out that video reflection can be supported by supplemental data such as children's feelings and the context of the scenes. Overall, the results imply that behavioral data has huge potential to be used for co-design. The next step of this research is to clarify the issues and benefits of using behavioral data for co-design by conducting a workshop among day care teachers and designers.

Keywords: Service Design · Behavioral data · Co-design · Early childhood education and care

1 Introduction

OECD defines the service quality of Early Childhood Education and Care (ECEC) as the features of children's environments and experiences that benefit children's well-being provided by an ECEC setting [1]. Since ECEC plays a significant role in forming the identity of an individual, there is a need to ensure and improve the quality of childcare. Improving the quality of childcare can be achieved by developing products and services for day care centers. To discover issues that will lead to improvement in the quality of

© The Author(s), under exclusive license to Springer Nature Switzerland AG 2023
A. Marcus et al. (Eds.): HCII 2023, LNCS 14034, pp. 255–268, 2023.
https://doi.org/10.1007/978-3-031-35705-3_19

childcare, it is important to consider solutions based on a deep understanding of practices at day care centers. Thus, empathizing with the people working in day care centers and the related stakeholders is necessary to allow designers to understand the different views on childcare depending on the specific context and facility.

Co-design is a promising approach that combines the values and capabilities of various stakeholders. In co-design, both designers and non-designers (i.e., people who have not been trained in formal design education) work together in design activities [2]. Non-designers are regarded as co-designers who play a significant role in design activities. In our context, day care teachers play a key role in design activities as co-designers, as they are constantly improving the quality of day care on a daily basis. For effective co-design, both parties are required to have a deep understanding of the field [3]. In other words, designers and co-designers need to understand the state of practice in day care centers.

To gain a deep understanding of a certain situation, design research communities have proposed many tools and techniques [4], such as written diaries [5], video observations [6], video diaries [7]. In the video diaries method, co-designers are asked to film videos responding to a list of questions presented to them. The recorded videos were used to understand the situations of co-designers. Co-design approaches also try to understand the values of the co-designers using various methods, such as cultural probes, which asks co-designers to take photographs of specific objects, and generative toolkits, which allows co-designers to express their latent values while working with their hands [8]. Another approach is to observe how co-designers behave in actual contexts. However, for day care centers, allowing designers to be on-site to observe may be considered disturbing the workplace. Therefore, methods to support co-creation design activities with materials from the facility, even when designers are restricted to access, need to be established. Video-based methods could be effective.

The recent development of information and communication technologies (ICT) has allowed the acquisition of plenty of in-situ behavioral data. Behavioral data, which is defined as "a collection of specific information, referring to data from sensors, self-logging, telemetry, or social networks which capture people's behaviors and patterns" [9], has been used for personal reflection such as smartwatches for personal healthcare. Although behavioral data has not been widely used in design [10], co-designers' behavioral data has the potential to play an important role in supporting co-design by providing a common ground.

Improving the quality of ECEC has been done by day care teachers through reflection of childcare activities. Reflection can be divided into two categories: reflection-in-action and reflection-on-action. Reflection-in-action is defined as a reflection carried out while the action is taking place. On the other hand, reflection-on-action is defined as reflection on the action after the action and verbalizing future responses [11].

Many tools have been developed to support self-reflection in the field of childcare. The tools use materials from the field, such as descriptions of episodes, pictures, and videos for supporting reflection-on-action [12]. The materials generally provide a common understanding of the scenes for reflection. For example, Cherrington (2014) [12] developed an interview technique based on videos of childcare situations that have been edited by researchers. Cherrington (2014) presented the effectiveness of using videos, but it required a significant amount of time to extract scenes for reflection out of the vast amount of recorded data. In reflection-on-action, when presenting information from the scene, such as videos, the scenes are generally extracted from the recorded video, which is very time-consuming to prepare. On the other hand, reflection-in-action takes place during childcare and is therefore difficult to record. Linking reflection-in-action and reflection-on-action may be a promising approach to creating materials for reflection-on-action with reduced efforts.

Reflection is closely related to co-design; reflection-on-action is looking back at what happened in the activities and thinking about improvements. In co-design, when those who were in the field are looking back at what happened, the behavior is similar to reflection-on-action. Thus, the use of in-situ data, such as those used in reflection-on-action, in co-design may promote a common understanding of the field. In co-design, outsiders (i.e., those who are not directly involved on site) also need to analyze in-situ data. However, in context-dependent childcare, it may not be possible for the outsiders to fully understand the situation simply by watching a cut-out video.

Although many methods for reflection have been developed, methods that apply to the field of childcare have not been well-studied. Therefore, in this study, we propose a reflection workshop utilizing in-situ childcare data. Through the workshop, the potential uses of behavioral data taken from day care centers for co-design is investigated. Specifically, this study investigates the effect of using selected recorded videos for reflection. We conducted a two-hour workshop with nine day care teachers at a day care center.

2   Method

2.1   Workshop

We conducted a workshop using video recordings triggered by the teachers' awareness on-the-job (reflection-in-action) for reflection-on-action. Figure 1 shows the preparation of video recordings and this workshop flow.

Video Preparation.   Before the workshop, video data for reflection were obtained using a reflection support system, VisRef [13]. With cooperation from a day care center, a one-year-old class was recorded for seven weekdays in May 2022. Five smartphones were installed as fixed-point cameras in the classroom. The five teachers in charge were the recording subjects and asked to wear smartwatches throughout the recording period.
When a teacher wants to reflect on a certain moment, they can start the app on their smartwatch and record a voice note. In addition to voice notes, they can also choose to save video data. Whenever a video save is initiated, three-minute videos (two and a half minutes before, and one minute after saving is initiated) are extracted from all five iPhones and posted to Slack through VisRef. In this manner, the day care teachers were able to extract and record their own observations as video data.

The workshop was structured so that the five teachers who recorded the videos would be able to do reflection-on-action using the videos they chose. Therefore, after the recording period, the teachers were asked to review the videos posted on Slack and selected one video to reflect.

Finally, the five teachers were interviewed after the recording period about the reflections they were carrying out in their classes to determine the structure of the workshop.

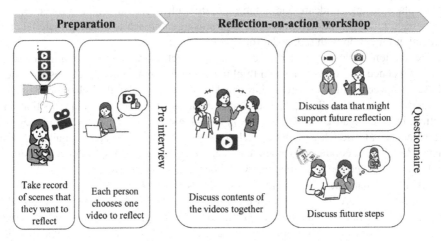

Fig. 1. Preparation of video recordings and workshop flow

Workshop Design. A total of nine day care teachers from the same center participated in the workshop. The participants were divided into groups of three teachers and one facilitator (researcher). The details of the participants and the composition of the group members are given in Table 1. Members who participated in the video preparation are marked with an asterisk (*) at the end. Audio recordings of each group's discussion were taken for analysis.

The workshop timeline is shown in Fig. 2. The workshop was mainly divided into two sessions, one for video-based reflection, followed by one for data exploration. In the latter, participants discussed data to be collected in the future to support the understanding of the childcare situation.

1. At the beginning, the purpose of the workshop was explained. In the ice break session, the group shared interesting and heart-warming moments of their experiences in childcare.
2. Then, as a preliminary preparation, each teacher shared with the group the video that they selected, along with the reasons for their selection. The group then reflected on the videos in groups and shared their findings and impressions.
3. Next, the participants discussed what they had learned from conducting the reflection part, their ideal method of reflection, and data to support future reflection.
4. Participants were asked to discuss data to support reflection-on-action. To help their discussion, six premade idea cards (see Fig. 3) were used.
5. Finally, as a summary of the day as a whole, the feelings and insights gained were shared within the team and shared with the whole team by the facilitator.

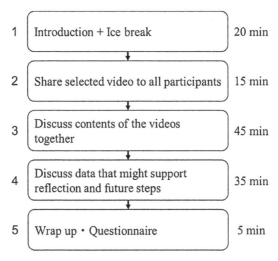

Fig. 2. Timeline of the workshop.

2.2 Data Analysis

Preparation. To find out what the teachers focused on in-situ, we analyzed the contents of the videos saved by the day care teachers during the pre-preparation period. The titles and contents of the videos saved by the teachers were labeled and classified according to category.

Pre-interview. All of the audio data for each interview was transcribed and organized by content, extracting the intentions of the teachers for initiating saves and what they felt during the preliminary preparation.

Workshop. All audio data taken during the workshop was transcribed. Relevant content from video-based reflections and discussions on potential future data were extracted. Then, they are labeled and categorized based on similarities in content.

3   Result

3.1   Contents of Saved Video Data and Voice Notes and Videos Selected for the Workshop

Over the seven days, the five teachers saved a total of 167 voice notes and video data. They were labeled and categorized based on content, as shown in Fig. 4. The results showed that they were most interested in children's behavior. Children's behavior refers to their observations of their play and development, with many contents relating to what the children were able to do, such as using milk cartons as toy trains and pushing in their chair when they finish their meal and get up from the table. The next most common item was injuries, with cases such as running into each other in the classroom and losing their balance while walking.

Table 1. Composition of workshop participants HT: Homeroom teacher

Group	Group members	Code
A	HT for 1 year old class*	A-1
	HT for 1 year old class	A-2
	HT for 1 year old class*	A-3
	Facilitator	-
B	HT for 0 year old class	B-1
	HT for 1 year old class*	B-2
	HT for 3–5 year old class	B-3
	Facilitator	-
C	HT for 1 year old class*	C-1
	HT for 2 year old class	C-2
	Senior Teacher	C-3
	Facilitator	-

Most of the categories are focused on children's activities, with "Trouble dealing with children" being the only category that concerns the teacher's actions. For that category, only two videos were saved.

Five videos were selected for reflection during the workshop. In the workshop, three videos were picked by each team for discussion. The reflection for each video took 15–20 min. The exact duration for discussion varied depending on the group. A summary of the videos selected by the day care teachers and the discussions that took place during the workshop is presented in Table 2.

3.2 Effect of Using Videos for Reflection-on-Action

The results of the workshop were analyzed in terms of the effectiveness and challenges of using video data and reflecting over the videos in groups, based on the comments made in the latter part of the workshop: 'What I gained from the reflection part', 'What I would like to do in the future', and 'Summary of the workshop'. We categorized the results into four categories.

Deepen Understanding of the Children and Caring Methods. As video data before and after a save is initiated are taken, the participants were able to understand the context of each video, which led to new insights. In addition, since they could play the video repeatedly, they were able to observe more children and the environment, gaining new information.

"I am much more aware now that each child has their own thoughts and feelings. Usually, I'm so occupied with things like making sure no one gets hurt." [C-1]

"I feel I was able to make new discoveries, much more than what I noticed at that moment in the video." [C-1]

Analyze playing

Attach sensors on toys that are popular amongst the children to observe and record their playing styles

- Who played with which toy and for how long?
- Which areas of the room do they play with the toy?
- How do they play with the toys?

Understand the environment inside the nursery

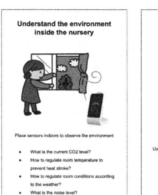

Place sensors indoors to observe the environment

- What is the current CO2 level?
- How to regulate room temperature to prevent heat stroke?
- How to regulate room conditions according to the weather?
- What is the noise level?

Analyze crowd movement

Use cameras to record movement and crowdedness in the nursery

- Where do children tend to group together?
- What are in the crowded areas?
- How does the crowding change at different times of the day?

Identify urgent situations

Use cameras to record events that cause the nursery teacher to rush urgently somewhere

- What is happening with the children when the teacher wants to go check?
- What positive things have happened?

Record child development

Use cameras and sensors to record situations where the teacher senses the children's learning progress and development

- What kind of development can be seen?
- How are the children enjoying preschool?
- What kind of behaviors are praised?

Understand teacher-children relationships

Use voice recognition systems and cameras to record the teachers' interactions with the children.

- To what extent do they talk with the children?
- How well do the teachers respond to the children when they are called?
- What kind of tone do the teachers use to respond?

Fig. 3. Idea cards.

"I think it's great that I could notice things other than what I noticed by just watching the video." [A-3]

"I thought it was great that you could look back many times, changing where you focus your attention. When I saw the two children moving earlier, I could look this way and that way." [A-2]

Consider Other's Situation as One's Own. The workshop was also attended by teachers in charge of other classes and the head of the day care, who did not participate in the video preparation. By watching the videos, those who were not involved in the workshop were also able to reflect from their own perspectives.

"I was able to look back and watch scenes where I wasn't present, and think, 'Oh, I have had that happen to me, too.'" [C-2]

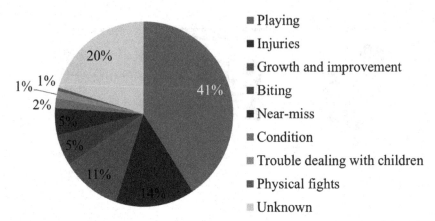

Fig. 4. The result of video categorization. "Condition" refers to situations in which the teachers were concerned about the condition of children (e.g., child looked sleepy). "Trouble dealing with children" refers to situations in which the teachers were worried about how to respond to the children.

"Even as I watched various other videos, I thought, oh, I shouldn't be here at this time, (...) what was I looking at that time, (...) I realized these when watching other videos, and I was able to reflect on that." [A-1]

Learning from Others. Teachers were able to gain insights from other teachers, which broadened my own perspective. Some said that watching videos selected by others helped them to understand their perspectives and ideas in childcare and doing so stimulated their own previous viewpoints and ideas.

"I was only focused on this part of my own reflection, but I think it was great that I was able to hear so many different voices. I think it will help me to improve myself" [B-2]

"I was able to notice how the seniors looked at the situation, and I think it would be good if I could look at it in this way." [A-1]

"I usually focus only on the development of my children, and I never thought of looking back on myself, so I think I was able to look at what I did wrong there." [C-1]

Empathizing with Others. Some participants were pleased that they got to see videos of other classes and conduct reflections together. Others also mentioned that this could lead to a sense of camaraderie and increase group motivation. They were able to understand how things were going in other classes and what the homeroom teacher thought was important.

"I think it's interesting to be able to see on video that the class has a great class atmosphere, and that this teacher values this kind of thing and this kind of childcare." [B-1]

Table 2. Summary of video content and discussions.

	Video Content Summary	Discussion Summary	Comments made by day care teachers
①	A child who was playing by the toy shelf was putting his feet in a Tupperware. A teacher saw that it was dangerous and removed the Tupperware from the child's feet	Other teachers said that it is difficult to judge what kind of actions are dangerous and presented solutions	*"It is quite difficult to judge. (...) Also, I made shoes from milk cartons. I would suggest something else."* [B-1]
②	When A was playing pretend, B brought the same toy and started playing pretend next to her. However, A realized that one of the toys B had brought was missing, so she brought the toy and handed it to B and continued playing	There was discussion on the power of children's interaction. A variety of other perceptions and ideas were shared	Child Development *"Maybe A realized that B wants to do the same thing? The fact that A went to get it voluntarily must be? I feel like I see a lot of differences in development."* [C-1] Playing areas *"The fact that there's a lot of playing on the mat is, for having fun, (...) very good I guess."* [B-1]
③	C was inviting a friend, D, to dinner with him, but D was lying down, drowsy, and fretful. Even so, C talked to D, and C put away the toys that D had dropped on the way to the dining table with the teacher	There was an in-depth discussion about why C was able to take such action. By watching the whole video, there were comments on other teachers and the situation at hand	*"Things like having someone to eat together with, eating after putting the toys away, eating together after waking someone up, these are actions backed with a plan in mind. I think it's something that they learn through repetition."* [B-1] *"They are concerned about things like where we are standing. Or things like picking up a dropped toy on the way."* [C-3]
④	When the children come back after playing outside, the day care teachers were not able to encourage playing, so the children started running inside the room	Reflections on the matter, empathizing words on the teachers' feelings, and interpretations of the situation were shared	Discussion of the situation *"The kids don't understand my situation, or that I'm cleaning up, so they do whatever they want."* [C-3] Interpretation of the children's behavior *"They couldn't find a game that involved just sitting, so they entertained themselves by running. I was a bit taken aback by how fun they were having by just running. (...) I think it's not really a bad thing"* [B-1]

(continued)

Table 2. (*continued*)

Video Content Summary	Discussion Summary	Comments made by day care teachers
⑤ E saw F playing on top of a teacher's lap. After F got off, E imitated F and played on the lap in the same way. After that, F and E looked at each other and they played together	In addition to the insight, opinions on the teacher were shared	Praise "*I think the teacher deserves a thumbs up for noticing that E also wants to be treated the same way.*" [B-1] Advice "*So, the two of them (...) leave, right? I guess it would have been better if the teacher could have given them toys to play with.*" [A-3]

"*Even though we use different methods, we can see that what we value is the same in the end, that we are not just colleagues, but that our thoughts are the same. So, I think it can lead to motivation and a sense of security.*" [B-1]

3.3 Drawbacks of Video Reflection

Although having video data for the workshop had many advantages, several drawbacks were also seen. Asking the day care teachers to start video recording during their work drastically reduced the time for preparing videos. However, initiating saves and selecting videos for the workshop was a burden for the teachers.

"*It was difficult to examine (the videos) when there's a ton of them. Just looking at it (the pile of videos), was enough to make me want to stop.*" [C-1]

'*To be honest, the voice input is not accurate, so we have to re-do it, but then we lose sight of the children. Some accidents might happen. It worries me.*" (From a pre-workshop interview)" [A-3]

The participants also commented that being recorded was stressful during childcare.

"It's (being filmed) just a bit stressful." [C-1].

While group reflection can lead to new insights, it can also lead to negative feelings of those who were present in the video recordings. The participants felt as if they were being blamed although the purpose of the workshop was to consider ways to improve the quality of childcare.

"*If you look at a recording of a class and say, 'This kind of attitude is not acceptable' or bla bla bla, then the person would feel rejected.*" [C-3]

3.4 Data to Support Future Reflection

In this study, fixed-point cameras were used for video data acquisition. During the discussion, some participants stated that it would be easier to communicate if the children's finger movements and actions were recorded from a certain angle. Those videos might enable the teachers to accurately understand children's behavior. Additional opinions are summarized in Table 3.

Table 3. Summary of discussion of data to support future reflection.

Data category	Opinion	Comments made by day care teachers
Video	Communicate one's point of focus	*"It's not easy to convey what I see from my own viewpoint. If I can't communicate well, […] it's not going to do any good for the children and the other teachers […] won't understand, so […] it's kind of easier to communicate if we can have pictures taken by camera."* [C-2]
	Zoom in	*"Not only the children, but also the environment surrounding the child is very important, so (…) it would be great if the whole room, the whole space, could be captured and recorded, and we could pick out certain spots."* [B-1]
	Add points of view	*"Record from a teacher's point of view, somewhere that's closer to the children."* [B-3]
		"What is it (the child) really looking at?" [B-1]
Others	Child's personality	*"Maybe it depends on the person, but I think ○○ cried a lot at the end. She's quite temperamental, so if it's someone she doesn't like, then, you know, absolutely."* [B-1]
	Locational information	*One teacher is here, one is in the pretend play area, one in the building blocks area and one free teacher is here. [C-3]*
		"If we could see, at the same time, where the teachers are and where the children are, it might be useful to improve the facility." [B-1]
	Mood changes	*"It would be interesting to see the fluctuations in a child's mood during eating, playing with toys, etc."* [B-1]

4 Discussion

4.1 How Reflection-in-Action Videos Support Discussion

The results suggest various advantages to conducting video reflection in groups. By using videos for discussion, the teachers were able to deepen their understanding of children and gain insights from situations where they were not present. This is influenced by the following two elements:

Video angle

- The iPhone cameras were installed by hanging them on the ceiling of the classroom, giving the video a wide perspective and a bird's eye view. This allowed the participants to observe various scenes from different viewpoints, which may have increased the number of insights gained. Seeing the situation from a third-person's point of view allowed the teachers to analyze their own behavior.
- Replay

As the teachers were able to play the videos repeatedly, they could observe a wide variety of scenes, which increased their viewpoints.

The reason some participants considered the workshop a learning experience is because the group discussed the insights they gained about specific situations while watching the video. Since each group member had different experiences and oversaw different classes, their different ways of thinking and skills led to distinctive insights. Sharing of insights through discussion provided an opportunity to incorporate perspectives that had not been available to the participants before. There are two possible reasons for this.

- The participants were able to share a situation accurately and objectively through video. Since there was evidence to back up their statements, they were more persuasive, and this made it easier for participants to be convinced of their findings. As a result, a mutual understanding within the group can be created.
- The discussion was able to proceed in accordance with the purpose of the workshop. In the introduction, we told the participants that the purpose of the workshop was to share their insights. The facilitator took notes of what the day care teachers discussed, summarized them on a large canvas, and passed the conversation around so that each member had a chase to speak up.

The teachers were able to empathize with each other because by watching the videos used in this discussion, the other participants were able to sense the work ethic of the child caregivers who conducted the reflection-in-action. In addition, reflection was conducted not only when recording them, but also when selecting videos to be used in the workshop. Among the many videos that were available, the videos that were selected for reflection with multiple participants were those that expressed what the teachers themselves thought was important. Therefore, the other participants were able to discuss each other's views on childcare and the state of the class from various perspectives.

4.2 Video-Selection

By linking reflection-in-action and reflection-on-action, the time spent selecting the video data was short. However, several disadvantages were found. First, day care teachers needed to take their eyes off the children when initiating a save. In childcare, it is difficult to divert one's attention away from children even for a single moment. Second, the smartwatches were often considered uncomfortable. The teachers often had to pay extra-attention not to damage the watches and keep them clean throughout the recording. Possible solutions include using devices that do not require displays, and to use quantitative indicators to automatically generate video data.

Some teachers mentioned that it was hard to select one video for selection. Due to the long recording period, many videos were posted to Slack. In addition, the user interface was not suited for such a task. To reduce this burden in the future, a video viewing platform could be developed to allow efficient video selection. The length of the videos could also be reduced to speed up viewing time during video selection. Developing an automated selection or a semi-automated selection method is also a promising future research.

4.3 Addressing Emotional Burden

Some day care teachers felt stressed because they were constantly being recorded. Possible solutions include shortening the collection period and properly stating how the data will be utilized. Some also mentioned that watching and discussing the videos in groups was a challenge. The videos can also be seen as objective evidence to condemn someone's behavior. To resolve such concerns, workshop facilitators should clearly state that the focus of workshops is to share insight, and design group work that encourages day care teachers.

4.4 Potential Use of Videos for Co-design

The simple presentation of the videos was found to be inconvenient. For example, information on why a day care teacher was at a specific location was deemed necessary for reflection. It is likely that other stakeholders in co-design will also need this information to understand childcare.

We also found that the reflections were highly focused on children. Thus, having insights from various perspectives might promote a better understanding of children and help day care teachers communicate in detail with parents. In future co-design, day care teachers may be more likely to accept ideas on improving the day care facilities and methods that can enable them to increase understanding of children.

Reflection also allowed day care teachers to come up with data that might be helpful for their work. For example, we found that they want to know the status of a child's development. Thus, reflection itself can be an effective technique for co-design with day care teachers.

5   Conclusion

To improve the quality of childcare using co-design, we held a reflection workshop with childcare workers using selected reflection-in-action video data. Our proposed method is considered effective as the workers were able to gain valuable insights about the children in their day care, which helps them improve their methods of childcare. We plan to organize a co-design workshop with a more diverse range of participants to solve problems in childcare. Further studies are planned on data and presentation methods to support understanding of the childcare situation at the co-design workshop.

Acknowledgements. This research was supported by the Tokyo Institute of Technology Department Research Grant (Research Project 20K20116) and JST-Mirai Program Grant Number JPMJMI22H3, Japan. The authors would also like to express their sincere appreciation to the day care center for their cooperation.

References

1. OECD: Starting Strong IV Monitoring quality in early childhood education and care. OECD Publishing, Paris (2015)
2. Sanders, E.B.N., Stappers, P.J.: Co-creation and the new landscapes of design. CoDesign **4**(1), 5–18 (2008)
3. Pirinen, A.: The barriers and enablers of co-design for services. Int. J. Des. **10**(3), 27–42 (2016)
4. Sanders, E.B.N., Brandt, E., Binder, T.: A framework for organizing the tools and techniques of participatory design. In: 11th Biennial Participatory Design Conference. ACM Press (2010)
5. Steen, M., Manschot, M.D., Koning, N.: Benefits of co-design in service design projects. Int. J. Des. **5**(2), 53–60 (2011)
6. Lee, J.J., Jaatinen, M., Salmi, A., Mattelmäki, T., Smeds, R., Holopainen, M.: Design choices framework for co-creation projects. Int. J. Des. **12**(2), 15–31 (2018)
7. Rose, E., Cardinal, A.: Participatory video methods in UX: sharing power with users to gain insights into everyday life. Commun. Des. Q Rev. **6**(2), 9–20 (2018)
8. Sanders, E.B.N., Stappers, P.J.: Convivial toolbox: generative research for the front end of design. BIS Amsterdam, the Netherlands (2012)
9. Gomez, A., Kollenburg, J., Shen, Y., et al.: SIG on data as human-centered design material. In: Extended Abstracts of the 2022 CHI Conference on Human Factors in Computing Systems, pp. 1–4 (2022)
10. Machchhar, R.J., Bertoni, A.: Data-driven design automation for product-service systems design: framework and lessons learned from empirical studies. Proc. Des. Soc. **1**, 841–850 (2021)
11. Schön, D.: The Reflective Practitioner: How Professionals Think in Action. Basic Books, New York, USA (1983)
12. Cherrington, S., Loveridge, J.: Using video to promote early childhood teachers' thinking and reflection. Teach. Teach. Educ. **41**, 42–51 (2014)
13. VisRef: 保育カメラと省察, https://hoikutech.com/camera/. Accessed 10 Feb 2023

Digital Health Twin in the Prevention Era for Personal and Corporate Wellbeing

Giacomo Galuzzi[1], Alessandro Nizardo Chailly[1], and Giuseppe Andreoni[2,3](✉) ⓘ

[1] Capsula s.r.l., Milano, Italy
[2] Dipartimento di Design, Politecnico di Milano, Milano, Italy
giuseppe.andreoni@polimi.it
[3] Bioengineering Laboratory, Scientific Institute IRCCS "E.Medea", Bosisio Parini, Lecco, Italy

Abstract. The availability of new miniaturized technologies for measuring the health status in self and remote conditions is rapidly pushing the development of new digital health solutions. The new AI and Metaverse era is also targeting the health field. This requires the evolution of new integrated models for health data fusion and representation. This paper presents development of a novel Digital Health Twin dedicated to prevention and implementing a cardiovascular risk index. Cardiovascular pathologies are the most diffused and relevant in the society. The model is combined with a Heath Pod solution for a territorial medicine approach even through corporate welfare solutions. This setting was adopted for the validation of the Digital Health Twin model and its User eXperience. A panel of 1314 subjects participated to the pilot test: they carried out a total number of 3755 test, that meant and average of 2,72 test per subject. Very good and promising results were obtained. The DHT model was well appreciated by 90% of subjects with excellent (about 70%) or good (about 20%) positive answers. Also the collective dashboard demonstrated to be a useful representation and tools to identify a status of health of a population, capable to highlight both individual issues and problems in specific category of people (by age, by gender, by occupation or section in the company).

Keywords: Health Twin · Digital Health · Prevention · Muti-domain representation · Health Pod

1 Introduction

Digital health is emerging as a priority for many public and private healthcare systems as a way forward to drive value for every global citizen, to ensure healthcare is accessible and equitable, and high performing [1]. In addition, recent scientific literature findings describe how 84% of pathologies are in direct correlation with lifestyle so that a new clinical branch is the so-called 'Lifestyle Medicine' where definition, promotion and personalization of coaching interventions are the most promising strategies. To achieve this proactive healthcare promotion goal, the most important action is said to be the patient empowerment that is defined as the process which people can gain a better control about decisions and actions related to his/her own Health through digital biomedical technologies [3]. This is also the 5-P Medicine vision adopted by the European Union recommending to push on Digital Transformation and towards Predictive, Preventive, Personalized, Participatory, and Psycho-cognitive Healthcare that is the target for 2030 [3–6].

Lifestyle diseases share risk factors like prolonged exposure to four modifiable lifestyle behaviors, that are responsible for about 60–65% in their development in comparison with the genetics that impacts only for about 30–35% [6–9]. Fortunately, most of the risk factors mentioned above are reversible and, if corrected in time, so are the diseases they trigger. The measurement of signals related to these factors allows for identifying and quantifying the risk so to produce the necessary awareness to promote a behavior change able to correct the situation. In this perspective an active role of the subject is needed before he/she becomes a patient. This action for the proactive healthcare promotion, is also called patient empowerment, in a multidimensional approach needed for a successful outcome [9]. New systems like Health Pods [10] offer a new typology of innovative check-up points to provide self-measurements of the main bio-signals related to lifestyle and health status, but a new digital twin model is needed.

2 Materials and Methods

The basic human domains [11] were selected and described in term of main features, parameters, and correlations among them: cardiovascular, metabolic and nutritional systems, physical state and psychological status have been identified as key bricks of human health, and the main non-invasive parameters for their measurement have been identified to build the corresponding health pod for their self-measurement (Fig. 1).

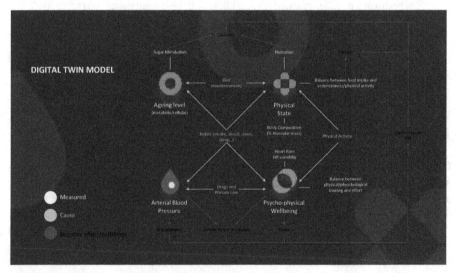

Fig. 1. The Physical-Physiological model underneath the Digital Health Twin general health and cardiovascular risk computation.

The domains are described by one of the most representative parameter, a physiological bio-signal that could be measured non invasively and through a device supporting a self-procedure i.e. without the presence or assistance of a clinical operator:

- Arterial blood pressure for the cardiovascular system;
- Advanced glycation endproducts (AGEs) for nutrition and metabolic functions describing the ageing level;
- Heart rate variability (HRV) for the psychological wellbeing;
- Body weight and body composition for the physical status.

The human model underneath the Digital Health Twin describes the complexity of human health through a set of correlations between the different domains. In Fig. 1 these links are represented by lines and arrows and the model is also able to identify the relationships with the most relevant and diffused pathologies, whose measured parameters are indicator of.

At the same time, these domains have been identified to provide information on lifestyles in a simple and intuitive way: data about nutrition, sleep and stress, exercise and blood pressure are combined with information on users' habits, such as alcohol consumption, smoking, diet, allow different data to be collected and express the psycho-cognitive and physical well-being of the individual in a holistic way. The basic set of measurements available to the user entering Capsula health Pod, provide her/him a quantitative assessment of the general health status. At the end of it, by means of a QR code, the individual has access to the Capsula web app which assimilates further information in order to build the user's Digital Me. This information is acquired in three ways:

- by means of binary or numerical input questions;
- by means of validated questionnaires (in particular, questionnaires were identified to detect physical activity, perceived stress and sleep quality of the individual);
- by means of questionnaires formulated by Capsula's partners, i.e. offering a service within the web platform (such as a questionnaire formulated by nutritionists to assess the individual's diet).

These data integrate the measurement and provide a more complete view of the health status. The Digital Health model or Digital me, is the digital integrated representation of this individually tailored and "smart" electronic health record. It is smart because it is not a simple database but the linking functions can be used for the computation of a global health index or of a risk index.

There are many ways to represent the heterogeneous set of these data, ranging from the more classical tabular to the more structured like radar charts or block sections as in the iOS health app. The choice that has been made is to develop a more intuitive representation, i.e. one that is capable of identifying human complexity in a simple way, but without framing it in a tabular format. For this purpose, the 'Digital Me' representation was chosen, i.e. a Health Digital Twin (HDT) prototype, implemented within a web app. The Digital Me (Fig. 2) can express the multifactorial organization of the human body in a clear, intuitive and authoritative manner, representing it as a kind of digital avatar.

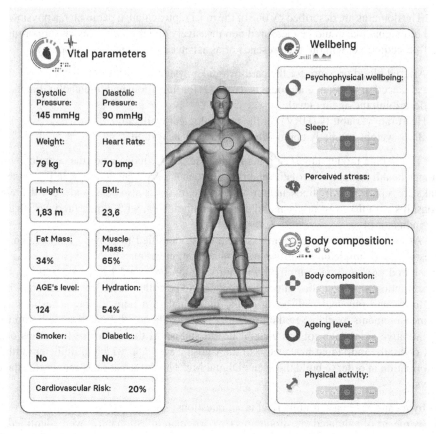

Fig. 2. The DHT or Digital-me representation in the mobile App, providing all the quantitative information measured or input by the user. An intuitive representation of the assessment of the global health in each domain is provided by means of an emoticon.

The Digital Me is an example of "data fusion", which is the integration of heterogeneous data from sources that were not designed to be brought together. This virtual representation of the user remaps his features on three levels:

- a vital parameters tab that identifies and blatantly expresses the individual's measured characteristics, assigning the most up-to-date numerical value (each box then encloses the measurement history). This card is intended to briefly represent some specifications that characterize the person, also assigning a cardiovascular risk by means of computational models;
- a "physical twin" that represents with semaphore scales the user's level of physical well-being due to his/her physical activity, fitness and nutrition;
- a "psycho-cognitive twin," which represents with semaphore scales the user's level of psychological well-being due to his or her mindfulness activity, sleep quality, and stress.

A preview of the mobile visualization of the "Digital Me" is shown below (Fig. 3).

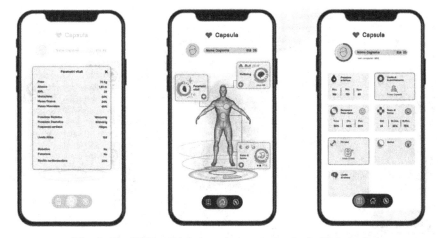

Fig. 3. The DHT or Digital-me representation in the Web-App.

A pilot tests on a large sample of healthy volunteers was conducted. The first goal of the test was dedicated to the verification of the acceptance and usability of the individual "digital health me model". The second objective was dedicated to the validation of the implementation of a digital health collective model for a small homogeneous community. To this goal a corporate welfare application was implemented for its well-fitting characteristics: adult healthy volunteers in a common workplace and conditions, and digital skills to have a community of people. An individual and collective representation was then studied, designed, and implemented to match this application field and case study. This collective analysis was synthetized into a global score to evaluate the overall wellbeing status in the company: this index has been computed considering the average scores in the four tests (corresponding to the human domains), weighted by the number of trials for each test and the percentage of subjects with low values in the CAPSULA assessment. This CAPSULA index aimed at evaluating the community wellbeing level.

3   Results

The pilot study involved a court of healthy adult volunteers working in a multinational company in the period running from June 2022 to 14 February 2023; the CASPULA system was installed in the entrance of the office building and employees were noticed by email of this opportunity; the participation was free and when a subject entered into CAPSULA she/he was asked to carry out at least one test and evaluate the user experience (Fig. 4).

General data about the test are reported in Fig. 4. In the testing period, 1314 subjects participated to the survey: they carried out a total number of 3755 test, that meant and average of 2,72 test per subject. The sample population was composed by women for 35,2% and 64,8% by men with a similar mean age of 50 years.

All the tests were successfully executed to evidencing the technical reliability of the Health Pod solution with very good intuitiveness of the commands (Fig. 5).

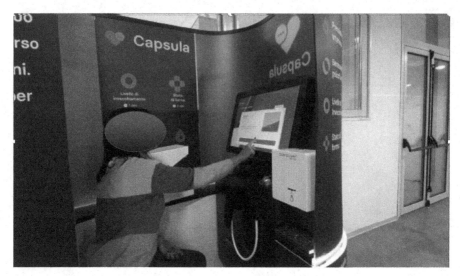

Fig. 4. A test subject executing the health assessment in the CAPSULA Health Pod in the company selected for the pilot experimentation.

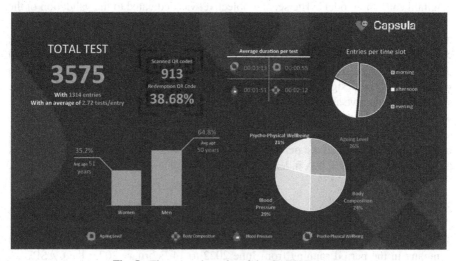

Fig. 5. The general results of the CAPSULA test.

The choice of the test is well balanced among all domains, with just a small preference for blood pressure, probably due to its well know significance and maybe for the mean age of the participants.

From the performance point of view the average time for the total subject experience is about 5 min; for the single test, the quickest one was the ageing level assessed by AGEs (mean duration: 55 s), followed by blood pressure (mean duration: 1 min and 51 s), Body weight and composition (mean duration: 2 min and 12 s), and finally psycho-physical wellbeing measured by HRV (mean duration: 3 min and 13 s).

At the end of the experience the users received a QRcode where they could find a detailed report and explanation of the meaning of the measures; a indirect assessment of patient empowerment and user engagement was given by the number of scanned QR codes (N = 913) corresponding to a QR Code Redemption rate of 38.68%.

The Individual Model well fitted to the general health conditions and the biomedical devices used for the measurements have provided the necessary reliability.

3.1 Acceptance and Usability

The evaluation of acceptance and usability was carried out through an automatically administered questionnaire composed by 4 items/questions investigating easy of use, satisfaction, and the willingness to repeat the experience as measure of the acceptance:

- Q1: I found use and understanding CAPSULA functioning EASY
- Q2: I found useful for my health and wellbeing this CAPSULA experience
- Q3: I would participate again in this experience
- Q4: I'm satisfied with this experience.

This short usability questionnaire was displayed on the screen of CAPSULA Health Pod at the end of the set of measurements, and the subject is asked to to select her/his answer evaluating the level of agreement according to the following scale: level of agreement score: 1 = no, 2 = poor, 3 = neutral, 4 = good, 5 = excellent.

The results were very satisfying with an average excellence level scored by 70% of participant for all questions and a positive assessment in 90% of subject for all factors (Fig. 6).

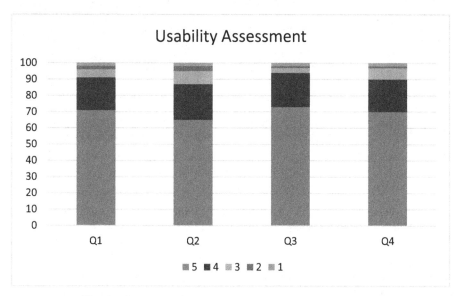

Fig. 6. The results of the usability and acceptance test on DHT.

From the answer to Q2, it could be also argued that for 88% of users, the individual model well fitted to the general health conditions and the biomedical devices used for the measurements have provided the necessary reliability.

3.2 Community Health and Wellbeing Test

In the same company the CAPSULA experience was proposed for the screening of the general health status as a corporate welfare intervention in the same period. The general outcomes (in Fig. 7) were proposing a division of the population by gender and by age. The threshold was set (also in accordance with the company management and in relation to the employees age range) at 45 years. For highlighting situation worth of consideration, a health threshold of 10% of respondent was identified: this meant that an attention level to poor health condition is obtained when more than 10% of the population has a value below the normal reference provided by the scientific literature findings. This situation is shown in the community dashboard through a red color for the corresponding datum.

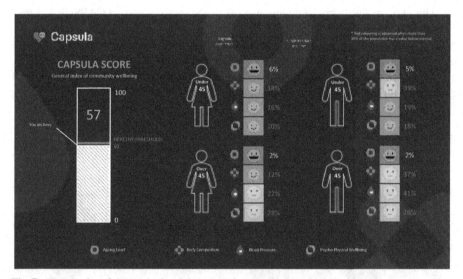

Fig. 7. The results of the analysis of the general status of the population in a corporate welfare setting using the DHT and its computational model for cardiovascular risk.

The Collective Dashboard was appreciated by the management and its outcomes were qualitatively coherent with the general perceived health conditions.

It was interesting to consider that 3 out 4 domains showed low healthy values in an appreciable amount of population. In particular, 41% of male over-45 subjects had blood pressure values (systolic and diastolic) higher than the recommended ones. This datum is also coherent with a not appropriate body weight and body composition for 37% of the tests.

In general, the best conditions are recorded for female subjects under 45 years.

The best domain is the ageing level measured by AGEs.

All these data led to a general index of community health and wellbeing of 57 on 100, meaning that the overall company health level is slightly below the normality value (60 points).

4 Discussion and Conclusions

This study aims at highlighting Digital Twin development for future personalized preventive healthcare matching individual needs in terms of ubiquitous health and better, high quality, care services and improved quality of life. For our society resources optimization and cost reduction of the healthcare expenditure are the expected outcomes.

The DHT model was well appreciated by 90% of subjects with excellent (about 70%) or good (about 20%) positive answers.

Also the collective dashboard demonstrated to be a useful representation and tools to identify a status of health of a population, capable to highlight both individual issues and problems in specific category of people (by age, by gender, by occupation or section in a company).

The proposed solution has many advantages: it has a good integration capability allowing for the aggregation of fluid and heterogeneous data such as those from the patient's electronic record, data measured in real time with wearable devices, and those from decentralized Capsule units. Continuous, point-in-time, vital and lifestyle-describing data coexist in the DHT.

The potential applications of the combination of a distributed network of sensing points like the CAPSULA Health Pods and a DHT technology can be several and somewhat disruptive, in prevention strategies, in epidemiological analyses, in fast checkups in clinical settings, and many others.

Currently some exploitation activities are dedicated to the evaluation of the effectiveness of treatments and/or therapies, response to medications or lifestyle changes, to the cost-effectiveness analysis in the implementation of medical and/or lifestyle solutions in the market, to the cost-effectiveness analysis in identifying the population for a clinical trial, for precision public health based on anticipating the needs of the individual and capable of responding productively.

The development challenges are in the realization of AI models capable of aggregating data so as to formulate personalized recommendations and suggestions or alerts in real time and for a wider list of pathologies, as well as in the integration with a set of digital therapeutics in the vision of the future e-Medicine.

References

1. Snowdon, A.: Digital Health: A Framework for Healthcare Transformation, HIMSS Report (2020)
2. Awad, A., et al.: Connected healthcare: improving patient care using digital health technologies. Adv. Drug Delivery Rev. **178**, 113958 (2021). ISSN 0169-409X. https://doi.org/10.1016/j.addr.2021.113958

3. Flores, M., Glusman, G., Brogaard, K., Price, N.D., Hood, L.: P4 medicine: how systems medicine will transform the healthcare sector and society. Per. Med. **10**, 565–576 (2013)

4. Pravettoni, G., Triberti, S.: A "P5" approach to healthcare and health technology. In: Pravettoni, G., Triberti, S. (eds.) P5 eHealth: An Agenda for the Health Technologies of the Future, pp. 3–17. Springer, Cham (2020). https://doi.org/10.1007/978-3-030-27994-3_1

5. Gorini, A., Caiani, E.G., Pravettoni, G.: Psycho-cognitive factors orienting eHealth development and evaluation. In: Pravettoni, G., Triberti, S. (eds.) P5 eHealth: An Agenda for the Health Technologies of the Future, pp. 109–121. Springer, Cham (2020). https://doi.org/10.1007/978-3-030-27994-3_7

6. World Health Organization: Ottawa Charter for Health Promotion. World Health Organization, Geneva, Switzerland (1986)

7. World Health Organization: Global Health Risks: Mortality and Burden of Disease Attributable to Selected Major Risks. World Health Organization, Geneva, Switzerland (2009)

8. Chiuve, S.E., McCullough, M.L., Sacks, F.M., Rimm, E.B.: Healthy lifestyle factors in the primary prevention of coronary heart disease among men. Benefits among users and nonusers of lipid-lowering and antihypertensive medications. Circulation **114**, 160–167 (2006)

9. World Health Organization: Global Status Report on Noncommunicable Diseases 2010. World Health Organization, Geneva, Switzerland (2011)

10. Andreoni, G., Caiani, E.G., Castaldini, N.: Digital health services through patient empowerment: classification, current state and preliminary impact assessment by health pod systems. Appl. Sci. **12**, 359 (2022). https://doi.org/10.3390/app12010359

11. Andreoni, G., Mambretti, C. (eds.): Digital Health Technology for Better Aging. RD, Springer, Cham (2021). https://doi.org/10.1007/978-3-030-72663-8

Improving Pediatric Medical Prescription to Promote First-Time Parent's Comprehension Through an Information Design Approach

Mariel Garcia-Hernandez[1]([✉]) [iD], Fabiola Chavez-Cortes[2] [iD],
and Alberto Rossa-Sierra[2] [iD]

[1] Universidad de Monterrey, Av. Ignacio Morones Prieto 4500-Poniente, Zona Valle Poniente,
66238 San Pedro Garza García, Nuevo León, México
mariel.garciah@udem.edu
[2] Universidad Panamericana Campus Guadalajara, Calzada Nueva 49, Granja, 45010 Zapopan,
Jalisco, México
{fcortes,lurosa}@up.edu.mx

Abstract. Studies indicate that parents consider pediatric medical encounters as stressful. One of the things they feel stressful is the uncertainty that revolves around the information in the medical prescription provided by the pediatrician since the information presented is not clear, confusing, and ambiguous. However, this feeling is more pronounced in new parents, since they do not have previous experience handling this type of health issue, it can be a significant trigger to face this type of situation and, above all, information. Based on this, a graphic restructuring was carried out from the perspective of the information design of the said medical document, that is, based on multi-scenarios and the cognitive, informational, and emotional needs of the users who interact with this design object. It was considered, in addition to the information that by law must appear in said documents, the ailment or symptom solves the medicine prescribed by the pediatrician, in such a way that, in addition to making these documents more understandable, it was sought to alleviate the stress and uncertainty that the user could feel. To validate the fact that the pediatric medical prescription was understandable and generated less stress, a questionnaire was applied to this user, the A/B Test and PSSUQ Questionnaire tool.

Keywords: information design · medical prescription · user experience

1 Introduction

Becoming a parent for the first time is one of the biggest changes a person can experience in their life [9]. First-time parents, as the newborn grows, become familiar with the management of each stage of it and with the tasks that are related to its upbringing and good development of the child [2, 9]. Within these activities related to the care of the firstborn, there is pediatric medical care. Studies reveal that this medical interaction is an activity that first-time parents find stressful [11].

1.1 First-Time Parents' Perception and Stress During Pediatric Medical Consultation: Outcomes

Studies have shown that is very common that first-time parents to experience stress and anxiety when they face medical information, particularly when it comes to the administration and monitoring of medical treatment of their children [6]. In the same way, other factors intervene, like a lack of prior medical knowledge, concerns about the effectiveness and the safety of the medication, and complex medical instructions [11].

Medical prescription plays and important role to treat diseases or conditions in children, for them, these documents should be clear and specific enough to be able to administer the medication correctly. This document is taken home by parents and serves as a guide for administering medication to their children [13]. It is important for parents to follow the instructions provided on the prescription, including the correct dose, frequency, and method of administration, to ensure the safe and effective use of the medication [1, 3].

However, a study indicates that during the administration of medications at home in children by their parents, especially first-time parents, there are a series of errors related to the incorrect measurement of doses, incorrect administration techniques, and misunderstandings about the medication regimen. These errors can result in ineffective treatment or even harm to the child [1]. It is important for parents to receive clear and concise information about the medication and the administration process from their doctor or healthcare provider, and to ask questions if there is any confusion, in addition, keeping regular communication between the doctor, and other healthcare providers can help to minimize medication errors and ensure the best possible health outcomes for the child. However, according to a study, there are barriers in said communication that prevent this from happening [11], therefore, the medical prescription becomes a true tool for the prevention of errors and safeguarding the physical integrity of the patient.

2 Information Design for Medical Documents

Information design theory is concerned with the effective and efficient presentation of information, considering cognitive, communication, and aesthetic principles [12]. The cognitive principles focus on how people process and understand information, while communication principles aim to ensure that information is presented in a clear and accessible manner. Aesthetic principles deal with the visual appeal and overall look of the information being presented. These three principles work together to ensure that information is not only effectively communicated but also visually appealing and engaging to the audience [12].

Information design in medical documents is especially important because medical information can be complex and technical, and it's crucial that it be presented in a way that is easy for patients and healthcare providers to understand. Effective information design in medical documents can improve communication, increase patient understanding and engagement, and ultimately improve health outcomes [5].

In the context of a medical prescription, information design can play a critical role in preventing errors and improving patient safety in medical prescriptions. By using clear, concise, and easy-to-understand language and visual aids, information design can help ensure that the instructions on a prescription are accurately understood and followed. This can reduce the risk of medication errors and adverse reactions, and ultimately lead to improved patient outcomes.

2.1 Intervention and Development of the Information Design Proposal

Based on what is indicated in the previous sections of this research work, an area of improvement was detected in the design of information presented by the medical prescriptions that are issued to first-time parents each time they take their child for a consultation.

The development of this proposal was based on what was found in a study where the design and structure of 384 medical prescriptions were analyzed [1]. Being a study developed based on a large sample of medical prescriptions, it was possible to identify the best practices and areas for improvement in the design and structure of these documents (Table 1).

Table 1. Prescription information from health establishments. Alvarez-Risco, Aldo, and S. Del-Aguila-Arcentales. *Errores de prescripción como barrera para la Atención Farmacéutica en establecimientos de salud públicos: Experiencia Perú.* Pharmaceutical Care España 17.6 (2015): 725–731

	Pediatric medical office 1	Pediatric medical office 2	Pediatric medical office 3	Pediatric medical office 4	Pediatric medical office 5	Pediatric medical office 6	Pediatric medical office 7	Pediatric medical office 8	Pediatric medical office 9	Pediatric medical office 10	Pediatric medical office 11	Percentage of data compliance by regulations
Expedition date	343	320	322	322	352	340	352	347	336	345	334	87,90%
Patient name	328	354	341	339	321	334	341	333	343	322	351	87,76%
Age	320	351	345	345	339	337	324	355	323	340	324	87,67%
Weight	99	93	90	86	87	92	104	85	92	88	99	24,03%
Diagnosis	130	121	131	140	145	125	108	151	109	154	131	34,21%
Drug concentration	350	322	328	351	351	323	343	340	331	345	325	87,81%
Pharmaceutical form	348	354	323	338	347	354	338	344	352	349	327	89,35%
Dose	285	277	243	275	225	318	328	221	338	295	354	74,79%
Administration route	34	32	49	30	50	50	51	40	51	39	53	11,34%
Frecuencie	204	156	184	139	115	200	176	148	131	110	186	41,41%
Treatment duration	300	282	206	242	270	296	286	264	252	246	226	68,02%
Signature	333	344	322	347	326	323	327	324	333	344	325	86,36%
Seal	341	321	352	326	351	352	328	342	331	329	337	87,83%
Expiration date	12	36	30	7	8	7	7	15	37	42	40	5,71%

The findings of this study could be used to inform the development of the proposal to improve the design of information in medical prescriptions, with the aim of reducing errors and improving patient safety. Something important to mention is that this study was carried out in Mexico, for which the regulations that establish the National Commission of Medical Arbitration of the Government of Mexico [4] had to be implemented regarding the data that this type of document doctors must present.

The design of the pediatric medical prescription design proposal was carried out by students of Information Design and Digital Communication from the University of Guadalajara, Mexico, in 2022 in the User Experience Research course, in three teams of two people. The design proposals were developed based on the principles of information design [12], from information collected based on research tools in the information design process [10] and under the regulations established by the National Commission of Medical Arbitration of the Government of Mexico [4]. The final proposals were as follows (Images 1 and 2):

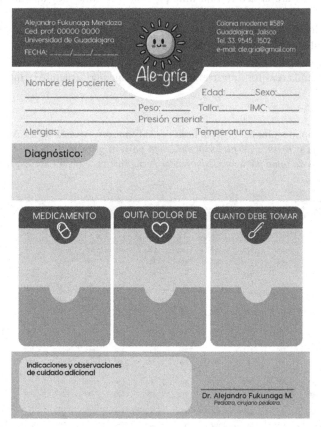

Image 1. Pediatric Medical Prescription Proposal A. Design by Cynthia Natalie Cano Medina and Laura Aramara Hernández Guajardo, (2022).

Based on those established as part of the information design, the formal considerations of design are shared below, considering the principles of information design and the information that, by regulation, must be presented.

Cognitive Principles. Regarding these principles, a hierarchical and segmentation strategy was used for the information presented to imply that the data presented in each section shared the same nature. In the same way, data such as dose, drug, route of administration, pharmaceutical form, and dose frequency are directly related through graphic

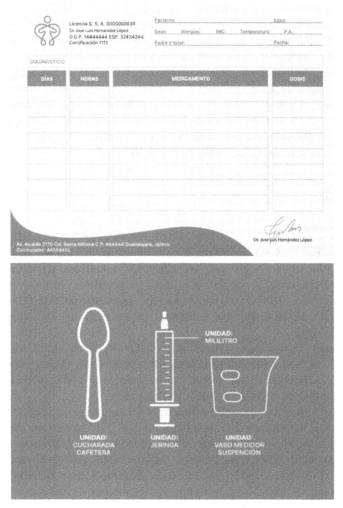

Image 2. Pediatric Medical Prescription Proposal C, front and back. Design by Michelle Anaya Chora and Carlos Josué Marquez García, (2022).

elements that coined familiarity with the information. The color and typography strategies were also planned in order to ease the cognitive load when reading the information presented in the recipe; geometric fonts like *Lato*, *Inter Tight* and *Visby Sans Serif* and sober colors were implemented, mostly in the cold range.

Communicative Principles. The tone of information was concise and to the point. The use of long sentences and phrases was avoided. Priority was given to handling clear information without falling into technicalities.

Aesthetic Principles. Regarding the aesthetic principles of the design proposals developed, geometric figures are observed, where the circle and rounded corners predominate. Slightly organic illustrations were implemented to represent some type of icon related to health and its care, without falling into medical symbols.

After having developed the previous proposals, a validation study was applied, which measures the degree of usability of each of the three proposals in order to identify the one that best complied with the information design principles (cognitive, communicative, and aesthetic), in addition, to know which was the most efficient (quick to read, cognitive principle), efficient (easy to understand, communicative principle) and satisfactory (aesthetically more pleasing, aesthetic) proposal [8].

3   Method

3.1   Study Design

Participants: For the validation of the three proposals from what is stated in previous sections, 385 first-time parents were evaluated, this sample size corresponds to 95% reliability and 5% error in correlation to the total population of these users, which corresponds to the 1,912,178 newborns that were registered in 2022 [7]. Participants were in Mexico, where gender was indifferent, as were their marital status, education level, and age range.

Experiment: This process corresponds to a cross-sectional study, where the A/B Test method was used, where the sample size was divided into three groups consisting of 128 people each. Each of these groups was presented with a different design proposal and the time it took to read it completely was measured.

After being exposed to the medical prescription design proposal, a PSSUQ questionnaire was shared with them via Google Forms, which seeks to measure the immediate perception of usability that the user had of the assigned proposal. The reagents found in this instrument were: 1) The organization of the information provided by the recipe was clear to me 2) I was able to understand the doses of the medication, frequency, and route of administration. 3) I have a clear diagnosis of the disease. 4) The doctor's data, such as telephone, address, and professional license are visible to me. 5) The organization of the information on the recipe seems pleasant to me. 6) I find the general design of this medical document aesthetic. Items 1 and 3 correspond to the efficiency variable, items 2 and 4 to the effectiveness condition, and statements 5 and 6 to the degree of satisfaction. Users were asked to select a value between 1 and 5, with 1 being strongly disagreed and 5 being strongly agree based on the degree to which each of the questionnaire's premises was close to what they considered to be true.

3.2   Results

Con base a las herramientas implementadas para hacer la validación de las propuestas de diseño de información se obtuvieron los siguientes resultados:

In Table 2 we can see the results of the validation tools, in the first parameter to be evaluated in the experiment we can see that the proposal that was faster to read was C,

Table 2. Data provided by the A/B test and the PSSUQ questionnaires for the validation of the proposals. Own elaboration.

	Proposal A	Proposal B	Proposal C
Average Reading Time	15 seg	22 seg	13 seg
1) The organization of the information provided by the recipe was clear to me	80%	85%	87%
2) I was able to understand the doses of the medication, frequency, and route of administration	83%	86%	90%
3) I have a clear diagnosis of the disease	85%	86%	97%
4) The doctor's data, such as tele-phone, address, and professional license are visible to me	88%	90%	90%
5) The organization of the information on the recipe seems pleasant to me	90%	87%	80%
6) I find the general design of this medical document aesthetic	91%	85%	75%
The percentages presented represent the score that oscillates between totally agree and agree**			

■ Efficient Variable   ■ Effective Variable   Satisfactory Variable

however, in addition to the fact that said proposal presents the coincidence percentages with the positive response (totally agree and agree) of the users, so it could be considered that it is the most efficient of the three proposals. Similarly, it should be noted that the proposal that presents the highest percentages of positive responses (totally agree and agree) in the effective variant is C. Finally, regarding the variant related to satisfaction, the test with the highest percentage is A. Therefore, we can conclude that the most usable proposal is C.

3.3   Discussion

To begin this section, we proceed to present a comparative table of the elements that make up the visual configuration of each of the proposals (Table 3):

Reading Journey. The reading route that turned out to be more efficient (because of its speed, 13 s on average) was the one presented in proposal C, since it is a configuration that alludes to the natural shape of the ocular route, it turns out to be more comfortable and easier for the user, unlike proposal B, which presents a configuration contrary to this conventional way of reading, where this proposal was where the user took more time to read it (22 s on average). From what we can say, reading efficiency is related to respecting the normal and conventional path of reading of the human eye in the design.

Layout. Proposal C presented four columns used for convenience according to the amount of information that was wanted to be presented, we can say that the grid gave rise to a more geometric configuration, therefore, cognitively it was a less heavy task, and this made said information better understood. Based on this, we can point out that

Table 3. Analysis of the visual configuration of each of the proposals developed. Own elaboration

	Proposal A	Proposal B	Proposal C
Reading journey	Top down reading	Reading from left to right	Reading from right to left
Layout	One column and 5 floors of information	Two columns, one wider than the other	Four columns and three floors of information
Typography	Two variants of the same font family in three different points	Three variants of the same font family in three different points	A typeface and four variables of it
Color/Color Contrast	Blue and orange accent color	White, blue and pink accent.	White and green in different opacities
Visual Emphasis	Information related to the drug, spectrum of relief and dosage	Patient and doctor information	Information related to the drug, spectrum of relief and dosage
Support graphic elements	Boxes, half circles and straight lines	Rectangles, straight lines and negative space	Rectangles, straight lines and negative space

for a better understanding, the implementation of geometric and harmonic arrangements would be sought to increase the understanding of the data that is presented to the user.

Typography. Based on the typographic strategy, we can mention that the fonts used shared the characteristic of being geometric and condensed, so the difference within this strategy lay in the fact that more variants of the same font family were used to increase cognition. And establish hierarchies of the same information that was presented in proposal C, which was the one that turned out to be the most effective. According to this, we can establish that the implementation of different variants of the same font helps to group information without overloading its processing by the user.

Color/Color Contrast. In the case of the color strategy, proposal C, being the most usable, was the one that implemented the fewest colors. Somehow, we can infer that this influenced having fewer visual distractors and made reading more pleasant, which we consider being related to the effectiveness of information comprehension.

Visual Emphasis. Something that enriches the usability of the piece of information design is the visual empathy that is made to the most relevant information in the compositional space, in this case, the information related to medical treatment. This was the strategy that was implemented in the design of proposal C, so we can argue that directing all the visual weight to what is most important in terms of the information presented is beneficial for the user's cognition and understanding.

Support Graphic Elements. In proposal C, it can be identified that there is a balanced amount of negative space, which helps to focus and delimit where the most relevant information of the design piece is located. In this case, it is considered that the fact of using negative space to visually help to outline areas that give the sensation of being a structure.

4 Conclusion

The correct decision-making and health care management are subject to the degree of understanding of the person in charge of managing these logistics. In the case of dosing and administration to children by parents who have no experience and are first-timers, it could become complex, due to ignorance of the said situation, additionally, to the stress that they could feel when facing this type of situation for the first time. There are studies that reveal that there are certain errors that are made in medication and medical treatment, due to a lack of understanding due to poorly designed prescriptions without sufficient data to guide the proper management of medication administration, which is why It is important to design this type of medical documents under the information design approach, which seeks to establish a good understanding of it, as well as to reduce the user's mental load when processing said information, without leaving aside the design aesthetics.

This approach that prioritizes the needs and understanding of the user can help ensure that medical prescriptions are clear, accessible, and easy to understand. This can involve using simple language, and visual aids, highlighting key information and providing clear instructions.

Based on this study, information design should be considered as an important tool to safeguard patient safety when the patient interacts with documents of a medical nature or other types of information design products that are contextualized in the field of health.

References

1. Alvarez-Risco, A., Del-Aguila-Arcentales, S.: Errores de prescripción como barrera para la Atención Farmacéutica en establecimientos de salud públicos: Experiencia Perú. Pharmaceutical Care España **17**(6), 725–731 (2015)
2. Carvalho, J.M.N., Gaspar, M.F.R.F., Cardoso, A.M.R.: Challenges of motherhood in the voice of primiparous mothers: initial difficulties. Investigacion y Educacion en Enfermeria. **35**(3), 285–294 (2017)
3. Cerezo de la Vega, M.A., Espinoza Cerezo, O.E., Techalotzi Amador, A., Tlalpan Hernández, R.M.: Elaboración Y diseño De La Receta De Enfermería/Development and Design of Nurse Prescribing. RICS Revista Iberoamericana De Las Ciencias De La Salud **5**(10), 67–97 (2016). https://www.rics.org.mx/index.php/RICS/article/view/39
4. Comisión Nacional de Arbitraje Médico. "Elementos básicos de una receta médica". Gobierno de México, 14 de febrero de 2020. www.gob.mx/conamed/articulos/elementos-basicos-de-una-receta-medica?idiom=es. Acceded el 1 de febrero de 2023

5. Garcia-Hernadez, M., et al.: Emotional design and human factors design as tool for understanding efficiency in information design process at medical documents. In: Advances in Industrial Design: Proceedings of the AHFE 2020 Virtual Conferences on Design for Inclusion, Affective and Pleasurable Design, Interdisciplinary Practice in Industrial Design, Kansei Engineering, and Human Factors for Apparel and Textile Engineering, July 16–20, 2020, USA. Springer (2020). https://doi.org/10.1007/978-3-030-51194-4_21

6. Hughes, R.G., Edgerton, E.A.: Reducing pediatric medication errors: children are especially at risk for medication errors. AJN Am. J. Nurs. **105**(5), 79–84 (2005)

7. INEGI: Estadísticas de Nacimiento en el 2021. Comunicación social. 21 de septiembre de 2022. Comunicado de prensa

8. Jordan, P.W.: An introduction to usability. CRC Press (2020)

9. Nelson, A.M.: Transition to motherhood. J Obstet Gynecol Neonatal Nurs. **32**(4), 465–477 (2003)

10. Pontis, S.: Making Sense of Field Research: A Practical Guide for Information Designers. Routledge (2018)

11. Street, R.L., Jr., et al.: How does communication heal? Pathways linking clinician–patient communication to health outcomes. Patient Educ. Couns. **74**(3), 295–301 (2009)

12. Visocky O'Grady, J., O'Grady, K.V.: The Information Design Handbook. How Books (2008)

13. Walsh, K.E., et al.: Medication errors in the homes of children with chronic conditions. Arch. Dis. Child. **96**(6), 581–586 (2011)

Development of Interactive Visual Communication Tools to Assist Caregivers

Mami Hayashi and Ari Aharari[✉]

SOJO University, 4-22-1, Ikeda, Nishi-ku 860-0082, Kumamoto, Japan
info@ahrary.org

Abstract. The number of people certified as requiring nursing care increases due to the aging of the population, a wide variety of products have been developed to support those requiring nursing care and their caregivers. Currently, systems such as nurse call systems have been developed in which a caregiver comes to the patient when the call button is pressed. However, caregivers with memory impairment who require nursing care need to remember the call's content by the time the caregiver answers the call.

In this research, we developed a system to support people who classify as levels 1 to 3. The proposed approach is designed based on the caregiver's basic needs support by selecting one of four options: "toilet," "eat/drink," "hot/cold," or "call" from the specially designed user interface. The proposed friendly user interface in this research can easily be modified and clarify the individuality of each user and the needs of the nursing care site. The requested information will notify the nursing care site smartphones through the LINE account. We also evaluated the proposed system by doing experiments in the daily support center.

Keywords: Care-receiver · Caregiver · Communication Tools

1 Introduction

The world's population is aging rapidly, and Japan's aging population is severe among them. According to Japan's Ministry of Health, Labor and Welfare (MHLW), the aging rate in Japan is expected to reach 38.4% by 2065 [1]. In addition, the number of people requiring nursing care is increasing every year as the population ages; as of July 2022, the number of people certified as requiring nursing care or support was 6.97 million, accounting for about 5.5% of Japan's population [2].

Japan's total population peaked at 128.08 million in 2008 and has begun to decline and is expected to decrease to 86.74 million by 2060. On the other hand, the elderly population is expected to continue to increase, peaking in 2042 [3]. The number of people certified requiring nursing care or support is expected to increase continuously until 2060, as the population of the elderly increases with the rate of those requiring nursing care [4].

With the increase in the number of people certified requiring nursing care or support, the number of people receiving nursing care at home without moving into nursing homes

© The Author(s), under exclusive license to Springer Nature Switzerland AG 2023
A. Marcus et al. (Eds.): HCII 2023, LNCS 14034, pp. 289–298, 2023.
https://doi.org/10.1007/978-3-031-35705-3_22

or other facilities is increasing. In addition, the MHLW (2013) is promoting home medical care and nursing care because the number of people certified as requiring nursing care and support is expected to continue to increase, and more than 60% of the population wants to receive care at home in their final days [5]. Currently, 58.9% of those certified as requiring nursing care or support receive care at home [6].

However, home care places a heavy burden on family members, as they are the principal caregivers at home. According to the MHLW (2016), 68.9% of caregivers of home caregivers feel worried and stressed [7]. In addition, the fatigue and stress caused by caregiving, as well as mental tension and anxiety, can lead to a chronic mental burden on caregivers, which can lead to strain on physical and cognitive functions, depression, and other mental health issues.

Therefore, this research targets caregivers who provide care at home and those who need care and conducts research and development of a communication tool between caregivers and those who need care, which supports the expression of the caregiver's intention, allows the caregiver and his/her family to maintain a moderate distance, and improves work efficiency and reduces stress for the caregiver.

2   Interactive Visual Communication Tools

Interactive visual communication tools have become increasingly important for caregivers and care-receivers, particularly in light of the COVID-19 pandemic, which has limited the ability of many individuals to have in-person visits with loved ones receiving care. These tools can help bridge the gap between care-receivers and their caregivers, allowing them to maintain meaningful connections and facilitate better care delivery.

One of the most widely used interactive visual communication tools is video conferencing software. Platforms like Zoom, Skype, and Microsoft Teams allow caregivers and care-receivers to have real-time video conversations, making it easier for them to stay in touch and share information. For instance, video conferencing can be used for remote care consultations, allowing healthcare professionals to diagnose and treat patients from a distance. It can also be used to help care-receivers stay connected with their family and friends, allowing them to see and hear from loved ones even if they cannot visit in person.

Another tool that can be useful for interactive visual communication is telehealth technology [8]. Telehealth technology enables caregivers and care-receivers to have virtual appointments, where they can see and speak with each other in real-time. This technology is particularly useful for those who have mobility issues, live in remote areas, or have difficulty accessing traditional healthcare facilities. Telehealth technology can also be used to facilitate remote monitoring of care-receivers' health, allowing caregivers to monitor their condition and respond quickly if needed.

Another important tool for interactive visual communication is the use of wearable devices [9]. Wearable devices are small, portable devices that can be worn on the body, allowing care-receivers to monitor and track various aspects of their health and wellbeing. These devices can be used to track vital signs such as heart rate, blood pressure, and temperature, as well as physical activity levels, sleep patterns, and medication compliance. Wearable devices can also be linked to mobile apps, allowing caregivers to access this data in real-time and respond quickly if needed. Another wearable technology that can be useful for interactive visual communication is smart glasses. Smart glasses, such as Google Glass, can be used to provide real-time information and support to care-receivers and caregivers, allowing them to access critical information and receive care and support from a distance. For example, smart glasses can be used to provide visual aids for individuals with visual impairments, or to provide real-time translation for individuals who are non-native speakers of a particular language.

Interactive visual communication tools are also being used to support care coordination and communication between caregivers and care-receivers. For example, many healthcare organizations are using mobile health applications to improve patient engagement and communication. These applications allow patients to communicate with their healthcare providers, view their medical records, and access health information. Additionally, these applications can be used to send reminders for appointments, medication, and other care-related activities. Some of the popular mobile health applications include MyChart [10], Heal, and Zocdoc.

Another tool that is becoming increasingly popular for interactive visual communication is virtual reality (VR) technology. VR provides an immersive experience for users, allowing them to feel as if they are in the same room as their loved ones, even if they are separated by distance. This can be especially beneficial for care-receivers who are isolated due to illness or disability, as it can help reduce feelings of loneliness and provide a sense of social connection. Some VR headsets, like the Oculus Quest, are specifically designed for use in healthcare, offering a range of features and applications that are tailored to the needs of patients and caregivers.

Finally, artificial intelligence (AI) and machine learning (ML) technologies are also being used to support caregiving. For example, AI-powered chatbots can be used to provide care-receivers with personalized health information, as well as respond to their questions and concerns. Additionally, machine learning algorithms can be used to analyze large amounts of data generated by wearable devices, allowing caregivers to identify patterns and trends in the care-receivers' health and wellbeing, and respond proactively.

Interactive visual communication tools are transforming the caregiving process, enabling caregivers and care-receivers to better understand each other's needs and collaborate more effectively. These tools are helping to improve the quality of care, increase access to care for those who live in remote areas or have mobility issues, and reduce the burden on caregivers by providing them with more information, support, and training. As technology continues to advance, we can expect to see even more innovative tools emerge that will further improve the caregiving experience for everyone involved.

3   Proposed System

In this research, we developed a system to support people who classify as levels 1 to 3. The target users are caregivers who provide care at home and caregivers who are certified as requiring 2–4 years of care and receive care at home.

The proposed approach is designed based on the caregiver's basic needs support by selecting one of four options: "toilet," "eat/drink," "hot/cold," or "call" from the specially designed user interface. The proposed friendly user interface in this research can easily be modified and clarify the individuality of each user and the needs of the nursing care site. A sketch of the proposed system shows in Fig. 1.

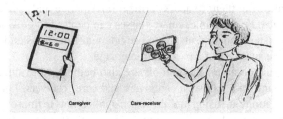

Fig. 1. Sketch of the proposed system.

3.1 System Configuration

The system configuration of the proposed interactive visual communication tools shows in Fig. 2. The proposed friendly Graphic User Interface displayed buttons created by applying Tkinter and the touch screen of a Raspberry Pi. When the button is pressed, the information on the controller is sent to Google Apps Script via an HTTP request, and the Google Apps Script sends a message request to the LINE API server, which sends a notification to the user via the LINE API server. The Google Apps Script then sends a message request to the LINE API server, and the user is notified via LINE through the LINE API server. A webhook containing user IDs is sent from the LINE API server to Google Apps Script. By recording the user IDs to be notified in a Google Spreadsheet, it is possible to set up notifications for specific users.

Tkinter. Tkinter is a standard Python library for creating graphical user interfaces (GUIs). It is one of the most commonly used GUI libraries in Python, and it is available for Windows, macOS, and Linux. Tkinter is built on top of the Tcl/Tk GUI toolkit and provides a convenient way for Python developers to create graphical interfaces for their applications.

Tkinter provides a variety of widgets such as buttons, labels, text boxes, check boxes, radio buttons, etc. that can be used to create a user interface. It also provides geometry management methods, which can be used to arrange the widgets in a particular layout. The widgets in Tkinter are highly customizable, allowing developers to change their appearance, behavior, and functionality.

Google Apps Script. Google Apps Script is a platform for automating tasks and extending the functionality of Google Workspace products like Google Sheets, Google Docs, and Gmail. It is a cloud-based JavaScript scripting language that enables you to create custom scripts and macros for these products. With Google Apps Script, you can easily automate repetitive tasks, create custom workflows, and integrate with other Google Workspace and third-party services.

Google Apps Script provides a convenient and easy-to-use development environment, with a familiar syntax and intuitive interface. It enables you to access and manipulate data stored in Google Workspace products, making it possible to perform operations like generating reports, automating email responses, or extracting data from spreadsheets. You can also use Google Apps Script to create custom add-ons and integrations that can be used within Google Workspace products.

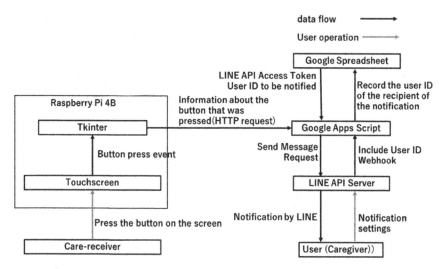

Fig. 2. Proposed System Configuration.

3.2 User Interface Design

User Interface Design for the elderly refers to the design of interfaces and technology that is easy to use and accessible for older adults. This includes designing interfaces with large, easy-to-read text, precise visuals, and simple navigation.

It is important to consider that older adults may have declining vision, dexterity, and cognitive abilities. Therefore, UI design should be created with these factors in mind and take steps to mitigate any challenges they may present. For example, large touch buttons, clear visuals and audio cues can help individuals who have difficulty with dexterity, while font choices and high-contrast colors can help with visual impairments.

Another important aspect of UI design for the elderly is ensuring the interfaces are intuitive and easy to understand. This can be achieved by using familiar, predictable patterns and layouts, as well as providing clear instructions and guidance. For example, using simple language and avoiding complex jargon can help older adults understand how to use the technology.

In addition, UI design for the elderly should also consider accessibility features such as the ability to adjust text size and font, the ability to navigate the interface using keyboard controls or alternative input methods, and the ability to use the interface with a screen reader for those with visual impairments.

Finally, it is important to conduct user testing with older adults to ensure that the design meets their needs and expectations. This can help identify any issues with the interface, such as unclear instructions, confusing layouts, or inaccessible features, and allow designers to make adjustments as needed.

In this research, we focus on the point that UI design for the elderly is an important consideration for creating technology that is accessible and usable for everyone and can easily be customized based on the needs of caregivers. By designing interfaces with large, easy-to-read text, clear visuals, and simple navigation, and by including accessibility features, we can help ensure that older adults are able to use technology effectively and comfortably.

The proposed approach is designed based on the caregiver's basic needs support by selecting one of four options: "toilet," "eat/drink," "hot/cold," or "call" from the specially designed UI. These four words were commonly necessary options while providing care to the care-receivers. (see Fig. 3).

Fig. 3. User Interface of the proposed system.

The proposed friendly UI in this research can easily be customized and clarify the individuality of each user and the needs of the nursing care site. Figure 4 shows the proposed UI's customized color and button, which can be quickly done on-site by the end users.

3.3 User Interface Notification Methods

An effective user interface for elderly support should use multiple notification methods to ensure that important information is communicated effectively. This can help to improve the quality of life for elderly users and provide them with peace of mind.

1. Visual notifications: Visual notifications, such as flashing lights or large pop-up messages, can be used to immediately grab the user's attention. These types of notifications can be particularly useful for emergency situations, such as a fall or health incident, where quick action is needed.
2. Auditory notifications: Auditory notifications, such as spoken messages or sound alarms, can be used to alert the user when they may not be looking at the screen. This can be useful for medication reminders, for example, when the user may be engaged in a different activity.

Fig. 4. Customize the design of the proposed UI.

3. Vibrations: Vibrations can be used as a discreet notification method, especially in public spaces where auditory notifications may not be appropriate. For example, the user's device could vibrate to remind them to take their medication, without disturbing those around them.
4. Email or text message notifications: For those who prefer to receive notifications remotely, email or text message notifications can be sent to a mobile device or computer. This can be useful for reminders about doctor's appointments or other important events, such as birthdays or anniversaries.
5. Repeat notifications: Repeat notifications can be used to ensure that important information is not missed. For example, if the user misses a medication reminder, the same reminder can be repeated at a later time.

The interface should also allow the user to customize the notification methods they prefer, so that they can tailor the interface to meet their specific needs and preferences. In conclusion, an effective user interface for elderly support should use multiple notification methods, including visual, auditory, vibrational, email or text message notifications, and repeat notifications. By using a combination of these methods, important information can be effectively communicated and the elderly user can be provided with peace of mind.

We focused on the "Email or text message notifications" and applied the LINE apps to design the UI notification. A diagram of the user registration process is shown in Fig. 5. An account can be easily added using a QR code, and a confirmation message will automatically send after a successful registration.

After the user registration is successfully done, then the system is ready to use. A restart can activate the device, and the UI, including four buttons, will pop up. If the care-receiver presses the button on the touch screen, then the information about the button will transfer to the Google Apps Script via HTTP. Next, the notification message will send through the Line API server to the registered caregiver's LINE account. A diagram of the notification process is shown in Fig. 6.

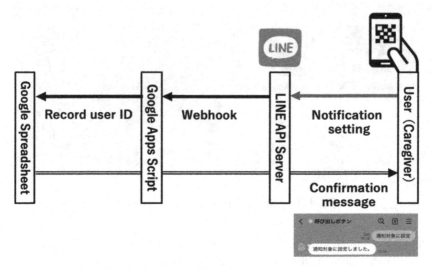

Fig. 5. A diagram of the user registration process.

We added a new function to the system to prevent the care-receiver from pressing the button repeatedly. When the button is pressed and the information is sent, the screen turns white and cannot be pressed. When the button information is transmitted, the button can be pressed again.

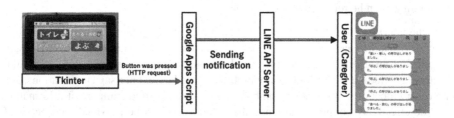

Fig. 6. A diagram of the notification process.

4   Evaluations

A demonstration experiment was conducted with home caregivers and care-receiver to determine the evaluation of validity of using the proposed interactive visual communication tools.

We also administrated a questionnaire to assess the level of satisfaction of the users with the usage of the proposed tools. The questions in the questionnaire are points to usability such as convenience, work efficiency and stress reduction, current good points, dissatisfaction, and points to be improved.

The output from the questionnaire allows us to confirm the satisfaction of the proposed communication tool for caregivers and care-receivers, and evaluation of leads to improved work efficiency and reduced stress for caregivers.

The environment of this experiment is described in Fig. 7. First, we registered the caregiver's smartphone to receive the notification. We also installed the User Interface to the left side of the care-receiver bed where she can easily touch the screen. Then we let the caregiver and care-receiver use the proposed interactive visual communication tools, and finally, we request them to answer the questionnaire.

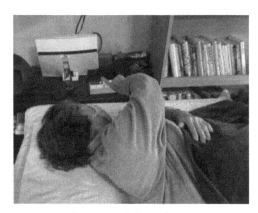

Fig. 7. The environment of the experiment.

The following table shows the questionnaire results by caregiver and care-receiver (see Table 1).

Table 1. Results of the questionnaire answered by caregiver and care-receiver.

Items	Answers
Was this device convenient?	Yes
Has it improved work efficiency and reduced stress?	Yes
Advantage	• History can be kept • Can be adapted for children and people with disabilities • Individualized support is possible
Disadvantages Improvement points	• Some elderly might not use the touch screen • It is difficult to understand how to press the buttons • The visually impaired cannot use the touch screen

From the results of the questionnaire, we can assume that the proposed tools are accessible for caregivers to use, and it helps to improve caregivers' work efficiency and reduces stress. In addition, the proposed tools' advantages were that they keep a history, can be used for children and people with disabilities and can be personalized. Besides, the disadvantage points need to be improved where the elderly are unfamiliar with using such touch screen devices.

5 Conclusions

Recently the number of elderly who needs nursing care in Japan has been increasing, and most of them wish to receive support at home rather than move into a nursing home or other facility. Since the primary caregivers' in-home care are family members, the burden of caregiving tends to fall on family members, and many family caregivers feel fatigued and stressed.

In this research, we developed a communication tool between caregivers and care-receivers that helps to express their intentions by using an especially designed interface. The proposed UI is designed based on the caregiver's basic needs support by selecting one of four options and can easily be customized and clarify the individuality of each user and the needs of the nursing care site. Also, an experiment was conducted to evaluate the validity of using the proposed tools. From the results of the questionnaire, we can assume that the proposed tools are accessible for caregivers to use, and it helps to improve caregivers' work efficiency and reduces stress.

References

1. Tokyo: Cabinet Office Homepage. https://www8.cao.go.jp/kourei/whitepaper/w-2022/zen bun/pdf/1s1s_01.pdf. Accessed 10 Aug 2022
2. Tokyo: Cabinet Office Homepage. https://www8.cao.go.jp/kourei/whitepaper/w-2021/html/ zenbun/s1_2_2.html. Accessed 10 Aug 2022
3. Tokyo: Ministry of Health, Labor and Welfare Homepage. https://www.mhlw.go.jp/wp/hak usyo/kousei/15/dl/1-00.pdf. Accessed 10 Aug 2022
4. Tokyo: Ministry of Health, Labor and Welfare Homepage. https://www.mhlw.go.jp/file/05-Shingikai-12601000-Seisakutoukatsukan-Sanjikanshitsu_Shakaihoshoutantou/0000163525. pdf. Accessed 12 Jan 2023
5. Tokyo: Ministry of Health, Labor and Welfare Homepage. https://www.mhlw.go.jp/seisakuni tsuite/bunya/kenkou_iryou/iryou/zaitaku/dl/zaitakuiryou_all.pdf. Accessed 12 Jan 2023
6. Tokyo: Ministry of Health, Labor and Welfare Homepage. https://www.mhlw.go.jp/topics/ kaigo/osirase/jigyo/m22/2207.html. Accessed 10 Aug 2022
7. Tokyo: Ministry of Health, Labor and Welfare Homepage. https://www.mhlw.go.jp/toukei/ saikin/hw/k-tyosa/k-tyosa16/dl/16.pdf. Accessed 10 Aug 2022
8. Brian, K.H., George, D., Karen, L.C.: Defining obtrusiveness in home telehealth technologies: a conceptual framework. J. Am. Med. Inform. Assoc. 13(4), 428–431 (2006)
9. Dittmar, A., Axisa, F., Delhomme, G., Gehin, C.: New concepts and technologies in home care and ambulatory monitoring. Stud. Health Technol. Inform. 108, 9–35 (2004)
10. Ramsey, A., Lanzo, E., Huston-Paterson, H., Tomaszewski, K., Trent, M.: Increasing patient portal usage: preliminary outcomes from the MyChart genius project. J. Adolesc. Health 62(1), 29–35 (2018)

Light Therapy Headset Model for Seasonal Affective Disorder Group

Qinxin He[1(✉)], Stephen Westland[1], and Yuan Feng[2]

[1] University of Leeds, Leeds, UK
ml20q2h@leeds.ac.uk
[2] East China University of Science and Technology, Shanghai, China

Abstract. With seasonal affective disorder currently affecting 10% of the population in northern latitudes and temperate regions and this statistic continuing to grow, light therapy is becoming the first treatment choice for seasonal affective disorder because of its lesser side effects and faster efficacy compared with other treatments. However, the light therapy products currently on the market are almost always in the form of table lamps, which require half an hour of exposure in front of a 10,000-lx light every morning. This treatment has does have some disadvantages; prolonged exposure to bright light can cause eye irritation, headaches and nausea, and it can also disrupt the patient's normal rhythm of life, especially for those who work on a regular schedule. Therefore, exploring alternative light therapy products is valuable and may have great market potential. Firstly, this paper explores the literature and finds that light can be transmitted to the brain through the ear canal, which may greatly reduce the probability of side effects. Secondly, through questionnaire research and the construction of a KANO model, this article identifies the acceptance of a light therapy headset among the target group, as well as its main functions and product usage process. On the basis of the research, the design schemes were completed. Finally, evaluation and selection of the design schemes were conducted through 3D modelling and printing techniques, user interviews and usability testing.

Keywords: Seasonal affective disorder · Light therapy headset · Medical and health product · Design model

1 Background

Seasonal affective disorder is a depressive disorder with seasonal patterns, the symptoms of which are characterised by periods of depression in the fall and winter, with remission in the spring and summer, and generally recurrent episodes (Fonte at el. 2021). Seasonal affective disorder is usually triggered by the shorter winter daylight cycle and is therefore predominantly prevalent in people living in northern latitudes and northern temperate zones (Tonello 2008). According to statistics, the prevalence of seasonal affective disorder ranges from 2 to 5% of the population in temperate regions and can reach up to 10% of the population in northern latitudes (Fonte at el. 2021).

A. Marcus et al. (Eds.): HCII 2023, LNCS 14034, pp. 299–317, 2023.
https://doi.org/10.1007/978-3-031-35705-3_23

In terms of the market for seasonal affective disorder, differences in the perception of the disease and the development of healthcare are the main reasons for the differences in the seasonal affective disorder market in different regions. North America has the largest seasonal affective disorder market in the world, with 38% of the market dominated (Future Market Insights 2022). The European seasonal affective disorder treatment market accounts for 29.5% of the market in 2022, second only to North America (Future Market Insights 2022). Other regions such as East Asia and South Asia, which account for 18.5% and 7.5% of the market respectively, are predicted to increase significantly in market share for seasonal affective disorder due to growing recognition of anxiety and depression (Future Market Insights 2022). The Oceania and MEA regions are slow in growing treatment demand for seasonal affective disorder due to lack of awareness, insufficient research activity and underdeveloped healthcare infrastructure, with market shares of 1.5% and 1% respectively (Future Market Insights 2022). From a global perspective, the global market for seasonal affective disorder is valued at USD 880 million in 2022 and will increase sharply in the post-epidemic era due to the influence of Covid-19 (Future Market Insights 2022). Therefore, the seasonal affective disorder market is expected to consistently grow and the market prospect will be prosperous.

The main treatment options for seasonal affective disorder are light therapy, medication and psychotherapy (Mayo Clinic 2022), while light therapy is becoming the first treatment choice for seasonal affective disorder due to its faster efficacy and less severe side effects compared to medication (Lam et al. 2006). As the prevalence and market valuation of seasonal affective disorder continues to grow, the use and acceptance of light therapy is also increasing.

However, against this backdrop, the form of light therapy products currently available on the market is relatively limited, generally in the form of light therapy table lamps (Cnet Health and Wellness 2022), which require sitting in front of a 10,000-lx bright light lamp for 30 min each morning (Pail et al. 2011). Although this form has its advantages, such as helping to illuminate the user's room and allowing the adjustment of lighting patterns, it also has disadvantages that cannot be ignored. One of the disadvantages is that the current light therapy table lamps are not easily portable, which can be inconvenient for users with busy schedules or for users who have travel needs. Furthermore, although the side effects of light therapy are relatively mild compared to medication, prolonged exposure to bright light can still lead to side effects such as eye problems, headaches and nausea (Meštrović 2021), and the probability of these side effects is particularly high in new patient groups who are beginning light therapy for the first time (Melrose 2015). Kogan et al. (1998) mentioned that in the light therapy side effect experiments, 45.7% of the 70 participants reported experiencing side effects, with headache and eye problems being the two side effects that occurred at the highest rate, typically within the first two days of light therapy. These side effects are partly caused by looking directly into bright light (Delgado 2019), and partly due to the bright light taking up the patient's full attention and energy during a 30-min treatment session (Botanov et al. 2013).

Therefore, designing an alternative light therapy product that allows portability and avoids the requirement for patients to look directly into bright light will be necessary and may have a great market value. This project conducted in-depth research on alternative forms of light therapy and through literature review it was found that there are organs or body parts of the human body that are able to receive light and transmit light information to the brain without the eyes. Audi launched a head mounted light therapy product for indoor workers in 2016, which was designed to supplement vitamin D for indoor workers (Alba 2020), as shown in Fig. 1. This light therapy product works by using the thinnest part of the human skull to transmit light, which changed the way traditional light therapy products are used. Although there was no user feedback to support the effectiveness of this head mounted light therapy product from Audi, it gave an inspiration for this paper. Thus, after an extensive review of the literature in this direction, it was found that some studies suggested that light can be transmitted through the ear canal to the brain and be perceived (Sun et al. 2016), as shown in Fig. 3. Jurvelin et al. (2014) indicated that light can be transmitted through the ear canal to the brain and can have effective antidepressant and antianxiety effects in patients with seasonal affective disorder (Fig. 2).

Fig. 1. Audi head mounted light therapy product (Alba 2020)

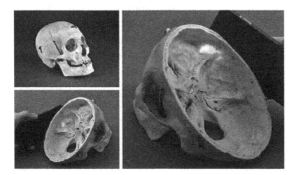

Fig. 2. Pterion is the thinnest part of human skull which allows light transmission (Alba 2020)

Based on the above theoretical support, the project decided to develop a product to provide light therapy to patients with seasonal affective disorder through the ear canal, aiming to improve the disadvantages of traditional light therapy which is not portable and has side effects due to exposure directly to bright light.

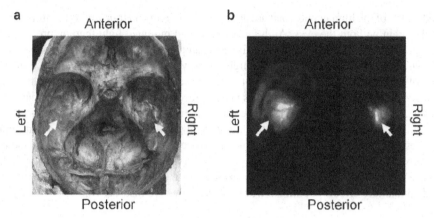

Fig. 3. Light can transmit into the skull through the ear canal (Sun et al. 2016)

2 Method

After researching the background and developing an initial design concept, the design development of this project went through seven stages: analysis of the target group, design of the usage flow of in-ear light therapy headset, creation of primary sketches, making primary models and conducting usability tests, headset shape improvement, drawing the final concept, 3D modelling and 3D printing and final concept presentation.

2.1 Questionnaire and Kano Model

Firstly, a questionnaire was sent to the target user group regarding their acceptance and expectations of light therapy and the innovative in-ear light therapy headset. The questionnaire was targeted at people living in areas with a high prevalence of seasonal affective disorder, which are northern latitudes and temperate regions (Tonello 2008). There were 151 participants who provided valid feedback, of which 62% said they have experienced or might have experienced seasonal affective disorder and 80% said they would prefer light therapy to medication and psychotherapy if they had seasonal affective disorder. In terms of acceptance of the innovative concept of in-ear light therapy headset, 82% of participants said they would be very willing to try or want to try this light therapy headsets.

Regarding the functionality of the headset, the questionnaire included the following seven questions about the functionality of in-ear light therapy headset, as shown in Table 1. Based on the results of the following questions, the Kano attributes of each function were calculated, and a better-worse coefficient diagram was created, as shown in Fig. 4, from which the main functions of the in-ear light therapy headset were confirmed.

From the better-worse coefficient diagram, priority should be given to the fourth quadrant, which is the Must-be quality. In-ear light therapy headset should therefore first have a high level of safety and good efficacy. Secondly, the first quadrant of One-dimensional quality should be achieved, which is portability, ease of use and a high level

Table 1. Questionnaire question numbers and corresponding content.

Question No.	Question content
Q1	A high degree of safety of light therapy products (e.g. little or no side effects)
Q2	The product has a good therapeutic effect
Q3	Portable and easy to carry
Q4	High level of comfort
Q5	Bluetooth connectivity, which allows to connect to mobile phones and has a corresponding app for intelligent control of light therapy time and intensity
Q6	It is multifunctional and can replace normal headphones in addition to the light therapy function
Q7	High functionality of accompanying app (e.g. have functions for socializing, product maintenance appointments, monitoring body status such as heart rate, blood pressure, body temperature, etc.)

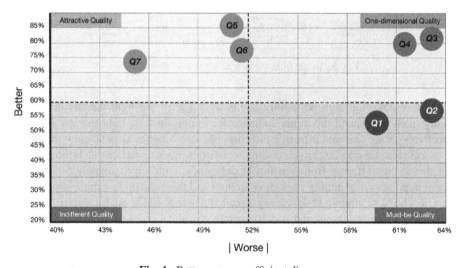

Fig. 4. Better-worse coefficient diagram

of comfort, and when these qualities are provided, user satisfaction will increase significantly. Finally, the second quadrant of Attractive quality also needs to be considered, which is to provide a supporting app and the light therapy headset can replace the normal Bluetooth earphone function.

The findings of the questionnaire indicate that there is positive feedback from the target group regarding the concept of light therapy headset and that in-ear light therapy headset would be attractive to the target consumers and may have a great market in temperate and northern latitudes. This research confirms the feasibility of the concept of in-ear light therapy headset and provides some reliable direction and guidance for the further design of in-ear light therapy headset.

2.2   Establishment of Product Usage Processes

After the user questionnaire research, the project designed the usage process of the light therapy headset and visualised the comparison with traditional light therapy. As shown in the Fig. 5, when the users wake up, they can quickly start the light therapy by opening the charging case, wearing the light therapy headset and opening the mobile phone app to set the intensity of the therapy light and start/end time. The process is simple and easy to operate, with the headset on and the start/end times set the users can do whatever they want to do without disrupting their normal daily schedule. When the light therapy is finished, the mobile phone app will remind the users to take off the light therapy headset and put it back into the portable charging case to complete the light therapy, which makes this light therapy product highly portable and solves the disadvantage of traditional light therapy table lamps that are constrained by space and location.

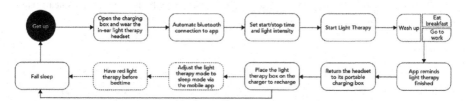

Fig. 5. In-ear light therapy headset workflow diagram

Furthermore, the high portability and ease of use of the light therapy headset is highly likely to expand the target audience for the product, as light therapy not only effectively treats seasonal affective disorder, but also vitamin D deficiency and sleep disorders (Smykowski 2022). According to statistics, approximately one billion people worldwide are suffering from vitamin D deficiency, with approximately 50% of the global population not getting enough vitamin D and there are up to a third of people in the UK who have vitamin D deficiency already (AIRIUS 2022). As for sleep disorders, it is one of the most urgent and widely prevalent medical problems in modern society (Walker 2017), with statistics showing that eight out of ten adults worldwide expect to improve their quality of sleep, and 44% of adults worldwide report that their sleep quality has become worse during the last five years (Koninklijke Philips 2019). And there was research showed that exposure to red light at night can effectively improve the quality of sleep for humans (Zhao et al. 2012). Therefore, as shown in the Fig. 6, the function of the in-ear light therapy headset is not only limited to the daily morning light therapy in autumn and winter, but users with poor sleep quality can also set the red light mode to improve quality of sleep through the mobile phone app, and users who work indoors for long periods of time can also use the product in summer to supplement the body's vitamin D needs.

2.3   Sketching, Modelling and Usability Testing

Following the progress of the above research, this project began to develop the product design of in-ear light therapy headset, starting with research into the structure of the

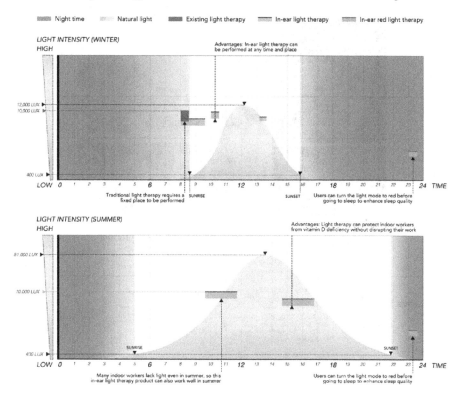

Fig. 6. Comparison of in-ear light therapy headset and traditional light therapy products

human ear canal and the in-ear products currently available on the market, as shown in Fig. 7. As in-ear light therapy headset is a product that needs to be worn for long durations every day, the product structure requires ergonomics and the material used for the in-ear part of the product needs to be soft and skin-friendly.

Based on the above research, the project developed primary concept sketches, as shown in Fig. 8, from which five achievable forms were selected and primary models were made in clay, as shown in Fig. 9, which were then tested in the first usability test. In the first usability test, three participants were invited to evaluate these five clay models in terms of comfort, ease of use and aesthetics. As shown in Fig. 10, model number 5 received a relatively high score and evaluation, so the project decided to use model number 5 as the base model for the light therapy headset for the next usability test and shape improvement.

The second usability test focused on the comfort of the clay model number 5 during long wearing durations. After wearing the model number 5 for 2 h, the tester noticed discomfort in tragus, because the model number 5 slightly squeezed this structure and although it was not felt in a short time, the tester felt clear pain in the tragus part after 2 h of wear. Therefore, model number 5 needs further improvement (Fig. 11).

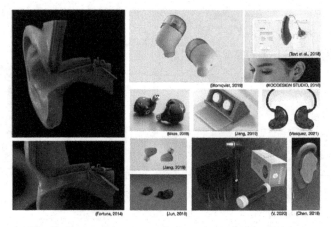

Fig. 7. Research on ear canal structure and in-ear products

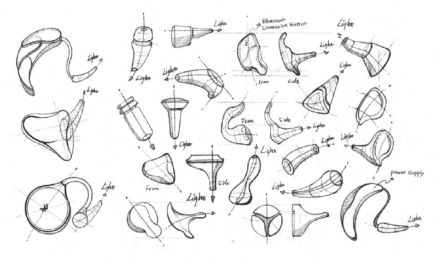

Fig. 8. Primary sketch of light therapy headset

2.4 Product Shape Improvement and Final Solution

As shown in Fig. 12, the shape improvement of the light therapy headset has progressed through three stages. The first stage was the model number 5 decided after the first usability test. In the second stage, in order to solve the problem of model number 5 squeezing tragus, which was found in the second usability test, a part of the structure of model number 5 was removed, which led to the enhanced model. The enhanced model fitted the human ear structure closely and was comfortable to wear. But a new problem arose, as the enhanced model fitted too well to the structure of the ear and was therefore difficult to take out. Therefore, the final version of the model extended the structure from the outside part of the ear of the enhanced model to make it easier for users to

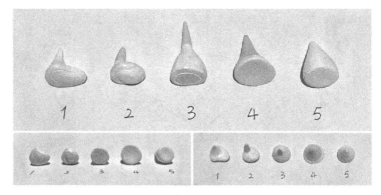

Fig. 9. Clay model photography

	Comfort	Ease of use	Aesthetics	Overall Feedback
Participant A	5 − 2 − 1 − 4 − 3	5 − 4 − 3 − 1 − 2	5 − 1 − 4 − 2 − 3	I found the No. 5 model is the best for me in terms of both comfort and ease of use, and it has a rounded look without being aggressive or sharp.
Participant B	2 − 5 − 1 − 4 − 3	5 − 4 − 3 − 1 − 2	1 − 4 − 5 − 3 − 2	I would relatively prefer the comfort of the No. 2 model, but the No. 2 is a little difficult to take out. The No. 5 is similar to the No. 2 in terms of comfort, but easier to put on and take away. But I think No. 1 model looks best in appearance, with a more graceful shape.
Participant C	5 − 4 − 2 − 1 − 3	5 − 4 − 3 − 1 − 2	4 − 5 − 1 − 3 − 2	I like both No. 4 and No. 5. The No. 5 model is comfortable and the No. 4 is beautiful.

Fig. 10. Feedback of the first usability test

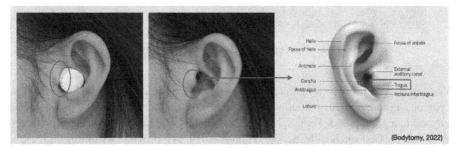

Fig. 11. Second usability test photos with ear structure analysis

hold it. Thus, the final version of the light therapy headset model was confirmed and its photographs are shown in Fig. 13.

The project then created a concept sketch of the final product based on the confirmed final version of the clay model and developed the materials for the various parts of the product and the position of the functional buttons. Furthermore, the project developed the colour scheme of the product. The product is available in three colour options, yellow,

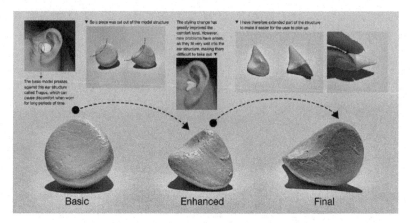

Fig. 12. Shape improvements for the light therapy headset

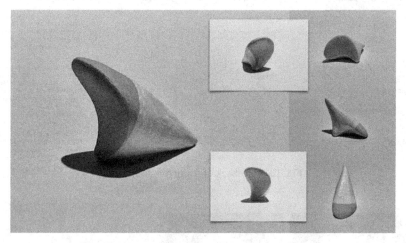

Fig. 13. Photographs of the final version clay model

blue and Very Peri. According to research on depressed groups, bright yellow can boost a person's mood, and this colour is also the one most preferred by healthy groups when they are in a good mood (Pappas 2010). Blue, on the other hand, is the colour preferred by both depressed and healthy people (Pappas 2010), as it provides a calming and restful effect (Boh 2021). And Very Peri is the colour that Pantone has announced as the trend colour for 2022 (Pantone 2022), it is a blue with a reddish-violet hue, which means hope, peacefulness and creativity. This colour not only meets the preferences of the target group of this product, but also appeals to a wider group of customers (GoVisually 2022) (Figs. 14 and 15).

According to the previous questionnaire research with the target group, how easy it is to carry and charge the light therapy headset was one of the design priorities for this product. This project presented three options, option one was inspired by Apple's magnetic card case and Apple Pencil (Apple 2022), as most people nowadays have to

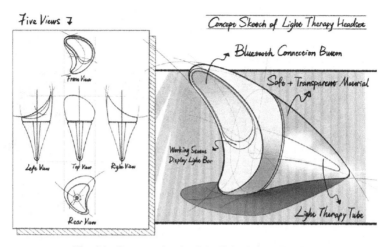

Fig. 14. Concept sketch of the light therapy headset

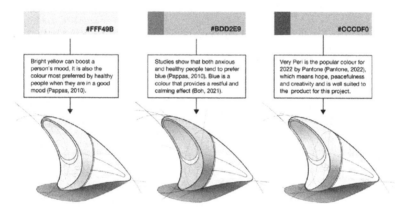

Fig. 15. Colour scheme of the light therapy headset

carry their mobile phones with them when they go out, so option one designed the light therapy headset with a portable case that can be used together with the mobile phone, the headset portable case can be attached magnetically to the back of the phone. There are three advantages to this method of carrying, the first is that it prevents the user from forgetting to carry the light therapy headset, the second advantage is the lightweight design, which reduces unnecessary handling and the number of items the user has to carry when on the go, and the third advantage is that attaching the light therapy headset to the back of the phone will maintain the power of the light therapy headset to a certain extent, so this was the solution that was finally chosen (Figs. 16 and 17).

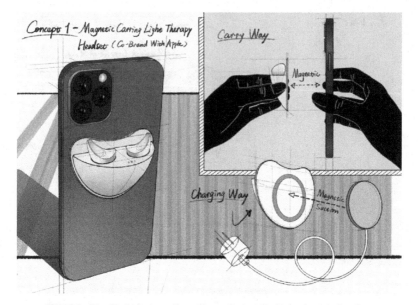

Fig. 16. The final choice of carrying solution for light therapy headset

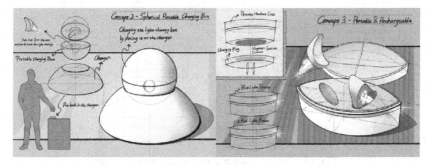

Fig. 17. Carrying options for light therapy headset

3 Results and Discussion

3.1 Design Outcome and Evaluation

The final output of this project is an in-ear light therapy headset prototype. The in-ear light therapy headset was modelled by using Rhinoceros software and the physical prototype was produced by using 3D printing technology for evaluation, after which the 3D model was rendered and displayed by using KeyShot software.

Figure 18 shows an exploded diagram and five views of the in-ear light therapy headset, showing the main components of the in-ear light therapy headset, its functions and the materials used for each part. The in-ear light therapy headset consists of five main parts, the first of which is the Bluetooth button, which will connect the headset to the mobile phone when the user presses it in order to set the intensity of the therapy light and start/end time via the mobile app. The second part is the status bar, which is adjacent to the Bluetooth button and will change colour according to the current light therapy status once the product has started working. The third part is the handheld part of the light therapy headset, which is made of non-slip resin as well as the Bluetooth button, this material was chosen because resin is an environmentally friendly material in a stable state, it is non-slip and can enhance the user's grip stability, on the other hand the resin is a lightweight material that will not be too heavy for the user's ears (Yorkshire Resin Company 2022). The fourth and most essential part of the in-ear light therapy headset is the light therapy tube, which can provide light of different intensities and colours, with the intensity of the light adjustable between 5,000 to 10,000lx, which is designed because although 10,000lx is the recommended intensity of light therapy (Pail et al. 2011), the adjustable intensity of light is easier to adapt to for first time users. Users can start with a lower intensity light at the beginning of the treatment and after a period of adaptation then move on to the standard treatment light intensity of 10,000lx may reduce the risk of side effects experienced by first time users. The final part of the in-ear light therapy headset is the protective shell for the in-ear part, which encases the light tube and is designed to protect the user's ear canal from direct contact with the light tube. The protective shell is made of transparent and soft silicone, which was chosen firstly because it is a smooth and stable material that will not cause discomfort or allergies when directly touching the ear canal and is ideal for use in medical products (Silclear Limited 2022). Secondly, the material is transparent and will not impede light transmission in any way, making it the appropriate material for this part of the product.

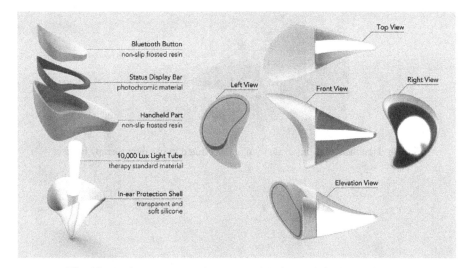

Fig. 18. Exploded view and five views of the in-ear light therapy headset

This project then used 3D printing technology to print the in-ear light therapy headset prototype and evaluated it in terms of handheld comfort and wearing comfort. As shown in Fig. 20, the in-ear light therapy headset is accurately sized and the curvature of the handheld part fits the curvature of the human finger, making it stable and comfortable to hold. The part where the thumb fits is the position of the Bluetooth button, which can be turned on with a tap of the thumb to connect to the phone while wearing. This design allows the user to wear and turn on the Bluetooth in one movement, enhancing the convenience and ease of use of the product. Figure 21 shows the wearing evaluation of the in-ear light therapy headset prototype, which shows that the headset is stable to wear. However, due to the material limitations of the 3D printed product, the material of the in-ear part is hard rather than the soft silicone material as designed, so the test of the 3D printed in-ear light therapy headset is of low value in terms of wearing comfort and this is one of the limitations of this project (Fig. 19).

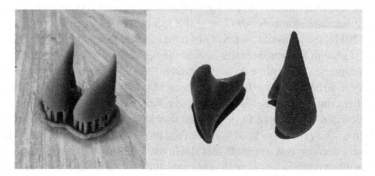

Fig. 19. Photograph of the 3D printed in-ear light therapy headset

Fig. 20. Handheld comfort evaluation of 3D printed in-ear light therapy headset

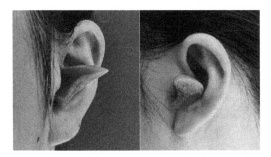

Fig. 21. Wear comfort evaluation of 3D printed in-ear light therapy headset

After the evaluation of the 3D printed in-ear light therapy headset prototype was completed, the project produced renderings and concept images of the product to demonstrate its usage and selling points to the target user group, as shown in Figs. 22, 23 and 24.

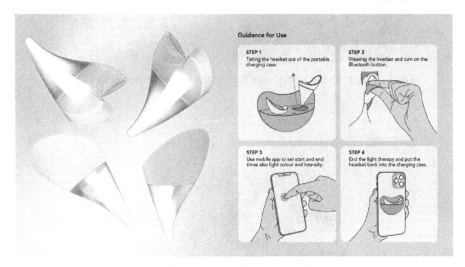

Fig. 22. Final concept rendering with guidance for use

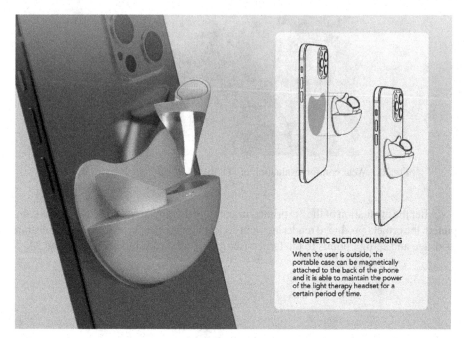

Fig. 23. Final concept rendering of the portable case with instructions for use

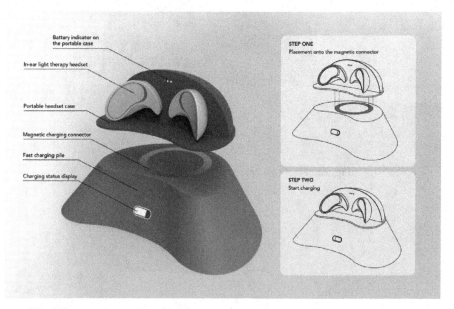

Fig. 24. Rendering and instructions for in-ear light therapy headset charging device

3.2 Conclusion

The project has achieved the following findings: firstly, in-ear light therapy headset is a convenient and effective alternative to traditional light therapy. This product solves the time, space and location constraints of traditional light therapy and greatly enhances the convenience of light therapy. The high portability and ease of use of the in-ear light therapy headset will enhance the well-being of those suffering from seasonal affective disorder and is highly desired by this target group.

Secondly, in-ear light therapy headset has the potential to broaden the range of applications for light therapy. The questionnaire research conducted in the regions where the target users are living shows that there is a large potential group of people living with seasonal affective disorder, who are not diagnosed and do not seek medical treatment due to lack of relevant knowledge, lack of attention or thinking that the traditional light treatment is troublesome. The in-ear light therapy headset is an easy to use and portable form of light therapy that this group is willing to purchase and improve their health. It is also useful to those who do not suffer from seasonal affective disorder but work indoors without sufficient light all year round. Anyone who needs supplemental light or to adjust their circadian rhythm can use this in-ear light therapy headset to enhance their health. This will have a positive impact on human health and well-being and the product has value for continued development.

Thirdly, in several rounds of usability testing, it was found that participants first selected models that are aesthetically beautiful to test, but the final ranking was based on the comfort and ease of use of the model. This shows that for wearable devices such as in-ear light therapy headset, the aesthetics of the device can inspire users to explore, but the decision of whether to buy or not depends mainly on the comfort and ease of use of the product.

This project also has some limitations. Firstly, current research has only shown that light through the ear canal has an antidepressant effect in the seasonal affective disorder group, however, there is still a research gap in terms of the intensity and colour of light to be used. This project therefore can only follow the existing standard light therapy recommendation of 10,000lx (Pail et al. 2011) and compensate for the uncertainty of the research by setting up the function of adjustable light intensity. Secondly, in the final evaluation of the 3D printed product, the in-ear part should have been made of a soft material, but due to the limitations of the 3D printed material this part was made of a relatively hard material. Thus, although the comfort of the product shape has been verified by several rounds of user testing, the 3D printed final product prototype is not of high value in terms of comfort evaluation. Therefore, in future research, the material of the evaluated object should be as close to the intended design as possible, so that the evaluation results will be more reliable and have a higher reference value.

Overall, the research and findings of this project is forward-looking and meaningful. The findings will enhance the health and well-being of humans, both those suffering from seasonal affective disorder and healthy individuals, and there is still further potential for exploration and development in this research direction and related products. In the future, the project will conduct in-depth research on in-ear light therapy to solve the limitations of the current phase of the project and develop a more scientific in-ear light therapy treatment system to provide more effective and reliable services for human health.

References

Fonte, A., Coutinho, B.: Seasonal sensitivity and psychiatric morbidity: study about seasonal affective disorder. BMC Psychiatry **21**, Article no. 317 (2021). (no pagination)

Lam, R.W., et al.: The Can-SAD study: a randomized controlled trial of the effectiveness of light therapy and Fluoxetine in patients with winter seasonal affective disorder. Am. J. Psychiatry **163**(5), 805–812 (2006)

Market Research Future. Seasonal Affective Disorder Market information: by type (fall and winter SAD, and others), by diagnosis (physical exam, lab tests, and others), by treatment (light therapy, medications, and others), by end user-global forecast till 2027 (2022). https://www.marketresearchfuture.com/reports/seasonal-affective-disorder-market-4123. Accessed 6 May 2022

Sun, L., Peräkylä, J., Kovalainen, A., Ogawa, K.H., Karhunen, P.J., Hartikainen, K.M.: Human brain reacts to transcranial extraocular light. PLoS ONE **11**, Article no. e0149525 (2016). (no pagination)

Jurvelin, H., Takala, T., Nissilä, J.: Transcranial bright light treatment via the ear canals in seasonal affective disorder: a randomized, double-blind dose-response study. BMC Psychiatry **14**, Article no. 288 (2014). (no pagination)

Tonello, G.: Seasonal affective disorder: lighting research and environmental psychology. Light. Res. Technol. **40**(2), 103–110 (2008)

Future Market Insights. Seasonal Affective Disorder Therapeutics Market (2022). https://www.futuremarketinsights.com/reports/seasonal-affective-disorder-therapeutics-market. Accessed 28 Aug 2022

Mayo Clinic. Seasonal affective disorder Diagnosis and treatment (2022). https://www.mayoclinic.org/diseases-conditions/seasonal-affective-disorder/diagnosis-treatment/drc-20364722. Accessed 16 Aug 2022

Cnet Health and Wellness. Best SAD light therapy lamp for 2022 (2022). https://www.cnet.com/health/best-sad-light-therapy-lamp/. Accessed 16 Aug 2022

Pail, G., et al.: Bright-light therapy in the treatment of mood disorders. Neuropsychobiology **64**(3), 152–162 (2011)

Meštrović, T.: Light Therapy Safety and Side Effects (2021). https://www.news-medical.net/health/Light-Therapy-Safety-and-Side-Effects.aspx. Accessed 16 Aug 2022

Melrose, S.: Seasonal Affective Disorder: An Overview of Assessment and Treatment Approaches. Hindawi Publishing Corporation (2015). Article no. 178564 (no pagination)

Kogan, A.O., Guilford, P.M.: Side effects of short-term 10,000-Lux light therapy. Am. J. Psychiatry **155**(2), 293–294 (1998)

Delgado, A.: What Causes Light Sensitivity (2019). https://www.healthline.com/health/photophobia. Accessed 16 Aug 2022

Botanov, Y., Ilardi, S.S.: The acute side effects of bright light therapy: a placebo-controlled investigation. PLoS ONE **8**, Article no. e75893 (2013). (no pagination)

Alba, J.: This Audi-inspired light therapy wearable aims to resolve your vitamin d deficiency (2020). https://www.yankodesign.com/2020/10/20/this-audi-inspired-light-therapy-wearable-aims-to-resolve-your-vitamin-d-deficiency/. Accessed 16 Aug 2022

Smykowski, J.: Does Light Therapy For Depression Work (2022)]. https://www.betterhelp.com/advice/therapy/does-light-therapy-for-depression-work/?utm_source=AdWords&utm_medium=Search_PPC_c&utm_term=PerformanceMax&utm_content=&network=x&placement=&target=&matchtype=&utm_campaign=16929735023&ad_type=responsive_pmax&adposition=&gclid=EAIaIQobChMI16WBvqOr-AIVGO3tCh1mlgCBEAAYASAAEgII2fD_BwE. Accessed 16 Aug 2022

AIRIUS. LED LIGHTING AND VITAMIN D (2022). https://ourworldindata.org/mental-health. Accessed 17 Aug 2022

Walker, M.P.: Why We Sleep. Ginkgo (Beijing) Books Co., Ltd., Beijing (2017)

Koninklijke Philips, N.V.: The global pursuit of better sleep health (2019). https://www.usa. philips.com/c-dam/b2c/master/experience/smartsleep/world-sleep-day/2019/2019-philips-world-sleep-day-survey-results.pdf. Accessed 20 Aug 2022

Zhao, J., Tian, Y., Nie, J., Xu, J., Liu, D.: Red light and the sleep quality and endurance performance of Chinese female basketball players. J. Athl. Train. **47**(6), 673–678 (2012)

Fortuna, P.: Ear (2014). https://www.behance.net/gallery/15846843/Ear. Accessed 10 May 2022

Blomqvist, V.: BUDS - A pair of in ear headphones (2019). https://www.behance.net/gallery/752 23611/BUDS-A-pair-of-in-ear-headphones. Accessed 10 May 2022

Tovt, T., Kroogman, I., Molotov, A.: Hearing Amplifier (2018). https://www.behance.net/gallery/ 72487061/Hearing-Amplifier. Accessed 10 May 2022

KOODESIGN STUDIO. Dearear Oval (2018). https://www.behance.net/gallery/67892413/Dea rear-Oval. Accessed 10 May 2022

Meze, A.: RAI PENTA - audiophile in ear monitors (earphones) (2019). https://www.behance.net/ gallery/30135655/RAI-PENTA-audiophile-in-ear-monitors-%28earphones%29. Accessed 10 May 2022

Jang, S.: 2019. BOOK. https://www.behance.net/gallery/74962339/BOOK. Accessed 10 May 2022

Vasquez, L.M.: MODELADO IN EAR - CLIENTE AYR (2021). https://www.behance.net/gal lery/132029115/MODELADO-IN-EAR-CLIENTE-AYR. Accessed 10 May 2022

Jun, S.: CF2_CT5. https://www.behance.net/gallery/70977425/CF2_CT5. Accessed 10 May 2022

V, A. Otoscope bundle set model (2020). https://www.behance.net/gallery/90167437/Otoscope-bundle-set-model. Accessed 10 May 2022

Chen, C.: Making In-ear Monitor. https://www.behance.net/gallery/60703799/Making-In-ear-Monitor. Accessed 10 May 2022

Bodytomy. Different Parts of the Human Ear: Which Ones Have You Heard Of (2022). https:// bodytomy.com/different-parts-of-human-ear. Accessed 10 May 2022

Pappas, S.: Different colors describe happiness, depression (2010). https://www.nbcnews.com/id/ wbna35304133. Accessed 10 May 2022

Boh, P.: What Colors Do Dementia Patients Prefer (2021). Available from: https://reamentia. com/what-colors-do-dementia-patients-prefer/. Accessed 10 May 2022

Pantone. PANTONE COLOR OF THE YEAR 2022/SHOP PANTONE VERY PERI (2022). https://www.pantone.com/color-of-the-year-2022-shop-pantone-very-peri. Accessed 10 May 2022

GoVisually. Very Peri - everything about Pantone color of the year 2022 (2022). https://govisu ally.com/blog/very-peri-pantone-color-of-the-year-2022/. Accessed 26 Aug 2022

Apple. Apple Pencil (2nd Generation) (2022). https://www.apple.com/uk/shop/product/MU8 F2ZM/A/apple-pencil-2nd-generation?fnode=7e3abefbaef96ccd5dea523fe69eaadd3fc3 dd46d819c572781abc1a8ea4c1221573ff450c860fbd3ef460f6c84276cc8db3b81e6264618 b4989fc5d154833342c5bc80b2000d1f0f475a0c7ea7fb0c51175216026559cef688099da0d 8cd92b. Accessed 28 Aug 2022

Yorkshire Resin Company. Why Choose Resin (2022). https://www.yorkshire-resin-company.co. uk/about/why-choose-resin. Accessed 28 Aug 2022

Silclear Limited. Silicone rubber benefits (2022). http://www.silclear.co.uk/about-silclear/sil icone-rubber-benefits/. Accessed 28 Aug 2022

Female Menstrual Emergency Service Experience Design for College Students

Yunrui He, Zhen Liu, Qihan Sun[✉], Xin Tu, and Yong Ma

School of Design, South China University of Technology, Guangzhou 510006, People's Republic of China
285071883@qq.com

Abstract. Irregular menstrual periods are common, many female college students ignore the physiological feelings of menstrual symptoms and forget to prepare sanitary supplies in advance. With humanistic care, this paper focuses on women's issues, observes and cares about the distress of female college students' menstrual problems on campus. The paper mainly refers to the double-diamond model as methodology guidance to our design research process, and has carried out a series of more detailed and comprehensive user research. At the same time, this paper improves the user research methods in the designing process, and innovatively applies them to Irregular menstrual problems on campus, while analyzing and dissolving user needs, and provides help to them through user interface and user experience design, which would make campus periods no longer embarrassing.

Keywords: Design Research Methodology · Menstrual Experience · User Interface and User Experience Design · Campus

1 Introduction

Menstruation is a normal physiological phenomenon that all women of childbearing age experience every month, one of the Physiological manifestations is menstrual bleeding, and it usually lasts from 2 to 7 days. During this period, women will have a variety of psychological and physiological reactions due to different physical conditions, such as fear of cold, backache, fatigue, depression and anxiety, sensitivity and so on. All these will have negative impacts on their normal studies and life. Meanwhile, Irregular menstrual periods are common. Many female college students ignore the physiological feelings of menstrual symptoms and forget to prepare sanitary supplies in advance and they can easily face embarrassment when their period suddenly comes, and they can't get help in time. This paper focuses on college girls' menstruation issues, observes and cares about the problems from their menstrual experience on campus, following the methodology guidance of the double-diamond model and carrying out three detailed and comprehensive user research sessions, employing a combination of product design, user interface and user experience design to improve their menstrual experience.

2 Literature Research

2.1 Worldwide Research for Menstrual Experience Service

In this paper, worldwide study has been conducted as follows: The Web of Science (WOS) database has been used as the data source. The Science Citation Index Expanded (SCI-Expanded), Social Sciences Citation Index (SSCI), Conference Proceedings Citation Index – Science (CPCI-S), Conference Proceedings Citation Index – Social Sciences & Humanities (CPCI-SSH) were selected as the sources. With the themes "social mentality" AND "health", 146 articles were collection in the WOS core database for macro analysis, and were selected and imported into the VOSviewer software for keyword clustering analysis, and we explored the relationship between menstrual experience and service, and its development worldwide.

Keyword Analysis. In the Network Visualization diagram generated by VOSviewer, items are represented by labels and circles. The size of the item label and the circle determines the weight of the item, and the distance between the two items or the strength of the connection represents the strength of their affinity. Circular nodes of different colors indicate different clusters. As shown In Fig. 1, associated with color change, all the keywords are divided into three clusters: menstruation; menstrual experience; and service. It can be seen in cluster 1 that several keywords closely related to "experience", namely: woman; access; depth interview; menstrual irregularity; fear; misconception; and provider. In cluster 2 there are keywords correlated to "menstruation", such as menstrual experience; reproductive health; school; girl; adolescent girl; young woman; menarche; menstrual product; focus group discussion; availability; and accessibility. In cluster 3 keywords that connected with "service", such as menstrual experience; reproductive health; school; girl; adolescent girl; young woman; menarche; menstrual product; focus group discussion; availability; and accessibility.

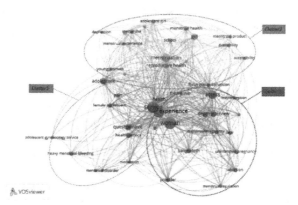

Fig. 1. Three clusters of "menstrual experience" and "services" themes in the Network Visualization diagram generated by VOSviewer (devised by the authors).

It is apparent (as shown in Fig. 2) that during 2010–2014, most of the research topics focused on serious menstrual problems, such as menstrual disorders, severe menstrual bleeding, health management and other relatively popular experiences. By 2016–2020, the research topics in recent years have increasingly focused on the menstrual problems of minority groups such as developing countries, "Bangladesh", "schools", "girl", "adolescent girl", and combined with the menstrual poverty problem in some regions of China, the quality assurance and "availability" of "menstrual products" also deserve attention. Combined with the above literature research and the enlightenment from our own campus life experience, we find the menstrual experience of female college students on campus an intriguing research topic.

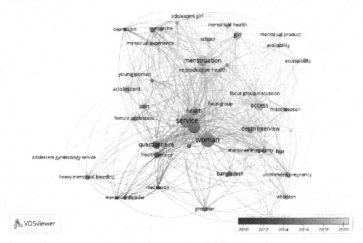

Fig. 2. The overlay visualization diagram generated by VOSviewer (devised by the authors).

The above-mentioned studies contribute to our understanding of menstrual experience and services, although our desk research information indicates that some menstrual research projects in some developing countries, such as the public welfare project, provide free sustainable and environmentally friendly sanitary napkins to young women and girls in Bangladesh and India. However, there are few studies on menstrual experience services, and most of the existing literature still focuses on the menstrual problems of special female groups in some regions, such as the unmet menstrual needs of homeless people in New York City [9], and the research on reproductive health and fertility issues, such as the issue of menstrual regulation in Bangladesh, the international outlook on menstrual and reproductive health [12], and few studies focus on menstrual experience and related products. Only a few researchers reached conclusions through actual research via interview. In terms of research methods, most researchers only use in-depth interviews and questionnaires, lacking in-depth application research methods such as situational inquiry, and lacking comprehensive and logical user research system guidance on the whole.

2.2 Domestic Research and Design

The CNKI academic journal database has been used as the data source and the themes were "social mentality" and "health". The time span of literature retrieval was set to all years. A total of 37 articles have been collected and selected for analysis (see Fig. 3).

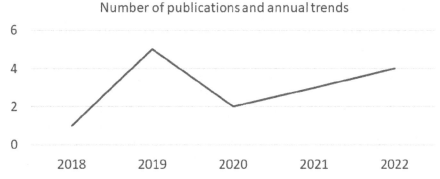

Fig. 3. The cart for the number of publications and annual trends.

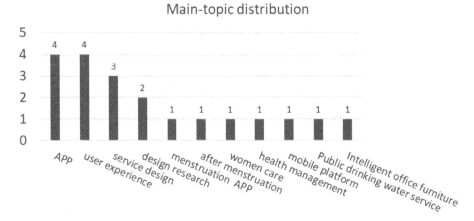

Fig. 4. The chart for main topic distribution.

From 2018 to 2022, the number of documents related to menstruation, service and experience design topics retrieved from CNKI showed an overall upward trend. (As shown in Fig. 4) Among them, the most popular topics were: APP, user experience, service design, design research, menstruation APP, post-menopause, women's health management, mobile platform. With the rapid development of science and Internet technology, mobile health applications have provided great convenience for real-time medical treatment and healthy life [7]. In recent years, more attention has been paid to women's health, with management APP conforms to women's health management needs [6–8]. However, in the context of smart city technology, they also have limitations. Most studies ignore the importance of women's experience. Existing studies limit the technical background of women's health management subject to personal data processing [7, 8] with a relatively narrow vision. They do not consider some organic combination of personal experience and specific group experience, even community and urban experience. How to design a more applicable and socialized APP has become our current research direction.

3 Methods

3.1 Methodology Overview

The paper mainly refers to the double-diamond model as methodology guidance to our design research process, and has experienced Discover, Define, carried out a series of more detailed and comprehensive user research. At the same time, this paper improves the user research methods in the designing process, and innovatively applies them to Irregular menstrual problems on campus, while analyzing and dissolving user needs.

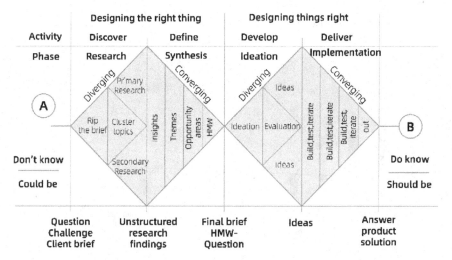

Fig. 5. The double-diamond model (generated by the authors).

As shown in Fig. 5 and Fig. 6, there are four stages in the double-diamond model: discover, define, develop and deliver. The flow chart of the research methodology is as follow:

1. In the "Discover" stage, five methods, namely: focus group, user diary, desk research, questionnaire and depth interview, are mainly used to obtain primary and secondary research data.
2. In the "Define" stage, five methods are mainly used: participant board, personas, affinity diagram, opportunity areas and HMW, to integrate and analyze research data.
3. In the "Develop" stage, the solution is generated by Brain storming, and then the solution is selected by evaluation.

4. In the "Deliver" stage, prototype and Product usability test is mainly conducted, and detailed improvement is made on this basis.

Fig. 6. The flow chart of the research methodology.

Discover Stage
Focus Group and User Diary

Materials: Sticky paper, camera.

Executive Routine: Step1. Record: Take out all the items. Record twice on the weekday (blue sticky paper) and weekend (red sticky paper). Step2. Return Visit.

Questionnaire and depth interviews

Materials: Sticky paper, camera.

Executive Routine: Step 1. Make an online questionnaire. Step 2. Distribute Issued to target users (female college students on campus), collect information. Step 3. Process information, and modify and make an interview outline according to the results of the questionnaire.

Define Stage
Participant Boards and Personas

Materials: Sticky paper, camera.

Executive Routine: Within this research method, the initial step is the collection of participants' interview information, following which they are transported to sticky notes with different colors (indicting different categories) for further processing. Then those sticky notes with information are sorted to single out those that can be categorized into interrelated themes, and then sorted into different clusters. Subsequently, they are divided into different categories. Participant boards and personas can be generated with above processed information.

Opportunity Areas and HMW

Materials: Sticky paper.

Executive Routine: Extract opportunity points and sort out the design framework and key points.

Develop Stage
Brainstorming and modeling

Materials: Sticky paper, Cardboard, tape, scissors.

Executive Routine: Make models and iteratively improve the design scheme.

Deliver Stage
Prototyping and usability test

Materials: Sticky paper, Cardboard, tape, scissors.

Executive Routine: Make models and iteratively improve the design scheme, make paper prototype for detail discussion.

4   Conduct

4.1   Participants

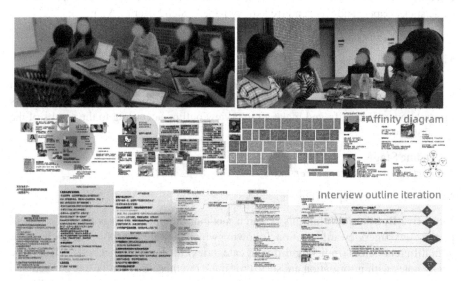

Fig. 7. Ten participants for user interviews.

5   Consequence

5.1   Focus Group and User Diary

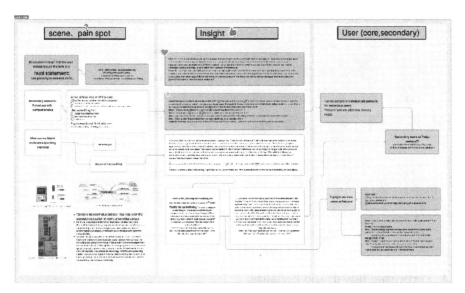

Fig. 8. The flow chart of pain spots and insights

5.2   Questionnaire and Depth Interviews

We first discussed and sorted out the relevant behaviors and reactions of women during the whole menstrual period, and then collected further information through questionnaire collection, preliminary interviews and desktop research (see Fig. 7). Finally, we learned that the above conditions are also common on campus: They often complain about suffering from the inconvenience and embarrassment caused by the lack of supply of sanitary products for women's periods during their study routine, which makes them feel particularly at a loss and arouses a deep sense of helplessness. On the issue of menstrual experience and needs, we made a questionnaire and issued it to fill in. Until the time 22: 00, November 29, 2022, we collected a total of 109 questionnaires from female college students. Among them, there are 26 valid questionnaires with reference value to our sanitary napkin help question and vending machine use design, and 10 students are willing to conduct further in-depth interviews. 33 of whom said that their menstruation was irregular, 63 of whom did not have the habit of preparing spare sanitary napkins in their bags when they went out, 86 of whom occasionally had menstruation without sanitary napkins, and 12 of whom often. 68 people said that menstrual period would cause dysmenorrhea. During menstrual period, 43 people needed analgesics and 41 people needed warmth (as shown in Fig. 8). After sorting out the collaboration chart according to these answers, we further clearly adjusted the characteristics and needs that distinguish the core user and the secondary user.

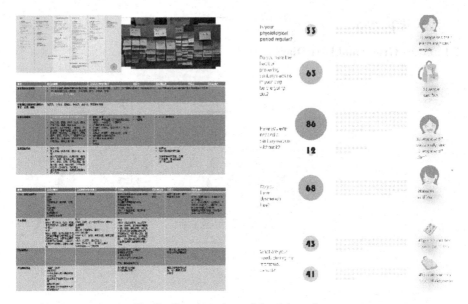

Fig. 9. Questionnaire and depth interviews

5.3 Participant Boards and Personas

Participant boards (as shown in Fig. 9, Fig. 10, and Fig. 11) for core users and secondary users, participants 1–3 are categorized and abstracted as our core user. And participants 4–6 for our secondary users.

The menstrual period of the pain point of the core user is irregular, and it will also be accompanied by the physiological reaction of hypoglycemia and dysmenorrhea. Whenever the menstrual period suddenly "visits", the user will feel extremely distressed. Because of carelessness, he often forgets to prepare the sanitary napkin in his schoolbag because he is embarrassed, it is always difficult to ask for the sanitary napkin. It is not convenient for users to buy a lot of backpacks for painkillers and warm babies, and it is easy to forget to take a small bag of grief sanitary napkin. And for our secondary users, It is not convenient to buy a lot of backpacks for painkillers and warm babies, and it is easy to forget to take a small bag of grief sanitary napkin.

1 - Careless and careless/irregular eating/premenstrual syndrome/gentle and kind.

2 - Irregular menstrual period.

3 - Dysmenorrhea/Do not tend to borrow from others/Value brand.

4 - Lively personality/Pay attention to the length of sanitary napkin.

5 - Clear menstrual period planning/Helpful/Large demand for warmth.

6 - Have the habit of taking spare sanitary napkins/need warmth and medicine chest.

5.4 Opportunity Areas and HMW

After a series of research, summary and discussion, we finally decided to carry out the project theme of "menstrual emergency assistance" for female college students who

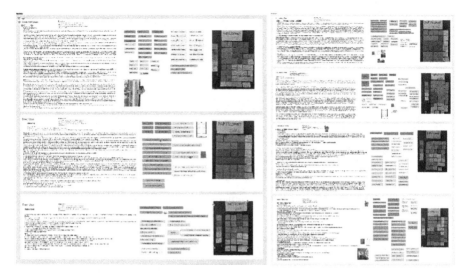

Fig. 10. Participant boards for core users and secondary users

Fig. 11. Personas for core users and secondary users

mainly solve problems like lack of menstrual planning and carelessness. Due to the particularity of sanitary napkins, it also takes into account certain environmental protection properties. First, taking individuals as the research object, combining with the current national policies and industry development status. Secondly, aiming at college student's menstrual problem, we use multipole research methods to decide our functions, interfaces, needs and interactions, and summarize the characteristics, advantages and disadvantages of their personal menstrual experience, so as to more accurately locate the target users and core functions; Thirdly, the interaction design and interface design methods of this topic are further clarified, and the ultimate goal is to build an intelligent mobile application platform that integrates personalization, informatization and convenience, and pays full attention to women's physical and mental health. Our design output are: assistance APP, and supporting sanitary pads vending machine (see Fig. 12).

Fig. 12. Chart for opportunity areas and HMW

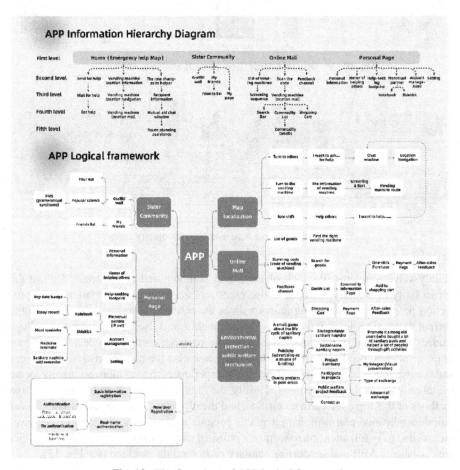

Fig. 13. The flow chart of APP logical framework

5.5 Brainstorming and Modeling

With the flow chart of APP logical framework (as shown in Fig. 13), we decided that our APP's most important function are girl help girl function zone, and sister community to help with each other for available sanitary napkins. Secondly, we also have vending machine purchasing for menstrual sanitary products, with the corresponding function online mall. Considering with the sustainable developing goals (SDGs), we also provide environmentally friendly sanitary napkins for emergency service (see Fig. 14, Fig. 15, Fig. 16, Fig. 17, and Fig. 18).

APP Core Function: sanitary napkin providers and "girl help girls".

Asking for Help: send out help/point-to-point help/the APP will notify the three nearest girls around to seek help - find the exact location/offer explicit navigation.

Offering Help: each active help can accumulate points, exchange the sanitary napkin in the vending machine, and other incentives, and encourage everyone to lend a helping hand/- trigger the accumulation of public welfare funds to alleviate the "sanitary napkin poverty".

With the Vending Machine: Storage/sales of sanitary napkin. With the app, users can make purchases from self-service vending machines for single piece independent packaging.

Additional Function: graffiti wall for emotional comfort - personal physiological/psychological diary.

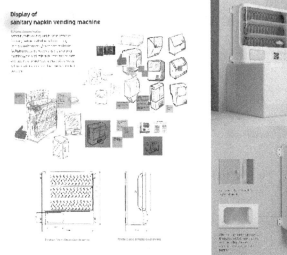

Fig. 14. Sketch and vending machine modeling

5.6 Prototyping and Usability Test

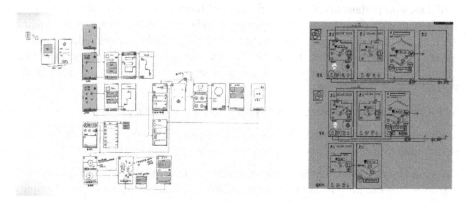

Fig. 15. APP frame and paper prototype

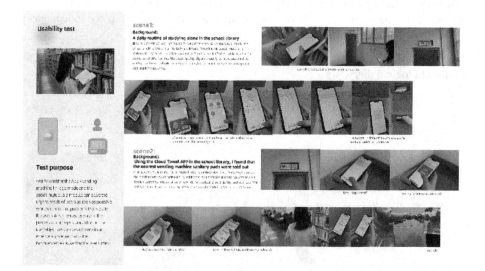

Fig. 16. Usability Test

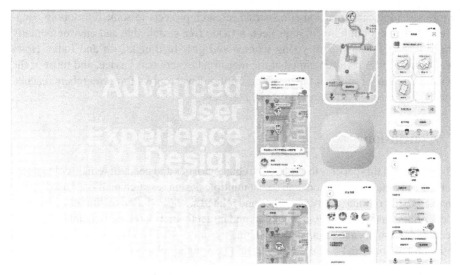

Fig. 17. APP high-fidelity prototype

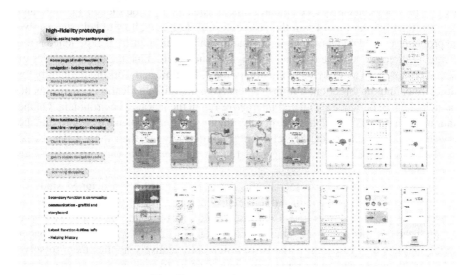

Fig. 18. APP high-fidelity prototype

6 Discussion

We learn that many women in different ages lacking in menstrual knowledge and corresponding practices, for example some low-Income Women and female adolescents with menstrual regulation (MR) services in Bangladesh, urban Karachi and Pakistan. Some concludes that there are unhygienic practices and misconceptions among girls and requiring action by health care professionals [19–21]. Although our desk research information indicates that some menstrual research projects in some developing countries, such as the public welfare project, provide free sustainable and environmentally friendly sanitary napkins to young women and girls in Bangladesh and India. However, there is little research aimed at the menstrual experience service, and most of the existing literature remain at the direct description level, only a few researchers reached conclusions through actual research via interview.

7   Conclusion

The purpose of this paper is to explore the characteristics and needs of female college students during menstrual period, and select multiple design research methods based on the characteristics of menstrual experience and related services (based on literature review): focus groups, user diaries, questionnaires and in-depth interviews, participant boards and personas and so on, and organically combine the double-drill process model with design research methods, and based on gender and personality characteristics, Eleven typical users were selected from female college students with menstrual problems for in-depth study. Through research, this paper found that many female college students ignore the physiological feelings of menstrual symptoms and forget to prepare sanitary supplies in advance and they can easily face embarrassment when their period suddenly comes, and they can't get help in time. From the perspective of designers, how to help them solve the problems caused by menstrual period and optimize their menstrual experience is the intriguing direction. On the one hand, designers should combine the characteristics of special groups, such as studying in the library for a long time and working frequently for a long time, find the direction of improvement from their life and learning environment, and help them experience social and interactive fun in the learning environment. On the other hand, designers should help them solve their menstrual problems by improving the services they receive, and put themselves more comfortably into their study and work, so that the menstrual period will no longer be troubled and become a warm and interesting experience.

On the basis of existing research, this paper has carried out a detailed study of menstrual experience, and conducted a more extensive survey of the three dimensions of users and products, users and users, users and environment, and found the more specific needs of this group in certain specific scenarios. At the same time, this paper flexibly applies user research methods to design and creatively applies them to solve gender problems. Typical users replace big data statistics to conduct more in-depth user research, making the user image more vivid and the research level more diversified.

To some extent, it expands your user research with a new idea. In addition to strengthening the more specific research of external environment interaction. Future research can also explore "women's power" from menstrual problems. Designers can enhance their experience in special periods from the perspective of design, help women to transcend themselves from troubled groups, enjoy convenient smart city experience, and provide more humanistic care and detailed insight data and user research support for the technological development of future life.

Acknowledgements. The authors wish to thank all the people who provided the time and efforts for the investigation. This research is supported by South China University and Technology, and Guangdong Provincial Department of Science and Technology 2022 Overseas Famous Teacher Project: "Behavior and Service Design Course for Sustainable Youth Development City Construction (SYCBD)".

References

1. The double-diamond model. https://outwitly.com/blog/human-centered-design-series-1/
2. Mob Tech: White Paper on Chinese Women's Health (2020). https://www.mob.com/mobdata/report/94
3. Rowland, C., Charlier, M.: User Experience Design for the Internet of Things. O'Reilly Media, Farnham (2015)
4. Cooper, A., Reimann, R., Cronin, D., Noessel, C.: About Face 4: The Essentials of Interaction Design. Wiley, New York (2014)
5. Wang, Y.: Research on User Experience Design of Adolescent Women's Health APP. Donghua University (2022). (in Chinese)
6. Zhu, Y.: Research on perimenopausal health management service design based on service contact point. Jiangnan University (2021). (in Chinese)
7. Cheng, Y.: Innovation and practice of personalized health management APP for women. Chongqing University of Posts and Telecommunications (2020). (in Chinese)
8. Xu, S., Duan, K.: Exploration of APP optimization design in physiological period based on psychological model. Ind. Des. **5**, 26–27 (2021). (in Chinese)
9. Gruer, C., Hopper, K., Smith, RC., Sommer, M., et al.: Seeking menstrual products: a qualitative exploration of the unmet menstrual needs of individuals experiencing homelessness in New York City. Reprod. Health **18**(1), 77 (2021)
10. Alam, A., Bracken, H., Johnston, H.B., et al.: Acceptability and feasibility of mifepristone-misoprostol for menstrual regulation in Bangladesh. Int. Perspect. Sex. Reprod. Health **39**(2), 79–87 (2013)
11. Power, R., Wiley, K., Muhit, M., et al.: 'Flower of the body': menstrual experiences and needs of young adolescent women with cerebral palsy in Bangladesh, and their mothers providing menstrual support. BMC Womens Health **20**(1), 160 (2020)
12. Holst, A.S., Jacques-Aviñó, C., Berenguera, A., et al.: Experiences of menstrual inequity and menstrual health among women and people who menstruate in the Barcelona area (Spain): a qualitative study. Reprod. Health **19**(1), 45 (2022)
13. Carlson, G., Wilson, J.: Menstrual management and women who have intellectual disabilities: service providers and decision-making. J. Intellect. Dev. Disabil. **21**, 39–57 (1996)
14. Robinson, H., Barrington, D.: Drivers of menstrual material disposal and washing practices: a systematic review. PLoS ONE **16**(12), e0260472 (2021)
15. Alda, C., Browne, A.: Absorbents, practices, and infrastructures: changing socio-material landscapes of menstrual waste in Lilongwe. Malawi 1057–1077 (2021)
16. Abu, J.I., Habiba, M.A., Baker, R., et al.: Quantitative and qualitative assessment of women's experience of a one-stop menstrual clinic in comparison with traditional gynaecology clinics. BJOG **108**(9), 993–999 (2001)
17. Ghandour, R., Hammoudeh, W., et al.: Coming of age: a qualitative study of adolescent girls' menstrual preparedness in Palestinian refugee camps in the West Bank and Jordan. Sex Reprod. Health Matters **30**(1), 2111793 (2022)
18. Speroff, L.: The perimenopause: definitions, demography, and physiology. Obstet. Gynecol. Clin. North Am. **29**(3), 397–410 (2002)

19. Sebert, A., Peters, E., Danjoint, D.: Unmet menstrual hygiene needs among low-income women. Obstet. Gynecol. **133**(2), 238–244 (2019)
20. Ali, T.S., Rizvi, S.N., et al.: Menstrual knowledge and practices of female adolescents in urban Karachi, Pakistan. J. Adolesc. **33**, 531–541 (2010)
21. Hossain, A., Moseson, H., Raifman, S., et al.: 'How shall we survive': a qualitative study of women's experiences following denial of menstrual regulation (MR) services in Bangladesh. Reprod. Health **13**, 86 (2016)

Objectively Assessing and Comparing the User Experience of Two Thousand Digital Health Apps

Maciej Hyzy[1,2(✉)], Raymond Bond[1], Maurice D. Mulvenna[1], Lu Bai[1], Robert Daly[2], and Simon Leigh[2,3]

[1] School of Computing, Ulster University, York St, Belfast BT15 1ED, UK
maciejmarekzych@gmail.com
[2] ORCHA, Sci-Tech Daresbury, Violet V2, Keckwick Lane, Daresbury WA4 4AB, UK
[3] Warwick Medical School, University of Warwick, Coventry CV4 7AL, UK

Abstract. There are more than 350,000 digital health apps in the app stores today. There is an average of around 250 digital health apps being added daily to the app stores. This indicates a public appetite to consume digital health apps, and a potential to decrease the pressure on healthcare providers by promoting digital technology. However, for this to be a viable option, digital health apps must be effective and safe to use. The quality, defined as "compliance with best practice standards", of such apps must be of the highest standard for these to be recommended by healthcare professionals. One crucially important aspect of the quality of an app is user experience (UX). The UX of digital health apps is important to assure that the technology is being used safely and as intended. The objective of this study was to describe common practices related to the UX for digital health app design. This study analysed a sample of 2,053 digital health apps with a focus on the UX practices in the digital health app design. The data included in this study was collected using the Organisation for the Review of Care and Health Applications (ORCHA) assessment tool. ORCHA is a United Kingdom (UK) based digital health compliance company that specialises in assessing the quality of digital health apps, which includes UX. The ORCHA UX assessment consists of 15 polar questions (Yes/No) and 3 multiple selection questions. A score of 65 is considered a 'threshold score' and a starting point, based on answers this score will increase, decrease, or stay the same.

Keywords: Digital health · mHealth · User experience

1 Introduction

There are more than 350,000 digital health apps in the app stores today. With an average of around 250 digital health apps being added daily to the app stores [1], in 2020 digital health apps saw 25% increase in downloads for different categories of health apps [2]. This indicates a public appetite to use digital health apps, and a potential to alleviate the pressure on healthcare providers by promoting digital technology. However, for this to be a viable option, digital health apps must be effective and safe to use. Meaning quality, defined as "compliance with best practice standards", of such apps must be of the highest standard for it to be recommended by health professionals.

One crucially important aspect of apps' quality is user experience (UX). UX of digital health apps is important to assure that the technology is being used safely and as intended. For example, a study from 2020 that examined user reviews with the aim of improving mental health apps engagement found that poor usability was the most common reason for abandoning mental health apps [3].

This study analysed a sample of over 2000 digital health apps with focus on UX practices in digital health app design. The data included in this study was collected using the Organisation for the Review of Care and Health Applications (ORCHA) assessment tool [4]. ORCHA is a United Kingdom (UK) based digital health compliance company that specialises in the assessment of quality of digital health apps, including UX.

ORCHA UX assessment tool assigns UX score (0–100) to digital health apps based on the answer to the questions in the assessment tool. An overall performance of digital health apps regarding UX has been examined in this study, as well as more tailored analyses regarding user involvement and guideline compliance. This study used descriptive statistics to analyse the findings and get an overview of common UX practices for digital health apps allowing for the identification of areas where improvements could be made.

In contrast to other UX, usability or accessibility assessment tools such as the mobile application user experience checklist (MAUX-C) [5] or system usability scale (SUS) [6], ORCHA UX assessment is specifically designed for digital health apps measuring compliance with standards and practices. This means that the assessment should be more objective rather than subjective, as it is compliance to practices and standards that is being measured.

This study has one objective: Describe common practices related to the UX of digital health app design. Practices such as: end-user involvement in digital health app development, what guidelines have been followed and what are the most common methods of user support etc. This will shed a light onto practices and guidelines digital health app developers have considered when developing digital health apps and how well they have performed in the ORCHA UX assessment. Out of 2053 digital health apps used in this paper, 469 apps had Android and iOS versions counted as separate, resulting in 938 assessments.

2 Methods

2.1 The Dataset and Statistical Analysis

In this study we conducted a secondary data analysis on the provided ORCHA dataset. The dataset included ORCHA UX assessment question answers, UX assessment score. R language and R studio has been used for descriptive statistics and generation of figures for data visualisation. 2053 of digital health apps have been assessed using ORCHA UX assessment tool. The assessment consists of 15 Yes/No questions and 3 multiple selection questions. Each question has been examined on its own and in conjunction with one another to gather information indicative of UX practices in digital health app design. The score of 65 is a starting point, based on answers this score will increase, decrease, or stay the same. Each assessment has been carried out by at least two trained reviewers, where in the case of a dispute, a third reviewer would resolve it. All reviewers have undergone the same training to use the assessment tool. The assessments were carried out between 18th January 2021 and 6th January 2022. *P*-values of < .05 were considered statistically significant. Shapiro test was used to determine if the distribution of UX scores is normal. ORCHA UX assessment tool's questions vary based on scene setter questions and selected categories [4]. This means that sample size of reported UX practices may vary with each ORCHA question analysis, the sample size can go up to 2053 digital health apps.

2.2 Ethical Approval

This secondary data analysis study gained ethical approval by Ulster University (ethics filter committee, Faculty of Computing, Engineering and the Built Environment). The process undertaken by ORCHA ensures that digital health apps' developers are aware of their score and are given time to contest findings of the assessment which may be amended if developers provide additional relevant information. All reviews, unless explicitly asked to be removed by the developer, are covered as suitable for research in ORCHA's privacy policy [7].

3   Results

Table 1 contains the details of ORCHA UX assessment score distribution. The median and interquartile range (IQR) of the ORCHA UX assessment results was 75.2 ± 8.42 out of 100. Standard deviation (SD) was 8.08 and standard error of the mean (SEM) was .178. These results indicate that there is little variance in the distribution of UX scores, this can be seen in Fig. 1.

Table 1. UX score distribution

Min	1st Qu	Median	Mean	3rd Qu	Max	SD	SEM
27.4	71.2	75.2	74.6	79.6	94.2	8.08	.178

Figure 1 depicts the density plot of the UX score distribution for the 2053 health apps. From the plot the majority of the apps fall to the right of the red line (indicating UX score of 65).

This means that most of the apps have achieved UX scores ranging from satisfactory to high. UX scores are not normally distributed according to Shapiro-Wilk test ($P < .001$).

Table 2 depicts health apps' compliance with guidelines (mutually inclusive) for the 2053 health apps in the dataset. Most apps did not comply with any of the guidelines (97%). The most common guideline that was followed was Web Content Accessibility Guidelines (WCAG) 2.1 AA (1.3%).

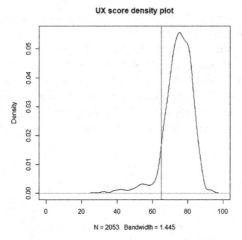

Fig. 1. UX score density plot

Table 2. Guideline compliance, percentage (%) out of 2053

Guideline	Sample size (n)
None	1989(97.0%)
WCAG 2.1 AA	27(1.3%)
WCAG 2.0 AA	21(1%)
W3C	13(.6%)
Other	13(.6%)
Android App Quality Guidelines	6(.3%)
Apple HIG	5(.2%)

Out of all apps, 692 (~34% out of 2053 digital health apps) of digital health apps did not comply with any guidelines and did not involve end-users in testing or had a statement about user feedback. Of those 592 had a UX score > = 65 (~29% out of 2053 digital health apps).

Table 3 depicts methods of support to end-users. These are the methods in which an end-user can contact organisation/developer of the app to ask questions and get support. The most common method to give support to end-users was via email (78%).

Table 4 depicts the basic functions of digital health apps in the sample of 2053 apps. It can be seen that 'search button' (n = 829) is the least provided function and back button is the most often provided function.

According to the data,

- 99% (out of 1996) of the digital health apps in the sample provided support for end-users with poor sight.

Table 3. Methods of support to end-users, percentage (%) out of 2053

Method	Sample size (n)
Email	1607(78%)
eTicket	1121(55%)
Helpline/telephone number	495(24%)
Live chat	220(11%)
None	118(6%)

Table 4. Digital health app functions

Functions	Sample size (n)
Back button	1883(92%)
Home/Menu button	1627(79%)
Help/About button	1467(71%)
Search button	829(40%)

- 98% (out of 1994) of the digital health apps in the sample provided support for end-users with hearing impairment.
- 97% (out of 2053) of digital health apps reported that there was no evidence of bugs during a review.
- 92% (out of 2051) digital health apps provided a statement about how to report issues to the developer.
- 87% (out of 1517) digital health apps allowed end user to change the presentation theme.
- 80% (out of 351) of digital health apps that had a forum, had a statement within the app that the forum content is moderated.
- 75% (out of 1959) of digital health apps clearly explained any medical terms used in the app.
- 74% (out of 1566) digital health apps give the end user options to manage the notification settings (push/email) within the app for convenience/privacy.
- 60% (out of 2031) of digital health apps allowed end user to change the font size in-app or responded to device preferences.
- 57% (out of 2053) provided some evidence of user involvement in testing.
- 48% (out of 1564) of digital health apps had a statement informing the end user how to manage notification settings for convenience/privacy.
- 32% (out of 2053) of digital health apps included a statement about user feedback during design/development
- 21% (out of 1909) of the digital health apps provided a statement about the developer's commitment to addressing problems reported to them.
- ~1% (out of 2053) digital health apps published or made available unedited user feedback data.

- ~1% (out of 2053) digital health apps published or otherwise made available any unedited user usage data.

4 Discussion

At the first glance looking at high UX scores of digital health apps, i.e. 75.2 ± 8.42 (median and IQR), it would appear that there is no further need for improvement. However, on a closer examination of the data, areas of concern where improvements could be made have been identified.

The majority of the digital health apps 97% (out of 2053) that have been assessed using ORCHA UX assessment in this study did not comply with any UX, usability or accessibility guidelines, as stated in Table 2. Nevertheless, the median and interquartile range of the digital health apps was 75.2 ± 8.42 on the assessment, see Table 1. The scarce use of guidelines and high median score on the assessment indicates that there is little use or uptake of UX, usability or accessibility guidelines in digital health app design. This may be since the guidelines in question are general mobile design guidelines and not tailored to digital health apps. Also, digital health apps have high heterogeneity, meaning that more tailored guidelines may be needed. Of those 3% of digital health apps that did comply with guidelines, WCAG 2.1 AA was the most popular 1.3% (out of 2053).

34% (n = 699) out of 2053 of digital health apps appear not to involve end-users at any stage of app development or testing, indicating that a greater public patient involvement (PPI) is needed in digital health app development. A study from 2019 [8], stated that many patient end-users stop using a health app two weeks after they download it. It is likely that the lack of end-user involvement led to lack of alignment with the preferences and goals of the intended end-users, resulting in poor user retention. This highlights the need for end-user involvement in digital health app development.

Around 29% (out of 2053) digital health apps had a UX score $>= 65$ yet did not comply with any guidelines and did not involve end-users in testing or had a statement about user feedback. This could indicate that the ORCHA UX assessment tool should consider changes to its question weightings given that digital health apps in general are able to achieve high UX scores without any end user feedback or adherence to guidelines. 92% (out of 2051) digital health apps provided a statement about how to report issues to the developer. This indicates that although end-user feedback has not been sought for by most digital health app developers (as 34% of digital health apps did not involve end-users at any stage of development), most apps had an option for the end-user to provide feedback by reporting issues. Furthermore, 21% (out of 1909) of the digital health apps provided a statement about the developer's commitment to addressing problems reported to them.

Many of the digital health apps allowed changes to the interface of the app for the convenience of the end-user: 87% (out of 1517) digital health apps allowed end-user to change the presentation theme. 60% (out of 2031) of digital health apps allowed end user to change the font size in-app or responded to device preferences. 99% (out of 1996) of the digital health apps in the sample provided support for end-users with poor sight. Giving end-user the ability to manage app interface could possibly remove struggles they might have with the app and increase usability and accessibility.

Moreover, 98% (out of 1994) of the digital health apps in the sample provided support for end-users with hearing impairment. 74% (out of 1566) digital health apps gave the end user options to manage the notification settings (push/email) within the app for convenience/privacy. As can be seen in Table 3, most apps used Email as method of support for end-users 78% (out of 2053). If a digital health app had a forum 80% (out of 351) had a statement within the app that the forum content is moderated. Moderation of such forums could prevent patient end-users from spreading misinformation on the forums. Table 4 states that many of the common function of mobile apps, such as home and back buttons have been used in digital health apps. However, only 40% (out of 2053) of digital health apps included a search button, but this could be since most digital health apps simply did not need it. Many of the digital health apps' allowed end-user to manage user interface and notifications, provided accessibility features, made use of well-known mobile functions (such as home and back buttons) and moderated content on forums (if applicable). Many of the digital health apps allowed for the modifications of the apps to suit end-users' preferences. And many earned points for allowing such modifications, resulting in high UX scores on the ORCHA UX assessment tool.

Although there is guidance such as International Organization for Standardization (ISO) [9], currently there appears to be no gold standard for digital health apps' UX assessment [10–13]. The current literature [10–13] suggests that improvements could be made in the development and evaluation of digital health apps in terms of clinical assurance, data privacy and UX.

Although a 2021 scoping review [10] examined the domain/criteria needed to evaluate digital health apps found that UX together with information validity has been the most evaluated criteria. This scoping review included frameworks such as system usability scale (SUS) and system usability measurement inventory (SUMI). These frameworks are designed to evaluate usability and are not tailored to digital health apps. In their 'count', if a framework evaluated an aspect of UX - it was considered a scale for evaluating UX. Usability is an aspect of UX evaluation, however counting frameworks that measure usability and UX together as one and the same has skewed the result.

Another 2021 scoping review [12] found that most evaluation frameworks for digital health apps were concerned with evidence, clinical foundation, and privacy. This study suggests that it is unclear if engagement has been adequately predicted with the existing frameworks. The study also suggests that balance between objective and subjective questions is a challenge for evaluation frameworks.

4.1 Related Work

A paper from 2022 [14], showed that a widely used SUS distribution for benchmarking of mean 68 (SD 12.5) can be used to reliably assess the usability of most health apps. However, exception occurred for physical activity apps that showed higher than expected usability of 83.28 (SD 12.39) when using SUS.

A paper from 2020 [15], conducted a systematic review focusing on of postoperative care health apps. The study found the usability of these apps to be above industry average, with median SUS scores ranging from 76 to 95 out of 100.

A paper from 2020 [16], examined long term UX of health app through an in-app embedded conversation-based questionnaire. The study found that the most satisfying experiences occurred mainly within the first weeks, those were treatment of monitoring and features. And the less satisfactory experiences were "technical problems on the application, and the effort and difficulty of use". This is like the findings of a different study from 2019 [8] that found many end-users of mental health apps stop using digital health apps after two weeks due to usability issues.

4.2 Limitations

This study has been conducted on the data gathered solely from ORCHA UX assessment tool. Their data collection for this study concluded in 2021, some of the digital health practices may have changed since then. ORCHA UX assessment tool does not assess long-term UX or undertake user testing, meaning that issues related to continued use or many aspects of the usability of an app would not have been identified with the tool. Out of 2053 digital health apps used in this paper, 469 apps had Android and iOS versions counted as separate, resulting in 938 assessments.

5 Conclusion

Overall, digital health apps appear to be scoring well on the ORCHA UX assessment tool. However, there is a place for improvement in terms of compliance with app design standards, statements of user involvement in design/development stage of app, evidence of user involvement in testing and medical terms explanations. The results of this study are significant as it uncovers the state of UX practices among digital health apps and suggests what improvements can be done to the design practices and UX assessment of digital health apps.

Acknowledgements. This research is done in partnership with ORCHA, a UK-based digital health compliance company. This work is supported by a Northern Ireland DfE CAST award / PhD scholarship. We would like to acknowledge the contribution of the many digital health app reviewers and developers who worked with ORCHA that allowed for the review of digital health apps and consented for their data to be used for the purposes of research. Without their contribution and consent this research would not have been possible.

Data Sharing. This study conducted secondary data analysis on the ORCHA dataset (Excel format). The data from this dataset (and for more DHIs) is freely available to registered users (registration is free) at ORCHA library [17]. However, the data will be presented for individual DHIs and not in Excel format.

Conflicts of Interest. This study is funded by a DfE Cast award and ORCHA. Simon Leigh and Robert Daly are employees at ORCHA.

References

1. Kern, J., et al.: Written consent of IQVIA and the IQVIA Institute. Digital Health Trends (2021)

2. ORCHA. COVID-19: Digital Health Trends Report - ORCHA (2020). https://orchahealth. com/covid19-digital-health-trends-report/
3. Alqahtani, F., Orji, R.: Insights from user reviews to improve mental health apps. Health Informatics J. **26**(3), 2042–2066 (2020). https://doi.org/10.1177/1460458219896492
4. Hunt Sophie. Review Documentation - Review Development & Resources | Exte. Accessed 13 Mar 2022. https://confluence.external-share.com/content/b6055aac-83e4-4947-be0e-ebb 8c39559ef
5. Brooke, J.: (PDF) SUS: A quick and dirty usability scale. ResearchGate (1995). https://www. researchgate.net/publication/228593520_SUS_A_quick_and_dirty_usability_scale
6. Richardson, B., Campbell-Yeo, M., Smit, M.: Mobile application user experience checklist: a tool to assess attention to core UX principles. Int. J. Human- Comput. Interact. **37**(13), 1283–1290 (2021). https://doi.org/10.1080/10447318.2021.1876361
7. ORCHA Privacy Policy. Accessed 11 Aug 2022. https://appfinder.orcha.co.uk/privacy-pol icy/
8. Torous, J., et al.: Towards a consensus around standards for smartphone apps and digital mental health. World Psychiat. **18**(1), 97 (2019). https://doi.org/10.1002/WPS.20592
9. ISO - ISO/TS 82304-2:2021 - Health software—Part 2: Health and wellness apps—Quality and reliability. Accessed 7 Feb 2023. https://www.iso.org/standard/78182.html
10. Hensher, M., et al.: Scoping review: Development and assessment of evaluation frameworks of mobile health apps for recommendations to consumers. J. Am. Med. Informat. Assoc. **28**(6), 1318–1329 (2021). https://doi.org/10.1093/JAMIA/OCAB041
11. Henson, P., David, G., Albright, K., Torous, J.: Deriving a practical frame-work for the evaluation of health apps. Lancet Dig/ Health **1**(2), e52–e54 (2019). https://doi.org/10.1016/ S2589-7500(19)30013-5
12. Lagan, S., Sandler, L., Torous, J.: Evaluating evaluation frameworks: a scoping review of frameworks for assessing health apps. BMJ Open **11**, 47001 (2021). https://doi.org/10.1136/ bmjopen-2020-047001
13. Torous, J.B., et al.: A hierarchical framework for evaluation and in-formed decision making regarding smartphone apps for clinical care. Psychiat. Serv. **69**(5), 498–500 (2018). https:// doi.org/10.1176/APPI.PS.201700423
14. Hyzy, M., et al.: System usability scale benchmarking for digital health apps: meta-analysis. JMIR Mhealth Uhealth **10**(8), E37290 (2022). https://Mhealth.Jmir.Org/2022/8/E37290. https://doi.org/10.2196/37290
15. Patel, B., Thind, A.: Usability of mobile health apps for postoperative care: systematic review. JMIR Perioper Med **3**(2), E19099 (2020). https://Periop.Jmir.Org/2020/2/E19099. https://doi. org/10.2196/19099
16. Biduski, D., Bellei, E.A., Rodriguez, J.P.M., Zaina, L.A.M., de Marchi, A.C.B.: Assessing long-term user experience on a mobile health application through an in-app embedded conversation-based questionnaire. Comput. Hum. Behav. **104**, 106169 (2020). https://doi.org/ 10.1016/J.CHB.2019.106169
17. Digital Health Libraries - ORCHA. Accessed 19 Jan 2023. https://orchahealth.com/services/ digital-health-libraries/

Facilitating Empathy for Care Recipients

Analyzing Care Behaviors Towards Person-Centered Care

Masayuki Ihara[1]([✉]), Hiroko Tokunaga[1], Tomomi Nakashima[1,2],
Shinpei Saruwatari[1,3], Hiroki Goto[1,4], Yuuki Umezaki[1,5], and Masashige Motoe[1,6]

[1] RIKEN, Wako 3510198, Japan
ihara@acm.org
[2] Yamanami Kaiteki Seikatsu, Co. Ltd., Omuta 8360091, Japan
[3] Shirakawa Hospital, Omuta 8370926, Japan
[4] Medical Corporation Meikikai, Kagoshima 8920871, Japan
[5] Shinjikai Medical Association, Omuta 8370924, Japan
[6] Tohoku University, Sendai 9808579, Japan

Abstract. The well-being of care recipients is an important issue in health care domains, while demand for higher work efficiency through data and information technologies is increasing. Data and technology utilization without a focus on individuals may lead to disregard for human dignity. This paper introduces a design principle for person-centered care services that prioritizes individual well-being on the basis of patient life backgrounds. We extracted problematic care behaviors with 6 typical categories, employed the person-centered care principle to design a co-creation workshop, and qualitatively evaluated the effectiveness of the workshop with care workers. A qualitative analysis using the Grounded Theory Approach revealed the effectiveness of visualization and shared viewpoints in the workshop design; however, we found that the design should be improved so that participants could deeply empathize with the recipients. We also extracted the 66 attitudes and behaviors expected of care workers and analyzed the requirements for their work environments. We discuss two important requirements in designing workshops. The first is care recipient centered design to provide each recipient with person-centered care service. The second is service-provider centered design to provide care workers with experience in empathizing with care recipients so that they could deeply understand them and effectively provide the created care service.

Keywords: Person-Centered Design Methodology · Nursing Care · Empathy

1 Introduction

In health care fields, there is demand for work improvements or novel care service developments because labor shortages are a significant problem. The well-being of care recipients is also one of the important issues in health care domains, while demand for higher work efficiency through data and information technologies is increasing. The utilization of data and technology without a focus on individuals may cause disregard for human dignity. It is not easy to increase the satisfaction of each care recipient while sustainably operating a workflow created as a result of work improvements or service developments. For sustainable operation, co-design approaches done with care workers can be effective in terms of defining reasonable operations for the workers. For increasing the satisfaction of each care recipient, a focus on his/her life background is essential. This is because each recipient has their own unique background in life and has their own perspective on happiness. This paper introduces a design principle for person-centered care services that prioritizes individual well-being on the basis of life background.

2   Issues Addressed

2.1   Work Improvements and Individual Cares

The number of users of nursing care services is increasing in aging societies due to the advancement of medical technologies. However, most nursing care providers suffer from labor shortage problems and expect work improvements or new care services that utilize data and information technologies to solve these issues. Data and information technologies are expected to be effectively utilized in health care domains in the future [1–4]. In Japan, regarding data utilization at small nursing care providers, fact data on care workers' operations, which is necessary for the insurance system, is registered, but there are few other uses of data even though such data has the potential to contribute to work improvements or better care services.

In addition, individual care is important because each care recipient has his/her own unique life background as well as diseases or disabilities. Care workers are so busy under labor shortage situations that they are required to do many tasks efficiently. A balance between work efficiency and individual care is required.

2.2   Problematic Behaviors by Care Workers

As mentioned in [5, 6], behaviors at care sites indicate several problems. Care workers experience psychological burdens under labor shortage situations because they have to quickly finish their assigned tasks with few staff. They may prioritize the efficiency of their tasks over understanding the feelings of the care recipient. That is, care workers may act in a self-protective way at work as a result of perceived psychological and workload burdens. Even if care workers have in their minds the desire to provide care in consideration of the feelings of care recipients, as a result of the above psychological burden, there is a discrepancy between the ideal and reality. To reduce this gap, it is important to be able to provide information that can serve as hints for the care workers' thinking processes and decisions.

In this study, we extracted 30 care behaviors that display a lack consideration for the care recipient (See Table 1) through a discussion with managers of nursing facilities (third, fifth, and sixth authors). The extracted care behaviors were categorized into 6 problems in care workers' minds: prioritizing their own convenience (C), disregard for patient's wishes (W), disrespect for the individuality of patients (I), disregard for the dignity of patients (D), depriving patients of opportunities (O), and overestimation of risk (R). These are based on self-defense in care workers' minds. Note that "X" and "x" in Table 1 mean the main and other related factors, respectively.

Table 1. Care behaviors that lack consideration toward patients.

Behaviors	C	W	I	D	O	R
Roughly assist with excretion worrying about time	X	x				
Restrain patient's body	X	x	x	x	x	x
Prioritize their own convenience without confirming patient's intentions	X	x				
Prioritize workers' time availability	X	x				
Prioritize efficiency during health checks	X					
Do nothing for situations where patient is just sitting	X					
Determine meal time according to workers' convenience	X	x				
Lie that patient's family will pick them up later	X					
Force reluctant patient to come to facility	x	X				
Ignore patient's mood and carry out routines and roles	x	X				
When doctor gives order to rest, ignore patient's will and force it	x	X				
Enforce their own values that it is better not to be at home in this state	x	X				
Respond to restless patients without thinking about patient's reasons		X				
Prioritize their own convenience without confirming patient's feelings	x	X				
Decide how workers will provide care without considering patient's opinions	x	X				
Force patient to eat who does not want to eat	x	X				
Ignore patient's calls	x	X				
Do not listen to patients	x	X				
Force bath even if patient does not like it	x	X				
Keep wallet to prevent wasteful spending and deprive patient of what she/he want to do	x	X			x	x
Do not provide patients with opportunities for social engagement					X	
Do not provide role to patient				x	X	
Manage patients while ignoring lifestyle habits such as drinking and smoking	x	x	X			
Organize recreational activities that treat all patients same	x		X		x	
Tell patient to go to restroom in loud voice that can be heard by others				X		
Listen only to specific patients	X				x	
Forcibly put patient who says she/he wants to walk home into a car and send her/him home	x	x				X

(continued)

Table 1. (*continued*)

Behaviors	C	W	I	D	O	R
Encourage patients to stay at facility due to excessive concern	x	x				X
Restrict patient with words and actions due to excessive awareness of danger	x	x				X
Excessively concerned about risk, saying what to do if something happens	x	x				X

Prioritizing Their Own Convenience

Care workers need to do many tasks in a limited amount of time due to an increase in the number of users of care services and labor shortages. To work efficiently, workers sometimes give priority to their own convenience when considering the time to spend on work and the order of work. For example, one example of such behavior is not carefully providing excretion assistance or health check due to worrying about time. As a result of the mindset to avoid troublesome situations, workers sometimes act unfavorably for their own convenience. For example, there are cases where workers do not speak to patients to whom they should speak, or listen only to specific patients with no difficulty.

Disregard for Patient's Wishes

As mentioned above, patients have their own backgrounds and circumstances in addition to diseases and physical disabilities, and these are reflected in their wishes. Some of these wishes are expressed in words, actions, and attitudes, but others are not. For example, there are behaviors such as ignoring a patient's call because of busyness and forcing a patient to take a bath even though the patient says he/she does not want to take a bath. These are care behaviors that disregard the wishes of the patients even when their wishes are expressed. In addition, keeping a patient's wallet in order to prevent them from wasteful spending is a behavior that neglects the patient's wish to buy what he/she wants and live a fulfilling life in the same way as a healthy person, even though the patient may not express this wish.

Disrespect Toward Individuality of Patients

Even if a patient uses nursing care services, he/she has individuality as a human being. However, individualized care given in consideration of the individuality of each patient is often inefficient in practice, so individuality tends to be neglected. For example, lifestyle habits such as drinking and smoking are often judged as "bad habits", but these habits can also be interpreted as representing the patient's individuality. In another example, nursing facilities may organize recreational activities for entertainment, but they may be designed to treat every participant the same, without considering each participant individually.

Disregard for Dignity of Patients

The dignity of patients is important. The Long-Term Care Insurance Act in Japan insists on providing benefits pertaining to necessary health and medical services and public aid services so that people are able to maintain dignity and an independent daily life routine according to each person's own level of abilities. Restraining a patient's body to prevent them from wandering due to dementia is an easy-to-understand bad example. As another example, there are cases in which a care worker calls out loudly to a patient, even though it may be embarrassing for the patient, such as when guiding the patient to the restroom, which can be heard by the people around them. In particular, for dementia patients, the inability to act like a healthy person may lead to their dignity being disregarded, which is a serious problem regarding caregiving behavior.

Depriving Patients of Opportunities

If a patient is unable to do something due to a disease such as dementia or a physical disability, care workers may deprive the patient of the opportunity to act independently. It is important for elderly people who use nursing care services to maintain their relationship with society. However, due to a disease or a disability, care workers sometimes do not actively create opportunities for dialogue with other users of the same nursing facility or with members of the community in a town. On the other hand, even though a patient has some remaining ability, care workers may not assign the patient a role that makes use of the ability. For example, care workers may deny a patient with mild dementia the opportunity to cook even though he/she can cook.

Overestimation of Risk

Nursing facilities have many physically disabled patients, and care workers are always at risk of injuring them due to falls or other causes. Due to cognitive decline, a patient may go out alone and have an accident. Care workers are often concerned about these risks, but their predictions can be overestimated. For example, when there is a patient who wishes to walk home from a nursing facility, the patient may be forced into a car and driven home as a result of worrying that he/she will have an accident on the way home. Although it depends on the patient's walking ability and cognitive ability, comprehensive judgment should be made by considering both the rehabilitation effect of walking and the risk of getting into an accident. However, care workers may make judgments based on self-defense in the face of difficulties in the event of an accident.

3   Person-Centered Design

3.1   Person-Centered Care

In the health care domain, a user-centered approach is often used to satisfy each patient's demands [7, 8]. The COPM, Canadian Occupational Performance Measure, is an evidence-based outcome measure designed to capture a client's self-perception of performance in everyday living and is used in many countries [9]. However, high work efficiency will be more prioritized than this user-centered approach at care sites.

As one principle to deeply understand each patient, person-centered care was introduced by Kitwood [10]. The principle is derived from the context of dementia care but can be applied to other health care domains. The notion of personhood in the principle means that each person should be accepted as his/her being in terms of the social relationship even though strange behaviors caused by dementia might be present. Person-centered care is used in limited health care fields [11], and its practical framework is called DCM, Dementia Care Mapping [12]. The framework is utilized in many case studies [13]. However, it is not easy to operate under the framework at care sites due to there being too many operations in the DCM cycle.

3.2 Utilization of the Person-Centered Principle in Design

DCM is a framework for operating a service, not for designing it. To use the person-centered principle for designing a service, another approach is needed. In our project, we used this person-centered principle to design processes on the basis of design thinking. Given the fact that DCM is not easy to implement, there is demand for business improvements and new services based on the person-centered principle and that consider the operation of on-site workers. Considering sustainable operation at a site, it is effective to design improvements and services through co-creation with workers who actually work at the site. From the perspective of person-centered emphasis, how care workers can empathize with each patient is an issue in designing a process and implementing it in practice. With the long-term goal of constructing a methodology for person-centered design using the person-centered principle, we started designing and implementing person-centered design from the empathy process of design thinking. In the following sections, we will introduce the co-creation project.

4   Co-creation Project

4.1   Project Overview

Aiming to create a nursing care service based on the person-centered principle, we decided to implement a co-creation project with a living lab approach. This co-creation project was proposed by a research institute (RIKEN, to which the first author of this article belongs), and is to be carried out over a period of about three years by researchers and care workers ("Living Aeru," a nursing care facility to which the third author of this article belongs). The care service provided by the facility is a small-scale multi-functional in-home care service that includes commuting, accommodation, and visits by care workers, and users who are suffering from dementia are included. We started the project by listening to the voices of care workers in a workshop (WS) and investigating the actual activities of patients and the awareness of the workers.

4.2   Designing the Workshop

As the initial stage of the co-creation project, we designed and implemented a WS (See Fig. 1) that encourages empathy for patients according to design thinking. The participants of the WS are a total of 5 people, the third author of this article (representative of Living Aeru) and 4 workers appointed by the representative (4 people in their 50s, 1 person in their 40s, gender composition ratio = 1 male: 4 females). Three of the five have experience participating in WSs for training, but they have no experience participating in WSs as a designer. All four workers nominated as a WS participant are middle managers with a title. They were judged to have the possibility of understanding and accepting the person-centered principle while knowing the actual situation of work in the field. The first author of this article designed and operated the WS as a facilitator and designer. The results of the WS were brought home by the facilitator, transcribed, organized, displayed on a large display at the next WS or distributed as printed matter, and they were visualized and presented to the participants in the co-creation space.

Fig. 1. A scene of the workshop.

1st Workshop: Extraction of Care Recipient's Behaviors and Backgrounds

We held a 3-time co-creation WS with the care workers so that they could understand the concept of person-centered care and sympathize with care recipients. The first workshop was to extract the care recipient's unexpected behaviors and their backgrounds. We expected the WS participants (care workers) to think about how they should care for the recipients through introspection. In this WS, participants were asked to recall their experiences in past care work where their own assumptions were different from the care recipient's actions and remarks and to write them down on sticky notes. The participants were asked to verbally talk about episodes related to the contents of each written sticky note. After that, all the participants voted for the sticky notes that they sympathized with. The reason the WS was designed to focus on unexpected behaviors was to focus on episodes in which the care recipient reacted unexpectedly to the caregiving behavior of the worker and to have the worker reflect on the care behavior. Next, we asked the participants to write down the background information they thought was behind the care recipient's actions and then asked them to vote on sticky notes that they could sympathize with. The purpose of having them write down the background information was to focus on the "personal background" that is emphasized in the person-centered principle.

2nd Workshop: Discussion on Recipient's Loneliness

The second WS was a free discussion on the issue of recipient's loneliness, which was extracted in the first WS. The purpose of the second WS was for the participants to externalize their opinions on "patient loneliness", an issue identified in the first WS. The participants were asked to speak out their opinions which were not expressed on the sticky notes of the first WS from a subjective point of view.

3rd Workshop: Lecture on Person-Centered Care Principle

The third workshop was a lecture on the person-centered care principle followed by participants reflecting on their own care behaviors through a care episode introduction. Even if care workers have learned the person-centered principle in other trainings, they tend to forget it in their daily field work. It was important for the participants to recognize the fact that they are unable to provide appropriate caregiving behavior due to their self-protective mentality. Therefore, in this WS, we aimed to make the participants aware of the importance of person-centered care by having them talk about specific care episodes.

5 Results

According to the results of the first WS, some background information related to feelings of loneliness was extracted, such as "feelings of wanting someone to be with," "loneliness of not having someone to talk to," and "feeling of alienation from not being able to have someone to talk to." At the WS, not only unexpected behaviors but also expected behaviors such as frequent phone calls from the care recipient at home were a topic of discussion. In terms of sympathizing with the loneliness of care recipients, a certain effect was seen in the first WS.

In the discussion in the second WS, there was the opinion that there is a difference between not having a conversation partner and having a conversation partner but not being able to talk. It was pointed out that care workers, who should be conversation partners, ignore care recipients. In addition, the participants recognized the fact that elderly people who had spent their lives working hard were retiring and receiving less attention from those around them. They pointed out that it is important for the elderly to be needed by society through the defining of their roles in their interactions with others.

In the third WS, we lectured that care recipients have their own backgrounds and personalities, which do not necessarily surface, and that even if they suffer from dementia, they still have latent abilities and possibilities, so that it is important to make use of them and maintain connections with society. One of the participants stated that there was a care recipient who used to be a taxi driver, so the participant asked him to take on the role of washing the car. There were also comments such as "Why don't you take advantage of his knowledge of the road and have him play a role?" The implication from these statements is that field care workers are experimenting with person-centered care practices. Unfortunately, although the above car wash work was implemented, it has not been continued, and thus, it has not been adopted on the site as it was not sustainable among the daily busy work. Maintaining opportunities for this recipient to demonstrate his remaining abilities in a social setting through the role of car washing declined in priority due to busy work and because the care workers focused on protecting themselves.

6 Analysis

In this section, we analyze the results of implementing the design process in the WS through the questionnaire responses of the participants. To analyze the design process, we qualitatively analyzed the participants' evaluation comments on the designed WS. The analysis was conducted using the Grounded Theory Approach (GTA) [14], which is a qualitative analysis method, for the free-text responses to the questionnaire conducted for the five participants. We analyzed the results of empathy for care recipients, that is, the results of the questions asked regarding the effects of the first WS and the reasons for them. Open coding of the GTA analysis was performed, and axial coding was performed on the results of the open coding. The results were classified into "Phenomenon," "Action/Interaction," and "Consequence," and they are shown in Fig. 2 as a category diagram.

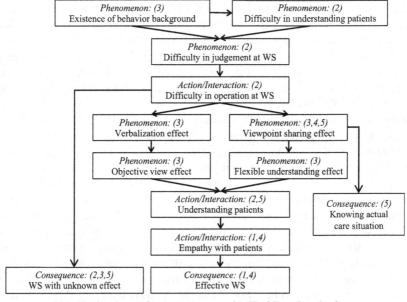

Note: Numbers in parentheses represent respondent ID of dimension related to category.

Fig. 2. Category diagram of GTA analysis on empathy for patients.

An interpretation that can be drawn from the result in Fig. 2 is as follows.

A patient's behavior has a background, which is not easy to understand. Therefore, even in WSs in which care workers participate, they sometimes find it difficult to make decisions and to operate. Depending on the design of the WS, we can expect the effects from objective observation by verbalizing thoughts and effects of flexible understanding by sharing viewpoints with other participants. These effects lead to understanding and empathizing with patients. In addition, the sharing of various viewpoints by the participants will lead to understanding of the actual situation of on-site care.

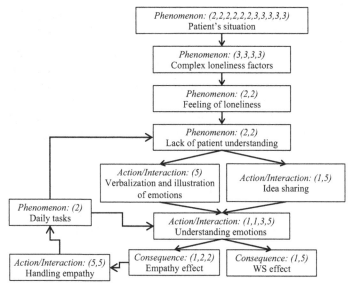

Note: Numbers in parentheses represent respondent ID of dimension related to category.

Fig. 3. Category diagram of GTA analysis on empathy for patients' feelings of loneliness.

Next, we conducted a GTA analysis in the same way on the results of the questionnaire on empathy for patients' feelings of loneliness at the second WS (See Fig. 3). An interpretation for Fig. 3 is as follows.

The patient's background includes facts that are easy for care workers to know, as well as various other circumstances. There is a feeling of loneliness as a result of the complex influence of those factors. It is not easy for care workers to understand this in their daily work. It is expected that WS design in which the patient's emotions are verbalized and illustrated, the opinions of the WS participants are shared, and daily work is reviewed by care workers will promote the understanding of the patient's emotions. One of the effects is empathy toward patients. However, care must be taken in how empathy is handled in supporting patients in their daily work.

These analyses suggest the importance of verbalizing, illustrating, and sharing opinions and perspectives. In future process design, it will be important to encourage care workers, who are overwhelmed by daily work, to get away from their busyness and flexibly understand patients from an objective point of view. Regarding the patients' unexpected behaviors, there were the following comments in the questionnaire responses.

- What is a patient's unexpected behavior?

- In the first place, what is the expected and normal behavior?
- Although I thought that it would not be an unexpected behavior if it was treated as a symptom of dementia, I thought that the patient's unusual behavior was an unexpected behavior and worked on the WS.
- The patient himself/herself does not know why he/she behaves in such a way, and in some cases, the symptoms are caused by dementia rather than by their own will.

From the above comments, it seems that the participants were confused about the interpretation of "unexpected." We intended to design the WS with the expectation that the care workers themselves would reflect on their own caregiving behavior, but there is room for design improvement in this regard. In addition, as can be seen from the interpretation of Fig. 3, the patient's background information is based on complicated personal circumstances, and the feeling of loneliness is the result of these complex factors. There were the following comments in the questionnaire responses.

- Background information is only speculation on my part.
- Only the patient himself knows how he really feels.

In person-centered care, even if there are symptoms of dementia, care workers are expected to proactively capture and understand the patient's background information and reflect the results in caregiving behavior. However, the above comment can be interpreted as half giving up, and there are still points to be improved as a design process that encourages empathy by care workers.

7 Discussions

7.1 Expectations for Worker's Behavioral Changes

According to the results of the WS, there is still room for improvement in the WS design, so it is necessary to obtain perspectives that should be emphasized for future WS improvement and service design. The WS mentioned above was not designed specifically considering the problematic care behaviors described in Sect. 2.2. Rather, it was expected that the care workers would proactively reflect on their own behaviors and think about these behaviors by themselves. To obtain perspectives for improving the WS, we extracted expectations for care workers to prevent these behaviors. The extraction work was carried out in a brainstorming manner by three nursing facility managers who were members of our research team. We asked those managers to write down the thoughts, behaviors, and skills they expect from care workers to prevent problematic care behaviors. Table 2 shows the extraction results.

Problematic care behaviors are often the result of workers' individual defensive psychology. Care workers often engage in these behaviors as a result of trying to avoid problem solving and taking responsibility in the face of troubles. One solution to this problem is to reduce the excessive sense of personal responsibility by engaging as a team of workers. In Table 2, as one of expectations regarding prioritizing one's own convenience, the importance of talking among workers, sharing tasks, and supporting each other is pointed out. Moreover, regarding depriving patients of opportunities, the importance of working as a team, not as a single worker by oneself, is pointed out.

Providing nursing care as a team could have the effect of making it easier to understand and use different criteria for judging behavior.

7.2   Care Behaviors as a Service Element

To provide care services that satisfy patients, care behavior is as important as care plans. When designing a new care service, it is necessary to design not only the service itself but also the care behaviors according to the necessary operation. Figure 4 shows the relationships between stakeholders and activities in our service co-creation project. Care workers are expected to deeply understand patients on the basis of empathy through participation in co-creation workshops. This deep understanding provides a subjective

Table 2.   Thoughts, behaviors, and skills expected to prevent problematic care behaviors.

	Expectation		Expectation
Prioritizing their own convenience (C)	• Have room to listen to the patient • Understand who the support behavior is for • Have empathy for the patient • Talk among workers, share tasks, and support each other • Flexibly adjust their hours • Do not blame patient families and care workers • Have leeway through stress care • Think flexibly • Make patient-centricity a common understanding among workers • Acquire independence without relying on instructions • Do not mind being labeled as incompetent • Dispel failure avoidance consciousness	Disregard for dignity of patients (D)	• Recognize that workers are in a stronger position • Know and consider the patient's values • Know the dignity of workers themselves • Learn the meaning of dignity • Think about the meaning of dignity through work • Understand patient rights protection • Understand respect and disrespect for dignity from the patient's life • Be in awe of the patient • Ask myself if I would do the same for healthy people • Increase opportunities to consider dignity

(continued)

Table 2. (*continued*)

	Expectation		Expectation
Disregard for patient's wishes (W)	• Confirm patient's intentions • Understand the need for work from the patient's perspective • Understand patient-centered care • Consider the patient's feelings • Be interested in the patient • Understand the lives and wishes of patients • Cherish patient's present moments • Do not judge patients negatively • Throw away the mindset of working in a uniform way • Be tolerant of each patient value • Create patient-oriented solution • Acknowledge a patient's selfishness in a crowd • Consider a patient's remaining abilities • Do not think it is a hassle to know the patient deeply	Depriving patients of opportunities (O)	• Understand independence support and patient freedom • Do not treat patients as elderly • Think about solutions, not depriving patients • Think about the meaning of one's own work • Consider possibilities and see them as opportunities • Work in teams, not self-contained • Create opportunities for discussion • Do not be judgmental and instead ask the patient • Review case studies • Know patient's strengths

(continued)

Table 2. (*continued*)

	Expectation		Expectation
Disrespect for individuality of patients (I)	• Work on the premise of respect for the individual • Understand that each patient is different • Deal with the patient's values and life • Understand the protection of patient human rights • Do not run away from difficulties or give up • Do not take it as someone else's problem • Understand the patient as a person • Think of the patient in place of oneself • Recognize a person who is different from others as one with unique personalities • Do not take the patient's personality as a nuisance • Respect patient dignity	Overestimation of risk (R)	• Assess risks correctly • Review risks with other workers • Do not use risk as a reason not to work • Imagine the patient's smile and joy • Consider both when to do the work and when not to do it • Talk to the patient about the risks • Consider the balance between risk and freedom • Talk to other workers about risks • Actively or passively solve the problem depending on the risk

view of care behaviors, and the care workers are expected to make behavioral changes in care delivery and appropriate behaviors according to newly designed services. It is assumed that the problematic care behavior list and expectations for care workers obtained through the cooperation of care facility managers will be used in future service design. The list and expectations are important in service design as an objective view from the manager's perspective. The care workers are expected to contribute to both design cooperation from the field's point of view through workshop participation and appropriate care behaviors according to the designed service.

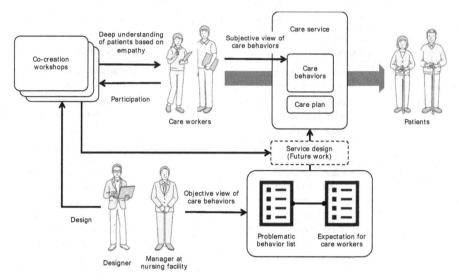

Fig. 4. Stakeholders and activities in our service co-creation project.

7.3 Contributions

In this study, we determined the issues in the nursing care field, interpreted the ideal nursing care under the concept of the person-centered principle, and applied it to the design. We believe that the contributions of this study are the following three.

1. Introduced the person-centered principle and applied it to the service design process from the perspective of design science
2. Organized and analyzed problematic care behaviors based on defensive reactions of care workers
3. Practiced the empathy process of design thinking with on-site care workers and qualitatively analyzed their comments

   User-centered design is fundamental in the field of service design. However, the person-centered principle, which originated in the field of nursing care, is hardly dealt with in the field of design. Person-centered design is based on a human view that focuses on individuals. It makes it possible to understand people in a more in-depth manner than user-centered design and to think about individual lives and needs and available resources for service design [15]. The unique life backgrounds of each patient such as their life environment, work history, hobbies, and sense of values could be a valuable resource for designing a person-centered care service.

   Even if a person-centered care service were well-designed and its effectiveness confirmed through experiments, care workers may not accept it. To design a sustainable service, it is important for both those workers and designers to co-create the service with agreements on issues addressed and ideas to solve them. Of course, customizing services to each user may cause service operation to be inefficient. This is why we also focus on the behaviors of care workers who will be service providers after the service is launched. Person-centered services bring value to care recipients through both appropriate design of the care service and appropriate care behaviors by the workers. Therefore, it is important to extract the problematic care behaviors due to defensive reactions of care workers and consider service design including correcting them.

In general, care workers are not familiar with design processes and are not motivated to join in design projects. Thus, designers should motivate them to cooperate in projects. In particular, the process of empathy is one of the important steps in design thinking. Empathy is also important from the perspective of person-centered design, which values the individual. Therefore, it is worthwhile to analyze the effects of care workers' participation in a co-creation WS and issues related to the WS design. The WS introduced in this paper was the first trial, and was designed with the main purpose of empathizing with care recipients. We believe that it is possible to design workshops aimed at raising awareness of problems and behavioral changes among care workers themselves.

8 Conclusion

In the practice of person-centered design introduced in this paper, there is room for improvement in terms of getting care workers to understand and empathize with the background information of care recipients. However, we confirmed the effects of verbalization, illustrations, and the sharing of opinions and viewpoints in a workshop. We also analyzed problematic care behaviors due to defensive reactions of care workers and discussed the discrepancy between the ideal and reality of nursing care based on the workers' psychology and behaviors. Future work will involve practicing the process of definition, creation, prototyping, and evaluation of design thinking toward person-centered care services as well as building a design methodology by generalizing the know-how obtained in the process practice.

Acknowledgements. We would like to thank the employees of the nursing facility "Living Aeru" for participating in the workshop and answering the questionnaire.

References

1. Hu, Y., Wang, Y.: HSAACE: design a cloud platform health status assessment application to support continuous evolution of assessment capabilities. In: 2022 The 5th International Conference on Software Engineering and Information Management (ICSIM) (ICSIM 2022), pp. 132–137. ACM, New York (2022). https://doi.org/10.1145/3520084.3520105
2. Karim, S., Gide, E., Sandu, R.: The impact of big data on health care services in australia: using big data analytics to categorise and deal with patient. In: Proceedings of the 2019 International Conference on Mathematics, Science and Technology Teaching and Learning (ICMSTTL 2019), pp. 34–38. ACM, New York (2019). https://doi.org/10.1145/3348400.3348414
3. Li, H., Cheng, Y., Li, Y., Ma, X., Li, D.: Health assessment system based on big data analysis of meridian electrical potential. In: Proceedings of the 3rd International Conference on Biomedical Signal and Image Processing (ICBIP 2018), pp. 75–80. ACM, New York (2018). https://doi.org/10.1145/3278229.3278235

4. Taweel, A., Speedie, S., Tyson, G., Tawil, A.R.H., Peterson, K., Delaney, B.: Service and model-driven dynamic integration of health data, In: Proceedings of the First International Workshop on Managing Interoperability and Complexity in Health Systems (MIXHS 2011), pp. 11–17. ACM, New York (2011). https://doi.org/10.1145/2064747.2064752

5. Grissinger, M.: Unresolved disrespectful behavior in health care: practitioners speak up (again)-part 1. Pharm. Therpeut. **42**(1), 4–23 (2017). PMID: 28090154; PMCID: PMC5215268

6. Grissinger, M.: Disrespectful behavior in health care: its impact, why it arises and persists, and how to address it-part 2. Pharm. Therpeut. **42**(2), 74–77 (2017). PMID: 28163550; PMCID: PMC5265230

7. Pais, S.: Integrating patient-generated wellness data: a user-centered approach. In: Proceedings of the Australasian Computer Science Week Multiconference (ACSW 2020), Article 35, pp. 1–8. ACM, New York (2020). https://doi.org/10.1145/3373017.3373052

8. MacCaull, W., Jewers, H., Latzel, M.: Using an interdisciplinary approach to develop a knowledge-driven careflow management system for collaborative patient-centred palliative care. In: Proceedings of the 1st ACM International Health Informatics Symposium (IHI 2010), pp. 507–511. ACM, New York (2010). https://doi.org/10.1145/1882992.1883073

9. Carswell, A., McColl, M.A., Baptiste, S., Law, M., Polatajko, H., Pollock, N.: The canadian occupational performance measure: a research and clinical literature review. Can. J. Occup. Ther. **71**(4), 210–222 (2004). https://doi.org/10.1177/000841740407100406

10. Kitwood, T., Bredin, K.: Towards a theory of dementia care: personhood and well-being. Ageing Soc. **12**(3), 269–287 (1992). https://doi.org/10.1017/s0144686x0000502x

11. Håkansson Eklund, J., Holmström, I.K., Kumlin, T., Kaminsky, E., Skoglund, K., Höglander, J., et al.: "Same same or different?" a review of reviews of person-centered and patient-centered care. Pat. Educ. Couns. **102**(1), 3–11 (2019). https://doi.org/10.1016/j.pec.2018.08.029

12. University of Bradford: Dementia Care Mapping. https://www.bradford.ac.uk/dementia/training-consultancy/. Accessed 31 Jan 2023

13. Brooker, D.: Dementia care mapping: a review of the research literature. Gerontologist **45**(suppl_1), 11–18 (2005). https://doi.org/10.1093/geront/45.suppl_1.11

14. Glaser, B., Strauss, A.: The Discovery of Grounded Theory: Strategies for Qualitative Research. Aldine, Chicago (1967)

15. Kimura, A., Hayashi, M., Akasaka, F., Ihara, M.: Sustainable person-centered Living Lab for regional management as extension of Japanese dementia care activities. In: Proceedings of OpenLivingLab Days 2019, pp. 312–321 (2019)

A Mobile Application to Support Arm Ability Training for Occupational Therapy Patients

Virendra Kadam, Nishit Kadam(✉), Pooja Kudche(✉), Swati Chandna(✉),
and Eliane von Gunten(✉)

SRH University Heidelberg, Heidelberg, Germany
{virendravijay.kadam,
Nishit.Kadam}@stud.hochschule-heidelberg.de,
kudchepooja20@gmail.com, {swati.chandna,Eliane.Gunten}@srh.de

Abstract. Occupational theory is an essential branch of science that aims to aid individuals in performing their daily activities and tasks. Occupational therapists use this theory to improve physical and mental health, treat injuries, and address the disabilities of patients [2]. This paper focuses on a mobile application that is designed to help people after Stroke in their recovery process through games and exercises based on Impairment-Oriented-Training (IOT) principles. This paper begins by providing a comprehensive overview of the concepts of occupational therapy and highlighting its significance in today's world. It then identifies the shortcomings of the first version of the application and suggests improvements based on competitor analysis, literature review, and user feedback. This paper also provides detailed information on the technologies used to develop the application, including the frontend and backend, and includes prototypes, user interfaces, and the results of interviews and usability tests. The application development is conducted iteratively, with continuous feedback and improvement at each step. This approach helped to achieve the project's goals and resulted in a more user-friendly and efficient application. The development's final result, along with the usability tests and interviews, provides valuable insight into the application's success and serves as a guide for future improvements and upgrades. It is important to note that the paper's focus is to ensure that the end-users receive the best possible experience while using the application, and the development process is designed to achieve that goal.

Keywords: Occupational Therapy · Impairment-Oriented-Training (IOT) · Mobile Application · Design Thinking · User Interface · Usability Testing

1 Introduction

Occupational therapy is a form of treatment designed to enable individuals to engage in meaningful daily life activities, despite any physical or mental limitations they may experience. It is based on employing and engaging patients' minds and attention in occupation-based activities to improve their ability to perform various tasks [2]. It is a comprehensive approach to overcoming many difficulties, encompassing cognitive

© The Author(s), under exclusive license to Springer Nature Switzerland AG 2023
A. Marcus et al. (Eds.): HCII 2023, LNCS 14034, pp. 361–373, 2023.
https://doi.org/10.1007/978-3-031-35705-3_27

abilities, motor skills, visual perception, sensory processing, and self-help abilities. It is a beneficial practice for individuals of all ages, including children who are learning new skills, adults recovering from injuries or accidents, and older adults looking to maintain their independence and ability to carry out daily activities [9].

Occupational therapists (OT) work closely with other professionals in speech-language pathology, audiology, nursing, psychology, physical therapy, and assistive technology [9]. Despite the importance of occupational therapy in promoting independence and functionality, access to quality therapy services remains a challenge for many people, especially those living in remote areas or with mobility issues. In-person visits can be time-consuming and expensive, and traditional therapy methods may not always be tailored to an individual's specific needs and goals. There is a need for a solution to improve the delivery of occupational therapy services and make therapy more accessible, convenient, and personalized for patients. An occupational therapy application for smartphones and tablets has the potential to address these challenges and improve the overall therapy experience for patients.

The occupational therapy process begins with assessing the patient's daily activities and their challenges in performing those tasks. Based on this assessment, the OT creates a customized treatment plan that is tailored to the patient's strengths, weaknesses, and specific needs. This plan is designed to help the patient overcome any barriers in their physical, social, or mental environment and achieve goals.

The OT must track the patient's progress throughout the therapy process, from the first day to the last. Additionally, the patient needs to have a way to track their progress for self-motivation. In today's technology-driven world, where the COVID pandemic has created a need for greater connectivity between occupational therapists and their patients, a smart Occupational Therapy mobile application can provide a solution for tracking progress and staying connected.

2 Related Work

In recent years, various applications have been developed and gained popularity to support Occupational Therapy and their patients. MedBridge is a healthcare technology company that provides online patient education and therapy tools for rehabilitation professionals [4]. The application allows therapists to prescribe interactive patient education and therapy activities, track patient progress, and communicate with patients through a secure messaging system. The app also offers a library of evidence-based resources and educational content to help therapists stay current with the latest developments in their field. While MedBridge provides many benefits for occupational Therapy, Physical Therapy, and speech therapy professionals, it also has some limitations and drawbacks. The cost of using the MedBridge [4] app may be a barrier for some therapists, especially small practices or solo practitioners. Like any technology, the MedBridge app may encounter technical issues such as slow loading times or compatibility problems with certain devices. The content offered by MedBridge may not be comprehensive or updated regularly, and the platform may only provide access to some of the information and resources that therapists need to be effective. Some users have reported that the platform can be confusing to navigate or that the user interface could be improved.

Fun Bubbles is an iOS mobile application that can be best used to help children with their fine motor skills from a very early age [3]. However, the following were found to be its limitations: The application may need to effectively teach the skills it claims to or may not have a clear educational goal. In addition, the application may be expensive or use in-app purchases or advertisements to generate revenue, which can be distracting or disruptive for children.

Piano Tiles is a cross-platform free mobile application focusing mainly on accuracy and coordinated movement speed [5]. It has been established that the following are its drawbacks: The game may need to teach musical skills or have a clear educational goal effectively. Rapid tapping motions required by the game may lead to repetitive strain injuries. The game may be expensive or may use in-app purchases or advertisements to generate revenue, which can be distracting or disruptive for players.

To solve the limitations, we developed the application "Ihr Therapeut" [9]. The initial version of the application underwent an intensive usability study that revealed its strengths and weaknesses. This review served as the foundation for enhancing the current version of the application. Subsequently, an examination of comparable applications in the market was conducted to generate ideas and draw inspiration. The following are some of the features that were identified during the review performed on the first version of the application:

- First version of the Occupational therapy application based on the end-user's pain points is created.
- Usability test sessions with the therapists have been conducted and the feedback has been analysed.
- The colour scheme of the application fits the end-users needs.
- Most of the exercises required for occupational Therapy have been implemented with accuracy.

As a result of intensive usability testing, the following limitations were discovered.

- Hampered user experience due to the lack of easy accessibility to all the screens.
- No usability test sessions conducted with real patients to get their feedback for further improvement.
- The logic implemented for two of the exercises were less accurate.
- The exercises can be performed without tracking a patient's progress, as no data is recorded for training and tests conducted.
- Scores of the exercises performed are not stored in the backend.

A comprehensive analysis of the current application and its documentation led to the plan for the next version of the application. This research work elaborately outlines the design. The outcome is an extended version of the application "Ihr Therapeut" [9] with effective and efficient user experience, facilitating the occupational therapy process for patients and enabling continuous communication between patients and therapists to monitor progress.

2.1 Improvisations Required in the First Version of the Application

To enhance the first version of the occupational therapy mobile application, the researcher studied the existing application in terms of its code, functionality, and user experience.

Upon careful examination and consultation with the occupational therapy department at SRH, the researcher identified the following aspects that can be improved in the current version of the mobile application:

- **Patient authentication:**

The first and foremost feature which was missing in the application is the user authentication for the patient's side. Due to this shortcoming, any patient who is not already registered in the app by a therapist could get into the application and play the games. This shortcoming also allowed any end user to play on behalf of the patients, which in turn might hamper the scores and progress of the actual patient.

- **Screen accessibility:**

After studying the code and using the application first-hand, the author noticed that all the screens of the app are not accessible to the end users. In order to access various screens in the app, the users had to restart the application repetitively which hampered with the user experience of the app.

- **Training section for all the games:**

The first version of the application just had the implementation of the games. After interviews with the SRH Occupational therapy department, the author understood the two parts most important in the entire process of the therapy viz., testing and training. The application missed the training section of the therapy process. The progress made in the training section of the application is one of the most important steps in the process and the patient's recovery.

- **Storing game scores:**

In order to set a goal for the patients to work towards during the training, it is important to have the scores of the games played in the testing period of the process. Even though the games were implemented, the score of the games were not stored in the backend. As this feature was missing in the first version of the app, it failed to serve the purpose of the application.

- **Statistical dashboard to track progress:**

In order to track a patient's progress throughout the duration of the therapy, it is important to represent the scores of each training of the patient in a visual graph which is easy to understand in the first glance. This dashboard should give the details of the goals set for the patient during the testing period and represent the scores of the patient achieved during the training phase along with the dates. This dashboard would be very useful for the therapists to change the therapy program if required and for the patients to track their progress, stay motivated and focus on his/her weakness.

- **Game Logic for Tippen and Zielen:**

The logic implemented for Tippen and Zielen was incorrect in the first version of the application. This hampered with the actual purpose of the game thus slowing the process of healing via occupational therapy for the patients.

Taking into consideration all the above shortcomings of the application, throughout the duration of the thesis, the author has tried to improve the application and add in all the necessary features required to enhance the usability of the application in turn improving the user experience of the application.

3   System Design and Implementation

3.1   Software Architecture:

The layered architecture pattern involves organizing components of a software system into horizontal layers, each having a specific function within the application such as handling presentation logic or executing business logic [1] (Fig. 1).

Fig. 1. Patient screen

In the presentation layer, the patient screen serves as a front-end interface that receives requests for patient information and displays the relevant details to the user. It operates independently of the underlying data sources, retrieval methods, and the number of database tables involved in obtaining the information. When a request is made for a specific patient, the patient screen forwards it to the API Gateway, which is a business layer.

The patient data is retrieved by the component DAO (Data Access Object) module in the persistence layer, which makes a call to the patient's object in the business layer. The DAO module for orders is also consulted to obtain order information. These DAO modules execute queries to obtain the required data and return it to the patient's object in the business layer. The patients object combines the data from both sources and passes it on to the API gateway, which then transfers it to the patient information screen for display.

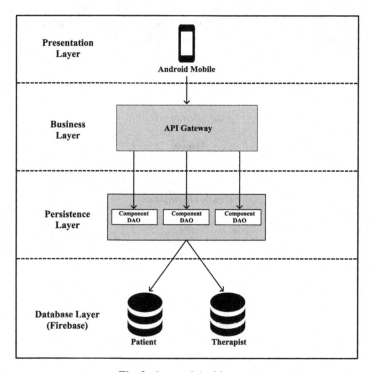

Fig. 2. Layered Architecture

Firebase [7] utilizes a data storage system where information is placed within documents and these documents are grouped into collections. This allows for efficient and organized storage and retrieval of data. As depicted in Fig. 2, the firebase database has two primary collections, patients, and therapists, each consisting of various documents representing individuals who can either be a patient or a therapist. These documents contain key-value paired data, such as age, id, name, remarks, as well as complex objects in the form of maps, such as test and train (Fig. 3).

The object "test" contains key-value pairs of data elements, including "attempt1," "attempt2," "attempt3," and "attempt4," which hold the scores of four attempts made during the testing period. The dates of the tests are stored under the "date" key, the name of the exercise under the "name" key, and the average score of the four attempts, which

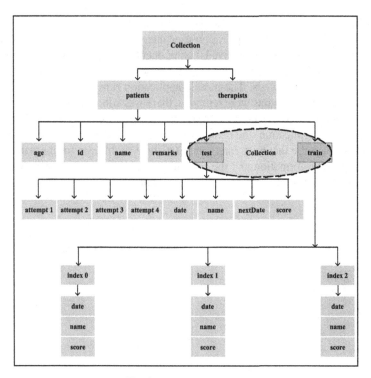

Fig. 3. Database structure

will serve as a target during training, under the "score" key. The object "train" contains the key "date" to record the date of the training session, "name" to store the name of the exercised trained, and "score" to store the amount of time it took to reach the target [6].

Apart from the UI changes made in the application, a new statistical dashboard to track a patient's progress was designed in this improved version. The discussed requirements for this feature were outlined as follows:

1. The ability to display and update patient details.
2. The ability for a therapist to delete patient records.
3. Differentiation between cognitive and motor exercises.
4. Displaying patient progress in the form of a training score graph.
5. The ability to view statistical graphs for all exercises.
6. Displaying therapy information such as goal, last test date, next test date, and start date of training.

Based on the inputs from the SRH Occupational therapy department [9] and using Figma [8] as a design tool, the application prototypes were designed. The department wanted a statistical dashboard for the therapists and students, designed using Figma [8]. The Occupational therapy department of SRH did not need cognitive and motor skills development for the application. They were only looking to have the Motor skills section. Hence, the two big sections on the first screen were not required.

In this technology stack, React Native [14] is used as the primary front-end framework for building the mobile application user interface. JavaScript [15] is used as the programming language, and the native UI components of the Android platforms are utilized to create a native user experience. The database component is firebase [7], depending on the application's needs. The mobile application runs on the Android operating system. As the two big buttons were removed, there was still a lot of space remaining on the screen. Therefore, to reduce the number of clicks for the user and improve the user experience of the application, the contents of the second screen were added to the first screen. Thus, once the therapist enters the Statistical dashboard for the patient, all the patient's required information and the patient's progress for each exercise can be seen at once with the minimum clicks possible (Figs. 4 and 5).

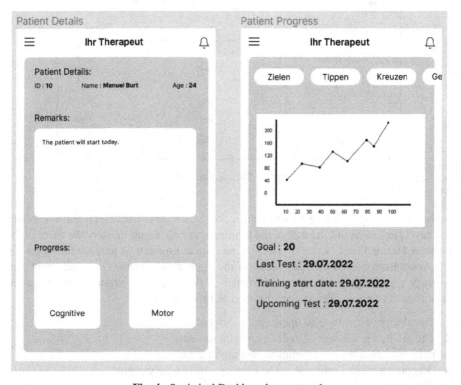

Fig. 4. Statistical Dashboard prototype 1

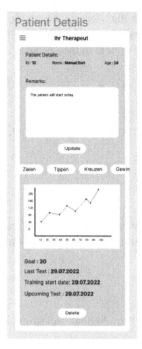

Fig. 5. Statistical Dashboard prototype 2

4   Results and Evaluation

4.1   Usability Testing

A usability testing [12] session was carried out with four patients from the Occupational Therapy Department at SRH. The patients were undergoing therapy to overcome the effects of their strokes and regain independence. The application under test consists of two types of motor exercises, with one being performed using the application and the other being performed physically, for which the application serves as a score-keeping tool. A moderator's guide was created for the usability test session, which included tasks specific to the Occupational Therapy application.

Facilitator/Moderator: The moderator oversees conducting the usability test session and creating a relaxed atmosphere for the participant. They guide the participant through the entire process, asking questions skillfully to identify any problems with the prototype without revealing the answers. The moderator's role is crucial in ensuring that the usability test session is productive and provides valuable insights into the application's performance.

Participant: Participants in the usability test are real-world end-users. They complete tasks assigned by the moderator and provide feedback on the product to evaluate the user experience and identify areas for improvement.

Tasks: Task analysis is a method used in user-centered design to evaluate a product or system by observing users as they complete specific tasks. Participants are asked to perform a series of tasks while the moderator records their behavior and interactions with the product. This provides valuable insights into the user experience and can be used to identify areas for improvement in the design.

Background Scenario

1. You have consulted an OT for therapy, and it is your first session today.
2. Your patient id is 80.

Task 1

1. You are starting your therapy with the exercise "Zielen." Please perform the testing as well as start with your training process for this exercise.

Task 2

1. Please perform the exercise "Umdrehen" and store your scores in the application.

General Questions

1. What do you feel about the overall concept of the application?
2. How can you check your progress using the application?
3. What according to you is missing in the application?
4. Would you prefer such an app over the traditional therapy process?

Result

1. Lack of pictorial representation of games.
2. Wrong logic implementation for Zielen & Tippen
3. Participants did not realize when the timer stopped for testing.
4. The screen had a lot of information which cannot be consumed at once.
5. Users clicked on the "Testing" heading instead of "Nachste" button.
6. Users needed step by step guidance to perform exercises.

4.2 Evaluation

The SWOT analysis [11] is a useful tool for evaluating the strengths, weaknesses, opportunities, and threats of a product or application. By identifying these factors, a business can gain insight into the advantages and disadvantages of their offering, as well as potential external threats and opportunities.

Strengths

1. The main objective of the application is to assist patients in their therapy by providing a comprehensive range of exercises for them to perform.
2. The application features a dashboard that allows patients to monitor and track their progress over time.

Weaknesses

1. The application requires an internet connection to function, limiting its accessibility in areas with poor or no internet connectivity.
2. The application does not have a virtual assistant feature that can interact with the patients in a dynamic way.
3. The application is not compatible with multiple operating systems and can only be used on a specific platform.

Opportunities

1. The application allows patients to perform their therapy exercises in the comfort of their own home, eliminating the need for regular visits to a therapist.
2. The application's progress tracking feature can be accessed by both patients and therapists, enabling them to monitor and adjust treatment plans as needed.

Threats

1. The presence of a large number of similar applications available on various platforms, globally, could pose a challenge for the success of the application, as it may have to compete with established and widely used alternatives.

5 Discussion

Individuals with physical, mental, or developmental disabilities, injuries, or illnesses that affect their ability to perform daily living and work-related activities. This can include but is not limited to, children, seniors, individuals recovering from strokes or other neurological conditions, and people with mental health conditions.

During this thesis project, various improvements were made to enhance the current version of the application. Despite these enhancements, further limitations have been identified. Currently, the app is not accessible globally and requires a stable internet connection to operate. Furthermore, it is dependent on the Expo CLI, which means any changes or updates to the CLI can negatively impact the functionality of the app. Currently, the application is only available on Android devices and does not support iOS. These limitations provide a solid foundation for the next version of the occupational therapy application to make it more accessible and user-friendly globally, offline, and across different platforms.

6 Conclusion

The previous version of the application was lacking in several ways, including a lack of detailed descriptions for exercises, inability to track scores, missing database structure to store testing and training data, and incorrect logic implementation for certain exercises. The new version of the application has addressed these issues by providing step-by-step instructions, the ability to track progress through a statistical dashboard, and improved accessibility and consistency in the UI. The current version of the application is more suitable for both patients and therapists to complete the required tasks and has been improved to meet the end user's expectations. The application should provide several benefits to the therapeutic process by adding YouTube links for the patients and being designed to run on multiple operating systems, including both Android and iOS, for consistent user experience. The User Interface should be flexible and updated regularly to remain visually appealing and introduce new features. The implementation of Maze and Kreuzen game should be thorough and complete, providing a fully functional and engaging experience with engaging storylines and captivating animations. The app should also allow patients to communicate and schedule appointments with their therapist easily and be accessible through the Google Play Store for easy downloading and usage on Android devices. The usability of the application has been improved for both patients and therapists by making all screens easily accessible, providing a consistent UI, and enabling users to achieve their goals. This has ultimately contributed to an improved user experience of the application.

References

1. Richards, M.: Software Architecture Patterns. O'Reilly Media, Inc. (2015). Accessed 04 Jan 2023
2. Merriam-Webster.com Homepage. https://www.merriam-webster.com/dictionary/occupatio nal%20therapy. Accessed 27 Jan 2023
3. Fun Bubbles – kids & toddlers Game. https://apps.apple.com/us/app/fun-bubbles/id4180 79933. Accessed 01 Feb 2023
4. MedBridge Education LLC Game. https://apps.apple.com/us/app/medbridge/id1003848915. Accessed 04 Feb 2023
5. Cheetah Technology Corporation Limited Game. https://piano-tiles-2.en.uptodown.com/and roid
6. Fong, G.: How to build your app using firebase database. https://blog.devgenius.io/how-to-build-your-app-with-cloud-based-database-using-firebase-5e458aeaeb07. Accessed 17 Jan 2023
7. Cloud Firestore Data Model Database. https://firebase.google.com/docs/projects/learn-more. Accessed 27 Jan 2023

8. Twago, A.: Figma. https://www.freecodecamp.org/news/figma-crash-course/
9. Dsouza, R.C., Chandna, S., von Gunten, E.: Ihr therapeut: a smartphone based user interface for people with sensorimotor injuries. HCI International 2022 Posters. Springer, Heidelberg (2022). https://doi.org/10.1007/978-3-031-06417-3_66
10. Mlambo, T.: World Federation of Occupational Therapists (WFOT) (2017). https://wfot.org/programmes/education. Accessed 04 Feb 2023
11. SWOT analysis (strengths, weaknesses, opportunities and threats analysis). https://www.techtarget.com/searchcio/definition/SWOT-analysis-strengths-weaknesses-opportunities-and-threats-analysis. Accessed 28 Jan 2023
12. NNGroup.com. Usability Test 101. https://www.nngroup.com/articles/usability-testing-101. Accessed 10 Jan 2023
13. Wikepidia.org. Human factors and Ergonomics. https://en.wikipedia.org/wiki/Human_factors_and_ergonomics. Accessed 07 Jan 2023
14. React Native framework. https://reactnative.dev/docs/environment-setup, last accessed 2023/01/14
15. JavaScript Programming Language. https://www.javascript.com/. Accessed 15 Jan 2023

Experience Design to Alleviate Social Anxiety in the Playground Under Smart Campus

Meng Li, Yuqian Yan, Yile Liu[✉], Zhihao Cheng, and Yixin Liu

School of Design, South China University of Technology, 510006 Guangzhou, People's Republic of China
995535656@qq.com

Abstract. This study is based on the background of smart campus, and mainly discusses the experience needs of college students in social activities around the playground. According to the existing research findings, 87.8% of college students in China have different levels of social anxiety. The cognitive behavior model of social anxiety considers that the primary internal factor of social anxiety can be summarized as the fear of individuals' negative evaluation of others. Due to the fear of negative evaluation of others, college students tend to pay too much attention to their own image in social interaction and are afraid to express their feelings in social interaction, so it is difficult to obtain positive emotions in social interaction and generate social anxiety. Social anxiety will seriously affect college students' studies, interpersonal relationships, individual well-being and even increase their suicidal ideation. The main users of this study are college students who have strong social needs but have social phobia. By exploring the needs of college students in social activities on the playground, we can alleviate their social anxiety. The research follows the people-oriented design concept, and adopts the double-drill model theory and scene research method, excavates the deep needs of users through in-depth interviews with users, field observation of user behavior, analysis of user playground social experience, and analyzes user portraits through tools such as affinity map, empathy map, and user journey map, so as to determine user needs. Finally combine the Internet with the development of smart cities GPS positioning and other technologies to design an application that can improve college students' campus playground social interaction, and alleviate college students' social anxiety.

Keywords: Smart campus · Social anxiety · Double drill model · Scenario research · Experience design

1 Introduction

The rise of the concept of smart city has attracted worldwide attention. The word first appeared in the early 1990s, which mainly emphasizing technology, innovation and globalization. In 2008, with the launch of IBM's Smart Planet project, scholars began to explore the definition of smart cities. Harrison and others defined smart cities as instrumentalized, Internet of Things and intelligent cities. Giffinger and Gudrun proposed six

A. Marcus et al. (Eds.): HCII 2023, LNCS 14034, pp. 374–388, 2023.
https://doi.org/10.1007/978-3-031-35705-3_28

characteristics to be considered for Smart: economy, governance, environment, people, mobility and life. The definition of smart cities continues to develop and emerge, although there is no clear definition of smart city at present, it is certain that smart city must be smart, which provides a comfortable and convenient living environment for people based on existing technology. It is a combination of human-environment-technology.

Smart cities are smart, and the derivatives of Smart are the objects of Smart. The Smart's objects are divided into three parts: smart functions, smart scenes and smart industries. This research is a smart campus under smart scenes, which is a branch of smart cities. After brainstorming, this research focuses on the social activities of Sit Around in the campus playground.

According to the existing research, 87.8% of college students in China have social anxiety problems of different degrees. The factors that affect social anxiety are diverse, which can be roughly divided into external factors and internal factors. External factors such as social exclusion, internal factors such as self-esteem, body image and personality traits. The cognitive behavior model of social anxiety considers that the primary internal factor of social anxiety can be summarized as the fear of negative evaluation of others. Due to the fear of negative evaluation of others, college students tend to pay too much attention to their own image in social interaction and are afraid to express their feelings in social interaction, so it is difficult to obtain positive emotions in social interaction and generate social anxiety. Social anxiety will seriously affect college students' studies, interpersonal relationships, individual well-being and even increase their suicidal ideation. The main users of this study are college students with strong social needs but social phobia.

The survey found that the playground is one of the most common social places for college students, and it is also the place with the highest proportion of social places in the school. College students like to gather in the playground for the new group building of the class, the first group building of the group members, and making friends on campus. But in the face of unfamiliar atmosphere such as making friends and breaking ice, most students will have social anxiety, they will pay too much attention to their own image, and are afraid to express themselves. It is also difficult for organizers to penetrate the emotions and needs of participants, resulting in poor experience of each activity. Faced with this situation, they usually choose to play with mobile phones and try to relieve embarrassment and boredom. Over time, mobile phones have gradually become the media for college students to socialize. In real life, they have different levels of social anxiety.

The main users of this study are college students who have strong social needs but have social phobia. The purpose of this study is to explore the needs of college students in social activities on the playground to alleviate their social anxiety. The research follows the people-oriented design concept, adopts the double-drill model theory and scene research method. It excavates the deep needs of users through in-depth interviews with users, field observation of user behavior, and analysis of user playground social experience. It analyzes user portraits through affinity map, empathy map, user journey map and other tools, so as to determine user needs. And it combines with the Internet, GPS positioning and other technologies under the development of smart cities. Finally designed an application that can improve college students' campus playground social interaction and alleviate college students' social anxiety.

2 Method

This topic focuses on the Sit Around situation in the school playground, it follows the people-oriented design concept, and discusses user needs according to the double-drill model (see Fig. 1). In the exploration stage, interview users to preliminarily understand user needs and then conduct situational research to observe user behavior on the spot. Through the development of affinity map, user journey map and user portrait to excavate the deep needs of users. In the definition stage, the design opportunity points are determined according to the user requirements, and then develop user demand model; At the conception stage, it could develop the app functional architecture, then evaluated the it and build a low fidelity model. Conduct usability testing at the low precision stage, and finally complete the app design.

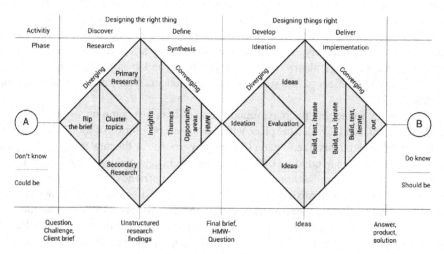

Fig. 1. Double dill model.

2.1 Discussion Topic

Before the user interview, explore the research topic through brainstorming. Then prioritize the four quadrants in the user definition section, and analyze from the two dimensions of necessity and influence. Users of the playground social activities can be initially divided into organizers and participants. In the course of playground design activities, it can be determined that the purpose of the activity is from unfamiliar to familiar. Users want to have a good emotional experience, be able to socialize, and have fun after class.

In order to deeply study the needs of users in the playground social scene, the study randomly invited 8 college students who had participated in the playground Sit

Around social activity to participate in the interview. And that can make preliminary assumptions about user needs for scenario research. The research conducted interviews from the following aspects: User's motivation to participate in playground activities, preferences in the process of activities, expectations of activities, attention to activities and experience of previous activities.

According to previous user interviews, hunt statement is defined as a social activity scenario of Sit Around in the playground. The purpose of the research is to enhance the experience of graduate students in this social activity. The preliminary definition of 5W1H is as follows:

When: In the evening, after about 20:00 (the playground after dinner).Duration: 1.5 ~ 2.5h.

Who: 1. College students in their spare time.

2.Postgraduate students who don't like to stay in the dormitory all the time.

3.Students who are interested in social interaction.

What: Social activities around the playground.

Where: School playground.

Why: 1. After the closure of the school due to the epidemic, graduate students are under great pressure for scientific research and need outdoor recreational activities.

2. The activity of Sit Around in the playground attracts graduate students who do not like to stay in the dormitory all the time.

3. The light in the playground is dim, there is a stereo playing, drink a little wine, and the state is relatively relaxed.

4. Graduate students who like to come out to participate in activities want to make new friends. Sit Around in the playground is a way to make friends.

How: Improve the activity experience of Sit Around and relieve social anxiety.

2.2 Scenario Research

In order to study user behavior in depth, the research adopts the survey method of field observation, records the user's words and behavior in the social activity of Sit Around on the playground, and analyzes the user's needs through affinity map and empathy map combined with the user's situation. According to the empathy map, the following user characteristics can be summarized:

1. Users reject activities with strong purpose.
2. College students have social needs, but are not willing to show them.
3. Although some users do not want to be the focus of language expression, they are already the focus of activities.
4. The user said that the main purpose of participating in the activity was to decompress and relax.
5. Self-introduction is necessary, but this link is usually awkward and can't remember many people's information at the same time.
6. When participating in social activities, they will pay too much attention to their own image.

2.3   Insight into User Needs

According to the user profile survey, users can be divided into primary users and secondary users. Among them, primary users are users who have strong demand for playground social activities, and secondary users are users who like to participate in playground activities. According to the situation research, the user journey map (see Fig. 2 and see Fig. 3) has been established based on the sorting of Empathy Map to gain insight into the potential needs of users.

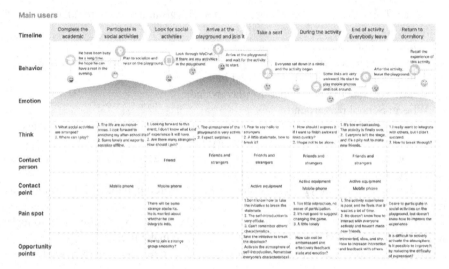

Fig. 2.   User flow chart of main users.

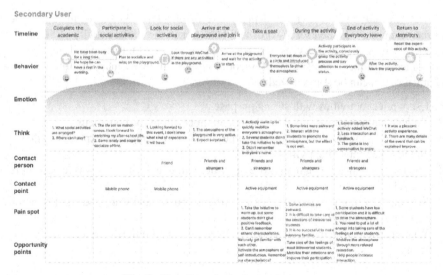

Fig. 3.   User flow chart of secondary user.

3 Build User Requirements

3.1 User Demand

Based on the situation research and in-depth analysis of the double-drill model, the User Persona can be created to build user needs (see Fig. 4 and Fig. 5).

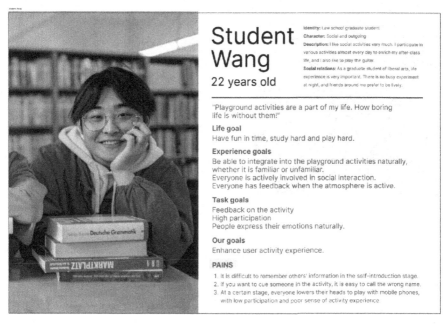

Fig. 4. Portraits of main users.

3.2 Design Opportunity Point

According to user portraits and user records, users' pain points can be listed, user needs can be established. The following Table 1 gives a summary of design opportunities.

According to user pain points, user needs and design opportunities, the app functions can be conceived. The following Table 2 gives a summary about the functions.

Student Zhang

23 years old

Identity: Graduate student of Automation College

Character: Introvert and a little shy

Description: I prefer social activities. I participate in social activities on the playground almost every week to enrich my after-class life, but I feel nervous about introducing myself

Social relations: The pressure of scientific research is high, and I like to decompress and relax in offline playground activities. My friends are relatively single, and I hope to meet new classmates.

"The people I know in the scientific research circle are too monotonous. I want to know different people!"

Life goal
Scientific researchers are not divorced from life.

Experience goals
Be able to express yourself naturally.
Don't worry too much about the image.
Can be noticed, will not be marginalized and independent; I hope everyone can interact with each other.

Task goals
Easily express opinions.
Easily participate in activities.
Be able to make friends.

Our goals
Decompression, happiness and making friends

PAINS
1. It's a bit unnatural in strange places.
2. If no one pays attention for a long time, he will feel boring.
3. It is difficult to remember others' self-introduction.
4. Want to meet new friends, but there is no good way.

Fig. 5. Secondary user portrait.

Table 1. User interviews and user observation records

User pain points	User requirement	Process assumption
Unable to quickly integrate into unfamiliar groups	Close social distance and ease embarrassment	1. Start of the activity: Break the deadlock by completing several simple tasks
Can't remember many people's information	Self-introduction is more natural and distinctive	2. Self-introduction: Deepen memory by setting distinctive personal image
Feel bored and don't know how to express	Can easily express the experience	3. Social link: Share activity experience and accept feedback through expression buttons
Left alone, hopping to get other's attention	Can be noticed by others	4. Add interested people

Table 2. Function concept

Scenario requirements	Design opportunity point	Functional assumptions
Relieve the embarrassment between strangers	Provide users with opportunities to participate in interaction through topic	Function 1: Pop up topic Function 2: Maintain common objectives Emotion: Provide a good atmosphere and enhance the sense of participation
Self-introduction is more natural	1.User personality selection, providing representative roles for user selection 2. Recommend appropriate role names and characteristics to users 3. User-definable	Function 1: User personality input/test Function 2: Recommend corresponding names Function 3: Virtual character Emotion: Don't be embarrassed by forgetting other's name
Express oneself during the activity	1. Users make suggestions anonymously 2. The user can edit the role status, and the avatar will also be changed to the corresponding status	Function 1: Provide anonymous feedback channel Function 2: Editable role status Emotion: Improve user participation
Pay attention to the status of others	Provide user interaction mode	Function 1: Provide interaction channel Function 2: Diversified interaction modes Emotion: Close social distance

4 Solution

4.1 Functional Architecture

According to the user's use process, the following functions are determined, and these functions are discussed in proportion according to the four directions of interest, practicality, realizability and innovation. The four directions are discussed and scored four times. The ranking is based on the proportion of the score to the comparison function to determine the priority of the function (see Fig. 6).

4.2 Scenario Research

The functional architecture can provide a logical architecture for the low fidelity design. According to the functional evaluation results, the app functions can be divided into five parts: Playground information, virtual character construction, real-time scene, activity dynamic release and personal information (see Fig. 7). According to the user flow chart, user requirements and functional architecture, using flow charts can be constructed.

Functional evaluation	Pop-up topic	Create image	Small Fire atmosphere performance	Situational simulation	Condition of playground	Share Moments	Change position	Status feedback	Send a private message	Add friends	Interactive mode	Interaction bonus	Anonymous feedback card
Rank	8	3	1	5	2	9	7	4	11	12	7	10	6
Interest (10) 30%	8	8	9	9	8	7	7	7	6	5	7	8	8
	7	9	10	9	10	8	8	9	6	6	9	7	7
	6	10	9	9	9	8	7	8	6	5	9	8	9
	7	10	10	8	8	7	7	8	6	6	7	7	8
Practicality (10) 30%	6	9	7	9	9	8	10	9	8	8	8	7	9
	8	9	7	8	9	8	7	9	8	7	8	7	8
	8	9	8	8	8	7	7	9	7	7	8	7	8
	8	9	8	8	8	7	8	8	7	7	7	7	8
Realizability (10) 20%	9	6	9	7	9	9	9	8	9	9	8	8	9
	9	6	8	6	8	9	9	8	8	8	9	9	9
	9	6	8	7	7	7	9	9	9	9	9	8	9
Innovation (10) 20%	8	8	9	9	9	7	9	7	7	7	8	6	7
	7	9	9	9	8	8	8	7	6	6	7	6	7
	8	7	9	7	8	7	8	7	7	6	8	7	7
	8	8	9	8	8	6	7	7	7	6	8	7	7
Total score (after averaging)	30.2	33.1	34.4	32.4	34.1	30	31.9	32.5	28.4	27.3	31.9	29.2	32.3

Fig. 6. Function evaluation.

Fig. 7. Information architecture

4.3 Low-Fidelity Model Display

The low fidelity function page has five modules: live playground activities, virtual image, virtual scene, dynamic circle, and personal home page (see Fig. 8).

The Live Playground Activities can be understood at any time and place. By using navigation and positioning, users can focus on the specific location of the playground. Users can know the specific location of the playground in one scene without worrying

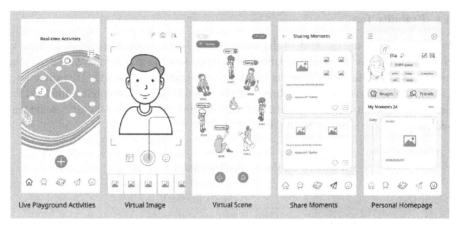

Fig. 8. Main pages of low fidelity prototype.

about not finding the location. Among them, the operation activity can be displayed, so everyone can see the activity through the app. If users choose not to display, then the activity can only be participated by specific people.

The Virtual Image function page is mainly used to solve the embarrassment of self-introduction in the social process. Participants can't easily remember other people's information, and it is difficult to interact with others during social interaction which resulting in a reduced sense of activity experience. In addition, when college students participate in unfamiliar social scenes, they will pay too much attention to their own image and fear the negative comments of others, and it resulting in social anxiety. While virtual images can make participants pay less attention to the real person, and can alleviate excessive anxiety with the help of social media. The virtual image function also provides MBTI and personalized 3D images so that participants can better understand each other, find common ground and increase social distance. Among them, 3D virtual images can intelligently analyze users' self-photos through big data, and finally generate virtual images that fit with personal images.

The Virtual Scene will restore the playground activities online to the maximum extent. Using the navigation and positioning system, it can simulate the real-time position of the characters in the offline activities into the virtual scene. The position of the users in the virtual scene will also be replaced according to the real-time position, as a bridge for online and offline social connection, it provides more interactive functions and personal experience feedback channels for participants with different personalities and social habits.

The Share Moments function is similar to the WeChat. Users can share their activity status at any time, and friends can see their dynamics.

Personal homepage is a self-management center, which can display user information and manage social friends.

4.4 Usability Test

In order to verify the usability of the user process, seven major users were recruited to participate in the usability test, and they were asked to complete six situational tasks in the low-accuracy model. The following Table 3 gives a summary of the ASQ questionnaire, and the scores were scored from three aspects: The difficulty of completing the task, the time of completing the task and the task support information. And the SUS scale was scored as a whole (see Fig. 9, 10 and 11).

Table 3. ASQ Summary.

Single task	User feedback
Create virtual character cards (take photo)	1. The overall process is easy to use and conforms to usage habits 2. Self-image generation button is not easy to find
Create playground activities	1. The use is smooth 2. Creating an activity for the first time is a little cumbersome
Edit status, anonymous feedback and viewing activity feedback	1. The private message and event notification icons are too similar and easy to be confused 2. There is little difference in their own virtual images, and it is difficult to find their own image 3. Need the guidance of novices. Some functions are not obvious and they are unknown
Social interaction	1. The meaning of fire is not direct enough to understand 2. The private message function is expected to be multi-channel, which can be accessed from the dialog box 3. The overall performance is relatively smooth
Event invitation	1. The use is smooth 2. The friend invitation interface needs to be searched for a while
Release dynamics	1. Don't know where the dynamic circle is 2. The release dynamics conform to the usage 3. The use is smooth

SUS availability scale score.

Descriptive statistics of SUS(n=7)						
Statistics	n	total	Mean	sd	min	max
	7	535	76.4	9.225998462	37.5	97.5

Fig. 9. Total score.

Descriptive statistics of Usability(n=7)						
Statistics	n	total	mean	sd	min	max
	7	528.1	75.1	6.099375456	25	96.9

Fig. 10. Usability score.

Descriptive statistics of Learnability(n=7)						
Statistics	n	total	mean	sd	min	max
	7	562.5	80.4	22.65817418	50	100

Fig. 11. Learnability score.

According to the score results of the sus scale, the total score of the app function test is 76.4, and the score is Good. The usability score is 75.1, so the rating is Good. The equal score of easiness to learn is 80.4, and the score is also Good. Therefore, the usability score of the app is Good and the research and design product is in line with users' social needs.

4.5 High-Precision Use Situation

User Scenario 1. Customized 3D virtual image (see Fig. 12).

When users download the app for the first time, they can generate images randomly, synthesize images by self-shooting and fabricate their own characters. In social interaction, people can remember their personal characteristics so that they can interact with each other later.

User Scenario 2. Find playground activities and create playground activities (see Fig. 13).

Users can learn about the existing social activities in the playground through this app, and they can also choose to join the activity or create a social activity by themselves.

User Scenario 3. Virtual character interaction (see Fig. 14).

When users feel bored in social activities, they can edit their status as Bored, and the virtual characters will also become bored, which can show the activity status. The feedback emotion can let the organizer adjust the activity content. If users are embarrassed

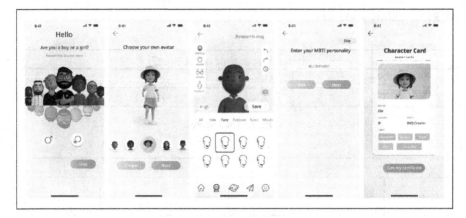

Fig. 12. Virtual image.

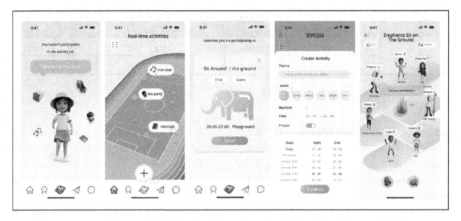

Fig. 13. Live Playground activities.

to express their feelings in the event, they can also give suggestions through anonymous feedback so as to enter a better social state. Users can also view other people's feedback through the activity message bar.

User Scenario 4. Interact with others and send private messages (see Fig. 15).

Users can interact with people who are far away from them by taking a photo or by private mail. At this time, the small fire in the virtual scene will become vigorous.

User Scenario 5. Share moments (see Fig. 16).

After the event, users can post an activity to share their feelings. This activity is open to the campus. And campus users can see these and participate in likes and comments.

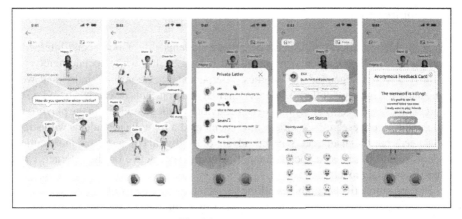

Fig. 14. Virtual scene.

Fig. 15. Personal homepage.

Fig. 16. Share Moments.

5 Conclusion

Social interaction affects all aspects of college students' life. Good social interaction contributes to college students' physical and mental health, while social anxiety will seriously affect college students' studies, interpersonal relationships, individual well-being and even increase college students' suicidal ideation. This research is based on the smart campus, and deeply study the social behavior of college students in the playground through the scene research. Provide offline social media for college students with strong social needs but social anxiety. With the advent of the digital era, more and more college students regard online as a social channel, which is very active on the Internet, while offline has social anxiety.

The app innovatively combines offline social interaction with online interaction. The design provides virtual character images and virtual situations. Users won't to be afraid to express and show themselves when they are in unfamiliar scenes. They can show their interests and characteristics by combining online media. In addition, virtual characters are big data systems in the context of smart cities, which can provide users with personalized virtual images. The virtual scene is supported by real-time navigation technology, which can accurately display the activity location. When the user participates in the activity, GPS technology will display the user's location in the virtual scene in real time. When the user changes seats, the characters in the virtual scene will change positions. With the support of intelligent technology, this playground social app is designed to alleviate college students' social anxiety. It can alleviate users' social anxiety by improving the playground social experience. The ideal social experience design promotes college students' healthy social interaction could have important practical significance.

References

1. Li, D., Yao, Y., Shao, Z.: Big Date in Smart City. Geomatics and Information Science of Wuhan University, China (2014)
2. Yin, C.T, et al.: A literature surver on smart cities. Chinese science: information science, China (2015)
3. Qian, X., Song, Ziyun., Huang, B.: The complexity of immersive intelligent university: cost of practical analysis. Chongqing Higher Education Research, China (2013)
4. Xu, L., He, S., Zheng, J., Wangm G., Yang, Y., Ye, T.: The connotation and evolution of the concept of Intellectualization Industrial technological innovation. Industrial technology innovation science, China (2022)
5. Xu, L., He, S., Zheng, J., Wang, G., Yang, Y., Ye, T.: The connotation and evolution of the concept of Intellectualization. Indust. Technol. Innovat., 50–54 (2022)
6. Li, K., et al.: Analysis of hot spots and frontier trends in the study of college students' social anxiety based on CiteSpace. Chinese general practice, China (2022)

Research on the Design of Weighing Scale Based on Health Management During Pregnancy

Yunzhu Li[✉] and Rongrong Fu

College of Art Design and Media, East China University of Science and Technology, Shanghai,
China
liyunzhu2085@qq.com

Abstract. A good health status during pregnancy is an important guarantee for
the health of the baby and the eventual smooth delivery of the pregnant woman.
Pregnant women have a strong health concept, and a strong health awareness will
motivate them to engage in appropriate health management behaviors. The special
psychological and physiological needs of pregnant women require corresponding
health management products to monitor maternal health, while the current maternal health management products lack attention to the emotional problems of users.
To efficiently record and manage weight and mood data during pregnancy, and
to meet users' psychological and physiological needs. In this study, GSR detection was adopted to measure the mood fluctuations of pregnant women. The final
design of a scale and health management app for measuring and recording the
weight and emotional changes of pregnant women, prompting them to manage
their health and their provision of scientific health advice.

Keywords: electrodermal signals · health management · pregnant women

1 Introduction

According to WHO 2020, in developing countries, the probability of experiencing maternal mental disorders during pregnancy and postpartum is 15.6% and 19.8%, respectively,
and is mainly depression. Pregnant women may suffer serious consequences such as miscarriage, premature birth, and suicide due to negative emotions such as depression, and
emotional problems are becoming one of the risk factors for the contemporary pregnant
population. It has been found that the physiological indicators during pregnancy are
different from the usual state. At the same time, pregnant women are subjected to great
psychological stress, and if they do not regulate their mood during pregnancy, it can
have an impact on the growth and development of the fetus and the health status of the
pregnant woman. Due to the non-popularity of bioelectric devices and high equipment
costs, it is difficult to provide scientific and accurate emotional monitoring methods for
pregnant women through professional devices such as EMG and EEG in every family.
Therefore, this study chooses to monitor pregnant women's mood fluctuation using GSR
detection. Since weight is one of the important indicators of pregnant women's health,
and pregnant women's weight and emotion are also correlated, the weight scale is chosen

as the design vehicle for emotion measurement, which can measure both physiological and psychological values, and develop the corresponding software design to provide accurate data basis for monitoring the weight and mental-emotional state of the target users.

2 Research Subjects

Using literature research methods to analyze the current situation of users during pregnancy and their demands for emotional and weight management. It also identifies the shortcomings of existing health products to find design opportunities and provides references and a basis for the design of weight scale software and hardware. The flow of user requirements and design opportunity points analysis is shown in Fig. 1.

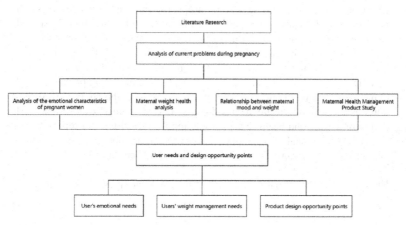

Fig. 1. User needs and design opportunity point analysis process

2.1 Problems During Pregnancy Status Study

Women can suffer from distress during pregnancy, which is associated with physical changes, psychological changes, identity changes, and lack of social support [1, 2]. In addition, body image, hormone levels and life role changes during pregnancy can make pregnant women more prone to mental disorders, such as pregnancy stress, anxiety and depression [3]. This may lead to poor pregnancy outcomes as a result [4]. Pregnant women are more sensitive and crave the company of others than non-pregnant women. They are insecure and want more respect and recognition from others. Therefore, pregnant women have special physiological and psychological needs. Physically, pregnant women need to know about pregnancy health care and reasonable health management. Psychologically, pregnant women need to take certain measures to relieve stress and bad mood during pregnancy.

Research on the Emotional Characteristics and Effects of Pregnant Women. Women's mood swings during pregnancy can be more frequent and intense than when they are not pregnant. Most women experience negative mood swings during pregnancy due to physical, psychological and environmental changes, resulting in negative emotions of anxiety, depression and worry. According to the American College of Obstetricians and Gynecologists, pregnant women in the perinatal period have a several-fold increased risk of developing psychological disorders [5]. The living environment during pregnancy also contributes to the unstable emotional state of pregnant women. According to relevant studies, the psychological state of pregnant women is closely related to family status, eating habits, living environment, and economic status [6].

Pregnant women with severe mood swings have abnormal estrogen levels. E2 deficiency and a large abnormal increase in FSH can lead to an increased probability of anxiety and depression and other adverse emotions [7]. Especially in the perinatal period, their hormonal changes and mood swings are more dramatic and they are more likely to fall into extreme emotional states. When emotional states are unstable, pregnant women's symptoms of pregnancy vomiting can worsen [8]. Poorer emotional states also lead to higher self-perceived stress, lower quality of life, and greater risk of preterm delivery [9]. Pregnant women with high emotional dysregulation, usually show insensitivity to parenting styles that are detrimental to child development [10]. Therefore, regulation of emotional state is a prerequisite for the health of the mother and child. A good mental health status during pregnancy is an important factor influencing the health management of pregnant women.

Study on the Characteristics and Effects of Weight during Pregnancy. Changes in maternal weight will reflect the physical health of the mother and fetus from the side. Pregnancy complications and neonatal complications are associated with maternal weight gain levels, and abnormal weight gain levels during pregnancy can put the health of the mother and fetus at risk [11]. Excessive maternal weight gain can also lead to adverse pregnancy outcomes for the mother, such as miscarriage, giant babies, and cesarean deliveries. There is also a risk of hypertension, diabetes, persistent postpartum obesity, and an increased chance of childhood obesity in the postpartum period [12, 13]. In contrast, pregnant women who gain too little weight during pregnancy have a higher probability of delivering a low-weight baby than those in the normal weight range, affecting fetal development. According to the BMI classification of the WHO, pre-pregnancy weight is divided into low weight, normal weight, overweight weight and obesity, and for pregnant women with different pre-pregnancy weights, the standards for weight gain during pregnancy are different: with 15.2 to 18 kg recommended for low weight pregnant women, 11.5 to 16 kg for the normal weight group, 70 to 11.5 kg for the overweight group and 5 to 9 kg for the obese group [14]. Therefore, reasonable weight management during pregnancy should also be performed according to the pre-pregnancy physical status to reduce the probability of maternal and infant morbidities.

Study on the Relationship between Maternal Mood and Weight. Relevant medical studies have shown that negative and stronger mood swings can lead to low interest and vigor in physical activity among pregnant women, thus reducing exercise management behaviors [15]. When depression and anxiety mood scores are high, their participation in weight management is reduced [16]. Negative emotions can also lead to irregular eating in pregnant women, such as excessive calorie intake in the diet, which affects weight health status [17]. Conversely, maternal weight also has an impact on mood, with maternal pre-pregnancy weight and pregnancy weight gain being the main factors for negative mood in pregnant women, and obesity (BMI > 27.9 kg/m2) and overweight (BMI > 24–27.9 kg/m2) hurting mood [18]. Therefore, there is a need to eliminate the interaction between mood and weight, and it is particularly important to maintain a healthy emotional state and weight management habits.

2.2 Research on Maternal Health Management Products

Under the background of "Internet+ ", pregnant women can make use of intelligent products to carry out scientific health management. Through research and analysis of existing products, pregnant women's health management products are divided into the following two categories: the first category of intelligent pregnant women's products includes fetal heartbeat and fetal movement detectors, fetal education machines, glucose meters, smart bracelets for pregnant women, pregnancy weight scales, fitness products and so on. These products are mostly used to display and record physiological values such as heart rate, blood pressure, weight, body fat, blood sugar and body temperature of pregnant women, which can meet the basic physiological measurement needs of users. The second category is pregnant women's health management applications, which can be used according to the supporting equipment or manually input data.

Research on Smart Weight Scales and Software Applications for Pregnant Women. Weight measurement during pregnancy is a very important task, and weight changes will reflect the physical status of the pregnant woman. Analysis of existing products for maternal weight monitoring needs. It was found that, in terms of function, most of the smart weight scales on the market are based on weight-body fat dual measurement, which can presume bone mass, body shape, muscle mass points, and water content through weight and body fat. The electrode scale can measure body fat by calculating the hand resistance value, but its mode of operation and accuracy is to be considered. Some smart scales can be connected to the supporting app to view measurement data and provide database analysis to generate health recommendations. In terms of shape, mostly square and rounded rectangles, the color is mainly white, black and pink. Existing scales can better meet the weight management needs of pregnant women, but they lack attention to the user's emotions.

Many smart scales will be combined with health management apps for data monitoring and recording, through a survey of the health management apps for pregnant women in the APP store, such applications can be divided into detection, record, knowledge, e-commerce, fetal education and sports. Measurement apps mainly focus on fetal heart rate monitoring and weight monitoring, which need to be used with hardware products. Recording applications are subdivided into manual input categories and automatic recording categories according to the data record method, which can be used to record values of fetal heartbeat, fetal movement, contraction, weight, abdominal circumference, and so on. Knowledge apps are the most common, and most of them have the function of maternity knowledge learning. At present, the following problems still exist in the app: the information is cluttered and the interface is not clear; the professionalism and accuracy of the content are not high; there is a lack of information exchange and transmission between software and hardware, which requires manual input of important data; there is a lack of personalized service, and only data storage is achieved.

Opportunity Point Analysis. According to the research on pregnancy health management products, there is still room for improvement in the design of weight scales as follows: First, pay attention to the emotional needs of users and add the function of emotion measurement. Third, it is convenient for pregnant women to measure their weight and emotions at the same time. Fourth, pay attention to the way people interact with the product and the convenience of the interaction between the product and the user. For the design of the supporting APP, the design should meet the following requirements: First, the interaction interface is logical and clear, simple to operate and reduce unnecessary information. Second, with personalized targeted services to generate daily health advice. Third, the measurement data is directly entered into the application. Fourth, enhance the communication between users and pay attention to their psychological needs.

2.3 Summary

Through literature research to analyze the special physiological and psychological characteristics of pregnant women, the analysis learned that pregnant women do have special physiological and psychological problems, and need to use corresponding health management products to solve emotional and weight regulation problems. And then research and analysis were conducted on health management products and health management applications for pregnant women to provide design opportunity points for weight design and supporting apps. Existing smart weight scales for pregnant women take weight and body fat measurement as the main function, and also need to take into account the psychological needs of pregnant women and take care of their emotions in terms of appearance and function. The existing pregnancy management app has a lot of room for improvement in terms of interaction, information visualization and personalized services.

3   User Needs Questionnaire

3.1   Purpose of the Questionnaire

According to the above studies, pregnant women have psychological and physical health management needs. To gain insight into the effects of mood and weight on maternal health and the evaluation of existing products, a questionnaire was used to determine the actual situation and needs of maternal health management and to understand the shortcomings of existing products.

3.2   Questionnaire Design

The questionnaire was set up with 14 questions, divided into four dimensions, as shown in Table 1. The first dimension is to investigate the basic information of users. The second dimension is to understand the user's pregnancy health management situation and clarify the specific needs of the user. The third dimension understands users' usage of related health management products, and the fourth dimension understands users' expected functions of weight scales and mobile apps.

Table 1. Questionnaire on pregnant women's needs for emotional and weight health management

Dimensions	Question content
Basic user information	Your age?
	Your pregnancy status?
Health management during pregnancy	Do you have regular health management when you are pregnant?
	Your weight status at the time of your pregnancy?
	Is it difficult to control your weight during pregnancy?
	Your emotional state during pregnancy?
	Did you have any of the following bad moods during pregnancy?
Product Usage	Have you used any of the following health management products?
	Do you use any of the following pregnancy health management applications?
	Do you think the current management products help relieve your emotions?
	Do you think the current products have addressed your weight management issues?
	What do you think are the shortcomings of the current products
Product Desired Features	What would you like to know about pregnancy health?
	What features do you think pregnancy-based management products should have?

3.3 Analysis of Questionnaire Results

A total of 61 questionnaires were collected in this survey, and 61 valid questionnaires were returned. Analysis of the questionnaire results showed that the vast majority of pregnant women would regularly perform health management, and most of them would use the scale for health management. Some pregnant women think that the product does not have a communication service and the interactivity of the product is weak. The recording and monitoring of body indicators is the primary demand of users, and learning, health reminder, data sharing and social services should also be added to meet the different needs of pregnant women groups. The health management needs of pregnant women were classified, and a total of five categories of needs were summarized, namely measurement needs, recording needs, psychological needs, cognitive needs communication needs and sharing needs, as shown in Table 2.

Table 2. Summary of maternal health management needs

User requirements	content
Measurement requirements	Average weight health management
	Presence of perinatal depression
Records	Need to record daily physical indicators
	Personalized assessment report required
Cognitive	Lack of maternity knowledge
	Need for professional health guidance
Communication	No "social circle"
	Lack of communication services
Share	Want to share data with family members

4 GSR Experiments

4.1 GSR Signals

When the body is subjected to external stimuli or changes in an emotional state, the activity of its vegetative nervous system causes changes in vasodilation and contraction of blood vessels in the skin and secretion of sweat glands, resulting in changes in skin resistance, a process known as the galvanic skin response. This process is referred to as the electrodermal response. Electrodermal is an important indicator of emotional arousal, and changes in the magnitude of emotional arousal can produce a significant electrodermal response [19].

4.2 Experimental Purpose

To detect the difference in electrodermal response between pregnant and non-pregnant women and to verify the existence of significant mood fluctuations in pregnant women, this experiment uses the detection of electrodermal signals and measures the mood changes of pregnant and non-pregnant women using the GSR electrodermal sensor under the same experimental conditions and completes an interview to verify the validity of the experiment after the experiment is completed. Finally, the data differences between pregnant women and non-pregnant women were analyzed according to the experimental data collected, and it was demonstrated that the scale can be used to measure the mood fluctuations of pregnant women using the method of electrodermal detection.

4.3 Experimental Setup

Experimental Subjects. A total of 8 participants were invited to the experiment, and 5 women who were not in the state of pregnancy and 3 women who were in the period of pregnancy were selected as subjects. The subjects all participated in the experiment independently, were in good health, in a good mental state and had stable daily emotions before the experiment.

Experimental Equipment. The device used in the experiment is the GSR skin conductivity sensor, which can measure the skin conductivity value as well as the mood change by connecting the finger electrode. As shown in Fig. 2, the device contains four parts, namely a GSR sensor, Arduino nano development board, finger sleeve, and USB download cable. As shown in Fig. 3, the electrode part of the finger sleeve is placed towards the palm while wearing the device. In this experiment, Arduino IDE is used as the data transmission platform, and sensor value and motion change are used as the evaluation indexes for the subjects.

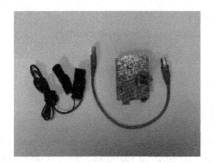

Fig. 2. GSR sensor

Fig. 3. Wearing method

4.4 Experimental Process

This experiment tests the mood changes of pregnant and non-pregnant women in a normal healthy state, respectively, and the measurement lasts for one minute. After the subjects gave their consent, the experiment was explained. Before the start of the experiment, the subjects were required to sit calmly at rest in a reclining chair and were instructed to wear the GSR device correctly, with their arms placed horizontally, and to maintain emotional stability and even breathing. Timing started at the same time as the measurement started, and the data was graphed after data recording was completed and the interview was finalized.

4.5 Experimental Data

By comparing the fluctuations of electrodermal signals between pregnant and non-pregnant women under the same experimental conditions, it was found that there were significant differences in mood changes and sensing values between the two groups. As shown in Fig. 4, the fingers of the pregnant women group had lower electrical resistance values, with sensor value values all below 300, while the non-pregnant women were all above 300. The five subjects in the non-pregnant group showed more stable ups and downs in their conductance values whenever their mood changed, with a difference

(a) non-pregnant group   (b) pregnancy group

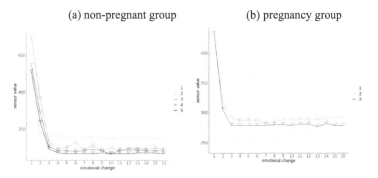

Fig. 4. GSR signal

between 0 and 12. Subject 1 in the pregnant group showed a high fluctuation in conductance value, with a significant decrease in conductance value and a difference of 48, and her mood fluctuated significantly.

Related studies have shown that skin conductance activity is easily influenced by emotions, psychological state and environment, and that the human body shows significant fluctuations in conductance values when under the influence, with the lower the conductance level, the stronger the conductance response [20]. The data from the present experiment showed that whenever the GSR device tested a change in mood, its conductance values changed. Under the same experimental conditions, there was a greater fluctuation in conductance values and lower conductance values in pregnant women compared to the group of non-pregnant women. This indicates that pregnant women have a more pronounced conductance response and significant mood swings. Mood swings are more pronounced compared to non-pregnant women.

4.6 Experimental Questionnaire

After the above experiments were completed, interviews were conducted with the participants as shown in Table 3. The purpose of the questionnaire was to do a perceptual analysis of the above experiments and to record the subjective feelings of the subjects. The results showed that the interviewees were all in good health and emotionally stable.

Table 3. Interview content

Question content
1. Are you in good health
2. What is your mood state (before the test)?
3. Was your state stable during the test?

4.7 Experimental Conclusions

After the above experiments and combined with the analysis of pregnant women's mood studies, pregnant women are more prone to mood swings, and severe mood swings can bring health problems to pregnant women, so it is necessary to monitor pregnant women's moods. In this study, the weight scale was used as a carrier for mood monitoring, and by measuring the electrodermal data of pregnant women, the mood fluctuations of pregnant women could be known, and finally, health guidance was provided to pregnant women according to their weight status and mood fluctuations.

5 Design Practice

Based on the above experiments and research, this section first summarizes the design transformation of the health management needs of pregnant women, then develops corresponding design principles for the scale and app, and finally carries out specific design practices.

5.1 Design Transformation

According to the user requirements, the corresponding design transformation relationships were summarized to provide a reference basis for the design direction and principles of the product. As shown in Table 4.

Table 4. Design transformation

Product Category	Demand	Design Conversion
Weight Scale	Measurement	Weight monitoring function
		Electrodermal monitoring of emotions
APP	Records	Daily signs data recording
	Cognitive	Maternity knowledge
		Personal health report
		Knowledge of fetal education
		Nutritional health
	Communication	Doctor Consultation Service
		Pregnancy Communication Circle
	Share	Data Sharing

5.2 Design Principles

Principle of Safty. Consider the safety of pregnant women in using the product, to facilitate the safe use of pregnant women, will be designed with rounded corners, and the height should be reasonable.

Principle of Universality. Suitable for pregnant women of all ages, the size of hardware products should be appropriate, and the software interaction mode should be easy to understand.

Principle of Unity. The software interface style is unified, and the color, font and icon have consistency.

5.3 Design Solutions

The product adopts a combination of software and hardware, and the interaction flow is shown in Fig. 5. The hardware part meets the user's measurement needs, measuring the user's weight and emotional state, and the software part is responsible for the analysis and recording of the data, and finally provides effective health advice. The product design process is shown in Fig. 6. According to the preliminary demand analysis and research results, the following design scheme is derived.

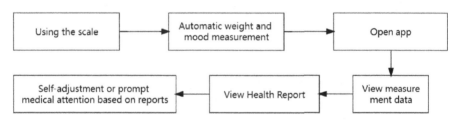

Fig. 5. Product-user interaction flow

The Size Design of the Weight Scale. According to the basic values of adult body size, we know that the foot length of women aged 18 to 25 years is between 208 and 251 mm, and the foot width is between 78 and 97 mm. The foot length of women aged 26 to 35 years is between 207 and 252 mm, and the foot width is between 79 and 98 mm. Due to swollen feet of pregnant women, their foot length, foot width and circumference will change. According to the relevant data, the amount of swelling in the feet of pregnant women is between 10 and 25 mm, so the size of this scale is sized to take this change into account.

As shown in Fig. 7, the final size of this scale is 356 mm*310 mm*57 mm, which meets the foot size requirement of pregnant women.

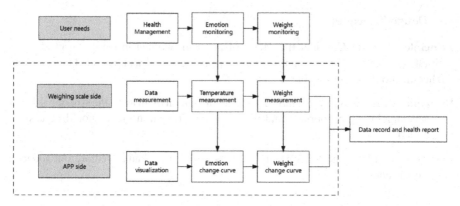

Fig. 6. Product design flow.

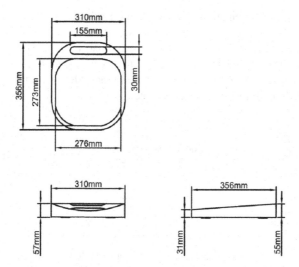

Fig. 7. Size of the weight scale

The Functional Design of the Weight Scale. The main function of the weight scale is to measure the weight and emotional state of pregnant women to meet their measurement needs. With the weight measurement module and foot dermatography measurement module, after the measurement is completed, the data is automatically imported into the mobile app. In addition to the record function for pregnant women there is also a printing module, pregnant women can choose to print out their daily weight data. The product features are shown in Fig. 8.

Weight Scale Appearance Design. The weight scale adopts a sleek exterior shape and a yellowish-beige color to give a soft visual impression. Its appearance and details are shown in Figs. 9 and 10.

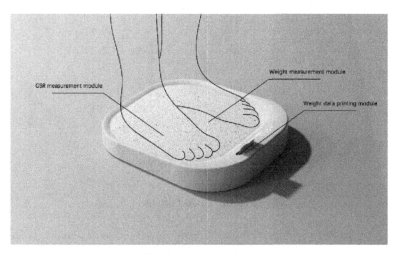

Fig. 8. Product features

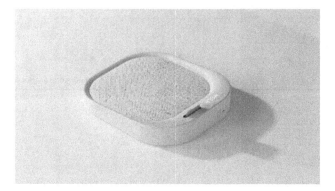

Fig. 9. Appearance of the weight scale

APP Interaction Design. The mobile app should meet the needs of recording, cognition, communication and sharing of pregnant women. The use process is that the user enters the interface to log in, opens the Bluetooth to search for the scale, binds the scale, improves the basic information, enters the home page to view the weight data and mood fluctuations, and if abnormal weight and mood fluctuations are monitored, the app will automatically make a pop-up window to remind. The specific app information architecture and interaction flow are shown in Fig. 11 and 12.

App Interface Design. The interface adopts a flat design style, following the principle of wholeness, and the visual style uses red as the main color and light red as the secondary color. As shown in Fig. 13 and 14.

Fig. 10. Product details

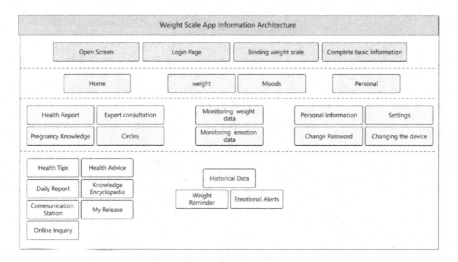

Fig. 11. Information architecture of the weight scale app

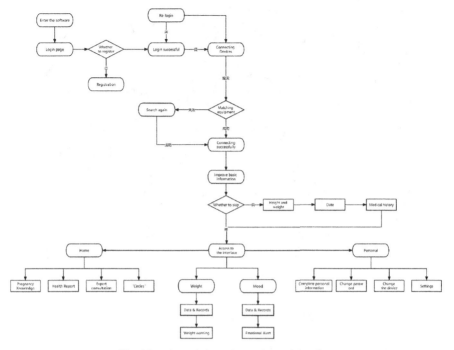

Fig. 12. The weight scale app interaction flow

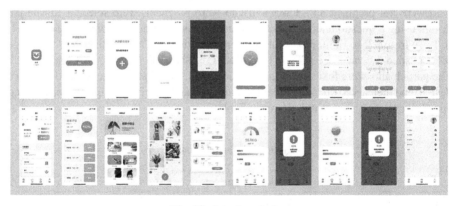

Fig. 13. Interface design

Fig. 14. Interface display

6   Experimental Validity Assessment

6.1   Evaluation of the Product Design

To assess the validity of the product design, a total of 9 participants, including 6 women who were not pregnant and 3 women who were pregnant, were selected to rate the design using a questionnaire. The questionnaire was rated on a 5-point scale (-2, -1, 0, 1, 2), from left to right, representing "very dissatisfied-2," "dissatisfied-1," "average 0," "satisfied-1," "average 0," and "satisfied-1." "Satisfied 1" and "Very satisfied 2". The participants were first shown the product effect, function, interaction and interface design, and then asked questions about the function and interface design of the scale and app. The evaluation content is shown in Table 5.

Table 5. Evaluation content

	Evaluation content	Average value
Product Features	Functionality	1.64
	Safety	1.62
	Usefulness	1.55
	Fun	1.63
Product Interaction	Visual style	1.8
	Interface Layout	1.74
	Icon Recognition	1.74

By rating each dimension of product functionality and product interaction, the results of each evaluation were between 1.5 and 2, with the pregnant women group being more demanding of product safety than the non-pregnant group. According to the average value, the respondents have a more positive evaluation of the final product.

7 Summary

For the design of the weight scale for pregnant women, this study first analyzed the basic physiological and psychological needs of the pregnant women group and the opportunity points of the existing products through the study of the emotional and weight characteristics of pregnant women and the research of related health management products to provide a theoretical basis for the subsequent design. And to further verify that pregnant women have special emotional needs, this study used GSR electrodermal sensor test to compare the emotional changes of pregnant and non-pregnant women. Finally, a weight scale during pregnancy and an accompanying app are designed to provide a more scientific approach to the health management of the pregnant women group.

References

1. Yali, A.M., Lobel, M.: Stress-resistance resources and coping in pregnancy. J. Anxiety Stress Coping 15(3), 289–309 (2002). https://doi.org/10.1080/1061580021000020743
2. Furberc, M., Garrod, D., Maloney, E., et al.: A qualitative study of mild to moderate psychological distress during pregnancy. J. Int. J. Nurs. Stud. 46(5), 669–677 (2009). https://doi.org/10.1016/j.ijnurstu.2008.12.003
3. Verreault, N.: Rates and risk factors associated with depressive symptoms during pregnancy and with postpartum onset. J. Psychosom Obstet Gynaecol. 35(3), 84–91 (2014). https://doi.org/10.3109/0167482X.2014.947953
4. Xiaojie, H., Junbo, Y., Lin, L.: A study on the correlation between pregnancy outcome and adverse emotions. J. SE Univ. (Medical Edition). 34(02), 226–230 (2015)
5. American College of Obstetricians and Gynecologists Use of psychiatric medications during pregnancy and lactation. Clinical Management Guidelines for Obstetrician-Gynecologist. Obstet. Gynecol. 111, 1001–1020 (2018)
6. He, P., Huang, Y., Lu, M., Huang, L.H.: Analysis of psychological status and influencing factors of 419 pregnant women during pregnancy and postpartum. J. China Matern. Child Health Care. 29(23), 3731–3735 (2014)
7. Yoman, R., Xuemei, M., Xiaowei, Z., Dingxi, Z.: Comparison of anxiety and depression in pregnant women with different estrogen levels during pregnancy. J. Int. J. Psychiatry. 43(04), 605–607 (2016)
8. Nakamura, Y., et al.: Positive emotion and its changes during pregnancy: adjunct study of japan environment and children's study in Miyagi prefecture. J. Tohoku J. Exp. Med. 245, 223–230 (2018). https://doi.org/10.1620/tjem.245.223
9. Pesonen, A.K., et al.: Maternal prenatal positive affect, depressive and anxiety symptoms and birth outcomes: Te PREDO Study. PLoS ONE 11, e0150058 (2016). https://doi.org/10.1038/s41598-022-04990-w
10. Leerkes, E.M., Su, J., Sommers, S.A.: Mothers' self-reported emotion dysregulation: A potentially valid method in the field of infant mental health. Infant Ment. Health J. 41(5), 642–650 (2020). https://doi.org/10.1002/imhj.21873

11. Baoyi, S., et al.: Effect of pre-pregnancy height and weight and weight gain during pregnancy on pregnancy outcome in women. J. Chin. J. Obstet. Gynecol. **2**, 6–8 (1998)

12. Nehring, I., Lehmann, S., von Kries, R.: Gestational weight gain in accordance to the IOM/NRC criteria and the risk for childhood overweight: a meta-analysis. J. Pediatr Obes. **8**(3), 218–224 (2013). https://doi.org/10.1111/j.2047-6310.2012.00110.x

13. Stotland, N.E.: Gestational weight gain and adverse neonatal outcome among term infants. J. Obstet. Gynecol. **108**(03), 635–643 (2006). https://doi.org/10.1097/01.AOG.0000228960.16678.bd

14. Fei-Fei, Z., Haidong, C., Chun-Fang, W.: Effect of pre-pregnancy body mass index and pregnancy weight gain on pregnancy process and outcome. J. Mod. Adv. Obstet. Gynecol. **26**(10), 756–759 (2017)

15. Swencionis C., et al.: Weight change, psychological well-being, and vitality in adults participating in a cognitive-behavioral weight loss program. J. Health Psychol. (Official Journal of the Division of Health Psychology, American Psychological Association). **32**(4), 439–446 (2013). https://doi.org/10.1037/a0029186

16. Jones, R.A., et al.: The impact of participant mental health on attendance and engagement in a trial of behavioural weight management programmes: secondary analysis of the WRAP randomised controlled trial. J. Int J Behav Nutr Phys Act. **18**(1), 146 (2021). https://doi.org/10.1186/s12966-021-01216-6

17. Avalos, L.A., Caan, B., Nance, N., et al.: Prenatal depression and Diet quality during pregnancy. J. Acad. Nutr. Diet. **120**(6), 972–984 (2020). https://doi.org/10.1016/j.jand.2019.12.011

18. Qingqing, F., Juan, D., Heng, Y.: Effects of obesity and maternal overweight on maternal perinatal mental health. J. Chin. J. Mod. Med. **32**(02), 80–85 (2022)

19. Ge, Y., Chen, Y.N., Liu, Y.F., Steady, L., Xianghong, S.: Application of electrophysiological measurements in user experience. J. Adv. Psychol. Sci. **22**(06), 959–967 (2014)

20. Yuanzhao, W., Shuxian, G.: Dermal electricity and its applications. J. China Rehabil. **1**, 41–44 (1992)

Impact of Healthcare Mobile Apps for Smoking, Sugar Intake, and Obesity on Maintaining Healthy Behavioral Activation

Xiaotong Li[1] and Ao Jiang[2,3(✉)]

[1] Sapienza, Rome, Italy
[2] Imperial College London, London, UK
aojohn928@gmail.com
[3] EuroMoonMars at ESA, Zuid-Holland, Netherlands

Abstract. The purpose of this paper is to explore the impact of healthcare mobile apps for smoking, sugar intake, and obesity on maintaining healthy behavioral activation. We conducted a three-stage experiment with a preliminary survey, a PAM survey, and interviews and found that healthcare mobile apps for smoking, sugar intake, and obesity can improve health behavior activation in healthy people, but these apps should help users improve their ability to prevent and self-manage disease in a simpler and more understandable way. Also, the discussion function of the apps can give users an intuitive perception of the disease and the design of the user discussion area can be enhanced in the future. In addition, the existing apps in the market contain content mainly for people who are already sick, future development of apps can add a prevention module to help users improve their poor health behaviors early and improve their disease self-management skills early.

Keywords: Maintaining healthy · Activate · Healthcare app

1 Introduction

With the end of the Covid-19 pandemic, e-healthcare is increasingly seen as a key development area for paramedicine and telehealth, as it can reduce potentially preventable deaths [1, 2] and promote equal access to quality healthcare resources for citizens. E-health is the provision of health information through the Internet to improve public health, which allows individuals to obtain information about diagnosis and treatment without visiting a medical facility. The potential of e-health technologies to educate patients and improve their health self-management skills is enormous. 43.5% of all global Internet searches in 2022 will be for health or health-related information. A growing number of users are expressing a desire to use the Internet to access information related to the prevention and treatment of disease. Electronic health records, electronic prescriptions, decision support systems, electronic management of chronic diseases, and barcoding of drugs and biologics have been shown to reduce healthcare costs and medical errors [3]. At the same time it allows users to decide for themselves whether to allow other institutions to access their own electronic data, which protects user privacy to a certain extent and emphasizes user data autonomy, and therefore makes more users willing to use electronic medical records of their own data; and medical institutions that have gained access can monitor the health status of users at any time and solve health problems before they become emergencies [4]. E-medicine allows users to gain more health-related knowledge, allows more users to participate in the process of developing management plans for their own health [5], and increases awareness and ownership of health management in the minds of users. This greatly reduces the appearance of inappropriate medical regimens and increases the likelihood that users will actively cooperate with health management plans. It also increases the possibility of long-term co-management of health by users and healthcare professionals due to the continuous and convenient online access to relevant medical resources. Currently, there is a plethora of digital health technologies available to deliver healthcare interventions, including apps, SMS texts, email, the Internet, interactive chatbots, and voice agents [6–8]. The large number of mHealth apps available for download proves their popularity [9].

Smoking, sugar intake and obesity are three of the major issues affecting human health globally. In 2020, 12.5% of U.S. adults (an estimated 30.8 million people) currently smoked cigarettes [10]; Nearly 40% of American adults aged 20 and over are obese.71.6% of adults aged 20 and over are overweight, including obesity [11], Most consumers are not aware of the WHO upper limit of sugar intake, while their estimation of the amount of sugar is not accurate [12]. Although these three health problems do not produce fatal health problems in a short period of time, they can cause health risks in a long term, such as lung disease due to smoking [13], cognitive impairment and cognitive decline [14], oral disease due to excessive sugar intake [15], and diabetes due to obesity [16]. However, people with these three behavioral habits are often unaware of the negative health consequences of such behaviors [17]. Some studies have shown a significant association between the lack of pleasure and smoking [18, 19]. Whereas sugar intake may have an impact on people's reward mechanisms, the intake of sweet foods (generally palatable) leads to addiction-like molecular and cellular changes in the reward system that drive habitual consumption [20, 21]. And overweight and obese people have very different views on diet and exercise compared to their normal weight peers [22]. So groups with these three types of behaviors do not have a strong motivation to prevent disease and stay healthy. However, with the development of cell phone features, many phones are now able to passively collect a variety of health data - including physical activity, social interactions, sleep, and mobility patterns - and infer information related to physical and mental health, such as sleep duration, exercise steps heart rate, etc. [23, 24], so users can be more conveniently and timely informed about their current physical condition and health issues. Combining these features with active user interaction, mobile applications can provide many different behavioral interventions by developing health management plans about users based on their characteristics. And users can use their cell phones to monitor data at any time and place, and share this data with healthcare applications, so it is widely loved by users. A large number of mobile applications for the treatment of chronic diseases (e.g., diabetes, hypertension, asthma, etc.) have been launched, and they mainly use the data collection capabilities of cell phones to instantly analyze the user's physical condition and give feedback and recommendations [25]. Further research into healthcare applications will not only help developers examine the accessibility and effectiveness of current healthcare applications, but will also help them develop more valuable healthcare applications.

2 Objective

While a variety of digital health programs exist to help users stay healthy and prevent disease, or to provide medical support and telemedicine for patients with pre-existing conditions, it is unclear whether these digital programs can increase users' behavioral activation to stay healthy. It is especially worrisome that a large number of users (healthy people) do not have a good sense of prevention and protection in carrying out some potentially negative health behaviors or in the development of chronic diseases. Therefore, the aim of this study was to analyze whether the currently more widely used healthcare digital programs enable people to have higher activation of health behaviors. We asked two questions: 1. The extent to which the use of healthcare digital programs activates healthy people in terms of their health maintenance concepts and experiences. 2. to measure the impact of existing healthcare digital programs on the knowledge, skills, and beliefs involved in health maintenance behavior activation.

3 Method

3.1 Research Design

The experiment was conducted in 3 phases. Phase 1 used a snowball method to collect current user usage of healthcare apps for smoking, sugar intake and obesity through various channels, such as app stores, social media and email. The final sample of 9 most widely used apps was identified for testing. Phase 2 uses the PAM questionnaire to measure whether the test sample can influence the user's health behavior and how each group influences the user's separately. Phase 3 randomly interviewed 2 participants from each app, asking them how they felt about using the healthcare app.

3.2 Participants

The survey was conducted in China (Mainland and Hong Kong) between December 10 and January 20, 2022 through an online questionnaire on the Questionnaire Star platform (https://www.wjx.cn/). Participants were recruited through social media platforms such as WeChat, Weibo, Xiaohongshu, and QQ, and participants should have a cell phone and not currently under treatment for a disease. All participants agreed to answer the question based on their consent, honesty, and the instructions in the questionnaires. The final sample consisted of 307 participants with a mean age of 37.15 years, including 161 males and 146 females. 83.1% of the participants had used smoking, sugar intake, and obesity-related healthcare apps, and 16.9% had no current smoking, sugar intake, and obesity-related healthcare apps. The overall demographic characteristics of our sample are shown in Table 1..

Table 1. Socio-demographic data of participants who completed the initial survey (N1 = 307).

Characteristics	N1
Age	
Mean(SD)	37.15
Range	22–51
Sex,n(%)	
Male	161(52.4)
Female	146(47.6)
Educational level,n(%)	
Low	90(29.3)
Middle	126(41.0)
High	91(29.7)

3.3 Materials and Procedure

The snowball method is a good method for collecting data from hard-to-reach or "hidden" populations (Atkinson & Flint, 2001), and this study used the snowball method to identify the sample of healthcare applications. The other material used in the experiment was the PAM questionnaire, a 13-item measure to assess patients' knowledge, skills, and confidence in self-management. The scale was specified using Rasch analysis and is an interval-level, unidimensional, Guttman-like scale. The 13-item scale is a simplified version of the original 22-item scale with similar psychometric properties to the original 22-item version. Participants were asked to indicate their level of agreement with statements by selecting answers from four options (strongly disagree to strongly agree), with a theoretical range of 0 to 100 on the PAM, with higher activation scores associated with higher levels of activation [26–28].

The study was conducted in mainland China and Hong Kong. Two men who had already used a health care application related to smoking, sugar intake, and obesity distributed study flyers and were contacted through acquaintances of the researchers who did not know the researchers and were not involved in the study. Snowballing occurred, and people passed on information to friends by word of mouth (Platzer & James 1997, Morse & Richards 2002), and the researchers asked them questions about their use of smoking, sugar intake, and obesity-related health care apps ("What are your most familiar smoking, sugar intake, and obesity-related health care apps? obesity-related health care apps?"). The final tally identified the nine most commonly used mobile apps related to smoking, sugar intake, and obesity as the test sample for the healthcare digital apps in this study. After an initial screening, they were randomly and equally divided into 9 groups of 10 people each, each using a mobile app related to smoking, sugar intake and obesity. Participants were surveyed with the PAM before using the app to measure the current users' mastery of the knowledge, skills and beliefs involved in maintaining health behavior activation. A longitudinal survey was conducted with PAM after 1 month of app use and 3 months of app use, respectively. The purpose was to determine whether there was an impact on the user's health behavior activation due to the use of the relevant healthcare app and the change in the degree of impact on the user. At the end of the 3-month experiment, two participants were randomly interviewed for each app and asked how they felt about using the app.

3.4 Data Analysis

All statistical data analyses were performed on SPSS v24.0 and MS Excel for Windows. The extent of activation of health care applications on participants' health behaviors and the effect of different health care applications on participants' health behavior activation were determined based on the data results of the PAM.

4 Results

4.1 Use of Healthcare Apps Related to Smoking, Sugar Intake, and Obesity

Preliminary survey data results indicate that the majority of people (83.06%) have used (including are now using) smoking, sugar intake and obesity related healthcare apps. And there are three reasons most likely to cause users not to use healthcare apps, "apps are not user friendly/not clearly described how to use (23.53%), apps push too many notifications (21.57%) and apps do not meet users' needs (16.86%)", as shown in Table 2..

Table 2. The use of health care applications related to smoking, sugar intake and obesity among participants who completed the preliminary survey (N1 = 307).

	N1,n(%)
Have used (including currently using) healthcare apps related to smoking, sugar intake and obesity	
Yes	255(83.06)
No	52(16.94)
Do you know the dangers of smoking?	
Yes	237(77.20)
No	70(22.80)
Do you know the dangers of excessive sugar intake?	
Yes	195(63.52)
No	112(36.48)
Do you know the dangers of obesity?	
Yes	223(72.64)
No	84(27.36)

(continued)

Table 2. (continued)

	N1,n(%)
Reasons to stop using smoking, sugar intake and obesity-related healthcare apps	
Apps do not meet user needs	43(16.86)
Apps are not user-friendly (unclear description of how to use it)	60(23.53)
Too many push notifications from apps	55(21.57)
The apps are always down	26(10.20)
Apps may compromise user privacy	20(7.84)
Apps are not easy to navigate	17(6.67)
Apps take up too much memory	16(6.27)
Apps don't gain user trust	18(7.06)

4.2 Evaluate Participants' Health Behavior Activation After Using Health Care Apps Related to Smoking, Sugar Intake, and Obesity

After the preliminary investigation, we used the PAM scale to measure the activation degree of the health care application on the participants' healthy behaviors. The data results (Fig. 1) show that the degree to which participants had the beliefs, knowledge, and skills to manage their condition, work with their providers, maintain their health, and receive appropriate and quality care was not high at baseline, with a score of 48.1, While the Score for "When all is said and done, i am the person responsible for managing my health condition " scored the lowest, with a score of 1.86.

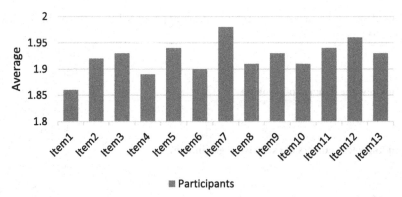

Fig. 1. Health behaviour activation measures for participants (N2 = 90) at baseline (T1) using the PAM.

We then divided the participants into three groups, each containing three different apps, and after one month the results showed (Fig. 2) that the activation of health behaviors significantly increased in all three groups, as evidenced by a significant increase in each score and a significant increase in the total score. Meanwhile, there was little difference in the activation levels of the three apps among the participants in the Smoking group, the difference in activation levels among the participants in the Sugar Intake group was higher than that in the Smoking group and lower than that in the Obesity group, and the difference in activation levels of health behaviors among the participants in the Obesity group was the greatest, as shown in Fig. 3. Over time, the scores at 3 months showed that participants' health behavior activation was significantly lower than their activation at 1 month, but still higher than their activation at baseline. Meanwhile, the data at 3 months (Fig. 2) showed that participants' health behavior activation levels remained similar across the three apps in the Smoking group, but the differences in health behavior activation between participants in the Sugar Intake and Obesity groups were smaller than those measured at 1 month (Fig. 4 and Fig. 5).

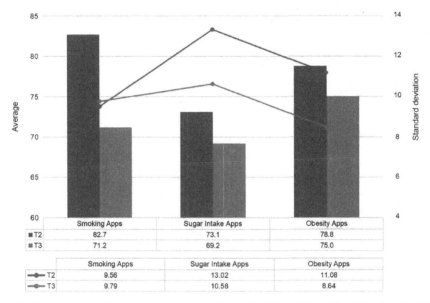

Fig. 2. Measures of health behavior activation at 1 month (T2) and 3 months (T3) using the PAM for the 3 groups of participants (N2 = 90).

The results show that the use of smoking, sugar intake and obesity-related healthcare apps increased participants' activation to maintain healthy behaviors, that different types of healthcare apps caused different effects on participants' activation of healthy behaviors, and that the degree of effect decreased over time.

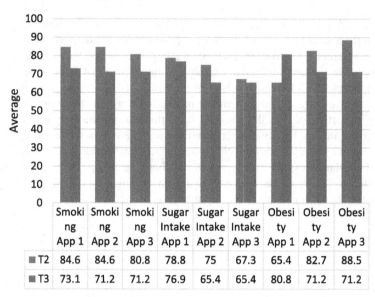

	Smoki ng App 1	Smoki ng App 2	Smoki ng App 3	Sugar Intake App 1	Sugar Intake App 2	Sugar Intake App 3	Obesi ty App 1	Obesi ty App 2	Obesi ty App 3
■ T2	84.6	84.6	80.8	78.8	75	67.3	65.4	82.7	88.5
■ T3	73.1	71.2	71.2	76.9	65.4	65.4	80.8	71.2	71.2

Fig. 3. Health behavior activation measures using PAM at 1 month (T2) and 3 months (T3) for participants (N2 = 90) using 9 apps.

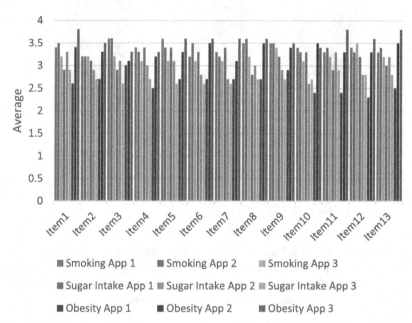

Fig. 4. Health behaviour activation measures for participants (N2 = 90) at 1 month (T2) using the PAM.

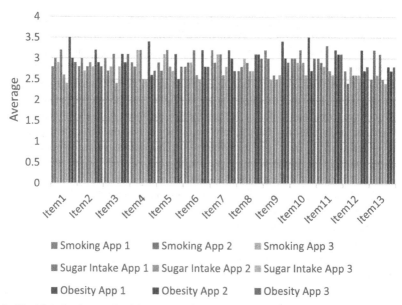

Fig. 5. Health behaviour activation measures for participants (N2 = 90) at 3 month (T2) using the PAM.

5 Discussion

In this experiment, we tested the impact of different smoking, sugar intake and obesity-related healthcare apps on users' activation to maintain healthy behaviors. With the spread of mobile health technology, more and more people tend to use more convenient and simple methods for disease treatment or disease prevention, thus a wide variety of healthcare apps are available in the market, especially in the field of chronic diseases [29], which is validated by the results of our experiment, where we found that the majority of participants had used healthcare apps related to smoking, sugar intake and obesity (83.06%). At the same time, the main reason why people abandoned the use of healthcare apps was that the apps did not describe clearly how to use them (23.53%), which may be due to the fact that users often do not have sufficient disease-related knowledge before using healthcare apps [30], so an interface full of specialized vocabulary may be difficult to understand, but having the necessary knowledge about chronic diseases is an important way to prevent and treat them [31]. However, having the necessary knowledge about chronic diseases is an important way to prevent and treat them [31], so helping users to acquire knowledge about chronic diseases in a simpler and more understandable way is an important issue for healthcare application developers to consider. After 1 month, the highest PAM scores were found in the Smoking group, which may be due to the high prevalence of diseases that may be caused by smoking in today's society, where both smokers and non-smokers are aware of the harms caused by smoking (77.20%), which is consistent with the findings of Sue Boney McCoy, 1992 et al. [32, 39, 40]. At the same time, most of the smoking apps set up user discussion forums, according to some participants' narratives, "active users discussing the pain of everyone quitting and the physical changes brought by smoking made me feel more real about the harm of smoking and more determined not to smoke", which proves that real interaction can enhance users' trust in the knowledge, skills provided by the app and have a stronger belief in choosing positive outcomes [33, 41, 42]. PAM scores in the Obesity group were lower than in the Smoking group, but higher than in the Sugar Intake group. This may be due to the cultural ideal of maintaining a good figure and people's stronger awareness of obesity prevention, many obesity-related apps are more well developed, and most obesity-related apps not only have knowledge popularization and online professional counseling for users by high-profile coaches [34], but also have corresponding reward mechanisms to help people develop good healthy behavioral habits [35, 43, 44]. The reason for the poor performance of the Sugar Intake group may be that most of the people who eat too much sugar are fond of sweet food. Their behavior habits have been formed and they are not clear about the harm of excessive sugar intake to the body [36.45]. Most of them only know that it will cause obesity and tooth decay. Therefore, it is difficult to change the concept of this group and cultivate their skills to prevent disease and maintain healthy behavior. After three months, the activation degree of health behaviors in the three groups decreased to different degrees, but the activation degree of Smoking group decreased the most. According to some participants, "I found that I could not directly feel the harm caused by smoking in the process of using the app. I knew that it might bring me some bad consequences, but I still felt that the bad consequences were far away from me". Therefore, smoking apps are more difficult to attract users continuously, especially for users who have not smoked and just want to prevent this bad behavior.

In addition, according to Fig. 1, we can see that the dispersion degree (SD = 10.62) and average score of PAM score at baseline are very low (48.1), which is because most of the participants' knowledge, skills and beliefs of preventing disease and maintaining healthy behavior at baseline are not strong, so the general score is low, but the average score is significantly improved after 1 month (78.8). Meanwhile, the Smoking group had the lowest dispersion (SD = 9.56) and the highest scores, and the three apps within the smoking group caused little difference in the impact of health behavior activation among participants, which may be due to the similar functionality of popular apps currently on the market. The data results may have been different if our participant sample was a younger group. Young people have poorer beliefs about smoking control [37, 46] and may have significantly increased health behavior activation after using smoking apps. The degree of dispersion (SD = 11.08) and mean scores of the Obesity group were lower than those of the Smoking group and higher than those of the Sugar Intake group. Nowadays, more and more cell phones can record the basic data of users at any time, so obesity apps are the most well developed and popular, but since the development of good behavioral habits requires long-term adherence and the related fields are very many and complex, such as diet, exercise, etc. [38], the activation of using obesity apps to improve participants' maintenance of healthy behaviors in the short term is less than that of the single-structured, pathway simple Smoking group, but after 3 months, we can clearly see from Fig. 2 that the participants' activation of healthy behaviors was higher than that of the Smoking group. The sugar intake group had the lowest PAM scores (73.1; 69.2) and the greatest dispersion (13.02; 10.58) in scores both after 1 month and 3 months of app use. Some participants described: "The apps for sugar intake are few and far between, have a single function, are cumbersome to use, and only present me with fixed food parameters, and most of the time I only use them when I am aware of a problem with my diet". Therefore, although the sugar-intake related apps in the current market can improve the activation of users' health behaviors, the effect is not obvious, and the ability to continuously improve the activation of users' health behaviors is poor. At the same time, the data results also reflect that people are not aware of the harm caused by sugar intake at present, and only 63.52% of people have relevant knowledge before the start of the experiment.

6 Limitations

This review has some limitations. First of all, the average age of participants in this study is 37.15 years old, belonging to older young people, but the results may be different if the experimental sample is younger young people. In addition, this article only focuses on health care applications for smoking, sugar intake and obesity. However, there may be differences between individuals using different types of health care applications. Therefore, the promotion of the results of this study is limited, and future research should consider these issues.

7 Conclusion

The results of the study suggest that healthcare apps can increase the activation of healthy people to maintain healthy behaviors. Healthcare applications should help users improve their ability to prevent and self-manage diseases in a simpler and easier-to-understand way. At the same time, the discussion function of the application allows users to have an intuitive perception of diseases, and the design of the user discussion area can be enhanced in the future. In addition, the existing apps on the market contain content mainly for people who are already sick, although it is helpful for healthy people, but it is not targeted. Future app design can add prevention modules to help users improve bad health behaviors earlier and improve disease self-management ability earlier.

References

1. Clancy, C.M.: Patient engagement in health care. Health Serv. Res. **46**(2), 389–393 (2011)
2. Sawesi, S., Rashrash, M., Phalakornkule, K., Carpenter, J.S., Jones, J.F.: The impact of information technology on patient engagement and health behavior change: a systematic review of the literature. JMIR Med. Infor. **4**(1), e1 (2016)
3. Mukherjee, A., McGinnis, J.: E-healthcare: an analysis of key themes in research. International Journal of Pharmaceutical and Healthcare Marketing **1**(4), 349–363 (2007). https://doi.org/10.1108/17506120710840170
4. Ball, M.J., Lillis, J.: E-health: transforming the physician/patient relationship. Int. J. Med. Inform. **61**, 1 (2001). https://doi.org/10.1016/S1386-5056(00)00130-1
5. Michael, A. , Ricci, M., Sahi, M.A., et al.: State of the Art and future directions: 2018, Privacy Preservation in e-healthcare environments. IEEE Access **6**, 464–478 (2018). https://doi.org/10.1109/ACCESS.2017.2767561

6. Stephens, T.N., Joerin, A., Rauws, M., Werk, L.N.: Feasibility of pediatric obesity and predia-betes treatment support through Tess. AI behavioral coaching chatbot. Transla Behav. Med. **9**, 440–447 (2019). https://doi.org/10.1093/tbm/ibz043

7. McKay, F.H., Wright, A., Shill, J., Stephens, H., Uccellini, M.: Using health and well-being apps for behavior change: a systematic search and rating of apps. JMIR Mhealth Uhealth **7**(7), e11926 (2019)

8. Jiang, H., et al.: A community-based short message service intervention to improve mothers' feeding practices for obesity prevention: quasi-experimental study. JMIR Mhealth Uhealth **7**(6), e13828 (2019)

9. Ferrara, G., Kim, J., Lin, S., Hua, J., Seto, E.: A focused review of smartphone diet-tracking apps: usability, functionality, coherence with behavior change theory, and comparative validity of nutrient intake and energy estimates. JMIR Mhealth Uhealth **7**(5), e9232 (2019)

10. Fast Facts and Fact Sheets | Smoking and Tobacco Use - CDC.https://www.cdc.gov/tobacco/data_statistics/fact_sheets/fast_facts/index.htm

11. National Health and Nutrition Examination Survey, 2017–2018; Harvard School of Public Health (2020)

12. Prada, M., Saraiva, M., Garrido, M.V., Rodrigues, D.L., Lopes, D.: Knowledge about sugar sources and sugar intake guidelines in portuguese consumers. Nutrients **12**(12), 3888 (2020). https://doi.org/10.3390/nu12123888

13. Yanbaeva, D.G., Dentener, M.A., Creutzberg, E.C., Wesseling, G., Wouters, E.F.M.: Systemic effects of smoking. Chest **131**, 1557–1566 (2007). https://doi.org/10.1378/chest.06-2179

14. Campos, M.W., Serebrisky, D., Joao, M.C.M.: Smoking and Cognition. Current Drug Abuse Rev. **9**(2) 76–79(4) (2016)

15. Moreira, A.R.O., et al.: Higher sugar intake is associated with periodontal disease in adolescents. Clin. Oral Invest., 1–9 (2020). https://doi.org/10.1007/s00784-020-03387-1

16. Chen, J., Lieffers, J., Bauman, A., Hanning, R., Allman-Farinelli, M.: The use of smartphone health apps and other mobile health (mHealth) technologies in dietetic practice: a three country study. J. Hum. Nutr. Diet. **30**, 439–452 (2017). https://doi.org/10.1111/jhn.12446

17. Kerawala, C.J.: Oral cancer: smoking and alcohol: the patients' perspective. Br. J. Oral Maxillofac. Surg. **37**, 374–376 (1999). https://doi.org/10.1054/bjom.1999.0183

18. McKennell, A.C.: Smoking Motivation Factors. British J. Soc. Clin. Psychol. **9**, 8–22 (1970). https://doi.org/10.1111/j.2044-8260.1970.tb00632.x

19. Leventhal, A.M., Waters, A.J., Kahler, C.W., Ray, L.A., Sussman, S.: Relations between anhedonia and smoking motivation. Nicotine Tob. Res. **11**, 1047–1054 (2009). https://doi.org/10.1093/ntr/ntp098

20. Hibbard, J.H., Stockard, J., Mahoney, E.R., Tusler, M.: Development of the Patient Activation Measure (PAM): conceptualizing and measuring activation in patients and consumers. Health Serv. Res. **39**(4 Pt 1), 1005–1026 (2004). https://doi.org/10.1111/j.1475-6773.2004.00269.x

21. Olszewski, P.K., Wood, E.L., Klockars, A., Levine, A.S.: Excessive consumption of sugar: an insatiable drive for reward. Current Nutr. Reports **8**(2), 120–128 (2019). https://doi.org/10.1007/s13668-019-0270-5

22. Mozes, A.: Why Obese People Find It So Tough to Slim Down, Diet & Weight Management, viewed 19 January (2023)

23. Trifan, A., Oliveira, M., Oliveira, J.L.: Passive sensing of health outcomes through smart-phones: systematic review of current solutions and possible limitations. JMIR Mhealth Uhealth **7**(8), e12649 (2019)

24. Harari, G.M., Lane, N.D., Wang, R., Crosier, B.S., Campbell, A.T., Gosling, S.D.: Using smartphones to collect behavioral data in psychological science: opportunities, practical considerations, and challenges. Perspect. Psychol. Sci. **11**(6), 838–854 (2016)

25. Leijdekkers, P., Gay, V.: Mobile apps for chronic disease management: lessons learned from myFitnessCompanion®. Heal. Technol. **3**, 111–118 (2013). https://doi.org/10.1007/s12553-013-0044-9

26. Anderson, K., Burford, O., Emmerton, L.: Mobile health apps to facilitate self-care: a qualitative study of user experiences. PLoS ONE **11**(5), e0156164 (2016). https://doi.org/10.1371/journal.pone.0156164

27. Fowles, J.B., Terry, P., Xi, M., Hibbard, J., Bloom, C.T., Harvey, L.: Measuring self-management of patients' and employees' health: Further validation of the Patient Activation Measure (PAM) based on its relation to employee characteristics. Patient Educ. Couns. **77**, 116–122 (2009). https://doi.org/10.1016/j.pec.2009.02.018

28. Hibbard, J.H., Mahoney, E.R., Stockard, J., Tusler, M.: Development and testing of a short form of the patient activation measure. Health Serv. Res. **40**, 1918–1930 (2005). https://doi.org/10.1111/j.1475-6773.2005.00438.x

29. Eugenio, S., Gianluca, C., Italo, Z., Giancarlo, M., Francesco, S.: Social media and mobile applications in chronic disease prevention and management. Front. Psychol. **6** (2015). https://doi.org/10.3389/fpsyg.2015.00567

30. Becker, S., Miron-Shatz, T., Schumacher, N., Krocza, J., Diamantidis, C., Albrecht, U.: 'mHealth 2.0: Experiences, Possibilities, and Perspectives. JMIR Mhealth Uhealth **2**(2) (2014). :https://doi.org/10.2196/mhealth.3328

31. Heggdal, K.: Utilizing bodily knowledge in patients with chronic illness in the promotion of their health: a grounded theory study. Californian J. Health Promot. **11**(3), 62–73 (2013). https://doi.org/10.32398/cjhp.v11i3.1542

32. McCoy, S.B., Gibbons, F.X., Reis, T.J., et al.: Perceptions of smoking risk as a function of smoking status. J. Behav. Med. **15**, 469–488 (1992). https://doi.org/10.1007/BF00844942

33. Ridings, C.M., Gefen, D., Arinze, B.: Some antecedents and effects of trust in virtual communities. J. Strategic Inf. Syst. **11**, 271–295, DOI:https://doi.org/10.1016/S0963-8687(02)00021-5

34. Yoganathan, D., Kajanan, S.: Persuasive technology for smartphone fitness apps. In: PACIS 2013 Proceedings, pp.185–195 (2013)

35. Feng, W., Rungting, T., Hsieh, P.: Can gamification increases consumers' engagement in fitness apps? The moderating role of commensurability of the game elements. J. Retail. Consum. Serv. **57** (2020). https://doi.org/10.1016/j.jretconser.2020.102229

36. Prada, M.: Perceived associations between excessive sugar intake and health conditions. Nutrients 22 **14**(3), pp. 640–652 (2022). DOI:https://doi.org/10.3390/nu14030640

37. Kreski, N.T., et al.: Adolescents' Use of Free time and associations with substance use from 1991 to 2019. Subst. Use Misuse **42**, 1893–1903 (2022)

38. Lang, A., Froelicher, E.S.: Management of overweight and obesity in adults: behavioral intervention for long-term weight loss and maintenance. Eur. J. Cardiovasc. Nurs. **5**(2), 102–114 (2006). https://doi.org/10.1016/j.ejcnurse.2005.11.002

39. Jiang, A., Foing, B.H., Schlacht, I.L., Yao, X., Cheung, V., Rhodes, P.A.: Colour schemes to reduce stress response in the hygiene area of a space station: a Delphi study. Appl. Ergon. **98**, 103573 (2022)

40. Lu, S., et al.: Effects and challenges of operational lighting illuminance in spacecraft on human visual acuity. In: Advances in Human Aspects of Transportation: Proceedings of the AHFE 2021 Virtual Conference on Human Aspects of Transportation, July 25–29, 2021, USA, pp. 582–588. Springer International Publishing, Cham (June 2021). https://doi.org/10.1007/978-3-030-80012-3_67

41. Jiang, A., et al.: Space habitat astronautics: multicolour lighting psychology in a 7-Day simulated habitat. Space: Sci. Technol. (2022)

42. Jiang, A., et al.: Short-term virtual reality simulation of the effects of space station colour and microgravity and lunar gravity on cognitive task performance and emotion. Build. Environ. **227**, 109789 (2023)

43. Jiang, A.O.: Effects of colour environment on spaceflight cognitive abilities during short-term simulations of three gravity states (Doctoral dissertation, University of Leeds) (2022)

44. Jiang, A., Zhu, Y., Yao, X., Foing, B.H., Westland, S., Hemingray, C.: The effect of three body positions on colour preference: An exploration of microgravity and lunar gravity simulations. Acta Astronaut. **204**, 1–10 (2023)

45. Jiang, A., Yao, X., Cheung, V., Taylor, L.W., Tang, H., Fang, Z.: The effect of body shape and swimsuit type on the comfort of Chinese women wearing swimsuits. Textile Res. J., 00405175221132012 (2022)

46. Zhang, N., Jiang, Ao.: Co-designing the next generation automatic driving vehicle HMI interface with lead-users. In: Krömker, H. (ed.) HCI in Mobility, Transport, and Automotive Systems: 4th International Conference, MobiTAS 2022, Held as Part of the 24th HCI International Conference, HCII 2022, Virtual Event, June 26 – July 1, 2022, Proceedings, pp. 231–243. Springer International Publishing, Cham (2022). https://doi.org/10.1007/978-3-031-04987-3_16

The Artistic Expression of Physiological Activities and Interactive Experience

Meng Li$^{(\boxtimes)}$

Harbin, Heilongjiang, China
monlimeng@163.com

Abstract. The communication function of art, instead of less significant as a record, has a role to play in the field of health. At present, artistic research, which include social welfare and aesthetic properties in the integration of art design and health care, still need to be deepened. This is a study that addresses the methods of artistic expression. To find a balance in feasibility and implementation between different dimensions of art mediums that can focus on physiological themes, message leading. The article examines the above issues through case studies and experiments. We select five groups of artworks to analyze the developable media, forms and their significance. Then, to discuss the production methods in terms of material, interactivity, performance and environmental factors through three art practices. After some experimentation, we select a few of works for public display. Through the exhibition and its feedback, we confirm the implementability of combining graphic and three-dimensional artistic approaches in the interdisciplinary creation of healthcare and art and design. Furthermore, we confirm that some scenarios can be applied, and the displayed ways are practicable. We try to bring the theme of art back to human beings themselves and provide aesthetic. And the physiological knowledge also can be applied feasibly in art. Art can simplify the profound knowledge make it easy to be understood and accepted. The integrated fields deep research about human aesthetics and health and wellness has further value.

Keywords: knowledge design · user experience · interdisciplinary practice

1 Introduction

With the great popularization of art and the broadening of the topic, the art topic gradually shifted from the individual to social, environmental, psychological, economic, and other long-term development issues (Robertson, J. & McDaniel, 2017) [1]. In recent years, medical research has made a lot of breakthroughs that allowed human to have a deeper understanding of the human body. However, the related artistic development has not fully kept pace with this development [2]. The original role of the dissemination and guidance of art has, to some extent, made no timely progress in the study and dissemination of human aesthetics.

The human body is dynamic stability. The bodies produce responses when they encounter outside stimuli. The body received the different substances stimulation and

© The Author(s), under exclusive license to Springer Nature Switzerland AG 2023
A. Marcus et al. (Eds.): HCII 2023, LNCS 14034, pp. 421–435, 2023.
https://doi.org/10.1007/978-3-031-35705-3_31

send the signals to brain, after judgment and analysis, the brain sends back instructions to perceptual organs and generate corresponding reaction [3].

The purpose of this research is to find an artistic expression form about human physiological activities in conjunction with the medical knowledge. The experiments compare different spatial forms orderly and balanced combination of art and communication. So that artworks can create an artistic environment to make the audience temporarily improve the recognition, care, and appreciation of themselves, and further to explore themselves. By visual art, the project expresses the reactions and manifestations occurred inside the human body, either microscopically or macroscopically, after being subjected to certain external stimuli or ingested certain substances and expresses a superficial educational conception and propaganda functions.

2   Methodology

1. To begin with, we analyze several groups of artworks with similar research themes in terms of form or material. After that, we integrate the analysis and present the basic ideas of the design.
2. We carry out the experiment regarding the form, interaction, and light in our three art exercises and come up with a few combined ways to suit the artworks.
3. Then, put the installations on display and observe the interactive behavior and feedback of the audience.

3   Theory

3.1   Case study

What Can the Specimens Show
The Mermaid De-Extinction Project [4]. Richard Pell uses specimens to summarize and illustrate past experiments in species improvement research. The specimens are stored in a "moment", which can be past or future, in process or conclusion. In his pavilion, there are also fantasy creatures like mermaids on display (Scc Fig. 1). Of them, the "mermaid" specimen is mixed with many existing species specimens, blurring the concept of time and showing people's continuous exploration of species' genes, so it stimulates the audience's curiosity and thinking.

Fig. 1. A diagram of The Mermaid De-Extinction Project.

How Can the Specimens Be Represented

THE WITCH IN THE LAB COAT (2019) [5], by WhiteFeather Hunter. She works with biologists using blood and serum and some muscle tissue to create a series of specimens or processes to preserve experiments. Some of them are also made of tools related to blood such as menstrual cups (See Fig. 2A).

In this work, she does not matter whether the objects need to be preserved under seal or whether the specimens are made following the regulations. Nevertheless, the sense of distance is created by the transparent protective case and liquid immersion, together with the clean white background and plastic gloves in the image record (See Fig. 2B). They render the work solemn and technological sense and relevance to life science together. And at the same time, the author puts some works openly in a normal life setting, reflecting their relevance to life and reducing the audience's alienation from the perception of the work (See Fig. 2C).

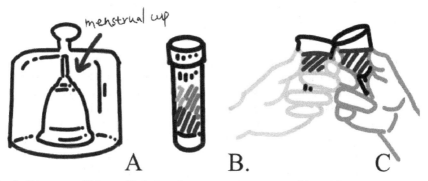

Fig. 2. Diagrams of Mooncalf. A: In using menstrual cups. B: With a white background. C: In the life scene.

How Can Projections Be Used

Surgeons' Hall Museum [6]. The museum displays thousands of specimens of limbs or organs with lesions classified by different parts of the human body and disease category (See Fig. 3A). The specimens are displayed in glass cabinets; the display panels are marked with magnification; the tissue structures are colored for easy identification; and some of those are modeled in plastic or resin only for presentation.

In the exhibition hall, there is a space that simulates a congress hall, in the middle lying a human body model on a display (See Fig. 3B). Every ten minutes, a video explaining the history of anatomy is shown here, and the anatomical process is projected on the mannequin while the explanation is going on. The static mannequin, as a projection screen, can represent the whole process of operation by projection, but without any change in itself. This educational presentation allows the audiences to immerse themselves in the atmosphere of learning as if they are last century students.

What Can Image Showcase

mEat me (for raising awareness of biopolitical issues) [7], Theresa Schubert. She

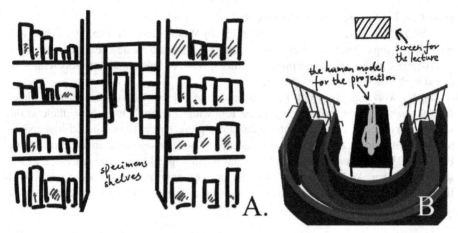

Fig. 3. Diagrams of Anatomy Demonstration Hall of Surgeons 'Hall Museum. A: Specimens of limbs or organs. B: Body model on a display.

extracted muscle fibers from herself thighs and cultured them into a piece of meat, then ate it in public. The live event was accompanied by an installation, projections of audiovisual documentation of the laboratory process, and presentations of machine learning models (See Fig. 4A). These models contributed to the development of complex narratives around the themes of bioethics, animal rights, and body politics.

Her manipulations and the growth of the meat under the microscope projected on the screen behind her during the performance (See Fig. 4B). The performance visually demonstrates the artist's active behavioral relationship with her flesh, while the video preserves this record and complements the microscopic deficiency that cannot be shown in a realistic public setting. The content of the video is not directly experienced by the viewer as the producer does, and it adds a wealth of behind-the-scenes information that helps the viewer to empathize with the artist's actions.

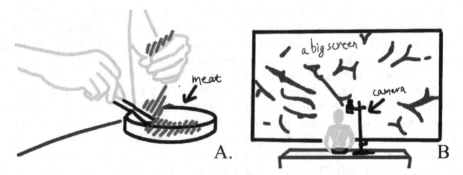

Fig. 4. Diagrams of mEat me. A: Performance. B: Projection.

- **How can the installation be interacted with.**

GENETIC HEIRLOOM: Guilt Adjuster & Interventionist Healer (installation and film that explore processes of production as cultural, personal and political practices, 2010) [8]. In their work, Revital Cohen and Tuur Van Balen express the popular understanding of genetics and the interactive installation They debate hereditary diseases, genetic defects, gender, and other blood ties between family members through the connection of liquid to the body (See Fig. 5). In the design concept, the authors wanted to use the installation to preserve and pass on the defective genetic information to their families and descendants in the future when medical treatments to cure the disease become available.

This design is not realistically possible for the moment, as storing genetic information requires special equipment and environments rather than art installations. But the art installation can send a signal that is a prerequisite for the behavior [9]. The impulse of the participant to engage in the act can reflect the need of the society, in which the process of participation is more important than its result. It is not necessary to design a highly specialized project with a message that the artists are incompetent.

Fig. 5. A diagram of GENETIC HEIRLOOM.

3.2 Analysis

The basic direction of the production is divided into two parts. The first part is a 3D sculpture or installation that occupies a space. The second part is a video. The dynamic flat image lacks a sense of space, but the moving images can better explain the principle and process of a certain reaction. Video can reflect chronological order and connect relatively independent sculptures or installations. The use of video can reduce the use of text to a certain extent, reducing the use of ancillary documents in the viewing of artworks and lowering the threshold of understanding. One of these two sections focuses on artistry and the other on the dissemination of knowledge. Aesthetics and knowledge are presented in an integrated manner.

The use of "specimens" can be extended into many forms. 1. Still sculpture. The use of hard materials and highly recognizable colors show the image of the designed object a sense of strength. 2. Objects are preserved in a closed manner to enhance the contemporary significance the work. 3. Containers that can sustain reactions and show how they occur. The viewer has two options: view it as a third party or experience it as a first party. Adding an interactive element to these specimens can allow participants to control the reaction, which can improve participation and entertainment but does not guarantee the orientation and quantification of the display.

Images are a soft indication. Humans have a strong ability to imitate and extract information from images [10]. Artworks require some specific steps to achieve an effect, in which, images are more likely to be noticed and understood by the viewer than to read them in words (the information in images is more loosely and simply). Audience perception and manipulation may be more demanding than in other parts. Such an approach can increase the success rate of the interaction.

The display of 3D objects and images can provide a different sensory experience (McTighe, 2012) [11]. The three-dimensional object provides a sense of space, while the flat image controls the angle and range of view with greater direction. The orderly combination of the two is a challenge to find a balance that complements each other without being cluttered.

4 Practice

4.1 Experiments

Morphological Experiments
Comparison of experience in four states for the same experimental model (from Drink Drank Drunk. The three reactions that occur inside the body after heavy drinking are represented through three interactive devices and an animation) [12].

1. The "exposed to the external environment" case applies to solid materials with a stable form, which be able to withstand the griping and tapping of the audience (See Fig. 6A).
2. The "in a closed environment" case model is better protected. However, the isolation from the outside world needs to ensure that the information is more obvious because it cannot be observed within a close range. Butters or levers are common mediums for connecting the inside and outside of protective enclosures in museums (See Fig. 6B).
3. The case of "intrusion in liquid" requires a high-water resistance material, at the same time, need considering whether the model information is allowed to be deformed by liquid refraction (See Fig. 6C).
4. "As the main component of a continuously operating installation" can enhance the sense of motion of the work. Moving objects are more likely to attract the viewer's attention than static ones, but it is important to consider whether the materials used can support repeated use (See Fig. 6D).

Different kinds of "specimen" display methods have their advantages and disadvantages, and the form of "specimen" needs to be considered according to its texture, strength, details, interactive needs, and other factors. The basic requirement is to keep the model display in line with the overall conditions of fun and experimentation.

Fig. 6. Human vascular nerve models. A: exposed to the external environment. B: in a closed environment. C: intrusion in liquid. D: As the main component of a continuously operating installation.

Interactive Experiments

During a workshop, two devices are set up and reactants are put in them, one of which is solid, and the other is viscous liquid. The front side of the device is labeled with a text description of the procedure and the other side with a brief description of the concept of the work (See Fig. 7).

Process: At the beginning of the exhibition, the author himself perform the usual operations on the installation followed the textual prompts as the role of an audience (See Fig. 8A). During the three hours of the exhibition, many visitors actively take part in the operation and experiment according to the texts. There was a noticeable difference between the two installations at the end of the exhibition, all the solid material are consumed while viscous liquid is left a lot, because in the middle and later stage of the exhibition, people started not to follow the prompts in order to see a different reaction (See Fig. 8B).

In the display, I showed the work Excessive Defense (Demonstrate the principles, prevention and treatment of common allergies) [13]. The surface of the work gradually becomes transparent caused by increased temperature and resulted in the text underneath to be emerged (See Fig. 9). But the display site was in a cooler environment, resulting in a cooler surface temperature for the work. So that some of the participants did not have enough body heat to complete the interaction in a short period of time.

It is necessary for the audience to be prompted that the installation is interactive, and the audience is very receptive to interaction. The interactive elements needed to be kept clean, tangible, and easy to operate.

Projection Experiments

Experimentation with different combinations of background materials and model-image relationships.

1. To play directly on the screen. This is a clearest presentation with little influence from ambient light (See Fig. 10A).
2. To play on a flat surface. That is a warm presentation, slightly more demanding on the surroundings (See Fig. 10B).

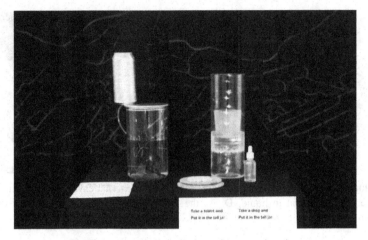

Fig. 7. Interactive installation with operating tips.

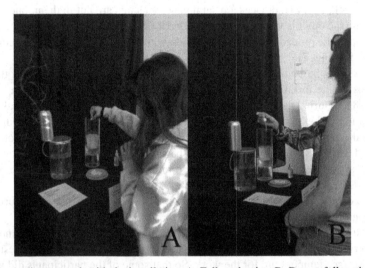

Fig. 8. Audiences work with the installation. A: Follow the tips. B: Do not follow the tips.

3. To play on a textured surface. This will distort the image and requires considering whether the location and volume are suitable, whether the texture has a strong relevance to the thereof the display (See Fig. 10C).
4. To play on a soft material. A black fabric is needed in the experiment. It will cause some information to be inconspicuous but create a natural sense of rhythm (See Fig. 10D) [14].
5. To play around the model. This will affect a sequential reading experience though the two are place separately without connection. The order of reading is related to the information depth of both (See Fig. 10B).
6. To play behind the model. The viewer receives a portion of the image, but the primary and secondary relationships are obvious (See Fig. 10E).

Fig. 9. The color or transparency of the surface of the work is altered by body temperature.

7. To play through the model. A portion of the image is distorted or left on the model in front of the participant. When a participant is manipulating the model, the body blocks the projection path, and the image is shown on the participant body (See Fig. 10F).

It is necessary to consider whether there is a strong connection between the model and the image and if so, projection mapping can be applied. The combination of model and image needs to be judged based on the complexity of both. How to present the necessary information in the image needs to be considered in order to avoid the image to be distorted or obscured. It is important to consider whether the model and images are information-rich to avoid displaying them in overlapping spaces.

Light and Shadow Experiments
This experiment tests the suitability of the artwork for display in different lighting environments (See Fig. 11)

1. In an illuminated environment, the image cannot be displayed in the form of projection, which it will make the projection invisible. So, it is better to use the screen directly to display the visual performance. People will generate a sense of vertigo in the lighting environment for a long time, so it is not suitable for works that require a long time to participate in the display.
2. In a color light environment, a brighter display cannot stand out from the visual point of view. However, if the display is too dark, it is needed to observe whether the theme of the work and the background is unified. Brighter light can reduce visual monotony. The video display has the same problem as Experiment.
3. In a natural environment, the warmth of the light will affect the surface color when it is projected onto the surface of the work or even inside (warm in a sunny day, gray

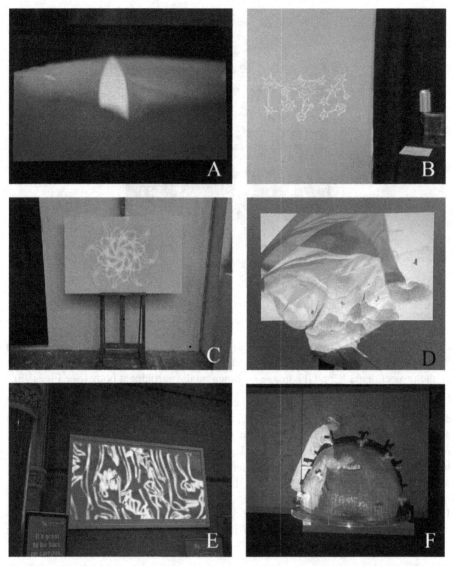

Fig. 10. Videos are displayed on different backgrounds. A: on the screen B: on a flat surface and around the model C: on a textured surface D: on a soft material E: behind the model F: through the model

on a cloudy day). So, the work is displayed outdoors or in a room facing a window would depend on whether the color of the work is an important message.

4. In a dark environment with distant light or back light, too much light spots will cause visual fatigue and blur the details. Lack of detail will lack information, so we should consider highlighting the key information. The clarity of the video is related to the distance and direction of the light.

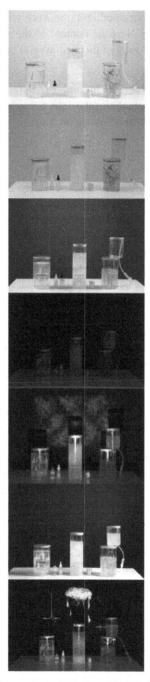

Fig. 11. The same set of works with different lighting.

5. In a dark environment without floodlight, the work will not be recognizable if it has no luminous elements, as well as the content of the video image will be relatively clear. So, if the image is the point of the display, you can consider removing the light source.

Image display is more influenced by ambient light and whether the operation is required, therefore, it is important to take into consideration whether the operating environment is suitable for human activities on display.

4.2 Performances

The three practical projects applied to this study were eventually adopted in different ways depending on the needs.

Project 1 Dream Overlap maps several levels of human thinking by showing the different stages of human dreaming. we display it twice. Once it is projected on the window in the display. The other time it was projected onto a projection screen with a glass cabinet around it (See Fig. 12). Both presentations were carried out in dimly lit environments with little light, where curtains and glass could somewhat blur a small amount of image information to achieve the effect of dreaming. It with some voice like breath and twittering but without clear sound. According to the chat, with no corresponding explanation, the audience choose to leave or discuss with others. Although there is design description, it is not integrated into the work and therefore go unnoticed.

Project 2 Drink Drank Drunk is showed in a controlled lighting environment where the lights are switched on at the start of the video playback and switched on afterwards. As the model welcomes hands-on work from the audience and the material is fluorescent which is stored in a liquid to simulate the in vivo environment. With the lights off the vision is focused on the fluorescent material and the video projected on that material, conveying a second layer of information. The video is divided into two parts, one with abstract graphics and the other with a hands-on demonstration. There are three sections of the work that require separate actions, but visitors do not follow the instructions exactly. This is caused by the instructional panels are not obvious enough: the video's time is long, and the three models do not do a unique job of operating. The frequent changes in lighting also make it difficult to see. We prepare a brochure for the audience, which includes cartoons on alcohol metabolism, image of the operation of the device and video screenshots. However, the handbook does not reflect the unity and necessity in the work and are often forgotten.

Item 3 Excessive Defense is explaining the basics about allergies, is displayed in the darkroom, there is lighting above the installation, but it does not affect the projection. The model is directly exposed to the outside world in order to complete the interaction. The influential content interacts with the installation, so it can be projected directly onto the installation with a strong sense of wholeness and direction. The device is triggered by simply throwing a prepared object into a designated cavity. The video has a little girl's voice explaining the knowledge and with subtitles. In the exhibition, visitors are significantly more motivated to watch the video than to participate in the interaction with the installation. The approachable voice that captivates the audience. The participation rate improves after we remove the cover from the entrance to the installation and expose part of the internal structure.

Fig. 12. Dream overlap reflected on glass cabinet.

5 Discussions

5.1 Application

Through the analysis of several artworks and scientific and educational displays, as well as our four sets of experiments based on three artistic practices, we found that, as the artistic visualization of physiological responses, the form of artistic expression needs to be determined by the content of the focused message. In practice, a variety of experiment forms can be matched and combined to achieve the purpose.

If the presentation focuses on the information of the model, we should try to accompany the model by a clear lighting environment to reflect a strong sense of interactivity and intimacy, which would attract audience to come into contact with them (e.g., direct exposure to the environment following the lighting guidance, etc.). We can also use luminous means to highlight the main body of the model, as in medical research, the researcher will reflect the object by fluorescent staining. Conversely, if the main message is to be communicated by images, the clarity of the presentation medium needs to be ensured. The ideal effects can be achieved by choosing to reduce the size of the screen, stagger the model, reduce the brightness and so on.

There needs to be a link between the image and the model in terms of pictures, dynamics, and text to provide a unified expression of information. During the production, we realize that the combination of images and models can better convey information in artistic visual representation of human physiological activity in practice. In order to get more targeted visual effects, we make specific adjustments to the volume, material, color, light, operation, position, order, information, and professionalism of the work according to the description of the object, the environment, the purpose and time of the display, and the audience groups. For example, fit may be needed to use bright colors and add funny guidance to children (visual system is not fully developed and ability to distinguish colors is weaker), however, for adults (better reading and comprehension skills), more professional and detailed are needed.

5.2 Interaction

During the presentation, some of the audience read the design instruction or manipulate the work following the note and ask questions or engage in discussions with the author. We observed that audience engagement is related to the dissemination breadth of the topic itself. The higher the popularity, the higher the attention. If the model can clearly provide topical information, the audience can be attracted faster.

In the art installations, the simpler the operation, the greater the involvement of the audience, like 'drop', 'put', 'press' for example. During the audience take part in the activity, the more obvious the changes triggered by the manipulation are, the more the work stimulates the audience's desire to explore and the more it helps with other modules presentation, such as interpretation, and the more the uniqueness of the operation, the easier the cooperation of the participants. For instance, 'Put A in B and press the button' is more limited than 'Just touch C'.

After the interaction, the more obvious the changes and the simpler the manipulation, the more positive the audience response are [15]. Certainly, physiological changes are relatively rigorous and complex, even if the viewer knows the subject matter of the work, it is not always possible to successfully interpret it without a systematic medical knowledge. So, explanations of text and voice can enhance the audiences' reception of the information and a short commentary would play a key role.

5.3 Significance

The study of artistic visual representations related to human physiological responses is an interdisciplinary study that combines the disciplines of biology and art. It combines the rigorous and rational science thinking with the natural and sensual art expression. From the artistic viewpoint, artworks should try to use knowledge to prompt people's visions of "human beauty" and hygiene and health, and the practical and philosophical meaning of art in social production can be expanded. From an intellectual point of view, artistic means can convey science information in a relatively gentle and interesting way, serving as an educational tool for both aesthetics and medicine. The exploration of art in a particular scientific field may solve not only some puzzles, but explore many breakthrough developments begin with art, and its attempts are valuable in their own fields. If the focus is on the dissemination of knowledge and displaying the principles and processes of the phenomenon, artistic techniques play a visually prominent role as means of expression (See Fig. 13).

5.4 Development

Knowledge could be disseminated through art, and this type of artwork is more suitable to exhibit in public area of laboratories or companies and science and technology museums to attract attention.

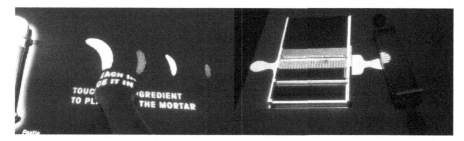

Fig. 13. Interactive projection installation in London Science Museum, photoed on 05/07/2022

According to the preliminary analysis of its interactive and fun performance, the deep research in this integrated field of human aesthetics and health and wellness has further value. In future art practice, this series of display forms can be applied to the art creation of science and nature communication.

6 Conclusions

Our research can make contributions to social education and welfare. The display and dissemination of these arts have the promise of being an aesthetic reminder to contemporary people to know themselves, appreciate themselves, protect themselves, and love themselves.

References

1. Robertson, J., McDaniel, C.: Themes of contemporary art: visual art after 1980 (2017)
2. Wilson, S.: Information arts: intersections of art, science, and technology (2002)
3. Marshall, E.: Medicine under the Microscope. Science (Am. Assoc. Adv. Sci. **326**(5957), 1183–1185
4. Rich Pell homepage. www.art.cmu.edu/people/rich-pell/
5. WhiteFeather Hunter homepage. https://www.whitefeatherhunter.ca/. Accessed June 2022
6. Surgeons' Hall Museum homepage, Edinburgh. https://museum.rcsed.ac.uk/
7. Theresa Schubert homepage. https://www.theresaschubert.com/. Accessed May 2022
8. GENETIC HEIRLOOM homepage. https://www.cohenvanbalen.com/work/genetic-heirloom. Accessed July 2022
9. Wilson, S.: Art + Science Now. Thames & Hudson, London (2010)
10. Eamon, C., Douglas, S.: Art of Projection. Hatje Cantz, Ostfildern (2009)
11. McTighe, M.E.: Framed spaces: photography and memory in contemporary installation art (2012)
12. Drink drank drunk homepage. drink-drank-drunk.mystrikingly.com. Accessed 27 Dec 2022
13. Excessive Defence homepage. excessivedefence.mystrikingly.com. Accessed 15 May 2022
14. Dream overlap homepage. dreamoverlap.mystrikingly.com. Accessed 13 Dec 2021
15. Nicholson, S.: Interactive Art and Play. Open University Press, Milton Keynes (1976)

Porous Ceramics for the Design of Domestic Ecologies

Enza Migliore[1]([⊠]) [iD], Zhennan Yao[1]([⊠]) [iD], and Xiaotian Deng[2] [iD]

[1] School of Design, Southern University of Science and Technology, No. 1088 Xueyuan Blvd., Shenzhen 518055, China
emigliore@sustech.edu.cn, 12233204@mail.sustech.edu.cn
[2] College of Design, National Taipei University of Technology, Taipei, Taiwan

Abstract. This study expands the knowledge of design for human well-being by exploring hygroscopic and microbial characteristics and deficiencies in domestic environments through ecological, interdisciplinary, and educative design lenses. This paper reports the literature review on quantitative and qualitative data from different fields to contribute to a multidisciplinary study. It generates a new understanding of ceramic materials and their use for sustainable and healthier household environments through the design of systems that control humidity, temperature, and microbial conditions.

The study assumes that the air quality in a domestic setting, along with the use of powered devices, needs the design of healthier and sustainable systems that provoke a change in behaviors and awareness, above all about the dependency on massive employment of energy.

The significance of this investigation is to produce interdisciplinary knowledge. Rather than having an exhaustive review of one specific aspect and field, we want to connect results in Materials Science and Engineering, Environmental Science and Building, and Design and Architecture to highlight opportunities and directions for design. It is a preparatory study for an applied research project. The goal is to provide new directions for designing porous ceramic systems to enhance the indoor quality of life under sustainability based on the environmental, economic, and social pillars. We map and analyze the domestic environment according to ecological considerations as guidelines to inform design, which contributes to human physical and emotional well-being. This result will involve education on new human behaviors, belonging, and connectedness with nature.

The key issues addressed are drying, cooling, and microbial properties for the design of domestic ecologies.

Keywords: Porous ceramic materials · Design · Domestic well-being · Future Ecologies · Hygroscopic and Microbial conditions

1 Introduction

Factors such as moisture, dust, and bacteria may change the condition of the domestic environment, affecting residents' health and well-being. For example, when someone lives in a high-humidity environment for a long time, the incidence of arthritis and other diseases may increase (Onozuka and Hashizume 2011; Ramos and Stephens 2014). In this regard, many residents adopt some devices, such as dryers, to absorb moisture in the air. Although such devices can improve air quality, they consume much energy, produce noise, and need maintenance. How to improve household conditions with less energy consumption is worth investigating.

Porous ceramics can contribute to reaching this goal. Porosity is the fundamental principle determining ceramic hygroscopic and microbial behavior (Jin-Xing et al. 2016). It is a strategy nature uses to optimize structures to cope with the demands of different functions. This principle can be used at different scales, from nano to macro, and modeled through innovative designs of materials and systems (Migliore 2016). Advanced manufacturing is used today to manipulate micro and porous macro features. Changes to porosity can impact a wide range of material properties and functions, from reducing weight and mechanical resistance to controlling interactions with fluid, sound, energy, and light. Porous ceramics can find many applications in high-tech fields (Zhang et al. 2012), in industrial filtration and separation, sound absorption and noise reduction, and thermal insulation; however, there is still much potential for exploring new possibilities in domestic spaces. The leading indoor presence of these materials remains confined to their impervious quality for aesthetic, waterproofing, and sanitizing functions, such as porcelain for tableware, tiles for the kitchen, bathroom fixtures, flooring, and wall surfaces. They become impermeable after glazing, a finishing procedure that makes the whole ceramic manufacturing and recycling process less sustainable. Glazing requires temperatures above 1800 degrees Fahrenheit and, most of the time represents an issue in the recycling stage. To be recycled, ceramics can be reduced to scraps or, for broader reuse, to dust. The glazed layer transforms the ceramics into a composite material, which is much more complex, if possible, to recycle fully.

This paper reviews studies on the ideal conditions for a healthy household environment based on the specific rooms' needs and features, categorizing and comparing porous ceramic and their applications in domestic spaces, and highlights untapped possibilities and alternative applications.

Our research question is how to exploit the extraordinary properties of porous ceramics in the domestic environment through design as an analogical, passive device for controlling ambient conditions.

Recent design investigations (Beckett 2021) and applications, such as the *Nave* terracotta cooling system, exist on the use of porous ceramics properties to enhance the household environment quality and on the analysis and experiments on indoor temperature, humidity, and microbial conditions through ceramics characterization in Materials Science and Engineering. We contribute a review that summarizes the state-of-the-art. We propose the early stage of a model that links the three factors of humidity, temperature, and microbiome and connects them to the needs of specific domestic environments to guide the selection of a type of ceramic material with distinguished functional and aesthetic properties for the design of objects, devices, and systems (see Fig. 1). At a future stage the authors will test the model in collaboration with Guangdong Dongpeng Holdings Company Limited, an expert in ceramics solutions for domestic surfaces, which is a partner in this project.

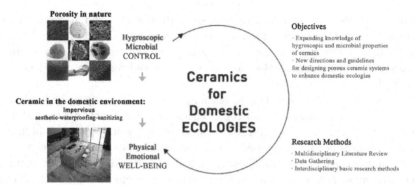

Fig. 1. Visual Abstract. The image on the top left is a collage of pictures from the web made by the authors with references to porosity from nature; the picture on the bottom left is a photo of ceramics surfaces from Guangdong Dongpeng Holdings Co., Ltd., which cooperates on the project.

2 Three Crucial Factors for the Well-Being of the Domestic Environment: An Interdisciplinary Review

Relative humidity, temperature, and microbial condition are three main features of the domestic environment (see Fig. 2). The three features in the primary functional partitions, such as the living room, kitchen, bathroom, and bedroom, are different. Identifying these features can be conducive to selecting the appropriate materials and their application for specific rooms. Today, massive amounts of energy are inevitably consumed to obtain comfortable indoor living conditions, and we want to explore new ways to contribute and encourage more sustainable solutions.

While the three critical factors of humidity, temperature, and microbial situation independently affect the indoor environment, they are also related. For example, relative humidity will affect the growth of microbial communities of different species. Arundel et al. (1986) summarized the growth conditions of specific microbial communities under different humidity conditions. They marked the optimal humidity range for human health Yu et al. (2013) studied the relationship between physiological equivalent temperature (PET) and relative humidity. Under low humidity conditions, the increase in humidity has little effect on the perception of human comfort, while when the relative humidity exceeds 60%, it inhibits the evaporation of human sweat. Thus, people feel discomfort. Rai et al. (2021) investigated the indoor environment's effect on microbial communities' growth. They showed that a temperature range of 10–30 °C and relative humidity of 40%–80% provided the most suitable conditions for airborne bacteria to survive for a long time and thus to spread over long distances.

2.1 Relative Humidity

The relative humidity is an important indicator to characterize the indoor wet environment. Changes in relative humidity affect residents' comfort. High relative humidity will increase the wetness of human skin and reduce the amount of sweating, thus reducing

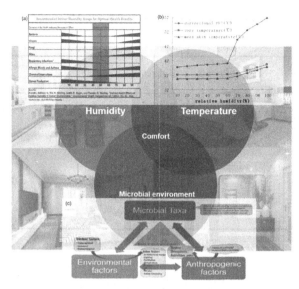

Fig. 2. Three main factors in the domestic environment. (a) Association between physiological equivalent temperature (PET) and relative humidity; (b) Relationship between the growth of microbial communities and humidity; (c) Effect of environmental factors on microbial growth (Arundel et al. 1986; Rai et al. 2021; Yu et al. 2013)

the efficiency of heat exchange between the human body surface and the external environment, thus making people feel overheated. According to a relevant study by Jing et al. (2013), the change in relative humidity will affect people's sensitivity to temperature. For example, a 10% decrease in relative humidity will increase people's feeling of indoor air temperature by 0.3 °C. Only under the combination of specific relative humidity and temperature will the relative humidity significantly affect the indoor personnel's heat feeling.

Tariku and Simpson (2015) explore the distribution of humidity in different functional areas in a home environment, where excess humidity in kitchens and bathrooms was significantly higher than in living rooms and bedrooms, implying that addressing excess humidity in kitchens and bathrooms is the focus of research in terms of indoor humidity control. The measured humidity data are presented in Table 1.

In a study by Zhang and Yoshino (2010) that summarizes indoor humidity conditions in nine different cities, it was concluded that high humidity and low humidity are common in Chinese homes and that most of the current ways to mitigate this situation require additional energy consumption. In addition, Mao et al. (2021) designed a new indoor humidity control system using a material coated with high adsorption capacity. Zheng et al. (2017) systematically analyze materials used for indoor dehumidification. Among them, MgO, gypsum, and diatomaceous earth are suitable for the current humidity control situation in the home environment. After summarizing previous indoor humidity control systems' design, selecting adsorbent materials is crucial. Luo Chenlu (2022) compared the moisture-absorbing properties of commonly used materials for indoor use, and the results are shown in Table 2. Compared with other materials, diatomaceous

Table 1. Excess Humidity Distributions within the Suites during Winter and Summer (Tariku and Simpson 2015)

Season room excess humidity	Living Room	Kitchen	Bathroom	Bedroom
Winter room excess humidity （g/m3）	2.6	3.3	4.1	2.3
Summer room excess humidity （g/m3）	1.9	3.0	3.7	1.4

earth ceramics have the potential to become the mainstream moisture-absorbing material for indoor use in the future by considering both moisture-absorbing properties and antibacterial properties.

Table 2. The performance of common indoor moisture-absorbing materials (Luo Chenlu 2022)

Type	Moisture absorption capacity	15 days breeding mold area	Moisture absorption duration
Laminated wood lumber	Good	Large	Bad
Plasterboard	Poor	Small	Poor
Sound-absorbing panels	Bad	Small	Poor
Diatomite ceramics	Excellent	Small	Excellent

2.2 Temperature Environment

Di and Wang (2013) field tests and calculations analyze the effect of indoor wind speed and temperature on occupant comfort under dynamic conditions. The presence of organic matter indoors often has a significant effect on indoor temperature, and Chen et al. (2017) study explores the effect of plants on indoor temperature, focusing on indoor green design (e.g., plant placement, sparseness, etc.). The results are shown in Fig. 3, where the plants placed on the window (Chinese roses) made the indoor temperature drop, and the double placement was more effective in cooling the temperature. In a study by Tham et al. (2020) that explored the effects of living environment temperature on human health, higher indoor temperatures may worsen the condition of people with underlying diseases, while for most people, uncomfortable temperatures can affect their health by affecting sleep. This blow is both psychological and physiological. Zhang and Wang (2021) studied occupant and environmental acoustics, indoor air, temperature, and lighting to find that the primary influence of indoor environmental design on occupant experience is indoor temperature. Djamila (2014) highlights that the most crucial thing for indoor temperature control is the appropriate application of passive cooling, shifting the goal from cooling the whole space to cooling the specific space where living activities are happening.

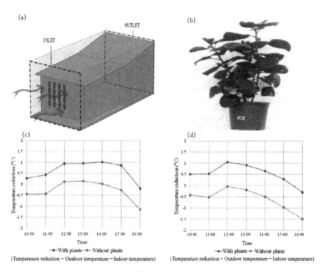

Fig. 3. a) Experimental environment b) Chinese rose c) Temperature reduction in the case of single-layer planting d) Temperature reduction in the case of double-layer planting. (Chen et al. 2017)

2.3 Microbial Environment

As our society becomes more urbanized, we now spend most of our time indoors, which has led to a change in the growth of indoor microorganisms. Some of the microbial populations hurt human health or are called pathogens (Liu et al. 2018), e.g., Staphylococcus aureus, but at the same time, some of them are also beneficial to human health (Gantzer et al. 2002; Ramos and Stephens 2014; Zocco et al. 2007).

Qi et al. (2020) studied the distribution pattern of indoor microorganisms through air sampling. The high-humidity areas indoors are often the cradle of bacterial growth, and bathrooms and kitchens usually have higher microbial levels than other rooms. Ramos and Stephens (2014) describe a large set of indoor environmental and architectural design and operational parameters that allow standardized methods for measuring multidimensional microbial data, providing methodological support for interior design. Frankel et al. (2012) studied microbial concentrations in many public indoor environments and identified environmental humidity as the most critical factor affecting microbial concentrations. Jeon et al. (2013) analyzed household microbial communities, focusing on the dominant microbial communities in the kitchen and bathroom.

3 Types of Porous Ceramics

Porous ceramic materials are inorganic materials with a certain number of pores in their internal structure, mainly characterized by equal pore size and uniform pore distribution. They are characterized by large pore surface area, high porosity, efficiently designed pore shape, and tunable pore size, which, together with their excellent thermal, magnetic, and physicochemical stability properties, make them widely used in chemical, metallurgical, and biomedical fields. Porous ceramics are mainly made of SiC and SiO2. Their porosity can reach 95%, and the distribution of pores can be flexibly controlled with the continuous updating of molding and foaming methods (Li Jiajia 2022).

Pore size, pore structure, original material, and porosity type are the four main features of porous ceramic materials (see Fig. 4). For pore size, Zhu Xiaolong (2000) classified porous ceramics into three types: microporous, mesoporous, and microporous; their pore sizes are less than 2 nm, between 2–5 nm, and greater than 50 nm, respectively. Yang (2004) classified porous ceramics into foamed, granular ceramics, and honeycomb ceramics for pore structure. For original materials, Zhengjian (1995) classified them into corundum, silicon carbide, aluminosilicate, quartz, glass, and others. For porosity type. Kaihui (2017) classified porous ceramics into open, closed, and interconnected.

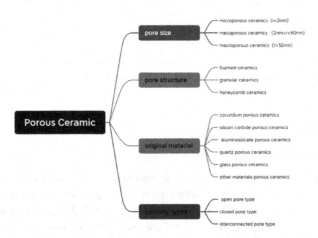

Fig. 4. Classification of porous ceramics, based on four criteria.

4 Design Research and Applications of Porous Ceramics in the Domestic Environment

Historically, and thus conventionally, design finds innovative and valuable applications for innovative materials and innovative applications for conventional materials (Manzini 1989; Karana et al. 2008; Chris 2013; Maine et al. 2005). Today, the discipline and profession of Design are actively participating in the experimental stage of manipulation, formulation, and definition of new materials (Brownell 2014; Karana et al. 2010; Ormondroyd and Morris 2019; Rognoli et al. 2015; Wilkes et al. 2014; Lin et al. 2012) and are committed to driving sustainable approaches and results, both in research and application (Lenau et al. 2015; Van Houten et al. 2022; Manzini 2016).

In this paragraph, we explore well-established and conventional design solutions and recent innovative investigations and proposals that use porous ceramics to regulate humidity, temperature, and microbiome environment.

4.1 Humidity Regulation by Design

Ceramics can be used to regulate the relative humidity through their porous properties in the domestic environment. They absorb extra moisture to lower the relative humidity in the environment.

Solutions exist, in our daily life, that contribute to the regulation of humidity conditions. A popular product is, for example, the drying stone by Marna Inc. (see Fig. 5a), used to reduce moisture in powdered and granular food, such as condiments, through porous ceramics' hygroscopicity. The relative humidity of the kitchen is high because water is often used. The corresponding problem is lumps in the seasoner (such as salt and sugar), which absorbs moisture from the air.

The unique porosity of ceramics is also used, through design, for the opposite condition, when diffused humidity in the air is required. Ceramics can quickly absorb liquids (water) that slowly volatilize through the micropores. For example, an application is a paper clay air-humidifier by Maxime Louis-Courcier (see Fig. 5b), made of the upper paper clay panel and the container at the bottom (https://maximelouis.com/paper-clay-air-humidifier). Users can drop the water on the container, that, absorbed by the microporous panel, will slowly volatilize, increasing the relative humidity of the domestic environment.

4.2 Temperature Regulation by Design

Ceramics can be used to regulate indoor temperature through their porous properties. Heat insulation is a passive system of temperature regulation. Heat insulation can protect the domestic environment from outdoor high-temperature environments and reduce heat loss. Turchenko et al. (2020) state that common passive temperature regulation is adding porous ceramic materials to building walls. Figure 6a shows porous ceramic plates used within building walls by Ibrahim et al. (2003). Such a wall can insulate external heat in the summer or reduce internal heat loss in the winter, which reduces the need for temperature-controlling devices.

Fig. 5. Humidity regulation of porous ceramics: (a) drying stone; (b) paper clay air-humidifier.

Consequently, it reduces energy consumption and noise in the domestic environment. Figure 6b shows another solution of passive temperature regulation by Manoj Patel Design Studio (https://www.manojpateldesignstudio.com/Dashboard). The vertical clay tiles absorb heat during the day and release it at night. However, although these solutions can affect temperature, it does not actively regulate the domestic temperature.

Fig. 6. Passive temperature regulation of porous ceramics: (a) materials in building walls; (b) vertical clay tiles.

A recent active solution is the ecological cooling system designed by Yael Issacharov (see Fig. 7). This project runs on an automatic irrigation system that starts working once water is poured into its hollow interior. Water passes through the permeable wall and is converted to water vapor by the heat of the air. This reaction absorbs heat from the surrounding air, cooling the water, the material itself, and thus the air in the room. The design works without power, and while user interaction with it is minimal, they can pause, turn off, or reprogram the temperature and humidity preset at any time. This project represents the new goal of contemporary design, which is dedicated to sustainability and extreme simplification of user interaction to educate about ecological behaviors and poetical manifestation and use of materials properties (Asyraf et al. 2022; Gaziulusoy and Erdoğan ÖÖztekin 2019; Manzini and Vezzoli 2002).

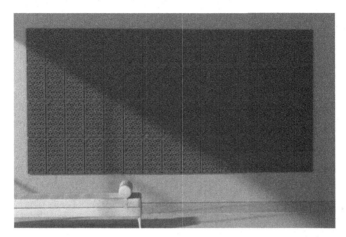

Fig. 7. Porous terracotta air conditioning system by Yael Issacharov. It is made of terracotta tiles combined with a water flow. (https://www.designboom.com/design/porous-terracotta-air-condit ioning-system-nave-yael-issacharov-10-03-2022/)

4.3 Microbiome Regulation by Design

The microbiome plays significant, although invisible, roles in the domestic environment. The traditional approach to the microbiome is elimination. A diffuse application is water filtration, which refers to eliminating microbiomes from drinking water. Porous ceramics can remove impurities from some substances (such as liquid or air). Drinking water filtration is a typical application of porous ceramics, which aims to remove impurities, especially microbiomes. Other materials (such as activated carbon) are often combined with porous ceramics to enhance filtration capacity. Researchers have added materials containing silver ions into the porous ceramic filter to amplify the efficacy of sterilization (Jackson and Smith 2018). The porous ceramic filter does not require electricity or generate waste; it can be cleaned easily and is reusable.

However, not all microbiomes should be eliminated. Novel approaches and explorations, such as in Beckett (2021), lead toward coexistence with the beneficial microbiome by controlling their amount and growth. A natural environment benefits people's health (Zocco et al. 2007; Gantzer et al. 2002; Beckett 2021). In a natural environment, there are many beneficial microbiomes. These microbiomes have little impact on the human body and can help humans eliminate harmful microorganisms. Control the balance of this beneficial microbiome can lead to a healthier environment for people to live in. Appropriate materials should be adopted and designed for such microbiomes (Lin et al. 2012). Figure 8 shows porous ceramics with fine grooves. Such porous ceramics can shape the indoor microbiome toward a healthier state; they have been demonstrated to inhibit the growth of pathogens and can also directly increase the presence of a healthy domestic microbiome (Vu et al. 2011).

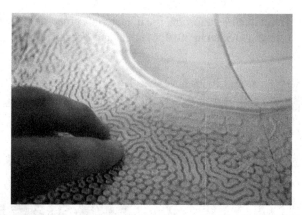

Fig. 8. Microbiome regulation of porous ceramics by Beckett (2021).

5   Discussion

5.1   Optimal Conditions for the Comfort of Household Environments

We summarize the data about the ideal indoor hygroscopic and microbial environment as a guide for designing healthier, sustainable, and comfortable domestic solutions (See Table 3). Due to the specificity of different geographical areas, we refer to our current location and use the subtropical conditions of South China as a pilot case study. This study will be used to implement a model and test it through design experiments and applications.

The first data is about temperature. The ideal indoor temperature for people to feel comfortable is 20 °C, and the humidity is between 20% and 60% (Jaakkola 2006; Tham et al. 2020). Today, this temperature should be set on the electric air conditioner. However, the temperature and humidity need to be adjusted slightly for the special functions of different areas. In the living room, the indoor area where people are most likely to work for a long time, a slightly higher temperature can help people focus; the bedroom should be relatively cool; people will lower their body temperature when they sleep, so properly lowering the bedroom temperature can help us adapt to the change in body temperature; the bathroom, it should be warmer to avoid walking into a relatively cold room after a hot shower and thus getting sick; and for the kitchen, corridors, and other spaces where people spend little time in the space should be slightly cooler than the general living space. In addition, due to the influence of outdoor temperature on the indoor environment, the comfortable temperature in summer will be 1–2 °C higher compared to winter, while for humidity, the best humidity in winter is between 30%–40%, and in summer is 40%–50%. This data is only needed to meet the minimum demand for those spaces where people spend little time.

For the summary of microbial communities inside the home (Adams et al. 2015), in bedrooms and living rooms, where the environment is more comfortable and people spend much time, Mycoplasma and Staphylococcus gold dominate; this is because they are mostly attached to the surface of human skin, and they are left on the furniture when you touch it. Moreover, the kitchen, a more complex environment, is full of moisture and grease, providing an excellent environment for the growth of Pseudomonas and Pantoea. In bathrooms with additional high humidity, Bacillus, Staphylococcus, and Streptococcus fared better than in bathrooms with extra humidity. A summary is provided in Table 3, **indicating** which microorganisms are safe and even favorable for human health. This gathered information is preparatory for the next step, where we will collect further information about the specific functions of each microbiome to inform the probiotic design of indoor systems, objects, and devices.

Table 3. Optimal temperature and humidity levels in each indoor space

Space	Temperature (°C)		Relative Humidity (%)		Microbial Environment P(Positive)/N(Negative)
	Winter	Summer	Winter	Summer	
Living Room	20-22	24-26	30-40	40-50	• Mycoplasma（N） • Bacteroides thetaiotaomicron (P)
Bedroom	16-19	21-23	50-60	50-60	• Mycoplasma（N） • Bacteroides fragilis (P) • Staphylococcus gold dominate (N)
Bathroom	22-24	22-24	<70	<80	• Bacillus (P) • Staphylococcus (N) • Streptococcus (P)
Kitchen	18-20	18-20	<70	<80	• Pseudomonas (N) • Pantoea (P)

Note: Positive/ Negative means good/bad for health

5.2 Hygroscopic and Microbial Classification of Porous Ceramic Materials

From the point of view of materials science, a summary of the structure and raw materials of porous ceramics allows us to summarize the properties of different types of porous ceramics (Wang 2021), as shown in Table 4. This table predicts the properties of porous ceramics by analyzing their structural parameters based on the raw materials used in their production. The smaller the particle size, the faster the porous ceramic absorbs water due to the capillary effect of the pore size; the porosity determines the water absorption and strength of the material; the higher the porosity, the more water is absorbed, and at the same time, the strength of the material decreases due to the presence of many pores inside the material. For biomass porous ceramics, the addition of some antibacterial substances (oyster shell powder, etc.) in the preparation process makes the prepared porous ceramics have moisture absorption and antibacterial properties at the same time, and this technology can be helpful in some specific scenarios (Abidin 2018; Ahmad et al. 2014; Lin et al. 2013; Vu et al. 2011).

Table 4. Classification of porous ceramics (Abidin 2018; Ahmad et al. 2014; Lin et al. 2013; Vu et al. 2011).

Type	Feature		Property				References
	Particle size (μm)	Porosity (%)	Water absorption	Absorption Speed	Strength	Anti-bacterial	
Alumina ceramics	0.3-0.5	90	Excellent	Good	Bad	Bad	(AHMAD R, HA J H, SONG I H.2007)
Volcanic ash ceramics	75	53-61	Good	Poor	Good	Bad	(Vu, D.-H., Wang, K.-S., & Bac, B. H.2011)
Diatomite ceramics	150	60-66	Good	Excellent	bad	Good	(Lin, K.-L., Lee, T.-C., Chang, J.-C., & Lan, J.-Y. 2012).
Antibacterial diatomite ceramics	5-7	49-55	Good	Good	Good	Excellent	(Ahmad N H, Abidin E Z, Zam H P, et al.2018)

5.3   Design Considerations: Deficiencies, Criticalities, and Opportunities

By connecting several fields of research and applications, this multidisciplinary review draws a broader overview of the state-of-the-art results in the field of porous ceramic for domestic applications. It helps to highlight deficiencies and opportunities in the different disciplines. This research wants to contribute to the field of industrial and product design. After analyzing and comparing data from Materials Science and Engineering, Building Construction, Environmental Science, and Design, we derive a series of considerations that can expand the knowledge and draw opportunities for Design.

The review highlights that:

- Most design and architectural investigations discuss the three factors of temperature, humidity, and microbiome separately.
- Although there are design applications of porous ceramics, which innovative materials are available, and which are more suitable are still being determined.
- Current designs in this field mainly consider the home as a generalized space and focus on something other than the different conditions and needs in specific rooms.

- On the other hand, some projects and investigations focus on a small portion of the space and contribute to improving marginal functions rather than aiming at both physical and emotional comfort.

These deficiencies drive several opportunities:

- The future design should consider the three factors together and select the most suitable materials, with an awareness and guide about the very innovative ones.
- There are hardly any devices made of porous ceramics for the domestic environment and humidity and microbial control.
- Since the focus here is on "passive" devices, people cannot control them, which can be a future opportunity for investigation, reflections, and experiments for design.

5.4 Suggestions for Porous Ceramics Selection and Design Directions

After summarizing the literature in different disciplines and understanding the state-of-the-art in the field of design, we highlight some findings from the interconnection and integration of data. These are the starting point for building a model for the design of ceramic domestic ecologies. Figure 9 provides an exemplification.

First, from the perspective of indoor humidity control, indoor environments are divided into two categories: direct contact with water and no direct contact with water. Spaces of the same category require the same or similar relative humidity conditions but different optimal temperatures. Their environmental characteristics are summarized separately, and we suggest design directions and decisions, referring to the performance characteristics in Table 4.

Most appliances and surfaces in the bathroom and kitchen are often in direct contact with water, so the water absorption rate and speediness of the material should be excellent. Due to the high humidity level created by the extensive use of water, these environments are easy to grow and host microorganisms.

We propose that 1) Novel ceramics made from Antibacterial Diatomite Earth (absorption and antibacterial rate) are suitable for this type of environment, 2) Integration with plants with no roots, high resilience, and adaptability, e.g., moss, can improve the water absorption while creating a healthy, balanced microbiome and improving the air quality; 3) Design systems based on functional geometry, adaptation to the specific room, integration of hygroscopic and microbial factors, and aesthetical characteristic to enhance the emotional and psychological wellbeing are suitable.

Besides the need for standard health conditions, bedrooms and living rooms have much more personalized uses and characteristics depending on the users' specific needs, preferences, and habits. At the same time, people spend most of their leisure and resting time in these spaces, so they ask for high comfort and excellent perceived temperature and humidity conditions. In these spaces, there is no regular direct contact with water. We suggest: 1) the use of ceramics with less adsorption rate and speediness (alumina and volcanic) while covering more space. The risk would be of making the environment dry; 2) integration with plants can improve emotional and psychological comfort, enabling the feeling of connectedness with nature while improving the microbial conditions; 3) design systems based on functional geometry, adaptation to the specific room, integration of hygroscopic and microbial factors, and aesthetical characteristic to enhance the emotional and psychological wellbeing are suitable.

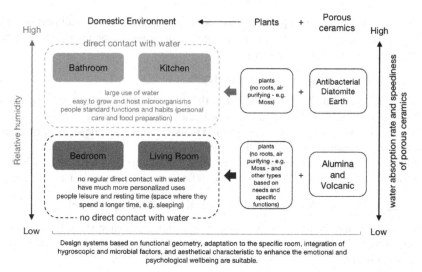

Fig. 9. An early model for the material selection and basic guidelines for future design directions

The discussion here is a demonstration of our design approach. We propose this early model for the material selection and basic guidelines for future design directions grounded on the data summary and as an exemplification of the goal and future use of our multidisciplinary review. We want to implement an exhaustive and practical model to support and drive design decisions based on ecological approaches. We will expand the review of the literature and case studies in different fields, create the model and make design experiments, prototypes, and tests around Shenzhen Bay (South China) in collaboration with Guangdong Dongpeng Holdings Company Limited. We aim to make a pilot test that is scalable and usable globally.

6   Conclusion

The future home will be more suitable for humans – and not humans - living under ecological development, awareness, and habits. From this perspective, using porous ceramics can reduce energy consumption in the domestic environment and improve living comfort. The current study does a multidisciplinary review that connects several fields related to the built environment, such as Industrial Design, Architecture, Materials Science and Engineering, Building, and Environment, on the topics of ceramic porosity, hygroscopic and microbial conditions, sustainable approaches, and human well-being in indoor spaces.

The research collects and summarizes three crucial factors related to the home environment: relative humidity, temperature, and microbial population, and identifies a range of optimal conditions for different home rooms.

We classify porous ceramics from the perspective of their chemical, functional, and structural properties, which can influence indoor moisture absorption, microbial environments, and, in general, hygroscopic, and thermal conditions. At this point, the study maps the related research and applications in the design field and highlights innovative approaches, deficiencies, and opportunities.

Finally, this paper proposes early guidelines for selecting porous ceramic materials and directions for designing systems that consider human comfort and emotional well-being while meeting ecological requirements.

Acknowledgments. The authors gratefully acknowledge Guangdong Dongpeng Holdings Company Limited for supporting this project.

References

1. Abidin, E.Z.: Development of porous ceramics as wall tiles with humidity controlling and antimicrobial characteristics from modified diatomaceous earth (de): potential to improve indoor air quality. Asia Pacific Environ. Occup. Health J. **4**(3), 41–49 (2018)
2. Adams, R.I., Bateman, A.C., Bik, H.M., Meadow, J.F.: Microbiota of the indoor environment: a meta-analysis. Microbiome **3**, 1–18 (2015)
3. Ahmad, R., Ha, J.-H., Song, I.-H.: Enhancement of the compressive strength of highly porous Al2O3 foam through crack healing and improvement of the surface condition by dip-coating. Ceram. Int. **40**(2), 3679–3685 (2014)
4. Arundel, A.V., Sterling, E.M., Biggin, J.H., Sterling, T.D., Anthony Arundel, by v: This content downloaded from 188.72.126.17 on Wed. (1986)
5. Asyraf, M.R.M., et al.: Product development of natural fibre-composites for various applications: design for sustainability. Polymers **14**, 920 (2022)
6. Beckett, R.: Probiotic design. J. Archit. **26**, 6–31 (2021). https://doi.org/10.1080/13602365.2021.1880822
7. Brownell, B.: From matter to x-matter: exploring the newfound capacities of information-enhanced materials. Mater Des. **90**, 1238–1247 (2014). https://doi.org/10.1016/j.matdes.2015.03.027
8. Chen, N., Tsay, Y., Chiu, W.: Influence of vertical greening design of building opening on indoor cooling and ventilation. Int. J. Green Energy **14**(1), 24–32 (2017). https://doi.org/10.1080/15435075.2016.1233497
9. Di, Y.H., Wang, S.C.: The research of indoor thermal comfort under dynamic conditions. Appl. Mech. Mater. **291–294**, 1752–1755 (2013). https://doi.org/10.4028/www.scientific.net/AMM.291-294.1752
10. Djamila, H.: Analysis of building materials for indoor thermal performance and thermal comfort. Adv. Mater. Res. **845**, 472–476 (2014)
11. Migliore, E.: Porositivity, il design della porosità (2016)
12. Manzini, E.: The Material of Invention: Materials and Design. The MIT Press, New York (1989)
13. Frankel, M., Bekö, G., Timm, M., Gustavsen, S., Hansen, E.W., Madsen, A.M.: Seasonal variations of indoor microbial exposures and their relation to temperature, relative humidity, and air exchange rate. Appl. Environ. Microbiol. **78**(23), 8289–8297 (2012)
14. Gantzer, C., Henny, J., Schwartzbrod, L.: Bacteroides fragilis and Escherichia coli bacteriophages in human faeces. Int. J. Hyg. Environ. Health **205**(4), 325–328 (2002)
15. Gaziulusoy, I., Erdoğan Öztekin, E.: Design for sustainability transitions: origins, attitudes and future directions. Sustainability **11**(13), 3601 (2019)
16. Gantzer, C., et al.: Bacteroides fragilis and Escherichia coli bacteriophages in human faeces. Int. J. Hyg. Environ. Health **205**(4), 325–328 (2002)

17. Ibrahim, E., Shao, L., Riffat, S.B.: Performance of porous ceramic evaporators for building cooling application. Energy Build. **35**(9), 941–949 (2003)
18. Jeon, Y.-S., Chun, J., Kim, B.-S.: Identification of household bacterial community and analysis of species shared with human microbiome. Curr. Microbiol. **67**, 557–563 (2013)
19. Jing, S., Li, B., Tan, M., Liu, H.: Impact of relative humidity on thermal comfort in a warm environment. Indoor Built Environ. **22**, 598–607 (2013). https://doi.org/10.1177/1420326X12447614
20. Jin-Xing, S., Bin, C., Pei-Sheng, L.: Preparation of light weight porous ceramics and sound absorption performance research. J. Inorganic Mater. **31**, 860 (2016). https://doi.org/10.15541/jim20150654
21. Jackson, K.N., Smith, J.A.: A new method for the deposition of metallic silver on porous ceramic water filters. J. Nanotechnol. **2018**, 1–9 (2018). https://doi.org/10.1155/2018/2573015
22. Karana, E., Hekkert, P., Kandachar, P.: Material considerations in product design: a survey on crucial material aspects used by product designers. Mater Des. **29**, 1081–1089 (2008). https://doi.org/10.1016/j.matdes.2007.06.002
23. Karana, E., Hekkert, P., Kandachar, P.: A tool for meaning driven materials selection. Mater Des. **31**, 2932–2941 (2010). https://doi.org/10.1016/j.matdes.2009.12.021
24. Chris, L.: Materials for Design (2013)
25. Li Jiajia, X.L., Zhang, F., et al.: Preparation and application of porous ceramics. In: 18th National Refractories Youth Academic Conference (2022)
26. Lin, K.L., Lee, T.C., Chang, J.C., Lan, J.Y.: Water absorption and retention of porous ceramics cosintered from waste diatomite and catalyst. Environ. Prog. Sustainable Energy **32**(3), 640–648 (2013)
27. Liu, Z., Ma, S., Cao, G., Meng, C., He, B.-J.: Distribution characteristics, growth, reproduction and transmission modes and control strategies for microbial contamination in HVAC systems: a literature review. Energy Build. **177**, 77–95 (2018)
28. Lenau, T.A., Keshwani, S., Chakrabarti, A., Ahmed-Kristensen, S.: Biocards and level of abstraction. In: 20th International Conference on Engineering Design (ICED 2015) Design Society. Milan, Italy (2015)
29. Luo Chenlu, C.W., Zhao, X., Liu, Q., Han, B.: Research on moisture absorption performance of commonly used interior materials. China Residential Facilities **224**(01), 108–109 (2022)
30. Maine, E., Probert, D., Ashby, M.: Investing in new materials: a tool for technology managers. Technovation **25**, 15–23 (2005). https://doi.org/10.1016/S0166-4972(03)00070-1
31. Manzini, E.: Design culture and dialogic design. Des. Issues **32**, 52–59 (2016). https://doi.org/10.1162/DESI_a_00364
32. Mao, Z., Zhang, H., Li, Y., Wang, X., Wei, Q., Xie, J.: Preparation and characterization of composite scallop shell powder-based and diatomite-based hygroscopic coating materials with metal-organic framework for indoor humidity regulation. J. Build. Eng. **43**, 103122 (2021). https://doi.org/10.1016/j.jobe.2021.103122
33. Onozuka, D., Hashizume, M.: The influence of temperature and humidity on the incidence of hand, foot, and mouth disease in Japan. Sci. Total Environ. **410–411**, 119–125 (2011). https://doi.org/10.1016/j.scitotenv.2011.09.055
34. Ormondroyd, G.A., Morris, A.F.: Designing with Natural Materials. CRC Press Taylor & Francis Group, New York (2019)
35. Qi, Y., et al.: Large-scale and long-term monitoring of the thermal environments and adaptive behaviors in Chinese urban residential buildings. Build. Environ. **168**, 106524 (2020)
36. Rai, S., Singh, D.K., Kumar, A.: Microbial, environmental and anthropogenic factors influencing the indoor microbiome of the built environment. J. Basic Microbiol. **61**, 267–292 (2021). https://doi.org/10.1002/jobm.202000575

37. Ramos, T., Stephens, B.: Tools to improve built environment data collection for indoor microbial ecology investigations. Build Environ. **81**, 243–257 (2014). https://doi.org/10.1016/j.buildenv.2014.07.004

38. Rognoli, V., Bianchini, M., Maffei, S., Karana, E.: DIY materials. Mater Des. **86**, 692–702 (2015). https://doi.org/10.1016/j.matdes.2015.07.020

39. Tariku, F., Simpson, Y.: Seasonal indoor humidity levels of apartment suites in a mild coastal climate. J. Archit. Eng. **21** (2015). https://doi.org/10.1061/(ASCE)AE.1943-5568.0000173

40. Tham, S., Thompson, R., Landeg, O., Murray, K.A., Waite, T.: Indoor temperature and health: a global systematic review. Public Health **179**, 9–17 (2020). https://doi.org/10.1016/j.puhe.2019.09.005

41. Turchenko, A., Davydova, T., Spivak, I.: Prospects for the creation of smart homes using energy-saving wall ceramic materials. In: E3S Web of Conferences, vol. 164, p. 02029. EDP Sciences, Les Ulis, France (2020)

42. Vu, D.-H., Wang, K.-S., Bac, B.H.: Humidity control porous ceramics prepared from waste and porous materials. Mater. Lett. **65**(6), 940–943 (2011)

43. Van Houten, F., et al.: Bio-based design methodologies for products, processes, machine tools and production systems. CIRP J. Manuf. Sci. Technol. **32**, 46–60 (2021)

44. Wilkes, S., et al.: Design tools for interdisciplinary translation of material experiences. Mater. Des. **90**, 1228–1237 (2014). https://doi.org/10.1016/j.matdes.2015.04.013

45. Yu, Y.J., Tan, J.G., Wang, H., Lin, C.C.: The effect of relative humidity on physiological equivalent temperature in hot environment. Adv. Mater. Res. **779–780**, 1266–1271 (2013). https://doi.org/10.4028/www.scientific.net/AMR.779-780.1266

46. Yang, G.-B., Cai, X.-H., Qiao, G.-J., Jin, Z.-H.: Fabricating technologies and progress of porous ceramics. Henan Keji Daxue Xuebao (Ziran Kexue Ban)/(J. Henan Univ. Sci. Technol.)(Nat. Sci.)(China) **25**(2), 99–103 (2004). https://doi.org/10.3969/j.issn.1672-6871.2004.02.025

47. Zhang, H., Yoshino, H.: Analysis of indoor humidity environment in Chinese residential buildings. Build. Environ. **45**, 2132–2140 (2010). https://doi.org/10.1016/j.buildenv.2010.03.011

48. Zhang, M.X., Tang, X.J., Zhu, Y.M.: Application of porous ceramic filtration on ballast water treatment. Adv. Mater. Res. **610–613**, 1505–1508 (2012). https://doi.org/10.4028/www.scientific.net/AMR.610-613.1505

49. Zheng, J., Shi, J., Ma, Q., Dai, X., Chen, Z.: Experimental study on humidity control performance of diatomite-based building materials. Appl. Therm. Eng. **114**, 450–456 (2017). https://doi.org/10.1016/j.applthermaleng.2016.11.203

50. Zhengjian, Q.: Handbook of New Ceramic Materials. Jiangsu Science and Technology Publishing House, Nanjing (1995)

51. Zhu Xiaolong, S.X.: Porous ceramic materials. Chin. Ceram. **36**(4), 36–39 (2000)

52. Zocco, M.A., Ainora, M.E., Gasbarrini, G., Gasbarrini, A.: Bacteroides thetaiotaomicron in the gut: molecular aspects of their interaction. Digestive Liver Dis. **39**(8), 707–712 (2007)

Visual Design Checklist for Glucose Monitor App User Interface Usability Evaluation

Chan Juan Tu[✉] and Alessio Russo

University of Gloucestershire, The Park, Cheltenham GL50 2RH, UK
`chanjuantu@connect.glos.ac.uk`

Abstract. Usability Evaluation is used for the graphical user interface of the glucose monitor apps. The interface visual evaluation methodology combines qualitative usability testing and quantitative usability evaluation to present a visual design checklist for the glucose monitor apps. The checklist was evaluated in two stages: the first evaluation phase with a professional designer of human-computer interaction, and the second evaluation phase with diabetes evaluating the product interface. The visual design checklist build, and the MiniMed™ Mobile app was selected as the visual design checklist test product for this study, demonstrated its capacity to assist development teams in meeting usability criteria. In conclusion, the checklist can be a valuable tool for evaluating the user interface of the diabetes apps, hence preventing errors and increasing patient acceptability of the glucose monitor interface overall. The results of the usability evaluation have led to recommendations for inclusive design and design for home medical device interfaces, which contribute to the design of medical product interfaces in a beneficial way.

Keywords: Usability Evaluation · Heuristics · Visual Design Checklist · Glucose Monitor Apps

1 Introduction

Usability is a priority in the product interface development process because it affects the system's acceptability to the user [1], especially for home medical products, where user safety is involved. Researchers have suggested that many available research resources, such as usability standards [2] and usability checklists [3], help this process by providing useful advice to teams during interface development. However, there needs to be more tools and resources specifically designed to aid in the usability assessment of Glucose Monitor Apps testing instrument interfaces. Current checklists frequently concentrate on the system's overall usability, including navigation [4], non-functional qualities [5], and even implementation difficulties. Such checklists are useful for evaluating an interface's general usability, but it may be helpful to have visual checklists specifically for glucose monitor apps that focus on basic visual elements.

© The Author(s), under exclusive license to Springer Nature Switzerland AG 2023
A. Marcus et al. (Eds.): HCII 2023, LNCS 14034, pp. 454–464, 2023.
https://doi.org/10.1007/978-3-031-35705-3_33

This study proposes a visual design checklist for assessing the user interface of glucose meters to bridge this gap. The checklist is based on a structured correlation exercise in which the visual checklist is tested in two stages [6]. The first phase involved gathering feedback from professionals and experts to improve the checklist. The second phase involved collecting feedback on Diabetes mellitus, taking a more practical approach, and analyzing how the checklist contributes to the user's security and satisfaction [7].

This study aims to elucidate the user-centered design of a glucose meter as an illustration for developing a highly usable and accessible usability assessment checklist for medical device interfaces. The visual usability checklist for a positive user experience will also include the following two questions:

- How to reduce the problem of information overload when too many functions are displayed on the interface of commercially available blood glucose me-ters?
- How to reduce the disorientation of diabetic patients who press alarms on the glucose meter interface when they feel discomfort, and how to ensure the effi-cient use of the glucose meter interface?

2 Present Study

The International Organization for Standardization (ISO) published IEC 62366–1:2015: Medical devices - Part 1, Application of usability engineering to medical devices in February 2015 [8]. It specifies procedures for medical device manufacturers to use in analyzing, specifying, developing, and evaluating the safety performance of their products. On the other hand, the user interface should be thoroughly tested and validated in the target audience [9]. In order to establish a visual audit standard for medical product interface specifications, scholars Murilo C. Camargo, Rodolfo M. Barros, and Vanessa T. O. Barros published a paper titled "Visual design checklist for graphical user interface (GUI) evaluation" in 2018 [10]. Our research expands on this work by refining the user interface visual assessment approach and focusing on guidelines for diabetic patients when using glucose monitoring app interfaces, content displays, or specific devices [11].

Heuristic assessment This study combines an expert-led product usability evaluation method proposed by Nielsen and Moclich in the 1990s to find ways to optimize the glucometer interface design process [12]. Furthermore, the study will consider usable product interfaces that correspond to the usage characteristics of the diabetic user community. This study investigates the information elements best suited for glucose monitor apps in the usability evaluation section [13]. It thoroughly investigates user preferences and comprehension. As a result, the usability study will no longer be restricted to particular commercial applications. This study examines the interface design of a glucose meter monitoring app from the perspective of diabetic patients, which will also address the two issues listed below in the visual design checklist (see Appendix A):

- How to reduce the disorientation of diabetic patients who face the blood glucose meter and press the alarm when they have discomfort symptoms to ensure the safety of using the blood glucose monitoring app?
- How to reduce the problem of information overload in the interface?

3 Methods

In this usability evaluation study, a thorough assessment of the user interface of a blood glucose monitoring instrument based on heuristics was d was conducted using heuristics in order to identify potential usability issues and determine how to fix them. This study's methodology included qualitative usability testing, focus groups, questionnaires, card sorting, desirability studies, customer feedback, and Desirability Studies.

Previous qualitative and quantitative research resources can assist interfaces in meeting recommended usability criteria, but medical product interface design tools are lacking. This study proposes a visual design checklist (see Appendix A) for evaluating user interfaces for home medical products to fill this void. The checklist was evaluated in two stages, the first of which included a questionnaire survey of HCI professionals and experts. The second phase involved visiting diabetic patients' homes and inviting them to complete a questionnaire after using the product. The MiniMed™ Mobile app from Medtronic served as the test interface, and its user interface was subjected to heuristic analysis.

Many traditional blood glucose monitors, such as One Touch VerioVue, FreeStyle Libre, Bayer Contour, and others, currently dominate the market, but researchers believe that the future will favor a mobile app approach to monitoring [14]. The MiniMed™ Mobile app was selected as the visual design checklist (see Appendix A) test product for this study because it displays key insulin and CGM data directly on the smartphone, allowing users to understand glucose levels better and view the history of diabetic patients [15].

3.1 The First Phase Usability Evaluation

The interface assessment Criteria consisted of 6 elements subdivided into 37 verification items (see the Table 1), which centered on the evaluation of the glucometer interface and included safety and repair criteria for medical product interfaces (e.g., contrast issues, poor readability, metaphorical failures, standardization issues, lack of overall consistency and uniformity, etc.). Twenty-five interface designers with ages ranging from 20 to 40 years old filled out the visual checklist form. The development team may use the proposed checklist, according to all responders, and all of the listed items are relevant. Table 2 shows the Usability Assessment Test Questions based on the interface evaluation basis.

3.2 The Second Phase Usability Evaluation

To collect feedback on user insights, and insight usability issues, the second qualitative usability testing invited 60 diabetic patients with a questionnaire (see Appendix A for full questionnaire). Patients were divided into three groups, with each group containing an equal number of patients of varying ages. Twenty patients in group A received a printed checklist and were instructed on how to use the blood glucose meter. Twenty patients in group B, who had not received the checklist, were unfamiliar with the meter's use. Twenty patients in group C, who only had a Chinese instruction manual, were instructed to use the meter at home to determine the environmental impact. This task required

Table 1. Interface Evaluation by Criteria.

Elements	Criteria
Color	(a)audience appropriateness; (b) digital environment; (c)continuity; (d)contrast (e)Primary colours;(f)brightness variation/neutral tones
Typography	(a) font definition; (b) suitability for display reproduction; (c) readability; (d) flexibility of use; (e) harmony; (f) suitability for the intended audience; (g) font size; (h) text alignment, line spacing, and column width; and I consistency
UI	(a) use of supporting graphics; (b) iconography; (c) iconographic metaphors; (d) uniformity; (e) rescaling; and (f) consistency
Layout	(a) grid definition; (b) grid flexibility; (c) general layout definition; (d) balance; (e) reading orientation; (f) negative space; (g) system feedback, error notification and help; (h) system positioning and status; and (i) standardization
Pattern	(a) target audience appropriateness; (b) menus and submenus; (c) web best practices; (d) button patterns; (e) visual design; (f) forms and data entry fields; (g) headers, subtitles, and body text; (h) required and optional fields, feedback, error, and assistance messages; and (i) links
Component	(a) harmony; (b) hierarchy; and (c) flexibility

Table 2. Usability Assessment Test Questions.

	Questions
Q1	Is the blood glucose meter application's interface content legible (readable)?
Q2	Is it the information you specify you need to see?
Q3	Is the interface navigate straightforward and user-friendly?
Q4	Is the layout order of the application's user interface apparent?
Q5	Is the interface a pleasure to use?
Q6	Is the organization of the information provided clear?
Q7	Is this APP easy to use?
Q8	Is the APP interface aesthetic?
Q9	Visually, does the interface largely meet your expectations and requirements?

one week to complete. During this time, the groups worked independently to prevent the exchange of information. Afterwards, the researchers gathered feedback from sixty patients and analyzed the interface based on a check list to produce Fig. 2's feedback results.

4 Result

Figure 1 bar graph in blue shows the results of satisfaction survey of interface designers with six elements of the interface of Johnson & Johnson Stable Glucometer, and the bar graph in red shows the results of satisfaction survey of interface designers with six elements of the interface of cell phone app (Health 160, WeChat). The graph shows that satisfaction with the interface of blood glucose meter is generally lower than that of mobile app interface, especially in the parts of color, interface composition and shape, which is related to the lower resolution of blood glucose meter display than cell phone interface. During the survey, the interface designer indicated that the simple interface design provides guarantee to ensure the safety of patients using blood glucose meters, and the interface should not contain irrelevant or unnecessary information, and appropriately increase or strengthen some information to make the main content more prominent.

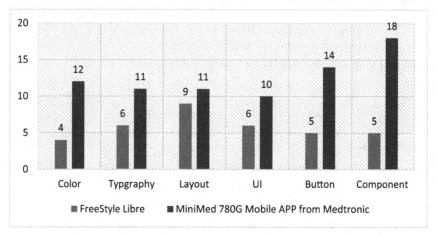

Fig. 1. Satisfaction survey on blood glucose monitor (Freestyle Libre) interface and diabetes app (the MiniMed™ Mobile app) interface.

Based on the facts obtained, group A fared much better than group B. The glucometer had a nice color scheme, accurate font use, only minimal reading concerns, appropriate icon metaphors, replicable layout, use of negative space and feedback system, and pattern definition of static components, according to Group A patients. Group B, on the other hand, failed to fulfill the majority of the evaluation criteria and was only effective in establishing the patterns of static components. With a few exceptions, group C patients were able to utilize the glucometer interface successfully by following the instructions. However, all three groups failed to match the recommended criterion for interactive components (e.g., buttons, links, menus, and forms). We analyzed the three groups stratified by three age stages, as shown in Fig. 2. Older patients had higher requirements for fault tolerance of interface operation, younger patients had higher requirements for visual aesthetics of the interface, and most patients thought that the glucometer interface should follow the principle of minimalist design so as to achieve ease of use.

Summary of the audit form for the use of MiniMed™
Mobile app in patients with diabetes

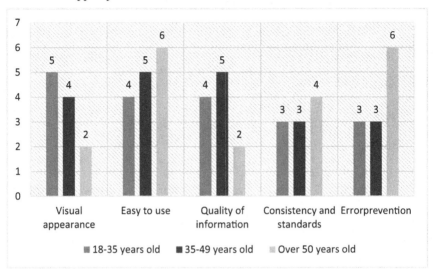

Fig. 2. Summary of the MiniMed™ Mobile app audit form for patients with diabetes.

5   Recording Issues

The above survey has certain defects, for example, in the second stage of evaluation, there is no segmentation for the group of survey users, such as the education, gender and occupation of users. The survey data of different age groups show the standard requirements of the visual interface of the glucose meter for the elderly, and of course the usability of the survey results is high among the middle-aged and elderly people who have a very large proportion of diabetes. A disadvantage of the method is that it sometimes identifies usability problems but provides no direct suggestions on how to address them. The method is influenced by the current mindset of the evaluator and does not usually produce breakthroughs in the design being evaluated. Figure 3 In response to the above evaluator survey data showing usability issues identified by different evaluators of the same glucometer interface, the current information layout of the glucometer interface is more likely to affect its usability than information overload issues.

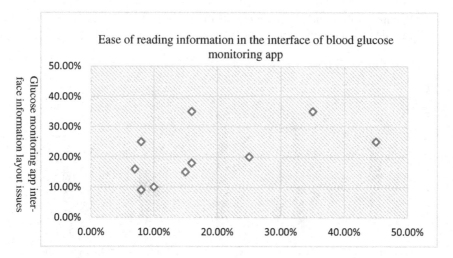

Fig. 3. The proportion of usability problems found by the different evaluators in the same glucose monitor interface.

6 Discussion

Many questions in Appendix A's visual design checklist emphasize interface design principles including rhythm, proportion, contrast, wholeness, harmony, continuity, closeness, continuity, hierarchy, resemblance, closing, and so on. Appropriate design elements and principles aid in meeting usability requirements, which are also considered when developing glucose meter interfaces. Lack of familiarity and poor page layout are two common usability issues in poorly designed glucose monitoring app interfaces. Interface design must create a good "Appearance and familiarity" and assist users in performing tasks, especially for medical monitoring products. Usability criteria such as consistency and standardization, flexibility and user control, feedback, error-proofing, matching the system to the real world, help, and documentation are used to reduce mistakes.

The first stage of the visual design checklist usability test focused on the visual orientation, buttons, information display, color, and other issues of the glucose monitoring app for questioning the type of test. The first stage was the interface designer's test data, and the data was unable to obtain the user's cognition and subjective feeling about the glucose monitoring app. As a result, in the second phase of the visual design checklist usability test for diabetic patients, over 50-year-old adults were easy to prevent errors, and senior patients were less concerned with the visual expression of the product interface and more concerned with whether the interface could effectively view blood glucose data and alert function. as well as notifications. Because senior diabetics constitute the majority of the world's population, development teams could benefit from using these checklists, and the MiniMed™ Mobile app should be designed to simplify the multifunctional approach to optimizing the visual interface of the historical data. This data result applies to all glucose monitoring APP interface usability optimization solutions.

7 Conclusion

This study demonstrates that heuristic evaluation is complicated and that we should rely on more than one person to examine interface results. When multiple experts evaluate heuristics together, the results are much better, and they should do so independently of one another [16]. According to the data, the following design principles for glucometer interfaces should be followed during the interface design process:(1) the principle of rationality, (2) the principle of dynamism; (3) the principle of diversity; and (4) the principle of commonality. The checklist can be a valuable resource for evaluating the user interface of glucose monitor apps, thus preventing errors and improving patient users' acceptance of the entire glucose meter interface. The results and findings of the usability testing led to recommendations for inclusive design and design for glucose monitor apps interfaces that provide useful contributions in targeting the design of medical product interfaces. The results concluded that the development team could gain from adopting the checklist, which would improve the general usability of the interface.

7.1 The Value

The results obtained in this study during two phases of evaluation revealed that using checklists to meet usability criteria yielded positive results. This audit sheet evaluation refers to some of the literature on the principles of ease of use and compares the organizational visual components of the handheld interface, such as colors, lines, shapes, textures, modularity, and grids, to improve the interaction between the diabetic patient and the glucose monitoring device interface.

The value of this study.

1) Helps usability evaluation of blood glucose monitoring device interfaces.
2) Serves as a useful and easy-to-use resource for design teams developing interfaces for blood glucose monitoring devices.
3) Provides control over interaction activities and evaluation.
4) The criterion can be applied to various home medical products and mobile medical interfaces regardless of audience target groups.

7.2 Limitations and Future Studies

This evaluation aims to improve user experience and standardization among development teams while keeping product safety and usability in mind and reducing the psychological stress associated with medical device use. The need for more data on current user experiences with new glucose monitoring systems is a limitation of this study. Glucose monitor apps should be integrated into how users interact with them. The device's perception of the user's immediate "environment" must be considered, and quantitative analysis techniques will become integral to user behavior and user experience research [17].

The future interface will emphasize design principles such as being obvious and simple to understand, having fewer and better components, and refined details [18]. Future work will include the use of checklists in the creation of real-world interfaces in order to analyze the behavior of checklists in adapting to workflows and different software development models. It is also possible to expand the checklist to include mobile interface development, as suggested by assessment experts. The future study will keep improving this checklist to improve the interface design's usability.

Appendix a

Visual Design Checklist for Glucose Monitor Mobile App User Interface
(Source: Developed by the authors, drawing on Microsoft Word, 2023)

Navigation	Compliance			
	Always	Sometimes	Never	Notes
The visibility of the interface state as well as the discoverability of interface information				
Clearly marked home page link				
A mobile app map is accessible if necessary				
The diabetes app interface structure is straightforward, with no extra tiers				
If needed, a simple search option is offered				
Functionality	**Compliance**			
	Always	Sometimes	Never	Notes
Every component is well labeled				
all required functionality is provided				
Clearly display insulin pump and CGM data				
Review your history convent				
Color	**Compliance**			
	Always	Sometimes	Never	Notes
Is the interface color harsh				
The interface overdoes font/color variation				
Text color is inaccessible with enough contrast ratio against the background color				
Typography	**Compliance**			
	Always	Sometimes	Never	Notes
More than 2 or 3 font faces on the interface design				

(*continued*)

(continued)

Navigation	Compliance			
No clear text hlerarchy and reader flow				
Text is legible and isn't too small				

Button	Compliance			
	Always	Sometimes	Never	Notes
Quickly find the alarm button				
Easy to find Insulin pump system notifications				
Clear of Displays of past and current insulin pump and CGM data				
Easy-to-use secondary display				

Content	Compliance			
	Always	Sometimes	Never	Notes
Text is concise, with no needless instructions or welcome notes				
Information is organized hierarchically, form the organization is clear and logical				
Content has been specifically created for the glucose mobile app				
The main titles are straightforward and descriptive				
The most important information is located above the "fold."				
Colors and styles are constant				
Emphasis (bold, italics, etc.) is employed sparingly				
Ads and pop-ups are not intrusive				
The main copy is brief and informative				

References

1. Hix, D., Hartson, H.R.: Developing user interfaces: ensuring usability through product & process: John Wiley & Sons, Inc. (1993)
2. Punchoojit, L., Hongwarittorrn, N.: Usability studies on mobile user interface design patterns: a systematic literature review. In: Advances in Human-Computer Interaction, 2017 (2017)

3. Camargo, M.C., Barros, R.M., Barros, V.T.: Visual design checklist for graphical user interface (GUI) evaluation. In: Proceedings of the 33rd Annual ACM Symposium on Applied Computing, pp. 670–672 (April 2018)

4. Hornbæk, K., Bederson, B.B., Plaisant, C.: Navigation patterns and usability of zoomable user interfaces with and without an overview. ACM Trans. Comput. Hum. Interact. (TOCHI) 9(4), 362–389 (2002)

5. Glinz, M.: On non-functional requirements. In: 15th IEEE International Requirements Engineering Conference (RE 2007), pp. 21–26. IEEE (October 2007)

6. Ji, Y.G., Park, J.H., Lee, C., Yun, M.H.: A usability checklist for the usability evaluation of mobile phone user interface. Int. J. Hum. Comput Interact. 20(3), 207–231 (2006)

7. Mi, N., Cavuoto, L.A., Benson, K., Smith-Jackson, T., Nussbaum, M.A.: A heuristic checklist for an accessible smartphone interface design. Univ. Access Inf. Soc. 13(4), 351–365 (2013). https://doi.org/10.1007/s10209-013-0321-4

8. Follette Story, M.: Medical device human factors standards: finding them and what they contain. In: Proceedings of the Human Factors and Ergonomics Society Annual Meeting, vol. 63(1), pp. 592–596. SAGE Publications, Sage CA (November 2019)

9. Quiñones, D., Rusu, C., Rusu, V.: A methodology to develop usability/user experience heuristics. Comput. Stand. Interf. 59, 109–129 (2018)

10. Camargo, M.C., Barros, R.M., Barros, V.T.O.: Visual Design Checklist for Graphical User Interface (Gui) Evaluation. In: Proceedings of the 33rd Annual ACM Symposium on Applied Computing, Pau, France. Association for Computing Machinery (2018)

11. Whitlock, L.A., McLaughlin, A.C.: Identifying usability problems of blood glucose tracking apps for older adult users. In: Proceedings of the Human Factors and Ergonomics Society Annual Meeting, vol. 56(1), pp. 115–119. SAGE Publications, Sage CA (September 2012)

12. Cafazzo, J.A., Casselman, M., Hamming, N., Katzman, D.K., Palmert, M.R.: Design of an mHealth app for the self-management of adolescent type 1 diabetes: a pilot study. J. Med. Internet Res. 14(3), e2058 (2012)

13. Garrett, J.: . The elements of user experience. Berkeley, CA: New Riders (2011). Nielsen, J.: Designing web usability. Berkeley, Calif.: New Riders (2006)

14. El-Gayar, O., Timsina, P., Nawar, N., Eid, W.: Mobile applications for diabetes self-management: status and potential. J. Diabetes Sci. Technol. 7(1), 247–262 (2013)

15. McVean, J., Miller, J.: MiniMedTM780G Insulin pump system with smartphone connectivity for the treatment of type 1 diabetes: overview of its safety and efficacy. Expert Rev. Med. Devices 18(6), 499–504 (2021)

16. Nielsen, J., Molich, R.: Heuristic evaluation of user interfaces. In: Proceedings of the SIGCHI Conference on Human Factors in Computing Systems, pp. 249–256 (March 1990)

17. Adikari, S., McDonald, C., Campbell, J.: Quantitative analysis of desirability in user experience (2016). arXiv preprint arXiv:1606.03544

18. Gould, J.D., Lewis, C.: Designing for usability: key principles and what designers think. Commun. ACM 28(3), 300–311 (1985)

The Impact of Technology Affordance of Short Videos on Users' Health Information Acceptance: A Study Based on Chinese Short Video Users

Wu Wei[1] and Yunjie Chen[2(✉)]

[1] School of Film Television and Communication, Xiamen University of Technology, Xiamen, Fujian, China
[2] School of Management, Ming Chuan University, Taipei, Taiwan
417167945@qq.com

Abstract. Health communication, as an independent field under communication science, has now gained a huge attention from the society, especially after the COVID-19 pandemic in 2019. On the one hand, human society attaches more and more importance to health, and health information plays an important role in improving people's wellness. On the other hand, with the development of media technology, the channels for health information communication have been constantly broadened. Short videos, as one of the major forms of new media, have been used to disseminate health information. Then, whether the media technology of short videos has an impact on users' experience became the concern of this study. More specifically, this study investigated the correlation between the technological affordances of short videos and the acceptance of health information by Chinese users.

This study adopted a quantitative approach. Through data analysis and structural equation modeling, this study found a positively correlation between technology affordances of short videos and users' experience of health information acceptance. Specifically, the association, visibility, and editability of short videos' technology affordances positively influence users' perceived ease of use and perceived usefulness of health information, and further positively affect users' continuous watching intention of health short videos. Based on these findings, this study suggested more targeted recommendations from a practical perspective.

Keywords: Technology Affordance · Health Information · Technology Acceptance Model · User Experience · Short Video

1 Introduction

Health-related issues have always been in the research field of humans. Ancient philosophers such as Imhotep (Egyptian), Socrates and Aristotle (Greek), and Avicenna (Persian), who also practiced medicine, are to be acknowledged for their contributions to communication that dealt with the health and wellness of their citizens [1]. In the Middle

A. Marcus et al. (Eds.): HCII 2023, LNCS 14034, pp. 465–479, 2023.
https://doi.org/10.1007/978-3-031-35705-3_34

Ages, people attempted to achieve immortality through alchemy, and now people use medical biotechnology to treat and prevent diseases. Human's pursuit and exploration of health reflect the development process of politics, religion, economy, culture, society, science and technology. In recent years, especially after the COVID-19 pandemic in 2019, health has once again attracted worldwide attention. The research on health only focused on the medical field at first, which has gradually attracted attention from more and more disciplines. Nowadays, health-related research has become a multi-disciplinary "crossroad" covering communication, public health, health care, sociology, psychology, social psychology, semiotics, anthropology, education, management, marketing, etc.

Academic research on the relationship between health and communication did not begin until the 1960s, mainly focusing on understanding the relationship between communication and health maintenance or disease prevention [2]. In 1971, the Stanford Heart Disease Prevention Program (SHDPP) implemented by Jack Farquhar (cardiologist) and Nathan Maccoby (communication scholar) at Stanford University was regarded as the threshold of health communication research [3]. At the annual meeting of the International Communication Association (ICA) in 1975, the Therapeutic Communication Interest Group decided to replace "therapeutic communication" with "health communicatio" and established Health Communication Division [4]. In 1988, the first academic journal in the field of health communication was published. Over the development of half a century, health communication has become a key area after the cross-disciplines area and also an important topic in current communication research.

According to Rogers, health communication is any type of human communication whose content is concerned with health [3]. The research on health communication can be roughly divided into six directions, including patient-provider communication [5], health communication campaign [6], mediated health communication [7], crisis/risk communication [8], health communication methodology [9], and new technologies in health communication. In particular, the new technology behind new media such as computers and mobile phones has not only changed the traditional ways people obtain information, but also quickly penetrated into all levels of health communication, such as using new technology to strengthen social support, improving eating habits, enhancing obedience, increasing safety behavior and screening, reducing health risks, and promoting communication between patients, consumers and medical personnel [10]. The influence of media technology on health communication is beyond all doubt.

As one of the main manifestations of the current new technology, short videos have accumulated a large number of users around the world. Taking China as an example, according to the statistics of the China Internet Network Information Center, the number of short-video users in China has exceeded 962 million [11]. Previous studies have shown that new media users in China always obtain health information through short videos [12]. Then, whether the technology format of short videos will affect the acceptance of health communication has become the focus of this research. Thus, this study adopts the perspective of technology affordance in combination with the technology acceptance model (TAM) to take the continuous watching intention of short video users in China as the embodiment of the influence, and discusses the impacts of short videos on health communication.

2 Theoretical Background and Hypothesis Building

2.1 TAM

TAM was put forward by Davis in 1986 and is mainly used to reveal the driving factors for individuals to accept new technology [13]. The original TAM was based on the theory of planned behavior (TPB), which included variables such as perceived usefulness, perceived ease of use, attitude, behavioural intention to use and actual use. The model indicates that perceived usefulness and attitude are are significant factors influencing users' behavioural intention to use new technologies, and attitude will be influenced by perceived usefulness and perceived ease of use, and perceived ease of use can explain the degree of perceived usefulness [14]. In 1996, Davis and Venkatesh thought that although the influence of belief on users' behavioural intention in TPB was all realized through the intermediation of attitude, the empirical researches of TAM showed that attitude could only partially explain the effect of perceived usefulness on intention to use [15]. Therefore, Davis removed the "attitude" from the TAM.

This study retains three key variables in TAM, namely perceived usefulness, perceived ease of use and behavior intention. Specifically, perceived ease of use refers to the degree to which individuals perceive to learn and master a specific new technology, while perceived usefulness refers to the degree to which individuals perceive that a specific new technology helps them improve their personal performance [14]. The positive correlation between perceived usefulness and perceived ease of use and users' acceptance or behavior intention has been substantiated in numerous studies. For example, based on 262 students' use of spreadsheets or calculators, Mathieson concluded that TAM's explanation of intention was 70% [16]; Taylor and Todd took 786 students' use of the computer resource center as the research background, and after three months' investigation, they concluded that TAM's explanation of intention was 52% [17]. Christopher et al. conducted a ten-month survey based on the use of smart cards by 176 businessmen, finding that TAM's explanation of intention was 33% [18]. Through previous research, it can be concluded that TAM has become a powerful simplified model to predict users' acceptance, which can not only predict users' behavior intention of new technology systems, but also study users' acceptance of new technology.

Based on the previous TAM researches, this study believes that perceived usefulness and perceived ease of use will affect users' acceptance of health short videos. At the same time, the degree of acceptance is reflected in the user's intention to continue watching such short videos, because if users do not accept such a way of delivering health information, they will choose not to watch them. Therefore, the following hypothesis is proposed in this study:

H1: Perceived ease of use is positively related to users' continuous watching intention.

H2: Perceived usefulness is positively related to users' continuous watching intention.

H3: Perceived ease of use is positively related to users' perceived usefulness.

2.2 Technology Affordance

Affordance is a basic concept in the ecological psychology founded by Gibson, which emphasizes the "complementarity between organisms and the environment" [19]. Gibson believes that there is objective information in the environment, and it marks the possibility of interaction between the organic bodies and the environment, so the "pickup" of the objective information shall become the main content of psychological research or sensory perception research [20]. With the development of the research, the concept of affordance gradually becomes clear, which emphasizes the relationship between the actor and his environment, the characteristics that the environment has to meet the needs of users [21], and the behavioral possibility provided for the actor [22]. Subsequently, such a concept was introduced into design psychology, information and communications technology and cultural studies. For example, from the perspective of cultural practice, Vyas pointed out that the affordance is not the attribute of artifacts, but a social and cultural relationship between users and artifacts is constructed in the real world, which pays more attention to the active participation and interactive operation of users, thus capturing the positive interactive relationship between users and artifacts [23]. Affordance has made research progress in computer, information interaction, and interface design, and has also been innovated and developed in practice. In terms of new media communication, affordance also has the same opportunities in theory and practice [24]. The technological affordances start from the properties of the digital technology itself. In other words, due to some natural characteristics, digital technology has a special effect affecting people's cognition, attitude, emotion and even behavior, and even some people think that this effect is dominant in many cases [25].

Prior literature has identified several affordances. These include: reviewability, recombinability, and experimentation [26]; persistence, visibility, association, and editability [27]; and network-informed associating, metavoicing, generative role-taking, and triggered attending [28] and have been shown to have different impacts such as organizational knowledge collaboration, socialization, flow of knowledge, power relations, and knowledge sharing [29]. At the same time, according to Treem and Leonardi [27], affordances are confirmed to promote knowledge sharing and transfer [30–32]. Therefore, this study takes association, visibility and editability from Treem and Leonardi's research as the presentation variables of short video availability, and believes that these variables will affect users' acceptance of technology during the use of health short videos.

According to Treem and Leonardi, associations are established connections between individuals, between individuals and content, or between an actor and a presentation [27]. It has been found through past researches that two forms of association affordance exist in social media: the first type of association, of a person to another individual, is most commonly referred to as a social tie; the other form is of an individual to a piece of information. In other words, association affordance refers to the possibility of establishing connections between individuals or between individuals and content [33]. This is consistent with the characteristics of short videos, such a new medium - interactivity. When users browse health short videos on the platform, they can not only see other users' comments on the short video, but also browse other videos of the same type due to the algorithm of the platform. Therefore, this research proposes that:

H4: Association affordance is positively related to users' perceived usefulness.

H5: Association affordance is positively related to users' perceived ease of use.

Visibility, according to Treem and Leonardi, is tied to the amount of effort people must expend to locate information [27]. Leonardi suggested that the consciousness of "who knows what" and "who knows whom" will increase through visibility, thus enabling users to identify experts in relevant fields and acquire related knowledge from other users [34]. Meanwhile, visibility affordance also makes users' behaviors and social information widely known within the organization [31]. And thus drives users to manage their self-presentation through information contribution to create a more favorable impression, which is helpful to gain access to key resources in organizations [35]. According to the findings of previous researches, this study argues that when users are browsing health short videos, they are looking for the experts they believe in from the video posters and commenters, and giving their own views and opinions. Therefore:

H6: Visibility affordance is positively related to users' perceived usefulness.

H7: Visibility affordance is positively related to users' perceived ease of use.

Editability refers to the fact the individuals can spend a good deal of time and effort crafting and recrafting a communicative act before it is viewed by others [36]. Sun et al. suggested that editability affordance allows users to codify their tacit knowledge into explicit knowledge, and also modify or revise content progressively, thus reducing the time and effort to organize and compile knowledge from scratch [29]. Editability can also refer to the ability of an individual to modify or revise content they have already communicated, including straightforward acts such as editing a spelling error or deleting content [37]. Thus, it is a function of two aspects of an interaction: communication formed in isolation from others, and asynchronicity [27]. In health short videos, editability is manifested as the function of users to modify and delete their own comments. At the same time, the published comments can be browsed by other users for a long time (unless the short video is deleted by the posters), so asynchronicity can also be reflected. Therefore, this study proposes that:

H8: Editability affordance is positively related to users' perceived usefulness.

H9: Editability affordance is positively related to users' perceived ease of use.

Based on the above hypotheses, Fig. 1 is the theoretical framework of the present study.

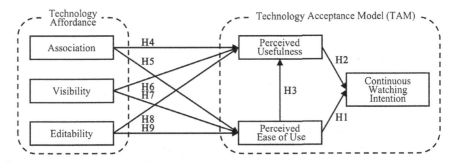

Fig. 1. Proposed theoretical framework

3 Methodology

3.1 Data Collection and Analysis

This study collected data through an online questionnaire. The questionnaire included a question designed to determine whether the respondent had experience in watching health short videos. A total of 350 questionnaires were distributed and 303 valid questionnaires (86.57%) were obtained. After the data collection, the respondents' demographic information was obtained through descriptive analysis. The sample comprised 150 (49.5%) men and 153 (50.5%) women (see Table 1). Exploratory factor analysis was performed to test the reliability and validity of the variables, and structural equation modeling (SEM), completed in AMOS 26.0, was used to determine the confirmatory factor analysis and model fit indices of the theoretical framework.

Table 1. Respondent demographics

Category		Frequency	%
Gender	Male	150	49.5
	Female	153	50.5
Age	Under 30 years old	233	77%
	31–50 years old	59	19%
	Over 51 years old	18	4%
Education	Under Bachelor	111	37%
	Bachelor	172	57%
	Master	12	4%
	Ph.D	8	2%
Monthly income	less than 3000 RMB	90	30%
	3000–5000 RMB	126	42%
	5000–7000 RMB	65	22%
	Over 7000 RMB	22	6%

3.2 Measurements

The questionnaire was developed on the basis of instruments described by other studies (see Table 2). The items were modified to improve their relevance to the problem investigated in this study and adherence to Chinese language habits. Specifically, perceived ease of use and perceived usefulness were measured using scales adapted from Venkatesh and Davis [38]. The scale used to measure intention to continue watchiing was from Davis [14]. The items for association and editability came from Rice et al.'s previous research [39]. And visibility was measured through a scale developed by Treem and Leonardi [27]. A 5-point Likert scale ranging from 1 ("strongly disagree") to 5 ("strongly agree") was used to measure the items of the constructs.

Table 2. Measurement scales

Construct	Measures	References
Perceived Ease of Use (PE)	In my impression, the health short videos are…	(Venkatesh & Davis [38])
	PE1: clear, logical and easy to understand	
	PE2: easy to find	
	PE3: easy to use	
	PE4:simply a way to help me get the knowledge I want	
Perceived Usefulness (PU)	I think that watching health short videos…	(Venkatesh & Davis [38])
	PU1: can increase my knowledge of health	
	PU2: can improve the efficiency of my knowledge acquisition	
	PU3: can accelerate the formation of my health knowledge	
	PU4: is useful to me	
Association (AS)	I think that through short health videos,…	(Rice et al. [39])
	AS1: I am able to connect with other members of the community	
	AS2: I am able to find new knowledge that I did not know or understand	
	AS3: it has enabled me to find other people I didn't know or understand	
Visibility (VI)	I feel that by watching health short videos,…	(Treem & Leonardi [27])
	VI1: it allows me to show others my knowledge about the subject	
	VI2: it allows me to show others my expertise	
	VI3: I am able to attract the attention of specific users in my community	

(*continued*)

Table 2. (*continued*)

Construct	Measures	References
Editability (ED)	In my experience, the process of using health short videos allows me to…	(Rice et al. [39])
	ED1: draft and edit posts before others view them	
	ED2: edit information in a post after it has been published	
	ED3: collaborate with others to create or edit a post	
Continuous Watching Intention (CWI)	In the future, I will…	(Davis [14])
	CWI1: get health information through health short videos	
	CWI2: watch health short videos more often	
	CWI3: recommend other friends to watch health short videos	

3.3 Reliability and Validity

Cronbach's alpha (CA), factor loadings (FLs), composite reliability (CR), and average variance extracted (AVE) were used to test the reliability and validity of the questionnaire (in Table 3). The CA, FL, CR, and AVE values were all within the acceptable range recommended by Hair et al. [40]. In addition, as indicated in Table 4, all square roots of the AVE (in **bold**) for the variables were greater than the intercorrelations of the variables, indicating discriminant validity. To test for common method bias, this study referred to Podsakoff et al. [41] and performed the Harman single-factor analysis [42]. The results revealed that 23.23% of the variance was explained by the first factor, which is lower than the cutoff value of 50%, indicating that this study was not confounded by common method bias.

Confirmatory factor analysis was conducted using AMOS 26.0, and the results are within a widely accepted range ($2/df = 2.079$, RMSEA $= 0.060$, GFI $= 0.907$, CFI $= 0.958$, NFI $= 0.923$, IFI $= 0.958$, TLI $= 0.948$, and AGFI $= 0.874$). All values indicated that model fit indices met the recommended values [43]. Therefore, the construct validity of the questionnaire was acceptable.

3.4 Structural Model

To further explore the correlations between the variables, a structural equation model was developed. The results of the fit indices are presented in Table 5. The results indicated that all model fit indices meet the recommended values [43]; therefore, the structural

Table 3. Reliability and validity

Construct		Loadings	Cronbach's alpha	AVE	CR
Perceived Ease of Use (PE)	PE1	0.81	0.839	0.57	0.841
	PE2	0.754			
	PE3	0.734			
	PE4	0.718			
Perceived Usefulness (PU)	PU1	0.872	0.911	0.72	0.911
	PU2	0.874			
	PU3	0.851			
	PU4	0.794			
Association (AS)	AS1	0.764	0.864	0.69	0.869
	AS2	0.805			
	AS3	0.916			
Editability (ED)	ED1	0.942	0.899	0.77	0.906
	ED2	0.731			
	ED3	0.936			
Visibility (VI)	VI1	0.925	0.944	0.85	0.945
	VI2	0.943			
	VI3	0.9			
Continuous Watching Intention (CWI)	CWI1	0.74	0.785	0.55	0.785
	CWI2	0.731			
	CWI3	0.753			

AVE, Average Variance Extracted; CR, Composite Reliability

Table 4. Mean, standard deviation, and correlation

	M	SD	1	2	3	4	5	6
1.PE	3.186	0.794	**(0.849)**					
2.PU	2.973	0.817	.396**	**(0.755)**				
3.AS	2.683	0.957	.421**	.428**	**(0.831)**			
4.ED	2.934	1.023	.318**	.315**	.270**	**(0.875)**		
5.VI	3.089	1.245	.358**	.261**	.287**	.226**	**(0.923)**	
6.CWI	2.875	0.803	.296**	.367**	.205**	.496**	.220**	**(0.742)**

*p < 0.05, **p < 0.01; PE, Perceived ease of use; PU, Perceived of usefulness; AS, Association; ED, Editability; VI, Visibility; CWI, Continuous watching intention; Bolded values indicate discriminant validity

equation model of this study was determined to have good fit. The β values derived for the proposed framework are presented in Fig. 2.

Table 5. Structural equation model

Fit Indices	Recommended Value	Value
$\chi 2/df$	<3.0	2.329
Root Mean Square Error of Approximation (RMSEA)	<0.08	0.066
Comparative Fit Index (CFI)	>0.90	0.947
Normed Fit Index (NFI)	>0.90	0.912
Incremental Fit Index (IFI)	>0.90	0.948
Tuckere Lewis index (TLI)	>0.90	0.937
Adjusted Goodness of Fit Index (AGFI)	>0.80	0.863

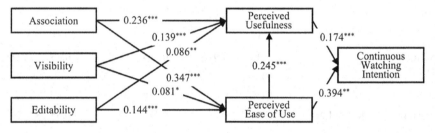

Fig. 2. Proposed framework with β values (*p < 0.05, **p < 0.01, ***p < 0.001.)

The data showed that users' perceived ease of use of health short videos was positively and significantly associated with their continuous watching intention (β = 0.394, p < 0.01). Also, users' perceptions of usefulness were positively and significantly correlated with their intention to continue watching (β = 0.174, p < 0.001). Therefore, H1 and H2 are supported. Furthermore, it was found that perceived ease of use was positively correlated with perceived usefulness during the user viewing experience (β = 0.245, p < 0.001), so H3 was supported. These findings suggested that users' intention to continue watching health short videos increases with their perceived experience with the technology, and also reflected the applicability of TAM in this study.

Regarding technical artifacts, association affordance with respect to health short videos experience was positively related to users' perceived usefulness (β = 0.236, p < 0.001). Thus, H4 was supported. Association affordance for health short videos was positively related to users' perceived ease of use (β = 0.347, p < 0.001). Thus, H5 was supported. In addition, visibility affordance in users' health short videos experience was positively and significantly associated with their perceived usefulness (β = 0.139, p < 0.001). And there is a positively impact in the perceived ease of use (β = 0.081, p < 0.05). Thus, H6 and H7 were supported. In the process of users using health short videos, editability affordance related to technical artifacts were significantly and positively associated with their perceived usefulness and perceived ease of use ($\beta = 0.086$, $p < 0.01$ and $\beta = 0.144$, $p < 0.001$, respectively). Therefore, H8 and H9 were supported. Taken together, the results of the data analysis demonstrated the positive impacts of technology affordance on TAM.

4 Discussion

The results of the data analysis showed that all the hypotheses proposed in this study were valid. The findings revealed that users' perceived ease of use will positively affect their perceived usefulness when they are watching health short videos; both perceived ease of use and usefulness will have a positive impact on the intention to continue watching. This is consistent with previous research findings [44, 45, 46], which indicates the applicability of TAM in the context of health short videos. At the same time, among the affordances of media technology, association, visibility and editability all have a positively influence on users' perceived ease of use and perceived usefulness. In other words, there is a positive correlation between technology affordance and technology acceptance, which verifies the previous related research results [47, 48, 49]. Therefore, during the use of health short videos, users' intention to continue using can be influenced through improving the affordance of technology and intensifying the acceptance of technology.

Based on the findings of this research, some suggestions can be made for the future development of health short videos from a practical perspective. First of all, service providers (including content posters, platform managers, system operators, etc.) need to design simple and easy-to-operate systems as much as possible to enhance users' perception of ease of use. This is because perceived ease of use can positively influence not only users' intention to continue watching, but also their perception of the usefulness of the product. In previous studies, many researchers have suggested improvement schemes for perceived ease of use, such as adding voice assistants [50], defining video titles [51], and ensuring high-quality images [52]. In combination with the findings of technology affordance and technological acceptance, this study can put forward clearer suggestions based on previous schemes.

As one of the first scholars to bring affordance into the field of product design, Norman once explicitly stated that designers should implement the concept of "user-oriented" design: the designer's job involves knowing the psychology of people in relation to how things work [53] to ensure that products can meet the needs and capabilities of target audiences. For example, service providers shall pay attention to the association and editability of short videos, so that users can search for high-quality information and health knowledge during their usage. Besides, the gamification mechanism [54] can be incorporated to encourage users to produce health short videos. It requires the association and editability of short video technology, and needs to take into account the creative needs of user generated content. In a word, the service providers may strive to design features that can afford or expand the association, visibility and editability affordances to increase possibilities for seeking and contributing healthy information using short videos.

Secondly, the service providers of health short videos also need to fully consider the needs of users in order to enhance their perceived usefulness. As suggested in previous studies, this can be started by accurately delivering health information [55], inviting authoritative experts [56], and focusing on the timeliness of users' needs [57]. This study found that the association, visibility and editability of the affordance of the short video technology can make users believe that the health information they have found is useful. Therefore, service providers can encourage users to actively access information through short videos, thus gaining user activity and maintaining the popularity of the platform or application. It is also feasible to use the characteristics of visibility to stimulate users to publish information (short videos, messages, or reposts). For example, it is practical to set specific themes, topics and activities to help promote the cohesion and communication of health knowledge. However, service providers need to strictly supervise the content of health short videos - especially the authenticity and scientificity - to prevent misinformation or meaningless disinformation produced by "content farms" from bringing negative perceptions to users or even having an adverse effect on their health.

Finally, there are some limitations that should be discussed in future study. First of all, the samples in this study are young in age. Although younger individals are usually have a higher acceptance of media technology, they may not pay much attention to health content. Therefore, future stduies can be conducted for the elderly groups. Secondly, the respondents of this study are all Chinese, which has restrictions. This is because people from different cultural backgrounds and social experience will have different understandings of the environment (including the technological context), making the affordance diversified [53]. In the future, the geographical scope of questionnaire distribution can be expanded. Finally, this study only picked association, visibility and editability as the dimensions of technology affordance. In addition to these, persistence [29], portability, availability, locatability, multimediality [49] modality, agency, interactivity and navigability [58], among others have also been used as dimensions in past studies. For the future, a more abundant and diverse composition of dimensions can be investigated to deepen the interpretation and use of technology affordance.

Funding. This Study Was Supported by the High-Level Talent Research Project of Xiamen University of Technology (YSK22019R).

References

1. Parvis, L.: How to benefit from health communication.(Learning from Experience). J. Environmen. Health **65**(1), 41–43 (2002)
2. Liu, Y.: A retrospective of research in health communication. J. Huazhong Univ. Sci. Technol. (Soc. Sci. Edn.) **25**(5), 99–106 (2011). (in Chinese)
3. Rogers, E.M.: Up-to-date report. J. Health Commun. **1**(1), 15–24 (1996)
4. Wang, D.: A review and foresight of health communication research. Soc. Sci. Abroad **5**, 49–52 (2006). (in Chinese)
5. Belle-Brown, J.B., Stewart, M., Ryan, B.L.: Out-comes of provider / patient interaction. In: Thompson, T., Dorsey, A., Miller, K., Parrott, R. (eds.) Handbook of Health Communication. Lawrence Erl-baum Associates, Mahway (2003)

6. Noar, S.M.: A 10-year retrospective of research in health mass media campaigns: where do we go from here? J. Health Commun. **11**(1), 21–42 (2006)
7. Kline, K.N.: A decade of research on health content in the media: the focus on health challenges and sociocultural context and attendant informational and ideological problems. J. Health Commun. **11**(1), 43–59 (2006)
8. Petts, J., Niemeyer, S.: Health risk communication and amplification: learning from the MMR vaccination controversy. Health Risk Soc. **6**(1), 7–23 (2004)
9. Thompson, T.L.: Seventy-five (count'em—75!) issues of health communication: an analysis of emerging themes. Health Commun. **20**(2), 117–122 (2006)
10. Suggs, L.S.: A 10-year retrospective of research in new technologies for health communication. J. Health Commun. **11**(1), 61–74 (2006)
11. China Internet Network Information Center: The 50th Statistical Report on China's Internet Development. http://www.cnnic.com.cn/IDR/ReportDownloads/202212/P020221209344717199824.pdf. Accessed 6 Jan 2023
12. Meng, W.: The hot spots, novelties and trends of new media research in 2021. Contemp. Commun. **1**, 10–14+50 (2022). (in Chinese)
13. Davis, F.D.: A technology acceptance model for empirically testing new end-user information systems: theory and results. Massachusetts Institute of Technology, Massachusetts (1986)
14. Davis, F.D.: Perceived usefulness, perceived ease of use, and user acceptance of information technology. MIS Q. **13**(3), 319–340 (1989)
15. Davis, F.D., Venkatesh, V.: A critical assessment of potential measurement biases in the technology acceptance model: three experiments. Int. J. Hum Comput Stud. **45**(1), 19–45 (1996)
16. Mathieson, K.: Predicting user intentions: comparing the technology acceptance model with the theory of planned behavior. Inf. Syst. Res. **2**(3), 173–191 (1991)
17. Taylor, S., Todd, P.A.: Understanding information technology usage: a test of competing models. Inf. Syst. Res. **6**(2), 144–176 (1995)
18. Christopher, R.P., John, S.H., Vandenbosch, M.: Research report: richness versus parsimony in modeling technology adoption decisions-understanding merchant adoption of a smart card-based payment system. Inf. Syst. Res. **12**(2), 208–222 (2001)
19. Gibson, J.J.: The Ecological Approach to Visual Perception, p. 127. Houghton-Mifflin, Boston (1986)
20. Gibson, J.J.: The Ecological Approach to Visual Perception, p. 239. Houghton-Mifflin, Boston (1986)
21. Hjarvard, S.: Ian Hutchby: conversation and technology. From the telephone to the internet. MedieKultur J. Media Commun. Res. **18**(34), 116–118 (2002)
22. Chemero, A.: An outline of a theory of affordances. Ecol. Psychol. **15**(2), 181–195 (2003)
23. Vyas, D., Chisalita, C.M., Van Der Veer, G.C.: Affordance in interaction. In: Proceedings of the 13th Eurpoean Conference on Cognitive Ergonomics: Trust and Control in Complex Socio-Technical Systems, pp. 92–99 (2006)
24. Jing, Y., Shen, J.: Introduction and expansion of the concept of new media affordance. Contemp. Commun. **1**, 92–95 (2019). (in Chinese)
25. Chang, J.: The Internet, technological affordance and the emotional public. Youth J. **25**, 92 (2019). (in Chinese)
26. Faraj, S., Jarvenpaa, S.L., Majchrzak, A.: Knowledge collaboration in online communities. Organ. Sci. **22**(5), 1224–1239 (2011)
27. Treem, J.W., Leonardi, P.M.: Social media use in organizations: exploring the affordances of visibility, editability, persistence, and association. Ann. Int. Commun. Assoc. **36**(1), 143–189 (2013)

28. Majchrzak, A., Faraj, S., Kane, G.C., Azad, B.: The contradictory influence of social media affordances on online communal knowledge sharing. J. Comput.-Mediat. Commun. **19**(1), 38–55 (2013)
29. Sun, Y., Wang, C., Jeyaraj, A.: Enterprise social media affordances as enablers of knowledge transfer and creative performance: an empirical study. Telematics Inform. **51**, 101402 (2020)
30. Ellison, N.B., Gibbs, J.L., Weber, M.S.: The use of enterprise social network sites for knowledge sharing in distributed organizations: the role of organizational affordances. Am. Behav. Sci. **59**(1), 103–123 (2015)
31. Evans, S.K., Pearce, K.E., Vitak, J., Treem, J.W.: Explicating affordances: a conceptual framework for understanding affordances in communication research. J. Comput.-Mediat. Commun. **22**(1), 35–52 (2017)
32. Oostervink, N., Agterberg, M., Huysman, M.: Knowledge sharing on enterprise social media: practices to cope with institutional complexity. J. Comput.-Mediat. Commun. **21**(2), 156–176 (2016)
33. Pee, L.G.: Affordances for sharing domain-specific and complex knowledge on enterprise social media. Int. J. Inf. Manage. **43**, 25–37 (2018)
34. Leonardi, P.M.: Ambient awareness and knowledge acquisition. MIS Q. **39**(4), 747–762 (2015)
35. Van Osch, W., Steinfield, C.W.: Strategic visibility in enterprise social media: implications for network formation and boundary spanning. J. Manag. Inf. Syst. **35**(2), 647–682 (2018)
36. Walther, J.B.: Impression development in computer-mediated interaction. Western J. Commun. (Includes Commun. Rep.) **57**(4), 381–398 (1993)
37. Rice, R.E.: Computer-mediated communication and organizational innovation. J. Commun. **37**(4), 65–94 (1987)
38. Venkatesh, V., Davis, F.D.: A theoretical extension of the technology acceptance model: four longitudinal field studies. Manage. Sci. **46**(2), 186–204 (2000)
39. Rice, R.E., Evans, S.K., Pearce, K.E., Sivunen, A., Vitak, J., Treem, J.W.: Organizational media affordances: operationalization and associations with media use. J. Commun. **67**(1), 106–130 (2017)
40. Hair, J.F., Gabriel, M., Patel, V.: AMOS covariance-based structural equation modeling (CB-SEM): guidelines on its application as a marketing research tool. Braz. J. Market. **13**(2), 169–183 (2014)
41. Podsakoff, P.M., MacKenzie, S.B., Lee, J.Y., Podsakoff, N.P.: Common method biases in behavioral research: a critical review of the literature and recommended remedies. J. Appl. Psychol. **88**(5), 879 (2003)
42. Harman, H.H.: Modern Factor Analysis. University of Chicago Press, Chicago (1976)
43. Arpaci, I., Baloğlu, M.: The impact of cultural collectivism on knowledge sharing among information technology majoring undergraduates. Comput. Hum. Behav. **56**, 65–71 (2016)
44. Nikou, S.: Factors driving the adoption of smart home technology: an empirical assessment. Telematics Inform. **45**, 101283 (2019)
45. Gefen, D., Straub, D.W.: The relative importance of perceived ease of use in IS adoption: a study of e-commerce adoption. J. Assoc. Inf. Syst. **1**(1), 8 (2000)
46. Saadé, R., Bahli, B.: The impact of cognitive absorption on perceived usefulness and perceived ease of use in on-line learning: an extension of the technology acceptance model. Inf. Manag. **42**(2), 317–327 (2005)
47. Tsai, J.P., Ho, C.F.: Does design matter? Affordance perspective on smartphone usage. Ind. Manag. Data Syst. **113**(9), 1248–1269 (2013)
48. Mao, C.M., Hovick, S.R.: Adding affordances and communication efficacy to the technology acceptance model to study the messaging features of online patient portals among young adults. Health Commun. **37**(3), 307–315 (2022)

49. Schrock, A.R.: Communicative affordances of mobile media: portability, availability, locatability, and multimediality. Int. J. Commun. **18**(9), 1229–1246 (2015)
50. Wang, M., Zeng, F.: Research on APP design of short video learning for the elderly based on user acceptance. Packag. Eng. **43**(4), 203–209 (2022). (in Chinese)
51. Kui, Q., Wang, L., Liu, Y.: Study on the factors of short video's influence on users' willingness to purchase books. China Publish. J. **6**, 8–14 (2020). (in Chinese)
52. Guo, H., Zhao, Y., Shi, H.: Research of the influence of short-form video display on customers' purchase intention on the E-commerce platform. Inf. Stud. Theory Appl. **42**(5), 141–147 (2019). (in Chinese)
53. Norman, D.A.: The Psychology of Everyday Things. Basic Books, New York (1988)
54. Suh, A., Wagner, C.: How gamification of an enterprise collaboration system increases knowledge contribution: an affordance approach. J. Knowl. Manag. **21**(2), 416–431 (2017)
55. Chen, Y., Pan, P.: Investigation on factors influencing perception of information usefulness of health short videos. J. Mod. Inf. **41**(11), 43–56 (2021). (in Chinese)
56. Zhang, D., Chen, Y., Wang, M.: Expectation and confirmation: a preliminary study on the factors influencing the continuous use of short video platforms - based on SEM and fsQCA. Mod. Commun. (J. Commun. Univ. China) **289**(9), 133–140 (2020). (in Chinese)
57. Zhao, X.: Research on the factors influencing users' willingness to participate in advertising on short video platforms. China Market **1111**(12), 27–30 (2022). (in Chinese)
58. Sundar, S.S.: The MAIN model: a heuristic approach to understanding technology effects on credibility. In: Metzger, M.J., Flanagin, A.J. (eds.) Digital Media, Youth, and Credibility, pp. 73–100. The MIT Press, Cambridge (2008)

A New Process Framework for Managing the Fuzzy Front End of New Healthcare Device Development

Fan Yang, Zhen Qin[✉], Min Lin, and Wa An

Guangzhou Academy of Fine Arts, 168 Waihuan Xilu, Higher Education Mega Center, Panyu District, Guangzhou, China
antony4d@hotmail.com

Abstract. Building on our pervious paper that concluded the poor usability of existing healthcare devices was largely attributed to the design innovation management issues occurring in the front-end stage of development cycles, the efforts in this study were devoted to develop a logically coherent framework managing the front-end activities in new healthcare device development. The conceptual foundation of this new process framework was laid from an investigation upon current healthcare device development practices, that was undertaken by surveying and interviewing twenty-eight company staff leading product innovations at five manufacturers. The proposed framework is outlined in three levels of definitions i.e., stages, implementation strategies, and output, to make the framework more prescriptive and easier to follow. There are six main stages i.e., requirements, project verification, project planning, designing, design solution verification, and preparation for implementation. Main development activities in each stage have been nailed down; and strategies driving the implementation of some key activities are also provided, to facilitate the enforcement of the whole process. The new framework maintains both the linear structure and the common development activities applied by the manufacturers in this study, thus users of the framework will not need to invent a complete new system in practice. While maintaining necessary flexibility to adapt to individual features of specific projects, the proposed framework gives a level of control to the fuzzy front end of healthcare device innovation processes.

Keywords: Innovation Management · Product Design · The Management Process · Healthcare Device

1 Background

1.1 Definition of the Front-End Stage

So far, there is neither a universally acceptable definition on the front-end stage of a new product innovation, nor is there a dominant framework to guide the activities in this stage. Researchers and practitioners use 'Phase 0', 'Stage 0', or 'Pre-Project-Activities'

The original version of this chapter was revised: Spelling errors in the names of two authors have been corrected and the acknowledgement section has been updated. The correction to this chapter is available at
https://doi.org/10.1007/978-3-031-35705-3_40

A. Marcus et al. (Eds.): HCII 2023, LNCS 14034, pp. 480–491, 2023.
https://doi.org/10.1007/978-3-031-35705-3_35

to make the same point. The front-end stage is generally described to begin when the project opportunity is firstly considered worthy of further ideation, exploration, and assessment; and to end when it is signed off to enter the subsequent development stages [e.g., 1–4].

Constant iteration and flow is the hallmark of the front-end activities including project initiation, product design, and design research (Koen et al. 2002). These complex, intuitive and reflective activities lead on to the chaotic, unpredictable and unstructured natures of the stage, in contrast with the typically structured and predictable subsequent development process. Thus, the front-end stage is also known as 'Fuzzy Front End (FFE)'. In literature, this term was early popularised by Reinertsen & Smith [1] in their book 'Developing products in half the time', and has been more widely recognised in recent years. In this paper, we adopt the term FFE, and further clarifies it to consist product development activities including Opportunity Identification, Selection and Assessment; Project Planning; Product Definition, Strategy Formulation and Communication; Design Idea Generation; and Design Concept Development (Fig. 1).

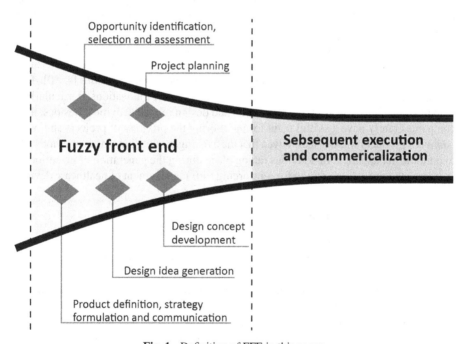

Fig. 1. Definition of FFE in this paper.

1.2 The Need for Reinforcing the FFE Management

The FFE stage of the overall procedure of developing a new product is the best opportunity to influence the product itself [5]. Existing researches have pointed out that FFE can consume up to 50% of development time [1]; and the decisions made during this stage affect 70% of the overall project cost [5]. Poor FFE management often lead to costly design modifications and other critical mistakes occurring in the later stages of projects, as well the total cycle time of product development and commercialization [4].

As a critical component of the FFE, product designing is also a 'fuzzy' process that involves iterative feedback loops among member from various corporate divisions like R&D, marketing, operations, and manufacturing. The team members embarking on designing are often unsure of their destinations, as well as the paths they are taking. While synthesising solutions to satisfy the given requirements from project leaders and/or clients, designers also produce questions and additional needs reflecting their evolving interpretations of the design tasks, building upon unexpected discoveries. Imprecision, ambiguity and abstraction characterise this continuous process of disclosing information and searching for insights to solutions [6]. However, the widely referenced product innovation methods, such as the Stage-Gate® Innovation method and the PACE® method, tend to focus only on the development activities occurring when the generation of invention has completed, and hence do little to guide the execution of the FFE activities, in particular, the designing process. The models of designing [e.g., 7, 8], on the other hand, tend to rely too much on intuition and experience; and are still ambiguous and fragmented [9].

The healthcare device sector is dominated by Small and Medium-sized Enterprises (SMEs) that are typically under resourced, or believe that they themselves are under resourced, to carry out front-end research and product designing activities [4, 10]. They generally lack skills and experience to embark on product innovations, particularly in planning, managing, and executing research and design related activities. Besides, these companies rarely have a skilful team for monitoring the progress of projects and/or the quality of products and services. Given that the existing product innovation methods tend to omit the management of activities taking place during the generation of inventions, it is essential to provide a solution for reinforcing FFE management of healthcare devices.

1.3   Research Context and Purpose

Our previous work [11] identified that the poor usability of existing healthcare devices was largely attributed to the design innovation management issues occurring in the FFE of development cycles. The issues were centralised in the two areas i.e., the sources of data, and the application of data. They led to ineffective team work during projects, and false and /or insufficient user input into the creation of final design solutions. In regard of this, our efforts in this study were devoted to create a FFE explicit, logically coherent, and cost-effective approach that aids project team members in both obtaining credible and effective data, and properly applying the data in product de-signing as well as the subsequent innovation stages. This paper presents a new FFE management framework driving the process of developing new healthcare devices, and also elaborates its conceptual foundations. This framework pays particular attention to reinforcing the ways of acquiring, processing, and delivering FFE data. Besides, it attempts to stimulate reflection, conversation, and achieving a better ideation.

2 Method

In Regard of the revelatory ability of qualitative methods, particularly the social scientific tradition of using qualitative data in investigating complex issues regarding new product development [e.g., 12–15], we opted for a mix of quantitative and qualitative methods, leaning more towards the latter. The innovation management approaches of six healthcare device manufacturers (including the two involved in the previous study [11]) based in the three Chinese cities i.e., Guangzhou, Shenzhen, and Nanjing were investigated by combining a survey with follow-up interviews. The selected participants were the twenty-eight company staff actively participating in or having critical influences on the FFE i.e., thirteen senior product/project managers, three innovation directors/consultants, four design engineers, three sales managers, and one quality manager. The survey questions were developed based on the results from our previous study [11], and were extensively piloted to establish the conceptual foundations from which a new process framework was then established. The questions contained multiple choice, yes/no answer questions, and longer qualitative questions, although these were limited to maintain a sufficient response rate and prevent fatigue effects. The follow-up interviews remove any ambiguity in the survey results and ensured the validity of information. Then, The collected data was analysed thematically by both the first author and the second author, as defined by Braun and Clarke [16].

3 The Conceptual Foundation

Building on the lessons learned from the previous study, this paper further synthesised the FFE process issues in healthcare product innovations into five groups: (i) the need of a formal tool for managing the FFE; (ii) the need for systematic FFE research; (iii) the need for formal design briefing; (iv) the need for governing project data centrally; and (v) the need for governing project data centrally.

3.1 The Need of a Formal Tool for Managing the FFE

Our results showed that there was a lack of formal governance of healthcare device development procedures. Only three of the six manufacturers had established their own principal product development process frameworks to guide everyday innovation practices. Even for the three manufacturers having formal development processes, the research participants indicated that the models were frequently and randomly modified in practices; and this issue was centralised in the front-end stage of projects (79%, n = 15).

As described by Achche & Appio [17], new design innovation project commonly rolls out without a clear definition or analysis of the process to go from opportunity identification to concepts; and the team embarking on the project is unsure of its destination and the path it is taking at the beginning. Along the way, the team will uncover new information that requires changing direction and often backtracking. Although the FFE is complex, intuitive and reflective, and the iterative feedback loops within the process may not be amenable to project management techniques, a level of structure and control is necessary, to ensure quality and to reduce risks.

Existing researches have revealed that successful product innovations usually go through calculated processes from concept to launch [e.g., 18–20]. For example, the Product Development & Management Association (PDMA) has sponsored best practice research projects since 1990, to identify trends in product innovation management practices and to discern which practices are associated with higher degrees of success. Their studies conclude that formal processes for new product development are now the norm – a total of 69% of the reporting firms indicate use of formal, cross functional process for NPD [5].

3.2 The Need for Systematic FFE Research

Almost all of the participants (93%, n = 26) said that the devices they developed were tagged as 'user friendly' or 'user based' when being brought onto the market. However, as recalled by the participants, the development teams rarely carried out any systematic front-end research with the purpose of gaining a deep understanding of the target audience's behaviours, habits, abilities, or any other factors that contributed to the designing process. Even when the users were involved in some of the projects, but only in the later stages and with the purpose of taking finalised design concepts forward into engineering; moving established prototypes forward into production; or delivering ready products onto the market.

The six manufacturers in the study tended to be reluctant in carrying out FFE research and design activities to disclose these factors. Around seventy-five percent (n = 21) selected 'not motivated' (n = 21); twenty-one percent were neutral; and only four percent (n = 1) selected 'motivated'. The participants further pointed out that the development of new healthcare devices was driven mainly by customer demands, new technologies, and legislation and regulation changes. Among these factors, customer demands were believed by the leaders of the manufacturers to be most common and influential (82%, n = 23).

Ironically, customer demands do not necessarily reflect the factors influencing the usability of the end-devices. The users of medical devices and the device buyers are frequently two distinct groups, unlike other industries like automobile and electronics. For example, the decision of purchasing a MRI scanner is often made by the board of a hospital or a public sector, not the medical practitioners operating the device (direct users) or the patients taking medical examinations (indirect users). As a result, most of the participants believed that the major influential factors determining the commercial success of medical device manufacturers was a company's relationship with the public sector and/or the government (79%, n = 2). The other success factors incorporate other key stakeholders in the supply chain, business flexibility, and added value and services to products. None of the participants included design-related FFE activities like user research and design contract management into the list.

It needs to be noted that healthcare device innovations are perplexed by the human factors and environmental factors that emerge during the use of the devices. For example, motor restriction can disrupt the users' ability to perform simple functions on a product interface, such as turning a knob, moving a slider, or pushing a button; visual decline may prevent them from reading check-up results or following colour indicator. While complex hospital medical devices are generally used in a controlled and supportive milieu, home healthcare devices were used in heterogeneous, unpredictable and uncontrolled household and community settings. The potential for errors, and the accidents that result, are ever present. Therefore, design-related research occurring in the front end is essential, to ensure that development teams give full attention to factors influencing the performance of final products.

3.3 The Need for Formal Design Briefing

None of the six companies' principal process model elaborated when and how to create design briefing documents, and by whom. This fact partially explained why only twenty-one percent (n = 6) of the participants deemed design briefing as a critical part of the whole development processes. A design brief is a documents that clarifies the scope of a design assignment and sets the plan of the design process. Engaging in design briefing provides designers, design commissioners and other stakeholders with an essential opportunity to communicate at the start of a project cycle. This aids designers in properly understanding the problems that they are requested to solve. An effective briefing process requires key stakeholders to reach a consensus on the fundamental questions of a task, and hence helps to everyone aligned with the same understanding throughout a project cycle.

The participants indicated that all of the six companies in this study relied on subtracting the design process to an external designer or a design team in the majority of the projects. This manner of developing new products further reinforces the need of engaging in a robust design briefing process. This is because that external designers are less likely than the design commissioner's own staff to be aware of the company's history, culture, business strategies, product lines, and technical abilities. The briefing process is essential in bridging the gaps in communication between the two parties.

3.4 The Need for Governing Project Data Centrally

There was a common lack of effective governance of project information in medical device development, as suggested in our previous paper [11]. This point was affirmed in this study. According to the participants, two of the six manufacturers did not manage the information from different projects centrally. Four of the manufacturers established their own company drives to store project information. However, in only two of the manufacturers, company central drives were used routinely. For the rest, team members preferred to user their own project folders in managing project information.

Any FFE output contributes to the design of the end-product on the premise that valuable information can safely reach the users of information, and be properly applied in downstream applications. Poor management erodes data quality and credibility, thus hinders creativity and leads to errors in later stages of development.

Issues were also present in the area of data format. Important information like the project briefing documents were presented and communicated in nonstandard and random formats i.e., a template, an interactive presentation, an email, or even a verbal agreement. Such information was too 'loose' to define the whole project, and led to inconsistency between team members as well as company divisions. Without central governance, project information is often fragmented and difficult to trace. This create difficulties for device maintenance, support services and future device upgrades. Besides, Knowledge and insights gained from individual projects can serve as reference data that is supportive to other/future projects.

3.5 The Need for Greater Stakeholder Engagement

Most project/product managers surveyed were not motivated to engage more stakeholders during project cycles (85%, n = 11). The primary cause as explained by these managers was that greater engagement would consume more resources during the enforcement of a project process. This 'demerit' of engaging greater stakeholders is immediate and manifest while any profit would only become apparent over time.

On the other hand, many existing studies have revealed that the designing of effective healthcare devices requires interdisciplinary stakeholder participation that can involve medical practitioners, psychologists, end user patients, project/product managers, designers, researchers, engineers, marketers, sales person, service engineers, and architects [e.g., 21–23]. The lack of knowledge and skills in other disciplines can strangle creativity and produce problems in decision making, which is likely to lead to ordinary solutions, loop-backs in the project cycle or even the failure of the project. For example, a medical engineer having an idea of using a touch screen to replace the conventional interface of a computed tomography may not realise that the motion of pressing physical buttons helps to prevent mistakes in operating the device. Similarly, a product designer may not be aware of the recent development of fibre sensors, and hence did not take this technology into considerations when designing a household heart failure monitor.

As a result, how to enable cost-effective cooperation between team members who think, work and communicate by different methods, and often lack understanding of other, presents a challenge to development process management.

4 The New FFE Framework

4.1 An Introduction to the Framework

In this section, we propose a new framework that illustrates how the FFE of general healthcare product development cycles can be constructed to facilitate ideation, information discovery, information application, and product designing.

As illustrated in Fig. 2, the framework comprises three levels of definition; with the first containing six main stages, the second containing nineteen development activities, the third containing some strategies supporting the enforcement of the corresponding activities, and the fourth contacting the process output.

The six main stages of the framework are 'requirements', 'project verification', 'project planning', 'designing', 'design solution verification', and 'preparation for implementation'.

(i) **Requirements:** The first stage, is to explore potential project opportunities or to define a given product development task by collecting, analysing and synthesising information of different types. To ensure that essential information is not omitted, the proposed development activities in this stage incorporate 'market positioning & segmentation', 'user study', 'regulatory requirements', 'competitor analysis', and 'self-assessment'. Building on this information the project proposal document would be established, and the information contributes to the overall project cycle.

(ii) ***Project verification:*** In this screening stage, a project proposal will be handed over to the company's board for assessment. It decides whether the proposal will become a real project.

(iii) ***Project planning:*** This stage sets the course of the whole project. It is composed of four proposed activities, namely 'internal communication', 'forming project team', 'project briefing', and 'design briefing'. Given that the briefing processes have been found to be poorly executed, the framework specifies the criteria to be applied for project briefing i.e., 'design fit', 'market fit', and 'business fit'. It further suggests considering whether the contents of a project brief meet the design fit requirement from the viewpoints of 'user fit', 'cultural fit', 'customer fit', and 'brand fit'; market fit from 'Saleability'; and business fit from 'economic feasibility', 'marketing & advertising fit', and 'technical feasibility'. The output of project briefing should include the documents of project plan, commercial specification, and procurement specification. To ensure the establishment of an effective design brief, the framework determines several essential activities, i.e., 'market segmentation & positioning', 'user study', 'regulatory requirements review', 'competitor review', and 'self-assessment'.

(iv) ***Designing:*** This stage is composed of 'design commissioning' and 'design iteration'. Design commissioning is described in the framework as a separate and formal component, to ensure that proper resources are allocated to reaching mutual understanding and agreement on the design task between the design commissioner and the designer. This activity leads on to two important documents defining the designing process i.e., the design contract and the design specification. Design iteration is the process where design concepts are created.

(v) ***Design solution verification:*** To select the most appropriate design concept and to decide whether the concept is mature enough to be implemented, the development team is requested to engage on 'design validation', 'technical review', and 'manufacturing validation'. In order to properly validate the concept(s) from the design perspective, the framework determines the three criteria i.e., 'aesthetics', 'functionality', and 'feasibility'. It further suggests considering functionality from the following facets: 'brand fit', 'user fit', and 'cultural fit'; and feasibility from 'economic feasibility', 'technical feasibility', 'manufacturability', and 'saleability'. Design concept(s) approved in this screening stage will be tagged as the final design solution, and then enter the subsequent implementation stages.

(vi) ***Preparation for implementation:*** This stage wraps up the FFE process. To prepare for implementing the design solution, the proposed activities include, but not limit to, 'engineering', 'supply chain development', 'manufacturing preparation', and 'supply chain development'.

It needs to be noted that this theoretical framework should be adjusted in practice, based on individual projects' features. For example, the criteria to evaluate a radical design concept will differ from those applied to assess incremental innovations; and the use of a very flexible structure may decrease the operation efficiency while a too linear and rigid process is likely to restrict the creativity and flexibility required for radical innovations. Certain stages and development activities outlined in the framework can be simplified accordingly.

Stages (Level 1)	Activities (Level 2)	Implantation Strategies (Level 3)	Output
Requirements	Market positioning & segmentation		1. FFE data 2. Project proposal
	User study		
	Regulatory requirements		
	Competitor analysis		
	Self-assessment		
Project Verification	Project review		Project contract
Project Planning	Internal communication		
	Forming project team		
	Project briefing	1. Design fit (User fit, Cultural fit, Customer fit, Brand fit) 2. Market fit (Saleability) 3. Business fit (Economic feasibility, Marketing & advertising fit, Technical feasibility)	1. Project plan 2. Commercial specification 3. Procurement specification
	Design briefing	1. Market segmentation & positioning 2. User study 3. Regulatory requirements 4. Competitor review 5. Self-assessment	Design brief
Designing	Design commissioning		1. Design contract 2. Design specification
	Design iteration		Design concept(s)
Design Solution Verification	Design validation	1. Aesthetics 2. Functionality (Brand fit, User fit, Cultural fit) 3. Feasibility (Economic feasibility, Technical feasibility, Manufacturability, Saleability)	The final design solution
	Technical review		
	Manufacturing Validation		
Preparation for Implementation	Engineering		
	Supply chain development		
	Manufacturing preparation		
	Supply chain development		

Fig. 2. An illustration of the new FFE process.

4.2 Features of the Framework

Compared with the existing innovation management models, our FFE process framework has some salient features:

- This logically coherent framework focuses explicitly on the FFE stage of the new product development process; and is based on the conceptual foundation that has been developed through studying the healthcare device sector.
- This framework gives a level of structure to the 'fuzzy' front end phase of new product innovations, while maintains necessary flexibility to adapt to individual features of specific projects. This helps to ensure that critical, limited resources are allocated to the product opportunities of most importance to the business, and to reduce the overall time to market of new technologies and the products they enable.
- The framework is outlined in three levels of definitions (stages, implementation strategies, and output), to make the framework more prescriptive and easier to follow.
- It has been recognised that, without defining the activities of each stage of the framework, it would be difficult for the framework to be implemented in either a live design project or an experimental workshop [24]. Thus, in addition to the basic structure consisting of six stages, main activities in each stage have been nailed down; and strategies driving the implementation of some key activities are also provided. This facilitates the enforcement of the whole framework.
- The framework maintains the common development activities applied by the manufacturers in this study. Besides, the framework is structured in a linear fashion, given that the manufacturers in this study were organised in a traditional hierarchical 'family tree' data governance; and their present new product development processes tended to be established in the nature of the widely used stage-gate process. Thus, the users of the framework do not need to invent a complete new system in practice.
- It supports the management of the design process by pining down the briefing activities; and also by elaborating how to review the project progress from a design perspective. This design-oriented framework helps to enforce design considerations throughout the traditionally technology-driven healthcare device development projects.
- In the execution of some key activities, the corresponding implementation strategies require valid input from different company divisions. This can enable alignment, synchronisation and integration across the whole project team, and hence promotes intimate collaboration between stakeholders at the start of a project.
- It is not only a design problem-solving guideline, but also a project management tool, since it both addresses the general factors that directly influence the design of a new healthcare device and the factors in other areas e.g., verifying project opportunities.

4.3 Limitations and the Next Step

The conceptual framework presented in this paper helps in improving people's understanding about the FFE stage of healthcare device development, and also provides a solution for improvement. Besides, it can serve as a theoretical foundation for the future design research.

The study is based on relatively small-sized sample, and the framework has not yet been tested in real projects. Some future work will be to evaluate this framework with a broad range of manufacturers in the healthcare device sector, and more experts from the companies. In light of the results the framework will be revised, and then put into evaluation in real healthcare device development projects. Afterwards, some computer-based tools may be developed to enable the adoption of the framework in every day product innovation practices.

Acknowledgements. This study was funded by the grant 'Research on Usability Testing Methods of Health and Medical Devices (23XSC11)' provided by Guangzhou Academy of Fine Arts. The funding source had no role in the design of the study and collection, analysis, and interpretation of data and in writing the manuscript.

References

1. Reinertsen, D.G., Smith, P.G.: The strategist's role in shortening product development. J. Bus. Strateg. **12**(4), 18–22 (1991)
2. Khurana, A., Rosenthal, S.R.: Towards holistic "front ends" in new product development. J. Prod. Innov. Manag. **15**(1), 57–74 (1998)
3. Kim, J., Wilemon, D.: Focusing the fuzzy front–end in new product development. R&D Manag. **32**(4), 269–279 (2002)
4. Yang, F., Renda, G.: The design briefing process matters: a case study on telehealthcare device providers in the UK. Disabil. Rehabil. Assist. Technol. **14**(1), 91–98 (2019)
5. Koen, P.A.: The fuzzy front end for incremental, platform and breakthrough products and services. In: PDMA Handbook, pp. 81–91 (2004)
6. Visser, W.: Designing as construction of representations: a dynamic viewpoint in cognitive design research. Hum. Comput. Interact. **21**(1), 103–152 (2006)
7. Beitz, W., Pahl, G., Grote, K.: Engineering Design: a Systematic Approach, 2nd edn. Springer, London (1996)
8. Suh, N.P., Suh, N.P.: Axiomatic Design: Advances and Applications, vol. 4. Oxford University Press, New York (2001)
9. Chen, Y., Zhao, M., Xie, Y., Zhang, Z.: A new model of conceptual design based on Scientific Ontology and intentionality theory. Part II: The process model. Des. Stud. **38**, 139–160 (2015). https://doi.org/10.1016/j.destud.2015.01.003
10. The Department for Business Innovation and Skills-GOV.UK: Strength & Opportunity - the Landscape of the Medical Technology, Medical Biotechnology and Industrial Biotechnology Enterprises in the UK (2010). https://www.gov.uk/government/uploads/system/uploads/attachment_data/file/31810/10-p90-strength-and-opportunity-bioscience-and-health-techno logy-sectors.pdf. Accessed 4 Sept 2017
11. Yang, F., Wang, L., Ding, X.: Why some "User-Centred" medical devices do not provide satisfactory user experiences? An investigation on user information factors in new device development processes. In: Soares, M.M., Rosenzweig, E., Marcus, A. (eds.) HCII 2022, pp. 314–324. Springer, Cham (2022). https://doi.org/10.1007/978-3-031-05897-4_22
12. Glaser, B.G., Strauss, A.L., Strutzel, E.: The discovery of grounded theory; strategies for qualitative research. Nurs. Res. **17**(4), 364 (1968)
13. Kumar, S., Wallace, C.: Among the agilists: participant observation in a rapidly evolving workplace. Paper presented at the Proceedings of the 9th International Workshop on Cooperative and Human Aspects of Software Engineering, Austin, Texas (2016)

14. Strauss, A., Corbin, J.: Basics of Qualitative Research: Techniques and Procedures for Developing Grounded Theory. Sage, Thousand Oaks (1998)
15. Yang, F., Al Mahmud, A., Wang, T.: User knowledge factors that hinder the design of new home healthcare devices: investigating thirty-eight devices and their manufacturers. BMC Med. Inform. Decis. Mak. **21**(1), 166 (2021). https://doi.org/10.1186/s12911-021-01464-3
16. Braun, V., Clarke, V.: Using thematic analysis in psychology. Qual. Res. Psychol. **3**(2), 77–101 (2006). https://doi.org/10.1191/1478088706qp063oa
17. Achiche, S., Appio, F.: Fuzzy decision support in the early phases of the fuzzy front end of innovation in product development. Portland State University (2010). http://pdxscholar.library.pdx.edu/cgi/viewcontent.cgi?article=1031&context=etm_fac. Accessed 20 Aug 2022
18. Booz, A.: New Product Management for the 1980s, 1st edn. BAH, New York (1982)
19. Cooper, R.G.: Predevelopment activities determine new product success. Ind. Mark. Manage. **17**(3), 237–247 (1988)
20. Griffin, A.: The effect of project and process characteristics on product development cycle time. J. Mark. Res. **34**(1), 24–35 (1997)
21. Vandenberg, A.E., et al.: Making sense of DialysisConnect: a qualitative analysis of stakeholder viewpoints on a web-based information exchange platform to improve care transitions between dialysis clinics and hospitals. BMC Med. Inform. Decis. Mak. **21**(1), 1–13 (2021)
22. Agouridas, V., Marshall, A., McKay, A., de Pennington, A.: Establishing stakeholder needs for medical devices. In: International Design Engineering Technical Conferences and Computers and Information in Engineering Conference 2006, pp. 541–551 (2006)
23. Coulentianos, M.J., Rodriguez-Calero, I., Daly, S.R., Burridge, J., Sienko, K.H.: Medical device design practitioner strategies for prototype-centered front-end design stakeholder engagements in low-resource settings. In: Proceedings of the Design Society: International Conference on Engineering Design 2019, vol. 1, pp. 957–964. Cambridge University Press (2019)
24. Macmillan, S., Steele, J., Austin, S., Kirby, P., Robin, S.: Development and verification of a generic framework for conceptual design. Des. Stud. **22**(2), 169–191 (2001)

Applying Motivational Interview in Designing a Pulmonary Rehabilitation Unit

Fan Yang, Rusheng Li[✉], and Chunhui Zhang

Guangzhou Academy of Fine Arts, No. 257, Changgang East Road, Haizhu District, Guangzhou, China

787389088@qq.com

Abstract. Although pulmonary rehabilitation has been well-recognized and recommended by the medical sector as an effective treatment to control and even prevent Chronic Obstructive Pulmonary Disease (COPD), a generally low level of compliance across patients taking pulmonary rehabilitation often prevents the program from delivering satisfactory outcome in practice. Motivational interviewing (MI) is frequently used as a directive, client-centered counselling style to promote adherence to treatment in patients with COPD. This study explored the effectiveness of MI in eliciting the real needs and requirements of patients with COPD, as required to create design inventions with satisfactory usability.

In the first stage, twenty patients with COPD were interviewed. The interviewees were randomly divided into a control group and an intervention group of 10 each. The control group (n = 10) underwent an unguided interview, while the intervention group (n = 10) was interviewed using the MI technique. The results were analyzed using comparative analysis. The number of effective answers acquired from the intervention group was significantly larger than those from the control group. In the second stage, a conceptual pulmonary rehabilitation unit was designed based on the user insight established from the interviews results. This unit was then tested with the interviewees and three physicians, and received positive feedback. This pilot study showed that MI aided the designers in establishing rich and credible insights into patients with COPD, by disclosing user information that traditional interview techniques tended to omit. It also provided a reference for on how to apply MI results properly in new product inventions.

Keywords: Product design · Interview Technique · Chronic obstructive pulmonary disease · Pulmonary rehabilitation · User insight

1 Introduction

Chronic obstructive pulmonary disease (COPD) is a significant cause of increased chronic morbidity and mortality worldwide. According to Adeloye et al.'s assessment of global, regional, and national COPD prevalence and risk factors, the global prevalence of COPD among people aged 30–79 years was 10.3% in 2019 [1]. COPD is expected to be the third leading cause of morbidity and mortality worldwide by the end of 2030, yet this serious problem remains unnoticed by the general public [2]. Today, COPD has

© The Author(s), under exclusive license to Springer Nature Switzerland AG 2023
A. Marcus et al. (Eds.): HCII 2023, LNCS 14034, pp. 492–503, 2023.
https://doi.org/10.1007/978-3-031-35705-3_36

become a more significant drain on health resources than asthma, not only because of the patient's lung disease but also because the disease, usually caused by smoking, often requires patients to receive multiple medications and long-term treatment [3]. Pulmonary rehabilitation is a non-pharmacological intervention that usually consists of exercise training, education, and psychosocial/behavioral components to increase patients' functional exercise capacity and quality of life [4]. In pulmonary rehabilitation programs, breathing exercises are often used as an intervention in the treatment of patients with COPD. Studies have shown that pulmonary rehabilitation programs such as respiratory retraining and chest physiotherapy for COPD patients can improve dyspnoea, functional exercise capacity, and HRQL [5]. To help patients train more accurately, therapists also use relevant medical products to assist with treatment. For example, in the study by (Almen et al., 2014), the NI LABVIEW-Based Breathing Trainer with Biofeedback and Plethysmography was used to guide patients through correct breathing exercises and monitor their pulse rate to help them keep track of their condition [6]. However, these medical devices are highly specialized, and it is challenging to complete breathing exercises without the guidance of a healthcare professional. There is, therefore, a need to explore the development of medical products to meet the therapeutic needs of this group. This paper will focus on the needs of people with COPD for respiratory training and explore the real needs of users, which are needed for the innovation of related medical products.

In the past, user interviews were typically used to obtain user information and explore user needs in the design process, in which the interviewer communicates directly with the interviewee to obtain the interviewee's relevant experience and psychological demands. The advantage of this method is that the interviewer can listen directly to the user's inner feelings and understand more about their psychological motivations. However, a disadvantage is that the interviewer can easily deviate from the interview topic [7]. In the study conducted by Han Yancui et al. (2021), a combination of the 'interview method and guided narrative' was used to help the interviewer return to the topic and guide the interviewee into a deeper narrative to obtain more useful information if the interview deviates from the topic or the research is not deep enough [8]. Miller introduced Motivational Interviewing (MI) in 1983 [9]. It is a vehicle for mapping out a personal plan for behavior change based on patient preferences and priorities that can help them become aware of their ambivalence about their behaviors and motivates them to make a behavioral change [10]. Initially, MI was mainly used to treat patients with alcohol addiction, and as it developed, MI was also applied to the treatment of COPD. Many studies have reported significant effects of MI in promoting self-efficacy, lung function, quality of life and reducing COPD-related hospitalizations in COPD patients [11]. Moreover, it has been found to be effective in improving medication adherence in adults with chronic disease [12]. In contrast, less attention has been paid to the effectiveness of MI in eliciting the real needs and requirements of COPD patients and collecting information from users. Such in-depth user research is needed to design relevant medical products.

Therefore, this study introduces the theory of MI to collect patients' demands in a guided consultation approach. As a guided interview method, it allows for a more comprehensive, objective, and clear understanding of the user and builds mutual understanding and trust, which is difficult to achieve with the traditional interview method. In order to gain a clearer understanding of how MI collects information from its users, this study will focus on two main areas of validation: comparison of interview information and the design of product solutions. It is hoped that the motivational interviews will not only yield potential information about the users that cannot be obtained from other interview methods, but will also lead to valuable conclusions for the design of a breathing exercise product that meets the real needs of the users and provides a reference for the innovation of related medical products.

2   Methods

2.1   Interviews with the Patients with COPD

The study population consisted of treated COPD patients in a stable stage at Nanhai People's Hospital, Guangdong Province, China, with diagnostic criteria by the Guideline for the Diagnosis and Treatment of COPD [13]. The participants were randomly divided into a control group and an intervention group of 10 cases. Inclusion criteria were the ability to communicate verbally, care for themselves, and an understanding on how to perform breathing exercises. People with severe cognitive impairment (e.g., Alzheimer's disease) and a history of related medical conditions that may affect their understanding of the content of the interview, were excluded from the study. Additionally, demographic aspects such as age, gender, education level, and smoking status of both groups of patients were not counted in the statistical analysis.

We used an interview sheet containing ten yes/no questions and four open-ended questions for the control group. Meanwhile, we used a motivational interviewing method for the intervention group, with open-ended questions, affirmations, reflective listening, and summaries as the core of the interview. Initially, to fully understand and gain the patient's trust, we encouraged them to express their views and opinions on breathing training, e.g., 'How do you feel about breathing training?'. Appropriate guided interventions were needed if the interviewees' answers strayed from the topic during the interview. After getting to know each other, we explained respiratory rehabilitation and disease information to interviewee willing to do breathing training. Finally, we gave feedback to interviewee on what we had heard to ensure that the information came from them and to help them resolve their ambivalence.

In order to be able to compare the effectiveness of the two interview methods in eliciting the patients' real needs, the intervention group was asked the same four open-ended questions as the control group. The research questions used to understand users' needs for respiratory rehabilitation training were RQ1: 'What are the difficulties you encounter in your usual treatment/rehabilitation training?' and RQ2: 'What kind of help would you like to get when doing rehabilitation exercises?'. To avoid limiting user responses to aspects of respiratory rehabilitation training, we extended the research questions to the entire stage of the patient's treatment (RQ3: What do you feel is most needed in the current stage of treatment?). We also asked users about their expectations of treatment products (RQ4: What kind of products would you like to have to complement your treatment?). At the end of the interview, data were collected and compared between the open-ended questions of the two groups. We grouped responses with similar meanings into one category to extract keyword representations. Then multiple response frequency cross-analysis was used to compare the frequency of responses between the two groups. For data processing, we used the SPSS 26.0 statistical package for data analysis. The chi-square test was used to compare the frequency of responses to the open-ended questions between the two groups ($p < 0.05$ was considered statistically significant).

2.2   The Design Experiment and Evaluation

Based on the initial findings from the first stage of interviews, a design concept for a pulmonary rehabilitation unit was derived. We used this conceptual design solution to verify the accuracy of the interviewees' needs collected by MI. In the second stage, we translated the answers with a higher frequency of interviewee responses into design requirements, which guided the development of the design program. With this design experiment, our goal was not to present a distinctive design but to examine whether the MI could support the design decisions for the relevant medical product. In the third stage, we undertook an evaluation of the conceptual design of a new household intelligent breathing trainer, with reference to the study undertaken by Yang and Al Mahmud [14]. Firstly, we created a satisfaction rating scale for this conceptual design, with a rating scale ranging from 1 (for 'very negative') to 5 (for 'very positive'), with higher scores indicating approval and lower scores indicating doubts about the concept. Interviewees were then shown the product's interactive interface and functional modules and asked to rate them. The ratings were made among 20 respondents and three doctors.

3   Results

3.1   Results from the Interviews

Table 1 reports the control group's responses to the ten yes/no question visit sheets. Eighty percent of these patients were unaware of breathing training, but all (100%) indicated they were willing to try them. In addition, 70% of all patients reported that they could not perform breathing training without supervision and could not ensure the training was correctly performed. 80% of patients said they could not actively observe and evaluate the effects of breathing training. They all wanted guidance on breathing exercises (100%) and were willing to share their training methods with others (70%).

The frequency of the two groups of patients answering the four open questions and the response rate of each option were as follows (Table 2). The frequency of responses was higher in the intervention group than in the control group, 105 versus 78, with a statistically significant difference ($p < 0.05$). The results indicated that the intervention group collected more valid user information in the interviews than the control group. In the first question (RQ1), the main difficulties encountered by patients with rehabilitation exercises were not knowing how to treat them and frequent review, with a response rate of 7.7%, the highest value for this dimension. In the second question (RQ2), the most important thing patients wanted to receive during rehabilitation was professional guidance and communication about their condition, with the highest response rate of 6.6%. In the third question (RQ3), the highest response rate was 5.5% for patients most needing knowledge about the disease at the time of treatment. However, it is worth noting

Table 1. Frequency analysis of the ten yes/no questionnaires

Questions	Options	Frequency (%)	Average	Standard deviation
1. Do you know anything about pulmonary rehabilitation?	Yes	6 (60%)	1.40	0.52
	No	4 (40%)		
2. Do you know anything about breathing training?	Yes	2 (20%)	1.80	0.42
	No	8 (80%)		
3. Would you like to try breathing training?	Yes	10 (100%)	1.00	0.00
	No	0 (0%)		
4. Are you willing to spend at least 20 min a day on breathing training?	Yes	6 (60%)	1.40	0.52
	No	4 (40%)		
5. Are you able to perform breathing training unsupervised?	Yes	3 (30%)	1.70	0.48
	No	7 (70%)		
6. Are you able to ensure that your breathing training are regular?	Yes	3 (30%)	1.70	0.48
	No	7 (70%)		
7. Are you able to actively observe and evaluate the effects of your breathing training?	Yes	2 (20%)	1.80	0.42
	No	8 (80%)		
8. Would you like guidance on breathing training?	Yes	10 (100%)	1.00	0.00
	No	0 (0%)		
9. Would you like to share your training method with others?	Yes	7 (70%)	1.30	0.48
	No	3 (30%)		
10. Do you seek medical help when you encounter difficulties in training?	Yes	6 (60%)	1.40	0.52
	No	4 (40%)		

that the intervention group also mentioned the need for supervision and companionship, and encouragement, information that the control group did not mention. In the fourth question (RQ4), patients were asked what they wanted in addition to medication, and they felt that products for complementary treatment should be portable (7.1%).

3.2   The Conceptual Design of a New Household Intelligent Breathing Trainer

The results of the interviews showed that most patients had a strong desire to do breathing training but did not know how to carry them out. Therefore, our design goal mainly focused on the guidance of breathing training. In addition, the MI interviews revealed

Table 2. Frequency of responses in the two groups before and after the intervention

Open questions	Keywords (options)	Control group	Intervention group	Response rate	results
RQ1	Difficulty in finding medical care	5	4	4.90%	$x^2 = 36.692$ $P = 0.004$
	How to treat	7	7	7.70%	
	Frequent review	8	6	7.70%	
	Complex training tasks	3	7	5.50%	
	Psychological problems	0	7	3.80%	
RQ2	Professional guidance	5	7	6.60%	
	Communicate	7	5	6.60%	
	Training advice	4	6	5.50%	
RQ3	Understanding your health	6	2	4.40%	
	Good Mindset	5	4	4.90%	
	Disease Awareness	6	4	5.50%	
	Diet advice	5	1	3.30%	
	Supervision	0	9	4.90%	
	Companionship	0	9	4.90%	
RQ4	Effective drugs	8	9	9.30%	
	Portable Products	6	7	7.10%	
	Multifunctional	3	5	4.40%	
	Expectorant products	0	6	3.30%	
Total		78	105	100.00%	

that the patients were most interested in being supervised and accompanied by others during the treatment to motivate them to complete the exercises. Taking these results together, we have devised the design requirements into four groups: 1) visual breathing guidance function for completing training programs; 2) adding the patients to establish a training program with real-time reminders and supervision; 3) recording training data to exchange information and adjust the training program; 4) portability. In the following step, we applied these design requirements to the design of the household intelligent breathing trainer and showed how it had been derived.

Feedback modality has been shown to influence a person's learning behavior, with audio-visual feedback being more effective than auditory feedback when learning intonation [15]. Similarly, audio-visual feedback was critical to providing user guidance when designing a breathing training product with guidance. In France, Gila Benchetrit designed a breathing exercise device that collects breathing signals and guides the subject through respiratory rehabilitation exercises based on graphics [16]. Such visual feedback of breathing signals effectively guided the user through the breathing training. After referring to Dong and Liu's research [17], the user's breathing values and rhythm were a form of visual presentation in our design solution, in addition to voice guidance. When the user exhales through the breathing trainer, the product terminal interface displays the current user's exhalation value and training phase (see Fig. 1). To differentiate between the user's exhalation and the guidance signal, we used different colors to indicate this, with the blue progress bar in the inner circle indicating the user's current breathing signal and the colored progress bar in the outer ring being the breathing guidance signal. In this case, the user has to try to exhale in rhythm with the guidance signal; the higher the exhalation value, the faster the progress bar will be, and vice versa. When the user's breathing rhythm coincided with the guidance signal, there was a feedback signal for the user (see Fig. 2). Because in many breathing training studies, different breathing training has differences in the control of time and rhythm [18]. Therefore, the visual signal presentation could significantly help users understand their breathing state and guide them to control the proportion of breathing time and breathing rhythm.

Fig. 1. Visualization of the user's exhalation values and training phases

Setting specific guidelines for goals could improve goal attainment while minimizing patient and provider frustration [19]. Factors we obtained from the MI interviews that influenced users to discontinue breathing training were a lack of both an understanding of how to conduct the training and specific guidelines to follow. If specific guidelines were important for patients to engage in breathing training, what needs to be done to get patients involved? Firstly, patients needed to complete a CAT score in the product in the form of a questionnaire to determine the severity of their current illness. Moreover, an appropriate breathing training program with an online doctor assessment (see Fig. 3) could help patients to establish short and long-term training goals with real-time

Fig. 2. Visualization of the user's exhalation values and training phases

reminders and monitoring. At the same time, the user could view their daily training schedule and the current status of completed and uncompleted items in the product interface and be constantly reminded by voice to continue completing their goals (see Fig. 4).

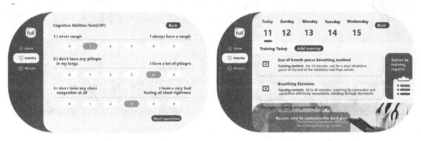

Fig. 3. User CAT scoring and training program development

Fig. 4. Users' task completion

In information management, each time the user uses the product, data such as the number of breathing exercises, duration of the training, and lung capacity values were recorded to provide further guidance. Such data can also be shared with family members and a dedicated doctor (see Fig. 5). In order to meet the patient's need for portability, we designed the product appearance with the proportional size of the product in mind. After extensive testing, we finally printed a 1:1 model of the product. (see Fig. 6).

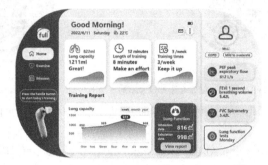

Fig. 5. Back-office data management for users

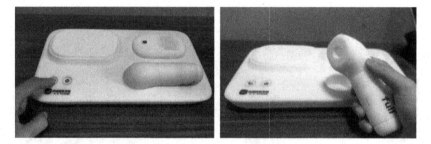

Fig. 6. Product models (product base, respiratory trainer, lung function tester)

3.3   The Evaluation of the New Household Intelligent Breathing Trainer

Our user evaluation aimed to provide information on the availability and satisfaction of home breathing training systems for people with COPD [20]. Therefore, we presented the conceptual design to three specialists treating chronic respiratory disease to obtain feedback. One of the experts stated that the concept was designed as a product to assist patients with breathing training, just like a family doctor. In his opinion, the breathing trainer with visual feedback was very suitable for patients to understand the status of their training and for patient guidance during breathing training. Another expert expressed a positive attitude towards intelligent data management, believing that data recording could provide valuable information to patients and doctors about disease treatment. However, the accuracy of the measurements needs to be studied in depth.

Table 3 shows the results of our satisfaction survey of 20 patients with three doctors. On a 5-point scale, the mean overall satisfaction score for the conceptual design program was 3.6 (SD = 0.64). Visualization guidance function averaged 4 (SD = 0.77); training plan development averaged 3.4 (SD = 1.03); and training data management averaged 3.4 (SD = 0.73).

Table 3. Conceptual design scheme satisfaction scores

	N	Minimum	Maximum	Average	Standard deviation
Q1: Visual guidance	23.00	3.00	5.00	4.0	0.77
Q2: Training program development	23.00	2.00	5.00	3.4	1.03
Q3: Training data management	23.00	3.00	5.00	3.4	0.73
Overall satisfaction	23.00	2.67	5.00	3.6	0.64

4 Discussion and Conclusion

4.1 The Interview Results

Our results showed that MI could significantly improve the interviewees' motivation in providing effective answers, and aid researchers in capturing the interviewees' latent needs that the interviewees themselves might not be aware of. This could be attributed to two factors. Firstly, during the unguided interview, the interviewees had less time to provide answers, less opportunities to communicate with the interviewees, and received less guidance, compared with the motivational interview. Secondly, through conducting motivational interviewing, we obtained much more responses, thus could achieve a better understand of the patient's psychological ambivalence. For example, when using motivational interview to find out what were the difficulties the research participants encountered in usual treatment/rehabilitation exercises, the research participants mentioned difficulties in finding medical services and psychological problems such as low self-esteem and anxiety due to a lack of knowledge about the disease and the financial burden on the family.

There was variability in the information obtained from the two groups of patients interviewed. This variability was not only in the amount of information obtained but also in the type of information obtained. Among the patients of Unguided interviews, their requests for treatment were more in the areas of appropriate medication/diet and knowledge of the disease. For those who received the MI interview, their treatment requests were more psychological, such as the companionship and encouragement of others. Patients with COPD are often asked to do breathing rehabilitation exercises in addition to taking medication, but these exercises are usually dull and often lead to a lack of motivation to complete them. Therefore, the companionship and encouragement of others are vital to maintaining their training. All in all, motivational interviewing provides us with more valuable user information during the design process.

4.2 The New Household Intelligent Breathing Trainer

The concept product we designed using MI interviews was also used for the first evaluation by medical professionals and related patients. Almost all participants in the program satisfaction survey indicated that they would like to use the product to assist them with breathing training. In addition, the conceptual design of household intelligent breathing trainers has certain technical issues but has a positive effect on the satisfaction of patients' needs. For example, we visualized breathing values and rhythm in response to the need for breathing training guidance, and this was assessed as very appropriate and helpful. This visual representation significantly reduced the cognitive load on the patients for breathing training and made the patients more willing to participate. In the subsequent development of the program, we tried to address patients' need for companionship and supervision, thus setting up functions such as breathing training program development and training task reminders. However, these functions seem only to meet the patients' need for reminders and supervision during training, not the psychological needs of patients for companionship.

In this study, we conducted separate unguided and MI technique interviews in patients with COPD to assess the effectiveness of MI in gathering the information needed to design COPD-related medical devices. The results showed that more interviewees' responses were collected from the intervention group, and most interviewees in the satisfaction survey for the conceptual design program agreed that the design program addressed their current needs for breathing training. We also described how the interviewees' needs obtained from the motivational interview guided design decisions, resulting in a three-part household intelligent breathing trainer consisting of training guidance, training program development, and data management.

Through the research in this paper, the MI interview method could help designers gain insight into the needs of people with COPD, which was difficult to achieve with traditional interview techniques. MI interview method mainly avoided the problems of inaccurate and imperfect data collection. Overall, as a pilot study, this paper should be used in conjunction with the results of other studies to help guide the design of products related to the development and stimulate future in-depth studies of MI in the design field.

Acknowledgment. The authors would like to express their sincere thanks to the participants and staff of the study. This study was supported by the Department of Education of Guangdong Province (Grant 2020GXJK135), and Grant 2020KZDZX1136. The funding sources had no role in the design of the study and collection, analysis, and interpretation of data and in writing the manuscript.

References

1. Adeloye, D., Song, P., Zhu, Y., Campbell, H., Sheikh, A., Rudan, I.: Global, regional, and national prevalence of, and risk factors for, chronic obstructive pulmonary disease (COPD) in 2019: a systematic review and modelling analysis. Lancet Respir. Med. **10**(5), 447–458 (2022). https://doi.org/10.1016/S2213-2600(21)00511-7
2. Wen, D., Wang, Z., Ma, X., Xian, B.: The worldwide progress of health related quality of life instruments for chronic obstructive pulmonary disease patients. J. China Med. Univ. **42**(3), 281–285 (2013)
3. Chapman, K.R., et al.: Epidemiology and costs of chronic obstructive pulmonary disease. Eur. Respir. J. **27**(1), 188–207 (2006). https://doi.org/10.1183/09031936.06.00024505
4. Hill, N.S.: Pulmonary rehabilitation. Proc. Am. Thorac. Soc. **3**(1), 66–74 (2006). https://doi.org/10.1513/pats.200511-121JH

5. Güell, R., et al.: Long-term effects of outpatient rehabilitation of COPD. Chest **117**(4), 976–983 (2000). https://doi.org/10.1378/chest.117.4.976
6. Almen, M.J.T.: NI LABVIEW-based breathing trainer with biofeedback and plethysmography. In: TENCON 2014–2014 IEEE Region 10 Conference, pp. 1–4 (2014)
7. Yang, F., Al Mahmud, A., Wang, T.: User knowledge factors that hinder the design of new home healthcare devices: investigating thirty-eight devices and their manufacturers. BMC Med. Inform. Decis. Mak. **21**(1), 166 (2021). https://doi.org/10.1186/s12911-021-01464-3
8. Han, Y., Jiang, K., Luo, T.: Feasibility study of combined application of survey methods: a case study of intergenerational communication design research. Design **34**(1), 111–113 (2021)
9. Rollnick, S., Miller, W.R.: What is motivational interviewing? Behav. Cogn. Psychother. **23**(4), 325–334 (1995). https://doi.org/10.1017/S135246580001643X
10. Droppa, M., Lee, H.: Motivational interviewing a journey to improve health. Nursing **44**(3), 40–45 (2014). https://doi.org/10.1097/01.NURSE.0000443312.58360.82
11. Wang, C., Liu, K., Sun, X., Yin, Y., Tang, T.: Effectiveness of motivational interviewing among patients with COPD: a systematic review with meta-analysis and trial sequential analysis of randomized controlled trials. Patient Educ. Couns. **105**(11), 3174–3185 (2022). https://doi.org/10.1016/j.pec.2022.07.019
12. Zomahoun, H.T.V., et al.: Effectiveness of motivational interviewing interventions on medication adherence in adults with chronic diseases: a systematic review and meta-analysis. Int. J. Epidemiol., dyw273 (2016). https://doi.org/10.1093/ije/dyw273
13. Wang, F.Y., Zhang, D.Y., Liang, Z.Y., Su, G.S., Zheng, J.P., Chen, R.C.: Interpretation of guideline for the diagnosis and treatment of COPD (2021 revision) for general practitioners. Chin. Gen. Pract. **24**(29), 3660–3663+3677 (2021)
14. Yang, F., Mahmud, A.A.: Issues in evaluating the user performance of new home medical devices: a field test of two devices produced by a leading provider. J. Des. Res. **16**(3–4), 196–213 (2018)
15. De Bot, K.: Visual feedback of intonation I: effectiveness and induced practice behavior. Lang. Speech **26**(4), 331–350 (1983)
16. Calabrese, P., et al.: A simple dynamic model of respiratory pump. Acta. Biotheor. **58**(2), 265–275 (2010). https://doi.org/10.1007/s10441-010-9108-7
17. Dong, Z., Liu, L., Li, W.: The interaction design of household intelligent breathing training system. In: Marcus, A. (ed.) DUXU 2016. LNCS, vol. 9748, pp. 309–318. Springer, Cham (2016). https://doi.org/10.1007/978-3-319-40406-6_29
18. Sharma, P., Thapliyal, A., Chandra, T., Singh, S., Baduni, H., Waheed, S.M.: Rhythmic breathing: immunological, biochemical, and physiological effects on health. Adv. Mind Body Med. **29**(1), 18–25 (2015)
19. Filoramo, M.A.: Improving goal setting and goal attainment in patients with chronic noncancer pain. Pain Manag. Nurs. **8**(2), 96–101 (2007). https://doi.org/10.1016/j.pmn.2007.03.005
20. Siering, L., Ludden, G.D., Mader, A., van Rees, H.: A theoretical framework and conceptual design for engaging children in therapy at home—the design of a wearable breathing trainer. J. Personalized Med. **9**(2), 27 (2019)

Whether Kangaroo Care Can Be Performed by a Device? A Conceptual Incubator Designed for Preterm Infants

Fan Yang, Chunhui Zhang[⊠], and Rusheng Li

Guangzhou Academy of Fine Arts, No. 257, Changgang East Road, Haizhu District, Guangzhou, China
260685587@qq.com

Abstract. According to the statistics of the World Health Organization (WHO), preterm infants account for 10% of all newborns on average globally. The developmental care method Kangaroo Care (KC), also known as 'Extra Contact', was first introduced by Edgar Rey and Hector Martinez in 1983. This intervention has been proven to provide many parent-infant benefits, such as parent-infant attachment, input for the infant's developing brain and more stable breathing. However, the need of the presence of both infants and their parents in the same environment can barely be realized in the NICU environment, thus greatly restricts the application of traditional KC in practice. The question arises: whether KC can be delivered by a device, in the absence of the parents. In this regard, we undertook this study to investigate the possibility of performing KC via a device, and how. We conducted a mix of face-to-face and online interviews with ten medical professionals from Guangdong Women and Children's Hospital and Health Institute, located at Guangzhou, china. The results led on to the creation of a conceptual preterm infant incubator that will be introduced in the later sections of this paper. This conceptual incubator incorporated three main essential features, i.e., 'skin simulation', 'heartbeat simulation', and 'smell simulation', in light of the critical elements of KC as concluded from the interview results. It was then evaluated with the ten interviewees, and received general positive feedback.

Keywords: Product design · Design innovation · Kangaroo care · Premature infants · Infant incubator

1 Introduction

Preterm birth is the leading cause of neonatal mortality, with a mortality rate as high as 20.8% [1]. Premature infants suffer from a series of diseases due to organ dysplasia and congenital diseases, so need long-term monitoring and treatment in NICU (Neonatal Intensive Care Unit) [1–3]. It is common in premature infants that hypoplasia and medical complications such as respiratory problems, vertebral paralysis and visual impairment. Although the development of modern science and technology can provide better life support for premature infants in neonatology [4], leaving their mothers after birth

© The Author(s), under exclusive license to Springer Nature Switzerland AG 2023
A. Marcus et al. (Eds.): HCII 2023, LNCS 14034, pp. 504–515, 2023.
https://doi.org/10.1007/978-3-031-35705-3_37

will inevitably affect the neural and physical development of premature infants [5]. To improve the well-being of the infants need care in the Neonatal Intensive Care Unit (NICU), current evidence suggests that skin-to-skin contact between infants and parents reduces recovery time, and hence helps the infants to leave the NICU sooner [24–27]. Kangaroo Care (KC) is a safe and effective method to care for premature infants, which means that premature infants have continuous skin contact with their parents at early birth, and take exclusive breastfeeding and follow-up after discharge [6, 22]. It can not only stabilize the physiological indexes of premature infants, promote the growth and development of premature infants, and relieve pain [7], but also promote maternal physical and mental recovery, reduce anxiety and improve satisfaction [8]. KC can improve behavior by promoting the stability of heart and respiratory function and reducing aimless exercise, further help mothers better contact premature babies [6]. This allows premature infants not only to maintain their body temperature, but also to significantly solve many clinical problems, such as stable vital signs, weight gain and prolonged sleep time [9]. As the development of KC is relatively perfect in the world at present [23], it has not been widely used in baby products, with many shortcomings. On the other hand, product innovations for premature infants are scarce. However, we have not yet found such devices on the Chinese market, nor did we find any existing publications exploring this topic. Therefore, this study aims to explore the effects of kangaroo nursing products on physiological indexes and growth and development of premature infants, then provide a reference for the application of kangaroo care products.

Previous research on kangaroo care for premature infants: The device measures the neonate's and caregiver's skin temperature and the neonate's relative position during KC. The device incorporates skin touch sensors to qualify the temperature readings, thus preventing false alarms [10]. Clothing design of KC can provide kangaroo care for mothers and newborns to improve comfort [11]. Integrated textile sensor for neonatal monitoring smart jacket meter [12]. A breathing mattress for the incubator is introduced, and a mattress motion actuating systems utilizing embedded electronic and pneumatic technology mimics the movements of the parents' chest to comfort infants and stimulate them to breathe regularly [13]. In addition to the above devices, the ergonomically-designed sofas for KC can also significantly increase the safety factor and reduce the risk for mothers [14].

Although KC has its positive effects, it can't be carried out when the life of premature infants is unstable in the early stage. Even if premature babies have stable vital signs, there will be certain risks when using KC methods, which makes KC methods very difficult. The purpose of this study is to develop revolutionary and innovative newborn detection and care solutions by combining existing advanced technologies, such as heartbeat simulation technology, electronic skin technology and odor simulation technology. We describe a new KC Infant incubator device to help mothers and premature babies interact with each other remotely in kangaroo care. We identified the heartbeat simulator, skin simulator and odor simulator needed for remote interaction. Our device replicates the mattress of premature babies by simulating the mother's skin, so that premature babies can feel the mother's temperature close to their bodies.

2 Methods

The parents of ten preterm infants aged 0–6 months were engaged in this study. We accessed these research participants between September 2022 and January 2023, with the support from *Guangdong Women and Children's Hospital and Health Institute*, located at Guangzhou city, China. At the start, we contacted the parents of thirteen infants; ten of the Thirteen infants' parents agreed to participate in this study. The infants were divided into four research groups: one complete term infant (gestational age 39–41^{+6} weeks), two early term infants (gestational age 37–38^{+6} weeks), five late premature infants (gestational age 34–36^{+6} weeks), and two early premature infants (gestational age 28–33^{+6} weeks). We included all of the four groups in this study to ensure that our results could represent the common features of preterm infants of different types, as defined by Fleischman et. al [29]. The sample size as well as the research manner were chosen with reference to some existing studies on kangaroo care i.e., Als et al. (2003) [27], Chen et al. (2011) [12], Karimi et al. (2016) [24].

This study could be divided into two phases: 1) the user exploration phase, and 2) the conceptual design phase. In the first phase, in total twenty interviews were undertaken with the infants' parents, either online or face-to-face (duration = 30–40 min each). The infants were observed at three different times of a day: 6 a.m. to 8 a.m. (early morning), 2 p.m. to 4 p.m. (early afternoon), and 8 p.m. to 10 p.m. (evening) as advised by the medical staff from the hospital, and during a total period of seven days. During each observation, the infants' breathing status, skin status, and sleep status were recorded. To determine the principles in performing KC as per medical requirements, a mix of face-to-face and online interviews with ten medical professionals *from Guangdong Women and Children's Hospital and Health Institute* were conducted.

To validate the knowledge obtained from the above research activities, we designed a conceptual incubator delivering KC. This design experiment drew on the seven stage design process proposed by Nigel cross [14]. The first stage was Clarifying Object, in which the design goal is to improve the comfort level of premature infants and promote emotional communication with parents in the NICU. The second was Establishing Function, to determine the function of achieving remote kangaroo care. The third was Setting Requirement. We interviewed the parents of premature infants and the medical staff of NICU to dig out the users' demand points, and determined the needs that can support the mothers to carry out continuous KC for premature infants. The fourth stage was Determining Characteristic. We measured the human body of premature babies born 0 to 6 months, and design an incubator product with heartbeat simulation function and ergonomics. The fifth stage was Generating Alternatives. The sixth stage was Alternative Evaluation, which tested and evaluated the heartbeat simulation, skin simulation and odor simulation respectively, and analyzed the fitness of each function of the incubator. The seventh stage was Improving Details. After designing the incubator, we interviewed relevant medical staff for product testing feedback, and realized function optimization and details improvement according to the interview results. In the end of the study, this conceptual incubator was evaluated with the medical professionals and the parents in this study, via interviews.

3 Results

3.1 Characteristics of the Participants

As illustrated in Table 1, thirty percent of the interviewed parents said that they would not accept KC, when being asked. They pointed out that kangaroo care required parents to hold infants for too long time. This led to stiffness and soreness in muscles of the arms, and could even led to tripping hazards of oxygen tubing.

However, KC could not be carried out in two families of early premature infants (gestational age 28–33^{+6} weeks). In one of the families, premature babies were born at 26 weeks, with a birth weight of just over 1 kg, so they could only stay in NICU. If parents wanted to see their children, they needed to queue up in advance. Parents entering the NICU were asked to wear sterile clothes and to see their children through windows outside the hallway. In another family, premature infants (gestational age 34–36^{+6} weeks) were out of danger after one week of treatment and could be taken care of with KC for a short time. We observed that gently touching the infants, calling the babies with soft voices, and letting the babies listen to their parents' heartbeats could make the babies fall asleep better.

Table 1. Interview questions and answers

Questions	Answers
Q1: Do you know anything about kangaroo care? (Yes/No)	Yes (n = 12, 60%)
	No (n = 8, 40%)
Q2: Would you like to do kangaroo care for your baby? (Yes/No)	Yes (n = 15, 75%)
	No (n = 5, 25%)
Q3: Are you aware of the key points of kangaroo care? (Yes/No)	Yes (n = 6, 30%)
	No (n = 14, 70%)
Q4: Do you know how to evaluate the physiological condition of premature babies in kangaroo care? (Yes/No)	Yes (n = 3, 15%)
	No (n = 17, 85%)
Q5: Have you ever encountered any emergencies in kangaroo care? (Yes/No)	Yes (n = 11, 55%)
	No (n = 9, 45%)
Q6: Do you have any requirements for kangaroo care environment? (Yes/No)	Yes (n = 16, 80%)
	No (n = 4, 20%)
Q7: Do you have any other nursing experience? (Yes/No)	Yes (n = 10, 50%)
	No (n = 10, 50%)

In ten groups of families, the premature infants were asked under what conditions they were most likely to fall asleep, under what conditions they breathed most smoothly, and from what help they were easy to fall asleep and breathe smoothly. Among ten cases of premature infants, two cases often fall asleep quietly, four cases usually fall asleep, three cases sometimes sleep, a case hardly go to sleep, and 0 cases never fall asleep quietly. In terms of investigation, we concluded that the main reason is that it is difficult for newborns to adapt to the existing environment without their mothers, resulting in inability to fall asleep. For this situation, we suggest making as much contact with parents as possible, such as touching the baby to feel skin-to-skin contact (8 answers), the most used strategies, holding the baby to stick to the chest (6 answers), listening to the mother's heartbeat and cordial call (5 answers).

The interviews with the senior NICU nurses with more than eight years of experience showed that premature babies should be given more necessary physical stimulation to promote the development of physical functions because they are not fully developed in the maternal body. As an intimate contact that premature infants need very much, touch helps them regulate their nervous, endocrine and immune systems to reduce their anxiety and increase sleep time and milk quantity (Fig. 1).

The results showed that effective KC, as defined in the medical area, required a proper combination of three key elements: 1) a sense of warmth and security realized by skin-to-skin contact between mother and child as soon as possible after birth, and the longer the better; 2) a sense of intimacy achieved by letting a child hear and feel his/her mother's heart beating, chest rising and falling with each breath, and voice; and 3) a sense of comfort obtained from giving pleasure as infants prefer the smell of their mothers and more likely breast milk over artificial smells such as perfumes or cigarette smoke.

Fig. 1. The existing incubator and environment of the hospital.

3.2   The Conceptual Incubate that Can Perform KMC

Building on the lessons learned from the above research activities, we developed an incubator that can deliver KC to preterm infants, by heartbeat simulation, skin simulation, and odor simulation. A mattress with heartbeat simulation is installed inside the infant incubator, and an artificial skin device is used in the heartbeat simulation mattress. It simulates the mother's skin and replicates a new tactile experience, so that premature infants can feel the mother's tactile feeling personally. A smell simulator is also installed inside the infant incubator, which can collect the body fragrance of mother or the smell of breast milk, so that premature infants can sleep more comfortably inside the incubator. Therefore, the need for heartbeat simulator, skin simulator and odor simulator in this design was discussed in this study.

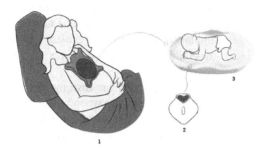

Fig. 2. Design Concept

Heartbeat simulation mattress includes three parts: induction module, replication module and process control module [15]. The design concept is shown in Fig. 2: Before kangaroo care, the sensing module is close to the mother's chest, and the mother's breathing frequency is sensed in the posture of skin contact, to replicate the mother's heartbeat frequency, as shown in Detail 1 in the Fig. 2. These collected data about the mother are synchronized to the mattress used by the child through the process control module (detail 2 in the Fig. 2). Then the mattress transmits the frequency of simulating mother's breathing to the mattress in the form of inflation and deflation for movement, as well as the sound of mother's heart beating and rhythmic breathing sounds come from the mattress (detail 3 in the Fig. 2). The hardware implementation of the KC device is given in the figure. At the same time, the types and positions of sensors in the device are explained [18–20].

Heartbeat Simulation Mattress: By imitating the chest breathing movement of parents during kangaroo care, the mattress will use inflation and deflation to change the ups and downs of the mattress according to the mother's heartbeat frequency. The internal process control module controls the mattress by storing and receiving data from the mother.

Skin Simulation: Artificial skin was added to the mattress surface close to the baby. Dae-Hyeong Kim and others developed a multifunctional wearable skin system [16]. We incorporate a multifunctional wearable skin system into the heartbeat mattress, including physiological sensors, and nonvolatile memory. Quantitative analysis of electronic, mechanical, heat transfer and drug diffusion characteristics verifies the operation of each component, thus achieving the true skin texture of mother.

Odor Simulation (see Fig. 3): It can imitate the smell of the mother's body and breast milk, so that premature babies can smell the mother's smell in the incubator. In addition, the function can also change the ratio of flavor molecules to different scenes, thus emitting different odors.

These mild stimuli provided in the auditory, tactile and thermal systems have a sedative effect on premature infants, resulting in a similar effect to that of incubators to keep the vital signs of premature infants stable [17]. More specifically, the simulation of the mother's skin was realised using sensors, micro-electromechanical systems, and new materials. A mattress mimicking the breathing of the mother's chest with embedded electronics and pneumatic technology for mattress motion actuating systems was used to calm the infants and to stimulate them to breathe regularly. To add to the immersive experience, the new incubator could also mimic the mother's scent, to make the baby feel more secure.

This remote kangaroo care can effectively improve the sleep quality of newborns [28]. Newborns can feel their mother's heartbeat when lying on the mattress, which is beneficial for newborns to enter deep sleep. While implementing remote kangaroo care, newborns can feel their mother's skin through the mattress of artificial skin, and reduce the crying time of newborns by placing the smell of mother's breast milk.

Fig. 3. Internal odor simulator

Kangaroo care proposed in this paper is suitable for the whole cycle of premature infant care. The product combines sheet metal and plastic materials on the main body to ensure compression while reducing weight and improving mobility. The outer frame of the incubator for premature babies is made of engineering plastics with strong resistance, the exterior is painted with metal paint to improve the texture, the lampshade is made of tempered glass to improve the transmittance, and the baby cabin cover is made of high strength plexiglass. In the details, the embellishment of metal frame gives the product a sense of technology and quality. In color psychology, pink can make people feel warm and comfortable, so the use of this product can also make premature babies get better comfort and warmth in body and mind. Figure 5 is an example of the application scenario.

In addition, based on ergonomic principles, the design of premature infant incubator should be as convenient and fast as possible to minimize the labor intensity of users, including medical staff and newborns. By referring to the Chinese human body height size table and adding the psychological distance of 200 mm on both sides, the length of the baby cabin should be 1000 mm and the width should be 800 mm (see Fig. 4). Therefore, KC proposed by us is suitable for the whole nursing cycle of premature infants.

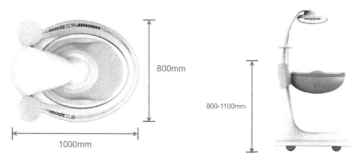

Fig. 4. Dimension of baby incubator

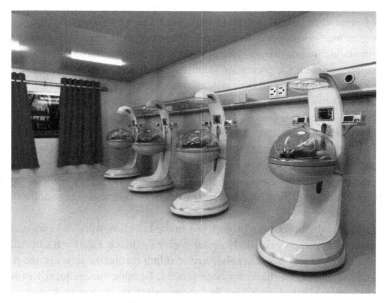

Fig. 5. Application scenario

3.3   The Evaluation of the Design Concept

All users interviewed (twenty) completed subjective evaluation. After content analysis, the interviewee put forward four specific items. The KC group had the following advantages: safety (75%, fifteen respondents) and humanistic care (35%, seven respondents). However, KC also has some disadvantages, including frequency of use (25%, five respondents) and inability to visually see results (25%, five respondents).

The concept product was scored by twenty-four medical practitioners, with the total score of ten, the overall satisfaction of sixteen medical practitioners is 8, the overall satisfaction of six medical practitioners is 5, and the overall satisfaction of two medical practitioners is 3. The support received was significantly higher than that of conventional nursing methods. The results indicated that KC infant incubator was recognized by most people.

The medical staff found the design concept valuable, but the components in the heart-beating mattress may need to be put in place. They suggested studying the range of motion of premature infants to determine where to install this device.

4 Discussion

After the design was completed, we carried out a simulation test on the product. The study showed that the implementation of remote kangaroo care had no effect on the respiration and heart rate of premature infants ($P > 0.05$), which were maintained within the normal range. In addition, compared with conventional nursing, the use of heartbeat simulation made the blood oxygen saturation level of premature infants higher and stable, the difference was statistically significant ($P < 0.01$), indicating that the sleep quality of premature infants had been improved. The reason may be that the remote kangaroo care method adopts 24 h uninterrupted influence on babies' dependence, which enables premature infants to have close contact with their parents, provides a comfortable and warm environment for premature infants, increases the emotional communication between premature infants and their parents, increases their sense of security, and helps to maintain the physiological indicators of premature infants in a stable state.

In this study, the close contact between parents and preterm infants was conducted through remote kangaroo care. The sound, smell, breathing, heartbeat, embrace and touch of parents were transmitted through the sensory organs of preterm infants, such as sight, hearing, smell and touch, which produced benign stimulation to preterm infants, made them feel the care and care of their parents, increased their sense of security and comfort, and stabilized their physiological indexes. Increase oxygen saturation levels [21].

In the first evaluation of the project, we invited doctors with 12 years' experience from Guangdong Women's Health Hospital to give feedback. Heartbeat simulation mattresses can be effective as an internal device of infant incubator, although the following advantages and limitations have not been proved. Because the frequency of heartbeat simulating mattress can make babies feel more secure by increasing parents' sense of existence.

The results show that heartbeat simulation makes premature infants fall asleep better and recover faster, further improving the experience of babies, mothers and nurses substantially. Heartbeat simulation mattress provides more convenient and humane solutions for nursing staff to enhance the survival rate and safety of premature infants. It also increases the sense of security and comfort of premature infants when feeling the care and care of their parents, and stabilizes physiological indexes to improve the level of blood oxygen saturation.

The possible limitation is that babies may rely too much on heartbeat simulation mattresses to get out of this environment. The solution to this problem can be used at an appropriate time, such as starting the heartbeat movement when the baby needs to rest, which makes them sleep more peacefully. When the baby is active, turn off the movement of the device, so that the baby can constantly adapt to normal environment. Another solution is to use the device continuously, and then reduce the frequency of use as appropriate as the baby recovers.

In the research, although a combination of many previous experiences, there are still some deficiencies in some theories due to its limited ability. Moreover, the neonatal intensive care unit as a high-risk ward, it is impossible to conduct in-depth field investigation, which brings some difficulties to the investigation. It is great promising for the development of KC products in the future, so the existing care for premature infants and the continuation of care will be improved in the long run.

5 Conclusion

KC has long been proven to be an effective method in improving the wellbeing of preterm infants. However, the technique cannot be broadly applied in practice be-because it requires the participation of both the infants and their parents during the whole process. This pilot study shows that traditional KC performed by the parents of the infants can be replace by a well-design device. As revealed by our results, the three key design features in simulating KC include 1)Heartbeat simulators help premature babies sleep better by mimicking the rate of a parent's heart beat and breathing rate during kangaroo care, 2)The Skin Simulator incorporates a versatile wearable skin system that allows premature babies to personally feel their mother's touch, 3) The odor simulator releases the scent of the mother's body and breast milk so that premature infants can better adapt to the hospital environment.

This paper presents a conceptual incubator, but it is only at the concept stage. Further research is required to further evaluate the three features, by developing a working prototype device and put it into field test.

6 Limitations and the Next Step

This pilot study showed that the Kangaroo Care practices which were traditionally performed in hospitals could to a large degree be realized by a device, without the participation of the parents of the infants or medical practitioners.

Acknowledgment. The authors would like to express their sincere thanks to the participants and staff of the study. This study was supported by the Grant Research on Usability Testing Methods of Health and Medical Devices (23XSC11). The funding sources had no role in the design of the study and collection, analysis, and interpretation of data and in writing the manuscript.

References

1. World Health Organisation, Preterm birth (2018). https://www.who.int/news-room/fact-she ets/detail/preterm-birth. Accessed 30 Apr 2020
2. Cao, G., Liu, J., Liu, M.: Global, regional, and national incidence and mortality of neonatal preterm birth, 1990–2019. JAMA Pediatr. **176**(8), 787 (2022). https://doi.org/10.1001/jam apediatrics.2022.1622
3. Gooding, J.S., Cooper, L.G., Blaine, A.I., Franck, L.S., Howse, J.L., Berns, S.D.: Family support and family-centered care in the neonatal intensive care unit: origins, advances, impact. Semin. Perinatol. **35**(1), 20–28 (2011). https://doi.org/10.1053/j.semperi.2010.10.004

4. Athanasopoulou, E., Fox, J.R.E.: Effects of kangaroo mother care on maternal mood and interaction patterns between parents and their preterm, low birth weight infants: a systematic review: kangaroo mother care, maternal mood, and parent–infant interaction. Infant Ment. Health J. **35**(3), 245–262 (2014). https://doi.org/10.1002/imhj.21444

5. Flacking, R., et al.: Closeness and separation in neonatal intensive care. Acta Paediatr. **101**(10), 1032–1037 (2012). https://doi.org/10.1111/j.1651-2227.2012.02787.x

6. Ludington-Hoe, S.M., Swinth, J.Y.: Developmental Aspects of Kangaroo Care. J. Obstet. Gynecol. Neonatal. Nurs. **25**(8), 691–703 (1996). https://doi.org/10.1111/j.1552-6909.1996. tb01483.x

7. Kostandy, R.R., Ludington-Hoe, S.M.: The evolution of the science of kangaroo (mother) care (skin-to-skin contact). Birth Defects Res. **111**(15), 1032–1043 (2019). https://doi.org/ 10.1002/bdr2.1565

8. Hynan, M.T., et al.: Recommendations for mental health professionals in the NICU. J. Perinatol. **35**(1), Art. no. 1 (2015). https://doi.org/10.1038/jp.2015.144

9. Karlsson, V., Heinemann, A.-B., Sjörs, G., Nykvist, K.H., Ågren, J.: Early skin-to-skin care in extremely preterm infants: thermal balance and care environment. J. Pediatr. **161**(3), 422–426 (2012). https://doi.org/10.1016/j.jpeds.2012.02.034

10. Joglekar, A., et al.: A wearable sensor for monitoring kangaroo mother care treatment for premature neonates. In: 2018 IEEE SENSORS, pp. 1–4 (2018). https://doi.org/10.1109/ICS ENS.2018.8589633

11. Zengin, H., Cinar, N.: Designing dress (Sarbebe) for kangaroo care, the effect of kangaroo care provided with this dress on mother and newborn's comfort. Health Care Women Int. **43**(6), 642–662 (2022). https://doi.org/10.1080/07399332.2021.1893733

12. Chen, W., Hu, J., Bouwstra, S., Oetomo, S.B., Feijs, L.: Sensor integration for perinatology research. IJSNET **9**(1), 38 (2011). https://doi.org/10.1504/IJSNET.2011.037303

13. Schets, M.W.M., Chen, W., Bambang Oetomo, S.: Design of a breathing mattress based on the respiratory movement of kangaroo mother care for the development of neonates. In: 2015 37th Annual International Conference of the IEEE Engineering in Medicine and Biology Society (EMBC), Milan, pp. 6764–6767 (2015). https://doi.org/10.1109/EMBC.2015.7319946

14. Saptaputra, S.K., Kurniawidjaja, L.M., Susilowati, I.H., Pratomo, H.: Ergonomic sofa design to support kangaroo mother care in Indonesia. J. Neonatal Nurs. **27**(6), 471–475 (2021). https://doi.org/10.1016/j.jnn.2021.06.013

15. Korja, R., et al.: Attachment representations in mothers of preterm infants (2009)

16. Jin, H., Abu-Raya, Y.S., Haick, H.: Advanced materials for health monitoring with skin-based wearable devices. Adv. Healthc. Mater. **6**(11), 1700024 (2017). https://doi.org/10.1002/adhm. 201700024

17. Jefferies, A.L., Canadian Paediatric Society, Fetus and Newborn Committee.: Kangaroo care for the preterm infant and family. Paediatr. Child Health **17**(3), 141–143 (2012)

18. Yang, F., Al Mahmud, A., Wang, T.: User knowledge factors that hinder the design of new home healthcare devices: investigating thirty-eight devices and their manufacturers. BMC Med. Inform. Decis. Mak. **21**(1), 166 (2021). https://doi.org/10.1186/s12911-021-01464-3

19. Yang, F., Al Mahmud, A.: Issues in evaluating the user performance of new home medical devices: a field test of two devices produced by a leading provider. J. Des. Res. **16**(3–4), 196–213 (2018)

20. Yang, F., Wang, L., Ding, X.: Why some "user-centred" medical devices do not provide satisfactory user experiences? an investigation on user information factors in new device development processes. In: Soares, M.M., Rosenzweig, E., Marcus, A. (eds.) Design, User Experience, and Usability: UX Research, Design, and Assessment. HCII 2022. Lecture Notes in Computer Science, vol. 13321, pp. 314–324. Springer, Cham (2022). https://doi.org/10.1007/978-3-031-05897-4_22

21. Diego, M.A., Field, T., Hernandezreif, M.: Preterm infant weight gain is increased by massage therapy and exercise via different underlying mechanisms. Early Hum. Dev. **90**(3), 137 (2014). https://doi.org/10.1016/j.Earlhumdev.2014.01.009

22. Khadivzadeh, T., Karimi, F.Z., Tara, F., et al.: The effect of postpartum mother–infant skin-to-skin contact on exclusive breastfeeding in neonatal period: a randomized controlled trial. Int. J. Pediatr. **4**(5), 5409–5417 (2016)

23. Roberts, K.L., Paynter, C., Mcewan, B.: A comparison of kangaroo mother care and conventional cuddling care. Neonatal Netw. **19**(4), 17–23 (2000). https://doi.org/10.1891/0730-0832.19.4.31

24. Karimi, F.Z., Khadivzadeh, T., Saeidi, M., Bagheri, S.: The effect of kangaroo mother care immediately after delivery on mother-infant attachment and on maternal anxiety about the baby 3- months after delivery: a randomized controlled trial. Int. J. Pediatr. **4**(9), 3561–3570 (2016)

25. Johnston, C., Campbell-Yeo, M., Fernandes, A., Inglis, D., Streiner, D., Zee, R.: Skin-to-skin care for procedural pain in neonates. In: The Cochrane Database of Systematic Reviews, vol. 1, CD008435 (2014). https://doi.org/10.1002/14651858.CD008435.pub2

26. Thapa, K., et al.: Feasibility assessment of an ergonomic baby wrap for kangaroo mother care: a mixed methods study from Nepal, pp. 1–16 (2018)

27. Als, H., Gilkerson, L., Duffy, F.H., et al.: A three-center, randomized, controlled trial of individualized developmental care for very low birth weight preterm infants: medical, neurodevelopmental, parenting, and caregiving effects. J. Dev. Behav. Pediatr. **24**(6), 399–408 (2003)

28. Abbas, A.K., Heiman, K., Jergus, K., et al.: Neonatal monitoring technologies: design for integrated solutions. Neonatal Infrared Thermography Imaging **1** (2012)

29. Fleischman, A.R., Oinuma, M., Clark, S.L.: Rethinking the definition of "term pregnancy." Obstet. Gynecol. **116**(1), 136–139 (2010). https://doi.org/10.1097/AOG.0b013e3181e24f28

Function and Visual Experience Design Strategy of Chinese Elderly Health Monitoring Smartwatch

Fangrong Yi, Delai Men[✉], Sijia Cheng, and Chen Liu

School of Design, Guangzhou Higher Education Mega Center, South China University of Technology, Panyu, Guangzhou 510006, People's Republic of China

mendelai@scut.edu.cn

Abstract. Since the 1990s, China's ageing process has accelerated. With the increase of age and the ageing of physiological functions, the elderly are more prone to diseases. At present, there are not many health-monitoring smartwatches for the elderly in the Chinese market, and fewer elderly people use health-monitoring smartwatches. The user experience of health monitoring smartwatches for the elderly in the Chinese market still has a large room for improvement. This study investigates the elderly population living in first and second-tier cities in China. The KANO questionnaire was used to investigate the functional requirements of the Chinese elderly for health monitoring smartwatches, and the results were analyzed. Five-level Likert scale was used to evaluate the visual elements that the Chinese elderly feel comfortable with the interface of the health monitoring smartwatch. Based on the research results, limitations, and future development of this paper, relevant suggestions are proposed, hoping to provide a reference for similar design cases and improve the quality of life of the elderly in the field of design.

Keywords: Elderly people · Smartwatch · KANO model

1 Introduction

Since the 1990s, China's ageing process has accelerated. According to the National Bureau of Statistics (NBS 2020), by the end of 2019, there were 176 million people over the age of 65 in China, accounting for 12.57% of the total population. Some scholars predict (Du et al. 2021) that the proportion of the elderly population in China will reach more than 29.8% in 2035 and about 37.8% in 2050. The increase in age leads to the decline of resistance, and the elderly are more prone to health problems. Liu (2019) said that the elderly are the main group of chronic diseases, and chronic diseases have a long onset cycle and are not easily detected in the early stage of the disease. The best approach is to make pre-disease health predictions, timely intervention during disease, and follow-up management after disease. Therefore, pre-disease health detection plays a crucial role for the elderly. At present, there are not many health-monitoring smartwatches for the elderly in the Chinese market. Compared with smartphones, tablets, and other smart

A. Marcus et al. (Eds.): HCII 2023, LNCS 14034, pp. 516–527, 2023.
https://doi.org/10.1007/978-3-031-35705-3_38

products commonly used in life, smartwatches are easier to carry, and the limitation of screen size makes its functions simpler and operation easier. Therefore, the smartwatch is friendly to the elderly with cognitive degradation and suitable for the elderly to use in their life after retirement. Due to the particularity of China's national conditions, with the acceleration of the growth of the elderly population, the empty-nest problem of Chinese families has become prominent (Wang 2016). Based on the particularity of the elderly group and the difference in living environment, there is a large room for improvement of the health monitoring smartwatch experience for the elderly group in China. This paper discusses the functional and visual needs of the elderly group living in first and second-tier cities in China for the health monitoring smartwatch.

2 Research Method and Process

This research uses various methods to complete the evaluation of Chinese elderly people on the functions and visual experience elements of smartwatches. Firstly, we investigated the literature and reports related to the ageing problem through secondary research, and then carried out a case analysis of several most popular watches for the elderly in the Chinese market and gave weight ratings within the group. In the first stage of the experiment, this study first adopted the interview method and questionnaire survey to determine the function preference of the elderly on the health monitoring watch, then supplemented and summarized the function list of the health monitoring smartwatch through group brainstorming, and finally investigated the function of the smartwatch through the KANO questionnaire survey and conducted data analysis of the results. In the second stage of the experiment, to make the elderly have a good experience when using smartwatches, we sorted the weight of the ageing characteristics of the elderly according to their influence on the smartwatch interface from the previous second-hand research. Based on the results, visual elements with the highest weight were tested and investigated, and the results were analyzed.

2.1 Literature Research on the Basic Characteristics of the Elderly

This study found that many people have put forward relevant conclusions in the physiological field of the elderly from specific secondary research on physiological and psychological characteristics. In terms of physiological characteristics: Fan (2015) analyzed the physiological characteristics and health characteristics of the elderly. He proposed that visually, older elderly people will see more and more blurred things, and their sensitivity to and ability to distinguish colours will decline. Auditory, with the increase of age, the perception of sound frequency will change, and the appropriate sound frequency for the elderly is 1000–2000 Hz (Wang et al. 2008).In terms of touch, due to the decline of sensory perception, Li (2015) proposed that the elderly's perception of cold, heat, and pain is not as obvious as that of the young. According to the Handbook of Disease Prevention and Health Management for the Elderly in the Community, memory, and thinking will decline with the age, people will become easy to forget things in daily life, and they will become slower to accept foreign news. According to Liu et al. (2013), chronic diseases such as hypertension, diabetes, heart disease, and senile dementia tend to occur with the decline of physical functions.

The research in the field of psychological characteristics of the elderly: after retirement, the elderly leave their jobs, suddenly feel idle, feel unable to stand in society, feel unvalued, and lack confidence and security. According to Liu et al. (2013), with the increasing incidence of chronic diseases, the elderly will feel insecure because of the threat to their lives and the threat of death.

2.2 Research on the Experience of Health Monitoring Smartwatches for the Elderly in China

This study collected, sorted, and analyzed the popular watches for the elderly in China to preliminarily understand the advantages and disadvantages of the current health monitoring watches for the elderly in China and guide the research direction. The research team scored the important functions of these watches according to the weight of whether the elderly use experience is friendly, interactive, and easy to use, whether there are appropriate functions and whether there is emotional care. The weight scores of the top three watches (Lianshuo V16, Lianshuo V4, Lianshuo F9) were analyzed in more detail, and the following conclusions were drawn from the detailed case analysis: In terms of interaction, the advantages of these three watches with higher weight are that they have good language interaction function, but the common functional level of the watch is placed deeper, need to click, slide and other interactive gestures combination use to achieve the purpose, and there are also difficulties in understanding the semantics of the function; In terms of function, their health detection function is relatively perfect, emergency and video communication function is relatively lacking, the daily use function is not perfect; In terms of user experience, their interface vision is relatively complex, and the user experience for the elderly is poor. In terms of emotional care, they rarely have the function of emotional care, and their children are not strong in contacting the elderly (Table 1).

Table 1. The weighting of market senior watches.

Senior Watch	Weight
Market Senior Watch	42.1
ASUS V16 4G Senior Watch	42.8
ASUS F9 Smart Health Watch	42.9
V23 Air Pump True Blood Pressure Health Watch	34.7
F3 Full Netcom 4G Senior Watch	8.6
Huawei New FIT6	34.4
Huawei Wath D Blood Pressure Watch	38.7
guàn Yi W3 Watch	25.1
dido Y2 Smart Watch	17.1

2.3 Interview Research

Since China was in the period of epidemic prevention and control during the study period, the team selected 6 elderly people aged 60–70 living in first-tier cities through online language and telephone recruitment through open recruitment. The deep demands of the elderly people were obtained through interviews, to understand the daily behaviour habits and preferences of the elderly group and help the team to sort out the functions of the elderly people on the watch. Before the interview, the participants were informed of the purpose of the interview, explained the importance of their contributions, and recorded the interview content for later collating. At the end of the interview, we would like to thank the participant and leave their contact information for follow-up communication. During the interview, we found that: the elderly people go out frequently after retirement, but they are not familiar with the new environment, and often can not find the place; The elderly can normally use the basic functions of smart devices, but when it comes to the deeper functions, they need to seek the help of people around them; And most of the elderly have chronic diseases, so they pay special attention to their health condition. Finally, we sorted out the daily life scenes and more detailed life information of the elderly from the interview records and set the questions for reference.

2.4 Questionnaire Survey

After the interview, researchers need to further obtain data support more detailed information about the health status, living habits, main activity places and environment of the elderly living in China's first-tier cities. Therefore, the team surveyed people over 55 years old in the form of online questionnaires. A total of 69 questionnaires were collected from people over 55 years old. Through the analysis and processing of the questionnaire data, the team found that 78.26% of the elderly do not live with their children, and 62.32% of the elderly contact their families every day. The group found that the elderly were lacking in emotional communication with their families, and most of them were eager to get emotional communication. In the survey on the health status of the elderly, 43.48% of the elderly suffer from chronic diseases, 39.13% suffer from memory deterioration, and 31.88% suffer from eyesight and hearing decline. Long-term chronic diseases mean that the elderly need to take drugs to control the condition at ordinary times. The decline of memory means that they often forget to do something in life.

2.5 List of Smartwatch Features

Due to the limitations of the questionnaire and the particularity of the elderly group, the researchers analyzed the questionnaire, based on the daily life scenes of the elderly people in the questionnaire results, carried out brainstorming around specific life scenes, supplemented and improved the relevant functions, and sorted out the preliminary function list of the smartwatch (Table 2).

Table 2. Interview outline of elderly users on the function of a smartwatch.

Type of requirement	Smartwatch functions
Daily life	Clock
	QR code payment
	E-card pack
	Radio
	Navigation
	Show health code
Emotional Care	Medication reminders
	Video cal
	Voice call
Health Screening	Record workout steps
	Record workout calories
	Record heart rate
	Record blood oxygen
	Sleep recording
Emergency functionsv	Fall detection

2.6 The Elderly Demand Analysis Based on the KANO Model

In the process of demand construction, this study mainly adopts the KANO model proposed by Japanese professor Noriaki Kano, which can reflect the nonlinear relationship between product performance and user satisfaction (Kano et al. 1984). After analyzing the collected data, the requirements can be divided into Must-be requirements(M), one-dimensional requirements(o), attractive requirements(A) and Indifferent requirements(I) Reverse requirements(R). Since user satisfaction will decrease after providing Reverse requirements, Reverse requirements will be removed in advance in this requirement screening. According to the attitude to increase function in the elderly and not to increase the function of attitude, according to five kinds of demand in the KANO model classification, this study based on the following table positioning smart watches a preliminary list of specific functions belonging to what kind of requirements for the elderly (Table 3).

2.7 Research on Visual Comfort Elements of Ageing Smartwatch Interface

The researchers conducted a weighted ranking (1–5 points) on the basic characteristics of the elderly obtained from the second-hand survey in the early stage of the study according to the degree of influence on the smartwatch interface. According to the ranking results, the visual factors with the highest weight were investigated (Table 4).

Table 3. KANO needs classification.

| | | This feature is not provided | | | | |
		Very much enjoyed	As it should be	Whatever	Grudging acceptance	Much disliked
Providing this feature	Very much enjoyed	Q	A	A	A	O
	As it should be	R	I	I	I	M
	Whatever	R	I	I	I	M
	Grudging acceptance	R	I	I	I	M
	Much disliked	R	R	R	R	Q

Table 4. The weighting **of basic physical characteristics of older people**

Feature	Category	Weight
Decreased sensitivity and discrimination to colour	Visual	4.67
Memory loss	Memories	3.67
Decline in reactive stress	Thinking	3.33
Increased incidence of chronic illness	Physical health	3.33
Altered sound frequency perception	Aural	3
Decreased perception of heat, cold and pain	Haptics	1.43

Since the visual elements closely related to the smartwatch interface include icon, font, and colour matching, this study surveyed these three visual elements using a five-level Likert scale according to these three dimensions. In this test survey, the valid data samples were 31, including 17 males and 14 females, all over 55 years old. Their occupations were concentrated in teachers and employees of national enterprises, indicating that the comprehension ability of the test group was relatively good. The researchers showed the elderly people tests about the visual elements of the smartwatch interface – icon, font, and colour matching. They were asked to place the test screen 45 cm vertically from their eyes in an indoor scene with natural light during the day and then rated the options according to visual comfort. Table 5 is font size, Table 6 is icon size and Table 7 is specific values of colour matching (background and foreground scenery) test samples.

Table 5. Watch interface visual element test element data-Font Size.

Number	F1	F2	F3	F4	F5
Font size	60 px	50 px	40 px	30 px	20 px

Table 6. Watch interface visual element test element data-Icon Size.

Number	I1	I2	I3	I4	I5
Icon size	220 px	140 px	100 px	70 px	40 px

3 Results

3.1 Retrieval and Analysis of KANO Questionnaire Data

The research team distributed the KANO questionnaire based on the function list to the elderly group over 55 years old. Finally, 94 questionnaires were collected and 55 valid questionnaires were obtained after the questionnaires were screened by the options screen of trap questions and age questions (age over 55 years old).

Berger et al. proposed to subdivide demand priorities by the available Customer Satisfaction Coefficient. The KANO model was used to analyze and count the user satisfaction coefficient of two dimensions of each demand item to determine the demand quality attribute. The specific calculation method is as follows:

$$\text{better coefficient} : \text{Better/SI} = (A + O)\big/(A + O + M + I)$$

$$\text{worse coefficient} : \text{Worse/DSI} = (-1) \times (M + O)/(A + O + M + I)$$

The better coefficient, the closer it is to 1, the stronger the improvement effect of user satisfaction will be, and the faster the satisfaction will rise. The worse coefficient, the closer it is to -1, which means the greater the impact on user dissatisfaction and the faster the satisfaction will decline. Therefore, demand items with higher absolute value scores should be given priority according to the Better-Worse coefficient in demand extraction (Table 8).

Draw the Better-Worse coefficient matrix according to the better-worse ranking table, adding the horizontal and vertical warning lines respectively, with the horizontal warning line being the average y = better and the vertical warning line being the average x = worse, as shown below. Finally, the following conclusions are drawn: (1)Desired functions: navigation, sleep recording, fall detection, record heart rate, language phone, electronic card package, and show the health code. (2) Necessary functions: clock, record workout steps. (3) Charm function: record blood oxygen, video call. (4) no difference function: record workout calories, radio, QR code payment, workout timing, medicine reminders (Fig. 1).

Table 7. Watch interface visual element test element data-Colour Brightness.

Number		C1	C2	C3	C4	C5	C6	C7	C8	C9
Background colours	Hexadecimal Code	#FFFFFF	#FFFFFF	#FFFFFF	#000000	#000000	#000000	#000000	#000000	#000000
	Transparency	100%	100%	100%	20%	20%	20%	30%	30%	30%
Button colours	Hexadecimal Code	#000000	#000000	#000000	#FFFFFF	#000000	#000000	#FFFFFF	#000000	#000000
	Transparency	10%	30%	60%	100%	30%	60%	100%	10%	60%

Table 8. Better-worse coefficient ranking table.

Fuction	Better/SI	Add satisfaction coefficient sort	Worse/DSI	Reduce satisfaction coefficient sort
Clock	0.6	11	−0.5090910	1
QR code payment	0.5094339	13	−0.2641509	13
E-card pack	0.72727273	6	−0.3454545	8
Radio	0.58490566	12	−0.1509434	16
Navigation	0.87272727	1	−0.3636364	5
Show health code	0.72727273	6	−0.4181818	3
Medication reminders	0.70909091	10	−0.3090909	10
Video cal	0.72222222	7	−0.2592593	14
Voice call	0.73076923	5	−0.4423077	2
Record workout steps	0.7037037	8	−0.3333333	9
Record workout calories	0.67924528	9	−0.2075472	15
Record heart rate	0.83636364	2	−0.4	4
Record blood oxygen	0.75	4	−0.3035714	11
Sleep recording	0.75	4	−0.3571429	6
Fall detection	0.75925926	3	−0.3518519	7
Workout Timing	0.7037037	8	−0.2962963	12

3.2 Data Collation and Analysis of Visual Comfort Elements of the Ageing Smartwatch Interface

Reliability analysis was used to measure the reliability of the sample answer results. The SPSS analysis results showed that the data reliability coefficient value of this test was 0.923, greater than 0.7, indicating that the core reliability quality of the research data was excellent, and the test items and results were reliable and effective (Table 9).

In the study on the visual comfort of the elderly smartwatch interface, this paper tested the font size, icon size and colour matching (background colour and foreground colour). The test questions were all set by a five-level Likert scale, and the data were descriptive analysis, including minimum value, maximum value, average value and standard deviation (Table 10).

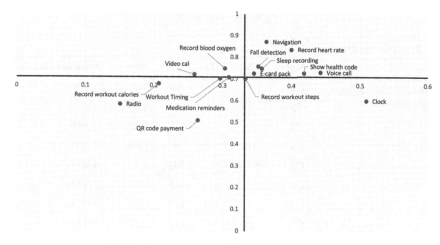

Fig. 1. Better-worse coefficient analysis matrix.

Table 9. The figure of Cronbach reliability analysis.

Cronbach reliability analysis		
Number	Sample size	Cronbach's alpha
19	31	.923

Table 10. The figure of descriptive analysis

The descriptive analysis						
	Number	Min	Max	Total	Average	Standard deviation
Font	F1	1	5	82	2.65	1.624
	F2	1	5	108	3.48	1.525
	F3	1	5	140	4.52	1.029
	F4	1	5	145	4.68	.832
	F5	1	5	145	4.68	.945
Icon	I1	1	5	103	3.32	1.469
	I2	2	5	133	4.29	1.006
	I3	2	5	144	4.65	.798
	I4	2	5	148	4.77	.669
	I5	2	5	147	4.74	.729

(*continued*)

Table 10. (*continued*)

The descriptive analysis

	Number	Min	Max	Total	Average	Standard deviation
Front view and background colour scheme	C1	1	5	94	3.03	1.779
	C2	1	5	110	3.55	1.480
	C3	1	5	111	3.58	1.385
	C4	1	5	83	2.68	1.620
	C5	1	5	105	3.39	1.453
	C6	1	5	113	3.65	1.450
	C7	1	5	113	3.65	1.603
	C8	1	5	117	3.77	1.477
	C9	1	5	81	2.61	1.542

As shown in the table above, a total of 31 valid data have been collected by the researchers. Through further analysis of the data, it is concluded that the distance between the watch interface and the eyes of the elderly is about 45 cm vertical in the indoor daytime natural light scene. Among the measured data, the highest average visual comfort is F4, F5, I4 and C8. Therefore, for the elderly, in terms of the comfort dimension of the smartwatch interface, the font sizes with high acceptability are 30 px and 20 px, the Icon size is 70 px, and the colour matching is #000000 with 30% transparency of the foreground scene and #00000 with 10% transparency of the background colour.

4 Summary and Discussion

4.1 Summary and Discussion of the Research Results of This Paper

In this paper, through the interview of 6 Chinese elderly people over 60 years old, the daily functional demand list of Chinese elderly health monitoring watch functions is extracted. Based on the KANO model, the demand for 15 functions is sorted. Through the analysis of 55 data, the expected function, essential function, charm function and undifferentiated function of Chinese elderly people for health monitoring watches are obtained. Then the research team sorted the basic features of the elderly obtained from second-hand research in the early stage of the study according to the degree of influence on the smartwatch interface. According to the sorting results, the visual factors with the highest weight were tested for the comfort threshold of the visual elements of the smartwatch interface. The most frequent visual elements were tested by 31 scores: Font size, icon size, and interface matching colour brightness value.

4.2 Limitations of This Paper and Possibilities for Further Research

The elderly subjects of the two tests live in first and second-tier cities with better economies and have higher educational backgrounds than the elderly of the same age. Since the economy of each city in China is quite different and the lifestyle of residents is also different, the results of this study may not apply to the elderly in all regions of China. At the same time, due to the influence of variables such as the number of subjects and individual life experience, the cross-regional collection of more sample sizes for design practice and verification of the effectiveness of the design strategy will also provide better suggestions for the product design of the elderly in China.

In the research process, we found that the elderly in China have frequent emotional communication with their children and friends, and the elderly and children have strong emotional communication needs for each other. However, the current smartwatch has not done enough to the emotional connection between the elderly and their children, and the relevant design and theoretical research need to be improved. If the emotional interaction can be further studied, It will greatly promote the experience of elderly people using smartwatches.

Acknowledgment. This project, Research on Elderly-Oriented Design Countermeasures based on the Elderly's Characteristics in Sensory Perception, is supported by Humanities and Social Sciences Research Planning Fund Program of the Ministry of Education of China (Grant No. 19YJA760043).

References

Du (杜鹏), P., Li (李龙), L.: Long-term trends prediction of population aging in China in the new era. J. Renmin Univ. Chin. **35**(1), 96–109 (2021)

Fan (樊秉义), B.Y.: Analysis of physiological characteristics and physiological health characteristics of the elderly. Old age world, p. 61 (2015)

Kano, N., et al.: Attractive quality and must-be quality. J. Jpn. Soc. Qual. Control **14**(02), 147–156 (1984)

Liu (刘灿), C.: Design and implementation of health monitoring software for intelligent elderly system. Chongqing University of Posts and Telecommunications (2019). https://doi.org/10.27675/d.cnki.gcydx.2019.000359

Li (李跃平), Y.P., Lin (林民强), M.Q., Wei (魏琴), Q., Lu (卢若燕), R.Y., Liang (梁栋), D.: Distribution characteristics and influencing factors of the health status of the elderly in China. Chin. Health Stat. 401–403 (2015)

Liu (刘晓红), X.H., Zhi (朱鸣雷), M.L.: Disease characteristics of the elderly and intervention strategies of geriatrics. Chin. J. Clin. (Electron. Ed.) 458–459 (2013)

National Statistics Office. Statistical Abstract 2020. China Statistics Press, Beijing, p. 33 (2020)

Wang (汪琪琦), Q., Cai (蔡萌), M., Wang (王希华), X.: Research on health communication strategies based on the physiological characteristics of the elderly. Mod. Biomed. Prog. **2**, 358–360 (2008)

Design of Preschool Children's Diet Education Products

Mingqi Zhang, Wei Wang[✉], and Shuai Sun

School of Design, Hunan University, Changsha, China
`wangwei1125@hnu.edu.cn`

Abstract. Children's diet has become a serious problem in recent years. "Healthy China 2030" published by state council also promotes the conduct of diet education for children. This project discusses about how to design the diet education products for children aged 3–6 years so as to effectively engage children in diet learning and improve the experience in acquiring diet knowledge simultaneously. The concept product Xueshi proposed in paper turns the obscure knowledge into a more intuitive way for preschoolers to understand, and can continuously attract preschoolers to learn with the combination of software and hardware. The tests of product with 3–6 year-old children showed that Xueshi could have a positive effect on diet education.

Keywords: Interactive design · Design for behavior change · Diet education · Children · User experience

1 Background

With the continuous improvement of socio-economic and living standards, the children in China gradually have three nutrition burdens: the problem of micronutrient deficiency, malnutrition, and obesity. Beside micronutrient deficiency and malnutrition, the problem of obesity is becoming increasingly serious [1]. 4.6% of the children between 3–6 years old are overweight, 9.2% of them are obese. And 14.4% of the children aged 6–12 are overweight, 20.0% of them are obese [2]. One of the most important reasons is children's unreasonable diet. According to the data of Chinese Nutrition Society in 2021, 51% of parents reported that their children had a significant problem of uneven daily dietary structure, and less than 30% of children reached the excellent level of balanced dietary structure. Most of the children have clear eating behavior problems such as picky and partial eaters [2]. In 2016, China State Council published the "Healthy China 2030" initiative, which is proposed to popularize the knowledge of dietary nutrition and guide the residents, especially the children and their families, to form scientific dietary habits. Consequently, it is necessary to carry out diet education for children. Through studying preschool children's eating behavior as well as their physiological and psychological behaviors, this paper extracts the design insights based on preschool children's need for diet education and proposes a concept of interactive products for preschool children's dietary knowledge learning. It carries out prototype development and further user testing of the prototype.

A. Marcus et al. (Eds.): HCII 2023, LNCS 14034, pp. 528–540, 2023.
https://doi.org/10.1007/978-3-031-35705-3_39

2   Current Situation and Features of Presently Available Diet Education Products

We studied the existing cases of diet education in the Chinese market. From the main initiators of diet education, there are mainly social groups, primary and secondary schools, and research institutes. From the object of diet education, there are education for eater and people engaged in diet education. From the main contents of diet education, the research results are shown in Table 1.

Table 1. The main contents of diet education in China

Approach	Introduction	Target population	Existing deficiencies
Training of diet educator	Knowledge training for people engaged in diet education	Diet educator	The content is usually dull and hard to absorb
Compile books on diet education	The books on food, nutrition knowledge and practice compiled by the institutes are used to guide practitioners to carry out teaching activities	Diet educator	The update cycle is usually long, and the practical guidance effect through direct communication will also be discounted
Food knowledge course	School health class or online courses offered, according to the food education textbook knowledge or PPT teaching materials for food to teach, usually mainly knowledge learning	Usually teenager and parents	Curriculum knowledge is relatively simple, lack of systematic content planning, teaching content without age subdivision and knowledge progression
Practice activities on diet education	Usually based on touching and making food (e.g. baking class and agronomy base experience). The knowledge dissemination is carried out by trained diet educators, mainly emphasizing the experience of children in practice	More participants in kindergarten and primary school	Most of them are single and low-frequency educational activities from which limited knowledge can be gained

(continued)

Table 1. (*continued*)

Approach	Introduction	Target population	Existing deficiencies
Sharing meeting	Held at certain intervals, usually start with popular knowledge and interest introduction	Usually teenagers and adults	Most of them are single and low-frequency educational activities with limited depth, focusing on public enlightenment and popular science
Picture books and cartoons	Usually in the family or kindergarten environment, help parents or preschool teachers to carry out popular explanation and enlightenment education of knowledge	Usually preschoolers, their parents and teachers	Mainly imported from abroad, lack of understandings of Chinese local food. Usually low intelligence, small adaptation crowd, difficult to continue to attract children
Teaching aids and toys	Tools with certain theme courses can help children to contact knowledge during play, which is usually not real food	Usually preschoolers, their parents and teachers	Low intelligence, interactive with pictures, stickers and other ways, rough production, large room for improvement

According to the research results, the diet education in Chinese society is still in the early stage, and faces the challenges such as the teaching knowledge is unsystematic and superficial, and current teaching method lacking attraction and interactivity for children. This study will further conduct the innovative design on the content of diet education knowledge and interactive way.

3 Identify Target User Group

The target population of this study are children aged 3–6 years. According to surveys, the detection rate of dietary behavior issues among preschool children is high [3–5]. Meanwhile, 3–6 years old is an important period for the growth and development of children, and their types of food and dietary structure are close to that of adults, which is a key period for the formation of eating behavior and lifestyle [6]. These eating behaviors and food preference are also closely related to their future eating habits in the whole life [7]. Due to preschool children's increasingly self-awareness and curiosity, they are easily distracted during eating, which leads to the formation of poor eating habits [8]. Therefore, it is necessary to conduct diet education for children in their preschool age.

4 Design Rationale

4.1 What to Be Delivered as the Content of Diet Education?

Through the observation of the eating behavior of children aged 3–6 years in the kindergarten, two aspects of diet problems have been identified. The first is poor dietary habits (e.g., spend too long to eat, lack of concentration while eating, and play while eating), which mainly occur in children aged 3–4 years. The other is unreasonable dietary choices (e.g., eat little vegetables and meat, prefer high snacks and drinks), which mainly occur in children aged 4–6 years. However, the dietary behaviors of preschoolers will be influenced by peers and their teachers when they are in school, usually better than when they are in home. Research shows that children aged 3–6 years all have the problem of poor dietary habits such as floating eating place and reject to new food [9]. Correspondingly, the diet education framework should consist of eating habits and education on nutrition during related education.

4.2 How to Deliver the Diet Education?

Study the characteristics of psychological development, cognition and behavior, and learning style of preschool children. Preschool children are easily distracted by surroundings, their attention span is about 10–15 min. Besides, their learning is based on direct experience and concrete image thinking, usually carried out in games and daily life. In addition, a better preschool education should be children-centered, and the education of children must follow their natural principles. It is necessary to comply with children's nature and carry out education according to the requirements and order of children's natural development to stimulate children's natural abilities. As a consequence, there are some principles that the diet education product should followed:

- provide rich interactivity and playability to continuously attract children to learn from exploration;
- enable children to understand knowledge through direct perception, which needs to transform related knowledge into language in line with children's cognition, rather than indoctrination and intensive training; and
- should not be designed in a way that forces children to learn, but rather in a way that stimulates their intrinsic needs to explore knowledge through content and formatting, which requires the product to be presented with sufficient hints and guidance in an appropriate form.

5 Concept Design: Xueshi

To demonstrate the education framework and the principles above, we applied them to a concept design of children's diet education products. The new product Xueshi (in Chinese 学食, Fig. 1) is a product-servie system that consists of a physical interaction model suit and an application in mobile device. The physical part includes the food model (Fig. 1a) for children interaction, and the food box base (Fig. 1b) for detecting the food module and providing acoustic-optic feedback. The application (Fig. 1c) presents related content of diet education, and provides feedback and display of interactive content.

Fig. 1. Physical Xueshi product suits (right) and rendering pictures (left)

5.1 Learning from Tangible Interaction

The concept Xueshi is based on the Five-link Curriculum Management [8] which is a process used to organize classes for preschoolers that follows the theory of children as standard for education and iterates according to the environment used by preschool children. The experience process of Xueshi includes five stages: A) introduction and stimulation, B) perception and exploration, C) feedback and stimulation, D) record and review, and E) focus and improvement. The specific operation process of the product is as shown in Fig. 2.

Children are firstly shown the animation in the mobile application. Each of the animation constructs a scene related to the problems of diet habits or nutrition and presents the bad influence of these problems, or raise the main character's positive expectations on

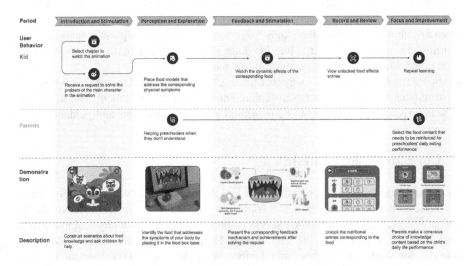

Fig. 2. Specific operation process of the concept Xueshi

body growth and health. Children then are asked to place the corresponding food model on the food box base to solve the problems or meet the expectations in the animation, in which process children watch the dynamic effects that the magic influence of food to the body when putting the correct food model on the box, gaining the nutrition knowledge of food. Children can review the known effects of food in the mobile application. And for children's parents, they can choose more targeted knowledge to let children practice more according to their children's daily diet performance, enhancing their children's understandings of dietary knowledge.

5.2 Technology Implementation

The hardware of Xueshi design consists of a ESP-32 Board, IC tags and a MFRC522 Reader Module (Fig. 3). The identification of food box base to the food model is based on the RFID technology. The tag of RFID system has been placed in the bottom of each food model, which means every food model has its own electronic coding; And the reader (MFRC522 Reader Module) of RFID system is placed under the top of the box.

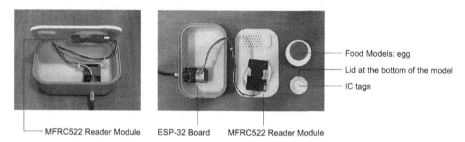

Fig. 3. The hardware of Xueshi design

When the food model is placed on the food box, the MFR522 reads the coding of IC tag put in the food model and transmits the information to the ESP-32 Board, telling which food model is placed on the box. The ESP-32 Board receives the information,

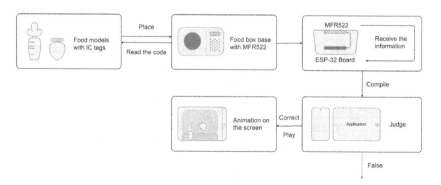

Fig. 4. The recognition process of Xueshi product

compiles it and sends it to the application. The application can make the decision whether the food model placed on the box is correct or not, and displays the corresponding feedback on its screen. The whole recognition process is shown in Fig. 4.

5.3 Insights Through Design Practice

Content Fits with Preschool Children's Cognition. The content of diet education takes the physical characteristics that children are more familiar with as an entry point. It transforms the obscure knowledge of nutrients into a direct understanding of the benefits of food to the body for children, which improves their understanding and association. The framework refers to the human organs and its eight systems. Children user could easily understood the content by selecting related parts (Table 2).

Table 2. The content of diet education

Main source	Chapter name	Learning objective	Represent food
Eye	The Bright Eyes	Know which foods can protect your eyes, know which foods have symptoms for your eyes, and learn to love foods that are good for your health	Blueberries, carrots, spinach, and egg yolks; Counterexample: Sweets
Tooth	The Great Dental Care Campaign	Learn the foods that are good for teeth, understand what foods will harm teeth, and reduce the consumption of these foods	Onion, kiwi, celery, mushroom; Counterexample: drinks with high acid content, cold drinks, sugar (especially hard one)
Nerve and brain	Let's Get Smart Together	Know which common foods will promote brain development, and make children love to eat these foods through product	Peanuts, walnuts, pumpkins, and fish
	I Love to Sleep	Know which foods promote sleep and encourage eating through the benefits of food	Edamame, tomato, milk, and banana
Lungs and respiratory system	Get Rid of A Cough	Know which foods can clear heat and detoxify, and are good for lungs and respiratory tract	Pear, yam, tremella, and radish

(*continued*)

Table 2. (*continued*)

Main source	Chapter name	Learning objective	Represent food
Stomach and intestines	Intestinal Cleaner	Knowing which foods promote digestion in the gut and where the food acts	Apple, sweet potato, corn, and yam
Immune system	Red Pimples Go Away	Know which foods can prevent allergies, and also let preschoolers know that they can't eat their own allergic foods	Carrots, onions, broccoli, and grapes
	It Doesn't Hurt At All	Show the different positions food effected and functions of food through animation demonstration. And let preschoolers roughly understand the effects of which kinds of food on wound healing and improving immunity. Understand that different foods have their own functions and the importance of a balanced diet	Bitter gourd, pig's hoof, kelp, and bass
Skeleton	The Secret of Growing Taller	Learn to grow tall that need a balanced diet, understand the disadvantages of eating snacks, guide children not to be partial to and picky about food, and understand which dietary behaviors will lead to grow tall through different situations	Eat a balanced diet, including several kinds
Blood and circulatory system	Nasty anemia	Know which bad eating behaviors will lead to the anemia, and know what food can improve this situation	Pig liver, animal whole blood, lean meat and other animal foods

(*continued*)

Table 2. (*continued*)

Main source	Chapter name	Learning objective	Represent food
Bone and endocrinology	A Fascinating Career	Know which bad eating behaviors lead to the growth retardation, and solve the problem by using the content learned before and matching a balanced diet	Balanced diet
Endocrine and digestive systems	Antagonistic Annoyance	Know which bad eating behaviors caused the character in animation to become fat/too thin, and solve the problem by using the food knowledge learned before and matching a balanced diet	Balanced diet

Intuitive Connection. The visual language of the product enables children to have intuitive cognition. Each animation adopts the more representative animal from Children's perspective of this theme as the main character, for example, the theme of eye pairs with owl, while the theme of to be taller pairs with giraffe. In the link of placing the food model, the graphics on the screen are also hinted. Similar to the metaphor of TV remote controls to new control units [10], Xueshi connects the food graphics with real objects corresponding to its function (Fig. 5) and helps children construct direct acquisition experience.

Tangible Interaction Beyond Screen. Xueshi does not take screen as the only means of interaction. The hardware design should not only pay attention to the modeling, CMF and human factors, but also the information design between physical interface and tangible interaction [11]. Xueshi uses the metaphor of the food box, where the food model is placed on the box base to establish tangible interaction beyond the screen. The combination of hardware and software strengthens the interactivity of children in the learning process, and allows children to learn while having fun, so as to achieve the purpose of attracting children continuously.

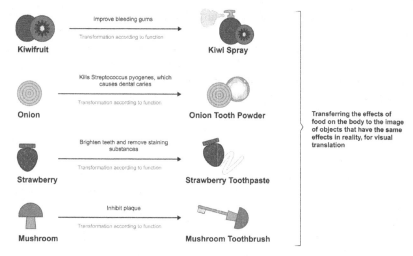

Fig. 5. The transform of food graphics in Chapter *The Great Dental Care Campaign*

6   User Evaluation

The design purpose of Xueshi is to educate children about diet effectively and improve children's learning of diet knowledge, and have an effect on guiding preschoolers to form a more scientific and healthier diet behavior. To verify this purpose and check the problem of product itself, a user test was performed over 8 children (4 boys and 4 girls) between 3–6 years (M = 4.6, SD = 1.06). The whole experiment was recorded, and conducted in the kindergarten with teachers and parents' permission.

Considering the attention span of preschoolers only about 10–15 min, the whole test lasted no more than 30 min. At the beginning of the procedure, researchers played with preschoolers for 5 min, during which preschoolers recognized food models and familiarized with the experiment environment. Then researchers introduced the process of playing the product approximately. For the next part, children explored and played Xueshi freely. The researchers observed children's behavior during playing, provided guidance when children needed and give positive feedback without influencing her/his

Fig. 6. Test process of Xueshi product

decisions when children tried to finish the task. At the end of each chapter's experience (the experiment task tested two chapters), there were some quick reviews to check children's acquisition of food knowledge, and questions to get the answer of willingness to try food (e.g., "Do you want to try this food afterwards?") and the product (e.g., "Do you like this game?" or "Do you want to try another one?"). Figure 6 presents a subject using the product (left) and the interface of application (right).

7 Result

Based on the video recordings and participatory observation, the researchers sorted out preschoolers' behaviors during the test, including the children's expressions, body language and the words they said. The result shows that Xueshi product did help preschoolers understand the food's functions on body.

On the acquisition of food knowledge on their body, all children aged 5–6 years could almost entirely remember the food's functions correctly only playing the product once, while children aged 3–4 years should play the product 2–3 times to remember all the food's functions (usually mixed up 1–2 types of food's functions when played once). And their retell of food function usually used direct description, for example, "Strawberries can make teeth white" "Kiwi, and the wound (point to the gingiva) is gone". On the acquisition of bad eating habits' influence on body, children aged 5–6 years also performed better than children aged 3–4 years. Children aged 5–6 years can understand what happened on the main character and what cause the situation, while 3–4 year-old children need some explanation. When children solved one symptom in the application, they would shake their heads, waved their hands and hurried to make the next attempt (put another food model on box). And there even were children experience the game chapters 3–4 times. On the willingness to try food mentioned in product, all participants gave the positive feedback. All these consequence shows that Xueshi could convey diet knowledge to children and engage them in learning.

The test also verified the intelligibility of graphics and dynamic effects on the screen when placing the food model. All participants can connect the graphics with real food models, and get the meaning of the relatively simple hints like "toothbrush" or "eye-drops", but have trouble in discover the dynamic effects when there are not much changes (like similar color changes or variation of brightness) or with short duration. There is an interesting finding that the younger children tends to put all food models one by one on the box to explore what would happen even they know the correct answer, which suggests the more exploratory and complete interactive feedback could engage young users better. On the guidance of position of placing food model on box, three of eight children did not know where to put the food model on the food box, and one child knew the position, but put the food model with hesitation, which needs further optimization.

8 Conclusion

This paper proposes Xueshi, a concept with tangible models and virtual application which aimed to provide diet education for children aged 3–6 years, improving preschoolers' acquisition of diet knowledge and guiding to promote their diet behaviors. This inter-active product-service system can effectively engage preschoolers in a better way of learning diet and food knowledge since its content is based on the common problems happened in preschoolers' daily diet. Moreover, the interactive way and visualization of these content are particularly designed for children aged 3–6 years due to their psychological characteristics and cognitive ability. Based on our design process, this paper also presents the design principles of diet education product. These outcomes can be used in related diet education products for children. The following aspects need to be promoted primarily in further optimization to provide children a more thorough and stimulating learning experience. First, it needs to provide multimodal feedback on the screen such as keywords sound, highlight or enhance the changes in visual when the correct food model is placed. Second, it needs to improve tangible interaction such as the shape of food box base to strengthen the intelligibility of position for putting food models. Third, the knowledge in animations could be easier for younger preschoolers to understand. The major limitation of this study is on the number of preschool participants in design evaluation part. And it lacks a long-term study by tracking its performance in real living environment.

Acknowledgments. This research was supported by the National Key Research and Development Program (2021YFF0900605), the Research Fund for Humanities and Social Sciences of the Ministry of Education (22YJA760082), the Science and Technology Innovation Program of Hunan Province (2022WZ1039), the National Foreign Cultural and Educational Experts Program of the Ministry of Science and Technology (G2022160013L), and the Fundamental Research Funds for the Central Universities and Lushan Lab. We acknowledge Feng Lan in Hunan University and Xufeng Lou in Huzhou University for technical support, Aosha Long in Hunan University and Ms. Liao in Mimi Kindergarten for advice of conceptual inspiration, and the reviewers in HCII 2023.

References

1. Yan, X., Ma, J., Song, Y., Xing, Y.: Report on the nutrition and health status of Chinese children in 2019. In: Annual Report on Chinese Children's Development, pp. 22–53. Social Sciences Academic Press (CHINA), Beijing (2020)
2. The 2021 Nutrition Knowledge and behavior Report for School-age and Preschool Children was released. Zhong Guo Shi Pin an Quan Bao, p. C02. Zhong Guo Shi Pin an Quan Press, Beijing (2021)
3. Li, C., Fang, Y., He, Y.: Analysis on eating behaviors and its influencing factors among 1057 preschool children in 5 provinces. Chin. J. Health Educ. **36**(01), 8–12 (2020). https://doi.org/10.16168/j.cnki.issn.1002-9982.2020.01.002
4. Jiang, Y., Zhang, Q.: Investigation on the status quo and development of preschool children's eating psychological behavior. Labor Secur. World **18**, 69–70 (2018)
5. Zhang, J.: Analysis on the status of dietary behavior problems of some preschool children in Changsha and its influencing factors. Mod. Prev. Med. **47**(14), 2555–8+62 (2020)
6. Ye, T., Hua, L., Qin, X., Zhu, Z., Hao, Y., Xiang, L., et al.: Eating behaviors of preschool children: a survey study. J. Nurs. Sci. **31**(05), 83–86 (2016)
7. Alles-White, M.L., Welch, P.: Factors affecting the formation of food preferences in preschool children. Early Child Dev. Care **21**(4), 265–276 (1985). https://doi.org/10.1080/0300443850210402

8. Zhang, H., Zhao, Y.: You er yuan Shi Yu Shi Yong Zhi Dao. Zhengzhou University Press, Zhengzhou (2021)
9. Shi, C., Li, X., Dong, J., Zhang, C., Tong, M., Guo, X., et al.: Prevalence of children's eating problems among 1 to 7 years old and its correlation with their physical development. Chin. J. Appl. Clin. Pediatr. **11**, 840–845 (2016). https://doi.org/10.3760/cma.j.issn.2095-428X.2016. 11.011
10. Ball, R., Chen, X., Wang, W., Overhill, H.: Merging motorcycle and smart phone controls for ride-share electric motorcycles. In: Bruyns, G., Wei, H. (eds.) [ ] With Design: Reinventing Design Modes. IASDR 2021, pp. 1474–82. Springer, Singapore (2022). https://doi.org/10. 1007/978-981-19-4472-7_96
11. Wang, W., Yang, Y.: The change of interaction in the age of intelligent products: a discussion on the design of physical touchable interaction. Art Panorama. (06), 129–133 (2022). https:// doi.org/10.3969/j.issn.1002-2953.2022.06.019

Correction to: A New Process Framework for Managing the Fuzzy Front End of New Healthcare Device Development

Fan Yang, Zhen Qin, Min Lin, and Wa An

Correction to:
Chapter "A New Process Framework for Managing the Fuzzy Front End of New Healthcare Device Development" in:
A. Marcus et al. (Eds.): *Design, User Experience, and Usability*, LNCS 14034, https://doi.org/10.1007/978-3-031-35705-3_35

In the originally published version of chapter 35 two of the author names had been misspelled and the acknowledgement text has been incorrect. This has been corrected.

The updated original version of this chapter can be found at
https://doi.org/10.1007/978-3-031-35705-3_35

Author Index

Printed in the United States
by Baker & Taylor Publisher Services